THE TUDOR AGE

THE
TUDOR AGE

by

JAMES A. WILLIAMSON

LONGMAN
London and New York

LONGMAN GROUP LIMITED
London
*Associated companies, branches and representatives
throughout the world*
*Published in the United States of America
by Longman Inc., New York*

First published 1953
Second Edition (with Appendices)1957
Third Edition 1964
*First published in paperback (with
revised Note on Books) 1979*

BRITISH LIBRARY CATALOGUING IN PUBLICATION DATA
Williamson, James Alexander
  The Tudor age. – 3rd ed., reprinted. – (A history of England).
  1. Great Britain – History – Tudors, 1485-1603
  I. Title   II. Series
  942.05   DA315   79-40216
  ISBN 0-582-49074-X

PRINTED IN GREAT BRITAIN BY
LOWE AND BRYDONE PRINTERS LIMITED, THETFORD, NORFOLK

INTRODUCTORY NOTE

THE present series was planned in the years immediately following the second world war, at a time when we were all vividly and gratefully aware of the capacity for survival of the British people and their interests and institutions. The physical destruction of book stocks during the war and the challenges of an incalculable future also pointed the case for a reassessment of the national evolution from early to recent times. The authors of the various volumes in the series were asked to give particular attention to the interaction of the essential aspects of national life and achievement, so that each volume might make a convincing contribution to the study of overall developments. Otherwise there was no attempt to secure general uniformity of style or treatment; each author was free to write in accordance with his own methods, tastes, and experience.

Dr Williamson was very much in accord with this approach, and in his admirable volume, first published in 1953, he treated the Tudor age as the decisive opening phase in the evolution of modern England. In the main his work was a study of the strengthening of the central authority, reform in the church and society, and the handling of external opportunities and challenges. The scale of the book and his own interests did not allow much space for the subtler aspects of Tudor administrative and constitutional development, but there was a correspondingly full treatment of what he regarded as the essential themes, including maritime and mercantile problems and foreign policy. The book has had many admirers, and has gone through three editions and four impressions. In this reprint in paperback the text of the last edition is unchanged, but there is a new bibliographical note by Dr D. M. Palliser.

W. N. MEDLICOTT

A HISTORY OF ENGLAND
IN ELEVEN VOLUMES

General Editor: W. N. Medlicott

*Already published
Some of the titles listed above are provisional*

PREFACE

THE following book is in the main a narrative history of the Tudor period, written with intent to balance the treatment of the various interests of the time and to evaluate their influence on the course of the national development. I have viewed the story as, first, a restoration of order and strengthening of administration; next, a reformation in the Church, the state, and the English society; and lastly, the opening phase in the growth of the new England that emerged.

The Tudor period has a distinctive characteristic in that some of its conflicts have left wounds that are still raw, which makes it difficult to avoid a personal bias in assessing its achievements; and it is useful to the reader that the historian should confess his bias at the outset. Mine makes me regard the period as a stage in the making of modern England and in the shaping of the national character and mentality. It has not, I hope, impelled me to distort the facts, but it has influenced the degree of emphasis allotted to them, and it has therefore led me to give greater attention to governing events in the economic, mercantile, and maritime spheres, and less to ecclesiastical transactions than some interpretations have done. I believe this to be in the interest of true presentation, for to my reading it seems that while the fortunes of churches fill a large place in the Tudor story, the people of England were in general more secular-minded during most of its course than they had been in former times and were to become in the Stuart century.

So I have tried to give an all-round view of the nation in active life, and in seeking to enlighten it I have borne in mind a circumstance that influences interpretation. The ethics of the age were not those approved to-day, and it is unfair to judge the actors too rigidly by our standards. A man esteemed worthy in Tudor times could do things that would exclude him from worthiness now. He could rob his neighbours by legal chicanery, take bribes in the performance of public duties, fawn and flatter with complete insincerity, burn his fellows for rejecting a creed, or hang them for necessity of state. Such things the age allowed, and before its last half-century there are few leading figures against whom some of these charges cannot be brought. But it is also true that conduct did improve. Elizabeth was more merciful than her father; Burghley was a more single-minded public servant than Wolsey; the later sixteenth century was less callous than the earlier. A seed of toleration was germinating, and the plant, of slow growth indeed, grew.

In writing this book I have had to follow in the footsteps of two great workers of the recent past, H. A. L. Fisher and A. F. Pollard, who covered the period in two volumes of *The Political History of England*. They are still outstanding guides to the Tudor story, the one for his happiness of style and broad grasp of history as a humane study, the other for his immense research and a knowledge of the sixteenth century, in highway and byway, that has not been surpassed. My debt to others also is so great as to cover all but a small portion of the field. The bibliographical note gives my acknowledgements in general, while the origins of specified points of information are given in the footnotes.

J. A. WILLIAMSON

PREFACE TO SECOND EDITION, 1956

I HAVE made various corrections and additions, drawn from criticism of the book on its first publication and from important published work which appeared too late for me to make use of it. I may, perhaps, here add one thing which might have been said in the original preface, namely, that the maritime enterprise of the period is in my view an essential part of its record; and that, while the origin of the British Empire is to be looked for in medieval commerce, its first effective chapter lies in the oceanic movement of the Tudor century, when Englishmen, few at first but many at last, were seeking a position in the world as distinct from a position in Europe.

Three Appendices have been added, to combine and elaborate treatment that has been dispersed or omitted in the text of the volume.

J. A. W.

NOTE TO THE THIRD EDITION, 1964

CORRECTIONS have been made in accordance with recent authorities on the period treated in this book.

J. A. W.

CONTENTS

CHAPTER III

HENRY VII'S CRUCIAL YEARS

CHAPTER IV

THE ACHIEVEMENT OF STABILITY

CHAPTER V

THE EARLY YEARS OF HENRY VIII: THE RISE OF WOLSEY

CHAPTER VI

THE DECLINE AND FALL OF WOLSEY

CHAPTER VII

ONE BODY POLITIC: THE ROYAL SUPREMACY

CHAPTER VIII

ONE BODY POLITIC: CONSOLIDATION AND DEFENCE

CHAPTER IX

THE BRITISH QUESTION

CHAPTER X

EDWARD VI: SOMERSET AND NORTHUMBERLAND

CHAPTER XI

THE REIGN OF MARY

PAGE

CHAPTER XII

THE ACCESSION OF ELIZABETH I

CHAPTER XIII

POLITICAL PERILS AND ECONOMIC RECOVERY

CHAPTER XIV

THE ELIZABETHAN AGE TAKES SHAPE

CHAPTER XV

THE FERTILE SEVENTIES

CHAPTER XVI

THE CONFLICT JOINED

CHAPTER XVII

THE ARMADA AND PORTUGAL

CHAPTER XVIII

THE ELIZABETHANS AT WAR

CHAPTER XIX

THE CLOSING YEARS

Contents

I

ENGLAND IN 1485

IN England and Wales the early Tudor monarchy had possibly three million subjects, the majority of them countrymen making their living by agriculture. London, with perhaps 100,000, was the only great town. Of the other towns, Norwich, York, Bristol, and Exeter were the largest, none of them probably with a population much exceeding 20,000. London was the greatest seaport, with a trade more than twice as valuable as that of Southampton, which came second in order of customs payments. By the same reckoning Newcastle, Boston, and Bristol in that order came next; but since Boston shipped a high proportion of raw wool, the most heavily taxed article, while Bristol shipped hardly any, it is possible that the payments may misrepresent the actual volume of shipping business and that Bristol's was the greater of the two. Newcastle's high place rested partly on the export of coal, already considerable. England's other towns were numerous but small, and some were growing smaller, since craftsmen were tending to desert them for the greater freedom of the countryside. In sum it may be guessed (for it is only a matter of guesswork) that not more than one-tenth of the possible three millions were townsmen, although their importance in the state was always greater than their numbers would indicate.

The population was for the most part rural, and it was not evenly spread. The moors and uplands of the north and west carried few people, much fenland was not reclaimed, and forests were not cleared. Only where good drainable soil clothed the structure of the landscape could men live in substantial village communities. In such favoured areas, commonest in the midlands and the south, but not altogether lacking in the north, the population must have appeared quite dense to fifteenth-century eyes, and would not seem scanty in comparison with that of the few completely rural areas surviving in our own time.

The society that occupied this land was not immutably fixed and resistant to change. It had undergone recent changes, and others were to come. The Black Death of the fourteenth century had been followed by a long decline of villeinage. The foreign wars and civil wars of the fifteenth century, and the growing complexity of trade, had been social solvents. The uppermost class consisted of the nobles, the bishops, and the heads of the more important abbeys. Next to them, and shading into them, stood the knights and country gentlemen, who held smaller estates but were much more numerous. For a long time the balance between these two categories had been changing. The knights and gentlemen, originally in pronounced subordination to the greater men, were gaining more freedom and security as independent possessors. The civil wars and conspiracies of Lancaster and York, with their long lists of casualties and executions, weakened the noble class more than the gentry. England in the thirteenth century had been a land of great fiefs subdivided into subordinate holdings that were tightly controlled. England in the fifteenth century contained many smaller independent properties. By 1485 the nobility were reduced in numbers and less powerful than a hundred years before. In the Church there was a loss of authority and a deterioration of the personal position of the higher ranks. Absentee foreigners held various bishoprics. The life was ebbing from the monastic system, whose leaders were men of less weight than in the past. The fifteenth-century abbot was less obviously a spiritual head than a member of the gentry, with the advancement of brothers and nephews as his main preoccupation. The decline of the great magnates had entailed, by some evidence, a loss of agricultural efficiency. Wide plans of clearance and reclamation were beyond the resources of the lesser landowners, and it is probable that the soil of England produced less than in the period of high medieval management. It is fairly certain that the population was smaller, not having recovered from the mass extermination of the Black Death.

Social change was in progress in the rural multitude. In the past it had been predominantly of an unfree lower order, but it was now throwing up in greater numbers a middle class of independent men, the yeomen of England, who were to reach their zenith in the two centuries that followed. Yeoman is not a term of strict definition. It indicated the substantial man with some security of tenure. He might or might not be a freeholder; but he owed no service other than the payment of rent, and if he were a copyholder or long lease-holder his rent could not be raised or himself legally evicted. There had always been such men, particularly in the eastern counties, but there were now many more of them. The yeoman class merged downwards into that of the cottagers and labourers. All had once been villeins, tied to their manor, bound to yield labour service to its lord and to submit to other exactions, answerable in the manorial court, and unfree to invoke the general law of the realm. By 1485 nearly all were free, enjoying their small holdings on payment or by the custom of the manor, taking wages for the work they did for others, free to sell their interest and depart, and to plead as equal subjects in the King's courts. Villeinage was not completely at an end, but it was ending, and its survivals were becoming exceptional.

The decline of villeinage was not an unmixed gain to the lower peasantry, for in practice it was accompanied by a decline of security. The peasants' tenures of such rights as they claimed were ill-defined and often invalid in law where they had been good by custom. Freedom and security were social incompatibles, and full security was only to be had by complete subordination. In England after the Black Death the general preference, slowly developed and held for centuries, was for liberty in spite of its penalties, and that view dominated the articulate society of the Tudor age. Economic change accentuated the penalties. Owners of land sought to alter its use in order to produce more wool. Insecure tenants were dispossessed, labourers turned adrift and their cottages pulled down. Destitution, vagabondage, and a drifting class of outlaws and criminals increased. They produced a social problem that cried more loudly for solution as the Tudor period progressed. The problem was not new or universal. In medieval society there had always been outlaws and beggars. In Tudor society there were many of them. But many does not mean all, or in fact anything more than a small minority. Eviction was not general, but patchy. It was a process for which a society determined to be free could find no sure prevention, and statesman-ship was to do its more constructive work in seeking remedies for the resultant distress.

The cloth manufacture was a social solvent. English wool was a high-grade material, but in early days was for the most part exported raw. Seeing the keen foreign demand, English kings levied heavy duties on its export, and the duties protected the infant industry of

cloth-making in England. By the Tudor period the industry was
established and advanced. Although more wool was being produced,
the export of raw wool was less than half what it had been in the
thirteenth century, and the growth of cloth manufacture accounted
for the difference. The trend continued until by the end of the Tudor
period there was very little raw wool for export. The demand for
wool caused the conversion of tillage into pasture and the insecurity
of the poorer peasants. A long-term effect was an improvement of
agriculture whereby the land, deprived of its pasture areas, was made
to yield sufficient food to supply the demand. There is evidence of
this improvement, especially in the reign of Elizabeth.

The countrymen provided the material for the cloth trade and did
some of the manufacturing, notably the spinning. Some weaving was
also done by people who were mainly land-workers. Most of the
further processes that produced the finished cloth were carried on by
whole-time craftsmen who dwelt chiefly in the towns. Towns,
however, were subject to oligarchic government, which maintained
injurious restrictions, and some also lacked the water-power which
was displacing manual labour in the fulling mills. In the late fifteenth
century these factors were causing craftsmen to move out of towns
in order to work in the freer countryside. Numerous towns complained of decay and desertion of houses and falling population, in
spite of the fact that the national population was slowly rising.

London suffered no such check. It was growing vigorously and
continued to grow throughout the period. By its close London had
with Westminster and the suburbs a quarter of a million people. Its
growth came partly from the increase of the personnel of government and its tendency to settle in the capital, partly from the growing
importance of the King's courts and the legal profession, but mainly
from increase of trade. The tendency, marked in the fifteenth century
and amplified in the sixteenth, was for London to absorb an ever-
growing share of the country's foreign trade. Southampton fell
quickly from its position as the second seaport when the spice-route
was changed by Vasco da Gama's discovery of the sea passage to
the Indian Ocean. The Venetians, the old intermediaries of the spice
trade, had landed their cargoes at Southampton, whereas the Portuguese, their supplanters, took theirs to Antwerp, where Londoners
bought for the English market. Bristol, Plymouth, and one or two
more of the larger outports improved their position, but the smaller
ones declined rapidly, lost their overseas trade, and became limited

to coasting and fishing. Larger ships unable to enter silting harbours partly accounted for it; but the greater cause was the increasing liaison between government and commerce, which gave the merchants of the capital a better chance. By 1485 London had attained a position in the kingdom which she had not held in earlier times. Thenceforward it became evident that who held London held England, a proposition repeatedly put to the test and demonstrated in the two centuries that followed.

The Church in the early Tudor time formed a great and in some respects a preponderant component of society. Ecclesiastics were, of course, much less numerous than laymen, but their influence permeated all ranks. The position of the higher dignitaries, and of the parish priests, the chantry priests, and the monks and nuns, was established and obvious: they formed the moral cement of the social structure. They were by no means the whole of the ecclesiastical population. There were more priests than benefices, and the surplus made their livings in various ways. In addition there were large numbers of men in minor orders, ranking legally as clergy, but following laymen's employments as scholars, tutors, and secretaries, and providing an outcast fringe of criminals and shady characters. The word clerk or cleric included for one important legal purpose everyone who could read; for the literate, if convicted in the King's court, could claim to be sentenced in the bishop's, which was unable to inflict the death penalty. The Church as a whole was in need of reform, and notably its section known as 'the religious', the professed monks and nuns. The disreputable fringes of the Church were a serious element in the social disorder with which governments had perennially to cope. But the good outweighed the bad. The regular clergy formed a social bond, their services inculcating beliefs and conduct without which chaos would have prevailed. The dignitaries formed a body of well-educated men of high rank, and the state appreciated their value and used their talents. The priests, especially the chantry priests, were the schoolmasters necessary to the civilization of the townspeople; and some of the religious houses were boarding schools for the children of the rich.

The merchants formed a town class parallel to the country gentlemen, taking the lead and furnishing magistrates and councillors. Although many were of gentle families and could describe themselves as *armiger*, they did not emphasize the social line that was clearly drawn between their country cousins and the yeomen.

In the towns wealth was the criterion, and the merchant class descended imperceptibly from magnates of foreign trade to substantial retailers, and thence almost to stall-keepers and hawkers. In London and the greater ports a merchant belonged to a recognized company, for entrance to which he qualified by apprenticeship or a fee. The companies were partly concerned with manufacture and retailing and partly with foreign trade. In London in the Tudor period the chief foreign traders were to be found among the Mercers and the Drapers, although earlier the Grocers, with their import of spices, had been prominent. It was not, however, as Mercers or Drapers, but as Merchants Adventurers that the Londoners bought and sold cloth overseas. Companies of Merchants Adventurers were formed in London and other English ports in the later medieval period, and their members were merchants whose status was already attested by their membership of companies dealing with internal trade. A foreign-trading merchant was therefore commonly a Merchant Adventurer and a Mercer or Draper. There has been some confusion about the term Merchant Adventurer, since it was used with more than one meaning. As a common noun it denoted anyone who traded anywhere by sea. It had also a restricted meaning, best indicated by the use of capital letters, limited to membership of the constituted companies. Early in the fifteenth century there were three main divisions of the properly constituted Merchants Adventurers, those trading to the Baltic, Scandinavia, and the Netherlands respectively; each of these divisions being recruited from merchants in all the English ports. By the end of the century wars and other misfortunes had reduced the Baltic and Scandinavian companies to abeyance, and the Merchants Adventurers as a proper noun meant those conveying English manufactures to the Low Countries. In 1485 they had their overseas headquarters at Antwerp, where they were ruled by a governor and assistants elected by themselves.

The merchants trading to Spain and Portugal, mostly west-country men although there were Londoners among them, probably had a similar organization in the late fifteenth century. Their earliest existing charter is dated 1530, but it may indicate a refoundation of a previously existing body. English merchants trading in France were not incorporated. Their greatest business was at Bordeaux for wines and woad; and Bordeaux, though no longer under the English crown, had such strong English affiliations that it hardly ranked as a foreign port. The purpose of the company organization was to regulate the trade in two ways, by supervising the conduct of the merchants, ensuring that they kept to agreed prices and rules, and by presenting a solid front in negotiations with foreign governments. The governor overseas was the man in authority for both purposes. At Bordeaux it may be supposed that the English were so well established that regulation was not needed, and the fact that they were rather buyers than sellers may have been relevant. In the ports of northern France and Brittany there was a diversity of traffic by small English vessels from a variety of English harbours. Regulation would have been difficult, and individualist trading was the method.

The most strictly controlled of all the foreign trades was that in raw wool, with wool-fells and hides. These were the oldest exports, antedating the cloth trade; and the company that handled them, the Merchants of the Staple, was older than the Merchants Adventurers. In 1485 the Staple had long been fixed at Calais, to which place alone the Staplers from all over England consigned their goods, and at which all foreign buyers from the north of Europe had to make their purchases. Italian buyers were exempt from the staple system, and might acquire wool anywhere in England and export it in their own ships, provided that they sold none north of the Alps. The English crown levied heavy duties on the outgoing wool. Its quantity was diminishing with the growth of the English cloth industry, but its quality maintained the demand in spite of its high price.

Seamen formed a distinct but small community within the nation. Their importance to defence and prosperity was recognized, but the imperfect statistics suggest that there were very few of them. About 15,000 men, not all of whom were seamen, formed the crews of the English fleet that fought the Armada in 1588, and they represented the transference of the greater part of the merchant marine to the naval service. Henry VIII's Navy at the end of his reign needed about 8,000 men, only two-thirds of whom were seamen, for full mobilization; and this was carried out in 1545 only by impressing every available man, so that it is on record that women were working the fishing boats that year. At the accession of the Tudor dynasty we have no figures. It is known that English shipping was depleted and that Henry VII took steps to foster it. We may guess that at the highest there were not more than fifteen or twenty thousand seamen in the country, or from $\frac{1}{2}$ to $\frac{2}{3}$ of 1 per cent of the population. There may well have been fewer. Throughout the Tudor period legislators and writers on public policy insisted on the need for obtaining more seamen and for conserving their lives by improving the methods of navigation.

Finally, the law contributed an important component to society. The former jurisdiction of the manor courts had nearly all gone to the various courts resting on the King's authority. The justices of the peace, overweighed by disorder in the previous turbulent generation, were about to increase and consolidate their importance, and their work was to become not only judicial but administrative. Serious crime was dealt with at the justices' quarter sessions and at the periodical assizes in the county towns. Conveyances and disputes about property gave occupation to attorneys spread throughout the country. The main force of the legal profession was concentrated in London, where the highest courts sat and where alone a good legal training was available. The Inns of Court provided for more than professional lawyers, and in the sixteenth century, if not earlier, it was the custom for young gentlemen to reside for a year or two in what was virtually a university of London in order to learn what they needed to know about the law as it concerned landed estate. Oxford and Cambridge were mainly ecclesiastical in their interests. The Inns of Court were for laymen.

So much for the structure of society. A more interesting subject is its quality. The social climate of the early Tudors gives the impression of freedom and harshness, as of a March wind in cold sunshine. Men were reckless and ruthless, guided rather by temper than foresight, doing things with their might and not knowing what they would do next. They were mostly young and undisciplined. That they were young is the factor that marks the greatest difference from society to-day. Apart from the great numbers that died in childhood, those who grew up did not see half the years to which their descendants look forward. The few who went to school were not long there. Those who went to the universities did so at fourteen or fifteen. The man of twenty-one was in his prime. At thirty he was becoming 'sad', the edge worn off his exuberance. At forty-five he was growing old, but most did not live to that age. Very few passed sixty. This at least was true of the nourished and nurtured higher ranks, and their inferiors were probably no longer-lived. Of all the sovereigns of Europe in the Tudor century only one or two exceptions, Queen Elizabeth and Philip II, lived to seventy or near it. No predecessor of Elizabeth in two hundred years reached sixty.

Among the nobles and gentry, the yeomen, peasants, and seamen, this short life of vigour was a component of character. On the average they lacked experience and obeyed their qualities more than their knowledge. Laws were pitiless and penalties dreadful, but men broke out and defied them and took the consequences. Few of these men had ever been to school in the modern sense and learned to keep their tempers. The higher ranks had grown up arrogantly among inferiors, the lower ranks accustomed to settle differences by blows rather than reason. They were all unruly and prone to expect evil of their fellows. Strong rule was needed to subdue their violence. The Tudor dynasty was to supply it, though not in overwhelming measure. If despotism implies slavish obedience there was never a Tudor despotism. Such considerations help to explain the treasons, riots, and rebellions of the time, when noblemen staked their heads and their lands for some pique or jealousy or hare-brained ambition, or when the commons could fight the King and risk the gallows for objects that they very hazily understood. Even the ablest and coolest men, like Wolsey and Thomas Cromwell, could play this game of fast and loose with a sovereign whose nod could destroy them. Gambling for the highest stakes was in the spring air of the time, with all to win and no mercy for the losers.

Paradoxically, although there was plenty of treason against kings, there was high reverence for the King. The rebels were no republicans, and when they sought to overthrow one monarch it was to set up another. Men thought always of the supreme authority as the King, not as 'the Government', still less as our bureaucratic 'They'. If things went wrong the people blamed the King, if well, they applauded him. It was in accordance with the facts, for the King was the ruler. His councillors gave advice which he need not take, and the whole responsibility was his. In legislation his power was limited by the necessity for Parliament's consent, but new legislation was not regularly called for, and the country could go for years at a time without it. In finance he was normally independent, needing Parliamentary grants only for the extra costs of war. The fact that the wearer of the crown was the working and responsible ruler of the country in the Tudor period must be kept always in mind. With it all there was no clear definition of right to the crown. When, as in the fifteenth century, there were various persons connected with the royal stock by descents from elder or younger sons of Edward III, complicated by illegitimacies or by female links in the chain, no one knew which claim was best, neither was there any means of obtaining

an impartial decision. It was agreed that the monarchy was hereditary, but it was not agreed who was the heir. That point was left
to be decided by personal ability and fortune. The family which
gained possession gained a separateness and sanctity as the royal
family, an invaluable attribute which it lay with them to preserve.
The Lancastrians, usurpers though they had been, had this royal
sanctity. The Yorkist brothers had been too unscrupulous and had
perhaps weakened it. The Tudors, as we shall see, knew how to be
at once human and royal. In the early Tudor period men referred to
the King as His Grace. Henry VIII regrettably altered the style to
His Majesty, but it was some time before the older form died out.

The religion of this English nation, and its attitude to the Church,
were destined to be cardinal factors in Tudor history. At the outset
a situation prevailed which had existed for some time, certainly since
the days of Wyclif. There was a general jealousy and dislike of the
Church as a propertied institution, and of ecclesiastics as a class.
Public opinion held that the Church was over-endowed and that
churchmen were worldly and grasping and gave little evidence in
their lives that theirs was a spiritual calling. This feeling was not the
result of hostile propaganda, but grew from the facts which were
open to common observation. Clerics who sought easy ways of
making money, who roystered and drank and broke the vow of
chastity, who exhibited no learning and did no work, were sufficiently numerous to be known to all; and the shining lights of whom
these things were not true were too few to mitigate the adverse
judgment. Earnest men among the dignitaries saw the need for
reform, but their efforts to achieve it were ineffectual. Abuses were
so well entrenched that little could be done. This was especially true
of the monasteries, which were able to defy the corrective moves of
the bishops.

Side by side with dislike of the churchmen there existed an
unquestioning belief in the doctrines they proclaimed and an urgent
desire for the services which they alone were qualified to give.
Englishmen believed in purgatory and the necessity of prayers and
offerings for the dead, in making material sacrifice for the remission
of sins, in the intercession of the saints, and in the merit of pilgrimage
to their shrines. The desire for the prayers of the Church was not
conventional but passionate. The dying man held himself lost without absolution. The priestly function transcended the individual,
and an unworthy priest was contemned, not for performing service

when unfit to do so, but for neglecting to do it at all. It is one of the greatest surprises as we follow the story of the time that these beliefs, so intense and fundamental, should have been shattered, as they were, by new ideas arising in the course of a single generation. In the old order there were, it is true, some dissidents who held few or none of the beliefs outlined above, the Lollard heretics who were descended from Wyclif. They were few, obscure, but pertinacious. The majority of the people had neither sympathy nor mercy for them. What they really taught is not well known, for the details of their trials are not preserved. All that can be said is that in scanty numbers they were denounced and burnt throughout the fifteenth century and into the reign of Henry VIII, and that public opinion approved of it.

The realm of England was unequally divided by the Humber and the lower Trent. The north contained much barren land and a thin population whose sentiments on government and religion tended to lag behind those of the midlands and the south. The plain of Lancashire, noted in pre-industrial times for its clear and pleasant air, and the south and east parts of Yorkshire were fair agricultural regions. North-country sheep provided material for a cloth industry that exported its wares through York and the Humber. The coastal coalfield of Northumberland was actively worked, sending fuel not only to London but to Europe in a multitude of foreign ships. But for the most part the north was poor and difficult country in which feudal lords had a greater command of the people than elsewhere, and the King's rule was less effective. The north was the most likely region to resist religious changes and the strengthening of the royal government. In the military sense it was an invaluable asset. Its rough going and its fighting people provided a deep zone of defence against invasion from Scotland. Century after century the northerners fulfilled their function of stopping Scottish armies and safeguarding the wealthy midlands and the south. In earlier times the Picts had raided far and deep and broken up the Roman province of Britain. In the later middle ages their descendants never got so far south, hardly ever into Yorkshire. The northern zone of defence was an important factor in the growth of English power. Scotland had no such zone. Its best regions were between the border and the central mountains, and its capital was open to a rapid stroke from the Tweed. Tudor history was to exemplify the disadvantage.

If the north was the bulwark of defence, the midlands and the

ENGLAND IN THE EARLY TUDOR PERIOD

MILES
0   50   100

Land above 600 feet shaded thus:—

The chief areas of old enclosure were in the South East, South West, Welsh Border and Lancashire, North Yorkshire and Northumberland. New enclosure was causing complaint in the Midlands and East Anglia.

south held the wealth of the realm. There, so far west as the Welsh marches, lay the homogeneous kingdom of England, divided into regions with different characteristics, but like-minded on the great questions of policy and progress. There were a few practicable main roads radiating from London, sufficiently good to enable the capital to be fed and to concentrate in it the merchandise which made it the greatest seaport. Areas between the main highways were variably served, some so ill that they were virtually isolated. Wool of differing qualities was widely produced, from the fine product of the Cots-wolds to the poor stuff yielded by Cornwall, contemned as 'Cornish hair' and hardly fit for manufacture. Broadly speaking, long-staple and short-staple wool formed two main categories and produced respectively the worsteds of East Anglia and the broadcloths of the country round Bristol; but there were many local variations and specialities. In agricultural organization there was a slow variation from the east with its open-field manors and nuclear villages to the west with its fenced fields and scattered dwellings. Anglo-Saxon as contrasted with mixed or Celtic ancestry may partly explain it, but difference of climate and terrain was probably the greater factor.

Beyond the marches Wales contained a quite separate society, modified by some English penetration in the south, tribal and pure Welsh in the north. The age of Anglo-Welsh warfare had ended, and Wales and England were about to join in a closer common life than ever in the past. West of the Tamar lay the smaller separate land of Cornwall, speaking its own tongue, but already more anglicized than Wales. Both Wales and Cornwall were destined to furnish a disproportionately large number of eminent subjects to the Tudor monarchy.

2

THE ESTABLISHMENT OF THE DYNASTY

HENRY TUDOR, Earl of Richmond, was the grandson of Owen Tudor, a Welsh gentleman who made a great marriage by taking to wife Catherine of France, the widowed queen of Henry V. The marriage was genealogically valueless to the Tudor family since it did not introduce the blood royal of England, but it did give them a prominence which Henry VI recognized when he created Owen's sons Edmund and Jasper Earls respectively of Richmond and Pembroke. Owen Tudor fought for Lancaster in the civil wars and was executed by the Yorkists in 1461. His son Edmund, the Earl of Richmond, had already died, but had first married a young girl named Margaret Beaufort, who was lineally descended from Edward III. One of that king's sons, John of Gaunt, and his mistress Catherine Swynford, had an illegitimate son known as John Beaufort. John of Gaunt subsequently legalized his union with Catherine Swynford and obtained an Act of Parliament declaring John Beaufort his legitimate offspring. Margaret Beaufort was the grand-daughter of this John Beaufort. She was married to Edmund Tudor, and on 28 January, 1457, three months after her husband's death and shortly before her own fourteenth birthday, she gave birth to Henry Tudor, destined to be King of England; so near a thing was it that the Tudor period ever came to pass. It may be added that she was twice married thereafter, but had no more children. Henry Tudor's English royal descent was therefore through his mother. In strict right it gave him no immediate claim to the throne in 1485, for the claim was hers, and she very much alive, a woman of forty-two in that fateful year, and destined to an active old age of piety and good works. One more fact is relevant to Henry's origins. The act legitimating the Beauforts had been passed under Richard II. His successor Henry IV, in confirming their rights by patent, inserted a clause excepting the right of succession to the throne. This clause was legally invalid, since letters patent did not override an act of Parliament; but it would obviously have been a talking-point for Henry's enemies if he should have emphasized too strongly his claim by descent. In fact he did not do so.

Until Henry Tudor was fourteen the chances of his being a candidate for the throne were remote, for the senior line of descent from John of Gaunt existed in the persons of King Henry VI and his son Prince Edward. In 1471, however, Edward was killed at Tewkesbury and Henry VI was murdered in London by the victorious Yorkists, in whose eyes young Henry Tudor at once acquired a new importance. It was advisable for him to leave the realm without delay. His uncle, Jasper Tudor, under whose care he had been brought up in Wales, sailed with him for France, but was driven by weather into a port of Brittany, whose Duke offered friendly hospitality. Brittany was then an independent country with only nominal subordination to the crown of France. But the power of France was growing, and the Duke of Brittany had no male heir. The future independence of the duchy was in peril, and Duke Francis may have reflected that the fourteen-year-old boy who had been cast on his shore might one day be in a position to show gratitude. Edward IV in England requested that Henry Tudor should be handed over to him, but the Duke did not comply.

So things remained until Edward IV died in 1483 and his brother Richard lost no time in seizing the throne and murdering the late king's two sons. The fact that Richard was a criminal usurper brought the Beaufort claim to life. A conspiracy to advance it failed in 1483 and cost the life of Henry's cousin the Duke of Buckingham. To co-operate with the movement Henry sailed from Brittany, but bad weather delayed him, so that only two of his fifteen ships got across the Channel; and when he sighted the English coast it was to learn that all was over and his friends dead or in flight. The failure in effect strengthened his position, for Buckingham was also a Beaufort and would have been no docile supporter, while a number of able men had declared themselves against Richard III. They were now refugees in France and Brittany, exiles intending to return as victors with Henry Tudor at their head. At Christmas 1483 he pledged himself to them that he would marry Edward IV's daughter Elizabeth of York and thus reconcile the factions of the civil wars and give peace to a reunited England. The Duke of Brittany gave his blessing and promised his aid.

In the end it was not from Brittany that they were to act. The Duke fell ill, and his ministers thought more of friendship with the existing than with the prospective King of England. In September 1484 Henry received warning that he was about to be given up to Richard III. In the nick of time he rode over the border into France, where the Regent Anne of Beaujeu promised him shelter. The Duke of Brittany recovered, regretted what had been done, and allowed Henry's friends to join him. Henry replied cordially, but remained in France. His adherents in exile numbered about three hundred men of middling or high standing. Their leaders were to be for the most part the ministers and councillors of his reign, and form a list worth noting: the Marquis of Dorset; the Earls of Oxford and Pembroke; John Morton, Bishop of Ely; Richard Fox, another churchman of great ability; and Reginald Bray, Edward Poynings, Richard Edgecumbe, Richard Guildford, and John Fortescue, all knights or soon to be knighted, together with Christopher Urswick, a trusty courier, who had brought from Morton in Flanders the warning that had enabled Henry to escape being given up to Richard III. With the exception of Dorset, who was a waverer, all these men were devoted heart and soul to Henry's service and remained in it to the end. They were not the usual hopeless *emigrés* of a lost cause. They were rather combatants who had made a tactical retreat and were bent on an early counterstroke. They maintained contact with numerous friends in England, where Buckingham's failure acted as a spur rather than a deterrent to a new effort to unseat the Yorkist usurper. The Regent of France and the boy king Charles VIII marked Henry as the coming man, and hoped by supporting him to lay the foundation of friendship with a powerful sovereign.

Henry Tudor was evidently a man whom men trusted. He was now twenty-eight, well educated in his Welsh boyhood by his uncle the Earl of Pembroke, not himself a scholar but appreciative of scholarship and all the arts, a good horseman devoted to hunting, and a soldier who fought with his head and made few mistakes in action. These were good qualities, but they would not alone have made him a great king after Bosworth Field, or even have enabled him to live to fight that battle. He was cool, humorous, and able to view things and men with detachment, wary and diplomatic, restrained by foresight of moves ahead, yet capable of instant decision and action, gifted with a financial sense surprising in one of his precarious way of life; and, above all, a man of his word. We may believe that when he committed himself to the adventure his main preoccupation was not, shall I win? but, how shall I proceed when I have won? This was the Henry Tudor of 1485. It is not, as will appear, an altogether just picture of the Henry VII of twenty years later.

The French lent him money, and he gathered a small expedition in the Seine estuary. Most of his 2,000 men were French, hastily enlisted in the Norman villages, although he had his faithful English and possibly a contingent of Scots, available by the good will of James III.[1] He was obliged to rely on gathering greater forces after landing, and wisely shaped his course for his native Wales. A quick passage with the ships of that time was a gamble on the weather. It was reasonably kind, and after a week at sea the expedition entered Milford Haven on the evening of 7 August. Richard III, who had seen what was coming although ignorant of the intended landing-place, was unable to intercept Henry. Richard had his royal ships in commission, but they were too few and too little organized as a fleet to counter an unlocalized threat of invasion. Richard gathered his land forces in the midlands in readiness to march against the enemy on whatever coast they might appear. Henry advanced through Wales to the Severn at Shrewsbury, and crossed into England without opposition. As Henry and Richard faced each other east and west, a northern force on the flank of either was a dominant factor. This force had been raised in Lancashire and Cheshire by Lord Stanley and his brother Sir William Stanley. The Stanleys were nominal Yorkists, but Henry expected their help, for Lord Stanley was his mother's third husband. Sir William Stanley visited Henry, but departed again. Lord Stanley had to be careful, since his son [2] was in Richard's camp, a hostage for the family's fidelity. The Stanleys therefore did not declare themselves, but hovered a little to the northward, while the chief combatants drew slowly nearer to battle.

The three armies at length converged at Bosworth Field in Leicestershire and fought on 22 August. Richard's force was the largest, but riddled with treachery. The Stanleys had disregarded his

[1] Agnes Conway, *Henry VII's Relations with Scotland and Ireland* (Cambridge, 1932), 5-7.
[2] By a wife previous to Margaret Beaufort.

orders and he had proclaimed them rebels. On the morning of the battle he ordered young Stanley's execution, but even in his own camp it was not carried out. Although now in contact with Henry, the Stanleys still did not place themselves under his command, and he attacked with only their assurance that they would support him in accordance with their own judgment. Sir William did strike in after Henry was hotly engaged, but Lord Stanley contented himself with watching a similarly inactive force on the other side under the Earl of Northumberland. This leader in fact betrayed Richard, who charged home in a fury of despair and was killed fighting. His crown was picked up on the field, and Lord Stanley placed it on Henry's head, while the victorious troops shouted 'King Henry!'

The Battle of Bosworth was decisive because it enabled Henry VII to show his talent for kingship. But it was the talent rather than the victory that opened a new passage in English history, and some troubled years were to elapse before that result should be apparent. To the men of 1485 Bosworth appeared as only one more battle in the long war of factions, and experience had proved that such victories were liable to be followed by defeat at no long interval. It was Henry's task to show his countrymen that all that was ended. He took up the task with mind prepared.

His method of securing the crown was important for the future, and a mistake might seriously have weakened his position. On the most favourable interpretation the Beaufort claim was not the best of the existing claims to the throne, since John of Gaunt, its originator, had been a younger son of Edward III, while the Yorkist line were the descendants of an elder son. There were two principal members of the House of York surviving, Elizabeth, the daughter of Edward IV, and the ten-year-old Earl of Warwick, son of Edward's brother the Duke of Clarence. But the kings of the House of Lancaster had been John of Gaunt's descendants, they had held the throne for over sixty years, and the Beauforts were their nearest surviving relatives. The Beaufort claim was therefore the Lancastrian claim, strong in history though weak in law. Henry did not argue it, but took the crown without argument, leaving men to choose whether he drew his right from John of Gaunt or the God of Battles, or from both. He had promised, and intended, to marry Elizabeth of York, which would satisfy many of the Yorkists. But he did not desire it to be said that he owed the throne to her, and so he deferred the marriage until he should first be fully acknowledged king in his own right. As for young Warwick, the new king seized him in Yorkshire and lodged him in the Tower.

Henry styled himself king from the date of Bosworth Field. Five days later he entered London amid general acclamations. At the end of October he was crowned by the Archbishop of Canterbury, and on 7 November he met his first Parliament. In the short interval since the victory he had established a well-chosen and hard-working Council in which his comrades in exile were prominent, and had taken a firm grasp of all branches of the administration. Considering the slowness of communications and the deaths of many prominent people in the first virulent outbreak of the sweating sickness,[1] it was rapid work. The Parliament reversed the attainders and forfeitures of many Lancastrians and attainted about thirty nobles and gentlemen who had fought on the losing side at Bosworth. Some of them, such as the Duke of Norfolk, had died on the field, and the object of the attainder was to place their lands at the King's disposal. By the standards of the age he was merciful. There were few of the executions that had always followed previous victories, and some of the forfeitures were afterwards remitted. Norfolk's son, the Earl of Surrey, also attainted, was pardoned and received into favour, to repay the King with faithful service and to win the battle of Flodden for his son. The above proceedings were preliminary to the main work of the session, which was threefold, to give the highest sanction to the King's accession, to provide him with revenue, and to begin the enforcement of the rule of law in a society which had become almost lawless.

The statute confirming the King's title was simple. Before it was passed, Henry made a speech claiming hereditary right. The measure itself adduced no hereditary claim, but enacted that the kingship should be with 'our now sovereign lord King Henry the VII' and should pass to the lawful heirs of his body and to none other. The Commons then granted to the King for life the duties known as tunnage and poundage, levied on imports and on certain exports. These were additional to the customs levied on the same trade, the customs being more ancient duties pertaining to the royal

---

[1] The sweating sickness was commonly said to have been introduced by Henry's French troops, but there is some evidence that it began before he landed. It reached London in September and killed two Lord Mayors in one week. It returned in four subsequent epidemics up to 1551, after which it was known no more. It was especially deadly to the well-living ruling classes.

prerogative and not subject to parliamentary grant. To describe all duties on commerce as the customs is convenient but inexact. Another statute empowered the King to resume, with some exceptions, all lands that had belonged to the Crown in 1455 but had since been granted away. The trade duties and the Crown lands provided the greater part of the normal revenue with which the King was expected to conduct his government in time of peace. Additional taxes might be granted by Parliament for warlike purposes, but as yet none was. The third purpose of the session, the strengthening of the law, was not effected by statute, but by a ceremony conducted by the King in person. He went to Westminster and administered to the Lords and Commons and to some other notables an oath that they would not aid criminals, keep retainers, give liveries or badges contrary to law, create riots or unlawful assemblies, or impede the execution of justice. No doubt some took the oath unwillingly and with silent reservations about keeping it. But its significance was great, for the news of it would be disseminated through the whole country when the members dispersed, and every subject would know what the King intended. Finally, the Lords and Commons together petitioned the King to marry Elizabeth of York, to which Henry answered that he was willing; and the Parliament was prorogued, in the following year to be dissolved.

In January 1486 Henry, already completely recognized as king, married the heiress of the Yorkist claim, having thus taken care that none could say that he owed his position in any part to her. Their mutual relations continued tranquil and presumably happy, with no recorded infidelities. The queen was the king's faithful and sensible wife, but hardly a great public figure. She bore him children and exercised little practical influence. The first child, Prince Arthur, was born eight months after the marriage.

Commercial policy was to be a dominant factor in the reign, and Henry's constructive mind was early at work upon it. Here he was at one with a people who were praying to be led. Half a century of national misfortune and unstable government had diminished English trade and shipping and transferred the greater part of the country's commerce to foreigners. No awakening to these evils was needed. They had long been recognized and discussed, but only a good government could abate them. England imported quantities of wine from Bordeaux, and the trade was falling into the hands of foreign carriers, whereas it seemed natural that English ships should conduct it. The Iceland fishery produced an appreciable proportion of the food supply, but a long quarrel with the King of Denmark, who owned Iceland, had reduced the English to the position of interlopers on its shores and hampered the exchange of English cloth for the dried and salted fish. Rich trade was being done with the Mediterranean, but almost all in Italian shipping, the occasional English venturers being penalized by discriminatory treatment. The cloth export to Flanders was not by any means a monopoly of the Merchants Adventurers, who complained that their Flemish rivals received greater government support. The activities of the Hanseatic League constituted an offence transcending all others. The League had almost driven English merchants out of the Baltic and Scandinavia. It fomented the Danish quarrel. Its ships were carriers of goods between England and Spain, England and Bordeaux, England and Flanders. The carrying trade (by foreigners) then and long afterwards excited English fury as something despicable and displeasing to heaven. But beyond this, the League was not triumphing in a fair field. It enjoyed excessive privileges which enabled its members to compete with Englishmen while paying lower duties than did the English themselves. Incredible as it may seem, a system of protection was in operation which protected foreigners against English competition in English ports. It was due to the generation of civil war. Edward IV had been expelled by the Lancastrians in 1470 and had come back next year with shipping and mercenaries supplied in part by the Hanseatic League. In repayment he had agreed in 1474 to the Treaty of Utrecht which gave the League its privileged position against his own subjects. Such treaties were liable to be repudiated, but the League knew that its sea power was strong and England's weak, and that its policy of promoting invasion and revolution could be tried again if need arose.

Such in outline was the situation that faced Henry VII, who knew that in default of remedy his reign would fail and he would fall. He had to expand the markets for the cloth export in order to create employment and profit. He had to transfer the export from foreign to English hands in order to satisfy his merchants. He had to build up a mercantile marine in order to provide naval defence by creating seamen, shipwrights, and shipyards. Only so could wealth grow and be enjoyed in safety. The measures which he was about to take were not for the most part original. They had been fitfully attempted before, but not persevered with. The doctrines of mercantilism were not a new gospel, but had long been agreed and desired, though not attained. In a country whose various regions were much isolated and in which there was no service of news and not even of posts, the general agreement on a mercantile policy may seem surprising. Parliament provides an explanation. For two or three months local leaders from all parts of the country were meeting, exchanging ideas, sharing information and urging action upon the King. Nearly all these men were interested in wool in one or other of its aspects, either as landowners, staplers, clothmakers, or cloth exporters. There was hardly a man in either house who did not draw part of his income from wool. Parliament was therefore a gathering of experts in England's predominant trade; and when the members went home to their counties they took with them information and ideas for the enlightenment of their neighbours.

In the shipping world the expansion of tonnage and employment of seamen could be promoted by a relatively simple policy which Henry adopted without delay. He revived and applied consistently a system of bounties to the owners of large ships. A merchant who built or acquired a vessel exceeding a specified burden received a remission of duties to a considerable amount on the goods shipped in her. At the same time he promoted in the Parliament of 1485–6 a Navigation Act requiring that Englishmen should not lade their goods in foreign ships when English ones were available, and decreeing that one entire and important trade should be reserved to English shipping. This was the Bordeaux trade. Henceforward Gascony wine and Toulouse woad were to be imported only in English, Irish, or Welsh ships with crews comprising more than 50 per cent of subjects of the King. The Navigation Act was of temporary application, but was subsequently made permanent by the Parliament of 1489.

Mercantile England awaited with interest the King's policy towards the Hanseatic League. He did not deal with this subject until the Navigation Act had been passed and Parliament dissolved. Then, in April 1486, he confirmed the existing Hanse privileges by letters patent. He must certainly have desired to repudiate the one-sided treaty which he had had no share in making, but he could not do it. The Hansa had ships, and Germany was the home of mercenary soldiers who could be hired for service anywhere. They had restored the Yorkists in 1471 and might try to do so again. England could not take the high hand with the League until she should have developed her own sea power. Nevertheless it was the ascendancy of the League that was stunting her sea power, and thus a dilemma was evident. Henry treated it by yielding nominal acquiescence to the Hanse privileges and at the same time utilizing every legal device to whittle them away. One such was the Navigation Act. The Hanse merchants quickly learned that it was of higher validity than a treaty or a patent, and that their carrying trade from Bordeaux must cease. At the same time a fruitful quibble was raised by the customs officers on the interpretation of *suae merces*, the phrase in the treaty describing the goods on which the League was to pay the lower duties. The Hanse merchants naturally claimed that it covered all the merchandise that they brought into England. Their opponents contended that *suae merces* meant only the wares produced in the Hanse cities, to the exclusion of those acquired elsewhere. This was another phase of the attack on the carrying trade. The *suae merces* controversy continued for decades.

After a winter of such occupations, Henry was obliged almost to take the field again, at any rate to take the road, by the disturbed state of the country, which required that he should show himself in as many directions as possible. The Yorkist party was by no means dead, and could not be, so long as the possession of valuable property was at stake. For a generation Yorkist partisans had grown rich on Lancastrian forfeitures and grants of crown land from the Yorkist kings. Now they were adjudged to give it all back, and their mood was pardonably combative. The surprising thing is that they did not make a greater fight of it; but there the King's central position, his swift methods, and his grasp of the administrative strings had a scattering effect. As the King travelled north in the early spring through Cambridge to Lincoln, an ill-managed movement developed against him. Francis, Lord Lovell, a survivor of Richard's army at Bosworth, gathered a force with which to challenge the King's entry into Yorkshire. At the same time the brothers Humphrey and Thomas Stafford, relatives of the late Duke of Buckingham, tried to raise the west midlands. Henry called out a sufficiency of his loyal subjects and advanced to York, whence his uncle, formerly Pembroke, but now Duke of Bedford, moved against Lovell's party. A promise of pardon caused them to disperse, and Lovell disappeared into some hiding-place from which he later escaped overseas. After due ceremonies at his northern capital, Henry turned south-westwards through Worcester, Hereford, and Gloucester to Bristol.

The Staffords also collapsed without a fight, and were made prisoners. Humphrey was executed and his brother pardoned. It was evident that the Yorkists had no hope unless they could get aid from without.

At Bristol, Henry was in the most progressive seaport of the country. It was a place of general trade and varied enterprise. From western France, Spain and Portugal, Ireland and Iceland, it imported wines, iron, sugar, hides, cattle, stockfish, salt fish, and such special products as dried fruits, oranges, Irish mantles, and brimstone from Icelandic volcanoes. It exported everywhere the cloth of the west country and distributed some of its imports in coastal shipping. Even so it was suffering from the depression caused by years of weak government. Its merchants entertained the King, and told him of decay of trade, losses by piracy, and the intrusions of foreign carriers. They were enterprising men, worthy of support. They already had business with the Canary Islands, only then in process of conquest by Spain, and with Madeira and the Azores, in the possession of Portugal. They had visions of island colonies of their own. In 1480 John Jay, a Bristol merchant, had sent out ships to look for the Island of Brasil, thought to lie west of Ireland. They had no success, but the attempts were continuing, or about to be continued. These men made an impression on the King, and throughout his reign he had a special care for Bristol interests. It was a kingly duty more congenial than coping with the feudal conspiracies that were to occupy so much of his time.

One of them was even now taking shape. It is commonly known as Lambert Simnel's rebellion, but the title gives a false emphasis. Lambert Simnel as a person is of little interest. He was merely a commonplace tool to be used for important ends, and the attempt to overthrow Henry VII would have taken place had Simnel never existed. The Yorkist leaders were determined on a serious push, rising of their party in England supported by as great a force as possible from overseas. To serve as an inspiration, a battle-standard in effect, they needed in their hands an alternative candidate for the throne, a prince of the House of York. Only one existed, the boy Earl of Warwick, and he was in the Tower. Two others had been in the Tower, the young sons of Edward IV, and they were dead. The fact that Richard III had murdered them was generally known, but no details had been published, and it might be just plausible to represent that one of them had been romantically preserved. Their bodies had not been seen and identified save by their actual slayers, who were keeping silence.

There was at Oxford a priest named Symonds who had as a pupil one Lambert Simnel, a joiner's son of promising intelligence. Symonds trained the boy to play a part. It is hardly credible that he should have done so without the instigation of powerful men, although no evidence of the origins of the plot has come to light. The part selected for Simnel was at first that of the murdered Richard, Duke of York, the younger son of Edward IV, who would have been twelve years old had he survived to 1486. But it seems to have been supposed that Henry VII would copy his predecessor's example by privily murdering the Earl of Warwick, and even that he had already done so; which would have made it difficult for him to expose a pretended Earl of Warwick without confessing his own guilt. The imposture was therefore altered, and Lambert Simnel was cast for the part of the Earl of Warwick, nephew of Edward IV and Richard III. The plot had three leading members who brought in many more. One of these was Lord Lovell, still lurking in England to the end of 1486. Another was John de la Pole, Earl of Lincoln, a Yorkist who had made his peace with Henry VII and had been received into his counsels. Lincoln's mother had been a sister of Edward IV, although this gave him no claim equal to that of the Earl of Warwick. The third was Margaret, the widowed Duchess of Burgundy, another sister of the Yorkist kings, a woman with an undying lust for vengeance upon the Tudor who had supplanted her family. Her dowager's court in the Netherlands was ever open to Henry's enemies. The Simnel scheme was early known in it, and may even have been hatched there. Henry's hold upon England was already such that a revolutionary movement could not get going within reach of his arm. The plotters therefore decided to make Ireland their place of assembly.

Before the end of 1486 the priest went over to Dublin with the boy Simnel. There were two Irelands, the coastal area of the four counties adjacent to Dublin, known as the English Pale; and the rest of the country, ruled in the main by chieftains descended from the Anglo-Norman adventurers of the twelfth century, Butlers, Fitz-geralds, and Burkes, who had become completely Irish in their affinities and way of life. Both the Pale and Celtic Ireland were Yorkist in sympathy, for the Duke of York, who had begun the English civil wars and had been beheaded in 1461, had ruled Ireland for several years as deputy for Henry VI. He had made himself popular, not least by a measure which declared Irishmen immune from writs issued in England, and the country revered his memory. Neither Edward IV nor Richard III had had much trouble in Ireland, and the Geraldine Earl of Kildare, whom they had made Lord Deputy, was retained in office by Henry VII. Most of the Irish notables, Kildare included, were therefore quite ready to support a Yorkist revolution. They accepted Lambert Simnel as the true Earl of Warwick and proclaimed him king; and they communicated with Margaret of Burgundy for the concentration of a joint military force for the invasion of England. Lord Lovell escaped out of England in January 1487, and went over to Margaret's court. A little later the Earl of Lincoln fled also to the Netherlands, to find the military preparations already in progress. Margaret had contracted with a German soldier of fortune named Martin Schwartz for a body of 2,000 experienced veterans. They collected sufficient shipping, quite possibly with the aid of the Hanseatic League, and at the beginning of May, Lincoln, Lovell, Schwartz, and the Germans landed in Dublin. Margaret and the English leaders knew without a doubt that Simnel was an impostor whom they could easily discard when he had served their purpose. The Irish lords seem to have believed in him. They crowned him as Edward VI, did homage to him, called a Parliament, struck coins and issued writs in his name. Waterford in the south held out for Henry VII, but for the moment he had lost all the rest of Ireland.

Henry had early knowledge of what was afoot. He arrested a few minor suspects, but failed to stop Lincoln. He distrusted the Queen's mother, the widow of Edward IV, and compelled her to retire into a religious house. He paraded the real Earl of Warwick through London in proof of the imposture. But in the main he had to wait. He had no naval force capable of intercepting his enemies at sea, and he could not take the risk of leaving England in order to attack them on Irish soil, since another force from the Netherlands might land on the east coast. The initiative was with them, and he could only gather an army and await their landing. Nottingham was his place of concentration, convenient for action towards any part of the western coasts.

The invaders might well have landed in the south-west, where Sir Henry Bodrigan, a turbulent Yorkist and sworn foe of Henry's councillor Sir Richard Edgecumbe, was ready to raise Cornwall in their behalf. They chose to make for Yorkshire, the home of their cause, and landed in Lancashire as the nearest way to it. Few joined them. Neither Irish nor Germans were popular in England, and it went against the stomachs of even the disaffected to receive a king at the hands of foreigners. Calculation was also against them. Henry's personality was already a factor. His imperturbable competence gave pause to hotheads.

The invaders did not risk an attack on York, but turned southwards to seek Henry on the Trent. They met him at Stoke, near Newark, on 16 June, 1487. The battle of Stoke was more bloody than Bosworth, but its details are almost all lost. The Irish fought with knives and spears and without armour, the Germans with their long pikes. They all stood to it bravely, but after three hours they broke under the shooting of the English archers and the pressure of the men-at-arms. Few of the Irish or the Germans escaped. Lincoln and Schwartz were killed, and Lovell was never found.[1] Lambert Simnel was captured. Henry was kind to the lad and made him a kitchen-boy and afterwards a falconer in his service, as good a living as if he had followed his father's trade and never been a king. He is known to have survived for nearly fifty years. Henry executed some of the more prominent among the disaffected, and imposed fines on a large number of the others.

The completeness of the victory discouraged such attempts for some years to come, and the King was able to pursue his constructive work for trade and public order, and to deal with some difficult questions of foreign policy. Before returning to London after Stoke Field, he sent Sir Richard Edgecumbe into Scotland to confirm friendship with James III by proposing a series of marriages between the House of Stuart and prominent Englishwomen. The policy ultimately bore fruit, but nothing came of it at the time, for James III was defeated and killed next year by a rebellion of nobles headed by his own son. The new king, James IV, was anti-English for the next decade, and the project of marriage-alliance had to wait. Henry called his second Parliament in the autumn of 1487. Its purpose was to pass attainders upon the principal Yorkists in the late rebellion, thus giving the King the disposal of their lands and fortunes. It also passed a measure which has been generally known as the Star

[1] Lovell's disappearance gave rise to stories that he escaped from the battle, and a body found in a secret chamber of one of his manor houses, in the eighteenth century was conjectured to be his.

Chamber Act, although it contained no mention of the Star Chamber.[1] The King's Council had long had jurisdiction in cases of political importance. What the new act did was to define and extend this work. The persons who were to compose the court were specified—the high officers of state, with a bishop and a peer and two judges—and the offences with which they were to deal were enumerated, those violations of law and order against which the King had made his members of Parliament take oath in 1485. The court was soon generally entitled the Star Chamber. It had also been occasionally so called before the act, which it is therefore untrue to represent as having created the Star Chamber either in name or in substance. The Star Chamber, like most of our institutions, was of slow growth from obscure origins. With Henry VII it entered its period of greatest usefulness. It could and frequently did take justice out of the hands of corrupt or intimidated local courts and administer it impartially with the weight of the King's authority. It curbed powerful men who could overawe justices of the peace or assize juries. It relieved and protected innumerable small men whose property had been seized by violence or corruptly sworn away from them. Its services were cheap and its methods swift, to the disgust of the men of the older law courts. It constituted a powerful engine of reform and contained possibilities of decline into an engine of tyranny.

In commercial policy the hostile attitude towards the Hanseatic League continued. The League deserved to be harshly treated for, while asserting its own privileges in England, it had not observed its promises to allow Englishmen free access to the Hanse ports, from which they had long been excluded. Henry's policy was to provide the Hanse merchants with sufficient grievance to make them willing to discuss the whole situation in a diet or conference. At such a diet he hoped to reopen the question of the treaty of 1474 and obtain a modification of its one-sided clauses. The customs officers therefore continued their ingenious interpretation of *suae merces*, English pirates captured Hanse ships and went unpunished, and public hatred of the Germans mounted so high that they could not walk safely in the streets of London. But these German traders had been hated for centuries and were used to it. They were tough nego-tiators, and when Henry brought them to a diet at Antwerp in 1491

---

[1] The words 'Star Chamber' occur only in an endorsement written long afterwards on a document reciting the act.

he obtained only a limited concession for English trade at Danzig at the price of renewing the whole treaty of 1474. Danzig, however, meant an opening into the Baltic, and the city was important as the mart for the naval materials, cables and cordage, tar and timber, which were known as Baltic stores and were indispensable to the fitting-out of ships in western Europe. At a later period, when the Tudor navy had become the first line of the national forces, we find a 'King's merchant' stationed at Danzig especially to buy for the fleet.

It was not only in England that the Hansa was unpopular. The King of Denmark, who also ruled Norway and Iceland, was equally under pressure from his overbearing neighbours, and responded gladly to overtures from England for the conclusion of the maritime war that had long been going on in northern waters. Henry sent a mission to Denmark which concluded a treaty in 1490. By this agreement Anglo-Danish friendship was re-established, and the English were given full facilities in the Iceland fishery and the right to hold premises of their own at the staple town of Bergen in Norway and in other ports. It was a new disappointment to the Hansa, which had profited from the English disabilities in Scandinavian trade. Danish goodwill meant also that English access to the Baltic would escape restriction in the bottleneck of the Sound.

The Mediterranean trade was another branch of business almost entirely in foreign hands. Although a few English adventurers had taken ships through the Straits of Gibraltar, their sailings were irregular and their trade unorganized. The Venetians, Genoese, and Florentines had almost all the business in their own hands. They brought to England spices from the Far East, purchased from Arab traders at Alexandria, textiles from the Middle East, currants and malmsey wines from the Greek islands, and superfine cloth, glass, armour, and other luxury goods manufactured in the cities of Italy, together with alum for the English cloth manufacture from some deposits owned by the Pope and then constituting the chief supply in Europe. The list of rich imports was paid for mainly by the export of English wool, an indispensable raw material for the Italian looms. The Italian merchants maintained business houses in London, but their shipping chiefly used the port of Southampton, which was safer for large vessels than the obstructed waters of the Thames estuary. Here came the Genoese carracks, and the Venetian galleys were regular visitors. The carracks were the largest sailing vessels then trading in Europe and were afterwards to give Henry VIII's ship-wrights the model for the great ships of his new Navy. The Venetian galleys were the largest oared vessels of their time, longer and narrower than the carracks, equipped with a sail-plan for use with fair winds and with long sweeps for progress at other times. They were not galleys of the kind used in Mediterranean warfare, but rather of the type afterwards known as galleasses, larger and stronger than the more nimble fighting galleys. They were also exceptional among merchantmen in being state-owned, and in keeping, by virtue of their oar-power, a fairly regular time-table like modern liners. Part of this fleet went on to the Netherlands while the remainder stopped at Southampton, and the whole was known as the Flanders Galleys.

The expenses of running this long-distance shipping, heavily armed and manned, were high, and the prices of the wares it carried were enormous. English merchants thought they could do better with their more economical private management, and Henry VII was prepared to back them. As a beginning a few English ships sailed to the Levant to lade malmsey at Chios and Candia, which were under Venetian control. In 1488 the Venetians imposed a discriminating duty against the English, to which Henry retaliated with an extra duty on Venetian-borne malmsey in England. Behind this was the whole principle of entry into or exclusion from the Mediterranean. In 1490 Henry approached Florence, a great cloth-weaving but not a great ship-owning city, with a proposal that the wool-supply for all Italy should be sent only to the Florentine port of Pisa and should be carried in English ships. Florence agreed, and consuls were appointed to be leaders of the English mercantile community in Pisa. The threat was sufficient, and the Venetians, fearing to see their wool-supply fall under the control of Florence, waived their opposition to English shipping in the Levant. The English trade was established, and continued lucrative until the mid-sixteenth century, when it was interrupted for a time by the growth of Turkish sea-power and piracy. This successful transaction was mainly of benefit to the merchants of London and was one among many of the factors that confirmed their loyalty to the Tudor government.

In the late fifteenth century a European states-system began to take shape with the consolidation of powerful monarchies in France and Spain. France recovered under Louis XI from the calamities of a century of Anglo-French war fought mainly on her soil. Louis carried out the first stage of the assertion of the authority of the crown over the great feudal nobles. He died in 1483, leaving his son Charles VIII a minor under the regency of an elder sister, Anne of Beaujeu. She was sufficiently skilful to tide over the minority without substantial loss of power by the crown. Spain had never been a single kingdom since the Moorish conquest. The royal authority in her two largest states was united in 1469 by the marriage of Ferdinand, King of Aragon, with Isabella, Queen of Castile, but either kingdom retained its separate system of government and administration. The Spanish sovereigns worked for consolidation against well-rooted local liberties and a turbulent nobility. France was more advanced than Spain towards the status of a strong and centralized monarchy, the future pattern for all the continent. The Germany of the Holy Roman Empire and the Italy of the city-republics, the papal states, and the kingdom of Naples, were at an earlier stage. Italy was destined to be conquered and partitioned without attaining any consolidation. In Germany the Habsburg emperors achieved some progress, which was to be arrested before the stage of united nationality was reached. Between Germany and France lay the remains of the fifteenth-century agglomeration formed by the Dukes of Burgundy, from the Netherlands through the Rhineland to Switzerland. These territories showed little power of cohesion. The Swiss established their separate independence. The rest were destined to be fought over by France and the Habsburgs for centuries to come.

England under Henry VII was interested in the process observable on the continent. The English already knew that their future depended on trade and sea-power, and that these would stand or fall by the fortunes of continental rivals. The pattern of diplomacy was shifting and complicated, and the objects sought by governments were many and various and of swiftly changing importance. To explain all the problems of Henry VII would be to write the international history of Europe in his time. In the years following his accession two demands seemed to him urgent, the preservation of Brittany from absorption by France, and the making of an enduring alliance with the united Spanish monarchy. He failed in dealing with the first, and succeeded in the second, which he considered the more important of the two.

Brittany was a highly maritime province, with numerous harbours, ships, and seamen. Its people were not, like the French, the traditional enemies of England. English and Bretons had sometimes fought side by side, they traded amicably, and between the Bretons and the western subjects of the English crown, the Cornishmen in particular, there was a sense of racial kinship and even a similarity of language which made mutual support seem natural.[1] Henry VII personally owed a debt of gratitude to Brittany, and he was not insensitive to such claims. The interests of England as a state would be prejudiced if France should acquire so large an accession of sea power, located at a point most threatening to England, fronting her Channel coast, flanking her southern trade routes. But Henry also owed gratitude to France, and in his personal views and tastes he was, as his contemporaries noted, a Francophile. France was quite determined to absorb Brittany, and almost the only means by which he could stop her would be a declaration of war. He knew how illimitable and unpredictable would be the extent of a hard-fought war with France. On personal and public grounds alike he could not consider it; the plan and purpose of his reign would be ruined. Yet he had to shape as though he would fight, whilst hoping to pull off a remote chance of success by the promotion of a state marriage. Brittany had at least an heiress.

The Anglo-Spanish alliance was a more hopeful undertaking. Both sides had real interests, permanent as well as temporary, in concluding it. The Spanish sovereigns were engaged in a final war to recover Granada, the southern province still remaining under Mohammedan rule. They were in sight of the end, after which Spain would be substantially united, with only the small Pyrenean kingdom of Navarre independent of them. Ferdinand was a man whose character resembled in some respects that of Henry VII, and whose tasks of curbing disorder and centralizing government were similar to his. Ferdinand foresaw that France might be the future enemy and ought to be prevented from growing too strong. He was mildly interested in preserving Brittany, and more immediately so in recovering the Pyrenean counties of Cerdagne and Roussillon, which had fallen into French hands in a period of Aragonese weakness. England was obviously capable of becoming a permanent ally against France. In addition there was an important Anglo-Spanish commerce that was worth fostering, with colonies of Spanish merchants in London and of English at Seville and its down-river

---

[1] See A. L. Rowse, *Tudor Cornwall* (1941), for details of the Breton-Cornish association in the fifteenth century. There were Breton settlers in the Cornish seaports, and a mutual acceptance unusual between peoples who were foreigners to one another.

port of San Lucar. Henry on his side desired Spanish aid in the Breton affair, and also something of much more enduring importance. He wished to secure for his new dynasty a status of recognition as one of the established European royal families. It could best be done by a marriage alliance. He had an infant son. The Spanish sovereigns had an infant daughter a few months older. An alliance with Spain, its permanence guaranteed by a contract for an ultimate marriage between the Prince of Wales and Catherine of Aragon, became the prime object of Henry's foreign policy.

The Breton affair remained active until 1491. The last Duke had no son, and was a sick man striving to preserve the inheritance for his daughter Anne. There was inevitably a French faction and a strong probability of French success. The Duke saw salvation in a powerful husband for his young daughter. Maximilian, son and successor-elect of the ageing Holy Roman Emperor Frederick III, was the chosen candidate. In 1486 Maximilian agreed to marry Anne of Brittany and preserve the duchy's independence. Maximilian, however, did little, being preoccupied by a struggle to assert his authority over the cities of Flanders. French infiltration into Brittany continued, and English adventurers, disavowed by Henry, went over to support the Duke. In 1488 the French party won a victory, and the Duke had to sign a treaty giving the King of France the control of Anne's marriage, shortly after which treaty the Duke died. Henry VII now offered mediation and at the same time raised money and men as a threat to France. Early in 1489 he made treaties of mutual assistance with Maximilian and with Brittany. He appeared to be very warlike, although there was no corresponding enthusiasm in England, not even for another bout with the ancient enemy.

Henry was giving everyone the impression that he meant action in order to further his main purpose, the alliance with Spain. He had already broached the marriage proposal to the Spanish sovereigns and they had agreed in principle. In 1489 he sent his envoys to Spain to conclude a comprehensive agreement. They landed in February, got to work on 12 March, and finished the whole negotiation on 27 March, quick work, considering that protracted and ungenerous haggling was the usual method even of friendly diplomatists. The Treaty of Medina del Campo was of first-class importance to the future of England, for it not only led to two royal marriages but founded an alliance which endured with some vicissitudes for eighty years, and contributed to English security amid unprecedented dangers such as the framers of the pact could not have foreseen. It was an example of the only kind of alliance worth making, that based on long-term mutual interests and the contribution of substantial services by either party.

The terms of the Treaty of Medina del Campo were as follows. The two powers promised to engage in mutual friendship and alliance, to protect one another's territories, and not to countenance or harbour any rebels against the other; to join in an eventual but not immediate war against France; to effect the marriage of the royal children when they should be old enough, with suitable stipulations about the princess's dowry; and to allow freedom of commerce and residence, each by the subjects of the other, in all their dominions, with safeguards against the increase of duties. 'All the dominions' included the Spanish colony of the Canary Islands, but nothing else outside Europe. Neither party foresaw the immense extension of the Spanish empire which was to begin with the first voyage of Christopher Columbus three years later. There were conditions about the making by either party of a separate peace with France which were more favourable to the Spanish sovereigns than to Henry. He was displeased at this and, although he had really gained most of his desires by the treaty, it is characteristic of him that he delayed his ratification for many months, whereas Ferdinand and Isabella had ratified on the day after the conclusion of the negotiations.

In 1489 there was some hard fighting between the English at Calais and the French who were upholding the Flemish resistance to Maximilian, but no war was yet declared; while English troops went over to Brittany, rather to establish themselves and watch events than to attempt a serious drive against the French. Meanwhile Maximilian deserted his friends by making a separate peace in order to further his Flemish aims, while the Spaniards showed signs of negotiating with France, and France sent ambassadors over to England. Everyone was hoping to score by chicanery, and no one was willing to fight. The play continued through the next year, 1490, at the close of which Maximilian, who had again taken a hand, was actually married by proxy to the Duchess of Brittany. It appeared to be a decisive event, but was not, for Maximilian never in fact saw his bride. The French moved into Brittany in sufficient force in 1491, defeated both the English and the Spanish contingents, and compelled the surrender of the Duchy. In December, 1491, exactly a year after her proxy marriage to Maximilian, the Duchess Anne was effectively married to Charles VIII of France and her territories united with his. The long Breton contest was over.

During the closing stages Henry had been making serious war preparations, and was not in a position to accept the accomplished fact and stand down. His third Parliament had met at the opening of 1489 and had granted war taxation to a considerable amount. The outcome was unpleasant. The returns from the whole country were not half the estimated yield, while in Yorkshire and Durham there was a minor rebellion against payment. The revolt cost the life of Henry's local deputy the Earl of Northumberland, and called the King north in person to suppress it. Parliament met for a second session at the end of 1489 and a third at the beginning of 1490, when it again voted substantial taxes. Henry collected the money and spent some of it on the forces in Brittany and Flanders, but let the season elapse without the large-scale invasion of France that was expected. In 1491 the same outline of events was repeated. It is possible that the King was serious in his warlike intentions but was waiting for Spanish aid, which he did not obtain.[1] With the consent of the Council he collected a benevolence during the summer, a levy on all persons of substance, as fairly assessed as was possible. In the autumn he called his fourth Parliament, gave it to understand that he would invade France in person, and again received a liberal grant. Next followed the total surrender of Brittany before the close of the year, and it might seem that the purpose of the war was at an end.

It was not. Henry, in his own mind, had already written off Brittany, and was about to fight for a financially advantageous peace or to gain it by a show of fighting. He did not take his subjects into his confidence, since any declaration of his policy would have frustrated it. The Parliament met again in January 1492, mainly in order to hear the King's detailed orders for raising a 'royal' force of invasion. He provided for the collection of fighting ships and a fleet of transports and for the levying of soldiers by commissions of array to chosen leaders. All were to concentrate at Portsmouth by mid-summer. The French reacted by demonstrations of an intention to invade England, but they were not in earnest. They did, however, disappoint Henry, who was looking for an offer of peace. After letting the summer pass he at length crossed the Channel at the beginning of October with a formidable army of 26,000 men. He

---

[1] See Gladys Temperley, *Henry VII* (1917), 104-6.

landed at Calais and laid siege to Boulogne. The town made a stout defence. Henry could very likely have taken it before winter, but he knew that this would not be the end but the real beginning of a great war. He elicited from his captains a statement of the difficulties of an autumn siege, a statement which in effect approved of negotiation for peace. The French were also anxious to conclude, for Charles VIII was already meditating the Italian adventure on which he was to embark eighteen months later, and was ready to buy peace on his northern front. So it all boiled down to a matter of money, as Henry had throughout intended. The negotiators met at Etaples and in four days concluded a treaty (3 November 1492). Its essence was that Charles agreed to pay in instalments a sum of approximately £150,000, an enormous amount for that time; and the war was ended. There was some disgust among the English lords and gentry who had spent largely in equipping their followers, with visions of plundering marches through France as in the great days of old. There was no doubt some cynical relief among the merchants and those with an interest in peace, tempered by a realization that the strong government they desired was becoming perhaps a little too strong. For that was the essential result. Henry had hitherto been almost as needy as his predecessors. He was now possessed of a financial surplus which was to increase steadily to the end of his reign and to make him unique among English rulers. It had all been done by patience and an accurate judgment of men.

3

HENRY VII'S CRUCIAL YEARS

THE character of Henry's reign was taking shape, and of its
shape he was to all appearance the sole architect. In all
transactions we have had to speak of the King doing this and
that, because, as contemporaries saw it and as history sees it, the
initiative was his. His deputies and envoys executed his instructions,
his councillors stood in the background. Yet it is possible that his
councillors had more influence than appears. Some of them were
men of exceptional ability, and it is reasonable to suppose that their
advice strengthened or modified the decisions that their master
made. The Council appears to have worked in the manner that has
been described as medieval, although there are well known medieval
exceptions to it, as a set of individuals giving their individual advice to
the King and separately undertaking such tasks as he allotted to them.

John Morton stands first among Henry's servants. He was an old
man when the reign began, and was over eighty when he died in
1500. Exceptional in that respect, he was great in the 'wisdom', the
practical knowledge of mankind, in which the King delighted. It
was generally agreed that in this he had no equal. Sir Thomas More,
who as a boy lived in his household, describes him as short in
stature, upright in bearing, amiable, gentle and earnest in conversation. To prove a man's wit and spirit he would engage him in a battle
of words and was pleased if he found him a worthy opponent, 'so
that therewith were not joined impudency'. He had a perfect
memory and a profound knowledge of the law. The King, adds
More, put much trust in his counsel, and the public also 'leaned unto
him'. A City chronicler, however, while admitting his wisdom and
his great services, says that 'he lived not without the great disdain
and great hatred of the commons of this land'. It seems that the
public associated him with the taxation and other financial exactions

which the King would allow none to escape, and that it was one of his services to bear the odium for these when in fact his counsel was for fiscal lenity. The story of 'Morton's Fork', the dilemma on which he was supposed to have impaled the contributors of the benevolence of 1491, was fastened on him over a century afterwards by Francis Bacon; but it was shown by Wilhelm Busch to have been a garbled version of an incident in which not Morton but Richard Fox was concerned. Morton was a Lancastrian and Bishop of Ely at the time of Buckingham's rebellion against Richard III. He escaped to Flanders, where he acted as the exchange for communications between the disaffected in England and Henry Tudor in Brittany. His work was indispensable to the success of Henry's Bosworth campaign. The King made him Lord Chancellor and Archbishop of Canterbury in 1486. The Pope made him a cardinal in 1493.

Sir Reginald Bray came next to Morton in the roll of the wise counsellors. He was described as a fervent lover of justice, but he had, like Morton, to bear some of the blame for the King's financial exactions. Henry's upbringing in foreign countries had not imbued him with the instinctive respect for the constitution which he might have had if he had been educated near the throne. Observers noted that he had leanings towards French (i.e. arbitrary) methods in government, and Morton and Bray more than any others of the Council strove to keep him in the right path. Bray moved in the background, content to serve and not to shine. One of his personal attainments was a taste for fine building. He was reputed to be the architect of Henry VII's Chapel at Westminster, but died in 1503 before its construction was far advanced. Richard Fox, Lord Privy Seal, held four bishoprics in succession, ending with Winchester. He also was a faithful counsellor, and was much employed in diplomatic work. He outlived the King by nearly twenty years. Sir William Stanley, Lord Chamberlain, was the only man of Henry's choice to turn out badly; and, from the circumstances of the opening years, it is possible that he was promoted rather from necessity than from judgment. Giles Daubeney, created Lord Daubeney, was one of the fighting men who had shared the exile in Brittany and France. The King employed his military talents on various occasions during the troubled early years of the reign. Sir Richard Edgecumbe and Sir Edward Poynings were two more men of action whose achievements will shortly be recorded. One other, neither an Englishman nor a member of the Council, may here be noticed, for he was in certain matters an adviser of the King. This was Roderigo Gondesalvi de Puebla, the resident Spanish ambassador in England. A permanent ambassador was then a novelty, and de Puebla was the first of any mark in our history. He was of somewhat lowly social standing, generally unpaid by his Spanish sovereigns, and chronically hard up. His detractors said that he lodged in a brothel and assiduously attended court for the sake of free meals, but he has found a modern defender who holds that he was a worthy and dignified figure.[1] Ferdinand and Isabella distrusted their representative, but found it worth while to continue him in office; for Henry evinced an apparent liking for the man, and occasionally told him things that were allowed to leak out in no other way. No doubt the King had his reasons, which may be evidenced by certain handsome payments to de Puebla recorded in the accounts of the Privy Purse. Henry and Ferdinand were the most astute monarchs of their time, and their use of penurious old de Puebla illustrates the sordid side of their diplomacy.

We take up the narrative in Ireland. The Earl of Kildare, an Irish nobleman of Yorkist promotion, continued in the office of Lord Deputy when Henry became King. In the Simnel rebellion his attitude was openly disloyal, and he took the lead in recognizing the pretender and launching his invasion of England. One of Kildare's kinsmen led the Irish contingent and perished with them in the battle of Stoke. It was time for Henry to reduce Ireland to obedience, but his means were scanty. Then and throughout the Tudor period the reduction of Ireland called for more money than any English government could afford. In itself it was a task not worth attempting, yet it had to be attempted on account of external factors; for unsubdued Ireland was the best base for a serious invasion of England. So, time after time, the Tudor sovereigns sent over their doughtiest servants to build castles out of sand, to bring a fighting country to allegiance with tiny handfuls of troops that could never make a permanent conquest. The military campaigns generally broke down at an early stage and were followed by negotiations designed to take advantage of disunion among the Irish leaders. In this game of statesmanship from a feeble hand Henry VII was more successful than might have been expected.

[1] Garrett Mattingley, 'The Reputation of Doctor de Puebla', in *English Historical Review*, Vol. lv (1940), p. 27.

In 1488 he sent over Sir Richard Edgecumbe with 500 men to secure the Irish ports and, if possible, the submission of the nobles. The ports, whose interests were in trade with England, were ready to obey the King, or rather to repudiate his enemies, if they saw hope of peace and quietness in doing so. Edgecumbe won them over, but achieved only a nominal success with the nobles. They took an oath of allegiance which sat lightly on their consciences, and Kildare remained Lord Deputy while refusing to obey Henry's command to come over to England and confer on Irish affairs. Everyone knew that Kildare was continued in office because it would have cost a war to unseat him.

So things remained until the prospect of an Anglo-French war revived the hopes of Yorkist partisans. As early as 1490 Yorkists in France were writing to their friends in England about a new move on behalf of the imprisoned Earl of Warwick. The unrest spread to Ireland, where some malcontents met at Cork. Opportunity placed a tool in their hands. A Breton ship entered the port, and in her crew was a handsome Flemish lad of seventeen, named Peter, Peterkin, or Perkin Warbeck. He was seen walking the streets in fine clothes as an advertisement of the wares the ship's merchant had to offer. The Yorkists noted him. Here was their Earl of Warwick. They asked him to impersonate the Earl and, by his own account, he refused, denying that he was of any exalted origin. They changed the plan and made him the Duke of York, one of the two young princes whom Richard III had murdered in the Tower. After long argument they overcame him and talked him against his will into accepting the part. The prime movers were not Kildare's noblemen, but a mayor of Cork and English Yorkists of the middle rank. Such is the ostensible story, and it may be true that Perkin Warbeck came in all innocence to Ireland without premeditation of conspiracy. Yet in other aspects the affair seems too coincidental for implicit belief, and it may well be that the plot originated in France, whence Warbeck was despatched for approval by the schemers at Cork. Once launched, the undertaking took a different course from that of the Simnel movement. Perkin Warbeck soon ceased to be a tool and became the genuine leader of his party. He developed into a daring adventurer, of high intelligence, ability, and charm of personality. He had a fatal weakness, which was to appear when the crisis came, but for five years he sustained the part of a serious candidate for Henry's throne, making half the statesmen of Europe believe that he was the veritable Duke of York, the missing son of Edward IV.

Before leaving Ireland Warbeck obtained the connivance of Kildare and the support of another chief, the Earl of Desmond, who opened communications on his behalf with James IV of Scotland. James IV was no friend to Henry VII, whom he regarded as an obstacle to the greater part which he desired Scotland to play in the affairs of Europe. The ill-will centred on the border stronghold of Berwick, held by the English, claimed as of ancient right by the Scots. James meant to have Berwick, a gateway of invasion in either direction by the east-coast route; and to further his ambitions he created a Scottish navy of good fighting ships supported by an auxiliary force built up as much by piracy as trade. James naturally saw possibilities in Perkin Warbeck, but they had to wait. The pretender's first destination was France. Charles VIII received him cordially and treated him as a prince, but did not unduly push him forward. Throughout the summer of 1492 the French kept Warbeck as a reserve in the diplomatic contest with England. When the contest ended in November with the Peace of Etaples, they discarded him and sent him out of the country. Charles VIII had cleared up his northern problems in readiness for a great adventure in Italy, and thenceforward wished for nothing but peace with Henry VII.

Perkin Warbeck betook himself to the Netherlands, where Margaret of Burgundy was ready to welcome another nephew delivered from the Tower. It is hardly likely that she believed in him, although she declared most positively that she did. If they ever had an interview without witnesses, their conversation would have been interesting to Henry VII. He on his part compiled a dossier of Warbeck's real origins and connections and sent it by the hands of an English mission to the Duchess. She answered acrimoniously, and diplomatic intercourse ceased. Margaret ruled only her own widow's portion of the provinces. Her step-daughter, now dead, had been married to Maximilian, King of the Romans, and their son was the Archduke Philip, a boy as yet under age, the true inheritor of the patrimony of the Dukes of Burgundy. Maximilian had many other concerns than the Netherlands, and we may regard their control at this time as shared between him and the Duchess Margaret. He considered himself injured by Henry's peace with France, and so also became a supporter of Warbeck.

Maximilian acted consistently as if he believed in the pretender's genuineness.

Warbeck in the Netherlands was even more of a menace to Henry than Warbeck in Ireland. The provinces were rich, and the *landsknechts* of Germany could always be had for pay, while the Hanseatic League with its formidable shipping had already reason to regard Henry as an enemy. Henry's necessity was to eject Warbeck as soon as possible. He could not do it by force of arms, but there were other means. The middle-class mercantile interest that ruled in the Flemish cities had no desire to foment revolution in England. The quarrel was dynastic and even personal, depending on the fact that Margaret and Maximilian had a feud with Henry Tudor. Henry therefore gave the mercantile interest a grievance against its overlords by causing an interruption of trade. After a summer of fruitless negotiation he struck in September 1493 with a prohibition of English trade with the subjects of the Archduke Philip, an expulsion of those subjects from England, and a transference of the Merchants Adventurers' cloth mart from Antwerp to Calais. The sale of English cloth to the Netherlands was thus suspended, and English merchants were hit, although they had some other markets for their wares. The cloth in question was woven but unfinished, not having been smoothed and dyed for the tailor's use. It was therefore raw material to the Flemish craftsmen and master-clothiers, and they had no alternative source of supply. Henry calculated that they would break before his men did, especially as the quarrel was not theirs. There has hardly ever been a more clear-cut and simple example of economic war.

The merchants of England gave Henry loyal support in spite of what it was costing them. They were, however, in no mood to tolerate any evasion of the arrest of trade by 'disordered persons' who might seek to dodge the prohibition. Persons obviously suspect were the members of the Hanseatic League, whose London factory, called the Steelyard, was obliged to deposit £20,000 as security that they would not trade illicitly. Suspicion mounted nevertheless, and a month after the beginning of the stoppage a mob of Londoners attacked the Steelyard. The Germans defended themselves stoutly, and the Lord Mayor came to the rescue after much damage had been done. He arrested eighty of the assailants, all of whom were released without serious punishment. The King never missed a chance of tacitly indicating his attitude towards the League.

The economic war needed time to be effective. Meanwhile Warbeck toured the Empire in the train of Maximilian, exhibited everywhere as the Duke of York and rightful King of England. His host brought him back to the Netherlands in 1494, where at Antwerp some loyal Englishmen tore down and trampled in the mud the royal insignia displayed outside the pretender's lodging. The fact that these demonstrators made their escape may indicate on which side lay the sympathies of the citizens.

Henry VII was keeping watch upon Yorkists and plotters in England, and determined at the same time to assert himself in Ireland, where the attitude of Kildare and his following was very unsatisfactory. In the summer of 1492, soon after Kildare had given countenance to Perkin Warbeck, the King suddenly dismissed the Earl from his office of Lord Deputy and appointed Irish opponents of his to that and other preferments. The stroke was evidently timed to coincide with some shift in the perpetual Irish feuds which placed Kildare at a disadvantage. He was unable to resist, and not only begged for the King's pardon but came to England in 1493 to seek it in person. Henry gave him hope and exerted his powers of diplomacy to obtain his permanent allegiance. Among these was a sense of the value of the practical joke in dealing with one who was really an undisciplined rustic. The King bade Kildare and his followers to a banquet and had their wine served by a cupbearer whose features they knew. It was Lambert Simnel, to whom they had once knelt as King Edward VI. For a moment their faces fell, and then an Irishman exploded in laughter, saying, 'So the wine be good, I will drink it!'—and the incident passed off with some suave prophecy by the King that one day they would crown apes in Ireland. Henry was less successful with Kildare at this stage than he had supposed. The Earl returned to Ireland apparently tamed, and soon came back to court for further pleading of his cause. He remained till late in 1494, but was to be guilty of yet another lapse before he became a loyal subject.

Before that stage should be reached there were to be reforms in the Irish government. In September 1494 the King appointed his second son Henry, a child of three, Lord Lieutenant of Ireland, and Sir Edward Poynings Lord Deputy. Trouble was brewing in Ulster, where the tribal chiefs were in communication with James IV, another possible invader of England in the cause of Perkin Warbeck. Poynings went over in October with 1,000 men and soon found, as others had done, that guerillas in their own country could be held down only by overwhelming force. The pardoned Kildare was with him and soon yielded to the intoxication of the native atmosphere. He intrigued with the rebels and wrote to the King of Scots. If Perkin Warbeck had been there the situation would have grown serious, but he was far away playing the king in Flanders. Poynings saw himself powerless for conquest. He arrested Kildare and split the rebel forces by friendly overtures. Ireland's strength was in irregular warfare, her weakness in the instability and mutual disloyalty of her chieftains. In December 1494 the Lord Deputy called an Irish Parliament at Drogheda. It passed the Statutes of Drogheda, the novel and long-enduring 'Poynings' Law'. By these measures all English laws were made valid in Ireland, the Irish Parliament was not to meet except on summons of the King and his Council in England, and no legislation was to be introduced in it without the previous approval of the same authority. These laws were destined to hold good for over two centuries and a half. In addition measures were passed for the defence of the Pale, the stoppage of livery and maintenance, and the tenure of important offices during the King's pleasure instead of for life. Not all of this proved effective, and the keeping of private armies was scarcely diminished. The Irish chiefs naturally abhorred Poynings' Law, but the people of the Pale regarded it as their safeguard.

Poynings shipped Kildare to England, to the Tower, and himself remained as Lord Deputy until the beginning of 1496. He grappled with the real problem, that of raising an Irish revenue sufficient to pay for an effective garrison. A good financial officer made a thorough survey of all the sources, and reported that they were inadequate. To hold Ireland by force the King must use English income. Henry made his decision, to return to the system of ruling through Irish leaders. He judged that Kildare had at last learnt his lesson, and he was right. In August 1496 the Earl passed from the Tower to Dublin as Lord Deputy, and held office without further offence for the rest of the King's reign.

When Maximilian returned with Warbeck to the Netherlands in 1494 it became evident that a push against Henry was soon to be made. Yorkists in England became expectant, and the prestige of the Emperor as patron of their cause led many to believe that at last they were going to win. A conspiracy was formed among ecclesiastics, the higher ranks of the gentry, and the middle-class malcontents, the common denominator no doubt being the forfeiture of family lands to the Tudor king. Sir William Stanley, a member of the royal Council and reputed the richest man in England, involved himself in it, a sign that he took its prospects seriously and was anxious to reinsure himself with the prospective Yorkist regime. Henry had efficient spies, one of whom was Sir Robert Clifford. This man had joined the conspiracy and gone over to Flanders, where he learned many secrets. Henry tempted him back with pardon and reward, to tell what he knew. Arrests were being made before his return at the close of 1494, and they continued after it. The most notable was that of Stanley, who was condemned for treason on Clifford's evidence and executed in February 1495, to the great advantage of the royal exchequer. His trial was public, and it is fairly certain that he was guilty. Other heads fell, and the English conspirators were neutralized before their foreign friends were ready to move.

The foreign friends, Margaret and Maximilian, regarded the affair as an investment. They supplied the pretender with ships and soldiers and exacted promises of great financial and territorial concessions in the event of success. At midsummer 1495 the expedition set sail and made for the coast of Kent, where the people were loyal to Henry and ready and alert. The local forces gathered at Deal as Warbeck's shipping anchored there. He behaved half-heartedly, sending 300 men ashore, but not landing in person to lead them. The men of Kent fell upon his three hundred, killed half of them, and captured the rest. The sheriff sent the prisoners to London. It was no time for clemency, and the King hanged most of them.

Perkin Warbeck tamely sailed away down Channel. He tried no further landing on English soil, but made for the comparative safety of Ireland. Part of his expeditionary force left him, and with the remainder he reached the Munster coast and joined his former friend the Earl of Desmond. Together they laid siege to the loyal town of Waterford. This was in July and August 1495, when Kildare was in the Tower and Poynings was still Lord Deputy. He took prompt measures and chased away the assailants of Waterford with further loss. Perkin Warbeck disappeared with a few ships, and was not located until two months later, when James IV received him with full honours in Scotland.

The failure of Warbeck's expedition made it possible to end the economic war with the Netherlands. English envoys went over at the close of 1495 to treat with the Archduke Philip, the heir of the

Dukes of Burgundy, while his father withdrew elsewhere. In February 1496 the parties signed the great treaty now known as the *Magnus Intercursus*, although it was not so called at the time. The arrest of trade had caused economic depression in the Flemish cities, and the government which rested on their prosperity had to relieve the situation. Liberty of trade by the merchants of both countries was restored, only the long-established duties were to be payable, mutual freedom of fishing in English and Flemish waters was recognized, and both sides were to put down piracy. All this was fair give and take, and some London merchants, expecting their King to turn the screw tighter, were disappointed. But Henry secured his political objects. Both governments agreed not to harbour or countenance any rebels against the other, and this provision was explicitly made applicable to the Duchess Margaret in the lands of her jurisdiction; so that thenceforward her teeth were drawn. The Emperor Maximilian was a consenting party, although the treaty was signed in the name of the Archduke Philip. The Merchants Adventurers duly returned to Antwerp, where the public received them with acclamation. The negotiators of the period were in the habit of easing their tasks by passing lightly over the details on which they could not agree and clothing the failure in ambiguous phrases. The financial and commercial provisions of the treaty thus left open points for dispute. Some of these were adjusted by supplementary treaties in 1497 and 1499. Others remained outstanding to a later date. But on the whole the *Magnus Intercursus* was an agreement of fundamental importance, governing in principle the resumptions of trade after later interruptions, and cited even in Anglo-Dutch negotiations in the seventeenth century, when the political position of the provinces had entirely changed.

Before concluding the story of the Warbeck pretendership, it is necessary to deal briefly with a development in the high politics of Europe which was to mould the international situation for more than half a century to come. Charles VIII of France, a romantic and adventurous but not a very able young sovereign, was determined to pursue a dynastic claim on the kingdom of Naples and thereby to achieve a French conquest of Italy. The desirability of delivering northern France from the likelihood of invasion while he was so engaged had moved him to agree to the Treaty of Etaples on terms very advantageous to Henry VII. In 1494 he led a powerful army into Italy and overran Naples with scarcely a blow struck. It proved to be only the beginning of an arduous struggle. The Pope, Alexander VI, and the north Italian powers of Venice and Milan, took alarm, as well they might. King Ferdinand saw a threat to Spanish interests in the growth of French power in the Mediterranean. Maximilian represented the ancient imperial pretensions to overlordship in Italy. All these combined early in 1495 in the Holy League, which pledged itself, in veiled language, to expel the French from Italy. The adhesion of Henry VII, with his ability to attack France from the north, was obviously desirable. He had no intention of attacking France, but the situation gave him the means of making his own profit from the necessities of the combatants. He played his hand cautiously while the continental war fluctuated. The north Italian powers threatened the French communications, and Charles VIII retreated from Naples in the summer of 1495, leaving part of his army behind him in garrisons. The Spaniards landed on the Neapolitan coast and captured most but not all of the French garrisons before the end of the year. In 1496 Charles was preparing a new expeditionary force to relieve the remnants and re-establish his conquest. Henry VII held the balance in the precarious position of contending princes, to whom loss of prestige seemed almost as dreadful in those days as loss of national independence seems to us to-day.

In Scotland James IV received Perkin Warbeck with open arms. He recognized the pretender as prospective King of England, married him to Lady Catherine Gordon, promised to assist him in open war, and demanded the cession of Berwick when victory should be achieved. The Scottish nobles and people were not enthusiastic, and the preparations for the adventure went slowly. A year elapsed before, in September 1496, an invading force of less than 2,000 men was ready to cross the border. No one supposed that such an army could conquer England, and the main reliance, that of all pretenders, was upon a rising of the English against their lawful King. Henry had taken his measures against it, and nothing of the kind was attempted. He had also good agents in Scotland, some of them in the very councils of James IV, and was well informed of the weakness of the undertaking. Meanwhile, Spain, anxious to smooth Henry's path to joining the Holy League, sent envoys to Scotland to dissuade James from his course and to talk of a marriage between James and a Spanish princess. At the same time the negotiations for the Anglo-Spanish royal marriage were resumed in earnest and entered upon their final stage. Henry, by simply being himself, an able and increasingly wealthy sovereign, in a position to fight but in no hurry to do so, was achieving his purposes and depriving Warbeck of effective aid. The long-heralded invasion from Scotland was all over in a week. James and Warbeck advanced a few miles across the border, perceived no vestige of English support, and retreated before the threat of 4,000 English troops marching from Carlisle. One of their performances had been the offer of £1,000 for the head of Henry VII, which must have amused him.

In the autumn of 1495 Henry had summoned a Parliament to assist him in dealing with 'the state of the country', which was still highly disorderly. It passed a variety of measures for improving the administration of the law. Justices of the peace were to notify the King's Council of riots. Assize judges were empowered to try offenders upon information, without commitment from lower courts which might have been corrupted. Poor persons complaining of wrong were to enjoy free legal aid. Persons accused were to be informed of the charges against them, and not fined in their absence due to ignorance. This Parliament also passed the well-known statute by which no man who obeyed the *de facto* sovereign could thereby incur the penalties of treason under his successor. Its explanation has been variously stated, and the advantage to the King does not appear to be unmixed. Possibly its origin was rather in his subjects' demand for insurance against troubles to come.

James IV's incursion was an act of war, and Henry was not inclined to pass it over, especially as Perkin Warbeck continued after it to be an honoured guest in Scotland. Immediately on receiving the news, Henry, without waiting for the formal election of a Parliament, summoned a great council of nobles and commoners and obtained from it a provisional grant of substantial taxation. This was confirmed by the legally elected Parliament which met in January 1497. The King's intention was in effect so to handle Scotland as to drive the pretender out of it, after which he would have no other friendly refuge.

The war taxation was payable in two instalments, in the middle and at the close of 1497. The collection of the first produced an unexpected and formidable rebellion in Cornwall, which made 1497 first the critical and then the triumphant year of the reign. The people of Cornwall were as conscious as the Welsh of their un-English nationality, they lived hard and poorly in their relatively barren peninsula, and their social structure and isolation made for a fusion of class-interests. There was no Cornish nobility, and the gentry had much the same political outlook as the farmers and seafarers. These Cornishmen were convinced that it was unjust to tax them for a war on the Scottish border. The war also was in one aspect a contest between Henry Tudor and Perkin Warbeck, a continuation of Lancaster versus York; and the Yorkists had been strong in Cornwall. But it was not as Yorkists that most of them rebelled. They did not proclaim that they would depose the King but that they would request him to dismiss his ministers, Morton and Bray, who were supposed to be the promoters of taxation. In the background was the recollection of the French war of 1492, which had served to fill the treasury and not to conquer the French. When the collection began, discontent was loud and general, awaiting only a leader. It found one in Michael Joseph, a smith mighty in muscle and courage, who took command of the men of his parish and was joined by the neighbouring ones until all Cornwall was up and ready. Local leaders, some of them gentlemen content to follow the smith, brought them together at Bodmin, where Thomas Flamank, a lawyer, clothed the movement with legality by telling them that the King was wrong to collect a tax without first using the feudal dues to which he was entitled for a Scottish war. It was Flamank who told them not to rebel against the King but against his false counsellors, and who enjoined them not to commit any pillage or damage against their fellow-subjects as they marched to London.

Flamank was a man of political acumen and Joseph an unselfish patriot. Together they turned their following into a sober and well-conducted army with a moral discipline surprising in an age of violence. They marched through Devon into Somerset, benevolently regarded by the people and collecting a few recruits. How they did it without pillage and without an organized supply service is unrecorded, but probably rich sympathizers provided them with food: it was midsummer, and east of the Tamar the countryside was fat. In Somerset Lord Audley joined them, with the blacksmith still in military command. Then they passed on through Wiltshire, Hampshire and Surrey to the edge of Kent. There Flamank expected strong support, for Kent had a tradition of popular risings; but the men of Kent were all for Henry Tudor, as they had shown two years before. The rebels turned north towards London.

Henry had strong military forces at command, although they were moving towards Scotland. He was taken by surprise, but he reacted in his usual ready fashion. The rebels were fighting men as all men were then. They had bows and blades, although little body armour, and a few pieces of artillery, taken perhaps from Cornish ships and coast defences. They lacked trained officers who had learnt to command in battle. The King had them, himself the best general in the country, Lord Daubeny, and the Earl of Oxford, who had fought at Bosworth and Stoke and seen many another campaign. The King had also the bigger army, in the proportion of nearly two to one. In these civil wars, however, numbers were deceptive, for they had often been neutralized by disloyalty. This time there was none.

The Cornishmen took post on Blackheath. The contemporary estimate of their numbers was 15,000, and may have been exaggerated. The King, by the same reckoning, had 25,000, consisting of Daubeny's troops called back from their movement towards Scotland, the militia of the home counties under their local leaders, and the citizens of London. The royal army poured over London Bridge and assembled in St. George's Fields, the King among them, inspiring them with his steady purpose. He meant the battle to be decisive and final. He sent Oxford round by the south to encircle the heath and block the roads of escape. Daubeny made the main attack from the westward across Deptford creek. Henry himself commanded the reserve with which to clinch matters. The Cornishmen on the heath knew that the game was up. They had intended their march as a demonstration rather than a revolution, and now the King had the initiative and called no parley. A good many deserted while yet there was time. Perhaps 9,000 stayed to fight it out. Even then this singular rising generated little hatred among these desperate men, or among their opponents. There was a sharp fight at the Deptford passage, and then Daubeny pressed forward to the heath. In a Cornish rally he was knocked down and captured, and released without hurt. Surrounded on all sides, the defence collapsed. About 200 of the Cornishmen were killed, very few of the King's. There was none of the evil massacre after victory which had stained the earlier wars. The common prisoners were dismissed for small ransoms to their personal captors, sometimes as little as a shilling. The three most prominent leaders were taken with the rest, and they had to suffer. Audley was beheaded on Tower Hill, Joseph and Flamank were hanged and mutilated at Tyburn. All others were pardoned by royal proclamation—pardoned as far as their lives were at stake, but not excused financial penalties.

Perkin Warbeck was still in Scotland when the Cornish insurrection took place. The Scottish king at once agreed with him to take advantage of Henry's difficulties, James to invade northern England, Warbeck to seek support in Ireland for a landing in Cornwall. Blackheath Field had already been fought before either was ready. James crossed the Border near Norham Castle, to which he laid siege. The Earl of Surrey advanced with a strong force to its relief, while a squadron of Henry's Navy, a new portent, sailed up the east coast. James retreated. Surrey followed, and carried out a sharp raid of south-eastern Scotland, with which James was unable to interfere. In the barren country and bad weather neither side could keep the field. A Spanish envoy, Pedro de Ayala, mediated a preliminary peace at the end of September, extended by a more permanent treaty signed in London in December; and James IV was out of the Warbeck adventure.

De Ayala had other tasks besides the making of this peace. Hard bargaining was going on about the Anglo-Spanish marriage, and the Spanish sovereigns decided that Warbeck in their keeping would be a useful counter. De Ayala tempted him to seek refuge in Spain and arranged that a Spanish merchantman should give him passage from Ireland. This was in July and August, when James IV was still actively at war; and it was therefore a betrayal of the Scot, besides being a somewhat sinister act of friendship towards Henry VII. It was in consonance with the diplomatic standards of the time, which may be likened to those of modern communism. In Ireland, however, Warbeck changed his mind, and nerved himself, after five years of postponement, to a decisive campaign. He opened communication with the disaffected in Cornwall and Devon. Inevitably this apprised Henry of his intention, for such things could not be hid. English ships patrolled the route from southern Ireland and actually boarded the vessel that carried Warbeck; but the master hid him in a cask and got him through. He landed in Cornwall on 7 September.

Within ten days he had a following of 8,000 men, most from Cornwall, some from Devon. They did not make the previous mistake of marching on London, but laid siege to Exeter, the fortified capital of the West. Its capture would have given Warbeck a strong position, although it would hardly have averted his fate; for the great mass of Englishmen, it is evident, were not for him. Exeter made a stout defence, while the trusty Daubeny advanced rapidly westwards and the King gathered overwhelming force to

follow. Perkin Warbeck raised the siege of Exeter and turned northwards into Somerset. A battle between him and Daubeny was
imminent, when the pretender's personal weakness averted bloodshed. He talked bravely to his troops to the last moment, and
deserted them secretly by night, riding for the south coast in the hope
of escaping overseas. All the ports were guarded, and he groped his
way as far as Beaulieu Abbey in the New Forest, where he surrendered on hope of pardon from the King. His wife, Catherine Gordon,
had been left behind at St. Michael's Mount. Henry treated her with
great kindness and sent her with an escort of ladies to the queen.
The disillusioned Cornishmen dispersed to their homes with curses
on cowardice. They had yet to learn more about their late commander, whom Henry brought westwards with him to Exeter.

As soon as he was confronted with Henry VII, Perkin Warbeck
made a full confession, acknowledging that he was not of noble
birth but the son of a Flemish waterman. He publicly repeated the
confession later in London. Henry treated him with generous
contempt and kept him in a confinement that was by no means
rigorous. All men of substance who had supported him, or had
failed to act against him, were severely fined, and it was some years
before they all paid off their arrears. Such was the contemporary view
of these matters that more executions and fewer financial penalties
would have been more popular. The people were used to bloodshed,
but they were beginning to say that the King was too fond of money.

Warbeck was an incurable optimist and was yet to get himself
hanged, but the back of armed insurrection was broken by the events
of 1497. That year was therefore the turning-point, as it was the
middle point, of the reign. For twelve years Henry had struggled and
prevailed against formidable forces, by his judgment, balance,
moderation, and speed of action. For twelve years more he was to
rule successfully, but less creditably, ageing rapidly, as men did then,
until his death was to evoke little regret from his people.

4

THE ACHIEVEMENT OF STABILITY

ALTHOUGH Henry VII worked to improve the old trades of England across the North Sea and with western and southern Europe, he was early acquainted with the fact that the ocean held possibilities of something new and revolutionary, which might yield a great addition to the wealth and sea power of the country that should achieve it. Two or three years after his accession there came to England a Genoese named Bartholomew Columbus on behalf of his brother Christopher, then an unsuccessful suppliant in Spain. Christopher Columbus proposed to lead ships westward across the Atlantic to Cathay, there to lade cargoes of the spices which were the world's richest merchandise and which the Venetians were then bringing from the Levant to Southampton. It is not clear why the negotiation with Columbus failed: we know only that Henry considered an agreement when it was too late and when Christopher Columbus had already concluded with Spain in 1492. There was shortly afterward, in England another projector, John Cabot the Venetian, proposing the same undertaking but seeking to achieve it in a somewhat different manner. The date of his appearance here is unknown, but was certainly not later than 1495. He settled at Bristol, whose merchants were more ready for exploring enterprise than those of any other port in the country.

There was nothing new in the idea of a westward passage to Asia. Europe had for centuries believed that the world held the three contiguous continents of Europe, Asia, and Africa, with possibly an unknown southern continent round the antarctic pole, and that all other lands were only islands of relatively small extent; and that these continents were disposed on the surface of a sphere. It was thus theoretically evident that a sea passage existed from the western coast of Europe to the eastern coast of Asia by a direct course along a parallel of latitude. Columbus and Cabot did not originate the theory. What they did was to bring forward arguments that the voyage was practically possible and that a ship of their period could make the westward passage to Asia and come back with a cargo of spices. The story that a learned commission in Spain answered Columbus that the earth was flat is fictitious. No learned men then believed that the earth was flat. What Columbus told the commissioners was that by his calculations the coast of Asia would be found where America actually exists, and what they told him was that Asia was much farther away than he supposed; and they were right and he was wrong. It was only the existence of the American continent, unknown to any of them, that gave him a subsequent vindication. Marco Polo and other medieval explorers had travelled east by land, but they had left no maps or accurate records of the distance traversed. Marco had spent many years in China and had written gorgeous accounts of its wealth and civilization, and he was especially eloquent about the adjacent island of Cipango or Japan, which he knew only by hearsay and placed in the tropics. Cipango, full of gold, gems, and spices, became the dream of adventurous merchants.

Columbus sailed in 1492 on a course west and a little south from the Canaries to the Bahamas. There he sighted his first new island and thence turned southward until he came upon the northern coast of Cuba. He assumed that Cuba was a great promontory of the mainland of Cathay, and so followed the coast eastward in order to round it. Off its eastern end he found the great island of Haiti, which he identified with Cipango and renamed Hispaniola. He returned to Spain in the belt of the westerly winds, in a higher latitude than that of the north-east trades which had taken him out. Columbus made his identifications of Cathay and Cipango only by ignoring some awkward facts, one of which was that the primitive savages dwelling there were obviously not the civilized orientals described by Marco Polo. Some of the Spaniards pondered these facts and were dissatisfied from an early date, but the Spanish sovereigns provisionally accepted Columbus's view.

John Cabot and the Bristol merchants did not admit that Columbus had found Cathay. The Bristol men must have learned the details in 1493–4, for they sailed their ships to the Andalusian ports where the discovery was common talk, and where numbers of

Englishmen were in residence. Cabot, a skilled geographer and a student of Marco Polo, was able to point out the discrepancies. His plan was to cross the ocean in English latitudes, in which, on the other side, he expected to find the nearest point of Asia. It would not be in the rich tropics, but from it he would follow the coast of the great continent until he came to the cities of Cathay and the island of Cipango. These, it is implicit in the argument, were beyond the lands of Columbus, which must be islands only part way across the ocean. The Bristol men hade made a preliminary discovery of a transatlantic country, which they named Brazil and located in what we should call Newfoundland or Nova Scotia.

How early the King came into the enterprise we do not know. He may have talked of discovery with the merchants when he visited Bristol in 1486. But in 1495 Henry was certainly interested, for his letters patent to Cabot, a document needing full deliberation, were issued in March 1496, before which date also de Puebla had reported the matter to the Spanish sovereigns. An English enterprise of Cathay was unwelcome to them, and Henry had no mind to break with them. But they were seeking his adhesion to the Holy League against France, and he skilfully interwove his oceanic purpose with the general bargaining which depended on his balance-holding position in European affairs. Knowing that Spain would take no active steps against him, he licensed Cabot and Bristol to do things quite at variance with the monopolistic privileges granted to Spain in the papal bulls of 1493. The royal grant was to John Cabot, his three sons, and their deputies, who were the Bristol merchants supporting the venture. They might sail east, north, or west and discover and occupy any lands previously unknown to Christians. They might monopolize the trade with their discoveries, paying the King one-fifth of the profits. They were to sail their ships only from and to the port of Bristol. The proviso about lands unknown to Christians was a prohibition against intrusion on the Spanish discoveries. The expected outcome was the transference of the spice trade from the old route through the Indian Ocean and the Levant to a much more economical route which would be an English monopoly.

Cabot sailed on 2 May, 1497, with a small ship and eighteen persons. His purpose on this voyage was not trade but the discovery of the way to Cathay. He crossed the ocean in English latitudes, in which he met with some unfavourable winds. On 24 June he made his landfall, perhaps on the coast of Newfoundland but more probably on that of Nova Scotia. He coasted south and west for

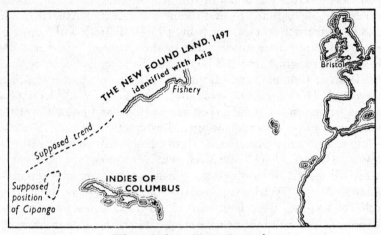

1. The Atlantic as seen by John Cabot in 1497-8

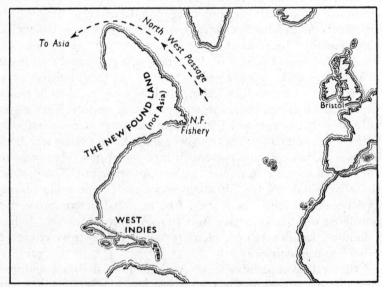

2. The Atlantic as seen by Sebastian Cabot after 1509

some distance, far enough to be certain that he had discovered a continent. Either going or returning he was on the banks of New-foundland, where he observed that the cod were so numerous as to constitute a richer fishery than that of Iceland. He was back at Bristol on 6 August and in London by the 10th. He asserted positively that he had reached the mainland of Asia, and it was the obvious inter-pretation. He had only to go again with a trading fleet, follow his coast west and south as he had found it trending, and attain the tropical Cathay and Cipango well to the west of the Spanish dis-coveries. The King was pleased and the public was enthusiastic. Then came a check occasioned by the landing of Perkin Warbeck and the final campaign in the west country. By December all was finished, peace was made with Scotland, and the King was again in London ready to take up the plan of Cathay. Henry made no concealment and allowed all to be discussed publicly. Spain was suspicious, and a Spanish envoy wrote to his sovereigns that he had seen Cabot's charts, which were false, and that what the English were seeking already belonged to Spain—'the cape which fell to your highnesses', an evident allusion to Cuba and what Columbus claimed for it.

By the spring of 1498 Ferdinand was more anxious than ever for Henry's co-operation against France, and it was therefore safe to disregard the protest and proceed with the adventure. Cabot sailed again with five ships laden by the merchants of London and Bristol. We know little of this voyage by direct evidence save that John Cabot himself was missing and never returned.[1] On circumstantial evidence it is reasonably clear that some of the ships reached the continent and coasted for some distance southwards. So much a Spanish map indicates, and the sovereigns were so much alarmed at the prospect of English intrusion in the tropics that they gave orders to their own pioneers in the Caribbean to discover as much as possible in anticipation. What the 1498 expedition did in detail is unknown. That it made an important negative discovery may be inferred; for in coasting southwards along the American shore, the English must have looked for the civilization of China and found only the savagery of the red men. There were no spices and nothing else of value. Commercially the expedition was so complete a failure that its return passed unrecorded. Geographically it may have done first-class work by discovering that the great mainland was not that

---

1 Denys Hay, 'The Angelica Historia of Polydore Vergil', Camden Series, vol. lxxiv, pp. ix - xi.

of Cathay but a continent hitherto unsuspected. America had been discovered in 1497, but its recognition as something new may well date from the voyage of 1498. This, however, is inference from facts that are ill recorded. English documents in subsequent years alluded often to 'the New Found Land', but never said that it was believed to be Cathay, as Cabot had so confidently claimed in 1497.

Meanwhile the King had more to think about than a speculation that had failed. He was gathering in the fruits of his diplomacy and of the overthrow of the Warbeck faction. He had already in 1496 nominally joined the Holy League, with a proviso that membership should not oblige him to go to war. It was an empty adherence that fell short of Spain's desires and continued Henry in his dominant position; for Spain sought above all things the liquidation of French claims in Italy. The royal children, Arthur and Catherine, were now ten years of age, and the marriage negotiations were resumed with a not too distant end in view and with Henry more able than the Spanish sovereigns to dictate the terms. So the position continued. In 1496 the details of the marriage settlement were arranged in a new treaty, which Henry refrained from ratifying until ten months had passed. A formal betrothal followed, and then the ratification of the treaty by the Spanish sovereigns in 1498. In the spring of that year Charles VIII of France died without issue. His cousin and successor Louis XII revived the Italian threat in a new form by asserting a claim to the Duchy of Milan. To clear the way for acquiring it he signed a peace with Ferdinand and informally undertook to cede half his Neapolitan claim by a partition. Henry at once demanded and obtained the renewal of the Treaty of Etaples with its guarantees of money payments by France. An uneasy peace prevailed, evidently unstable, because a French success in northern Italy would revive the rivalries not only with Spain but with the Emperor Maximilian. The English king could look on with comparative detachment and seek his profit.

After his capture Perkin Warbeck was kept in a very open arrest, with a lodging in the royal palace and a horse allotted for his exercise. In 1498 he suddenly made off, in an attempt to get out of the country. The ports were at once warned, and he was soon caught. Once again the King spared his life, but placed him in rigorous imprisonment in the Tower. The role of pretender was apparently so fascinating as to discount the risks of assuming it. At the end of the year yet another appeared, a young man named Ralph Wilford, who asserted that he was the Earl of Warwick. Some kind of conspiracy gathered round him, but the details are obscure, and he was captured before it had gone far. This time there was no mercy, and Wilford was hanged. The affair may have been more serious than we know. It seems to have brought the King to a terrible decision. The unfortunate Warwick, an innocent prisoner since the age of ten, was a standing danger to the throne. Nothing but his death, publicly effected, could dispose of it. So Henry seems to have decided, not without a struggle that set its mark on him. De Ayala wrote in the spring of 1499 that he had aged twenty years in a fortnight. The reason for his disquiet is, of course, only a matter of inference, and may have been quite other than that supposed. But the summer witnessed a tragic plot in the Tower.

Perkin Warbeck was soon intriguing with warders and, apparently, with outsiders who had access to him. He was so lodged that he could communicate with the Earl of Warwick. A few others, all obscure persons, are named as members of the conspiracy. This handful agreed that they would fire the Tower, seize the money it contained, and raise a rebellion, or at least give opportunity for Warbeck and Warwick to escape overseas. Poor Warwick, his wits weakened by long confinement, became their tool. Authority had been watching them, and, as soon as the evidence was complete, all were pounced upon. In November 1499 their public trials took place, that of Warbeck at Whitehall, that of Warwick before a court of more than twenty peers in Westminster Hall. Perkin Warbeck was hanged at Tyburn; the Earl of Warwick, to the sorrow of the people, was beheaded on Tower Hill. Ostensibly it was just retribution for a dangerous treason, but few thought so. It was said, but proof is lacking, that Henry yielded to pressure from the Spaniards, whose interest it was to dispose of Warwick before the marriage. Catherine of Aragon herself may have believed it, for she exclaimed long afterwards that her marriage was made in blood. The responsibility lay upon Henry, who may indeed have taken advantage of a foolish escapade instead of actually procuring it, but who knew that his prisoner was morally innocent.

After further protracted haggling and accidental delays, the Spanish marriage was at length effected. Catherine of Aragon landed at Plymouth in October 1501 and was married to Arthur on the 15th of that month. England received her with enthusiasm. She was a girl of fifteen, and she was to grow into a woman of courage, kindliness, and dignity, who never lost the popularity with which she began her English career. The marriage was short-lived, for Arthur died suddenly in 1502. His girl-widow remained in England. His brother Henry, born in 1491, became heir to the throne. It was expected that the Anglo-Spanish alliance would be cemented in due time by the procurement of a papal dispensation for him to marry Catherine. For the present he was too young, and in subsequent years Henry VII found reasons for delaying the match in order to profit by the suspense, all the while keeping his daughter-in-law in England.

Meanwhile another marriage, of even greater historical effect, was being made. The end of the Warbeck adventure removed a cause of quarrel with the King of Scots. In 1499 negotiations began for his marriage with Henry's daughter Margaret, which duly took place in August 1502. It was not a happy marriage, for James IV was something of a libertine and much older than his fifteen-years-old bride, neither was he reconciled to perpetual peace with England. But it did result a century later in the accession of James VI, King of Scots, descendant of Tudor and Stewart, to the throne of England.

For Henry VII, although politically the times were good, they brought heavy personal losses. His son had died in 1502. Less than a year afterwards his wife died. Elizabeth of York had wielded no political power, but she was well liked, and perhaps had a good influence on the King. Certainly his character grew harsher thenceforward, and he seemed to lose some of his talent of good leadership, although not of domination. Of their seven children four died young, leaving Henry, Margaret, and a younger daughter Mary to grow up. Old Cardinal Morton died in 1500, and Sir Reginald Bray in 1503. The quality of the reign was passing.

The failure to reach Cathay in 1498 did not deter Bristol from further enterprise. The Portuguese colonists of the Azores were interested in discovery and were also engaged in trade with Bristol. Three Azorean captains came to England in 1500–1 and concerted an exploring and colonizing project with the Bristol merchants. In 1501 and 1502 the King issued two patents to the Bristol combination, giving ample licence to discover, colonize, and monopolize trade. In the second of the patents the proviso that had limited the adventurers to lands unknown to Christians was omitted. The whole field of enterprise was thrown open to them, and many detailed clauses elaborated their rights to conquer and found colonies, to rule the King's subjects therein and to expel foreigners, and to trade with special and exclusive privilege. It reads like the plan for a colonial empire. The patentees became known as the Company Adventurers to the New Found Land, and that title yields the only clue we have to the locality of their operations.[1] What they achieved and exactly where they worked are unknown. They were active until 1505 and perhaps to a later date. There are indications that they did found a colony somewhere, and that they sailed both north and south on the American coast. Their earlier proceedings evidently promised success and pleased the King, for he granted money rewards to the Bristol men and pensions to two of the Azoreans for 'the true service which they have done unto us to our singular pleasure as captains into the New Found Land'. Then, after 1505–6, the records fall silent, the last being that of a lawsuit between members of the company. What their captains and colonists did can only be guessed: fishing, no doubt, for Newfoundland cod; fur-trading perhaps; seeking probably for the North West Passage to Asia, which became a project as soon as it was realized that the new land was a barrier on the road to Asia. We cannot say positively that it was so realized by 1505, although almost certainly it was. By 1509, as will be shown, there was to be no doubt of the fact. Hugh Elyot and Robert Thorne were the most prominent of the Bristol men, and their names ought to be remembered.

Other pioneers, of a different kind, were working in this period, with effects that were to be momentous. Throughout the Middle Ages English scholars had travelled south in search of learning, and the Renaissance after the dark times had long been in progress. In the reign of Henry VII the scholars found in Italy a new emphasis on what came to be called humanism, a keen and even rapturous appreciation of the art and letters of the ancient world, an enlargement of the scope of study, and a change in its aims and methods. Hence came a revolution in mental attitudes, and an enlightenment of the hard businesslike ability characteristic of the period after the Black Death with a wider care for the things of the mind and conscience and the graces of living. The newer humanism was not concerned only with the glories of writing, sound, and visual art. It turned to the religion which was the background and the envelopment of all men's lives. It realized that long-founded doctrines and practices were of questionable historical validity and that the familiar Latin texts of the scriptures were inaccurate and sometimes

---

[1] The term 'New Found Land' was then applied to the whole coast of North America.

misleading. To learn Greek and to study the sources of Christianity in versions as near as could be attained to the originals became the life-work of men who saw the corruption of the existing Church of Christendom. Many years before the Reformation came to mean revolt against the Church, these reformers sought to restore her purity from within. In England the reforming movement was specifically known as the New Learning, humanist indeed, but ardently religious.

Oxford produced the most notable English scholars of Henry VII's reign, as Cambridge was to do in that of his son. William Grocyn did much to further the study of Greek. John Colet combined scholarship with critical ability and broad-minded piety. While London in 1497–8 was enthusiastic for Cabot and Cathay, Oxford was listening to Colet's lectures on the epistles of St. Paul, which urged exact study of the scriptures through the original languages and contrasted the life of the early church with that of the money-getting fraternity who stood for 'the Church' in contemporary Europe. Thomas Linacre went also to Italy to read Greek texts, but his special study was of medicine, and his work in England led to the foundation of the Royal College of Physicians and the beginning of scientific treatment. Younger than these men was Thomas More, whose mind was intent on all learning and whose sympathy and practical humanism made him the centre of a circle of like-minded friends. Although intensely devoted to religion and reform, More remained a layman and became a lawyer. He sat in Henry VII's last Parliament and made himself prominent by fearless opposition to a royal demand. These are only the more prominent names in a movement of national importance. No one in Henry's reign foresaw how great that importance would become. The Church was being constructively criticized, as it had often been before, by some of its most devout members. It was not being attacked by heretics who wished to overthrow it. Yet there was one more man whom we must mention, of the same loyal and critical type, who was to provide high explosive for the use of future assailants—Erasmus of Rotterdam, whom it is an understatement to describe as a Dutchman, since he was a European at home in any land of Christendom. Erasmus was twice in England in Henry VII's reign, well known to all the scholars and their patrons, to the King's counsellors and the King himself. He was an ardent and outspoken reformer, favourably received by William Warham, Morton's successor as Archbishop of Canterbury, and by all men of leading in church and state. His greatest work, in historical effect, was to come after the reign had closed. Henry and his mother, the Lady Margaret commemorated in professorships, were good friends to both Oxford and Cambridge, as to all other well-doing institutions in the realm.

It is well known that Henry in his later years became rapacious in seizing the wealth of his subjects on unjust grounds, and that Edmund Dudley and Sir Richard Empson were his most prominent agents in the process. Henry's rapacity should be understood. If he was grasping on grounds of state policy, he was not miserly. He was convinced that to secure the peace and prosperity of his kingdom it was better that the state—which meant himself—should be rich and aloof rather than that it should be bellicose and consequently needy. In all aspects of affairs, diplomatic, military, and financial, his policy was one, that of the card in hand, never played until it should be absolutely necessary. A naval phrase of later times, 'the fleet in being', its mere existence a check on the enemy's plans, illustrates the King's attitude. He kept himself 'in being', rich and formidable, and stood unscathed in a troublesome world of competitors who were prone to fight with inadequate means for unnecessary ends. It was the essence of the wisdom for which the world admired him, the wisdom not of an ambitious conqueror but of a man content with his own and determined to hold it. He was no miser. He could spend with profusion when the occasion demanded it, as sometimes he judged it did. The wedding of Catherine and Arthur was such an occasion, when the King's money flowed like water; and there were others also. He was generous, too, within reason, to good causes, and to those, sometimes humble people, who served him well.

When we consider the means by which he made the state rich the picture is less pleasant. His first great coup, the foundation of his wealth, had been the sham fight with France leading to the Treaty of Etaples in 1492. There was little moral guilt in that, although it left an unpleasant taste in the mouths of those who had expected a jolly passage of plunder and rapine. Then came his humanity towards the rebels of 1497, for which they had to pay in swingeing fines and confiscations: some would have preferred to see some open-handed bloodshed in lieu of it. At the same time a much more sinister financial method became evident. The England of his time thoroughly disliked taxation by grant of Parliament, however much the England of later times regarded it as the keystone of liberty. Henry found it expedient to pursue the policy now known as soaking the rich, the individual rich being his victims, although the rich as a class felt themselves always within the scope of his vigilance. The Act of 1495, which enabled judges to try men on information without previous presentment by a grand jury, was his instrument. Whether it was designed to that end is not clear. There were numerous statutes, commonly dormant for the most part, against which almost all men of substance were technical offenders. Some, no doubt, were scarcely aware of their delinquency, and would never have been sent by the county justices to answer for it in a higher court. Informers were now invited to denounce such offenders and responded with alacrity, until informing became an undesirable new profession. Empson and Dudley were its organizers, skilled in the law, heartless and greedy, growing ever bolder under shelter of the King's favour. Empson seems to have been the senior in service, and Dudley did not become prominent until 1501. He was then about thirty, and in the next few years made a great fortune. He was much hated, but may not have been altogether as black as he was painted, or as Empson undoubtedly was.[1] Their importance developed rapidly from the middle years of the reign, in conformity with that ill-development in the King's character of which signs became apparent.

Tyrannical prosecutions with the purpose of extorting money were sufficiently numerous to make Empson and Dudley hated by the propertied classes. We should, however, beware of exaggeration, for they were not numerous enough to alienate the support of those classes from the King. The squires and burgesses knew very well that he was a good king to them and to the interests on which they throve, and he knew that they were the supports of his throne. A few very flagrant cases are known, but of how many others they were representative is not known. First, it may be mentioned that the oft-told tale of the Earl of Oxford being fined £10,000 for parading retainers before the King is possibly fictitious. It was narrated by Bacon, and there is no contemporary evidence to support it. Bacon repeated a tradition, but such traditional stories very easily arise without the least foundation in truth; and in Oxford's case the probabilities are against it. One of the first attested cases was that of Sir William Capel, a London alderman, who was fined £1,600 in

[1] See 'Edmund Dudley' by D. M. Brodie, *Royal Hist. Soc. Transactions*, 4th ser. vol. xv, 1932.

1495 for infringing trade regulations, and was again in trouble after he had been Lord Mayor in 1503–4, when he was once more fined a heavy sum. Two other Lord Mayors, Thomas Kneysworth (1505–6) and Sir Lawrence Aylmer (1507–8), were thrown into prison pending the payment of large fines for irregularities in their exercise of office. A very vindictive prosecution beginning in 1499 ruined Sir Robert Plumpton, a Yorkshire landowner, mainly, it appears, for the private benefit of Empson, although the King knew what was going on. Many men incurred fines which they were unable to pay at once and discharged by instalments spread over years. About fifty of these uncompleted payments were outstanding at the King's death, and all these fifty exactions were sufficiently unjust to be remitted by the new sovereign. The degeneration of the King's morality is evident, an example of the corruption of power. By the middle of his reign he would seem to have been wealthy enough for his security, but reasonable prudence then broke down into morbid fears, fear that some new crisis would empty the treasury, fear of the unruliness of 'over-mighty' men among his subjects. Meanwhile his genuine reforms in law and finance continued to yield better times to all but the most conspicuous.

The only political menace of the later period was the Earl of Suffolk, and he was never as dangerous as Perkin Warbeck. Suffolk was the brother of the Earl of Lincoln who had been killed at Stoke, and inherited the Plantagenet blood of his mother, a sister of Edward IV. He was discontented at the loss of some of the family estates by forfeiture for treason, and fled overseas in 1499. He was tempted back by promises of the King's favour, but fled again in 1501 as the leader of a Yorkist movement which could only gather strength beyond the reach of Henry's arm. The Emperor Maximilian, always Henry's enemy, received Suffolk and made him some promises of aid. Taught, however, by the Warbeck fiasco, Maximilian did not exhibit his guest about Europe as the rightful king of England, but kept him inconspicuously in the background, with a residence in the imperial city of Aix-la-Chapelle. Henry arrested Suffolk's fellow-conspirators in England and kept watch by means of spies on the small party at Aix. He offered money to Maximilian for the surrender of Suffolk, but failed to obtain it. Suffolk remained a potential but not an immediate danger, and his ultimate fate was bound up with the course of general diplomacy, in which he was never more than a counter.

Maximilian's son, the Archduke Philip, was now a grown man and through Mary of Burgundy, his mother, the effective ruler of the Netherland provinces. He was married to Juana, daughter of Ferdinand and Isabella, and was the father of a boy born in 1500 and destined to be the great Emperor Charles V. Juana, being older than Catherine of Aragon, was the prospective heiress of her parents in both Aragon and Castile; and her husband, who controlled the Low Countries and might one day control all Spain, was an object of diplomatic interest to Henry VII. Already Henry and Philip had met at Calais in 1500 to discuss marriage projects and the amendment of the commercial treaty of 1496, but no great results had ensued. In 1504 Queen Isabella died, and Juana became rightful Queen of Castile. She was not quite sane, and was incapable of governing. A contest at once developed between her husband Philip and her father Ferdinand for the rule of Castile. Ferdinand was on the spot and long established as a Spanish king; but Castile and Aragon were by no means united, and popular sentiment in Castile gave Philip an opening to challenge his father-in-law. Henry VII looked on, having, as usual, a masterly position in relation to both parties, marred only by the existence of Suffolk as a Yorkist claimant. It had been understood that Henry, Prince of Wales, should marry Catherine of Aragon when old enough to do so. They were betrothed in 1503, in which year Pope Julius II granted a dispensation allowing the young Henry to marry his brother's widow. The prospects that opened on the death of Isabella caused Henry VII to prepare a retreat from the contract: for, if Ferdinand should lose his hold on Spain, his daughter would be a less attractive bride for the future King of England. In 1505 therefore young Henry formally declared before the Bishop of Winchester that he held the betrothal to be void because effected against his will while he was under age. This act was kept secret, to be produced if required.

Henry VII had thus a card to play against Ferdinand. He provided himself with another against the Archduke Philip by stimulating a commercial quarrel arising out of the unamended clauses of the *Magnus Intercursus*. The English complained of unjustifiable exactions, and once more their mart was removed from Antwerp to Calais. Suffolk, meanwhile, tired of being kept in cold storage at Aix-la-Chapelle, unwisely quitted that shelter in search of other support. In the course of his travels he was made prisoner by the Duke of Guelders and fell ultimately into the power of the Archduke Philip.

Such was the situation when fortune presented Henry VII with a gift which he knew how to exploit.

At the close of 1505 Philip and Juana prepared to go in person to Spain and assert their rights to Castile. The Archduke was warned of the danger of a winter voyage, but chose to risk it. He and his wife set sail from the Netherlands in January 1506. Their ships were caught in a westerly gale and driven into Weymouth, where they took refuge. The royal pair would have done well to leave as soon as the gale abated, but the experience had been daunting and they stayed a few days to recuperate. An astute Dorset gentleman saw the possibilities, pressed hospitality on the foreigners, and sent the news post haste to the King. He at once invited Philip and Juana to Windsor, whither they were escorted with magnificent ceremony, and where they stayed a month as the guests of the wealthiest host in Europe. Henry spent his treasure with an open hand and an easy mind, for his guests were his prisoners. It was all done by kindness, but none the less effectively. Before he left, the Archduke signed a treaty of defensive and offensive alliance, with mutual repudiation of the rebels and enemies of either party, promised his sister Margaret in marriage to Henry VII, guaranteed to hand over the Earl of Suffolk on condition that his life should be spared, and gave powers to subordinates to conclude a new commercial treaty on England's terms. Then, flattered and befriended to the end, and recognized as King of Castile, he rode down to Falmouth to rejoin the ships which had preceded him thither. And so he sailed with Henry's blessing to win his kingdom. Suffolk was duly sent to England, and duly spared—a prisoner in the Tower, while the King lived—only to be executed by the next Henry, who declined to be bound by his father's word. The commercial treaty was concluded to English satisfaction and Flemish chagrin. It was known in after times as the *Malus Intercursus*, the revised version of the *Magnus* of ten years before.

Philip made some progress in Castile, but after six months died suddenly in September 1506. His sister Margaret declined to marry the elderly Henry, who, unabashed, proposed himself to Philip's widow Juana, in spite of the fact that her instability was now reported to be evident insanity. He was assured that she was capable of bearing children, and was prepared to overlook a trifle. It is possible, indeed, that Ferdinand exaggerated his daughter's disability, although there is no doubt that in some form it existed. The ambassador de Puebla concurred in recommending the match to King Ferdinand, saying that Henry would be so good a husband that she would soon recover her reason. However, marriage negotiations were then as slow as changes in the diplomatic situation were quick, and the project cooled away. Henry was still attracted by the prospect of gaining a footing in Spain, although how he would have used it can only be guessed. He had yet his daughter Mary to dispose of, a child, but within the scope of such bargaining. In 1507–8 it was arranged that she should be wedded to the boy Charles, the son of the late Archduke Philip and Juana, who would be the ultimate heir to Ferdinand's Aragon as well as Castile. The marriage never took place. Long before the project could be realized it faded away in the altered conditions of a new world; for six months after the conclusion of the pact Henry VII was dead. We may end this record of Renaissance wooings with the mention of one more of Henry's own. Shortly after the death of his wife Elizabeth in 1503 he had proposed to marry his eldest son's widow Catherine of Aragon. But marriage to the elderly King would have barred a subsequent union with his son and successor, and Queen Isabella denounced the project, which had to be dropped.[1] Catherine lived on in England as a widow, none too kindly treated, until the end of the reign. Matrimonial proceedings such as the above were not limited to royal and noble families. They were customary among all classes in a time when property was inherited by lineal descent rather than by will and testament, and the status of women was that of links in a genealogical chain.

The King's Navy, as a permanent and organized part of the national defences, took shape on a modest scale in Henry's reign. The Yorkist kings had possessed a handful of ships, of whose fighting powers nothing is known. These ships were not organized as a service, and their chief function may have been to make individual trading voyages for the royal profit. They played no part in the measures taken to resist invasions, such as that by which Henry VII began his reign. Henry himself placed chief reliance on diplomacy to avert a large-scale war, but he realized that a strong fleet might one day be wanted, and he laid the foundations. Early in the reign he built two great ships, the *Regent* and the *Sovereign*, each of about 700 tons, an exceptional size at the time. They carried few or no great guns, but were armed with numbers of little firearms called serpentines, whose small size can be inferred from the fact that the *Regent* had 225 of them. Henry built also three smaller vessels. His

[1] G. Mattingly, *Catherine of Aragon* (1942), pp. 52–3.

Clerk of the Ships, Robert Brigandyne, lived to fill the same office with a much expanded Navy in the first part of Henry VIII's reign. Brigandyne built at Portsmouth the first dry dock recorded in England, and some of his accounts and inventories have been preserved. The Navy of Henry VII began a continuous succession of ships, officers, and dockyard services, which has come unbroken to the present day. The medieval fleet, on the other hand, had died out completely in the days of Henry VI.

The records of Henry's reign give a general impression that trade was increasing and the country as a whole growing more prosperous. The customs receipts, with an advance of about 30 per cent from the beginning to the end of the reign, confirm this. If the actual growth of trade was in the same proportion, the population being almost stationary, it must mark a notable improvement in general well-being. Some of the customs increase, however, may have been due to the more efficient collection which we may assume to have resulted from Henry's methods of administration. As an offset to this, the transference of trade from foreign to English hands would have diminished receipts, for Englishmen paid lower rates than did most of the foreigners. Balancing one factor against the other, we may conclude that there was a considerable advance in prosperity. Various regulations aimed at preventing the carrying of coin and precious metals out of the realm. That they were really effective is attested by the observations of foreign writers on the extraordinary richness of the goldsmiths' shops in London and on the widespread existence of silver plate even in the homes of humble people throughout the country.

The Merchants Adventurers undoubtedly increased their business in the Netherlands, in spite of the two periods of stoppage, and their sales were an index of the expansion of the cloth manufacture. London was already growing more rapidly than the other towns as a centre of internal business and as a port of foreign trade. The rich London members of the Merchants Adventurers attempted in 1497 to increase their preponderance by enacting higher fees for membership, which they were better able to pay. The outports protested, and Parliament, with the King's approval, redressed the grievance by an Act reducing the fee from the £20 fixed by the Londoners to a maximum of ten marks, or £6 13s. 4d. In 1505 the King issued a new charter to the Merchants Adventurers giving full powers of control overseas to an elected governor and a court of twenty-four elected assistants, chosen by various guilds in and out of London. In one of his aims, that of forcing the Hanseatic League to admit Englishmen more freely to the Baltic, Henry failed. The trade which he obtained at Danzig was limited, and the Hanse cities were as obstructive to the English as Henry was to them For a time he secured another opening by a separate treaty with Riga; but the League forced Riga to come into line with its general policy, and English business in the Baltic remained severely restricted. One consequence was that no English merchants were allowed to pass through the Baltic provinces into Russia, which continued to be an unknown country for another half-century.

On the ocean, one more achievement coincided with the close of the reign. Early in 1509 Sebastian Cabot sailed with two ships to seek the North West Passage to Asia. It is entirely clear that this was his object, which makes it equally clear that by this date the English understood that the New Found Land was a new continent distinct from Asia; for Cabot was trying to turn the New Found Land by the north in order to reach Asia. The evidence for the course of his voyage consisted mainly in maps and writings which he left at his death long afterwards. These documents have now disappeared, but they were seen and described by Elizabethan students, from whose statements we have to reconstruct the story. From their testimony it appears that he sailed past the southern point of Greenland and thence north-westwards across Davis Strait. On its farther side he found an opening between 61° and 64° N. It was a channel leading westwards round the northern shore of what we now call Labrador and then broadening into an open sea extending south and west. Sebastian Cabot was convinced that he had rounded the New Found Land and was in the ocean stretching to Cathay, the Pacific Ocean as it was later named. The navigation was dangerous by reason of drifting ice, and at this point the crews insisted on turning back. Their commander had to submit. He spent the rest of the season in examining the Atlantic coast of America in case an easier channel might open there, and at the close of the year he returned to England. This story bears a remarkable resemblance to that of Henry Hudson a century later, except that Hudson's mutineers killed him instead of bringing him home. The conclusion is that Sebastian Cabot's west-going channel was Hudson Strait and that his new ocean was Hudson Bay. It was not the Pacific, and the Passage was not really opened, but Cabot had good reason for supposing that it was, just as Hudson himself died in the belief that he had found the way to Asia. When Cabot reached England it was to find that his royal patron was dead and that the altered circumstances were not propitious to further voyages of exploration. He lingered a while in England and then went to Spain in 1512 to take service with King Ferdinand. The Spaniards had other views than that of the quest for the North West Passage, and for the rest of his long life Sebastian Cabot was never able to follow up his discovery.

Henry VII died on 21 April, 1509. He was only fifty-two, but in appearance much older. In his earlier days as king he was liked and respected, in his later he was respected and feared. He had outlived the gratitude of the people for whom he had done so much. They admitted his wisdom, but resented his growing arbitrariness. They had even grown tired of the peace for which they had thirsted and of the economy in which their true interest lay. Henry himself was probably content with the retrospect, save that his conscience troubled him, as we know it did, over his injustices to individuals. He viewed his work as duty and had never unduly courted popularity. He was sincerely pious and without questionings of the religion in which he lived. He was the founder of the new England of the sixteenth century, but had no conception of himself as modern or an innovator, and no prescience of the revolutionary changes that were to ensue. His best epitaph is in Bacon's words: 'a wonder for wise men'.

5

THE EARLY YEARS OF HENRY VIII:
THE RISE OF WOLSEY

WITH the reign of Henry VIII Tudor history enters its revolutionary period; and the first and most intricate phase of the revolution was dominated by Henry himself. Revolutions, however, are not made by solitary men, and the condition of the English people, its religion, and its Church, worked upon by new forces common to all Christendom, were such as to create the upheaval whose early course was directed by a king of high ability. People, Church, King, and Renaissance are thus the elements of the story, whose comprehension will be helped by some preliminary description in anticipation of events.

Henry was born in 1491 and succeeded his father at the age of eighteen. We have no continuous story of his boyhood and youth, but only one significant picture and one no less significant silence of the record. The picture is from the pen of Erasmus of Rotterdam, who saw him as an eight-year-old boy in 1499. Erasmus and Thomas More were staying at a country house of Lord Mountjoy, an intimate of the royal family, and More took Erasmus to a neighbouring house to be presented to the children of Henry VII, who were all, except Prince Arthur, together there:

When we came into the hall, the attendants, not only of the palace, but also of Mountjoy's household, were all assembled. In the midst stood Prince Henry, now nine (*sic*) years old, and having already something of royalty in his demeanour in which there was a certain dignity combined with singular courtesy. . . . More, after paying his respects to the boy Henry, the same that is now King of England, presented him with some writing. For my part, not having expected anything of the sort, I had nothing to offer, but promised that on another occasion I would in some way declare my duty towards him. Meantime I was angry with

More for not having warned me, especially as the boy sent me a little note, while we were at dinner, to challenge something from my pen.

There is much history in that little passage: the social freedom which permitted a poor scholar to turn up thus informally at the royal table; the mature prince of eight, with qualities of mind and character already graved as they could not have been on ordinary childish clay; his friendship with More already formed, and neither knowing how friendship was to end.

Erasmus saw only a glimpse. Henry was no bookworm, although intelligent above the ordinary. He revelled in field sports and the open air. At sixteen he was an accomplished bowman. About that age there is the significant silence of the record already noted. The prince was entering exuberant youth, strong in body and mind. His father was ageing fast, and calculating men might look to his coming end. The position was that of Shakespeare's Prince Hal. We should expect to hear of a court faction urging the Prince of Wales to seek power before his time; and there is not a word of it. The prince was loyal and dutiful and proof against the temptation that must have been there. The negative suggests a good son and a good father. And so in due course Henry VIII became king, a horseman, a sportsman, a musician, a scholar, especially in theology, generous and accessible, good to look upon, the pattern of a sovereign after the English heart. He was Plantagenet as well as Tudor, for his mother was Elizabeth of York. He had her personal beauty and his father's vigorous brain. England rejoiced. The warring Houses were fused, and the outcome promised well.

Religion and the claims of the Church enwrapped the whole life of the people. Church courts had a range of jurisdiction additional to that of the ordinary law. They inflicted penalties for sins as distinguished from crimes, and the sins were numerous and the penalties severe. In town and country the man of normal conduct was much more likely to be fined or flogged by the court Christian than by the justice of the King. The Church took its dues on birth, marriage, and death, and controlled the probate of wills and much other nonspiritual business, always with substantial fees. Associations for secular purposes of craftsmanship and trade had always their religious side, their chapel and priest and services for the members. In towns the bells were always ringing for successive ceremonies. The conduct of everyday life was moulded and supervised by the clergy. For most people it was no hardship, since they had no conception of any other system. The average man enjoyed his church in many aspects. For the poor who had no houses, but only sleeping dens, it was their club and the centre of their social life.

But it was upon death and the idea of the hereafter that the vast power and activity of the Church was mainly concentrated. A rigid system of doctrine and practice brought home every day to every person that retribution for the faults and failings of life was inevitable and terribly painful. Heaven might be bliss, but before heaven came purgatory, an awful period of fire and torment, dreadfully prolonged without the intercession of the Church. None could escape it, and only by good works might it be shortened. Onerous penances for sin might help, pilgrimage to holy shrines, prayers to the saints for their favourable countenance. A good end with proper absolution was essential. Above all, purgatory might be mitigated by prayer for the soul after death. The rich man might buy hundreds of masses for his soul,[1] the poor man could only lament his inability to do the like. Although the Church practised much charity and kindliness, care of the sick and relief of the hungry, it is hard to avoid the conclusion that its hold upon the people was mainly that of fear, fear not so much of the Church itself as of what would come if it withheld its ministration. So men believed and, in proportion to the vividness of their imaginations, were uneasy or terrified. Then in the early sixteenth century a New Learning began to spread, at first among few, soon rumoured among the many. It told them that their fear was exaggerated, their propitiations unwarranted by holy writ. The majority did not quickly accept it: the majority's beliefs are never quickly shaken. For a minority it was joy and freedom, a load lifted that could never be replaced. In their new freedom they were crude, unmannerly, and aggressive. That was but an inevitable phase, most prominent in England about half way through the century. But the freedom spread as the old generation died out and the young grew in a world where the ancient fears were questioned. Such is the pattern of the English reformation of religion.

That is by no means identical with the material misfortunes of the Church, which constituted a revolution rather than a reformation. We are here on a different plane, not of religion but of lands and money. All over the country the wealth of the Church was apparent,

---

[1] Henry VII paid for 10,000 masses for his soul to be said in the month after his death and for others in perpetuity.—H. Maynard Smith, *Pre-Reformation England*, p. 8.

glebe, episcopal manors, and chantry lands; and, most noticeable of all, the great estates of hundreds of monasteries rich by the pious gifts of former generations and now accused of spiritual decay and failure to justify their wealth. Everywhere the rents of good land and the fees for a multiplicity of occasions supported the clergy. Most of them were poor and lived simply, but their numbers were excessive, and critics were saying that the whole profession was swollen out of proportion and that its work could be done by fewer men at less expense. Critics had been saying this for more than a hundred years, and the complaints had been fruitless, partly because the great nobles had a feeling that the stability of their order was involved with that of the Church. Now the old nobility was diminished and depressed. Middle-class men and newly created peers filled the King's Council, and squires and merchants were the favourites of the state. Merchants and squires were looking on Church land as something that might soon be ripe for development. Some of the clergy shared the same point of view. The Church as a body might be stout for its property, but many individual churchmen belonged to aspiring families. Once a serious attack should develop, they would not all be found on the side of the defence.

The Church owed obedience to the Pope more explicitly than to the King, a relationship that had caused high dispute in the past. In matters spiritual the Pope's jurisdiction was supreme, and these were not clear-cut from matters temporal, for there was a borderland between them. The Middle Ages had held the theory of Christendom united in fealty to Pope and Holy Roman Emperor, two aspects of a single divinely appointed authority. England had never given much recognition to the Emperor, but the papal claim was real. Once more the trend of the time was against it. National consciousness was taking shape, and the idea of 'England an empire' was in the air. An empire in this context meant a fully independent country owing neither duty nor tribute to any outside power. Yet large sums were taken every year in papal taxation. It was nearly all paid by the clergy, but the laity knew that indirectly it came from them, since the whole realm supported the clergy. The woolsacks that were shipped to the Pope's account brought no corresponding imports, and most men were economists enough to see that they lost by it. Taking all factors into view, it seems likely that the Church as a financial system and propertied institution would have been attacked in this Tudor century even had no New Learning questioned its doctrines.

The new King's Council in 1509 continued, with two notable exceptions, very much as Henry VII left it. The Archbishop of Canterbury, William Warham, was its senior member by rank, though not prominent in personality. Richard Fox, now Bishop of Winchester, and the Earl of Surrey came next. Poynings and some other veterans of secondary status remained. Sir Richard Empson and Edmund Dudley were at once removed. The young King gave favourable hearing to their victims, and public opinion demanded their heads. It was not feasible to put men to death for enforcing the law, which they could claim was all that they had done, and they were therefore tried and executed on a trumped-up charge of treason by gathering armed retainers with intent to resist the lawful authority on their old master's death. The accusation was transparently flimsy, but the whole country acclaimed the sentence and held that justice had been done. Their condemnation was not hurried, and more than a year elapsed before they were put to death. Among the King's advisers a new figure soon arose. Thomas Wolsey, an ambitious priest who had slowly made his way upward, was the royal almoner from the accession, having already been employed by Henry VII. In 1511, when nearly forty, he was made a member of the Council.

Henry VIII was not, like his father, a man of French sympathies, and it seems to have been expected that he would force a quarrel on France at the outset. After the long peace the country was ready to resume what many held to be a normal function of English existence, and the precedent of young Henry V a century earlier was remembered. Henry VIII may privately have so intended, but, high tempered though he was, he was not one to act upon impulse. Throughout his reign his seemingly sudden decisions are generally found to have been long premeditated: he could keep his intentions to himself until time was ripe. It was not ripe in 1509. Fox at least, and Warham, among his senior councillors, were disinclined for adventure; and there were preparations to be made. Three months after his accession Henry married his sister-in-law Catherine of Aragon, on the strength of the dispensation granted by Julius II in 1503. The holiday festivities of coronation and wedding satisfied the public taste for excitement. Parliament met early in 1510 without mention of war taxation, and granted for the King's life the usual duties on exports and imports. Later in the year the Treaty of Etaples with France was renewed, and the French continued to pay the instalments of money required by its terms.

Other things nevertheless were being done. A proclamation reminded all men of their duty to possess weapons and be exercised in their use. The King's Navy began to grow significantly. From his father Henry inherited the first-class ships *Sovereign* and *Regent* and three smaller ones. The *Sovereign* was rebuilt in 1509 and made effectively into a new ship. In that year and the next the King built two more great ships and purchased three others from merchants for conversion into ships of war. It was the beginning of a powerful Navy, quietly put in hand. Furthermore, he looked about for naval commanders. The Earl of Oxford had long been Lord Admiral, but the office was legal and administrative and not combatant, and Oxford did not go to sea. Henry, with a view to finding a successor with sea experience, picked out the two young Howards, Thomas and Edward, sons of the Earl of Surrey, and sent them to sea in 1511 to bring to account Sir Andrew Barton, a Scottish officer whose piracies were the complaint of English merchants. Barton was a servant of James IV and a commander of the new Scottish navy. The Howards fought and killed him and added his two privateers as prizes to Henry's fleet. Henry himself loved ships, understood the use of sea power, and acquired a technical knowledge of things generally unknown to landsmen. He was in fact his own minister of marine at a time when his senior advisers knew and cared nothing about the Navy.

European politics revolved round Italy. In the first years of the century the French under Louis XII made good their hold on the duchy of Milan, while leaving Naples to Ferdinand of Aragon. Julius II, a fighting Pope who personally led his forces in the field, sought to create a solid block of papal territory in central Italy. The Venetian republic held wide lands bordering on Milan and the papal states. Louis and Julius formed a league to attack and despoil Venice, which they accomplished by winning a decisive battle just as Henry VIII mounted the throne. The Venetians were influential in London and reconciled to English trading in the Mediterranean. Henry gave them his sympathy, but the Italian interest was not sufficiently important to England to justify a war with France. In 1511 the Pope grew jealous of the French ascendancy and changed his policy. With Venice and Ferdinand, who sought to extend Spanish power to northern Italy, he refounded the Holy League, whose real aim was to drive the French out of the country. Ferdinand's north Italian views were distant, and his immediate aim was to keep the French fighting there while he conquered the kingdom of Navarre, in the Basque country stretching on either side of the western Pyrenees. The adhesion of England would be useful to his purpose. Henry's vigorous new councillor Wolsey was eager to support the Roman cause. The Pope, hard pressed by the French, sent complimentary messages. Ferdinand promised full co-operation in an invasion of France. In November 1511 Henry decided on war and joined the Holy League. He gave out that he was reviving the English claim to France and the conquests of his ancestors. The campaign was to begin in 1512.

It is commonly said that in his youthful inexperience Henry was duped into a wildly impossible undertaking. It is true that his father-in-law duped him by playing false from the outset. But for this, the real undertaking would not have been impossible and gave promise of a great success. Henry could hardly have expected to conquer and hold the realm of France, still less would his veteran advisers have encouraged the idea. It was no more than propaganda to arouse the English people to a 'royal' war. The real objective, as the event showed, was the recovery of Bordeaux with sufficient surrounding territory to make it tenable. For the circumstances we must look back to 1491, when the kingdom of France absorbed the duchy of Brittany. In doing so it acquired a population of seafaring and ship-owning subjects and a variety of harbours, including Brest, spacious, landlocked and defensible. Brest and the Bretons gave France the opportunity of creating a naval power in the Atlantic, and already by 1512 a French navy was being formed there. French sea power was thus established on the flank of the English trade routes to the southward; and those southern trades, notably that with the Mediterranean, were offering an increase of national wealth more easily won than in the dour competition with the Hanseatic League in the North Sea. The Bretons were loyal subjects of the French crown. Bordeaux, on the other hand, had been for three hundred years in continuous possession of the English kings and had been lost for only half a century. The bulk of its trade was still with England, to which its citizens were bound by tradition and interest. many, indeed, must have been of English descent, as were those of Calais; and every winter, it was estimated, there were seven or eight thousand Englishmen in the port for the wine-shipping. It lay sixty miles up the estuary of the Gironde, where the swift tides aided the passage of the traffic up and down. Bordeaux, could it have been

taken and held, would have been a counterpoise to Brest in considerations of sea power, and an evident aid to the growth of English
commerce. The above is an explanation but not a justification of a
war that was aggressive and not immediately necessary. Wolsey was
in favour of it, Fox and Warham are said to have been against.
Henry VII would not have undertaken it.

The Anglo-Spanish arrangements for 1512 included naval and
military action. The English fleet was to command and patrol the
Channel and beyond Cape Ushant as far as Brest. Ferdinand's fleet
was to command the Bay of Biscay down to the Spanish coast.
England was to send an army to land at the Spanish ports close to
the Pyrenean frontier. Ferdinand was to furnish another, and jointly
they were to invade France and occupy Guienne, whose capital city
was Bordeaux. Guienne was to be an English and Navarre a Spanish
conquest.

First the English Navy took the sea. When war became certain it
was rapidly expanded, and in this year the King's ships comprised
eleven of over 200 tons and eight smaller ones. Sir Edward Howard,
the younger of Surrey's sons, sailed in command, and in August
received his patent as Lord Admiral of England, the first of a new
succession of the fighting Lords Admirals of the sixteenth century,
four of whom, it may be noted, were members of the Howard
family. The English army under the Marquis of Dorset left England
in June. Howard's duty was to see that it got safely to the Spanish
coast. He cruised off Brest, and the French did not challenge him.
When Dorset had landed, the fleet returned to Portsmouth, and
thence sailed to Brest again to look for the French. This time the
French came out. A battle ensued, which appears to have been a
running fight with 'innumerable shooting of guns and long chasing
one another'. The chased were evidently the French, who retreated
into Brest, with the exception of their great ship *Cordelière*. She was
grappled by the *Regent*, and after a terrific fight both were destroyed
by fire, with the loss of nearly all their men. The English were shaken
by this tragedy and spoke modestly of their victory, for such in the
general result it was, since the French remained thenceforward
behind their defences and did not again contest the command of the
sea. Two days after the battle the English destroyed thirty French
merchantmen. Howard returned to England in the late summer and
laid up his greater ships, leaving a winter guard of small ones to
patrol the Channel.

Meanwhile the land campaign went wrong. Dorset on the coast with his English archers waited for Ferdinand to join him with Spanish guns and cavalry and invade France. Ferdinand had the English where he wanted them and devoted himself to the conquest of Navarre. There were only two roads between France and Spain in this region, one along the coast between the mountains and the sea, the other through the centre of Navarre and over the pass of Roncesvalles. Ferdinand used the latter and conquered all Spanish Navarre by the end of the season. Meanwhile the English on the coast served to prevent any French attempt to work round his flank and take him in rear. It was not what the English had come for, and Dorset was loud in his complaints, although he exhibited no sign of independent enterprise. His men, with plenty of 'hot Spanish wines' and little to eat, grew unhealthy and discontented. Finally they broke into open mutiny, and the whole army took to its transports and came home without leave in the autumn. Ferdinand thereupon accused his allies of deserting him, and for Henry it was a dreadful fiasco.

Some voices were for peace, but Henry saw that it could not be thought of at such a moment. He determined to invade France in person in 1513, not in the south-west as Ferdinand still suggested, but across the Channel through Calais. Ferdinand decided to be content with his gains. In the spring he fell ill and, so he said, feared that his end was near. His confessor exhorted him to be reconciled with his enemies. He accordingly signed a truce with France whereby he was to keep Navarre, and afterwards assured Henry that he had done it in the English interest. However, another diplomatic veteran, the Emperor Maximilian, saw a chance of making something out of French difficulties, and joined Henry for the campaign of 1513. The preparations were expensive and complete, and Wolsey had much to do with them. Everyone was saying that it was his war, and he knew that failure would ruin him. Julius II died in February, and was succeeded by the Medici Leo X. Wolsey had ambitions at Rome, but his time was not yet. His policy was thorough-going support of the Pope, with England a favoured province of the holy see, and England's leading man a candidate for a future vacancy in it.

Henry sent Howard to sea in the spring with a stronger fleet than in the previous year, for the shipyards had been working hard. Louis XII, seeing the failure of his sailing fleet, had sent round a force of galleys from the Mediterranean under a good officer named

Prégent de Bidoux. Galleys were not often used in northern Europe, the reason being that they were rowed by slave labour and that slaves were chiefly obtained in the perennial fighting with the Mohammedans of the Levant and North Africa. Howard sailed at once for Brest and formed a blockade, preparing to go in and attack the French where they lay. Prégent, who had been lying in St. Malo, went to the rescue and forced his way through with his galleys, sinking an English ship in the process. He anchored the galleys in the shallows of Blancs Sablons Bay, north of the Brest entrance, unapproachable by the deeper English ships, and made ready with fireships and a concerted plan of defence to deal with Howard's expected incursion. Howard determined first to eliminate the galleys, which had produced an unpleasant moral effect on his men. He led a force of light rowing craft to assault them in their anchorage. From his own boat he boarded a galley, but was overcome and killed before his friends could follow; and the attempt was abandoned. So ended the first combatant Lord Admiral at the age of twenty-four. He had been the soul of his fleet, which he left in a difficult position with its victuals expended and exposed to the danger of a westerly gale. The captains returned to England, saying truly that they had nothing to eat. The seamen were unwilling to go back on account of the galleys. The moral ascendancy of the galley in coastal waters continued for seventy years to the days of Drake. The King appointed Thomas Howard as Lord Admiral and was at first determined to resume the blockade of Brest. But the invasion that summer was to be across the Straits of Dover, and second thoughts showed that it could be covered by a fleet cruising in the Channel. In fact the French made no move from Brest and did not contest their opponents' command of the sea.

Henry crossed the Channel at midsummer with an army of about 35,000 Englishmen, archers, cavalry, and men-at-arms, and a train of artillery; and took into his pay 14,000 mercenaries from Germany, together with some Swiss, the pikemen who were now supreme on the fields of Italy. It was an all-round force very different from Dorset's of the previous year. Wolsey was with them, and for Wolsey war was always a form of diplomacy. It was probably of deliberate purpose that the King and his nobles campaigned with the utmost pomp and luxury, demonstrating the wealth of England and building up the prestige that would double the value of a victory. Maximilian with a small force joined the English, rather as volunteers than as equal allies, and they laid siege to Terouenne on the Lys at the beginning of August. Louis XII, sick and old (he was entering his fifties, which few kings survived), hovered to the westwards with the main French army. On the 16th he sent forward a strong mounted force to interrupt the siege and throw supplies into the town. By good generalship the English swiftly outmanœuvred the French and forced them to retreat. The retreat became a rout in which the French horsemen lost several hundreds killed and a number of notable prisoners. This was the famous Battle of the Spurs, or of Guinegâte. Henry took part in the chase. His detractors say that he was always careful to avoid personal risk, but on this occasion he can hardly be sneered at if his opponents did not make a better fight of it. In fact the battle was won by the great men and their mounted retinues, and the infantry never had a chance to catch up. A contemporary remarked that the affair was much more dangerous to the generals than to their armies.

Terouenne surrendered a week later, while Louis still remained inactive. Henry turned next to the siege of Tournai, then the richest and most populous city of the western Netherlands. It was taken towards the end of September. Henry and Maximilian were still fast friends, for the inland conquests were mainly of benefit to the Emperor rather than to England. After the fall of Tournai the campaign was ended, with promises of resumption next year and a renewed agreement for marriage between Henry's sister Mary and Maximilian's thirteen-year-old grandson Charles.

In the north that September had seen a much greater battle than any in France. James IV, nursing a grudge for Barton's fate and bent on strengthening Scottish contacts with the continent in despite of England's new sea power, threw in his lot with France and declared war in the summer of 1513. He was much stronger than in Perkin Warbeck's day, richer probably by reason of his work for Scottish shipping and North Sea commerce. He crossed the Tweed in August with a great army and captured Norham Castle in a week. The King and Wolsey being in France, the defence of England fell to Queen Catherine and the old Earl of Surrey. Together they called up forces from the south, the midlands, and the north. Early in September, before James had moved far from Norham, Surrey was in contact with him, seconded by his son the Lord Admiral, who brought a contingent of seamen from the fleet. The armies were great and equally matched, too great for the foodless border country in which they must fight at once or tamely disperse. James was eager to fight, and chose the strong position of Flodden ridge. 'Skilful Surrey's sage commands' tempted him out of it. The English marched round to the north of Flodden, crossing the Till stream at two places, and Surrey at once embattled them and began the attack, the English army facing south and the Scottish north. James might profitably have struck while these moves were in progress, but did not. When they were complete and his enemies in order, he suddenly left the height of the ridge and moved down to the encounter. The fight began in the late afternoon and lasted far into the night. For either side it was all or nothing, with little hope of escape for the vanquished. After many vicissitudes and dreadful bloodshed the English prevailed. James IV and his nobles and 10,000 of his men were killed, and the survivors melted away in the darkness. Although both sides had some artillery at Flodden, it was characteristically one of the great medieval battles, fought, not by professional armies, but by the national levies, bowmen, billmen, and spearmen, undrilled and undisciplined, but filled with patriotic fire. Scotland was left to a boy-king, James V, whose mother, an unwise and unpopular woman, was a Tudor princess. In reward for the victory Surrey recovered the dukedom of Norfolk which his father had lost at Bosworth. He died in 1524. His son the Lord Admiral was then Duke of Norfolk for the rest of the reign.

Henry returned to share with his people the glories of the year. To the public mind it had been glorious, though the material results were small. Two border towns in Flanders captured by the most costly army that England had ever sent abroad yielded no hope of conquering France. The King and Wolsey knew it. But their prestige was high, some things not measurable in territory had been gained, and diplomacy had a fair field before it. King Ferdinand's diplomacy was already at work. His idea was to convert his truce with France into an alliance by means of a marriage between his younger grandson Ferdinand and a daughter of Louis XII. Louis would then make over his north Italian claims to the happy pair, and another of old Ferdinand's ambitions would be on the way to fulfilment. Meanwhile the equally untrustworthy Maximilian was making a truce of his own with France and finding reasons for postponing the marriage of his grandson with the Princess Mary. Henry VIII must have had the characters of these two old gentlemen from his father, but he had trusted them nevertheless; and now he found himself the sole member of the Holy League left actively at war. It was a lesson that he did not forget. He put a good face on it, and with sound policy continued to build up his fighting navy. By 1514 it numbered twenty-seven sail large and small, the most notable addition being the *Great Harry* of 1,500 tons, completed in that year. The effect was to give him the upper hand in the coming negotiations, since he could still strike France but France could not strike him.

Early in 1514 the death of the Queen of France gave Henry and Wolsey their opportunity. They offered the Princess Mary to the elderly widower on terms which mortified Maximilian and dissipated the schemes of Ferdinand for the acquisition of Milan. At midsummer the girl of seventeen was married to Louis XII, having, it was said, stipulated to her brother that in return for the sacrifice she was to marry next time according to her own will and pleasure. Louis repudiated the two grandfathers and made a military alliance with England, ceded Tournai (of which Wolsey became the absentee bishop), and promised greater money payments than those fixed by the Treaty of Etaples. Wolsey was triumphant. All Europe was talking of Henry's glory and England's power. All England resounded with congratulation, for the King was the country incarnate, and every man felt elated when his sovereign was great and feared. Wolsey had proved himself the trusty servant of the Pope, and was shortly to claim his rewards. Everyone had come well out of a risky adventure; but the treasure left by Henry VII was greatly diminished.

The satisfaction was soon modified by the death of Louis XII on the first day of 1515. His successor was his nephew Francis I, a young man of twenty, whose thirst for military glory was as great as the weariness and disillusionment of Louis. Henry sent the Duke of Suffolk to Paris to pay his compliments to the new sovereign. The Duke had only recently been advanced, having begun life as plain Charles Brandon, the son of a gentleman who had been killed fighting for Henry VII at Bosworth. He was a personal friend of Henry VIII and had served with credit in the campaign of 1513. While in Paris he made love to Henry's sister Mary, the widow of Louis XII, and they were married secretly and without the King's leave. It was a grave offence so to enter the royal family and at the same time to deprive the English state of the prospect of another continental marriage. For a short while Suffolk's position was doubtful, but Henry ended by forgiving the pair and presiding at a magnificent public wedding in London.

Henry disliked Francis I from the beginning. He soon had reason to be jealous of the French king's military achievements, which transferred some of Europe's admiration from himself. Francis renewed the treaty with England, but at the same time sent the Franco-Scottish Duke of Albany into Scotland to claim the regency during the minority of the young James V. He then collected a great army with speed and secrecy and marched into northern Italy, where he won a decisive battle at Marignano in September and recovered the duchy of Milan at a stroke. The next great event was the death of Ferdinand in 1516. The heir to both Castile and Aragon was Charles, grandson of Ferdinand and of Maximilian, a youth of sixteen who was ruling in the ancestral Burgundian provinces of the Netherlands. The cast of European personalities and prestige was changing, and three young sovereigns, Henry, Francis, and Charles, were to dominate the future. It needed only for Maximilian to go, and a new age would have begun. For the present there was a suspense in anticipation of things to come. After a period of hostility towards Francis on account of Milan, the King and Wolsey came to terms with him by a treaty of 1518. The English gave up Tournai for a disproportionately large sum of money, while Francis undertook to keep Albany in France and not to interfere with English plans in Scotland. This pact was supplementary to a treaty of amity signed earlier in the year between Francis, Charles, and Maximilian; and the inauguration of peace among Christians was ecstatically proclaimed, while the sovereigns professed to intend a joint crusade against the Turks. Even the experienced Bishop Fox thought the settlement to be of excellent promise, although there seemed to be nothing to guarantee its permanence. The statesmen gave every impression of believing themselves and one another, and it is difficult to fathom their true thoughts.

Wolsey's capacity for work was immense. Foreign affairs were only one branch of his activities, which included the administration of all the home affairs of the realm, and also of the English Church, which he governed much more intensively than had been done for centuries. Without intending it, he was conditioning the Church to be submissive when taken over by the Crown at a later stage. An efficient Tudor minister carried a greater load than a modern premier. He had, indeed, a smaller nation and a less complex range of business to deal with. On the other hand the people were unstandardized and wilful, the communications were poor and decisions slower to take effect, local customs were powerful against central regulation, the common law competed with ecclesiastical law, and there was no civil service and no police. Above all, the Tudor minister had no trustworthy colleagues. The other royal councillors were not his supporters but his critics and would-be supplanters. The minister had to take charge of all vital business himself and to attend to it in the smallest detail, with the assistance of inferior men who were nothing more than clerks and factotums, a staff of his own improvization. It could be done only by wide knowledge and correct judgment of men: it had to be his aim to know personally and assess accurately all the prominent men of every part of the country, and to collect reports through a service of agents of his own creation. Some of this business was done by correspondence, but the greater part by conference, representing an immense effort of memory and mental concentration never committed to writing.

After the war Wolsey rapidly established his control. In 1514 he became Archbishop of York. That he did not obtain Canterbury was due only to the fact that Warham, although an older man, outlived him. Warham, however, resigned the Lord Chancellorship in 1515, and Wolsey succeeded him. In the same year he was made a cardinal by Leo X. For the control of the Church which Wolsey had in mind something more was needed, and in 1518 Leo conferred it by appointing him Papal Legate, *legatus a latere*, with a higher authority than the Archbishop of Canterbury held as *legatus natus*. Wolsey's legatine power gave him jurisdiction over every ecclesiastic in England and made the courts Christian an engine in his hands.

As Lord Chancellor Wolsey's chief work was in matters of justice. Society in the new century was growing more complex, and many questions of contract, trade, and property were inadequately determined by the ordinary law, with expense and uncertainty to the litigants. The general demand was for less law and more justice, and the Court of Chancery was there to supply it. Chancery administered justice according to 'the King's conscience', as a court of equity to which the oppressed could appeal. It had long existed. Wolsey seems to have greatly extended its work and to have exerted himself to see that justice was really done. So also with the Star Chamber of which he, as the King's chief councillor, was also the head. The Star Chamber had been used by Henry VII as a means for the repression of violence, intimidation, and corruption. His success had not been complete. Retainers were still kept by powerful men, although no longer employed to resist the King. A certain amount of oppression and corruption of the courts still went on. Perhaps these practices increased in the early years of the new reign. At any rate, Wolsey found them in existence and was determined to stop them. He did so by an unsparing use of the Star Chamber jurisdiction, to such an extent that some who looked back on the record held him to be the substantial founder of the court. Two years after his accession to the Chancellorship he reported to the King that the realm was in such peace and good order as had not been known before. The good order was not absolute, but the improvement was great. At the same time the Court of Requests, also under his management, acted as a junior Star Chamber for the less important cases of humble men too poor to sue elsewhere. Wolsey saw to it that they had justice. For a few years he dealt personally with much of this business, and many had reason to feel gratitude for his efforts. As his work increased he was obliged to delegate to others, and the Court of Requests lost some of its original high motive. Later in the Tudor period it became a tribunal favoured by officials and servants of the Crown for the prosecution of their suits. There was no hard line of distinction between the jurisdiction of these courts. Cases of similar type are found in all three, and the choice of court lay with the initiator of the action.

Whatever his motive, Wolsey had a genuine determination to do justice to the oppressed. Enclosure of common land for one purpose, that of converting it into sheep pasture individually owned, had been frequent in the fifteenth century, and Henry VII had enacted in 1489 the first general statute in restraint of it. The defect of such legislation was that its enforcement rested primarily with the local justices, who might themselves be enclosers. The abuse therefore continued. It impoverished the evicted and enriched the evicters. Nationally it entailed increase of pauperism but also increase of the general wealth by expansion of the woollen industry, the evil being more immediate and visible than the good. Wolsey was impressed with the injustice. He attempted to check further enclosing of common land and to reverse enclosures already made. The Parliament of 1515 passed a very defective measure for this purpose, and Wolsey appointed commissions to enforce it. The result was only temporary, and the process of enclosure was soon resumed without effective interference from the state. Resentment is a stronger political influence than gratitude, and public opinion was largely shaped by men of property, with the result that Wolsey's anti-enclosure policy augmented the opposition against him.

Wolsey's legatine power came later and took longer to grow to its full authority than did the chancellorship. Its chief developments belong therefore to the next decade. The foundations were, however, laid in 1518. From the beginning he had been conscious that abuses in the Church demanded reform, abuses not of doctrine, but of jurisdiction and privilege and out-of-dateness in relation to a changing society. He spoke often of reforming the Church, and the loyal, non-revolutionary scholars, who wished to see it reformed from within, hoped that he would be the man to do it. Such reform must be with the authority of the Pope. He was far away, without personal knowledge of England, and occupied with many things. A papal legate, with full power to exercise the papal authority over all churchmen, was needed. The *legatus a latere* had hitherto been an ambassador, sent from Rome with full powers for some special purpose and withdrawn after its completion. He had generally been a foreigner with no special standing in English politics. Wolsey received his legatine commission as a resident Englishman already at the head of the secular administration and proposing in addition to exercise the ecclesiastical power, not for a limited time and purpose, but universally and indefinitely. The authority of the Pope was confided to the *alter ego* of the King. What if the King should liquidate his *alter ego*? That was a shadow of the future. For the present Wolsey had the ecclesiastical power. He used it less for reformation than for the inflation of his own magnificence. Power was his desire, before reform. All England must be in his obedience.

An affair of 1514–5 demonstrated the extent of Church privilege and its insecurity in face of a public opinion already surprisingly hostile. Richard Hunne, a London citizen, refused to pay a mortuary or fee demanded on the burial of his child by his parish priest. The priest sued him in the court Christian. Hunne answered that it was a court depending on a foreign authority, before which a subject of the King was not answerable, and invoked the Statute of Præmunire to that effect. It was a dangerous challenge to the clergy, who answered by charging Hunne with heresy and locking him up in the Lollards Tower. There he was discovered dead by hanging. His jailers said that he had hanged himself. Public opinion held that he had been murdered to stop his mouth, or rather, to stop his suit of *præmunire*. A coroner's jury returned a verdict of murder against the

Bishop of London's chancellor and two of the prison warders, one of whom confessed to the crime, although he may have done so under intimidation. Passion ran high for months. The Parliament of 1515 considered the case, Wolsey's authority was appealed to, and the King himself made a personal investigation. By his command the charge of murder was not proceeded with, but this did not amount to an acquittal, and the ecclesiastics concerned lay under strong suspicion. The historical importance of the case is that it showed the opinion of London to be violently anti-clerical and the jurisdiction of the Church ripe for serious attack.

This was one of Wolsey's reasons for seeking comprehensive legatine powers. He knew that reform must ultimately come, and he was determined that it should not be carried out by laymen, but by himself. In the end he did little. By controlling the courts Christian he prevented open scandals like the Hunne case, but the ultimate effect was to postpone the large question until it broke out with pent-up force after his fall. A parallel matter was that of benefit of clergy, whereby criminous clerks were immune from the King's law. The minor orders were not really priests in their lives or their functions and contained a good proportion of the criminal class. A temporary Act of 1512 partially deprived them of benefit. The Commons in 1515 sought to make it permanent, but the Lords under clerical influence threw out the bill. Again, Wolsey desired to have the abuse abated, but not by Parliament. His own suggestion was to the Pope, that recruitment to the minor orders should be limited and the criminal fringe of the Church thus gradually reduced. A papal bull decreed this course, but only for a term of five years, and the principle remained unsettled. Wolsey was impressed by the vigour with which the Commons stated their view. The result was that Parliament, which had been meeting frequently, was called no more for the next eight years. He would allow no power that could challenge his. The King was also impressed by these controversies. Their effect on him was different: he began to meditate on the fact that ecclesiastical jurisdiction was independent of his own.

Exercising by the King's permission vast executive authority, Wolsey attained in these years to an unexampled position of pride, power, and magnificence. Foreigners were particularly struck by it. Several of them have recorded the sumptuousness of his household, his furniture and service, exceeding that of any other subject; the numbers of gentlemen who attended him; his precedence over all the nobility; and his governance of the King. 'This cardinal', wrote an Italian, 'rules both the King and the entire kingdom.' 'He alone', wrote another, 'transacts the same business as that which occupies all the magistracies, offices, and councils of Venice.' They did not quite understand the source of his power, which was nothing but the pleasure of the King, revocable at any time. Wolsey had no support among the nobles or the higher ecclesiastics or even among the merchants. The nobles hated him as an upstart, the churchmen as a tyrant, while he never showed much appreciation of, or consideration for, trading interests. Even the humble folk, for whom he had some care and who did benefit by his enforcement of justice, were not grateful. They derived their political views from the talk which went on in the houses of the great, and which was gossiped and magnified by their servants. Even the intimacies of court life were thus made widely known among the people.

Meanwhile the position of the King was curious in these first half-dozen years of Wolsey's power. Henry was no idler, and every moment of his day was filled with occupation of body or mind. He exercised his muscular frame with hunting, jousting, leaping, and wrestling, thinking nothing of running thirty courses in the lists on successive horses and taking hard knocks in the process. He entered eagerly into banquets, masques, and ceremonials, always as the leader of the revels. He composed music. He devoted time every day to divine service. He read and disputed theology and listened with keen attention to the sermons of the best preachers he could find. 'Let every man have his own doctor; here is mine,' he said as he linked arms with Colet after a discourse in which the dean had criticized his war policy. He studied every detail of ships and artillery, questioning shipwrights, sea captains, and gunners, and bending his powerful mind to the comprehension of their arts. His personal acquaintance once saved a shipwright from a trial for heresy; examine the man if you will, he told the clerics, but do not press him too severely; you will find him simple in these matters.[1] Such things were retailed throughout the land, and account for Henry's hold upon his people. But why did he let Wolsey play the king? In foreign affairs, because he knew that Wolsey was his master in diplomacy, and was content to watch and learn. In home affairs, because it was convenient to have hard work efficiently done by one who could be displaced whenever necessary. Henry's was a

[1] M. Oppenheim, *Administration of the Royal Navy* (1896), pp 73–4.

developing character, as most are, not one subject to a sudden conversion; and the later Henry is incredible on the assumption that
the earlier was nothing but a pliant weakling.

The King's marriage was turning out unfortunately. Catherine of
Aragon was a woman of upright and dignified character, liked and
respected by all. But Henry and England wanted a prince to carry
on the succession, and the prince was not forthcoming. There was a
depressing series of premature births and infants that died soon after
birth, and the only survivor was the Princess Mary, born in 1516,
a disappointment because it seemed likely that no woman could
succeed to the throne without causing a renewed outbreak of civil
war. Some have surmised that the fatalities in the nursery were
traceable to the King's own state of health in these years. It is only
a surmise, which accords ill with the accounts of his general fitness
and well-being. Indeed, the medical history of the Tudor family
must ever remain an unprofitable subject, for lack of scientific
evidence. Catherine was some years older than her husband, and he
allowed himself some distractions, but he was never a libertine like
his contemporary Francis I. His one illegitimate child, a boy who
was made Duke of Richmond, was born in 1519. In politics Catherine
represented the Spanish alliance. Although a faithful wife, she was
also a faithful daughter, and in one letter written to her father she
alluded to England as 'your' kingdom. Ferdinand's perfidy in the
French war reacted on her position, and a rumour spread in 1514
that Henry was thinking of divorcing her. Such a plan may have
commended itself to Wolsey, but nothing came of it at that time,
although marriage projects still formed a prominent part of the
diplomatic stock-in-trade.

Scholarship flourished in England during the first decade of
Henry VIII. The King in his active life found time for it, Wolsey
wished to figure as its patron, and whole-time scholars found their
scope, although the age was not so exclusively theirs as they had
hoped. Colet remained Dean of St. Paul's until his death in 1519.
His influence was not that of writing and research, but of a Puritan
preacher who practised the strict life which he enjoined. If he did
not markedly reform his generation he at least made humbugs feel
uncomfortable and showed by contrast what humbug was. His
school for London boys, of which his duties did not permit him to
be high master, did much to spread the leaven of his way of life.
More was his disciple but not his counterpart, illustrating the good

life by genial friendship and a tolerance towards others combined with strictness to himself. More loved his life, his family, society, great business, and the court. The King loved him, but always with the reservation that the state, which meant the King, came first. More quite understood it. Long before the shadows of doom began to gather, he remarked that if his head could gain the King one castle in France it would fall. More lived in the world as it was, but for the world as it ought to be. He loved his England, full of the faults of which he could dream as one day to be amended. He was loyal to his Church, rampant as he saw it with folly and villainy, because these things were incidents which good men would correct. Loyalty was the toughest sinew of the inner character of More, as friendship was his greatest gift. In a sense we may reckon him the first great liberal, but not entirely, for his second greatest gift was humour.

Erasmus came again to England in 1509, and stayed five years. Lord Mountjoy invited him to share in the feast of humanism opening with the new reign. It was a disappointment, for high diplomacy and war were soon to take precedence, and the life of action to stand before the things of the mind. The King was gracious, but Erasmus got no high preferment. He taught Greek at Cambridge, making a poor living of it; but during those years he wrote the books that established his European fame, and prepared from Greek manuscripts his version of the New Testament, whose new renderings of certain words and phrases were ammunition for reformers of doctrine. In other writings Erasmus sought to kill the diseases of the Church with ridicule. Yet he had no wish to kill the Church. The outright rebels who were soon to arise in Luther's Germany hailed his ridicule as that of an ally and then denounced his churchmanship as that of a backslider. In truth he was consistent and never wavered from an attitude that the march of the times rendered sterile before his end.

More published his *Utopia* in 1516. In some ways the book is unlike its author, for there is little essential geniality or liberty in the society it depicts. The people's bodies are well cared for. All wear uniform, dwell in cities built as exactly alike as the ground permits, assemble to eat in public at the call of the bugle, discuss no politics except in open council, take their prescribed turns at town and country work, and sink into the slave-camp if they offend. Only in religion have their thoughts a qualified emancipation. To the nineteenth century, which lived in freedom and was alive to its defects, *Utopia* was an admirable essay in planning. To the twentieth century, which knows more of communism, *Utopia* is a cold hell in which Virtue reigns, all must seem virtuous, the things one may do are carefully prescribed, the things one may want to do are not done. There are no taverns, no betting, no money, no competition to improve one's position. Field sports are frowned upon, and the only game permitted is a sort of chess. *Utopia*, although its creator did not realize it, could not have lasted long without single-party elections and a secret police. But More did not mean his Utopians to be taken seriously. They are a peg on which he hung his satire of his fellow-Europeans, and his exposition of the moral principles which should inform government. Professor Chambers, in his fine biography,[1] explained those principles and showed how More sought to mould his own political life upon them; yet it must be said, though some have denied it, that in his later years, as Lord Chancellor, More did lend himself to persecution of heretics in accordance with the contemporary ethic and contrary to that expressed in his great book.

The hopes of explorers, like those of Erasmus, suffered under the King's preoccupations with war. Sebastian Cabot, returning in 1509, got no support for further work in the North West. In 1512 he was paid 26s. 8d. for making a map of Guienne, and went with Dorset's army to Spain. There, with his commander's consent, he transferred himself to Spanish service, in which he rose ultimately to be Pilot Major, or head officer of the mercantile marine. He maintained relations with England, which he revisited at least once in the ensuing years. In 1517 John Rastell, a lawyer and brother-in-law of Sir Thomas More, attempted a western expedition. American discovery was being discussed in More's circle, as the location of Utopia indicates. Rastell meant to explore the New Found Land with a view to pushing on thence to Cathay, which he placed a thousand miles beyond. He fitted out in the Thames, and Bristol played no part. The King gave him letters of recommendation to all Christian princes. He failed at the outset, for his mariners were unwilling. They wasted the season by putting into Channel ports on plea of defects, and when they reached Waterford refused to go any further and set Rastell on shore in Ireland. He came back and embodied the unhappy incident in a play in rhymed verse called *A*

---

[1] R. W. Chambers, *Thomas More* (1935).

New Interlude of the Four Elements, printed in 1519, which contains the first description of North America written in English.

In 1519 a greater interlude was ending, the halt in European rivalries since Wolsey had negotiated the general peace. Early in the year the Emperor Maximilian died, and the election of his successor began a new train of emulation and turmoil among princes; while in Saxony Martin Luther was already embarked on the course of protest and revolt that was to divide Christians in the centuries to come.

6

THE DECLINE AND FALL OF WOLSEY

At midsummer, 1519, the seven princely and ecclesiastical electors of the Holy Roman Empire filled the vacancy caused by the death of Maximilian by choosing his grandson Charles, then nineteen years old. Francis I had appeared to be a more or less serious candidate, and the electors required to be heavily bribed; but public opinion in the Empire made it necessary for them to elect a German prince, with schism and internal war as the alternative, and the senior representative of the Habsburg house had an unwritten right and a territorial eminence which placed him in advance of any possible rival.

Charles V, as grandson of Ferdinand and Isabella, was already King of Spain and of Ferdinand's conquest of Naples. As grandson of Maximilian and Mary of Burgundy, he was Archduke of Austria and the neighbouring provinces and the ruler of the Netherlands (henceforward 'the Emperor's Low Countries'), and of the County of Burgundy, with a claim to the Duchy of Burgundy, now incorporated in France. The imperial title gave him claim to the overlordship of Milan as a fief of the Empire, and to a vague pre-eminence in all Italy, actually divided among city states, ducal sovereigns, and the temporal possessions of the popes. The Spanish sovereignty included that of the Spanish conquests in the New World across the Atlantic. In 1519 they comprised the four great Antilles (Cuba, Hispaniola, Puerto Rico, and Jamaica), the Isthmus of Panama, and some weak holdings on the north coast of South America between the Isthmus and the island of Trinidad. As yet they produced little treasure or trade and were a disappointment to their owners. But in that very year Cortes was landing in Mexico, to achieve a conquest that would revolutionize conceptions of the wealth of America; and the pioneers in Panama were hearing golden rumours of Peru to the southward, although a dozen years were to elapse before Pizarro's conquest should prove them true.

At the time of his election Charles was in Spain, disliked and resisted as a foreigner by the nobles and townsmen who conceived themselves the victims of his greedy Flemish counsellors. He was obliged to leave Spain to take up his new responsibility, and after his departure the discontent became a civil war. Ultimately his lieutenants established his authority, although it was some time before Spain realized the advantage of having the greatest prince in Christendom as its king. While the claims of Charles in Milan and Burgundy were to territories in French possession, the French were similarly aggrieved at Naples and Navarre being in Spanish possession. The elements of a great war for supremacy between Francis I and Charles V were easily discernible. It could be averted only by fair give and take, which was not within the capacity of Renaissance statesmanship, and there was therefore no hope of averting it. This situation dominated Europe for forty years to come. Henry VIII and Wolsey, with questionable wisdom, allowed England to be drawn into the first stage of the conflict. In this they were men of their age, which regarded war as an exciting and pleasurable occupation natural to princes. Their people, with many individual exceptions, held the same view, although they reacted strongly against the taxation that was its logical sequence. Henry VII had followed a better way and had been less popular than his son.

Whether it was Wolsey's war or the King's has been debated, and the answer seems to be that they were agreed on it. The old idea that Wolsey tried to prevent it, but failed after two years, is now untenable. What may be called the romantic motive, that of figuring in great events, is the only one that can be found for the King's participation, and England then did not find the romantic motive so preposterous as she would do now. Wolsey, realist as he was, might also be willing to play to it, since his chief profession, in which it was essential to him to shine, was diplomacy, and the most spectacular diplomacy was that which accompanied war. Wolsey in addition aspired to be Pope, to which the war might open his path; and like most autocrats conscious of latent opposition he might calculate that war would distract criticism from domestic affairs. There appear to be no other reasons than these for the decision. It used to be thought that Wolsey worked for the balance of power, with England as the arbiter between the rival sovereigns or as the creator of a league against the stronger. But from the outset the Emperor was expected to prevail, and England nevertheless joined him, whereas her Navy in the Channel could effectively have cut his communications between Spain and the Netherlands. The decision to support Charles was taken on quite other grounds than those of a balance.[1]

In May 1520 Charles V landed at Dover on his voyage from Spain and had a preliminary interview with Henry at Canterbury. Henry was next engaged to meet Francis I in Picardy, to play the ostensible part of mediator for the preservation of peace. Such was not the real intention, and the gorgeous pageantry of the Field of Cloth of Gold in June was a gigantic sham serving only to bid up the value of English adhesion to the Emperor. Henry and Francis embraced like friends with enmity in their hearts, for their mutual dislike was inveterate. Their prestige was maintained by lavish expenditure on ceremonial entertainment, while all the time the English believed that Francis had troops concealed in the neighbourhood, and were on their guard against a treacherous attack. The constructive result of the performance was nothing. Afterwards Henry journeyed to meet the Emperor at Gravelines and Calais, and there the real business was done. Although the resulting treaty was in general terms, it was understood that England would join Charles V against France, if and when war should break out. It had not yet done so, and another year was to elapse before detailed plans and bargains would become necessary. Meanwhile it was publicly professed that Henry was seeking to restrain both sides from hostilities.

That year, 1520-1, produced some interesting events. Germany had long been discontented with the abuses in the Church, and more or less secret sects had existed whose tenets resembled those of the English Lollards in that they rejected Roman doctrine as well as criticized Roman practice. These ideas were already infiltrating eastern England by way of the trade routes, and may partly account for the anti-clerical attitude of London in the Hunne case of 1515. In 1517 Martin Luther, a Saxon monk, began his denunciation of the sale of indulgences in Germany. From that he proceeded to revolt on fundamental doctrines. In 1520 his writings incurred a bull of excommunication from Leo X, and at the close of the year he described the Pope as anti-Christ and publicly burnt the bull at

[1] See A. F. Pollard, *Wolsey* (1929) which discounts the balance theory.

Wittenberg. Luther gained powerful support from all classes in Germany, and his revolt was one of the important questions to be dealt with by the new Emperor in the imperial diet held at Worms in 1521. By that date the Pope had agreed to support Charles in the impending war, and Charles was therefore anti-Lutheran. At the diet Luther boldly asserted his opinions, and German adhesion to him was strong enough to save his life. He went into retirement for a time under the protection of the Elector of Saxony.

These things had their effects in England. The King and Wolsey were papalists, the King from theological conviction and sympathy with authority against rebellion, Wolsey because his legateship was the keystone of his position and because he expected loyalty to Rome to bring still higher reward. In 1521 the books of Luther and his associates were burnt in St. Paul's churchyard in a ceremonial at which Wolsey presided and the Archbishop of Canterbury was present. At the same time Henry was reading them and composing his answer on behalf of the Pope and the orthodox faith. His *Assertion of the Seven Sacraments* is judged by theologians to exhibit respectable though not profound scholarship and is known to have been substantially the King's own work. It was duly sent to Leo X, who rewarded the author with the title of Defender of the Faith. Thus England, the Emperor, and the Pope were ranging themselves on the same side.

A treason trial of 1521 testified to Henry's anxiety about the succession of his only legitimate child, the five-year-old Princess Mary. The Duke of Buckingham, who was, like the Tudors, a descendant of Edward III, had been speaking and acting unwisely. He ranked highest among the remnants of the feudal nobility, and he was jealous of Wolsey's ascendancy. Political observers thought that if the King died he would push his claim to the crown, and he was alleged to have spoken to that effect. The case against him amounted to little more than suspicion, and suspicion sealed his fate. His peers condemned him for high treason, and he was executed. There was some ineffective public sympathy; but the reasoned thought of the time held that the interest of the state transcended that of justice to an individual. Men remembered the civil wars and did not yet feel the importance of moral principle. Henry was the exponent of this view, which he was to push to extremes in time to come. The politician's trade was as dangerous as that of the soldier, and men entered it with their eyes open. Most dangerous of all was it to be a descendant of Edward III, and if, as is possible, that was Buckingham's only offence, he was deserving of sympathy.

A project of 1521 carried the development of the oceanic interest a stage forward. Hitherto the King and the cardinal had shown no concern for discovery and the new trades to which it might lead, and they had allowed Sebastian Cabot to transfer his services to Spain. The Newfoundland fishery was being frequented by the west-country seamen, and that was the sole gain realized from the discoveries already made. One explanation of the indifference was that Tudor policy had so increased the prosperity of the old trades that merchants were content to exploit them without seeking new. At this date a change took place in the King's views, and he became eager for oceanic expansion. Sir Thomas More and his learned friends were influential at court, and More's circle was interested in discovery. Stories of the promise of wealth in Mexico must have reached England through the English merchants resident in Seville, and from the same source it must have been known that the Emperor had despatched Ferdinand Magellan in 1519 with a fleet for the discovery of the westward route to Asia through the Pacific. Western exploitation was beginning a new chapter, and the age of the *conquistadores* was setting in. Henry VIII was always emulous of his brother sovereigns' achievements. It is possible also that he reckoned on the effect of an enterprise of his own in augmenting the value of the English alliance in the affairs of Europe.

Early in 1521 the King decided on the formation of a national company to be operated by the merchants of London and those of the outports. Wolsey approached the Mercers and Drapers and commanded them to subscribe to the equipment of a fleet of five ships, to which the King would add one, while Bristol had already promised two of its own. Sebastian Cabot had been in London and was to be the leader of the expedition. The objective is not clearly stated, but was almost certainly a voyage to Cathay by way of his passage through the New Found Land. Magellan had gone to seek a parallel passage round the southern end of South America, and Cabot knew more than the public knew about his intentions. The English project fell flat from the beginning, for the unusual reason that while the government was eager the merchants were opposed to the adventure. The merchants raised objections, one being that Cabot had never been in 'that land' (Cathay ?) himself and could not know the way, another that, if successful, the expedition would offend

Spain and draw retaliation on their established trade nearer home.
So lukewarm were the Londoners that Henry sent for their leaders
and personally rated them: 'His Grace would have no nay therein,
but spake sharply to the Mayor to see it put in execution to the best
of his power.' It certainly looks as though there was a diplomatic
motive which the citizens were thwarting. In the end passive resistance conquered, and the subscriptions were so meagre that no
expedition could be equipped. It is a curious incident; for the general
rule in such enterprises was that private adventurers were keen
while governments would do little to help.

As the year drew on it was evident that war was approaching and
that it was no longer advisable to send away good ships and seamen
who might serve with the Navy. The Spanish rebellion had proved
an irresistible temptation to Francis, who sent an expedition to
reconquer Spanish Navarre. It had little success, and the rebellion
was defeated in the summer. At the same time a Flemish noble
revolted against Charles and was assisted unofficially by French
soldiers. These events played into the hands of Wolsey, who went
over to Flanders in August to play the mediator while secretly
concerting measures of war with the Emperor. For three months
after concluding a secret treaty with Charles he pretended to be
seeking the preservation of peace, with his King as the arbitrator
of differences. Meanwhile Leo X confirmed his adhesion to the
alliance, Henry meditated a sudden attack on the French navy, and
the imperial forces made ready to invade Milan. They did so with
success in November, whereupon, in Pollard's words, 'Wolsey
rushed to the rescue of the conqueror'. In the August treaty it was
concluded that Charles should marry Henry's daughter and com-
pensate the English for the loss of the annual payments due from
France, and Charles promised his influence towards the election of
Wolsey as Pope at the next vacancy. Concealment of the pact until
November allowed the collection of the payments for 1521. The
papal vacancy occurred unexpectedly with the death of Leo X in
December. Throughout 1521 Francis I, himself an entirely unscrupulous man, had been treated with perfidy by Wolsey and his King.

In the diplomacy then fashionable Wolsey was unsurpassed. The
same can hardly be said of his statesmanship. He had displayed
immense ability in achieving results that were not worth having.
In 1522 Charles again visited England on his way back to Spain, his
safety assured by the English fleet. Later in the summer the English

declared war on France. The Earl of Surrey, although still Lord
Admiral, commanded the army of invasion, while Sir William
Fitzwilliam led the fleet. At the opening of his reign Francis I had
promised naval activity and had founded the new port of Havre de
Grace opposite the old Honfleur at the mouth of the Seine. Latterly
the French king had neglected his fleet, which was in no position to
challenge the imposing force that Henry had never ceased to build
up. Fitzwilliam sailed the Channel without opposition, raided coast
towns, and captured many merchantmen. It was as well that the
French could not fight, for the supply of victuals and stores to the
English Navy broke down, and confusion and corruption were
evident. Wolsey as the universal administrator was responsible. He
never showed any appreciation of the importance of sea power, and
there would have been no navy had not the King himself created it.
On land there was a fiasco. Francis, with Italy as his main theatre of
war, ordered his officers in northern France to act defensively and
avoid a decisive engagement. Surrey set out from Calais and marched
ravaging with great cruelty through the French districts of Picardy
but achieving no military objective, and that was all.

The treasure of Henry VII had long been exhausted, and the cost
of this futile war became a serious problem. War with France almost
automatically involved trouble with Scotland and further expenditure for northern defence. At Rome the cardinals in conclave showed
no disposition to consider Wolsey's claims. They elected as the new
Pope Adrian VI, formerly the tutor of Charles V, and the last non-
Italian to be chosen Pope. He was, however, in poor health, and
was not expected to last long, so that Wolsey continued to hope.
Wolsey's agent in Rome suggested that His Holiness should be
invited to England, where the climate would probably kill him.
The Emperor comforted Wolsey with pensions. In Scotland the
Duke of Albany reappeared from France in 1522 to bind the young
James V and the nobility to the French cause. Like the English
leaders in this war, he took the field too late in the season, and found
himself obliged to disband for the winter with nothing done except
to cause the English considerable expense in counter-measures.

Wolsey had no love for Parliament, and had not called it since
1515. In 1522 he tried to raise supplies for the war in the guise of a
loan. It was really an unconstitutional tax, for contribution was
compulsory, the mechanism of collection was that of taxation, and
no one expected repayment. The return was insufficient, and in 1523

it was necessary to summon Parliament. It met in April, and four months' haggling were needed before it would grant about half of the £800,000 that Wolsey demanded. That amount was unprecedented and staggering, and some declared that it represented almost as much coin as there was in the country. The Commons chose Sir Thomas More as their Speaker, and he did his best to bridge the gap between the House and the administration. Wolsey went in person to bully the members into acquiescence. He was received with defiant silence, for the Commons held that they were not required to debate with one who was not of their number. More humbly explained this to him, and he retired in dudgeon. A new man, Thomas Cromwell, was one of the members, and he was said to have made a speech declaring the folly and futility of the war, of which the alleged purpose was the reconquest of the former English possessions in France. It would be better, he said, to subdue Scotland first, and then it would be more feasible to adventure on the continent. It was a bold speech, but the King never resented bold advice when there was common sense in it. It is possible that this was the germ of the policy which he was to pursue in years to come. The clergy were not taxed in Parliament, but by their own convocations of Canterbury and York. Wolsey had no mind to suffer the intervention of Archbishop Warham, and used his legatine power to combine the two convocations under his own presidency. There, amid much resentment, he obtained the ecclesiastical contribution. The sunny days of Wolsey's rule were over. His violations of privilege and precedent were those of an angry and frustrated man, and the meeting of Parliament gave opportunity for talk against him and for its dissemination through the country.

While these things went on in London, two English armies were in the field, one under Surrey, the other under Suffolk. Surrey ravaged Scotland well beyond the border, until Albany returned from a visit to France bringing artillery and mercenaries. Albany advanced in force, and a great battle was expected on the Tweed. At Surrey's approach, however, Albany shirked the issue and retreated. The Scottish nobles reviled him and disbanded their forces, and the danger from Scotland receded. In France the Duke of Suffolk penetrated far southwards from Calais, but the imperial forces did not give the promised co-operation, and he had to retreat. In the south the Duke of Bourbon turned traitor to Francis I and joined the Emperor, but no great result came of it, and the French king substantially held his ground. For England this was effectively the last year of the war.

Adrian VI died in 1523, and then if ever was the time for Charles V to fulfil his promise to Wolsey. He did so by writing letters from Spain to recommend Wolsey's election and by retarding their transit until the election was over. The cardinals chose a Medici as Clement VII, and the Emperor had intended that they should do so. The papal throne was the real object, if there was one, for which England had poured out treasure and suffered humiliation, and it was lost. Clement VII turned out to be a poor investment for Charles, for he was so completely untrustworthy in an irresolute spineless way that neither friend nor foe could make anything of him.

So far Charles V had had the best of the war. He had recovered Milan and occupied Genoa, which went far to giving him command of the western Mediterranean; for the Genoese were famed for their mercenary fleets of fighting galleys, the counterpart of the Swiss pikemen on land. The English Navy had given him the still greater advantage of safe communication through the Channel from Spain to the Low Countries. The English themselves had gained nothing. In 1524 Bourbon led the imperial army from Italy to an invasion of Provence. It failed before the defences of Marseilles, and Bourbon retreated by the coast road of the Riviera. Francis I made a rapid counterstroke by crossing the Alps with a considerable army and coming down into the Italian plain. There, at the end of the year, he laid siege to Pavia. The garrison held out, and Francis held on too long while relieving forces were gathering. In February 1525 the imperialists surprised the French in their lines and won a really decisive victory, destroying the French army and taking prisoner the King of France.

For lack of money, Henry and Wolsey had done nothing in 1524. The news of the battle of Pavia moved them to an effort, not to restore the balance of power, but to strike in against defenceless France and claim a share of the spoil. The Emperor had other views. He was short of money, he had Italy, and he could force his royal prisoner to conclude a treaty which would give him his desires without further fighting. To consolidate his position he meditated marriage with an infanta of Portugal, which would involve breaking his engagement to marry Henry's daughter. Portugal, rich with the monopoly of the eastern spice trade, could afford a handsome dowry, and the union would be popular in Spain, where Charles was gradually improving his position. The English alliance was no longer vital to the arbiter of western Europe. Eastward he had yet to face a swelling wave of Turkish conquest, and here England could do nothing for him.

Before these things were apparent Wolsey was eager for a 'royal' invasion of France in the summer of 1525, with Henry moving magnificently in to assume the crown of the unlucky Francis. It was not practical politics, as the instinct of the English people realized. The truth was that England had no military power to sustain such a position, and had no means to pay for its creation. Effective armies on the continent were now composed of professional soldiers, organized and disciplined, expensively equipped with plate armour and an increasing proportion of firearms, and still more expensively accompanied by trains of artillery, which were growing indispensable in pitched battles as well as sieges. The age of the longbowman was over. His arrows would not penetrate armour, the nature of his weapon did not lend itself to close order and the steadiness of the disciplined mass, and he himself was not a regular soldier but an armed civilian, looking to plunder and a happy return after a short campaign. As for the finance of war, it was provided on the one side by the natural wealth of France, the most favoured land in Christendom, and on the other by the profits of oceanic adventure reaped by Portugal and now to a growing extent by Spain, and distributed through Europe by the Italian and German bankers and commercial houses. In this respect the conquest of Mexico was already improving Spain's position, and there was more of that kind to come. England had as yet no oceanic gains to show, but her real hope lay in her ships and sailors. The Tudor period was to be one of maritime greatness and not of military conquest. Wolsey had no glimmering of the truth, and his ideas were obsolete. Henry had more than a glimmering, as his royal fleet shows, but his mind was slow to mature.

The word, then, for 1525 was invasion of France; and the country refused to find the money for it. It was evident that another Parliament would be more recalcitrant than the last, and Wolsey resorted to a forced loan, to be levied like a tax at regular rates on every man's property. He called it the Amicable Loan, but it was certainly not amicable. Everywhere he met with refusal, from the city of London to remote villages. His own clergy opposed him. He was prepared to insist, even threatening the Lord Mayor and aldermen with the loss of their heads. The King was cooler. He had not lost his sense of what was possible. He called off the loan and abandoned the invasion. Whatever were Wolsey's feelings, he had to comply. He realized that the Emperor had not proved his friend. If France was not to pay in provinces she could pay in cash. And so, while Charles was extracting a dowry of 900,000 ducats from Portugal, Wolsey negotiated a treaty with the ministers of the captive Francis, whereby they were to pay 100,000 crowns a year during Henry's life as the price of peace with England. The first instalment arrived before the end of the year.

It is not easy to assess the condition of the people in the 1520's, the last decade before the social order was modified by the trans-ference of Church property to new owners. The evidence indicates that foreign trade prospered in spite of the wars, and the derivable impression is that the advance made under Henry VII was main-tained, but that further progress was less rapid. The cloth export provided the entire livelihood of many people, part-time employ-ment for many more, and an indirect effect on the prosperity of the landed interest as a whole, the combined categories representing virtually the whole nation. The greatest export was to the Low Countries and through them to Germany, the next greatest to Spain and thence indirectly to the Mediterranean. The importance of friendship, or at least the avoidance of war, with the Emperor was thus apparent. The Portuguese opening of the direct sea passage to the Indian Ocean, dating from the voyage of Vasco da Gama round the Cape in 1497–9, had revolutionized the spice trade, which was no longer in the hands of the Venetians and the Genoese. This caused the rapid decay and distress of Southampton, their port of entry. The products of Italy and the Levant remained important, and were being increasingly brought in by direct trade in English ships sailing chiefly from London and taking out English goods in exchange. Trade with Portugal, southern Spain, and the eastern Atlantic islands appears to have increased, and in general the old trade routes accounted for a genuine economic prosperity. It was subject to violent fluctuations. The war taxation of 1523 produced a slump, and Wolsey's loan of 1525 caused an acute crisis, with cloth-masters turning off their hands and merchants ceasing to lade their ships. The weakness lay in England's comparative lack of coined wealth or fluid capital. Merchants explained to Wolsey that though they might be rich in stocks they were bare of money, and the immediate effect on employment was considerable. But in all these matters the complaints of grievance are vociferous, and the voice of prosperity is silent. Men knew better than to advertise good fortune, and on the long view it would seem that the condition of England in the middle years of Henry VIII was much better than it had been at the accession of his father. Here Wolsey's solid work in the enforcement of law and justice was producing its effect. The need of the future was a share in the oceanic trades, and a few advanced minds, including the King's, were already making plans to secure it.

One remarkable plan proceeded from Robert Thorne,[1] a Bristol merchant resident in Seville. He knew the history of Magellan's expedition, whose sole surviving ship returned in 1522. Its main purpose had been to approach the spice islands by a west-going route which would be a Spanish monopoly, and then to claim that the islands themselves lay in the Spanish hemisphere of the globe as defined by the bulls of partition. To that extent the expedition had succeeded, but had found it impossible to return across the tropical Pacific in face of the trade winds. The surviving ship had therefore come home by the Indian Ocean and the Cape, thus circumnavigating the world and trespassing on the Portuguese monopoly. Charles V was at first inclined to exploit the discovery of Magellan's Strait and claim the spice trade, until another voyage emphasized the geographical difficulty explained above. At the same time the Emperor's marriage to the Infanta made it desirable not to quarrel with Portugal. In 1526 it appears that he was willing to sell his claim for what it was worth, either to Portugal or, surprisingly, to England. This caused Edward Lee, Henry's ambassador in Spain, to make enquiries among the English merchants about the value of the project. Robert Thorne answered by telling what he knew about 'The Spiceries', and then proceeded to unfold a different scheme of his own.

His plan was embodied first in a letter to Dr. Lee, and afterwards, more cogently, in a memorial addressed to Henry VIII and entitled 'A Declaration of the Indies'. Thorne's Indies were neither West nor East. They were the unknown lands and islands which he believed to exist in the tropical area of the Pacific. He expected them to yield gold and rich merchandise, and he held that they were divinely appointed to become an English empire beyond the seas. Even the route to them would be an English monopoly, for the ships would sail north from England to the north pole and thence follow the

[1] Son of the Robert Thorne of Henry VII's reign.

opposite meridian south to the mid-Pacific. Measured on the globe it was by far the shortest way, and he minimized the difficulty of the polar ice: 'there is no land unhabitable nor sea innavigable'. Nothing came of it at the time, but Thorne's memorial was known later to the Elizabethans, and had some effect on their enterprises.

Henry had already made trial of the North West Passage approach to the Pacific. In 1527, before the receipt of Thorne's project, he had sent out two ships under John Rut to seek Cathay by way of the New Found Land, the plan of which he had been baulked by the unwillingness of the Londoners in 1521. Rut lost one of his ships on the Labrador coast. Baffled by the ice, he turned southwards down the American coast, and appeared in the West Indies, the first English expedition known to have gone there. He tried to trade at Santo Domingo, but the Spaniards fired on him and he sailed away. It was a foreshadowing of much that was to come.

At home in these years Wolsey's legatine authority had important consequences to the Church. His full power was built up in stages by successive papal grants. When complete it amounted to virtually the whole jurisdiction of the Pope, to be exercised in England by a cardinal who was at the same time Lord Chancellor and the all-doing minister of the King. In times past kings and popes had disputed their respective powers over the English church. Now the royal and papal powers were combined. It was a golden opportunity for reform. Wolsey made little use of it for that purpose: he talked of more reforms than he effected. Power for its own sake was his aim, to satisfy his undying lust to do all and forbid any other man to do anything. He usurped the patronage of bishops in the appointment to benefices and in other exercises of administration. He ruthlessly invaded their jurisdiction and even that of Archbishop Warham in the various church courts, reducing every court Christian to his obedience. The bishops had by English law the collection of fees for the probate of wills. Wolsey increased the fees and made them payable to himself. He enjoyed the benefits of vacant bishoprics and collected most of the incomes of those held by absentee Italians, allowing them fixed stipends in lieu. He held in addition to his archbishopric of York another English bishopric (finally Winchester, the richest of all), and the abbey of St. Albans, the richest monastery in England. This was practical denial of a necessary great reform, that of pluralities and absenteeism. As archbishop he was himself an absentee, for he did not enter his province until the last year of his life, and his metropolitan city of York never saw him at all. He suspended the ecclesiastical work of the two convocations and performed it irregularly himself; and when the convocations met in time of Parliament in 1523 to grant taxation he combined them unconstitutionally under himself. In doctrine he and the King were papalists, and he professed no intention of reform. On the other hand, while he had by the combination of the spiritual and secular arms the opportunity for a great holocaust of Lollards and the newer heretics, he did not exercise it, and it is to his credit that not one heretic was burnt during his ascendancy. There were some imprisonments, and some of the culprits afterwards enjoyed his favour.

Reform could easily have begun with the monasteries, for everyone knew that they were in need of it. They were not subject to episcopal control, but Wolsey brought them under the legatine power by bulls which he obtained from Leo X in 1518–9. He used it to make appointments to the headships of houses, and to interfere in matters of detail, but he made no comprehensive investigation and reform. His patronage was not exercised to promote persons of high morality or learning. In one instance he appointed a woman of distinctly low morality to a nunnery, and earned thereby a rebuke from the King. He did not regard monastic endowments as sacred, and he suppressed about a score of the smaller houses in order to use their property for the support of his great new Cardinal College at Oxford and of another at Ipswich. Not long before his end he was contemplating the semi-suppression of a number of great abbeys by combining them with thirteen new bishoprics, the two foundations to exist side by side and the bishop to act as abbot; but this scheme did not come into effect.

All this power-accumulation by the legate was inevitably sterile, for it would perish with him. He could not found a dynasty of papal legates. Neither King nor Pope would allow any more such as he.[1] Reforms made by virtue of his power might have outlived him, but he did not make them. He did make the bishops and all influential clerics his enemies, so that they were to rejoice even more than the laymen at his fall. And when he should fall, the fruit of all his energy, ripe and ready for use, would pass 'on a plate' to the King.

The demand for the reform of Church jurisdiction and finance, and of the lives of churchmen, was left to accumulate until it became

---

[1] Wolsey's legatine powers were wrung from successive popes by persistent pressure and against their inclination.

irresistible in the next decade. At the same time the new learning, with heresy of the kind that was later called Protestant, was making headway in these last years of Wolsey's rule. Luther's writings began to have a serious effect in England in 1521. Henry's rejoinder has been noticed, and the burning of Lutheran books at St. Paul's. The books nevertheless continued to be imported and read, and their influence spread inland from the merchants of London and the east coast ports. The cardinal who was to become Pope Clement VII commented scornfully on the book-burning that the burning of heretics' bodies would be more effective; but to that Wolsey would not agree. In 1524 his new Oxford college was alleged to harbour Lutherans, and he did nothing to rout them out. Luther replied to Henry with scurrilous German abuse. The King laughed when he read it, but Sir Thomas More countered with equally regrettable abuse of Luther; and the general effect was to publicize heresy and undermine the age-old implicit faith. A body of opinion began to grow which was neither traditional nor Lutheran but, in a limited sense, sceptical, suspending judgment and awaiting an outcome. The Lutheran writings early reached Cambridge, reinforced by Erasmus's Greek Testament; and a group of students discussed them at a meeting-place that was known as Little Germany. Among them were Thomas Cranmer, William Tyndale, Hugh Latimer, Thomas Bilney, and others, who were to die in the flames in the fullness of their convictions. For the present they were feeling their way and making no spectacular pronouncements or defiances. Cranmer in particular was a man who thought deeply and moved slowly. About 1525, he said, he began to pray for the end of the Pope's jurisdiction in England, but he made no public profession to that effect.

Since the battle of Pavia there had been a pause in hostilities between France and the Emperor. The King of France was taken prisoner to Spain, and there in January 1526 he signed the Treaty of Madrid, by which he obtained his release on promising great surrenders of territory and leaving his two sons as hostages. Francis signed without any intention of observing the treaty, and probably Charles knew it, for he took quite coolly its subsequent repudiation. It was quickly made, and the question became that of a ransom for the French princes. France and the Pope and the Italian states formed the League of Cognac in May, ostensibly to promote peace, really to challenge the imperial preponderance in Italy. A terrible event, the conquest of Hungary by the Turks in the great battle of

Mohacs, gave momentary pause to Christian enmities, and Clement
VII was perhaps sincere in exhorting all princes to combine with
him in a crusade. But soon it was tacitly agreed that Hungary was
the Emperor's affair, and other terrible events were to follow in
Italy. The first was a battle in Rome between papal and anti-papal
factions, in which St. Peter's was plundered and Clement forced to
take refuge in the Castle of St. Angelo, his assailants being supported
by the imperialists. Wolsey, as ever, was anxious to aid the Pope
and to play a leading part in continental affairs. His plan now was a
league with France to moderate the dominance of the Emperor.
Charles, with the Turks and the Lutherans on his hands, wished for
a general settlement. Wolsey began with his French alliance as its
basis; and here the restoration of a balance of power may be regarded
as his aim, although it was a late conversion after the part he had
played in destroying the equilibrium.

Wolsey as usual dealt more in threats than in conciliation, and his
French alliance became an offensive league against the Emperor.
Early in 1527 the Bishop of Tarbes came from France to negotiate,
and proposals were discussed, the germ of much greater things, for
Henry's daughter to marry Francis, now a widower, and more
remotely for Henry himself, although not a widower, to marry a
French princess. There was naturally no allusion to the last matter
in the Anglo-French treaties signed at Westminster in April. These
provided for the first marriage and for a joint war against the
Emperor if he should refuse the terms of the allies. Once again
Wolsey was ignoring English opinion, which was anti-French and
pro-imperial. He had now the habit of regarding himself as pushing
all men into their places in his schemes, and was confident that he
could do it.

At this juncture the most terrible of events occurred in Italy. The
Duke of Bourbon, in command of an imperial army of German and
Spanish troops, moved south towards Rome in order to put pressure
on the Pope. The soldiers were unpaid and starving, and compelled
their commander to lead them to the assault of the city's walls.
Bourbon was killed at the opening of the attack, and thenceforward
there was no control. Rome resisted, and a thousand of the assailants
were killed. Then their comrades burst in and engaged in an orgy of
massacre, rape, profanation, and plunder such as the age had not
seen. The truth was bad enough, and it was exaggerated in the telling
throughout Christendom. The German Lutherans were naturally

not distressed, neither, a significant fact, were the people of London, who said that the Pope was well served. They hardly appreciated the importance of one outcome of the disaster, namely, that Clement VII fell into the hands of the imperialists and became the prisoner of Charles V. To Henry VIII and Wolsey that was a very serious matter, for the event was tied up with a business that was already secretly in agitation at the English court.

The secret business was of twofold origin. The King had long been worried by the insecurity of the succession to the throne. It lay with his only legitimate child, the girl Mary, not in robust health and not yet in her teens. Henry himself was thirty-six and his wife Catherine forty-two, and she could hope for no more children. That was one incentive to a drastic remedy. The other was that Henry, about the turn of the year 1526–7, had fallen in love with Anne Boleyn, the daughter of a rich and highly-connected knight of City origins who had recently been created Lord Rochford. Henry wanted a new queen to bear him a Prince of Wales, and was determined that she should be Anne Boleyn. Wolsey also wanted a new queen, but his plans demanded that she should be of the French royal house.

When Julius II gave his dispensation in 1503 for the marriage of Henry and Catherine of Aragon, there were doubts, shared by the Pope himself, of his competence to do so. In one aspect the doubts arose from the fact that a general council had pronounced against the papal power to dispense. In another aspect they concerned the nature and extent of the dispensation, whether in fact the previous marriage of Arthur and Catherine had been consummated, a matter incapable of proof or disproof. Henry VII had, for obvious political reasons, professed to entertain these doubts, but had ended by recommending his son to marry the princess. Her father Ferdinand had been keen for the marriage, and it took place in 1509 as part of the political alignment of the powers then being formed. Had a thriving family resulted all would have been well. The deaths of all but one of the royal infants were a disaster to a king who was the loyal servant of the Church and manifestly favoured by heaven in all other respects. They suggested to his mind a divine sentence on his doubtful marriage, a punishment for living in sin. Henry had these scruples of conscience before Anne Boleyn began to fascinate him. His theological learning and his faith in the doctrines of the Church made them inevitable. That he stifled them so long after the hope of a prince was dead testifies to a personal loyalty to Catherine which is to his credit and which would not have been shown for a moment by the cynical libertine who sat on the throne of France. With the passing years the succession problem became more urgent. The Buckingham trial was an act of injustice to promote a public good, to safeguard the child Mary from a probable challenge. Then came Anne Boleyn, and desire marched with conscience, sweeping the King down a muddy torrent in which his honesty was challengeable and he in his heart could scarcely have been certain how he fared. He was to emerge a worse man than he entered, with a conscience that he had learned to shape to his ends, and coarsened by some brutal actions. A fairly good man had been placed in a situation for which he was not good enough.

Anne Boleyn was the younger of two sisters, of whom the elder, Mary, had already been Henry's mistress, a fact which accounted for the ennoblement of their father in 1525. Anne herself went to France in 1519 as an English maid-of-honour to the French queen. She came back on the outbreak of war in 1522, being then about fifteen years of age and precociously experienced in the ways of courts. She was about twenty when the affair with Henry began, not very beautiful, but with a charm at least for him. She had no intention of succeeding her sister as his mistress, and Henry did not desire it. He wanted a queen and a legitimate heir. Behind her stood her father Rochford, whose wife was a sister of the Duke of Norfolk, the former Lord Admiral, Thomas Howard. Anne was therefore the Duke's niece. For the Norfolk connection the possibilities of political power flowing from a royal marriage were obvious, and promised Wolsey a severer tussle than he had experienced with Buckingham.

To describe the ensuing proceedings as a suit for Henry's divorce from Catherine of Aragon is to misrepresent the issue, but the word divorce has established itself and is convenient. Henry's contention was that he had never been lawfully married, and he sought from the Pope not a divorce but a pronouncement of nullity. In method Henry differed from Wolsey. The King proposed to marry Anne and then ask the Pope to confirm the accomplished fact. Wolsey was for obtaining the Pope's consent beforehand, and he had his way, intending that the new marriage should not be with Anne. He knew that his own position was growing precarious. Opinion was hardening against the French alliance, and many were expecting him to be dismissed by the King, with Norfolk succeeding him as minister.

His course was to trample down the incipient opposition and rouse the French to such a military effort that the Emperor should be overcome and all things set right by the triumphant Anglo-French league. It was a gamble by a desperate man who saw ruin as the alternative.

In February 1527 the Bishop of Tarbes had thrown out a hint that the Princess Mary might not be a brilliant match for France, since her legitimacy was questionable. This was by no means the origin of Henry's doubts, which had arisen long before, but it gave him an added incentive to proceed. In May the King was collusively summoned before Wolsey, in secret, and asked to answer as to the Pope's representative for living in sin with his brother's widow. Henry appeared to defend his position, but expressed readiness to accept censure if the case went against him. It was a mere rehearsal, and went no further; but the fact leaked out, and the Emperor was informed. He saw it, of course, as part of the Anglo-French plan against him, and was aroused more on that account than by indignation on behalf of his aunt. In June Henry himself informed Catherine that they must part, and her reaction was strong and uncompromising. Meanwhile Rome fell and Clement VII became the Emperor's prisoner. As such, he would not be allowed to facilitate the English plans, and Wolsey went to yet more adventurous lengths. From July to September he was over in France, attempting to conclude the Princess Mary's marriage (she was eleven years old), while knowing that he must shortly declare her parents to be unmarried, and seeking to anticipate all such objections by bringing on the decisive war. For the Pope's incapacity to aid him he had an answer. The Pope being under constraint, the cardinals must act in his place, Wolsey himself being appointed his vicar-general; and all cardinals were accordingly summoned to meet in France and take measures for the government of the Church during the captivity. Only four answered the summons, and the failure of the scheme was obvious. Charles countered it by allowing Clement the semblance of liberty by means of an arranged escape from Rome to Orvieto, a town whose geographical position precluded any access save by the goodwill of the imperial commanders.

In the latter part of 1527 Henry began to appreciate that Wolsey was playing for his own hand and was not to be relied upon as a promoter of the Boleyn marriage. The minister's three months' absence gave scope to Norfolk and the Boleyn faction to press their views, and Anne made no concealment of her dislike of the cardinal. The end, however, was not yet. Henry was one to ruminate on suspicions and allow them to ripen before taking action, and he gave little or no sign that his confidence was waning. In January 1528, at Wolsey's vehement instance, Henry declared war on the Emperor, and France did the same. Charles, who was informed of the opinion of the English people, published a damaging reply, in which he alleged that Wolsey had asked him to make him Pope, and on refusal had threatened revenge even though it should cost the ruin of England. True or not, it was what the English wished to hear, for a war with the Netherlands and Spain would cost the ruin of a great many of them. The cloth trade was an unanswerable argument for peace with the ruler of those countries. Feeling ran higher than in 1525, and it became plain that the people would not permit the war to be begun. The King also would not hold out for the war, which might cost him his throne. He could offend his people's wishes to a certain extent, but he knew when to stop. In three months trade was being resumed, and in six months a truce was formally signed. The French sent a strong army into Italy and marched the length of the country, but by the end of 1528 it had all come to nothing and Charles had restored his position. Next year Clement VII agreed to peace on the Emperor's terms and became his man, or 'his chaplain' as it was described by some. France also made peace by the treaty of Cambrai. Wolsey's great stake was lost, and England was well out of an adventure that was in no one's interest but his.

The fortunes of the matrimonial suit fluctuated with those of the war. At the beginning of 1528 Clement, not knowing who would win in Italy, refused to make any decision, and suggested that Henry should marry Anne at once, leaving the question of Catherine's marriage unsettled. Henry now had more sense of public propriety, if not of morality, and declined to be the husband of two wives at once. Then the French began to score their successes. In April the Pope commissioned Wolsey and Cardinal Campeggio, who held an English bishopric, to hear and decide the case in England, without any appeal allowed against their judgment. It was something, but not all that Henry wanted, for Campeggio at least might decide against him. He pressed for a commission in the form of a decree predetermining the case in his favour. At length, the French advance continuing, Clement issued this commission to Campeggio with orders that he was to show it only to Henry and Wolsey, to keep it otherwise secret, and not to let it out of his possession; and generally, to create all possible delay before bringing the case to trial.

Campeggio, elderly and in poor health, was not disposed to speed. He took nearly three months on the journey from Rome to England, and when he arrived in the autumn of 1528 the French victories had dissolved in defeat. It seemed that his master's master would prove to be the Emperor after all. That was also the view of Clement, who sent a message to Campeggio that he was not to give sentence without further orders, and another instructing him to destroy the secret decree. Campeggio occupied the winter in theological arguments with Henry and in joint efforts with Wolsey to persuade Catherine to deny her own position or to enter a convent. Catherine was unshakable in her determination to hold out to the end. By all straight reasoning she was Henry's wife, and so she would remain. Her hopes were raised by the sudden production in Spain of a hitherto unknown brief of Julius II, which cut away the grounds for challenging the validity of his famous dispensation. This new document was suspect for more reasons than one. There was no record of its issue in England or in Rome. The English representatives in Spain saw it and declared it a forgery, and they were not allowed to bring it to England for examination. The effect of this incident was to prolong the delay before the opening of the legatine court of the two cardinals.

The English of the Tudor period were in the mass a free people, their freedom tempered by the fact that the monarchy could act tyrannically towards individuals. Such individuals were generally members of the ruling class, participators in the dangerous political game, and the masses were not unduly sensitive to their misfortunes. When, however, the interests or sentiments of the people were really touched, the popular voice made itself heard with freedom and emphasis. Henry VIII had a keen ear for it, more especially when it was the voice of London, the citadel of the Tudor position. In 1528 the sentiments of London and of all England were touched by the ill-treatment of Queen Catherine. She was well liked for her honest and fearless character, in spite of her foreign blood. Her rival, Anne, although of London origin, was hated even by Londoners, who saw her as the King could not see. The expression of their views became loud and forcible. Henry deemed it well to explain himself. He called a representative meeting in the City and declared that his conscience was the mover of his action, that

Catherine was a noble woman of the highest qualities, and that nothing would please him better than that she should be adjudged his lawful wife. But he spoke also of the danger of a questionable succession to the domestic peace which the land had enjoyed for twenty years, and of the doubts expressed by the Bishop of Tarbes and other great clerics. He ended by asking them to declare these things to all men and to pray that the truth might be established. What are we to think of it? He was a complete egoist, as a man in his position, the centre of twenty years of king-worship, could hardly fail to be. But he was the state, and his egoism included the public interest as well as the personal. Perhaps, with the better part of him, he believed what he said while he was saying it. The cynical explanation is too easy. He was not all hypocrite.

In the summer of 1529 the two cardinals at length opened their court. Henry and Catherine appeared personally before it, Catherine to make an impassioned appeal for justice, kneeling in supplication before the King, and then to leave, denying the competence of the court. The case proceeded without her, the evidence and pleadings all in favour of the King. Sentence was expected on 23 July. Campeggio had orders from Rome not to pronounce it. He adjourned the court until October. Wolsey had expected this, but Norfolk and his friends were taken by surprise. Suffolk, the foremost of them, broke into abuse of cardinals and of Wolsey in particular, a new portent on a public occasion such as this. The Pope, as Wolsey knew, had already signed a 'revocation' of the trial to Rome, and there would be no autumn continuation. Campeggio departed. Agents searched his luggage for the secret decree, and did not find it; for undoubtedly he had destroyed it. The failure of the legatine court was in the outcome Wolsey's death-blow, and it came after a moment of extravagant hope earlier in the year. For then a report had spread that Clement was dead, and for the third time Wolsey had been confident of election and escape from the encirclement that was drawing round him. But Clement lived, and the Emperor kept tight hold of his chaplain.

A week after the adjournment the King summoned Parliament to meet in November. It was not Wolsey's policy, and the King was now in command. With his sense of the public will he had taken the strongest measure in his power. Indignation was now against Pope and Emperor, who were citing the King of England to plead before a foreign court, and Catherine's wrong was overwhelmed by a blast of national pride. In such temper, Parliament would debate more than the King's matter. The Pope and the Church and the legatine authority were open to attack, and for aid they could hardly look to the Defender of the Faith.

Wolsey's overthrow came simply and quietly before Parliament met. Nothing more was needed than a piece of legal routine, a writ of *præmunire* in the court of King's Bench. *Præmunire* was the opening word of the Latin writ, and became by that accident the name applied to the statute passed in 1392, of whose purport it gives no indication. The purport was that whoever should introduce papal bulls or other instruments into the realm, and by their means exercise authority which pertained to the King, should be subject to perpetual imprisonment and forfeiture of goods. It was easy to show in many detailed instances how Wolsey had broken the statute by his actions as papal legate, and it was no defence for him to allege that the King had consented to his so doing; for, as the law stood, the King had power to pardon an offence after it had been committed, but not to give licence for its committing in advance. Wolsey in fact made no defence, but only submission. The penalties of *præmunire* fell short of death, he had hopes that they would not be fully enforced, and with Parliament approaching, the alternative might be an act of attainder that would cost him his head. The Lord Chancellor understood the legal position as well as any man, and had to make the best of it. His hopes were justified in that he was not imprisoned and that the King, while taking the greater part of the immense fortune accumulated from the exercise of power, left him still a wealthy man.

He did not remain Lord Chancellor. He was required to resign the great seal, and just before the meeting of Parliament it was delivered to Sir Thomas More. As for the legateship, however the Pope's appointment might stand, it was gone with the wind when *præmunire* precluded its exercise. To Wolsey it had been the embodiment of all his greatness, transcending any office in the King's gift, and he well knew that not only he but the papal power in England had fallen in a common ruin. There were others who knew it too.

Wolsey had yet a year of life and fitful hope and restricted activity, but in those October days of 1529 his ministry ended, and with it the age of Wolsey in England's history. In his life-work he had been an administrator rather than a reformer. His pervading energy left little scope for the normal functions of the English state to act, or to develop on their historic lines. In that sense he was a fifteen-years interregnum. If we try to sum up, and ask whether his European prancings, his intrigues and wars, his mastery of the Church, his good work for justice, his waste of treasure, his light hand with heretics, his governance of the King, were for England's good, the answer, from one student, is—probably yes. Not long emerged from a period of anarchy, society's chief need was firm government, and Wolsey contributed to that.

7

ONE BODY POLITIC: THE ROYAL SUPREMACY

IN the years after Wolsey's fall a change, so rapid as to constitute a revolution, took place in the English realm. A biographer of Henry VIII might recount it in terms of his matrimonial affairs and the development of his character. In the history of the Church it comprises the overthrow of the Roman jurisdiction and the confiscation of ecclesiastical wealth. In the record of religion it includes denial of doctrines formerly accepted and some tentative steps towards the formulation of a new statement of belief. But in the moulding of the state the record is of all the above, and more. It is the story of the fusion of diverse elements in people and polity into a more compact and self-conscious nation, into 'one body politic', to use a phrase that was current at the time; and of the modification of institutions to that end. Henry's share of the work was quickly done in those years, although left ragged and incomplete. Two more decades of turmoil led to its rounding off in what is called the Elizabethan settlement. A further generation of uncertainty followed before it was evident that the settlement was established and that the English people could go forward from that basis to new advance, taking for granted the answers to the great questions of the past. Only in the retrospect of centuries does it appear that Henry's work was the root of all.

Throughout the Middle Ages the people had existed in the two great categories of clergy and laymen, with a more even balance than those terms suggest to modern minds. Statistics are lacking, but it is clear that the clergy were far more numerous in proportion than they are to-day, and that their corporate wealth and power were greater still in proportion to their numbers. In many respects they were independent of the King's governance, and in many they governed the King's nominal subjects. In the House of Lords the bishops and abbots usually outnumbered the lay peers. The Commons could grant the King taxes payable only by laymen, while the clergy taxed themselves in their convocations, sometimes at different rates. Episcopal courts dealt with laymen's property, and courts Christian competed with the common law in enforcing the discipline of ordinary life. The clergy were nearly all Englishmen, but they thought of themselves as churchmen, members of an organization that was not national but common to all Christendom. Their law was that of the universal church, their capital was Rome, and their supreme head was the Pope. In brief, the allegiance of about half the active opinion and political force of the country was to an outside authority, while that of the other half was to the national king. Men were conscious of the weakness of this system, illustrated by its past failure to stand the strain of a feeble monarchy and ambitious factions. The same strain threatened to occur again at any moment when the King should die. The incentive to strengthen the political fabric was therefore urgent, and it could only be done under the King's leadership while yet there was time. Allegiance to the national crown must supersede allegiance to Christendom as a whole. To make the decision involved a strife of opinion, and only by strong handling could a strife of armed forces be averted. Individuals suffered that cities should not burn.

The stratification of the lay and clerical estates was the major but not the only weakness. England north of the midlands was isolated and imperfectly controlled from the capital, given over to the feudal allegiances and special jurisdictions that had died out in the south, with lawless traditions fostered by border warfare. The marches of the Welsh border and Wales itself were another anarchical region where the King's writs often failed to run. Multitudes of small anomalies existed, particularly in the seaports, special rights and immunities, commonly entitled 'liberties', but really hindrances to the liberty and action of the people as a whole. The sting needed to be taken out of them, although, in English fashion, their vestiges were to remain innocuously for centuries to come; for their liquidation was not usually by abolition but by encroachment of the central authority.

The King and his later ministers were alive to these problems, but could not have dealt with them unless a great progressive section of the community had been fully as determined as they. The active forces of the time were agents of change. The New Learning bred reformers of religious doctrine, generally too forward for the taste of the crown, but playing their part in dissolving the conservative opposition to its aims. The secular education of the Renaissance produced open minds ready to consider new policies, and fastened the stigma of the obsolete upon unreasoning resistance to change. The great geographical discoveries began to interest seamen and merchant adventurers and to generate ambitions whose fulfilment could proceed only from the basis of a solid national state and stable government. It was a long-term factor, whose early workings nevertheless will be seen in the post-Wolsey decade. The merchant class as a whole was thriving and successful, acknowledging its debt and pledging its support to strong government. It saw what passed in foreign countries and was able to compare and think constructively. More than any other men the merchants abhorred the idea of civil war and placed their hope in national unity. They and their counterparts the country gentlemen were ready to co-operate, and to push their interests in the Parliament which henceforward the King was to make a more prominent part of the national system. In sum, the energy and intellect of the nation were with the King. A few first-class men were against him, seeing what havoc he was to work with the old world which they loved and would have reformed on different lines. The bulk of his opponents lacked resolution and initiative, their defence of a lost cause dissolving in fitful flurries and tame acceptances. To categorize, however, although easy, may be deceptive. Most men felt rather than reasoned, and their sentiments on diverse subjects pulled them in different ways. Ideas did not flow in smooth currents but in troubled cross-currents. The pattern is confused and contradictions abound. Out of them we have to pick the conclusions that are clear.

In the opening stage the King was dominated less by desire for reformation of Church and state than by determination to succeed in his marriage project. Apart from morality, his judgment was sound. The body politic needed a male succession to the crown, without which few expected to avert a breakdown. Until its solution in 1533 the marriage problem governed politics.

Under Wolsey hardly any other man had counted as of the first importance. With his fall half a dozen men acquired a new prominence. More as Lord Chancellor and Norfolk and Suffolk ranked as senior councillors. Stephen Gardiner, a rising political cleric who had once been intimate with the Cambridge reformers, succeeded to the bishopric of Winchester, compulsorily resigned by Wolsey. John Fisher, Bishop of Rochester, took the lead against the King's policies in the House of Lords, his choice made and his resolution steeled in advance even of More. William Warham, Archbishop of Canterbury, his long life drawing to its close, remained inactive and aloof as Wolsey had compelled him to be. Thomas Cromwell was not yet ostensibly a minister, although he may already have been an influence in the background. He had made his value known as Wolsey's servant. He cannot be said to have deserted his old master, for his employment was gone. He wasted no time on sentiment, paid court to Norfolk, and took care that his abilities should be known to the King. Henry was now in active control, with More, Norfolk, and Suffolk as his leading men of affairs. He had an uncomfortable time while they were striving to learn the business at which they had been onlookers rather than actors in the past, and he was tempted to regretful hankerings after the masterliness of Wolsey. Among secondary figures of rising note we may count John Stokesley, Bishop of London, Edward Lee, soon to be Archbishop of York, the Earl of Wiltshire (formerly Lord Rochford), father of Anne Boleyn, and, outside the English ranks, Eustace Chapuys, the able Savoyard ambassador of Charles V. Unknown to the public in 1529, unknown as a man of destiny even to himself, waited Thomas Cranmer, though he was not to wait for long. Before the Parliament met he had already let fall the opinion that was to launch him at the age of forty on a great career.

The first session of the 1529 Parliament endured for only a few weeks at the close of the year. The Commons met in a mood to give utterance to the anti-clericalism that was rising like a tide in the country, and in the King's mind also. The general feeling was spontaneous, and there is no reason to suppose that Henry unduly influenced the elections: he had no need to, although he did ensure the choice of certain individuals who would be useful. King and Commons were at one in their view of the Church as an organization. They were at one also in their adherence to Catholic doctrine. No leanings towards heresy were so far evident. The Commons passed bills restricting mortuary fees and probate fees, and prohibiting, with many exceptions, pluralities and non-residence of clergy and their participation in trade. Fisher in the Lords denounced this as incipient heresy, which the Commons indignantly denied. The King intervened and so managed the contestants that the bills were passed. The return of Wolsey to power still seemed possible. Among the Lords, lay and spiritual, he had no friends; and they passed a bill of exaggerated charges against him, which the King allowed to be smothered in the Commons after a speech for the defence by Thomas Cromwell. Wolsey 'in being', if not in office, had his uses. Parliament was then prorogued for more than a year. Viewed as a stage in the progress of the King's marriage plans, this session was, or should have been, a warning to the Pope that the King was capable of dealing him heavy blows, and an intimation that concessions might avert them.

Early in 1530 Henry sent Stokesley, Lee, and Wiltshire to Italy to seek the Pope's complaisance. They arrived to find Clement as tightly held by Charles V as ever, in process indeed of crowning him Holy Roman Emperor at Bologna. Far from granting Henry's desire, the Pope summoned him to appear at Rome to answer Catherine's appeal. Henry knew that the Pope was not a free agent, and sought by suitably increasing the pressure to convince him that it would be better to defy his imperial master than to lose England. At the same time Henry was careful to show his distaste for heresy, and so to make a bargain easier when the time for it should come. St. Paul's churchyard witnessed new burnings of heretical books, including William Tyndale's biblical translations, while pressure was being applied in a new form from which the King hoped much.

In August 1529, not long after Campeggio had shown the Pope's hand by adjourning the legatine court, the King set out on progress through the country and stayed a day or two at Waltham. Living there was Thomas Cranmer, as tutor to the two sons of a gentleman named Cressy. When the court came to Waltham, Stephen Gardiner was billeted in Cressy's house. Gardiner and Cranmer were old Cambridge acquaintances of the Little Germany days. They talked of the King's divorce and the intolerable delays of canon lawyers, so recently instanced by Campeggio's intervention. Cranmer with some diffidence gave his suggestion for a solution, that the King should turn his back on the canonists and appeal to the theologians on the question whether a man could marry his brother's widow. The appeal should be made to the doctors of divinity of the universities throughout Christendom. Gardiner reported this suggestion to the King, who was exceedingly pleased with it. He had himself the learning of a divine, and knew that his case was stronger in theology than in law. He was convinced that honest opinions would be in his favour. Their pressure on the Pope would be powerful, for the authority of the universities might be cited as more weighty than his.

Thomas Cranmer was a shy and diffident man. He ascribed it himself to bullying as a little boy by a brutal schoolmaster. Macaulay, whose boyhood had not been of that sort, wrote in his exuberant way that Cranmer was a slave to a tyrant king and base politicians. It was far from true. Reserved and slow and with an inly working mind, Cranmer did not seek danger, but he did form resolves and conceptions of duty that now impelled him to quit the life of meditative peace and take the risks of a life that held no attraction. If he had weakly sought escape England would have been the poorer. We may note also that his diffidence was with ambitious, thrusting men whom he simply had not words to answer. With those of his own calling he could be quietly firm. The King respected him and never threatened him, and they became personal friends; at the end, in fact, he was the King's only personal friend. He had the physical courage of a good horseman who loved to master a rough mount; it was noted of him that he would choose the most difficult horse in a stable, and a middle-aged scholar was not expected for his credit's sake to do that. When the King returned to London for the 1529 session of Parliament he appointed Cranmer to work out his proposals in writing, and lodged him in the house of Anne's father, the Earl of Wiltshire.

Cranmer 'did a book', as the phrase was, of his arguments to the divines, and went to his own university to try its effects. Opinion at Cambridge was divided, but it seems that Cranmer's views won over some dissentients and turned the balance to a qualified decision in the King's favour, although Cranmer himself had left before the issue was decided. Oxford also returned with some reluctance a majority opinion for the King's contentions. Cranmer meanwhile was attached to the mission, already mentioned, which Henry sent in 1530 to Clement VII. It failed in its approach to the Pope, but on its journey obtained favourable opinions on the theological point from the French universities. In Italy also some of the universities agreed with the English point of view in spite of the Pope's displeasure. In Germany the Lutheran universities were not so serviceable. They had little more reason for benevolence to Henry than to the Pope, and Lutherans in general took broader views on marriage restrictions than were useful in this particular case. In Spain, as might be expected, the divines were preponderantly against Henry. On a general view, discounting English and Spaniards as partisans and counting French and Italians as neutrals, Henry received considerable and genuine support from the learned men of the Catholic world, and some no doubt speculated on how a General Council of the Church would treat the matter. Such a Council was overdue and was dreaded by Clement, for it might deal with things that touched him closely, such as the territorial possessions of the papacy and the aggrandizement of papal families.

Early in 1530 Wolsey still had hope of some return to power. The King formally pardoned him for his offences, and in the summer he was allowed to take up his duties in his province of York. He performed them, as was his nature, efficiently, but they did not satisfy him, and he was soon dabbling in politics and communicating with foreign ambassadors. Norfolk and the Boleyns were on the alert and reported their suspicions to the King. By seizing and roughly treating a servant of the Cardinal's they obtained evidence of treasonable designs that are unlikely to have been true. In November Wolsey was arrested to stand his trial for high treason. He knew that for a man like him trial and sentence were synonymous terms. He died at Leicester Abbey on his way to the Tower. Henry, who had already written him off, affected no regret. The court indulged in merriment on the event.

A few days after the death of the great victim of *præmunire* the King had a writ entered under the same law against the whole order of the clergy, on the ground that they had accepted the legatine authority. It was a terribly simple law, the only limit to its reach being the King's will, and laymen perceived that it could be levelled as easily at themselves as at the clergy. The clergy had no defence, although most of them had been utterly unwilling offenders, since they had detested the legatine power while submitting to it. The two convocations had to buy their pardon of the King by a huge money payment and by something else of more enduring importance. In February 1531 Archbishop Warham put it to his convocation that they must acknowledge the King as 'singular protector, only and supreme lord, and, so far as the law of Christ allows, also supreme head of the English Church and clergy'. He did not ask for voices in favour, but accepted the assembly's silence as consent; and so it was passed. At the same time Parliament was meeting for its second session. Its business was to legalize the pardon which the clergy had bought so dear. The Commons were careful to claim similar pardon for the laity and obtained it for virtually nothing, the condition being that the King was absolved from repayment of Wolsey's Amicable Loan, which would not have been repaid in any case.

For the remainder of 1531 there was a lull in the divorce proceedings. Anne and her faction were highly unpopular in the country. Still more unpopular was the prospect of a quarrel over the matter with the Emperor, with a consequent stoppage of trade. Catherine was uncompromising as ever, and resistant to new persuasions to make way for her rival. The Pope was known to be unstable and at the service of him who could squeeze hardest. Henry paused to take stock of these factors and feel his way. A legitimate male heir was what he wanted, and he exercised considerable patience. The conception of him as the mere victim of amatory lust does not accord with the time factor in the story. He determined to marry Anne in the winter of 1526–7. He ultimately married her in that of 1532–3. In the six years between he could have had his way with her as a lover had he so chosen. What he did choose was to exercise the restraint of a statesman. The comparative inaction of 1531 was probably due to the slow maturing of a policy in the King's mind. By 1532 it was ready. At this time he lacked first-class advisers. More had brains enough, but was unwilling in the marriage matter, and the King used his service in other directions. Norfolk was willing, but lacked foresight and initiative. He was a cold-hearted time-server, sadly fallen from the promise of the gallant young man who had fought Andrew Barton and charged home at Flodden. Suffolk was a hearty, obstinate, out-of-doors man, of small use in diplomacy. Gardiner, who had no respect for the Pope, was ready to serve, but Henry seems never to have had a high estimate of his ability. Cromwell was the really necessary man, and it is possible that in this year the King began to listen to him.

However it was, Parliament met for serious business at the opening of 1532. Anti-clericalism was not satisfied with the small victories of 1529 and demanded greater things. Henry was ready to make it his instrument by appearing as a king importuned by popular zeal, doing his best to mitigate its excesses, and warning the Pope that unless he were reasonable nothing could avert a catastrophe. The part of the magnanimous mediator was one that Henry knew well how to play. In February someone initiated in the Commons a bill to stop the payment of annates, the first year's income of newly occupied benefices, to the papal treasury; and the King told the papal nuncio that it proceeded from the popular demand. Before the annates bill had gone far the Commons presented a petition to the King—'a supplication against the ordinaries'—praying redress of the injurious powers and exactions of the clergy. Without doubt it represented the views of the House, and undoubtedly also it was initiated by the King. There is evidence that Cromwell had a hand in it, even if he did not devise it. The petitioners deplored the spread of heresy but asserted that faithful men were unjustly condemned for it in the spiritual courts. They complained of clerical avarice and money-getting by many methods. They pointed out that convocation had power to make canon law repugnant to the laws of the realm, thereby diminishing the King's authority. The King accepted the supplication and referred it to convocation for reply. The reply was of course unsatisfactory, and the King required convocation to submit to new rules on its legislation. Henceforward they were to make no new canons without the royal consent; while the whole existing canon law was to be reviewed by a committee of the King's choosing, and all articles found contrary to the law of God or of England were to be eliminated. Convocation could only yield, and the surrender is known as 'the submission of the clergy'.

Part of the canon law thus to be amended related to the consecration of prelates, concerning which Henry blandly announced that he had made a discovery. 'We thought,' he said to a parliamentary deputation, 'that the clergy of our realm had been our subjects wholly. But now we have well perceived that they be but half our subjects, yea and scarce our subjects. For all the prelates at their consecration make an oath to the Pope clean contrary to the oath they make to us, so that they seem his subjects and not ours.' The implication was that he had had no previous knowledge of the oaths.

The Act of Annates was passed while the above business was going forward. It was not a measure against the clergy, who were indeed represented to have initiated it, but against the Pope. Henry intended to use it for pressure and secured the inclusion of a clause whereby the operation of the measure was suspended until the King should decide to enforce it. Clement, however, took little notice, and in November threatened excommunication if Henry should proceed with the divorce. Two other events of 1532 were important. Immediately after the submission of the clergy More resigned the

chancellorship and retired into private life; and in August the aged
Warham died, leaving a vacancy most opportune for the King's plans.

The patient work of years was now ready to bear fruit, and Henry
moved rapidly to victory. In Cranmer he knew that he had a man
convinced of the justice of his cause and abhorrent of the papal
jurisdiction. He decided that Cranmer should be the new Archbishop
of Canterbury. Gardiner might have served his turn, but he would
have done so as a matter rather of politics than of conviction; and
Henry appreciated conviction when he himself shared it. Cranmer,
in his sojourn in Wiltshire's house, had become an adherent of Anne.
'The gospel light that dawned in Boleyn's eyes' was the phrase of a
much later enthusiast, but it does perhaps express her command over
Cranmer, who was slowly turning in the Lutheran direction. She
seems to have had for those who knew her a magnetic quality that
outweighed her essential cheapness. That indeed was evident to the
women of the people, one of whom came up before the justices for
describing her as a goggle-eyed whore. But to Cranmer she was a
child of light, and he would do his best to make her queen. He did
not wish to do it as archbishop. He had no desire for money or place;
but it was the King's command, and he somewhat sadly obeyed. He
was away in Germany on the royal business when the vacancy
occurred, and so small was his respect for canon law that he brought
home with him a German wife, the niece of a Lutheran divine.
Henry did not boggle even at that. There was no time to be lost, for
by the end of 1532 Anne was with child.

In November 1532, or more probably in the following January,
Henry and Anne were married so secretly that neither time,
place, nor celebrant can be conclusively stated. Cranmer's name was
already before the Pope for the archbishopric, since it was essential
that his position should be completely regular. Clement saw no
reason to refuse. The vacancy had to be filled, and he himself had
seen Cranmer two years before and probably regarded him as a
harmless nonentity. The Act of Annates also was in suspension, and
a concession might keep it so. The requisite documents were therefore dispatched with unusual speed, and Cranmer was consecrated
with all the formalities on 30 March. Before taking the usual oath to
the Pope, he privately wrote and signed a statement that he held the
oath void if it should conflict with his duty to the King. Elaborate
arguments have been framed in defence of this deception. The best
that can really be said for it is that it was common form and

characteristic of churchmen. Lee, Stokesley, and Gardiner at this time took the same oath and broke it.

Concurrently with Cranmer's business an Act of Appeals was passing through Parliament. It declared that 'the body politic' of temporal and spiritual people in England was entirely subject to the King, that the English Church was competent to determine its own ordinances, that appeals to Rome caused damage, danger, and delay, and that all spiritual cases should henceforth be decided within the King's jurisdiction and nowhere else. Acute persons realized that this was a rupture on a major issue. London, moreover, knew more of Cranmer's theology than Rome apparently did; and there was some alarm and reluctance in the Commons for fear of reprisals from the Emperor if the act should pass. Henry managed the delicate matter effectively. He made a pet of the papal nuncio, a somewhat guileless man, and was publicly seen in friendly converse with him in order to allay the general fear that unpleasantness would ensue. He had his way and the Act was passed. A few days later convocation decided as the universities had done, that marriage with a deceased brother's wife was unlawful and the Pope's dispensation void. Fisher dissented and was at once sent to prison. The riposte smacks of Thomas Cromwell, who was always inclined to instant retaliation; and it was at this time that Chapuys notified the Emperor that Cromwell had become Henry's chief adviser.

The closing scenes of the great marriage case were devoid of emphasis and almost obscurely conducted. In mid-April 1533, before he had been a month archbishop, Cranmer opened a court in the quiet countryside of Dunstable, thirty miles from London, to determine the condition of Catherine of Aragon. She refused to appear, claiming that Rome was the place of decision and ignoring the recent statute. After a fortnight of uncontested proceedings Cranmer gave sentence that her reputed marriage had been illegal and that the papal dispensation was of no validity. Five days later, on 28 April, Cranmer pronounced that the King was lawfully married to Anne. On 1 June the archbishop crowned Anne as Queen in Westminster Abbey. Henry had won his six years' contest and had now only to await the birth of his child, which the astrologers assured him would be a boy.

A breath of cleaner air may remind us that the life of England in these years was not bound up solely with divorce-court evidence and political intrigue. The South Sea project of Robert Thorne of Bristol and Seville, of which he had written so cogently to the King, had languished. It depended on royal support, which was not available amid the preoccupations of the divorce. Thorne himself came back to England to work for it, but died in 1532 at the age of forty; and thenceforward this cause was lost for a generation. Meanwhile a Plymouth merchant, William Hawkins, was doing promising work entirely by his own initiative and resources. The coast of Brazil had been discovered by the Portuguese in 1500 and soon revealed a useful commodity in the brazil wood which gave the country its name. It was a dyestuff of high value to cloth-makers, and its collection from the natives provided a lucrative trade. French interlopers competed with the Portuguese in spite of the papal bulls of partition, and at the same time began to trespass on the other Portuguese monopoly of the Guinea coast of West Africa. In 1530 William Hawkins began to take part in both trades, bringing home ivory and probably pepper from Guinea and dyewood from Brazil in exchange for knives, hatchets, and arm-rings of English manufacture. In one voyage of which the customs records survive the goods brought home were assessed at twenty times the value of those taken out. Hawkins carried on this trade for at least ten years and perhaps longer. Robert Reneger and other men from Southampton followed his example. In 1542 they had a fortified station on the Brazilian coast near Bahia. Thereafter the records of the trade are silent for many years, but are found again in the reign of Elizabeth. The enterprise may or may not have been discontinued in the interim. In either case Hawkins under Henry VIII is entitled to the credit of having inaugurated the first regular oceanic trade of England and to have been the pioneer in the commercial challenge to the monopolies set up by the bulls of Alexander VI. Hawkins corresponded with Cromwell and was personally known to the King. The Newfoundland fishery discovered by John Cabot and the Bristol men was also bringing in good returns; and from the middle years of Henry VIII brazil wood and 'Newland' fish were articles of trade between England and her European neighbours. The economic effects were undoubtedly small as compared with those of the older wool and cloth trades. More important was the stimulus to new and daring thought, with action that was bound to call sooner or later for government support and to strengthen the bond between the crown and its merchant adventurers.

When Henry was managing the passage of the Act of Appeals he had some ground for expecting trouble with the Emperor. He therefore cultivated friendship with Francis I, who was then negotiating the marriage of his second son with Catherine de Medici, the Pope's niece. There was a fleeting prospect of winning over the Pope and creating a triple alliance against Charles V. It was not needed since Charles decided not to interfere in the English affair. The Lutherans were unsettled in Germany and Moslem power was threatening in the Mediterranean, while the Netherland traders were as reluctant for a breach of intercourse as those of London. The Emperor could not fight. The Pope, incensed by the summary ending of the marriage case, had meanwhile prepared a bill of excommunication against Henry, but was holding it in suspense. Henry retaliated to the mere threat, and again we may discern the counsel of Cromwell. At the close of the year 1533, when Francis and Clement met at Marseilles, Edmund Bonner, another of the King's new clerics, presented himself to the Pope and announced that the King of England would appeal from the papal sentence to a General Council of the Church. In one respect the move was clumsy, for it offended the French King; in another it was agreeable to the Emperor, who desired a Council for the settlement of the Lutheran schism. Henry's real object was to neutralize foreign distractions and concentrate upon his domestic plans, a complete reversal of Wolsey's outlook.

Thomas Cromwell had indeed succeeded Wolsey and drawn ahead of the ministerial miscellany operating since 1529. He was a man of humble and some said disreputable origins, his father a Putney blacksmith and brewer of doubtful honesty, and he himself a youthful traveller abroad under a similar cloud. Such tales were repeated, but not substantiated. It is established that Thomas Cromwell as a young man sought his fortune in the European wars. In a French army he took part in an Italian battle, and the experience convinced him that he was a fool to risk his bones in a quarrel not his own. He remained in Italy in mercantile employments and later went to Antwerp as a merchant's factor. Before he was thirty he was back in England, having learnt much of the seamy side of business life. He understood Italian and read in manuscript the *Prince* of Machiavelli, with entire appreciation of its picture of how things were done in high politics. He was endued with enormous drive and will-power and a keen financial sense, and devoid of pity and conscience. He had none of Wolsey's lust after magnificence, but preferred to live rather as a rich man of plain tastes. He could make himself agreeable with shrewd and witty conversation, but frowned upon lewdness; at least he did so on one occasion when a travelled student, thinking to flatter his knowledge of Italian, sent him a copy of improper verses in that tongue and received a blistering rebuke. His character and talents rendered him useful for the work that Henry had in prospect. His previous employments had provided the right sort of experience. He had served Wolsey in financial matters, and had managed for him the dissolution of the minor monasteries whose funds had endowed Cardinal College. He was in business in a large way as a money-lender and had thus acquired extensive knowledge of the private affairs of leading men. For himself he desired power, the power of the first minister of a despotic king. And yet we may discern a flaw in his seemingly matchless intelligence; for he seemed never to realize that the king who could make him could break him, and assuredly would when his phase of the king's work was done. But this is to reason from after-knowledge. To Cromwell it may have seemed that if the King should die with the work in progress a future of limitless power might be his.

His marriage settled, Henry proceeded rapidly with the completion of the royal supremacy over the Church by the abolition of the whole papal jurisdiction. His appeal to a General Council could be urged as a denial that he intended heresy or schism, and it was extensively placarded in England. At the same time the Pope was represented as a usurper whose power over the Church was unwarranted, and an order was made at the opening of 1534 that henceforward he was to be known simply as the Bishop of Rome. Parliament met in January, and by the end of March had completed most of the necessary legislation: the second Act of Annates, confirming the first and making new regulations for the appointment of bishops, Rome's part in which was eliminated; an act forbidding the payment of Peter's Pence and all other taxes to Rome; and an act embodying the decisions on canon law made in the submission of the clergy two years before. Beyond this, Parliament passed the Act of Succession, bastardizing the Princess Mary and making the issue of the new marriage the heirs to the throne. The Act further required the King's subjects to take an oath to observe it, and made it high treason to oppose the succession by deed or writing. In a second session later in 1534 Parliament passed the Act of Supremacy, declaring that the King was Supreme Head of the Church of England and endued with all the power hitherto exercised by the Pope.

The overthrow of the Roman jurisdiction was thus accomplished without a single official innovation in doctrine. There were heretics in England, but they were a small minority. The King and most of his subjects were conservative in belief, and the social disorders in Germany which had accompanied the rise of Lutheranism were a warning to the ruling classes in England to dissociate themselves from religious experiments. The breach with Rome was intended to strengthen authority, not to challenge it. But Cromwell perceived that authority was now so strong that it could afford in the years to come to attack beliefs that might stand in the way of its own interest. Under his guidance the revolution was not to be halted.

The child of Anne Boleyn, born in September 1533, was a girl, the Princess Elizabeth, destined to live for seventy years and to reign for forty-five with achievement as great and glory greater than her father's. No one could foresee it, and Henry was bitterly disappointed. The curse seemed to be on him still. This time his conscience did not tell him that he was to blame. His passion for Anne had cooled, perhaps even in the long years before their marriage. Her office for him was to be the mother of his son, and she was failing him. He began to console himself with other women and told Anne that she must put up with it as her betters had done.

While the breach with Rome won general acquiescence and the approval of most, the same could not be said of the domestic side of the King's conduct. Popular sentiment was against the Boleyns, who were hated also by most of the nobility. The national interest required peace with the Emperor's dominions, and the ill-treatment of his aunt caused continued uneasiness. Apart from interest, there was a general personal sentiment in Catherine's favour. The Boleyns again, in their resentment against Rome, were suspected of Lutheran views, which was more than public opinion would tolerate. Free speech was the ingrained habit of a free people, and men of all classes were extraordinarily unreserved in expressing their views. Chapuys, who came from the different tradition of the continent, took it for sedition of the sort that would lead to rebellion, but his interpretation was exaggerated. Cromwell, who also had continental ideas of politics, saw talk as a danger rather than a safety-valve and meant to suppress it by terror. For the next six years Henry, under his advice, struck right and left at prominent individuals known to hold dissenting views. For the preservation of the general design, which after-history has shown to have been in the greater interests of the nation, he conducted a limited reign of terror, limited because its victims, although mostly of high excellence, were few in number. While their heads fell the people as a whole lived in the old freedom and prospered under a rule whose value they appreciated. Henry's terrorism was not that of the modern totalitarians. There were no secret police, domiciliary raids, or detention camps. The terror of 1534–40 was in a limited circle of active men, personally known to one another and concerned to assert their views of the public interest in a difficult time. The charge against the King is that he acted in criminal wilfulness and vindictive passion against legitimate opposition. His defence is that the sacrifice of high-spirited individuals averted a conflict of masses. In the long perspective it is fairly clear that both contentions are true. By his middle age (he was forty in 1531) Henry had grown slowly into a ruthless egoist and a national statesman. And since a Renaissance sovereign bore all responsibility in his own person, the two descriptions are mutually compatible. If the terror was Cromwell's in method and detail, it was Henry's in authorship. The King wanted certain work done, and Cromwell was the man who could best do it. He was the minister, not the master.

In 1534 an affair known as that of the Nun of Kent or the Holy Maid of Kent came to its climax. For some years a girl named Elizabeth Barton, dwelling not far from Canterbury, had been falling into trances and uttering communications seeming to emanate from saints in the spirit world. A group of Canterbury priests took control of her and made her a nun, and her revelations became dangerously political, such as that if the King married Anne Boleyn he would be dead within a month. Notable people grew interested, and some interviewed her from curiosity and perhaps from political motives. The King had a talk with her, but did not disclose his impressions. Fisher of Rochester thought well of her. More also saw her, and was not attracted. Cromwell, the affair being notorious and unsettling to public opinion, brought her and her controllers to account for treason, and condemned them by attainder in Parliament. In the bill he included Fisher and More for misprision, in that they knew of a treasonable practice and had not revealed it; to which they answered that since the King had examined her there was nothing to reveal. After considerable argument More's name was struck out, but Fisher was sent to the Tower, condemned to imprisonment and a heavy fine. The Nun and her accomplices were executed. Cromwell's object had been to obtain incriminating material to be held *in terrorem* over persons whom he wished to coerce on other grounds. The recklessness of his victims is hard to understand. The poor woman herself was irresponsible, but surely the priests and the curious interviewers must have known that they were playing with fire.

More knew that his respite would be short. The oath to support the succession was being tendered to all men of consequence, and few were refusing it. As framed, it required not only the recognition of Anne's marriage and the priority of her children, but also the constructive repudiation of the Pope by declaration that the marriage of Catherine had been invalid. More would accept the first but not the second. Fisher concurred, and they were both sent back to the Tower in spite of Cranmer's plea that the succession only should be required of them. Henry gave no sign of compassion for the man in whose garden he had often strolled in friendly conversation. On the contrary, he considered that More was guilty of ingratitude for signal favours. The Pope must be abjured by all England without any exception. All other members of Parliament, of the two convocations, and of the universities swore as required. Merchants and gentlemen took the oath, and also monks and friars. Among these alone a few declined it. For contumacy the small order of Observants was suppressed and the members sent to other houses. John Houghton, the prior of the London Carthusian monks, was sent to the Tower and was there argued into submission by Stokesley, the Bishop of London.

The above proceedings showed Cromwell that something was lacking in the existing law, as it stood in the summer of 1534. The mere refusal of the oath of succession did not carry the death penalty. Acts of attainder were of course laws in themselves and independent of other law, but they could be passed only when Parliament was sitting; and there might be opposition, as there had been over More's inclusion in the Nun of Kent attainders. The autumn session of 1534, which passed the Act of Supremacy, therefore rounded off the powers of the executive by the Statute of Treasons, which made it high treason to deny the King's supremacy by spoken word as well as by deed or writing. The refusal of consent to what had been done thus became capital, even though unaccompanied by any overt act or persuasion of others. Opinion alone was treason, a 'bloody law' indeed, as Cromwell's accusers were afterwards to tell him.

Next year Cromwell used the recent acts to make some notable examples. The security of the succession and the repudiation of the Pope were associated principles, and the victims were challenged on the simple issue of the royal supremacy. In April John Houghton and the priors of two other Carthusian houses, together with the head of the monastery of Sion and the vicar of Isleworth, were thus brought to trial under the treason law and condemned by a very hesitant jury, who were said to have yielded only to Cromwell's intimidation. Execution at Tyburn followed immediately, with all the barbarity of hanging, drawing, and quartering. Fisher was next dealt with. He had been open in his criticism of recent policies and would probably have suffered in any case. But the new Pope Paul III, who had succeeded Clement VII a few months before, infuriated the King by making Fisher a cardinal. It has been said that this was not an intentional defiance, but that the Pope and his advisers were so ignorant of what was going on in England that they intended the promotion of a notable English bishop as a compliment to the country and its sovereign. But Henry had no doubt of what it meant, and remarked that when the hat arrived its recipient would perforce wear it on his shoulders. Fisher's case was quite simple. He had openly stated that the King was not supreme head of the Church, and he stuck to it. A London jury found him guilty, together with three more Carthusians, and they were all sentenced to death. The monks were hanged, and Fisher was beheaded on 22 June. An aged invalid, he had been consistently valiant through many trials and had declared his position without any shirking or subterfuge whenever a challenge arose.

Last came Sir Thomas More, whose name and fame were known through Europe. He was less easy to condemn than Fisher, for he had not paraded his opinions. Verbal denial of the supremacy was now treason, but he had not denied it; he had only refrained from asserting it. More was a lawyer and made the best of his argument. Yet it could not make away with the stubborn fact that he would not repudiate the Pope or admit the King to be the head of the Church. On that he was firm, and for that he was condemned. After the verdict he gave an unrestrained statement of his views: 'Since I am condemned, and God knows how, I wish to speak freely of your statute for the discharge of my conscience.' The statute, he said, meaning the Act of Supremacy, although the law of England, was invalid because it was contrary to the law of Christendom, which was that Christians owed obedience to the Pope. The supporters of the statute were in opposition to the general sense and practice of Christians past and present, and no country was competent to make such a law without the general consent of Christendom. The unity of Christendom and the authority of its officers over national sovereigns was the principle for which More would die. The opinion of his fellow-countrymen, then and four centuries thereafter, was in the main for the contrary proposition, that liberty and national sovereignty are intertwined, and that the nation demands allegiance before a larger union which in practice never has been in unchallenged operation and, if it could be, would destroy liberty. The question, like others of the troubled sixteenth century, is reviving in altered form in the troubled twentieth.

More gave his opinion and died for it, by the headsman's axe on 6 July 1535. His execution, with that of Fisher, rounded off the process of the breach with Rome, which had begun with the acknowledgment of the supremacy by the clergy in 1531, had grown manifest with the Act of Appeals in 1533, and had become irrevocable by the Act of Supremacy of 1534 and the treason trials of 1535. Fisher and More had made their protest and gone down, their cause hopeless because it had too few supporters. The terrorism of Cromwell and his master is but a superficial explanation of the fact; for there could have been no terrorism had the generality of free Englishmen been in favour of the Roman cause.

8

ONE BODY POLITIC: CONSOLIDATION
AND DEFENCE

THE days of Anne Boleyn were numbered. The King thought of getting rid of her in 1535, but to do so would have been a triumph for Catherine and for Rome. Popular hatred of Anne was as great as ever. Norfolk, whose niece she was, made ready to abandon her. Cromwell viewed her without sentiment, as a piece to be sacrificed at need. Cranmer was her only friend, but he was the King's servant first. Late in 1535 Henry was attracted by Jane Seymour. He brought her soon afterwards to court and began to promote her relations, and notably her brother Edward Seymour, destined to rise high. In the opening days of 1536 Catherine of Aragon died, to the King's intense relief, for her existence had been a brake on his freedom. Like many Englishmen of his century he made the law the keeper of his conscience and did without remorse whatever it permitted; and he could have judicially murdered Catherine under the treason act, but that it would have been too unpopular. But any unlawful stroke of death, as by poison, would have been abhorrent to him, and so Catherine's life ran its natural course. Her death brought no comfort to Anne. Within a month she miscarried, and her husband resigned further hope from her. The succession required another queen.

In the spring of 1536 the change was being secretly prepared. Cromwell collected evidence to incriminate Anne of adultery with several young men about the court. When it was ready the King struck suddenly, the arrests beginning half an hour after he had been sitting amicably with her to watch a tournament at Greenwich. The detailed charges are known, but little of the testimony on which they were based. Anne may not have been guilty; but if technically innocent, she had been a reckless fool, which accords ill with the general sophistication of her proceedings. One of her alleged lovers confessed under torture. The others denied the charge. All were found guilty. On 19 May Anne Boleyn was beheaded in the Tower. Two days earlier the five convicted men, including her own brother, had been executed. Norfolk presided at her trial and led the peers in their verdict of guilty. Henry exhibited his usual callousness on the occasion of her death, which was celebrated by the same exuberance of court revels as had marked that of Catherine five months earlier. Before the month was out he married Jane Seymour. At last he had a straight unquestionable marriage and could look to the future with new hope.

Such is a brief summary of an affair which illustrates the character of the King and his time. The view given above is that of most historians. For a different one, more favourable to Henry, Froude's pages should be read. Froude represents Henry as surprised and heartstricken by compelling evidence of his wife's guilt; and it should be noted that Cranmer, himself surprised and sorrowful, believed that such were his master's feelings. But Cranmer was something of an innocent in these matters, and had evidently not been made privy to the preliminary collection of evidence. The technique of the case—and it was typically Henry's technique as a destroyer—was thorough preparation in secret followed by a public exposure dumbfounding in its suddenness, and then a rapid trial and immediate execution. Froude gives an impressive list of the nobles and gentlemen who took part in the trials and contends that they would not have given so unanimously the verdicts they did give unless the case against Anne had been conclusive. That they should have sent half a dozen people to death without good proof is hard to accept but for the fact that there are other instances to show that gentlemen did do such things in the sixteenth century. Their intellectual and ethical outlook was entirely different from that of the nineteenth century. They made little discrimination between sound and worthless evidence; justice was what a vaguely-phrased law could be made to allow; public executions of unfortunates from all walks of life were an everyday spectacle evoking little pity; and necessity of state was a god to which all bowed down. *Ira principis mors est :* Warham himself had said it to his convocation.

Cromwell knew that strong government requires money and that the course on which the King was embarked might produce rebellion and foreign war. High taxation was more than the excitable England of the 1530s would endure. The alternative was for the crown to acquire a new mass of capital wealth, and it was lying ready to hand in the possessions of the religious houses. The monastic lands were ripe for confiscation. Suggestions for it had been made since the time of Wyclif, since when also the endowment of new foundations had almost ceased. Wolsey had set the example of confiscation, and several observers had believed from the moment of his fall that a total dissolution was imminent. The general anti-clericalism made the expectation obvious. In addition the monasteries were not popular with the mass of the clergy. They clung to privileges which made them almost immune to reform by the English bishops. Many of them were known to harbour fewer brethren than of old, and those of lower quality, who had ceased to practise the scholarly or ascetic life. They did much less than they might have done for the general education of the realm. Their secular interests, land-owning and even trading, took the monks out of doors and broke down the rules of a secluded life. Most of the communities were unintelligent and easy-going, many were slothful, some vicious; and these things were well known to their neighbours. They had in fact outlived the conditions for which they had been founded and had not adapted themselves to the new age of Tudor England. They could expect more assailants than defenders and were easy game to Cromwell and his master. The only question was how far the confiscation would reach.

In January 1535 Thomas Cromwell was appointed vicar-general and empowered to act for the King in the ecclesiastical matters which pertained to the head of the Church. The intention was a thorough investigation and reconstitution of the Church, to be carried out over the heads of the bishops. Included in it was a visitation of the religious houses. Cromwell, a man of method, first made an accurate survey of the value and revenues of all church property, and then appointed his subordinate visitors to report on the monasteries, whose wealth he had ascertained to be nearly half that of the entire Church. The wealth of the monasteries has sometimes been exaggerated. The absolute figures are fairly meaningless, owing to changes in values, and the position may be best indicated by stating that the total annual revenue of the houses (£140,000) was somewhat greater than the crown's annual revenue in normal years when there was no extraordinary taxation.

The visitation took place in the latter half of 1535. The visitors were lay or ecclesiastical lawyers, one of whom was notable for the zest with which he collected evidence of immoral living, and another for his narrow legalistic interpretation of rules which had been so long broken that they might be regarded as obsolete. Their condemnation of the houses was not universal, a fair number being reported as satisfactory. The loose living was of course the matter in which public interest was greatest. It was probably exaggerated in the reports, which have not been completely preserved, and by some writers on the subject. To some extent it was inevitable among 'single men in barracks' living a life that was dull and aimless to those who had no spiritual vocation for it. More common were bad temper, quarrelling, and evil speaking, which furnished the visitors with a rich crop of adverse evidence from within the houses. Lack of vocation was the great defect. Boys of fourteen were sometimes entered as novices and professed before they were twenty. As they grew up some became disgusted and miserable, feeling that life was passing them by. Among the youngsters there were many who wished to leave; the elderly accepted their lot and had less desire to change it. Although dissolution was in the air no decision had yet been pronounced upon it. The visitors acted as if their mission was reform, not destruction. They dismissed some of the younger monks and enunciated strict injunctions for the future conduct of the houses.

The King's activity was widespread. Contemporaneously with the ecclesiastical valuation and the visitation of the monasteries, he was taking steps towards the better government of Wales. Looking at the Welsh he might well have said, as he had said of the clergy, 'they are scarce our subjects'. The country was wild and little known to the royal officers. It had no representation in Parliament and was untroubled by Parliament's laws, or by any law at all, being in a worse state of crime and disorder than England had been in the civil wars. The Marcher lordships, one hundred and thirty-seven separate jurisdictions, some of which, however, were in the royal hands, occupied the borders and much of the country that is now Wales. Their lords administered 'the custom of the Marches', and the King's writs did not run, the lordships in general being notable as the refuge of outlaws and criminals. A Council of the Marches existed, but was ineffective for lack of administrative machinery, since there were no county courts, quarter sessions, or justices of the peace.

So large a patch of anarchy could no longer be tolerated in an age of consolidation. Henry's policy was not to create an effective Welsh government but to incorporate Wales and the Marches with England. In 1534 he appointed Rowland Lee, Bishop of Coventry, a severe but statesmanlike man, to be president of the Council, which became better known as the Council of Wales. Lee, armed with full powers, carried out the same operations against disorder as Henry VII had done in England after 1485, putting down offences of the livery and maintenance type and diminishing the criminal population, so it was said, by 5,000, the number of evildoers whom he was supposed to have hanged. His reports led to radical legislation early in 1536. This Act combined the unshired Welsh lands and part of the marcher lordships into the new counties of Monmouth, Brecon, Radnor, Montgomery, and Denbigh, the remainder of the lordships being added to the adjacent English counties. It established English law as the law of Wales and English as the legal language. It provided also for the representation of Wales in Parliament. A complementary Act of 1543 created two more counties, Glamorgan and Pembroke, but transferred Monmouth to England. It set up also the full mechanism of local justice and administration in the shape of sheriffs, justices, coroners, and the appropriate courts. The Act of 1536 was the key measure, and has been described as the act of union between England and Wales. Probably the population concerned appreciated the benefits of order, for there was no nationalist movement in opposition. National sentiment in fact inspired loyalty to the Tudor monarchy, among whose servants Welshmen were always prominent.[1]

The Welsh act was passed in the last session of the Parliament which had been elected in 1529 and is justly known as the Reformation Parliament. This session, in the spring of 1536, accomplished other important work. Much property was still under entail, heritable by the lineal heir of the last possessor and not devisable by will. This, if enforced, prevented heads of families from making provision for their younger sons or other dependants, and a custom had long prevailed of setting aside lands legally owned by one person for the 'use' of another; and these lands in 'use' were recognized as legally protected property. Their beneficiaries, however, not being the owners by feudal right, were not subject to the feudal dues payable to the crown. At its instance the Statute of Uses was

---

[1] See J. F. Rees, *Tudor Policy in Wales*, Historical Association pamphlet (1935), a valuable review of the subject.

therefore enacted in 1536, declaring that lands in use were to be regarded as the full property, for feudal purposes, of those who profited by them, and subject to the incidents of feudal tenure. The measure, a preventive of tax evasion, was unpopular with a section of the gentry, although others no doubt gained by it. It was substantially amended in 1540 by a law allowing some kinds of property to be left by will.

The last, and in social effects, the greatest act of this Parliament, dealt with the monasteries. It is highly probable that Cromwell intended to dissolve every one of them, but not so likely that at this stage the King did. Whether or not Henry had the full intention, he presented a very moderate measure to the House of Commons. In a personal visit to the House he introduced the bill, asking the members not to be influenced by himself but to weigh the matter carefully and decide as the common weal required. Several years afterwards Latimer declared that the visitors' reports on monkish enormities were read in the House and evoked a general cry of 'Down with them!' His statement has been discounted because there is no contemporary evidence of it and because a man's memory after the lapse of a dozen years may lead him astray. So it well may in points of detail, but hardly in so simple a prime assertion; and probability is in favour of the reports having been communicated to the House. The preamble to the bill states that 'manifest sin, vicious, carnal, and abominable living' prevail in the smaller monasteries, although the greater ones are well conducted. This was not in accordance with the reports, which implicated houses of all sizes. Probably the Black Book, so-called, in 1536, dealt only with those it was then proposed to suppress. The measure provided for the dissolution of the religious houses of all kinds having an income of less than £200 a year, although it empowered the King to spare such as he thought fit. The property was to go to the crown. The heads of the houses were to receive pensions. The monks had the option of being transferred to the greater houses, where there were many vacancies, or of taking 'capacities' to enable them to seek employment as secular clergy. The number of houses was 376, but about a hundred of them were respited, to share the fate, as it turned out, of the greater monasteries two or three years later. The total revenue of the houses involved in the first suppression was computed to be about one-fifth of that of the monasteries as a whole, so that the crown's policy was not as yet extreme. The debates of 1536 are not recorded, but it was said long afterwards that there was a good deal of opposition in the Commons. The general opinion was undoubtedly in favour of suppression, but individuals may well have been reluctant to see particular houses perish. On the other hand there were many individuals with an eye upon particular monastic properties, which they were anxious to obtain on the easiest terms they could get. To deal with the mass of complicated business which arose, a new Court of Augmentations was established. It received all the property into the King's hands and disposed of some of it by sales and leases. The property included buildings, plate, and jewels as well as lands. In all this there was much of what later times would have called financial irregularity or corruption, passing of bribes, enrichment of officials, too easy sales and leases amounting to partial gifts to great nobles and local gentry. Such was the common sixteenth-century method of doing business, and without such method the administration could have got nothing done. Wasteful irregularity did produce swiftness, where bureaucratic regularity produces wasteful delay. In any case, the latter method was impossible because there was no bureaucracy. Right on to the end of the century public servants were allowed and expected to pay themselves by a certain amount of peculation instead of being granted adequate salaries for the work they performed. In the event the crown did receive the mass of the monastic wealth. The disposal of it will be more conveniently considered at a later stage when the greater houses had also fallen.

Traditional pictures of jolly monks sitting in rows at long refectory tables tempt us to think of the monasteries as housing large communities. In fact the houses dissolved in 1536 had few members. They may have had altogether about 2,000 monks and nuns, an average of less than eight apiece. They gave employment to about four times as many laymen, most of whom, in so far as their tasks were useful and not superfluous, were needed by the new owners of the property. Their greatest public service was that of giving hospitality to travellers, and it is very unlikely that their successors kept up this service, although enjoined to do so. The monks were bound also to distribute alms to the poor, which in practice attracted undesirable hangers-on who lived idly instead of working. The deserving poor suffered by the change with the undeserving.

Although most members of Parliament welcomed the dissolution, they were representative of the more enterprising sections of the upper and middle classes. Among the mass of the people there were some, as shown above, who lost by the change, and many who could see no advantage in it. Local sentiment was shocked by the overthrow of a local institution, and to some it seemed that this was the presage of further changes that would shatter their world. One quarter of all the monasteries dissolved in 1536 were in the two counties of Lincolnshire and Yorkshire, and there the discontent was greatest. In October some spontaneous rioting grew rapidly into a formidable rising in Lincolnshire, a conservative region little touched by the new ideas of London and the home counties. It was known that Cromwell's handling of the monasteries was part of a larger overhaul of the entire Church; and the priests set rumours going that many parish churches were to be destroyed as superfluous, and their plate and vestments confiscated. Part of a subsidy granted by Parliament two years before was outstanding, and it was said that an inquisition of unprecedented strictness was to be made into goods and incomes, that diet was to be restricted and cattle confiscated. Cranmer's reforming tendencies were known, Hugh Latimer had been made Bishop of Worcester, and other reformers were receiving promotion, while Cromwell was believed to be a favourer of Lutherans. The Statute of Uses was disliked by many of the gentry. These things were stated by the rebels among their grievances. All professed loyalty to the King, but demanded the elimination of Cromwell and his agents and of Cranmer and the reformers. There was no criticism of the royal supremacy or demand for the restoration of allegiance to the Pope. The priests rather than the gentry originated the revolt, but the gentry joined it in half-hearted fashion, some from intimidation.

The Lincolnshire affair was all over in a fortnight. The Earl of Shrewsbury, the nearest magnate to the scene of disorder, called out the forces of the north midlands and assembled them at Nottingham. Henry sent the Duke of Suffolk to take general command with levies from the south. These leaders acted with good sense. They perceived that the gentry were not whole-hearted in the revolt and used them to pacify the commons. In the pacification there was no appeasement. On receipt of the grievances the King wrote an open reply to the insurgents rating them for their ignorant presumption and charging them to disperse. Such was his prestige that on hearing it they did disperse, without so much as a skirmish and without a single demand being granted.

But the fire kindled in Lincolnshire had already spread into York-shire, and this was a more serious business. In Yorkshire the over-throw of fifty-three religious houses almost amounted to a social revolution, and caused men of all classes to declare that knaves ruled about the King. As in Lincoln, a fire of revolt swept spontaneously over the county, while leaders with some power of organization and discipline took advantage of it. The chief leader was Robert Aske, a knight's son and a servant of the Earl of Northumberland. He was a Yorkshire lawyer who, riding towards London as Lincolnshire rose, fell in with a party of the insurgents and was induced to join their movement. From Lincolnshire he went back to his own county and was there compelled by the insurgents to take command. He must already have had a considerable reputation for leadership or for opposition to the royal policies. Many of the gentry joined the rebellion, and after some hesitation and show of resistance Lord Darcy and other nobles did the same, all under Aske's general command. The rebels took possession of York and gathered an army of more than 30,000 men at Doncaster. Their demands were similar to those of Lincolnshire—restoration of the monasteries, abolition of heresy, liquidation of Cromwell and the reformers. There were in addition strong economic and social reasons for discontent—enclosure, landlords' exactions, and rise of prices—and an authority holds that a revolt might have occurred even without the religious grievance.[1] The insurgents professed to be assembled to petition the King, not to resist him, and they called their move-ment a pilgrimage, the Pilgrimage of Grace, under the banner of the Five Wounds of Christ, a common religious symbol of the time.

Once again Henry had no mind to be intimidated. But as a states-man he did not desire the bloodshed of a civil war fought between armies of his subjects, and as a machiavellian he had no scruple in outwitting his opponents instead of fighting them. Their weak point was that they did not want war, while short of it they could hope to gain their ends only by the King's complaisance. His weak point was that the midland levies were distinctly tardy in rallying to his support, even under such well-known soldiers as Norfolk and Suffolk, while all the rest of the north was showing strong sympathy with Yorkshire. In essence it was a conflict between London and the North, due to the existence of a gap of half a century between their respective outlooks in politics and religion.

[1] R. R. Reid, *The King's Council in the North* (1921), p. 126.

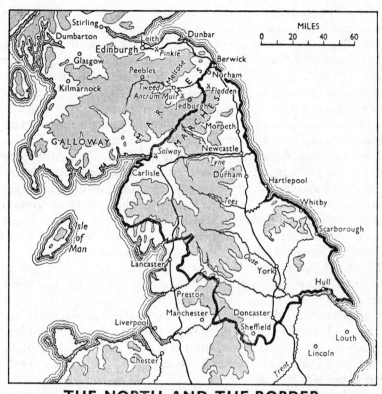

THE NORTH AND THE BORDER

———— *Main Roads* ━━━▶ *Boundary of Jurisdiction of Council in the North*

Land above 600 feet

The Duke of Norfolk, facing the rebels at Doncaster with only a quarter of their numbers, was not in a position to fight. He consented to receive their demands in writing for transmission to the King. The King answered that the complaints were misconceived, groundless, and devised by arrogant presumptuous men, but that if these ringleaders were given up to him he would pardon the rest. While these exchanges were going on, Norfolk and Aske had agreed to a military truce, which was bound to break down under mutual suspicions unless an end were quickly achieved. But discussion was protracted. The movement did not quickly subside as in Lincolnshire. On the contrary, large meetings of the rebel leaders at York and Pomfret in November and December stuck by their demands and expressed them in a detailed document to be presented for agreement as a treaty. Aske went with it to Norfolk at Doncaster. The Duke was still too inferior in force to think of fighting. He could not pledge the King to accept the demands, but he did promise a general pardon and the calling of a parliament to review all the recent objectionable statutes. Aske, who thoroughly disliked the role of rebel leader, was only too glad to agree. He removed his badge of the Five Wounds and professed his loyalty. Then he returned to his colleagues at York and told them that all was well. The rebel forces dispersed, while Aske was summoned to London to explain the rising to the King. Henry treated him graciously at a personal interview and confirmed Norfolk's promise of a parliament. So the affair might have simmered down, with the King committed to no concession but the calling of a special parliament. But some of the leaders began to suspect that Aske was deluding them or being himself deluded. Cromwell remained the King's minister and Cranmer the archbishop. The royal forces were being strengthened, and the categorical demands had not been granted. Against Aske's advice, the rebels attempted to seize Hull and Scarborough in January 1537, an act of folly now that the substantial army of the previous autumn was disbanded. It gave the King the opportunity to revoke his pardon. Relatively small royal forces arrested all the leaders and paralysed resistance. Darcy was executed in London and Aske at York. There were over two hundred other victims, including half a dozen heads of Yorkshire abbeys not yet dissolved. Henry had faced his greatest domestic crisis and demonstrated the strength of his position. It lay in the loyalty of the whole country, the North included, to himself as a person, and in the fact that to him as King there was no alternative candidate whose advancement would not cause anarchy and ruin. His own inner mind remains inscrutable. Did he really intend the general pardon and revoke it only under indignation at a breach of faith? Did he, while treating Aske with royal good humour and sympathy, meditate hanging him? No one can truly say. With all his apparently open exhibition of his character and motives, Henry kept his secrets. He kept them even from such a human gimlet as Thomas Cromwell.

The North was a region too remote and too specialized to be administered direct from London, and it was, moreover, as the Welsh marches had ceased to be, a military frontier against a foreign power. From the fifteenth century a system had existed whereby civil government was under a council at York and military defence under a lieutenant and three wardens, for the east, middle, and west marches along the border. The defect, revealed by the Pilgrimage of Grace, was that the council lacked both the prestige and the will to keep the local magnates in order even in Yorkshire, while in the other counties it scarcely operated at all. Cromwell was a believer in the efficacy of the council system, and, as in Wales, his remedy was to strengthen it rather than to try something different. Under his advice the King reconstituted the Council in the North in 1537, appointed able men to its membership, and increased its liaison with the Council in London. Thenceforward it effectively carried on the King's government in the five counties of Yorkshire, Durham, Northumberland, Westmorland, and Cumberland. Border warfare, and constant cross-raiding even in so-called time of peace, rendered the border counties disorderly by southern standards, but there was an all-round improvement. It was on the whole a successful step in consolidation and an example of the administrative skill which looked rather to getting the right men than to devising a new system.

Amid the crowded events of the 1530s Ireland, like Wales, claimed attention from a king who was consolidating his *imperium* with a view to the eventual domination of the whole of the British Isles. Henry VII, having decided not to spend the money necessary to an effective conquest of Ireland, had entrusted its rule to the leading Irish potentate, the Earl of Kildare, and had been satisfied with the Earl's renunciation of active sympathies with the enemies of the throne. This arrangement continued in the early years of Henry VIII, a second Kildare succeeding to the predominant position of the first. Wolsey neglected Irish problems, and the great Kildare connection, known as the Geraldines, became increasingly independent and disorderly. The second greatest faction, that of the Butlers, more English in its affiliations, was inferior in strength, while oppression and sporadic warfare became endemic. A Geraldine revolt in 1534 was indeed put down, and the contemporary Earl of Kildare executed three years later, but the trouble was not cured. Ireland quite naturally did not share the enthusiasm with which England repudiated the Pope. Spanish emissaries of Charles V, entering by means of the long-standing trading connection between Spain and the Irish coast, stirred up trouble for Henry. Similar Scottish emissaries were powerful in Ulster, which was more accessible from Scotland than from England. Altogether, an unsubdued Ireland was a threat in the event of foreign war to Henry's position in England, a springboard for an intervention in the troubled North as in the days of Margaret of Burgundy and Martin Schwartz.

The situation had to be dealt with. The preliminary was by Cromwell's method of investigation and collection of information as a step to framing effective measures. A commission under Sir Anthony St. Leger was at work on this from 1537, while Lord Leonard Grey, the Lord Deputy, was not only failing to cope with the Geraldines but falling under suspicion of co-operating with them, which led to his execution for treason in 1540. His successor was St. Leger, who carried out work comparable to that of Poynings fifty years before. He was given more money than his predecessors had enjoyed, and induced the Irish Parliament in 1541 to enact that Henry should thenceforth be styled King of Ireland instead of merely Lord. By force and prestige St. Leger obtained the allegiance of tribal chiefs and their assumption of English-sounding titles, together with an acknowledgement of the royal supremacy and a prospect of the use of English law and land tenures. The success was considerable, and lasted longer than might have been expected. Finance was the limiting factor, for Ireland could not be made to yield sufficient revenue to pay for efficient government; but with Henry's able administrators the country remained orderly for the rest of his reign.

Although Henry's policies in the decade after Wolsey's death did not involve him in foreign war, they threatened more than once to do so, and at its close he had to face a severe international crisis in which both commerce and religion were involved. Some commercial considerations may therefore be mentioned at this stage. The standing threat to English prosperity, a threat involving fatal consequences unless averted, lay in the chance of hostilities with Charles V. The cloth export to the Netherlands and thence to the German market was England's most vulnerable point. To interrupt it would have been the Emperor's obvious move in support of Rome and Catherine of Aragon had it not been a two-edged weapon; for its use would have inflicted equal or perhaps greater damage upon his own subjects in the Low Countries. Their local independence was considerable, as was their financial contribution to his treasury, and he was well aware that his care for their interests was the price of their support. So, in the matter of the cloth trade, he held his hand, and even left it to Henry on one occasion to threaten a stoppage which he had no intention of continuing. Henry fully appreciated the danger of an initiative from the Emperor's side, and this accounts for an improvement of English relations with the Hanseatic League. Wolsey had in the main continued Henry VII's ill-will towards the trade of the Hanse cities. After his fall the changed conditions caused a reconciliation in the form of a gradual easing of relations, until by the end of the decade England and the League were almost on terms of informal alliance. With one city, Lubeck, Henry went further, giving material aid to a factious democratic government that arose in it after a Protestant revolution. But the success of Henry's friends was ephemeral, and after two turbulent years big with promise of a new situation in Baltic trade their leaders were executed in 1536. The net result, however, was an improvement of the English position, aided by the fact that Denmark under a new King went Lutheran, an example followed by the rest of Scandinavia.

Elsewhere the commercial record of the 'thirties was of developments rather than of new departures. The English merchants in Spain received in 1530 their earliest recorded charter of incorporation from the English crown. By this instrument they became a body similar to the Merchants Adventurers at Antwerp, electing a governor and court of assistants to reside at San Lucar, the port of Seville, and bound to pay subscriptions and abide by the regulations made by the elected body. There is some reason to believe that this was a refoundation rather than a complete novelty, because thirteen years earlier the local grandee, the Duke of Medina Sidonia, had granted to the English merchants some privileges, including the right to build a church of St. George at San Lucar, which could only have been received by some kind of corporation. The Mediterranean trade, which Henry VII had set on its feet, flourished under his son. It was now a trade only in Mediterranean and Levantine produce, to the exclusion of the far eastern spices, which the Portuguese had diverted to the Cape route. The change caused the extinction of the once-important Flanders Galleys of Venice, which after two centuries of operation came to England for the last time in 1532. Venetian merchants remained important in London, but had to finance their wool-purchases by other imports. These, fine cloth, glass, and armour from Italy, sweet wines from Chios and Crete, sugar from North Africa, and various luxuries from the Turkish dominions, were brought to England in privately-owned ships, of which a growing number were English. There were English factors

at Candia and in Chios, and great men like Cromwell and the Duke
of Norfolk took part in the trade. Among the outgoing goods there
is record of the dyewoods that Plymouth and Southampton were
bringing from Brazil. Finally, the long-distance fisheries need
mention. From London and the east-coast ports more than a
hundred vessels went annually to Iceland, while Bristol and the west
country sent fleets to Newfoundland. These ocean fishermen were
especially valuable to naval defence, since they were all home in
England in the winter and available for impressment if the Navy
should be fitting out for a campaign.

Under Cromwell's ministry religious tendencies, as apart from
church organization, became significant of much that was to come.
The heretics of the New Learning were still a minority, but politics
were making them important. It will be convenient to refer to them
henceforward as Protestants, although the word was not common
in England until the reign of Edward VI. Strictly used, it still applied
only to the Lutherans of Germany. The transition from 'heretic' to
'Protestant' may be allowed to denote a small and very tentative
recognition of some of their views and practices, coupled with a
distinct slackening of zeal in the persecution that was still legally
valid. For this there were diplomatic reasons, as will be shown.
There may also have been a personal predilection on the part of
Cromwell. We are so accustomed by his general record to regard
him as a ruthless materialist that it is hard to credit him with religious
sentiments; but there is some ground for believing that he favoured
the Protestants more than policy required, an attitude that was both
disinterested and dangerous. Cranmer and Latimer were his friends,
and the Protestants certainly looked upon him as their protector.
The King acquiesced without conviction and only until circumstances should alter.

To circulate the Bible freely in the English tongue may not have
been contrary to the doctrine of the older Church, but it certainly
was not its practice. The Protestants on the other hand were eager
for an English Bible, and its progress marks to a certain extent their
progress. William Tyndale, the greatest of the translators, was a
Gloucestershire man, from a district where the Lollards had once
been strong. Born about 1495, he made it the single object of his life
to produce a worthy and scholarly English version in language
readable by the boy who followed the plough. He learned Latin at
Oxford and Greek at Cambridge, where he was an early member of

the Little Germany circle. He had no private means, and his problem was to find employment that would afford leisure and quiet for his real task. He failed to get preferment in England, being, as he described himself, 'speechless and rude, dull and slow-witted'. Such was his social quality, as it has been of many men who were far otherwise when setting pen to paper. In London he fell in with members of the Merchants Adventurers Company, who were imbibing the New Learning through their contacts with the Netherlands and Germany. These merchants appear to have financed his migration to Germany, his maintenance there, the printing of his translation at German presses, and its clandestine importation and distribution in England: 'it is to Big Business', wrote Maynard Smith, 'that we principally owe our version of the New Testament'. The detailed proof of the story is not complete, although it is obvious that expensive printing and organized book-running were beyond the capacity of a penniless and unworldly scholar, working alone. Tyndale's English New Testament, independently translated from the Greek, with some renderings that excited the wrath of conservative churchmen, was reaching England in 1526. Substantially it is preserved in the authorized version that is still the most widely read to-day; and no one has ever questioned that it is the work of a genius and a principal moulder of the character of modern England. The early date of its introduction to the country made it certain that authority would disapprove. The Church in fact burnt the book and would have burnt its author had he not been out of reach. But many persons failed to surrender their copies and read them in secret; and it is significant that Archbishop Warham had to buy a whole edition in order to destroy it, which enabled the producers to print a larger one out of the profits.

Tyndale went on with his work, and by 1530 was able to print his translation of the first books of the Old Testament. Events in England took a more favourable course, and with the advent of Cranmer and Cromwell the government no longer sought his blood. In fact Convocation petitioned the King in 1534 to sanction the issue of an English Bible. Tyndale's danger was not now from England but from the heresy laws of the Netherlands. So long as he remained in the English House (of the Merchants Adventurers) at Antwerp, its immunities protected him. In 1535 an Englishman betrayed him to the city authorities by tempting him out into the clutches of officers who were waiting to arrest him. After eighteen months in prison he was strangled and burnt at Louvain in October 1536. Charles V had expressed horror at the execution of More, and by his laws Tyndale was slain. There was no moral difference between the Emperor and the King of England, great and worthy sovereigns both by the standards of their age. Tyndale's inquisitors were also of their age. They described him as learned, pious, and good, and killed him nevertheless.

The ex-friar Miles Coverdale, personally known to Cromwell, and an associate of Tyndale's later years, turned to Protestant Switzerland for shelter, and completed the translation of the whole Bible for printing at Zurich. It was ready in 1535 to satisfy the demand already officially made in England. Coverdale was not an original scholar, and he used Tyndale's work so far as it went, his own portion of the translation being from inferior sources although in an almost equal felicity of language. The use of this Bible was permitted in England in 1536, although Cranmer thought that in parts it was unsatisfactory. Next year Cranmer approved a new version, combining Tyndale's work, unadulterated, with improvements in the other portion, by John Rogers, another protégé of the Merchants Adventurers, who published under the alias of Thomas Matthew. The work is therefore known as Matthew's Bible. The suitable text was thus established, but with notes and prefaces that were questionable. Cromwell had now convinced the King of the need for an official bible, printed in sumptuous style for authorized use in churches. English printing was not yet good enough, and so Matthew's text without the embellishments was printed in Paris and introduced as the Great Bible in 1538. When heresy-hunters in Paris interrupted further production, the types, presses, and French printers were brought over to London to continue.

We may now view these and cognate matters from the standpoint of the English government. In 1535 the King, in answer to the request of Convocation, agreed that an English Bible should be prepared, and the use of Coverdale's was permitted the next year as an interim measure. Heresy, or Protestantism, or the New Learning, by whatever name doctrinal reform might be known, was now raising its head. Cromwell's view of it was obvious from the thing he did not do, that is, burn heretics, while Cranmer and half a dozen bishops of recent promotion desired doctrinal reform of some sort. The King was Catholic, but many Catholics agreed that certain reforms might be made; and he had a personal liking for two at least of his new prelates, Cranmer and Latimer. So in 1536, while argument raged hotly in the country, the time was ripe for some pronouncement. Henry ordered the bishops to confer towards an agreed statement, and when they failed he dictated it himself, in the form of the Ten Articles. The first five dealt with faith and the others with ceremonies. The faith so defined was in the main Catholic, although with certain implications that would please Lutherans. The customary ceremonies were to be maintained, with explanations eliminating the abuses that had accompanied them, such as the distinction made between prayers to saints (commended) and worship of them (condemned), and the statement that prayers for the dead were charitable, although purchased pardons and masses had no power to deliver from purgatory. It has been noted by an ecclesiastical historian that most of the abuses corrected by the Ten Articles were subsequently corrected in similar manner by the Catholic Church at the Council of Trent. Henry's articles were thus not obnoxious to thorough-going Catholics. But Henry's new bishops and vicar-general undoubtedly were; and their continuance in favour was the main hope of the reformers.

Cromwell followed the Ten Articles with instructions to the clergy to preach against the usurped power of the Bishop of Rome, to discourage the veneration of images and relics and the making of pilgrimages, to teach children the Lord's Prayer, creed, and commandments in English, and to place an English Bible in every church. Next year, 1537, the government issued *The Institution of a Christian Man*, or *Bishops' Book*, explaining and amplifying the doctrine of the Ten Articles, and watering down the importance of purgatory and of means of deliverance from it. Finally, in 1538, Cromwell issued injunctions not only for the purchase and exhibition in every church of the Great Bible, but for the public reading in English every Sunday of the Lord's Prayer, creed, and commandments, and for the removal of images to which pilgrimages and offerings were customary. Practical New Learning speedily followed in the destruction of famous shrines throughout the country, where relics and wonder-working images had collected pilgrims for centuries. The most notable, and the richest, was that of Becket at Canterbury. The valuable jewels and gold plate which enriched the shrines passed into the keeping of the Court of Augmentations. Thus abruptly the medieval practice of making pilgrimages ceased.

These changes completed the advance of the New Learning, or more properly the attacks on the Old, made under Cromwell. They were carried out by the royal authority, in virtue of its supremacy, and not by Parliament. The Reformation Parliament, having lasted since 1529, was dissolved in the spring of 1536. The execution of Anne Boleyn necessitated the summoning of another in the summer in order to regulate the succession. It did so by enacting that the child of Anne was illegitimate and that the succession should be with the prospective issue of Jane Seymour. Jane fulfilled expectations by giving birth to a son in 1537, dying herself soon after. The new prince was destined to succeed as Edward VI.

After the fall of the smaller monasteries the dissolution of the remainder, more numerous and very much richer, continued piecemeal in the next four years. The attainder of the head of a house was held to involve the acquisition of the whole property by the crown. In this way several of the abbeys fell by the complicity of their abbots in the Pilgrimage of Grace. The great majority ended by an ostensibly voluntary surrender. In some cases it was in fact forced, in many it really was voluntary, for the abbots, seeing the trend of the times, made the best terms they could by accommodating the government. Not all of the newly enriched gentry received their grants from the Court of Augmentations, for in the closing stages the monks themselves anticipated the end by disposing of land to their friends and neighbours on easy terms, sometimes falsifying the dates of leases in order to evade the law. The abbots who surrendered received handsome pensions, and the monks, including those who had been transferred from the small houses, were also pensioned. The subsequent history of many of them has been traced, and it appears that the pensions were actually paid and that ex-monks and friars rose to good preferment in the succeeding English Church, some of them enjoying benefices in the Elizabethan Protestant régime. The old impression that the dissolution involved starvation to the rank and file of the religious is no longer tenable. On the other hand there were resistant abbots like those of Reading and Glastonbury whom Cromwell executed on hollow charges of treason, thus securing the dissolution of their houses; but even in these cases the brethren received their pensions. This appears to have been true for the rest of Henry's reign, although about 1552 there was a period when some of the pensions fell into arrears owing to the poverty and corruption of a later government. Payments seem afterwards to have been resumed.[1] The fruits of the later dissolutions were legally granted to the crown by an act of the Parliament of 1539, and the whole process was completed in 1540.

The movable wealth of the abbeys, like that of the pilgrim shrines, went into the royal exchequer. Some of the lands were retained as royal domain, but the greater part were leased or sold. From Alexander Savine's analysis of the evidence it appears that about 1,000 grantees obtained lands of £90,000 annual value by payments totalling £780,000, at the rate, that is to say, of eight to nine years' purchase. These were comparatively easy terms, partly necessitated by the fact that so many sales in a short period must have created a slump in values or buyers' market. A great many of the purchases were speculative, and the property did not long remain in the hands of the original buyers. The number of outright gifts by the crown was relatively small, about eighty, and the generalization that Henry 'endowed' a new nobility and gentry is not justifiable. Nevertheless nobles and gentry were the ultimate possessors of the abbey lands, and of these the gentry as a class were the greatest gainers. The period of liquidation of property allowed their ranks to be recruited from successful merchants, yeomen, and craftsmen, a process that has always gone on but was intensified in the mid-Tudor period. To this extent a new landed gentry was created by Henry's dissolution.

If Henry VIII had been able to keep all this treasure he would have died as rich as his father. Most of it in fact was to be dissipated in the wars of the next decade, unforeseen at the dissolution. But the King spent a considerable part in the successful prevention of a war which he did foresee, an attack by the continental powers on the English Reformation. From 1536 onwards he fortified the coasts and the seaports with the low-built thick-walled stone castles of which many still exist, embrasured for heavy guns, and sited to deny the anchorages to invaders' fleets. More important still, he rebuilt the Navy with more modern vessels than those that had played their part in the early wars of his reign. The reconstruction of the Navy has been obscured by the fact that many of the old ships' names were retained and bestowed on their successors. The *Great Harry* of 1,500 tons, for example, built in 1513, was broken up in the late

[1] 'The Edwardian Arrears in Augmentations Payments', by A. G. Dickens, *English Historical Review*, vol. lv (1940), p. 384. The author points out that few of the friars received pensions.

'thirties and succeeded by the *Great Harry* of 1,000 tons, a smaller but more formidable ship. The same was true of the *Mary Rose* and others. The Navy of Henry's last years was new and up-to-date in design and armament, and played its part in deterring the Catholic powers from a projected anti-English crusade. In another and better-known direction Henry spent monastic wealth in the foundation of six new bishoprics, of which five have remained. He did not, as he might have done, spare anything for education and social betterment; and here he might have heeded Wolsey's example in Oxford.

The religious and ecclesiastical matters already described were linked with foreign affairs. In 1535, after the executions of Fisher and More, the new Pope Paul III prepared a bull of excommunication and deposition against Henry VIII. The Pope knew that he could not expect Henry's subjects to act upon it, but hoped that Henry might be subdued by the joint intervention of France and the Emperor. At that juncture, however, Francis and Charles were on the point of falling out again, with Milan as the bone of contention. The last Sforza duke, a protégé of Charles, died in October, and the duchy lapsed to its overlord as an imperial fief. Francis was determined to recover it, and next year was again at war with Charles. The Pope suspended the publication of the bull to a more favourable time. Henry knew of its contents and lay under the threat that his brother sovereigns would make a bargain about Milan and turn their arms against him. His policy was to be friendly with Francis, who would be anti-papal if it paid him; to open negotiations with the Lutheran princes of Germany, who were increasing in numbers and confidence; and at the same time not to commit any irrevocable act of hostility against Charles, whose power to harm England was greater than that of any other sovereign. Henry, in short, worked to restore good relations with Charles, but to do it from strength rather than from weakness, by a display of support to Charles's enemies. It was a difficult policy, but Henry was by this time a master of diplomacy, greater than his tutor Wolsey, because less arrogant and with a finer sense of realities and a better judgment of the characters of those with whom he had to deal. Cromwell was inferior both in knowledge and judgment of foreign affairs. Henry kept the decisions in his own hands, but allowed Cromwell some scope in negotiating with the German Protestants, mainly because such negotiations would be easier to disavow if carried on by the minister rather than

by the King in person. In 1533 and again in 1535 English missions
went over to Germany to survey the possibilities of co-operation.
On the second occasion Edward Fox, Bishop of Hereford, and
Robert Barnes, one of Cromwell's Protestants, provisionally agreed
to an alliance with the League of Schmalkalde (the combination of
Protestant princes), on the basis that England should accept the
Lutheran creed and that Henry should be styled the Defender of the
League. If Cromwell really thought this possible he was deceived
about his master's views. Henry had no intention of forcing
Lutheranism on his mainly Catholic England, and did not see why
he should be committed to defending people who did not undertake
to defend him; although the affair nevertheless had its uses as giving
cause for anxiety to the Emperor. Henry therefore did not ratify the
agreement, but took his time before announcing his refusal in 1536.
Meanwhile the death of Catherine of Aragon removed the principal
barrier between him and the Emperor. Henry's most vigorous
enemy was thenceforward Paul III, who sought to make use of a
notable English exile, Reginald Pole.

Pole, through his mother the Countess of Salisbury, was the
grandson of the Yorkist Duke of Clarence, the ill-fated brother of
Edward IV. In spite of this unfortunate ancestry Henry had shown
him great favour as a young man, giving him a large income and
leave to travel and study abroad. Pole was a sincere and honest man,
too guileless to succeed in politics or diplomacy, resembling Thomas
More in recognition that abuses defaced the Church, and also in
uncompromising loyalty to the Pope as its head. When the dissolution of Catherine's marriage was mooted Pole took the view that it
was inadmissible and told the King so to his face. To this act of
courage Henry reacted generously and gave Pole leave to withdraw
again from England, still enjoying his pension. Pole returned to
Italy and there, on receipt of a demand from the King to state his
honest opinion in writing, he composed a book of unbridled denunciation and threats and exhortations to repentance. It was a regrettable performance in view of the benefits its author had received,
and very much in excess of the sober statement he was entitled to
make. Henry received it in 1536 and showed no anger, although we
may guess that his composure was ominous. He invited Pole to
return to England, but Pole went to Rome. There, before the end of
the year, the Pope made him a cardinal and legate to England, and
dispatched him to make what he could of Henry's difficulties with

the Pilgrimage of Grace. The hysterical quality in Pole's book should have told the Pope that its author was not the man for a mission requiring consummate ability and wisdom, and, as might have been expected, the cardinal-legate failed utterly. Fortunately for himself he never drew near England, and after having been expelled successively from the territories of Francis I and Charles V he returned humiliated to Rome. The French king and the Emperor were still at war, and neither would take the risk of serving the Pope by offending the King of England. Such was Henry's position in 1537.

Meanwhile Paul was preparing to summon a general council at Mantua. It was not to be the council which Henry had demanded at an earlier stage, a council which would not have met in Italy and at which the Pope would not have presided but would have appeared as a litigant on equal terms with the King. Henry therefore sent to the Lutheran princes to dissuade them from being represented, and they replied with a mission to England to seek the religious concord they desired. Henry played their deputies long and gently, and finally dismissed them with their wishes unattained. Cromwell and Cranmer both desired an Anglo-Lutheran pact. To their minds the price of the English Reformation might well be war, and a Protestant alliance was an obvious precaution. Henry saw his way to enjoying the fruits of victory without a war, and pursued his own course. It was yet to be a perilous one. The Pope had learned a lesson from the failure of Cardinal Pole, and devoted himself to ending the Franco-Imperial conflict. By his mediation Francis and Charles concluded the Truce of Nice in June 1538, and next month they met in conference at Aigues Mortes in Provence. A coalition of Pope, King, and Emperor was formed, professedly against the Turk, although a more obvious infidel was nearer to their thoughts; and in December Paul decided to launch the long-suspended bull of excommunication and deposition. Henry, having surmounted the domestic crisis of 1536–7, had now to face the diplomatic crisis of 1538–9.

He did so with his coast defences and his Navy. From Berwick south to Dover and from Dover west to Falmouth the harbours and landing beaches bristled with castles and bulwarks. The King supplied the guns and powder and kept a few professional gunners in pay at each defence. The local men formed the bulk of the forces, mustering for drill, digging entrenchments, staking the beaches, all ready to turn out in strength under their county leaders at the signal of the beacon fires. The gentry and yeomen provided horse, the rest were pricked as able archers or able billmen, and the muster rolls brought up to date. The new ships were manned with seamen and fishermen, and newer ones were on the stocks. This was an answer to a threat of conquest, and all knew it. Dissension was forgotten in determination to support the King, the King of England decreed deposed by the Bishop of Rome.

Among the nobles there were a surviving Yorkist remnant, who told Chapuys that the Emperor could strike Henry down with their approval. Plantagenet blood stirred hopes of a change of dynasty should Henry die and leave an infant successor. The Poles were the focus of this. Sir Geoffrey Pole, brother of the Cardinal, had been very loose-tongued. In the Tower, still talking, he turned King's evidence against his own clan, and talked his elder brother, Lord Montague, Henry Courtenay Marquis of Exeter, Lord Delawarr, and several others, to their doom. The Poles' mother, the Countess of Salisbury, was likewise condemned, but respited for the time in the Tower. Their treason had been mostly talk, but under Cromwell's law to talk treason was to be guilty of it, and all the men except Sir Geoffrey went to the block at the close of 1538. He was pardoned, tried to kill himself, and lived a haunted man. 'Imagining the King's death' was a dangerous day-dream, the more so as the King was not in good health, an ex-athlete growing corpulent, suffering from headaches and tormented by a chronic ulcer in the leg; and the eldest Pole had said, 'He will die suddenly. His leg will kill him, and then we shall have jolly stirring.' Of such anticipations the people thought as the King did, for his death was a spectre to all.

As 1539 came in the prospect was all of invasion. Cardinal Pole had gone to Spain to urge the Emperor to free himself for the enterprise by making truce with the Turks; and from Spain came complaints of English merchants that the Inquisition was imprisoning and racking them for refusal to deny the royal supremacy. An invading force was supposed, erroneously, to be mustering on the Dutch coast, and there was plenty of talk in the Low Countries to give support to the idea. The Scots were also hostile, and the Pope made David Beaton, the Bishop of St. Andrews, a cardinal, and sent him to work up Scottish fervour against Henry's iniquities. How far the fears were warranted is an uncertain question. The Pope was the principal enemy, and he could strike only by the hands of others.

The Emperor was the key man, without whom nothing could be done. He was still under forty, but weary with many cares and disillusioned of war. He made no decision, and at the right moment Henry gave him a material incentive to refrain.

In February 1539 proclamation was made that for seven years from the following April foreign merchants might trade from and to England on payment only of the duties paid by native Englishmen. A subsequent state paper showed that this concession entailed a reduction in revenue of about £10,000 a year, no great matter to the English treasury in comparison with what the Court of Augmentations was bringing in. Its importance was that the greater part of the gift went to the Netherlands, that it was in fact a neatly placed bribe to the mercantile houses of Antwerp. They were now enabled to buy cloth in London and ship it themselves instead of being forced by higher duties to purchase from the Merchants Adventurers at Antwerp. The English traders were of course prejudiced by having to ship on equal terms with the Flemings instead of doing so under the protection of differential duties, but it was the price they had to pay to avert a war that would have stopped their business completely. However disadvantageous economically, Henry's concession was a diplomatic success. The Emperor continued inactive, and by the summer the war-scare was dying down.

It is fairly certain that Henry had never relished the tentative negotiations with the Lutherans and the small encouragements given to the English Protestants under Cromwell's advice. He determined in 1539 to make clear his Catholic orthodoxy in matters of dogma, and by so doing to soften foreign discontents and please the great non-Protestant majority of his own people. A new Parliament met at the end of April. Cromwell had striven to secure the return of members amenable to himself and the King. But in truth a fissure was opening between Cromwell and the reforming bishops on the one side and the King on the other, who was turning now to the counsels of conservative leaders like Norfolk, Lee the Archbishop of York, Gardiner of Winchester, and Tunstall of Durham. These men were not papalists or advocates of sparing the monasteries, but they were Catholics who disliked much that had been done in the past three years. A Catholic reaction was setting in, to which Henry willingly lent himself. In character with this climate of opinion the new Parliament not only legalized the surrender of the greater monasteries but passed the Act of the Six Articles for the definition of religion or, in its own words, for 'abolishing diversity of opinions'. The articles were as follows: assertion of the doctrine of transubstantiation; and declarations that the sacrament should be administered to laymen in one kind only, that the marriage of priests was forbidden, that private masses should continue, that vows of chastity must be perpetually observed, and that auricular confession was to be made. These were all contrary to the wishes of Protestants, who named the Act the whip with six strings; but the articles were popular with the mass of the people, including the occupants of abbey lands. The penalties enacted were severe: for denial of transubstantiation, burning at the stake; for breach of the other five articles, ordinary hanging as for felony. In spite, however, of an initial outburst of persecution inspired by subordinate authorities, the Act was not in general severely enforced; and a subsequent amendment allowed offenders to escape the death penalty for infringement of all but the transubstantiation clause.[1] Henry's purpose was rather to make public declaration of his doctrinal position than to enter on a general persecution, and he disliked excess of zeal on the part of busybodies. In the passing of the bill, Henry used Norfolk and not Cromwell as his parliamentary agent. Cranmer showed some boldness in resisting certain clauses in debate, but his position as archbishop was unshaken. Latimer was uncompromising and had to resign his bishopric.

Although the expectation of war began to weaken after the spring of 1539 there was no formal reconciliation with France or the Emperor, and so long as the two papalist powers remained on good terms England could not feel at ease. As the summer drew on Charles V found occasion to travel from Spain to the Netherlands and Germany. In time past he had made such a journey by sea along the English coast of the Channel. Now Francis invited him to pass through France, and as he did so he was royally entertained in Paris, where the utmost cordiality seemed to prevail between host and guest. It was a portent that though the threat to Henry might be suspended it was not abolished. Such being the position, Cromwell urged upon Henry that a German alliance would be an insurance, and that, since Henry had been two years a widower, his marriage with the sister of the Duke of Cleves would be on all grounds desirable. The Duke of Cleves was not a Lutheran and not a papalist, but like Henry conducted the religion of his state on independent

[1] See J. D. Mackie, *The Earlier Tudors* (Oxford, 1952), p. 427.

and mainly Catholic principles. But he was the brother-in-law of the Elector of Saxony, the strongest of the Lutherans, and he had a claim to the Duchy of Guelders, on the Netherland border, which the Emperor did not admit. Cromwell assured Henry that Anne of Cleves was beautiful and personally a most desirable match. Here Cromwell exaggerated, and Hans Holbein, who painted her portrait, was much nearer the truth; but Henry chose to believe Cromwell. The negotiation went on through the summer, and the marriage treaty was signed at the beginning of October while the Paris hospitalities were emphasizing the Franco-Imperial accord.

Cromwell hoped that the Cleves marriage would strengthen his own position, shaken by the reactionaries in 1539, and so it would have done had the marriage been a success. But when Anne arrived at the end of December the King was bitterly disappointed on personal grounds. He felt that he had been deluded into a sacrifice that might prove unnecessary after all. On that point he was right, for after the Emperor left France and arrived in the Netherlands it soon began to appear that his cordiality with Francis had been more apparent than real. Francis wanted but one thing, the Duchy of Milan, and it became evident that he was not going to get it by fair words. Yet the lady was in England, ready for an immediate marriage from which Henry recoiled. He said so in blunt terms to his counsellors, but there was no way out. He unwillingly went through the ceremony early in January 1540, conceiving himself an ill-used man. Anne was no more enamoured of Henry than he of her, and this unfortunate marriage remained merely nominal.

It is highly probable that Henry began now to consider the liquidation of Cromwell. The minister had done useful work, but it was accomplished, and he had made a bad mistake and was becoming an encumbrance. His only real friend at court was Cranmer, who had little political weight and was supremely faithful to the King. Norfolk and the nobles hated Cromwell, as did Gardiner and most of the bishops. Among the people Cromwell was equally unloved, save by the small Protestant minority. His English Bible aroused no general enthusiasm, since it gave opportunities to noisy zealots; and the parish priests, to the content of their flocks, were slack and unwilling in performing the English innovations in the services. Abroad, Cromwell was a liability—obviously in any quest of good relations with the Emperor—and even in France, where his record was abhorred by powerful Catholic influences. Henry may well have revolved these circumstances, but after his custom he kept his counsel and gave no sign. He was not yet ready to strike. In judging him we should remember that he had never expressed any personal regard for Cromwell, as he had for Cranmer. The man had been always an instrument, not a friend.

Whatever may have been in the King's mind, observers in the spring of 1540 were predicting Cromwell's fall. Then Parliament met, and the minister was once more in his element as the great man of business. He extracted a useful subsidy from the Commons and the concurrent convocation of the clergy. He passed also a new Navigation Act, which cited and reinforced the old one of Henry VII making the Bordeaux wine trade a monopoly of English shipping, and went considerably further. The evidences of Franco-Imperial disaccord being now patent, it was possible to modify the free-trade concession of 1539. The new measure did so by enacting that foreigners who availed themselves of the reduction in duties must lade their goods in English ships, the merchants of the Hanseatic League alone being exempted. The Flemings of Antwerp were indignant, and Chapuys wrote bitterly of Henry's duplicity in making a concession when afraid of war and virtually revoking it when the danger had passed. It soon became apparent that Henry's purpose was to extort better treatment from the Emperor, and after two years of wrangling, as part of a general *rapprochement*, the Flemings and Spaniards were exempted from the obligation to employ English shipping.

To all appearances Cromwell was in the ascendant once more. Already a baron since 1536, he was advanced in April to the earldom of Essex. He arrested a batch of his opponents, including the Bishop of Chichester, for papal sympathies, and it was thought that Latimer was to be reinstated. But he could not yet touch his chief foes, Norfolk and Gardiner, who were working to win over the King. The French ambassador wrote that the two parties in the Privy Council[1] were bent on destroying one another. The atmosphere was

[1] The transformation of the earlier Council into the Privy Council of the later Tudor period may be represented by a change of title here. Dr. G. R. Elton, in his *Tudor Revolution in Government* (Cambridge 1953) credits Cromwell with the development whereby the Privy Council acted as a body, sitting regularly and tending to give corporate in place of individual advice to the sovereign, while undoubtedly acting corporately in a wide range of administrative matters. The development was achieved by no single decision and was somewhat masked under Cromwell's ascendancy. There were subsequent fluctuations, but the newer Privy Council is seen fully established in the reign of Elizabeth I. The adjective Privy was not invariably prefixed, and Cranmer's Prayer Book speaks of 'the Lords of the Council'.

electric, and a storm inevitable. Henry watched inscrutably, and at length, having kept all trembling, suddenly made his pleasure known. On 10 June he had Cromwell arrested in the Council chamber and sent to the Tower on charges of treason or, more explicitly, of conniving at heresy and of intending to force his will upon the King. The arrest was the decisive action, for with Parliament sitting an act of attainder was a matter of course. Cromwell answered angrily as his enemies rose upon him in the Council chamber, committing such paltry actions as snatching the decorations from his person while they taunted him with having made the bloody laws by which he would die; but once in the Tower he cringed for mercy, although he had never shown any. The King still wanted something from him, evidence to facilitate the divorce of Anne of Cleves; and having given it he went to the scaffold, regretted by the Protestants but by none others of the generality. Among the great men only one spoke for him, Cranmer, who urged his worthiness upon the King as he had that of Anne Boleyn, and with the like effect. Cranmer, called by some a time-server, never turned his back on a friend in need. Cromwell was credited by his enemies with a 'last speech' in which he declared himself a Catholic. It was widely held to have been a forgery, and Foxe in his *Martyrs* printed a dying confession of a very different tenor. Two days afterwards Barnes and two others who had served him were burnt as heretics, while three priests were executed for denying the royal supremacy.

Cromwell's execution rounded off the most eventful decade of the Tudor century. His policy, so far as it was not already achieved, was repudiated a few days before his death by the divorce of Anne of Cleves. Fitly enough, Gardiner was appointed to manage it, and did so without difficulty in convocation and Parliament, so handy a tool was the canon law to one who understood it. Henry settled on Anne a handsome income, and she lived happily in England for the rest of her days. Norfolk deftly supplied the vacancy by pushing forward one of his innumerable relatives, a young woman named Catherine Howard. She became the fifth queen shortly after the fourth's dismissal.

9

THE BRITISH QUESTION

THE events of 1539–40 throw light on the conception of Henry VIII as an irresponsible despot. Despotic in disposition he certainly became, but in action he was always responsible to the will of his people, and to ascertain that will he was keenly attentive to the manifestations of their opinion. The strife of parties that preceded Cromwell's death was a conflict into which principles entered as well as personalities. The King was the arbiter, and when he had well pondered he expressed his decision in so sharp a fashion as made men think that the decision was all his own. Partly it was his, and partly that of his people; and his merit as a king was that on fundamentals he and his people were one. They were content that he should give the decisive lead. Statecraft was his business, and he knew more and saw farther than they did. They expressed their wishes and accepted his judgment. Even in the most despotic years opinion was freely expressed. A few men died for dangerous speaking, while the great majority said what they pleased with impunity. The King's councillors were expected to speak their minds, and did so. As for the people, they approved of the King's government. They had cast their all into his cause in 1538–9 and were to do so again in 1544–5. To the English Henry was a master as the captain of the ship is the master of the crew. They knew that a master was necessary to their survival, and then and for long afterwards they held him for a good one. That he was a rough master may be granted, as that they were a rough crew.

After Cromwell there was no predominant minister. Henry took charge in all matters, and took counsel from various angles, from Norfolk and Gardiner the Catholics, and from Cranmer and Edward Seymour (whom he made Earl of Hertford) the reformers. He had had no real wife since Jane Seymour died, and indeed for many a year before he married her, since the Boleyn interlude had been an affair rather than a normal marriage. He was now genuinely fond of Catherine Howard and thanked God that he was living a good life. He grew for a time more healthy and cheerful, rose before six, and put in more hours at business than ever before. He still took exercise on horseback, but the days of jousting and wrestling were over. He was fifty in 1541.

As ever the succession was the most pressing care, both for king and nation; and events were to link the succession with the affairs of Scotland and the idea of carrying the consolidation of the state to a united kingdom of the British Isles. Young Edward was a child of three when the new decade opened. His early death was possible, and a minority and regency distinctly probable. Behind him were Mary and Elizabeth, both declared illegitimate, and in any case as women not seriously held likely to rule a turbulent people without disaster. The illegitimate son, the Duke of Richmond, had died in 1536. In Scotland was the next candidate of Tudor blood in the person of James V, nephew of Henry and son of Margaret Tudor.

James V had been born less than two years before his father died at Flodden, and consequently there had been a long minority. His mother was married again to a member of the Douglas family. She was unfaithful to him and generally unpopular with the nobles, and her conduct was such that her brother Henry VIII took occasion to reprove her for her matrimonial laxities. The outcome was that when the young James grew old enough to rule in the 'thirties he found many of the nobles hostile and was driven to rely upon the churchmen, of whom after 1536 Cardinal Beaton was the leader. Events in England had caused this division between the Scottish nobles and clergy. The nobles began to hanker after a spoliation of Church property and to form the nucleus of a pro-English party. The churchmen clung to the ancient French alliance, the Pope, and the Emperor; and in 1538–9 Beaton did his best to bring Scotland into the projected coalition of Catholic powers against England. There were native heretics in Scotland akin to the Lollards, and trade with the Netherlands introduced Protestantism into the east coast ports, while a few of the nobles were attracted by the New Learning. By 1540 the heretic element was sufficiently notable to call for persecution, which Beaton was ready to supply. The division between nobles and churchmen was not clear-cut and must be taken as a convenient approximation. Many of the high offices in the Church were held by noble families, and the ecclesiastical tone and code of conduct were lower than in England on the eve of the Reformation.

Henry early perceived that the defence of his anti-papal reformation against the probable attack on it would be greatly eased if Scotland could be brought into line. In 1536 he invited James to meet him at York, to be urged to a parallel confiscation of Church property. James declined to attend and went instead to France, where he married a daughter of Francis I. Within a few months she died, and he then married Mary of Lorraine, sister of the Duke of Guise, the most powerful of the papalist nobles in France. The marriage was the work of Beaton, who was determined to commit Scotland to a pro-papal and anti-English policy. In 1540 Henry tried again, sending Sir Ralph Sadler to make fresh proposals for a royal conference and a Scottish reformation. Henry desired a meeting at York in 1541, on the occasion of a northern progress which he intended to make, but again James refused, and it was plain that he was committed to the Pope.

Henry duly made his northern progress. He had not previously been north of the Trent, and he used all his magnificent power of prestige to confirm the authority which the Council in the North was establishing. The progress was a brilliant success and had solid results in strengthening the defence of the north against the stresses it was shortly to undergo. He returned to London well satisfied in spite of the failure of his Scottish approach. No sooner was he back than he suffered a personal misfortune. Evidence had been reported to the Privy Council that Catherine Howard before her marriage had led an immoral life and had been compromised with more men than one. To conceal such a story would have placed the councillors in a dangerous position. Yet Henry was attached to his wife, and none cared for the task of enlightening him. At length Cranmer was prevailed upon to do it. At first the King was incredulous; but the proofs were conclusive, and the culprits themselves could make no denial. It came out that even before Catherine's marriage these affairs were known to a number of people. Worse was to come, for on equally conclusive evidence it was shown that during the late northern progress she had continued in the same courses, carrying on her amours almost under her husband's nose. Only one outcome was possible, for a divorce had been the solution only in the two cases where a queen had had to be dispensed with for no fault of her own. The enormities of Catherine Howard amounted, in the contemporary view, to treason. Parliament passed a bill of attainder in January 1542, and she was beheaded a month later. The well-known portrait of Catherine Howard is that of a beautiful woman carrying gentleness and intelligence in her face. From it few would suspect her true history.

Norfolk, her uncle, manœuvred his way out of the disgrace, although some of his relatives were imprisoned for having held their tongues too long. The tragedy was a check to the ultra-Catholics, whose nominee Catherine Howard had been, a check emphasized next year when Henry married Catherine Parr, a widow of thirty, who held Protestant sympathies. She and Cranmer and Hertford formed a near-Protestant nucleus very close to the King and protected by his personal regard. The Howards were disappointed of the predominant influence for which they had hoped from the fifth marriage. Henry nevertheless did not forget his own Catholicism and that of the majority of his people, and the Catholic party was by no means driven from power. Their ultimate ruin was to be due more to dynastic considerations than to their beliefs.

The Six Articles marked the limit to which legislative reaction was carried. In 1541 the slackness of many parishes in providing English Bibles was remedied by a new order imposing penalties for further delay. The observance of several saints' days was abolished as tending to idleness, particularly at harvest time. Cardinal Pole's mother, the Countess of Salisbury, lying under attainder in the Tower for two years past, was executed at the same time, for reasons which are not on record. They are generally believed to have been the King's increasing brutality and suspicious habit of mind. All this took place before the fall of Catherine Howard. The next step was in 1543, when Henry issued *The Necessary Erudition of any Christian Man*, usually called *The King's Book*, of definitions and explanations of religious doctrines. Its tendency was to reinforce the Catholic view, and it did so more plainly than the earlier *Bishops' Book* by including matters that had then been omitted. Henry was deeply concerned to secure uniformity in religion, since differences on religion undermined the unity of the body politic. He disliked the strife of factions, but he sought to end it rather by management than by exterminating one faction and making the other preponderant. Gardiner and Cranmer both retained his favour. Cranmer was known to be virtually a Protestant, and his party was numerically smaller. His enemies sought more than once to overthrow him, but on each occasion the King took his part and snubbed them. Equally he protected Gardiner from a hostile advance by his opponents. The fact that men felt free to initiate such moves in the presence of a sovereign of autocratic temper shows that the actual position of English liberty was stronger than is commonly supposed. The best approach to an understanding of the true state of politics and the constitution in these years is to attempt to view them as Henry saw them and to appreciate his problems and his thoughts—by no means an easy undertaking.

A determination to obtain Milan was the constant factor in the unprincipled life of Francis I, and once again it led to a general war. Charles V did not wish to fight France again. His first desire was to settle with the Lutherans of Germany and his second to lead a great Christian armament to Constantinople there to deal with the Turkish menace at its source. But he could not give up for nothing the strategic key of Italy, which controlled his southern line of communications between Spain and the Empire. In the autumn of 1540, having failed in negotiations with the French, he conferred the duchy of Milan on his son Philip, thus deciding that it would thenceforth be attached to the crown of Spain. Francis determined to fight and slowly began preparations. He had formed an alliance in 1535 with Solyman the Magnificent, the conquering Ottoman sultan who had already inflicted severe losses on the Emperor. This act of infidelity had not lost Francis the regard of the Pope, Paul III, who was annoyed by the prospect of concessions to the Lutherans. Paul maintained ostensible neutrality, but supported Francis in his anti-English policy towards Scotland. In 1541 two French envoys travelling through Italy to Constantinople were killed by the Emperor's officers in Milan, and Charles refused to disavow their action. It was another step to war, which actually began in the following summer. These were in outline the European circumstances upon which Henry VIII had to found his policy towards Scotland. They ranged Francis and the Pope in the ranks of his enemies and made ultimately necessary an alliance with the Emperor, an alliance heartily approved by the mercantile element in the English people.

In the summer of 1542, not yet having declared himself for or against France or the Emperor, Henry renewed his invitation to James V to come to England for a conference. James again refused, and border fighting broke out. Sir Robert Bowes, warden of the middle march, led a raid which ended disastrously when he was

ambushed and captured at Haddon Rig. The affair was magnified
into a great victory for the Scots and seriously damaged Henry's
prestige on the continent. He demanded the release of the prisoners,
the signature of a perpetual alliance, and a meeting with James
before the end of the year. The Scots would not comply, since
Haddon Rig had strengthened Beaton's influence. In the autumn
Henry therefore ordered the Duke of Norfolk to invade across the
eastern border. Norfolk's movement was not a raid with the mobile
border horse, but an advance with a regularly constituted army. It
was therefore slow, and the lateness of the season made it a complete
failure. The country afforded no subsistence, and the transport broke
down on the soddened terrain. Within a few days Norfolk had to
fall back to Berwick, having achieved nothing. James and Beaton
were in the ascendant, although many of the Scottish nobles looked
doubtfully at the prospect of a regular war with England, to which
they were not yet irrevocably committed. James nevertheless
decided on a great raid across the western border to Carlisle. He
collected about 10,000 men, for the most part mounted, and launched
them across the border under the command of his favourite Sir
Oliver Sinclair. With them were several of the greater nobles, who
had expected the king to lead them and resented their subordination
to Sinclair. Yet the numbers were overwhelming, for Sir Thomas
Wharton at Carlisle could raise no more than 2,000 men, and
Norfolk's army was far away across difficult country at Berwick.
Strategically James had devised a shrewd stroke; tactically it
foundered on the unreliability of the border troops. These men, on
both sides, were individually hardy and enterprising soldiers, but
they were also thieves, with the thief's instinct to cut and run when
surprised. As Wharton with his small force advanced boldly on the
Scots, they were burning and plundering in their usual manner.
Their king was not there, and Sinclair was no leader. A panic broke
out, with cries that Norfolk was upon them. The whole army
dissolved in rout towards the Esk River and the bogs of Solway
Moss. Many were drowned and over a thousand made prisoners,
while the survivors struggled through the floods without their
ordnance, horses, arms, and standards. The panic was attested by the
fact that only seven Englishmen were killed. It was Haddon Rig in
reverse, but on a larger scale. Among the prisoners were seven
nobles and numerous gentlemen.

Such was the rout of Solway Moss, hardly a battle, but the

beginning of a chain of events that were in the next eighteen years to alter decisively the course of Scottish and British history. On hearing the news James V collapsed into moaning and grief from which he never recovered. Within a month he was dead. Two young sons had already been taken from him. Just before his end Mary of Guise gave birth to a daughter, destined to be the only survivor of his family and to be known to history as Mary, Queen of Scots. Scotland was left to the afflictions of another long minority, with the queen-mother to maintain the papal cause, which was also for some years to be the cause of national independence.

Before hearing of James's death, which was entirely unexpected, Henry VIII had determined to take such steps with Scotland as would end the perennial menace to his rear whenever his relations with continental powers were critical. He had informed the King of France of his intention. Francis, much as he desired Henry's aid against the Emperor, knew that in any event he was unlikely to obtain it, since such a course was against the interest and inclination of the English people. He would not throw away the Scottish alliance for the mere possibility of an English one. The papalist party were strong in his councils, and he replied to Henry that James was in the right and that France would support Scotland as a faithful ally. The news of James's death invigorated the purposes of both Henry and Francis. Francis prepared armaments in his ports to go to the assistance of Scotland, but severe winter weather delayed their sailing. Henry made use of the nobles captured at Solway Moss to form a pro-English party, and at the same time revived the ancient claim to the feudal overlordship of the English crown over Scotland. He would have done better to have kept that contention in the background, for its assertion was a mistake. It aroused Scottish patriotism against him and long delayed the pacification and co-operation which he desired. It would in fact have been permanently fatal but for the rise of Protestantism in Scotland, a force that was yet feeble in 1543. Henry had still to learn the toughness and tenacity of the Scottish people. He knew only their noble representatives and had a poor opinion of them, in which it must be confessed he was justified. The result of his misjudgment of the nation was that no settlement was achieved in his lifetime or for many years afterwards. In the long outcome the union of Great Britain was to owe as much to John Knox the Scottish Protestant as to the Tudor statesman; and Knox had not been heard of in 1543.

In Scotland the first results of Solway Moss and the king's death were the overthrow of Beaton by the opposition nobles and the choice of the Earl of Arran as regent, coupled with overtures for peace with England. Arran was a near-Protestant who did not believe in purgatory and was ready for the repudiation of the Pope and the suppression of the monasteries. He was also weak and unreliable. 'A soft God's man', a contemporary estimate, gives in four words the two essentials of his public character. Beaton was imprisoned, but retaliated by pronouncing an interdict of all religious ministrations, an interdict which the majority of the priesthood obeyed and the majority of the laity received with terror. In England Henry conceived that he had only to play one move to win. He released the prisoners of Solway Moss after a month in London, and sent them home, together with his ambassador Sir Ralph Sadler, to secure a treaty for the acknowledgment of his overlordship, the eventual marriage of the infant Mary to his son Edward, the up-bringing of Mary in England, the handing over of Beaton to English custody, and the garrisoning of Scottish fortresses by English troops. These prospects occupied the first half of 1543. But the favourable tide receded. Arran weakened and shuffled, released Beaton to allay popular clamour for the lifting of the interdict, and finally (in September) surrendered to the formidable cardinal and craved his forgiveness; while priests and patriots grew wrathful at the threat of heretic aggression. Sadler found himself in a quicksand of infirmity and duplicity in which he could discern no standing ground. He warned Henry of it, but Henry in London remained confident. He believed Scotland to be in his grasp, on the sole condition that he should be firm in warding off French intervention. It was the major error of statecraft in his career.

Meanwhile the French forces for Scotland were delayed, and their first contingent did not arrive until midsummer. Before that date Henry had lost patience or realized the truth of Sadler's reports. He threatened invasion in force, and the Scottish leaders gave way. Beaton was at the head of a party, but not yet restored to ascendancy. The others agreed to the Treaty of Greenwich, signed on 1 July 1543, the day after the French expedition had been sighted off Aberdeen. It provided that the marriage should be made in due time, but that the Queen of Scots should remain in her own country until she was ten years old, and that Scotland should preserve its laws and liberties. The surrender of Beaton and the garrisoning of the fortresses were dropped. This moderation of demands was six months too late. At the opening of the year it might have had a chance. Now Beaton was rampant and his French allies active, and national resentment against England was gathering strength as the Solway disaster receded into history. The Treaty of Greenwich, although useful as a talking-point in after years, did not even ensure the neutrality of Scotland in the approaching French war. Before the end of the year Beaton, with Arran in his pocket, declared formal war against England and renewed formal alliance with France.

On one point Henry had been clear-sighted, that even if he won Scotland outright he would have to fight France; for the French would never quietly consent to the loss of their chief weapon of offence against England. In February Henry secretly agreed to a military alliance with the Emperor. In June he came into the open with a virtual ultimatum to Francis, based on French support of Scotland, the cessation of the French payments due to England by former treaties, and the impiety of the alliance concluded between the French and the Turks. War began in July with the despatch of a contingent to serve with the Emperor on the Low Countries frontier. Henry's last and most serious French war thus arose out of his determination to unite the British kingdoms. How serious and how ruinously costly it was to be he probably did not foresee. To engage in it seemed natural on the standards of sixteenth-century conduct, which were like those of the aggressive dictatorships of the twentieth century. Peace might be economically desirable, but it was not a moral aim to which political ambitions should be sacrificed.

Henry designed two operations for the campaign of 1544. The principal one was to be his own invasion of France in co-operation with the Emperor. As a preliminary he purposed to safeguard his rear by a rapid stroke at Edinburgh, which should inflict sufficient damage to keep Scotland out of action for the summer. Norfolk had been sent the wrong way to work in the previous year, and he was now an old man losing his qualities as a commander. Henry therefore entrusted the Scottish command to the Earl of Hertford, and decided to make use of a strong naval squadron under Lord Lisle, who had recently been appointed Lord Admiral. Lisle was John Dudley, son of Dudley the extortioner executed in 1510. Lisle concentrated his fighting ships and a sufficiency of transports at Newcastle and the adjacent harbours. In March and April Hertford collected his army from the nine northern English counties (so far south as to include

Cheshire, Derby, and Nottingham), whose service was allocated to the northern front. By 1 May he had 12,000 foot on board the ships, while 4,000 horse were to invade by land from Berwick. Two days after its embarkation the expedition entered the Forth. Hertford found Leith undefended, and took it without loss. He then turned on Edinburgh, whose citizens put up a fight at the Canongate but were forced to give entry. The castle held out, but Edinburgh itself was pillaged and set ablaze. At this point Hertford was joined by his horse, who had ridden swiftly from the border under the warden of the east march. There was now no opposition, and it remained to complete the work of destruction as economically as possible. Hertford returned to Leith, shipped his guns and heavy gear, and prepared to march in light order back to Berwick. Before going he burnt the pier of Leith and every house in the town. Lisle had meanwhile destroyed all the merchantmen in the Forth and had captured two ships-of-war. Hertford then set out southwards, his army creating a broad band of destruction along the coast and through the eastern Lowlands. In eighteen days from the start he was again at Berwick, his mission accomplished with the loss of forty men. The whole affair, with its moderate force, amphibious method, and good staff work, was something new in Tudor warfare. Hertford was plainly a general to be reckoned with, while Lisle's fleet, the King's personal creation, had done all that was required of it. It should be added that Hertford had acted under orders, although he himself disliked the policy of devastation and would have preferred instead to leave garrisons to hold Leith and other places. The King, with the French war in prospect, thought the garrisons an ill-judged commitment, and overruled him. Hertford's view sprang not only from policy but from humanity, another new thing in that generation.

Meanwhile the forces of central and southern England were moving to the ports, and again we are struck by the excellent management of a complicated business. Henry's new, consolidated England was efficient, and its servants were capable men. The army was raised on a county basis, the number of men to be found by every gentleman in the shire having been first worked out, and their mustering places appointed. Here they gathered on the appointed day, received their coats and conduct money, and moved off under their local leaders to the port appointed to them. The army embarked at every seaport from Harwich to London and from London to Rye and Winchelsea, and its speed and good order depended upon the right amount of shipping being ready for the troops who were to use it. Other preparations were also necessary on an enormous scale: assessments on every county for its quota of horses, oxen, carts, sheep, grain, and malt, and their punctual collection and transport; the provision of 'playtes' or special flat-floored barges for ferrying horses; the construction of mobile bakehouses and brew-houses to accompany the army in the field; the concentration by native founding and foreign purchase of a great train of heavy guns, including fifty mortars to fire a new invention of exploding shells; and the covering of all by the shield of the Navy, the fighting fleet of the united nation, the monasteries afloat.

All went as designed. Towards the end of May the movement started, and by the middle of June nearly all were overseas deploying on the frontier of the Calais pale. By agreement with the Emperor, the King was to command an army of 42,000. Of these his English-men numbered 36,000, and the remainder were German mercenaries armed with hackbuts, a weapon in which the English were weak. They had field-guns and siege-guns in plenty, but for the personal missile they kept still to the longbow, while the majority of the foot, as of old, were pikemen and billmen. Hertford belonged to the newer school of officers who believed in firearms. He wrote that he would rather have 1,000 hackbutters on the Border than 5,000 spearmen. Lisle and Lord Russell, another coming man, held the same views. The bow had reached its last days.

Charles and Henry had agreed to join forces and advance to the capture of Paris. Neither seriously meant to do it. The object of both King and Emperor was not to conquer France but to compel France to make peace and cease from interfering with their other designs. Charles looked behind him to a religious settlement in Germany and a grand stroke at the Turk. Henry also looked behind him to the incorporation of Scotland in his dominions. He knew that the taking of Paris, even if possible, would be the opening of a limitless war with the spirit of France, and he preferred to fight not France but Francis, a different opponent. Moreover these Renaissance wars in western Europe did not usually end in captures of capitals and great territorial conquests. They were waged only in the summer, and during the winter communications withered and armies came home or perished. Henry had in view a more practicable objective in the shape of Boulogne, whose possession would double his powers of putting pressure on Francis, and whose loss would be a point of prestige on which a bargain might be struck.

Henry therefore with a part of his army laid siege to Boulogne, while Norfolk with the remainder attacked the inland fortress of Montreuil which lay on the road towards Paris. The Montreuil proceedings were useful as a cover to Henry on the coast, but were not seriously pressed for their own sake. The English duly blockaded Boulogne, battered its walls with 60-pounder cannon, and shelled its houses with the new mortars. After two months, on 14 September, the French commander yielded and the town passed into Henry's hands. Four days later Charles V signed a separate peace with France at Crespy. Henry knew what that meant, the concentration of all French forces by sea and land against himself. He recalled Norfolk from before Montreuil, manned the broken walls of Boulogne with his best troops, and himself returned to England to organize defence, having already sent orders that preparations should be made in every shire to muster every man under sixty at an hour's notice.

Charles V, whose objectives in the war resembled Henry's in lying behind him instead of in front, was equally half-hearted about the advance on Paris. In the conditions of the time it was not a sound operation, since there were numerous fortified strongholds between the Flemish frontier and Paris, and these unless taken would cut the invaders' winter communications and lead to a disaster; and there was no time to take them all. Francis understood the diplomatic opportunity and opened separate negotiations first with Henry and then with Charles. Henry notified his ally and refused to treat without him. Charles thought that he might none the less be let down and closed with Francis, having real or manufactured excuses for his conduct. Henry had occupied the best of the season at Boulogne without advancing to join his ally, and was alleged to have given a verbal consent that Charles should treat; and Charles had made an unwise military move that allowed the French to threaten his communications, and so could plead necessity. But, when all was said, the Peace of Crespy was a cold-hearted abandonment that left Henry to shift for himself when greater loyalty could have secured an all-round settlement. The Pope had a hand in it, desiring as ever to unite the continental powers against the heretic island, and to secure their assistance in dominating the general council of the Church that was at length to assemble at Trent in the following year. The bull convening the council was issued in November 1544. Its outcome was expected to be the closing of the Catholic ranks and the extirpation of the Protestants. England's position, opposed single-handed to France and Scotland, was serious. The summer's war had cost over half a million pounds, and taxation was already at dizzy heights. There was not much to spare for hiring foreign mercenaries, and the country's defence rested on the spirit of its free men in arms rather than on its wealth. France on the contrary commanded large bodies of professional soldiers, mostly foreigners, and paid them with the taxation wrung from her relatively huge population. In this age the French peasant did not fight in person, but paid and starved. The resulting military strength was impressive, but really less solid than that of amateur England. On the sea the forces of the two combatants also showed some important differences. Events on the sea in 1544–5 played the decisive part in shaping and terminating the war.

In 1544 Francis had engaged a force of galleys to co-operate with the Turks in the Mediterranean, but his naval effort in the Channel was too small to yield any chance of commanding the sea. Lisle's fleet effectively did that, while the private shipowners, particularly of the western ports, took out letters of marque empowering them to 'annoy the King's enemies' at their own cost and discretion. Thus licensed, the privateers swept the French merchantmen off the sea and enjoyed a profitable summer. With the signing of the treaty of Crespy, the Spaniards and Flemings became neutrals, and French merchants began to ship cargoes in their vessels, claiming that the neutral flag covered the goods. The privateers asserted the contrary doctrine and took enemy goods out of neutral ships, and sometimes made prize of the ships themselves. The neutrals thus became incensed and their neutrality the reverse of benevolent. Robert Reneger, the Southampton man whom we have seen pioneering in Brazil, was obliged to take a prize vessel into a Spanish port, where the authorities disallowed his claim and confiscated the goods. In retaliation he cruised off Cape St. Vincent, and in March 1545 captured a Spanish treasure-ship worth 30,000 ducats homeward bound from the Caribbean. Others, notably William Hawkins of Plymouth, and Thomas Wyndham, a naval captain who owned privateers, were active in seizing Spanish and Flemish ships on the like pretexts; and there were many more pursuing the same quarry. The result was to make the Emperor hostile. In January 1545 he arrested the Merchants Adventurers at Antwerp, and embargoed their goods. In March, after the Reneger capture, his Spanish government took parallel action, and the Inquisition again began to persecute the English residents in Spain. As the summer came in, war with the Emperor was distinctly probable. Henry sought to moderate the activities of the privateers, but he had loosed a force that he could not immediately control. With the Council opening at Trent, and the Pope, the Emperor and the French in prospective combination, the situation was critical. Henry recommenced the old move of overtures to the German Lutherans, who were equally in peril, but their irresolution, as of old, was insuperable. His only real friends were, curiously enough, the Hanseatic League, with whom he had come to amicable terms as the wars began. They supplied him with naval stores and even with large ships equipped to join his fleet. One of them, the *Jesus of Lubeck*, was destined to a notable career under the English flag.

Francis, then, held the initiative in 1545, and he designed a campaign to force England to her knees. Briefly, the plan was to concentrate a superior fleet in the Channel and by its means to land an army to take Portsmouth, the only Channel base of the English Navy; if this prospered, to make further conquests in England; and under cover of the attack, to recapture Boulogne and possibly to take Calais as well. The determinant factor was primarily sea power. Boulogne and Calais, nourished from the sea, could be held against all attacks; cut off, they would fall. But behind this there was land power. If the worst happened and the French got a footing in England, would that mean surrender? Henry and his people said no, and the year witnessed preparations for resistance on the total scale and in the 1940 mood. 'My lord,' said the East Anglian militia to their Duke, 'if they come, for God's sake *bring us between the sea and them.*' But sea power was the first consideration, and that of Francis I requires accounting for. France had a sufficiency of skilled seamen, with captains of courage and resource. They were drawn not only from her European trades but from Atlantic enterprises more extensive than those of England. Frenchmen had been fishing in Newfoundland and trading and fighting on the coasts of Guinea and Brazil in greater numbers than the English, and in all the wars since Charles V had been elected emperor they had been privateering in the Caribbean, and pirating in the intervals of peace between. The officers and men were there, of the same breeding and training as those of England who forty years later were to fight the Armada. Their ships were small but well armed and able, the counterparts of the English privateers who were operating in the Channel and the Bay. The royal fleet was weaker than that of England, for Francis had always put his money on his armies. He supplemented it by hiring or impressing great Italian merchantmen and bringing them round to Havre de Grace. More important still in contemporary judgment, he was able to bring round a fleet of twenty-five fighting galleys which he no longer needed to resist the Emperor in the south. All these, making up a hundred and fifty sail, he had concentrated at Havre in the early summer. It was a formidable force, whose weakness lay not in material so much as in mixed nationalities (the galleys were Italian) and in the chief command, held by Claud d'Annebault, Baron de Retz, a leader of no high quality. The army was ready to embark on board the fleet, and the secret of its destination was well kept. Henry did not know where the blow was to fall, and had to be ready on all his coasts.

The English fleet was smaller but of better quality. Henry gathered it at Portsmouth to the number of eighty sail, of which forty were described as large. His own ships numbered between fifty and sixty, including many small craft, so that some of the forty great ships were armed merchantmen. On the seas were about sixty privateers, mostly operating in the western Channel, and these were to be called in at need. Every available seaman was called up, leaving women and boys to work the coastal fishery. In summer weather the chief danger was expected from the galleys. To counter them Henry had constructed a new type of light craft called rowbarges, with oars and sails, and armed with two or three guns on the broadside as well as in the prow. He had also built greater ships called galleasses, up to 450 tons, equipped with auxiliary oars for mobility in light airs. His main strength lay in his carrack-built sailing battleships, of which the new *Great Harry* was the most splendid example. By land the newly created lords-lieutenants drew up muster-rolls of every man in every shire. On the warning of the beacon fires all knew where they were to fall in, each with his bow, bill, or pike. They amounted to four armies of roughly 30,000 men each, the northern one to look towards Scotland, the eastern, southern, and western to be ready to march towards the landing-place of the French invaders. Much would depend upon staff work and logistics, in which competence had already been tried and proved. The King himself was in chief com-

mand with his Council as his general staff. Every port had its forts
and batteries; from Berwick round to Falmouth there were forty-one
garrisoned places, and every landing beach was staked and
entrenched. Every man of standing down to yeomen petty-captains
was keen and eager: even peaceful Cranmer was raising a troop of
artillery for the defence of Kent.

The people were totally with the King. To them it was harder to
pay than to fight, but they paid cheerfully. The calls were staggering.
The militia were to serve without a penny, but all else was paid for,
and the bills mounted. Parliament had granted a subsidy payable by
the end of 1545, and its collection was brought forward by several
months. No one had time to sit in Parliament that summer, and so
for a further supply Henry resorted to a benevolence assessed on the
wealthy. The Privy Council issued a frank appeal setting forth the
peril of the country and urging everyone to pay. All did with one
exception, a London alderman who had forgotten that if he had the
rights of an Englishman he had also his duties, and was accordingly
reminded of the latter by being sent to serve as a private soldier on
the Scottish front. Elsewhere payment was prompt and cheerful;
'if this be too little, His Grace shall have more', said one set of
contributors; and it was reckoned that the benevolence would bring
in more than a subsidy.

The year opened with a defeat. On the border the wardens of the
marches had continued the policy of raiding into Scotland through
the autumn and winter. In February Sir Ralph Evers, 'a fell cruel
man' as the Scots said, led an incursion to Jedburgh, and in the course
of it sacked Melrose Abbey and wantonly desecrated the tombs of the
Douglases. It was an act of wicked folly, since the Douglas family
belonged in general to the pro-English party. Retribution followed
when Evers rode into an ambush at Ancrum Moor and his border
horse fled in panic like the Scots at Solway Moss. Ancrum Moor
checked the raiding policy and encouraged the Scots to draw
together, while 3,000 French troops got through the Irish Sea to
Glasgow. In France at the same time the French forces approached
Boulogne and established batteries to make the harbour untenable.
Hertford was in command of the garrison, from which he organized
a sortie and drove the assailants ignominiously out of their works.
After Ancrum Moor he was recalled and sent again to the Scottish
command.

At midsummer the invasion was imminent. The fleet was concentrated at Portsmouth, and there Henry and his Council betook themselves in July. On the 18th the French were seen approaching round the eastern end of the Wight, and they anchored for the night between Bembridge and Ryde. Next morning, in a dead calm, d'Annebault sent forward his twenty-five galleys. It was their perfect opportunity, the English ships lying immobile in the anchorage outside the harbour, their eastern flank covered by the forts along the shore to Southsea and their western by the shoals.[1] For an hour and more the galleys fired hotly, making a special mark of the *Great Harry*, but they did no vital damage. Then a breeze off the land sprang up, the English got under way, and the galleys were chased off in disorder, the little rowbarges being noticed for their good service. In these proceedings the *Mary Rose* was lost, caught with her gun-ports open in a sudden gust of wind, and heeled over and sunk with nearly all on board. D'Annebault, in superior force, ventured nothing further save some long-range firing. He talked of staking all on a great push into the Portsmouth anchorage, but the land batteries were a deterrent, and his seamen told him that the wind that would take him in would make withdrawal difficult. He then landed troops in the Isle of Wight. Here the streams and woods of the lower ground were bad for close-ordered mercenaries and favoured the English archers, and after two days the French were beaten out with loss. D'Annebault next moved eastwards and anchored off the shoals that fringe the coast from Portsmouth to Selsey Bill. Lisle saw that a south-west wind would place the French in a bag between the Chichester shore and the Owers shoals. He determined to attack when the right wind came, but the French realized the position and sailed clear away in time. Time indeed had been against them. The western privateers were coming in, and the forces of the southern shires were on the march for Portsmouth. Before many arrived the peril had receded. The whole country was mobilizing, but it was not needed. On the instant of learning of the French withdrawal the King sent orders to halt and disband. Hampshire and Sussex men reached Portsmouth, but those from London, Oxford, Berks and Wilts were stopped half-way.

D'Annebault, his crews already smitten by disease, passed eastwards along the Sussex coast, and landed some soldiers at Seaford. At once the defence came into operation, and the levies of Sussex

---

[1] So the authorities appear to indicate, but the exact arrangement must be doubtful, for the area seems small for the number of ships that were there.

and Kent raced to the scene. The landing-party fell under a storm of arrows, and few regained their ships. Then the French leader drew off to Boulogne, whose besiegers were making little progress. Boulogne in fact was secure against all but starvation, and against that was victualled for several months. D'Annebault landed part of his army to assist, and put to sea again. If he could hold the Channel to the end of the year the prize might fall. But he could not. The western ships were joining Lisle, who was now strong enough to seek battle. On 15 August the fleets met off Shoreham, again in very light weather. D'Annebault sent forward his galleys, and the English 'rowing pieces' (the ships with auxiliary oars) handled them so roughly that the pure sailing vessels had little to do. Both sides broke off and anchored three miles apart. Lisle made ready for a general action on the morrow, but when morning dawned the French were far away, hull down beneath the horizon. D'Annebault's galleys having failed him, he would not risk a battle with his ships. Typhus and plague were raging, and he went back to Havre, where an English spy saw the landing of his human wreckage in the sorriest plight imaginable. The English also suffered the penalties of bad food, overcrowding and hot weather, and fluxes and 'burning fevers' were rife among them. But the great peril had been defeated. On the border Hertford, having stood on guard in the crisis, began again in September the dreadful process of ravaging the Lowlands.

At the close of 1545 England and France were financially exhausted, although the extent of England's embarrassment was not patent to the world. Ostensibly she was still rich, her people full of fight and willing to pay new taxes, her agents able to negotiate loans on the Antwerp bourse. The King's councillors knew better and were aghast at the consequences of continuing the war, which had already cost nearly a million and a half of English money. They urged the King to restore Boulogne and thereby obtain good terms on all other matters. Boulogne, ran the argument, is not worth the cost of keeping; we have proved to the world that the French cannot recover it in arms; let us break off now, while our military prestige is high, and while our wealth and determination are apparent; so shall we secure the fruits of victory. Henry thought otherwise. He had learnt to distrust treaty promises unbacked by securities. The better the terms he could extract from the French the more likely were they to repudiate when they saw their chance. He meant to rack his brother Francis, and he would hold the lever in his hand. He would keep Boulogne as 'a Milan for the French king', a security for the performance of treaties. Negotiations failed that winter, while the English dockyards turned out new fighting ships.

In the new year there was reinforcement of Boulogne and skirmishing round it, while the fleet at Portsmouth made ready to turn out stronger than in the previous year. It came to nothing, for the French had shot their bolt and Henry had correctly judged the situation. In May his ambassador Sir William Paget formulated terms with the French. England had entered the war with one object, a free hand in Scotland. She closed it with two, Scotland and an indemnity. The terms agreed upon were that within eight years the French should pay two million crowns, and on completion should receive the restitution of Boulogne. In addition the French were to pay a perpetual pension to England of 50,000 crowns and a life pension to Henry of 100,000. The peace was to include Scotland, on the understanding that she was bound by the Greenwich Treaty of 1543. Although the Scots had not been consulted, Henry was satisfied with the French undertaking to hold off and leave him to deal with them, which was all that he could expect from France. These terms were formally concluded as a treaty on 7 June 1546, and the French war was over.

A week before the formal signature the Scottish affair had taken a turn which gave promise of a peaceful settlement. For two years Protestantism had been on the increase, surprisingly, since its interest lay in friendship with England rather than with France. Cardinal Beaton was its natural enemy, for his position bound him to France and the Pope. In 1545 George Wishart, preaching Protestant doctrines, with John Knox as his disciple, attracted many listeners. He was arrested and taken to the Cardinal's palace-castle of St. Andrews. There, in March 1546, Cardinal Beaton burnt George Wishart for heresy. Retribution came in less than three months. Before the end of May a band of avengers plotted their way into the guarded castle and surprised Beaton in his bed. Like some other proud men of that time he did not die game, but howled piteously to be spared as a priest. They hung the body over the wall for Scotland to see.

Beaton's death was good news for Henry VIII, who had been informed of a previous design to kill Beaton and had not reprobated it. Some have therefore believed that he contrived the murder, but of this there is no evidence, and the details bear all the signs that it was simply what it professed to be, an affair of blood for blood, limited to the actors on the scene. Knox was not one of them, but he recorded the tale with approval, and he was hardly more an admirer of Henry VIII than of Cardinal Beaton, who for him were but two sorts of Catholics. The political result was not peace with England, although there was some diminution of Scottish intransigence. The Protestants were as yet far from being able to assume power, and the country continued to be ruled by the Catholic majority. They did not accede to the terms of the Treaty of Greenwich, and for the remainder of 1546 matters stood in suspense, with the French holding aloof and Henry meditating a decisive stroke for the following year.

In England it was time to think of other things, and indeed some of them had not been neglected during the war. Henry's health was growing worse, and he knew that he could not last long. For years indeed he had been thinking and planning less for his own prospects than for those that lay beyond in the perilous time of his son's minority. In his last year the minority became his chief preoccupation. An essential to civil peace was the maintenance of religion in accordance with the balance of opinion. The balance was slowly shifting forward, the Protestants growing more numerous and more confident in demanding a recognition of their claims. Neither their claims nor those of the Catholics included toleration. For either side truth was absolute and dissent worthy only of extirpation. True statesmanship regardful of the public good was increasingly forced into the attitude later expressed in France as that of the *politiques*, to avoid extremes, to hold the balance, to appeal for charity and order. Henry had to seek these things not only in the country but in his own Council, and as his end approached found their attainment increasingly difficult.

Free access to the English Bible in the churches had led to contemptuous and insulting conduct by the zealots, who made it an occasion to interrupt the decorum of the services. Parliament in 1543 therefore limited the privilege of public bible-reading to noblemen, gentlemen, yeomen, and merchants. Cranmer meanwhile had defeated a move of Gardiner to have the Bible retranslated in a more Catholic sense, with its rhythms spoiled by the retention of many Latin words. In 1544 the King decreed that the Latin litany should be converted into English, and a temporary version was issued while Cranmer worked upon his masterpiece, the English

Litany that was first published in 1545 and has since endured. The Parliament of the end of 1545 passed an act transferring to the King's use the endowments of the chantries. It was a measure mainly of war finance, although some of the money was ultimately used for the refoundation of schools. At the same time it was a practical step towards Protestantism, and the reformers did not fail to point out that the abolition of masses said for dead men's souls was a constructive denial of the doctrine of purgatory. A remarkable scene took place at the close of this Parliament. Henry addressed the Houses on the subject of religious dissensions, speaking with emotion, 'so sententiously, so kingly, so fatherly' that it struck all as an unusual occasion. Charity, he told them, was the foundation of religion, yet it was being frozen by dissension and hatred arising from opinions only, and the names used to propagate them. Papist, Lutheran, Anabaptist, he said, were names devised by the Devil for severing one man's heart from another's. Charity was faint among them, and God never less honoured and served. He urged them to amend it. 'Then may I justly rejoice that thus long I have lived to see this day, and you by verity, conscience and charity between yourselves may in this point, as you be in divers others, accounted among the rest of the world as blessed men.'

The Six Articles were still the law, and in 1546, after Edward Crome had loudly emphasized the construction put by the Protestants upon the Chantry Act, the Catholics in the Council made use of them. Latimer was examined, but as he, though in most points a Protestant, still believed in transubstantiation, he was safe from the burning clause, and the King's protection covered him in the less heinous matters. Others were less fortunate and were burnt. The most famous victim was Anne Askew, a Lincolnshire lady whose heresy might have been passed over had she not made it a challenge to authority. Once brought to trial, her doom was inevitable, for she would abate not a jot of her creed. She was duly condemned to the fire, but there was something more. She was known to be a friend of certain suspected ladies of the court, and her inquisitors sought to extract evidence against the Hertford connection, and perhaps against Catherine Parr. The Lord Chancellor Wriothesley and Sir Richard Rich personally racked Anne Askew in the Tower without obtaining any incrimination of the victims they aimed at, after which this heroic woman was burnt in public. The torturing of a woman was done without the King's knowledge or permission and for the purposes of a faction, upon whom must rest the disgrace. As for the burning, it was no longer Henry's policy, but the Six Articles were one of the 'bloody laws' for which he was peculiarly responsible, and the law took its course.

As the year drew to its close the King's illness grew more serious, and the rival parties in the Council braced themselves for the decisive fight which should yield supremacy in the approaching regency. On the one hand were the Howards, Gardiner, and Wriothesley, on the other Hertford, Lisle, and Cranmer. Henry watched through the autumn and gave no sign of his decision. Would he leave a Catholic, a Protestant, or a balanced council of regency? His own stake was the survival of his line and the welfare of his country, which he held to be identical. We have it on evidence at second hand that he meditated a decisive move towards Protestantism if he should be spared for a few months longer. However that may be, he certainly liked Hertford, the boy Edward's maternal uncle and the man most to be trusted to play fair by him. He probably respected Hertford's honesty, but may have doubted his wisdom. Lisle was to prove selfish and untrustworthy, although as yet his reputation was good. As for Cranmer, he was loyal to the core, but of small political acumen. These men would be fairly certain to move towards outright Protestantism. They would have the support of London but not of the country, and the result might well be civil war. On the other side, Norfolk and his son the Earl of Surrey, haters of the new learning and the new nobility, with Gardiner, the ablest Catholic bishop, were likely to declare for the Pope if it should suit them, and again there might be civil war. Suffolk, a sensible, moderate man, had recently died. Henry must have longed for more time, but he knew that time would be denied him. Then, in December, the decision came, occasioned, although probably not determined, by the folly of Surrey and his father's lack of control.

Surrey, not the rash youth he has sometimes been described, for he was thirty and a soldier of some experience, was nevertheless capable of ungoverned foolishness. It had scarcely been dignified for an earl and the heir to the senior title in the peerage to lead a gang about the London streets breaking windows with catapults, and there had been other evidence of his lack of ballast. He began now to say that when the King should die no one would have a better claim than his father to be regent of the realm, and that when that should come to pass they would deal hardly with the upstarts who surrounded Henry. He also assumed arms with some royal emblems to which his claim had been forbidden by the College of Arms, a symbolism with more significance then than now. The King saw whither this would tend, and in the interest of peace during the minority he allowed the anti-Howard party to strike. There was evidence to colour a charge of treason, and more was soon forthcoming, of alleged communications with Cardinal Pole and of an alleged design to make Surrey's sister the King's mistress in order to advance the family influence. In mid-December Norfolk and Surrey were both arrested. On 13 January a London jury, after great hesitation, condemned Surrey for treason, and he was executed six days later. Parliament had already met for its winter session, and the Duke of Norfolk was proceeded against by bill of attainder. He knew well the futility of defence and had already pleaded guilty. The bill passed both houses, and he was condemned to die on the morning of 28 January. Whether guilty or not on the rather flimsy charges advanced, one can hardly feel much sympathy: he had borne his part in the deaths of greater men, from More to Cromwell, on no higher ground than reason of state, which was the reason for his condemnation. But he was not to die; for early on the fatal morning the King was no more.

Renaissance kings in their fifties were worn out in mind or body. Charles V, Francis I, and Henry VIII all died at about the same age (58, 52 and 55 respectively). Francis was badly diseased for several years and, losing will-power, ended much under the domination of women. Charles kept his physical activity later, but his mind lost its vigour and in his last years he was subject to spells of melancholy and loss of volition. Henry's body failed him. As the disease in his leg grew worse he became unable to take exercise, and would not at the same time moderate his hearty eating and drinking. His corpulence grew into a crippling handicap. Pain rendered him sometimes savage and unapproachable, but to the end he could call forth his innate courtesy and behave with gentleness and good feeling. His mind and his will remained vigorous. They drove him to drag his weary bulk to the French campaign in 1544 and to take station at the point of danger in 1545. To his last breath no one dominated him, and all waited on his imperious and unclouded intellect. Competent doctoring might have prolonged his life for years. In December 1546, after the arrest of the Howards and the concomitant eclipse of Gardiner, he made the final alterations to his will, which had been drawn before he went to the siege of Boulogne. After mid-January no one saw him except a small domestic circle and two or three councillors. His royal assent to the Norfolk attainder was given by commission. On the night of the 27th he was sinking, and sent for Cranmer. When the archbishop arrived the King was speechless and could show recognition only by a pressure of the hand. At two in the morning of the 28th he died.

Just over sixty years had elapsed since the foundation of the dynasty on Bosworth field. The last twenty-five of those years had witnessed the revolution that founded modern England, the repudiation of papal authority, the incorporation of the Church in the national system of government, the secularization of much of its property, the enrichment of the middle classes and release of their potential energies, the working of the Protestant leaven, the tentative steps to a combination of North and South Britain. It had been a grim and searching time, the autumn of the old order declining into winter, with biting frost and bitter wind to tone the social soil for a new season of growth. It was not a happy and generous age. Hardness and mercilessness were its characteristics, amid an unscrupulous freedom in which danger lurked and men strove and thrust their competitors down without a compassionate glance. The high religion of the middle ages had taught men not to value present life and comfort since they were as nothing compared with the soul's eternity. During two centuries that belief had been losing not its validity but its appeal. Tudor England revelled in earthly interests; and the war of creeds, as Henry had truly said, was killing what was left of the Christian example that should have been the corrective. But these things have their ebb and flow, and the years in store were to witness some intimations of the coming of a humaner age, the uprising of a more liberal spirit not seen since More's spark had been put out. A paradox also was visible in the quality of the community, that amid all the strife of individuals and the ruthlessness of factions the national spirit was growing stronger and more conscious of itself than it had ever been before. After the revolution there was beginning the youth of the new order, the second half of the story of Tudor England.

10

EDWARD VI: SOMERSET AND NORTHUMBERLAND

THE middle of the Tudor period was a time of continuous economic unbalance leading to social crisis and weakness of government. From beginning to end, roughly from 1540 to 1570, it occupied a generation. It was at its worst in the reign of Edward VI, there was a little improvement under Mary, and there was a steady and even rapid emergence in the first decade of Elizabeth. The causes lay mostly within the country, but some were external.

Just as the medieval Church had been the moral framework of society, so the tenure and use of land had been its material framework. Land had been held and worked under conditions hardened into custom and regarded as permanent, the manor and the village and the lives of their communities continuing for generations with alterations so gradual as to be hardly perceptible in the short span of years enjoyed by the individual. Custom had been the touchstone, and custom, so locally varied and so apparently malleable, had been effectively stronger than statute law. In the decline of the middle ages, the fourteenth and fifteenth centuries, the framework grew rickety and custom was sapped by economic forces. The point of view slowly altered. Land, from being the stage on which a coherent society enacted its predetermined parts, became something out of which the individual could make money and improve his individual status, a thing not much contemplated in the earlier view. The enterprising individual did not even need to be a member of the local community; he might come from outside and live mainly elsewhere and be quite unknown to it. Growing trade and manufacture were the causes of this fundamental change in outlook and practice. 'Enclosure' is the name loosely applied to some of its most important effects. Enclosure and capitalistic exploitation of land were going on before the advent of the Tudors, they continued in the first half-century of Tudor rule, and they were greatly intensified by the reformation as conducted by Henry VIII. They came with as much inevitability in the social world as do changes of climate and erosions of coastline in the geographical. Short-term arguments freely pinned the blame for them on one party and another. Society being what it was, no one was really to blame and no one really understood what was taking place. In any case, blame is the wrong word for a natural process that yielded good results as well as bad.

Enclosure meant more than one thing. It might be the consolidation of small holdings into larger ones without much change of use, it was in many instances the conversion of arable land into sheep pasture on a large scale, and in a usual and much hated form it was the fencing-off of community land to make private parks attached to manor houses. In almost every case it exemplified the use of fluid capital amassed in trade, the aggression of the money-power against the declining power of custom; and in almost every case it involved injustice to those whose position rested on ancient custom, the customary tenants, the commoners who lived partly by the use of common land, the cottagers who had been ploughmen and were not needed as shepherds in the same numbers as before. The dispossessed were turned off to swell the ranks of the vagrants and criminals, the 'poor' who were a perennial problem. The process was not universal, but took place here and there as capitalists succeeded conservative landowners; and it was widely spread in time. But time did not allay the resentments it aroused. Half a century might pass, and the village still looked vengefully upon the fences enclosing the ancient common field. New aggressions grew ever more numerous in the great boom in land-jobbing that followed the fall of the monasteries. Statesmen had been aware of the trouble, but unable to check it—Henry VII, Wolsey, and More. Henry VIII saw it, as his yeomen and merchants blossomed into squires, and a handful of his councillors and new nobles grasped widely scattered manors which they hardly saw and treated only as sources of income. Henry in his later years made little attempt to grapple with the problem. He had to consolidate defence and neglect social reform. With the statesmen inactive, the less responsible began to talk and protest, Hugh Latimer the dispossessed bishop, one or two men of House of Commons standing, some minor officials and Protestant pamphleteers.

Trade and manufacture were the chief causes of, and the partial offsets to, the distresses on the land. The wool which had formerly gone overseas in sacks to the Calais Staple, now went mostly as bales of cloth to the English House at Antwerp, and the people who made the cloth were an increasing element in the rural as well as the urban population. From the sheep's back to the merchant's warehouse there were many crafts and processes involved. The spinning and weaving had always been part-time rural occupations as well as full-time townsmen's jobs. The fulling and dyeing and several other stages had generally been carried out in the towns. The old chartered boroughs, overtaxed and over-regulated, were declining in the early Tudor period, while their industries sought the freer countryside. Capitalist control was increasing. The great clothiers put out the material and paid for its manufacture as piecework, and concentrated the finished article at the country's cloth-markets, of which Blackwell Hall in London was the chief. Some even collected many hands in factories resembling the mills of the nineteenth century in all save the employment of mechanical power. More than one dismantled abbey served as a cloth factory. The uprooting of the peasant was providing a labour force for industry. It remained to be seen whether industry could employ the whole force.

That depended on the export trade and the demand of foreign markets, and in the 1540s the demand appeared insatiable. It seems as though there must have been a rise of living standards in Europe, most likely the effect of American and Far Eastern developments of trade. In England, in spite of the wars, there was a cloth boom, and the exports climbed year after year. In the first fourteen years of Henry VIII the average annual export was of 85,000 cloths; in 1540–8 the average was 122,000.[1] This was a cause of inflation or rise of internal prices, and the wars aided the process by compelling Henry's government to raise loans abroad and so lower the rates of exchange and the real selling price of English goods in foreign money, and by compelling the King also to debase the English currency, with a further short-term effect of stimulating sales abroad. The Victorian writers, their lives and their outlook soundly based on the hard gold sovereign, decried Henry's folly, but the twentieth century can make allowances for him. Paper pounds unbacked by gold are equivalent to his debasement of silver coin. Rates of

[1] For an excellent treatment of this subject, and of the economic situation in general, see S. T. Bindoff, *Tudor England* (1950), Chap IV.

exchange deliberately pulled down to stimulate exports resemble in effect his Antwerp borrowings. Inflation and rising costs in both ages were inevitable and permanent. A simple set of Tudor figures may illustrate. The wages of seamen in the Navy (never higher than the men could be got for) were 5 shillings a month in 1509; in 1545 they were raised to 6 shillings and 8 pence; and in 1585 to 10 shillings. It is true that the men were often pressed and the service was not entirely voluntary, but the same was true of most employments; for any man the alternative to taking a job at the customary wage was corporal punishment as a vagabond.

The rise of prices continued after the economic fever had abated. It had not been caused solely by English circumstances. In the early part of the century there was an extension of silver mining in Germany; and from about 1540 the influx of silver into Europe from the mines of Spanish America began to have a marked and increasing effect on European finances, and the silver stream grew into a flood that had not diminished by the end of the century. The silver came primarily to Spain, but Spain was a sieve through which it passed to all Europe, and indeed to Asia as the import of eastern luxuries increased. Such were the social and financial problems confronting the successors of Henry VIII. As was natural, men were to react in accordance with their natures and prepossessions. A historical view should be objective. Sympathy for the uprooted static folk and dislike of their thrusting disturbers may distort appraisement of the facts. The custom-bound village was never an elysium, but rather an orderly pigstye, and its denizens had not the mentality that destiny was to demand of Englishmen; the freed force of active enterprise could alone achieve that destiny, and if at first it was mannerless and selfish, such attributes are characteristic of the newly liberated.

As Henry VIII lay dying the Earl of Hertford and Sir William Paget paced the gallery talking of the prospect. Paget was a new man who had risen by ability, the son of a nobody and now a skilled diplomatist and confidential secretary of the King. Edward Seymour was a new nobleman, but of an ancient family of the gentry. Before his sister had become Henry's queen he had had court and diplomatic training, and he had since shown himself the best general that England possessed, and a soldier moreover who was merciful and deplored the cruelties of war. He took liberal views also of social questions and was prepared to champion the underdog. He had been quite ready to acquire substantial estates by the dissolution, but he treated his tenants well. Like many liberal men in our history, he was autocratic as well as kindly, impatient with colleagues who did not take his views for granted, and disdainful of persuasion on what he held for right: a good man, but less subtle than politics required, a new type in the ruling ranks of Tudor England. Hertford was in possession of Henry's will, and the question was how to proceed upon it. The accession of a minor presented difficulties, since Henry had made no provision for a protector. In the general view the Council could only be the sworn servants of a living king and could exercise no power on the strength of appointment by a dead one: the Council, like Parliament, was dissolved by the demise of the Crown. Henry had however been empowered by an Act of 1536 to enumerate by will a set of executors and assistant executors, who were to continue the administration on the lines laid down in the will until his successor should be of age to appoint a Council of his own. It was not an arrangement of much promise in 1547, since nine years must elapse before Edward would come of age at eighteen. Among the executors were the Protestants Cranmer, Hertford, and Lisle; the Catholics Wriothesley and Tunstall, Bishop of Durham; and Paget, who may be classed as a *politique*. The Protestants preponderated in power and prestige. Wriothesley was distrusted as insincere, since he had been one of Cromwell's men and had changed his views on the minister's fall. Tunstall was sincere enough, but old and lacking in energy. The only Catholic leaders who could have balanced the Protestants were Norfolk and Gardiner, and both were omitted from the list. Norfolk was in the Tower, to be respited but not pardoned; and the exclusion of Gardiner was a pointer to the development which Henry looked for. Hertford and Paget decided that there must be a royal power, which in practice must be exercised by a regent, and a royally appointed Council. They agreed to keep Henry's death secret for a day or two, while Hertford should bring the young king to London, and that then Edward, in spite of his years, should authorize the measures they had in mind. They were no doubt right. England was a monarchy and required an active and responsible monarch. The example of Scotland showed how easily a minority could degenerate into anarchy. The English problem would be more difficult than the Scottish, for it included the royal supremacy over the Church. The spiritual power was identified with the Lord's anointed, and could not plausibly be exercised by a regent without a more obvious expression of secularization than had yet been admitted.

Parliament was in session at the time, and did business on the day after Henry's death in ignorance of that event. Not until 31 January was the announcement made, and with it Henry's last Parliament terminated. Immediately afterwards the executors met, and on Paget's proposition elected Hertford Protector of the realm. They then made themselves a properly constituted Privy Council by taking oath to the new King, who had already formally received Wriothesley's surrender of the Lord Chancellorship and had reappointed him. Paget declared that Henry had intended the creation of new peerages and promotions, and these were effected under the seal of Edward VI. Hertford became Duke of Somerset, Lisle Earl of Warwick, Wriothesley Earl of Southampton, the brother of Catherine Parr Marquis of Northampton, Sir Richard Rich and Sir Thomas Seymour (brother of the Protector) barons. Paget himself was not in the list, an omission which lent verisimilitude to his assertion. The transition to the new régime was completed when Edward was crowned by Cranmer three weeks later, and when in March Somerset obtained the royal letters-patent as Protector, in supersession of his selection by the Council. Everything had then been done to regularize a situation for which there was no recent precedent.

For the first months of the reign foreign affairs were in the ascendant. In principle Somerset continued to the best of his ability the policies of Henry VIII. He was bent on settling the Scottish question and maintaining the advantage of the French peace. Francis, with a respect for English arms, was complaisant, and negotiations were begun for an Anglo-French defensive alliance and a final delimitation of the frontiers round Calais and Boulogne. But Francis I outlived Henry VIII by only two months, and died at the end of March. His son and successor Henry II was incensed against England and was determined to have Boulogne without delay; and he had a son, the Dauphin Francis, for whom an active Scottish policy might win the young Queen of Scots as a bride, with the prospect of an eventual union of the French and Scottish crowns. Moreover, the early death of Edward VI, which seems in prophetic fashion to have been in everyone's calculations, coupled with the already declared illegitimacy of the Tudor princesses Mary and Elizabeth, would leave the Scottish queen heiress of right to the

English throne. The will of Henry VIII had indeed cut out the Scottish claim, but that was a domestic decision which international diplomacy would not respect; and for the Valois house under an able and warlike young king there opened the dream of a solid empire of France and the British Isles, cutting the Habsburg empire in two, and capable of giving law to all Christendom. The Valois future was indeed to be sadly different, but the dream of empire was to colour the policies of Europe for a dozen years to come. These considerations, foreseen, if not yet all articulated, faced Somerset. Not only the ambitions of England, but perhaps also her eventual survival as a free state, demanded that he must secure Scotland. He conceived that for Scotland there were two alternatives, union with France and union with England. Many Scots disliked the first, and he determined to make the second as palatable as he could. He talked no more of English overlordship, but played for union by royal marriage on equal terms, with all rights, laws, and liberties reserved. An Empire of Great Britain with mutual love for its garrison was the phrase he used. It was the ideal of a liberal with his eyes upon the heights, but his feet fated to stumble on the dirty facts of hatred and self-interest that cumbered the ground.

In the summer of 1547 the French strengthened themselves in Scotland, their naval forces eluding the English and passing troops up the east coast to the Forth. In July they took St. Andrews, where the Protestants had been entrenched since Beaton's murder; and the Protestants, John Knox included, were taken away to row as slaves in the French galleys. Raiding across the border began again, and it was evident to Somerset that fair words would not by themselves prevail. He gathered an army, and early in September advanced from Berwick. He had about 17,000 men, with Lisle as his second-in-command, and a fleet of thirty-five ships-of-war, with transports for his supplies keeping touch along the coast. Lisle had been succeeded as Lord Admiral by Lord Clinton, who commanded this fleet in person. Somerset's army was mainly of archers, pikemen, and mounted men-at-arms, but he had with him fifteen field-guns and 800 of the hackbutters whom he valued highly. The border horse, whose repute had fallen in recent campaigns, played a very minor part. Some of the Scots welcomed him. Arran and the queen-mother called out the rest in a larger but worse-equipped army, some 23,000 strong.

As Somerset advanced he found the Scots in a strong position east of Edinburgh. Seeing his inferior numbers, they quitted it and sought to outflank him and drive him against the seashore. They had some success against the English left or landward wing, whose ranks they broke with loss. But in the centre where the two armies faced each other across a swamp, Somerset's foreign hackbutters fired steadily at the close ranks of Scottish spearmen, while his artillery commander got his guns on rising ground behind the English line and tore the Scottish array with ball and hail-shot. English ships also stood close in and contributed their fire across the beach. Raw levies could not stand it, and the whole force broke and fled, pursued and killed for miles back to Edinburgh. The battle was known as Pinkie. Somerset viewed the rout and slaughter with misgiving and stopped his men as soon as he could; for his purposes required an acknowledged preponderance of his military force but not a bloody victory that would exasperate the hatred he sought to allay. Six thousand Scots were nevertheless recorded slain, for less than one-tenth that number of English. It was the last great battle between the kingdoms, and it was unlike Flodden in that the firearm had decided it, although the bowmen also played their part.

After Pinkie, Somerset pursued the methods that he had vainly urged upon Henry. He spared Edinburgh a second sack and made no move to occupy it, and checked the ravaging of the defenceless land. Instead, he garrisoned the strongholds from the Tweed to the capital and round it to Dundee, the islands of the Forth, and the towns across the western border that soon fell into his hands. He then did his utmost to inspire the spread of Protestantism from these centres by the distribution of Bibles and of an English propaganda designed to appeal to friendly feelings. The official account of the campaign by William Patten, quickly written and published in January 1548, was humane and not exultant in its tone, and included apostrophes to the Scots to sink enmity and join Great Britain: 'Seek we not the mastership of you, but the fellowship!'—'We covet not to keep you bound, that would so fain have you free from the feigned friendship of France.'

The Protector himself could not remain in the north, for his first Parliament was about to meet, and diplomatic business was urgent. He was back in London before the end of October, and never again saw Scotland. He had not secured that country or its heiress, nor evicted the French. His garrisons, however, were a base for future efforts, and his moderate use of the victory of Pinkie gave colour to his professions of persuasion rather than conquest. It is easy to exaggerate the influence of the ancient Franco-Scottish alliance. The Scots of this period did not like the French any more than they did the English, perhaps in their hearts they liked them less. The solution of independence from either domination and of peace and eventual union with England was to come through Protestantism, and here Somerset had done excellent long-term work with his Bible missions. Knox was in a French galley tugging at an oar, defiant in his misery to the extent of hurling overboard an image of the Virgin brought round for the veneration of the slaves; and he was to come back.

In the first months of his protectorate Somerset made no clear-cut moves towards religious change. Yet in various ways the tide flowed towards a Protestant advance. Persecution under the Six Articles ceased, to the annoyance of the Catholics; popular preachers denounced images, and in various places the Protestants broke them and interrupted the ceremonies of the established order. Wriothesley, the strongest Catholic in the Council, was got rid of, ostensibly not for religion but for a technical misuse of his jurisdiction as Lord Chancellor, whereby he lost his great office and his seat in the Council. In the summer of 1547 the Protector ordered a new ecclesiastical visitation, which there were abuses enough to justify, and Cranmer issued a set of injunctions to ensure more learning and better conduct. Bonner of London and Gardiner of Winchester, the strongest Catholic bishops, objected, and both were ultimately imprisoned after rejecting the Council's overtures. By the time Parliament met in November the colour and tone of the administration were Protestant. The impression was strengthened by the appearance of notable religious exiles from the continent, who sought and found a refuge in England which would have been precarious under Henry VIII.

The Protector had a real hatred of persecution and terror and, somewhat misjudging his time, thought it ripe for an impressive declaration of religious and political liberty. On his initiative the first act of the new Parliament was to repeal in a body the Six Articles and all earlier laws permitting religious persecution, all restrictions on religious teaching and on printing religious books, and much of the new treason legislation that had accompanied Henry's reformation. Treason by writing and overt act remained, but treason by word of mouth was swept away; and two witnesses were made necessary for a conviction. The preamble to the repealing Act enunciated its motives; the late king had rightly made severe laws in a time of crisis, 'but as in tempest or winter one course or garment is convenient, in calm or warm weather a more liberal case or lighter garment both may and ought to be followed and used'; and, the spring of a new age having arrived, a general relaxation is expedient. The practical distinction between the two sorts of treason may be illustrated by the fact that under the revised law the condemnation of Sir Thomas More would have been impossible. It is significant that the Church as a whole did not view the new religious tendencies as an offence. Many of the clergy were growing Protestant. Convocation, sitting contemporaneously with Parliament, petititioned for the sacrament in both kinds and for the legalization of marriage of the clergy.

The Chantries Act of 1545 had transferred to the Crown such endowments as had been made for religious purposes but had since been secularized, and had empowered the Crown to investigate the state of the remainder. A new Chantries Act in 1547 re-enacted the above and confiscated for the Crown all endowments providing for prayers of any sort for the dead and all the property of guilds or corporations set aside for religious purposes. Somerset avowed the religious principle that Henry had only tacitly indicated, namely that prayers for the dead were unnecessary. A first charge on the funds thus accruing to the Crown was declared to be the payment of pensions to displaced chantry priests. These pensions were paid. Their scale was not lavish, but neither had the lost employment been onerous. As a separate activity many chantry priests had conducted schools, and many corporations had mingled education, charity, and religious services in the portion of their endowments devoted to non-secular purposes. The Act provided that money from the confiscated property should be paid for the continuance of the educational work. How far this was in fact done is a matter of controversy, and obscure through lack of evidence. Some have held that most of the schools came to an end, others that there was considerable refoundation, but little or no new foundation. It is, however, pertinent to state that the generation that was of school-going age from about 1550 shows in its middle and lower ranks no sign of being any worse educated than its predecessors, and indeed some signs of being considerably better educated. One can find many instances in the narratives printed in Hakluyt's *Voyages*. Somehow many men had learnt to read, and Tyndale's Bible did the rest. The balance of the chantry endowments went to the treasury, and a large part of it ultimately to the landed gentry. They were the residuary legatees of the chantries, as of the monasteries.

In religious practice there was as yet no Protestant revolution directed from above. Somerset with his ideas of liberty had deliberately lifted the safety-valve and had found the Parliament of 1547 ready to abet him. The changes were mostly from below, with infinite controversy and confusion. Some parish priests observed old forms, others new; and, however hotly the parishioners might be divided, there was no authority to give a decision. The position was an outrage to the Catholics and distasteful to others who had no ardent conviction but desired peace and order. Order rather than liberty was really the dominant wish of the country, coupled with the partly contradictory proviso that order must be achieved without persecution. That is the clue to the otherwise irrational acquiescence in the changes of the next dozen years to the Elizabethan settlement. Soon it became obvious even to the Protector that complete liberty was farcical when accorded to violent-minded zealots. In 1548 he and his Parliament had to make some decisions. Parliament did not meet till the autumn. Before that the power of the royal supremacy was used to issue proclamations and injunctions. The Latin mass was retained, to be followed by a communion service in English with both bread and wine administered to the laity. The Litany was already in English, and other parts of the service were anglicized. Fasting in Lent was enjoined, but orders were given for the cessation of several ancient rituals and the removal of images from churches. These instructions were, to say the least, not universally obeyed. Parliament, when it met, legalized the marriage of the clergy, but it had greater work to do.

Cranmer had been working on a new English prayer-book to replace the various rituals that were more or less in use in the existing confusion. He himself was a Protestant, an English one not strictly identifiable with any of the foreign persuasions, but more akin to the Zwinglians of Switzerland than to the Lutherans. In his draft of the book he rejected the mass and the doctrine of transubstantiation. It was presented to Parliament at the close of 1548, and debated by both Houses in free speech uninfluenced by the administration. A majority of the bishops secured the alteration of certain phrases held to preclude a belief in transubstantiation, and their amendments were such as to leave the question open. With this compromise the use of the prayer-book became law as part of an

Act of Uniformity passed in January 1549. The Act required the exclusive use of the new book. Its penalties (mild for the time) were chiefly upon priests who refused compliance, and there were none upon laymen who absented themselves from the services. The extreme Protestants were disappointed, for the book prescribed service rather than doctrine, and its ambiguities enabled different doctrines to be read into the service. On the whole it was a statesmanlike appeal to the moderate opinion of the majority.

In Scotland things had not gone well in 1548. At the opening of the year Somerset published *An Epistle or Exhortation* to the Scots, emphasizing his desire for fellowship and not domination, and justifying his invasion as designed for the enforcement of the existing treaty and not for conquest. 'We intend not to disinherit your Queen,' he said, 'but to make her heirs inheritors also to England'; and he pointed out the danger to Scottish liberty inherent in marrying her to a Frenchman. But his garrisons were in the eastern lowlands and the western borderland, and he had left the control of Edinburgh, Stirling, and Dumbarton to Arran and the queen-mother. Their answer was to ship the girl-queen in the summer from the Clyde to Brittany. The expected result was that she would be married to the Dauphin Francis, the son of Henry II. This would give the French a definite claim to overlordship to back the forces that they were engaged in drafting into Scotland, and to counter it Somerset felt obliged to revive the claim to English overlordship. The move was less unwise than it had been when Henry VIII had made it, for with the spread of Protestantism many more of the Scots were now inclined to close with England on fair terms than to subject themselves to the imperialism of France. The Protector was unable to do more. Domestic difficulties were mounting, and the French were threatening war for the recovery of Boulogne.

One sharp difficulty was with the Protector's brother Thomas Seymour, a selfish ungoverned man without a spark of public spirit. Amid numerous changes of office he had secured that of Lord Admiral. He had also married Henry's widow Catherine Parr and had done his best by coarse advances to compromise the Princess Elizabeth (then aged fifteen) who was living in her care. When Catherine died in September 1548 he designed to marry the princess, and he was evidently a prospective disturber of the peace. As Lord Admiral he connived at piracy and gave ground of complaint to France. He had ostentatiously shown contempt for his brother by refusing to serve in the Pinkie campaign, and he was accumulating money for a following by piratical profits and by a clearly felonious manipulation of the mint at Bristol. Somerset was forbearing even to weakness, but he already had veiled enemies in the Council who perceived what capital could be made out of a family scandal. It was they—Warwick and his friends—who insisted on bringing Seymour to trial for treason. The Protector yielded but took no personal part. The proceedings were by bill of attainder, in the course of which all the evidence was heard in the Lords. The bill passed, and the Protector gave his consent to the execution. He could have refused, and afterwards regretted that he had not done so. He regarded consent as a matter of duty, for there is no doubt that reasons of state demanded his brother's death more cogently than in many other cases of that generation. His decision was open to moral condemnation, and his prestige and popularity suffered. Seymour was executed in March 1549.

Of more serious national import was the social question that came to a head in 1548-9. As has been explained, it was not new but intensified in the last years of Henry VIII. During those years Protestants who were advanced in religion were radical in politics, although their radicalism was of an English type that was to run on through the Puritan opponents of Charles I to Cobbett in the nineteenth century, harking back to an idealized past for remedy of the evil innovations of the present. Robert Crowley in those years complained of merchants owning farms and buying up streets of London houses and rack-renting both. Henry Brynkelow attacked the limited class-representation in Parliament and wanted members from the poorer classes, or at least elected by them: 'it is not riches or authority that bringeth wisdom.' When the new reign opened, Hugh Latimer, who had been silent after losing his bishopric in the Catholic reaction, began to preach again to large audiences who heard his biting descriptions of social oppressions, conceived as offences against God and always as the innovations of his own half-century. John Hales, a member of Parliament and a personal friend of the Protector, put the same into writing and enunciated remedies. Their followers were many and were known as the party of the commonwealth, the word having no republican meaning but its literal sense of the general good.

For many the position was already desperate. Rising prices and rising rents favoured some and ruined others. Roughly, it was the pastoral interest that went up and the agricultural that went down;

while the increase of pasture created unemployment, for it needed fewer hands for a given area. Hales faced the question with a moral proposition, an old one restated, that property must be used not only for private ends but with a sense of public obligation, for which aim there must be abandonment of enclosing and restoration of tillage. The peasantry needed no telling. In the spring of 1548 there were riots and commotions in several of the southern counties.

Somerset decided on reform. As a reformer there were joints in his armour. His campaign would be against the newly rich, and he was one of them. His estates were immense and acquired in less than twenty years. He was building himself a London palace between the Strand and the river on land confiscated with little disguise from the Church, and he had even thought first of a Westminster site at the expense of the Abbey and St. Margaret's. But he viewed the Church as an organ of the state, and to the head of the state the absorption of Church property was only a matter of bookkeeping. There were some to whom he appeared as thief and policeman, yet there is no doubt of his sincerity against social wrong to poor men. Great landlord he might be, but to his own dependants he was not an unjust one. As for his lavish expenditure, if he had lived otherwise there would equally have been critics of his beggarliness. Tudor England liked its rulers to be magnificent.

In June 1548 the Protector issued a proclamation against enclosures, setting forth at length his social and moral doctrine and constituting a creed of reform, and announcing that an enquiry would be held into breaches of the existing enclosure laws 'that a convenient and speedy reformation might be made'. The laws went back into the previous century, and the appeal was to the godly past against the ungodly present. Parliament met in November and imposed a tax on sheep, with the amount doubled on those kept on enclosed pasture. It also passed measures to check profiteering in foodstuffs and to prevent craftsmen from combining to limit their hours of work. It rejected other bills originated by Hales and the Protector for remedying abuses committed by landowners. The commissioners were duly appointed to examine the enclosures, their method being to take evidence from sworn juries in the various shires. They met with difficulties and evasions, packed juries and fraudulent ploughlands composed of a single furrow across a pasture. They imposed no penalties, since the object was to accumulate evidence for new legislation. The landowners were confident that it would all come to nothing. The oppressed commoners thought so too; and there lay the danger. The effect of the enquiry was not to arouse hope of orderly reform but to inflame the existing exasperation and touch it off into resistance. In the summer of 1549 the southern counties and East Anglia were in a ferment, and the government of Somerset and his Council was breaking down. The first undisguised rebellion, however, came from the south-west and from a different cause.

In Cornwall there had already been some resistance to the religious changes enjoined in 1548. The new Prayer Book was to come into use on Whitsunday 1549. Revolts against it began simultaneously in Devon and Cornwall. The Cornishmen crossed the Tamar, and the principal fighting took place in Devon. The rebels took the town of Plymouth, although the castle overlooking the harbour entrance held out. Exeter resisted and was besieged for a month by the combined insurgents. There was some parleying between them and the government, in the course of which the Cornishmen rejected the Prayer Book and required the restoration of the mass, because most of them knew no English; on which Cranmer remarked that more Cornishmen understood English than Latin. The revolt was mainly on religion, and the priests formulated the demands, which were return to the Catholicism of Henry VIII and suspension of change until Edward should be of age to exercise the supremacy in person; there was no demand for restoration of the Pope. In a broad sense the revolt had also social aspects, the country against the towns, the peasants against the gentry, even the ploughmen against the seamen; in a word, the old against the new. Lord Russell was sent by the Protector and Council to put it down. He had a handful of German ritters and Italian hackbutters engaged for service in Scotland, and he called out a considerable force of militia under the gentry of the adjacent counties. These county levies were not keen to fight their neighbours, and one of Russell's merits as a commander was that he induced them to do so. He won a small battle at Clyst St. Mary and relieved Exeter in August, finishing the rebellion by routing the diehards at Sampford Courtenay, the village at which the rising had begun. Somerset was for conciliation. He enjoined fair words and persuasion to the rebels while still in arms, and reproved Russell for the military executions by which the ringleaders were disposed of. The Council were already at odds with the Protector, and under Warwick's inspiration sent orders of a much more ruthless nature. Russell had extensive western estates, and acquired more, and the earldom of Bedford, as a result of the rebellion. His son, like him a Protestant, was godfather to a Protestant yeoman's son named Francis Drake.

Shortly after the opening of the prayer-book rebellion a formidable movement began in Norfolk. Its first stage was the destruction of the fences of an unpopular new landowner, followed by similar actions as the example spread. Robert Kett, a tradesman who had prospered and who had himself bought land, took command of an insurgent force that rapidly grew to a strength of 20,000. He did not regard himself as a rebel. He proposed to camp his men as a great demonstration in favour of the law—all the enclosure law—and to offer co-operation with the Protector's government against all the infringers and local wrongdoers of the county. This was to take Somerset at his word, but in a manner of which not even he could approve. The Council saw it as rank rebellion of the most dangerous kind, a challenge to the social order and the rights of property, each interpreted in the newest senses of the words. Kett led his men to Mousehold Heath, outside Norwich, from which for two months he dominated the countryside. The city contained a faction in his favour, and his men were admitted within the walls. The encamped host was orderly and not extreme in its treatment of the gentlemen whom it captured, although it victualled itself at the landowners' expense. It was not actuated by religious discontent, and regular services were held on the Heath in accordance with the new prayer-book. There was no question of the Protector or the Council viewing Kett's movement as anything but rebellion. A first attempt by Somerset to disperse it by the offer of a pardon failed, Kett replying that he had done nothing to require pardon. The Marquis of Northampton then advanced with a small force and was beaten. Somerset prepared to take the command, but handed it over to Warwick. At the end of August Warwick attacked the rebels in earnest and routed them with considerable slaughter. It was said that three thousand were killed, while from fifty to a hundred prisoners, including Kett, were subsequently executed. The severity was significant of Warwick's leadership, not Somerset's, and it caused the Council, which approved of it, to think of transferring their allegiance. Liberty, as Paget told Somerset, was being overdone, and reaction was in sight.

Foreign affairs completed the Protector's discredit. French troops continued to move into Scotland, and the transference of the young queen to France was a defeat for England that more than offset the victory of Pinkie. Somerset was willing to offer Boulogne for French consent to the Anglo-Scottish marriage, but Henry II believed that he could take Boulogne with ease and wanted Scotland as well. His ambitions even stretched to Ireland, to be entered through Ulster by way of Scotland. In August 1549, while the western and eastern rebellions were still unfinished, he declared war and laid siege to Boulogne. The English garrison fought with spirit and showed that they could hold out indefinitely, provided that their sea communications were maintained. But the money cost was more than Somerset could defray, and in Scotland his garrisons began to fall to Franco-Scottish attack.

Agrarian discontent in many counties besides Norfolk, the indignation of propertied men at what they held to be the treacherous weakness of government, the prospective loss of Scotland and Boulogne and fears even for Calais and Ireland, the cruel rise of prices in spite of all anti-inflationary expedients, and the depletion of the treasury raising fears of new exactions, all combined to produce disillusion with Somerset's protectorate and a readiness to end it. London, or at least its influential magnates, shared the feeling, and London's voice was probably the decisive factor. Warwick was ready to rise by Somerset's fall, but his followers were as yet a minority, and he allied himself with the Catholics, whose confidence had been raised by the west-country revolt. Gardiner and Bonner were in the Tower, the one for resisting the changes of 1548, the other for defying the Prayer Book; but Wriothesley was active and appeared to have as strong a faction as Warwick. They combined in September to plot the Protector's overthrow. Somerset at Hampton Court suddenly realized that the Council was against him and that he was in danger of being seized. He moved with the King to Windsor and called on the commons to rally to him. Many did turn out, but the gentry refrained, and the people without officers were of no value. He summoned Russell to bring the western army to his support, but Russell declared against him. The eastern forces were in Warwick's hands, and Somerset had nothing for it but to surrender. He did so on 10 October and was in the Tower four days later. The Protectorate was ended after an existence of two years and nine months.

Warwick was a good soldier and also a politician of diabolical cleverness. He saw his way to power, but did not choose to exercise it in the discredited office of Protector. Edward VI was now twelve years old, intelligent, pliable, and keen for public affairs. His name had increasing weight for those who could use it; and people were already looking forward to a resumption of active monarchy. Warwick decided that government should ostensibly be directly by the Council, to whose business the King should be progressively initiated. The Council chose Warwick as its Lord President, and he also resumed his old office of Lord Admiral. To facilitate his rise, council seats were allotted to Wriothesley and other Catholics, who expected that in payment for their support Warwick should initiate a Catholic reaction. He had no such intention. He judged that such an alliance would be unstable and that his purposes would best be served by the forward wing of the Protestants, who were strong in London and the home counties. Experience had shown that the west and north could not stand against the centre of wealth and administration. The Protestants were alarmed by the appearance of the Catholics in the Council and proportionately enthusiastic for Warwick when he got rid of them. He did so by February 1550, by which time five Catholic councillors were under arrest and expelled from their seats. The Warwick party then monopolized high office, in the persons of Northampton (Parr), Bedford (Russell), Wiltshire (St. John), and Lord Paget, the last three being new promotions in the peerage. Gardiner remained in the Tower and was deprived of his see of Winchester. Protestant bishops hailed Warwick as a shining light and a soldier of Christ and an instrument of the word of God. They were simple-minded men. Nevertheless his victory did mean something permanent for their cause. 'The unrecorded struggle between the Protestants and Catholics in the Council at the end of 1549', remarked Pollard, 'was a turning-point in English history.'

Parliament met in a new session a month after Somerset's fall. The mood of the majority was of disgust with the previous liberal policies and alarm at their results, although a minority did its best to resist the passing of panic legislation. The outcome was that treason was extended to include conspiring to imprison a privy councillor and to alter the laws, a ruling that made the treason laws of Henry VIII look mild. But this measure was passed at the instance of Warwick and the Council; and it was enclosure that principally interested the members. Here they re-enacted the thirteenth-century Statute of Merton, which enabled lords of manors to enclose common land at their own discretion, leaving 'sufficient' for the tenants' use. The lord was to be the judge of sufficiency, and persons who assembled to break down his resulting fences incurred the death penalty. The ascendant interest was further emphasized by the creation of new felonies in combining to lower rents and to lower the price of corn. Such legislation bears the mark of tyranny but not of tyrannical strength. It was a confession of fear. In these middle years of the century England was on the verge of a social war.

In these circumstances began the three-and-a-half years' rule of Warwick. He was an able man, but his essential lack of morality was discerned by all except the unworldly Protestant enthusiasts, and it had a debasing effect upon all. He was never popular and had no loyal friends. The story of his government is of a struggle for support by the lavish distribution of favours, and of a connivance at corruption that intensified the black cloud of bankruptcy overhanging the state. Yet his own temper was sanguine, and it is clear that he did not despair of surmounting his difficulties. It is hard to credit a man of his complete selfishness with long-term policies designed to benefit his successors; and the fact that he did initiate such policies shows that he hoped to enjoy their fruits.

There was nothing in the treasury, and the temper of the country precluded expectation of revenue from new taxation. It was therefore necessary to end the war with France and to abandon ambitions in Scotland. The Boulogne garrison had taught Henry II that he would not get the place for nothing. Early in 1550 he and Warwick concluded for its surrender for 400,000 crowns. It was a fair bargain as things stood, and Warwick gained credit by exacting the release of the Scots carried away from St. Andrews to serve in the French galleys; and thus John Knox came to England to join the ultra-Protestant refugees collected from all Europe. Scotland was a more serious matter. Somerset's garrisons were overcome by the Franco-Scottish forces or withdrawn by Warwick as the price of peace, while the dropping of any attempt to prevent the marriage of Mary Stuart and the Dauphin made a French conquest of the entire British Isles a possibility of the future. The 1550s were to be the decade of Valois triumph, and Henry II was only temporarily deflected from his British designs by new hostilities with the Emperor in 1551.

Warwick's reasons for carrying forward the cause of the Protestants are intelligible if somewhat inadequate. First, he secured a small but active body of supporters, whose unpopularity in some quarters was greater than the value of their aid; and second, he was able to collect a final gleaning of church property for the treasury and to use church lands as bribes to his followers. The first step was an undoubted reform, the promulgation of an ordinal or set of rules for admission to clerical orders. The ordinal of 1550 recognized only bishops, priests, and deacons, and abolished the more numerous minor orders whose members in the past had often been a scandal to the Church. By simplifying the ceremonies of consecration it gave offence to conservative Catholics. This and other controversies gave ground for proceedings against several bishops with a view to purging the bench of Catholic influence. In 1550 and the following year four bishops (of London, Winchester, Worcester, and Chichester) were deprived, while the death of another (Gloucester) and the resignation of Veysey (Exeter) gave six vacancies for Protestant appointments. The most notable case was that of Stephen Gardiner, to whom the Protestant historian Foxe was soon to attach the tag of 'wily Winchester'. Gardiner was not a papalist but a Catholic of Henry VIII's allegiance. He had been committed to the Tower for repudiation of Somerset's changes. In 1550–1 he was ready to submit to the Act of Uniformity, but Warwick designedly made the terms of submission so humiliating that the bishop could not subscribe to them; and he was accordingly deprived by a royal commission. The use of the royal supremacy while the King was a minor was objectionable to those Catholics who had themselves taken part in creating it. They contended that it should lie in abeyance until the King came of age. In the places of the Catholics the Council appointed Nicholas Ridley (London), John Ponet (Winchester), John Hooper (Worcester and Gloucester combined), Miles Coverdale (Exeter), and John Scory (Chichester). Hugh Latimer could no doubt have been reappointed to a bishopric had he so chosen, being by this time a full Protestant in the matter of transubstantiation on which he had long hung back. He preferred to retain his independence by refusing any office, and continued his preaching of radical sermons whose social rather than theological import was displeasing to the ruling class. All the new prelates had to surrender some part of the endowments of their sees, to be used by Warwick for distribution to his supporters. This was carried farthest in the case of Winchester, the richest bishopric, where Ponet gave up the whole mass of landed property and received a fixed salary in lieu. The aged Tunstall of Durham was the only notable Catholic bishop remaining, and he was deprived before the end of 1552.

Ridley at once began a campaign against the mass in the diocese of London. Some of the clergy had contrived to retain a Catholic form of service while ostensibly using the prayer-book of 1549. Ridley required a fully Protestant interpretation, with the disuse of the altars and their replacement by communion tables in the front of the chancel or in the body of the church. Here was no formal innovation in doctrine, but rather in ceremony, which was much more significant to most of the laity. Doctrines were of prime interest to the theologians, while ceremonial excited (as it has done many times since) the passions of the laymen. The Council found Ridley's example good and enjoined it upon all the bishops before the end of 1550. Hooper at Gloucester went even further. He was what would now be described as a Protestant nonconformist and objected to the use of any sort of vestments; and it was only under threats from the Council that he gave a grudging consent to the ceremony of his own consecration. Coverdale at Exeter held similar views but was by nature less of a combatant. These men, by their conduct in their offices, were effective propagators of the Protestant attitude through the length and breadth of England. Behind them was the steady, gentle pressure of Cranmer, least combative of men, but moving forward with slow serenity. In 1550 he published a treatise on the sacrament, repudiating the doctrine of the real presence.

The Prayer Book of 1549 had been amended against Cranmer's will and did not wholly represent his views. The use made by the Catholics of its ambiguities to perpetuate the mass was entirely displeasing to him. He began almost at once to consider a revision, and he was urged to this course by the counsels of the foreign Protestant divines resident in England. John Calvin, the French reformer, was already established at Geneva, and Cranmer was in correspondence with him. Edward VI was being educated in strictly Protestant beliefs, and his support, certainly of some weight, would be for change in the forward direction. Knox, whom Warwick designed to make an English bishop, was on the same side. Early in 1552, before Cranmer had completed his revision, Warwick anticipated the fact by passing through Parliament a second Act of Uniformity requiring adherence to the prospective new book and imposing penalties on laymen as well as churchmen for non-compliance. The book duly appeared before the end of the year. It so ordered the communion service that there could be no substitution of the mass in disguise. It simplified the other services by eliminating ritual and the use of vestments, and a last-minute addition while printing was in progress declared that no adoration was implied by the practice of kneeling at communion. Knox, Martin Bucer the German, and Peter Martyr the Italian, had all given counsel in these developments, which in sum may have gone even farther than Cranmer thought desirable. Altogether the book was Protestant, and services conducted on its requirements, in churches already stripped of images and paintings and equipped with communion tables in place of altars, were an unmistakable intimation to the people that Protestantism was established. Cranmer worked on two other tasks, the reform of the canon law and the definition of doctrine. The first had been several times mooted and suppressed since the 1530s, and now again it was laid aside by government after much patient work by the archbishop. The second was achieved by the publication of the Forty-Two Articles of religion in 1553. They appeared too late to become effective before the complete Catholic reaction of Mary's reign set in.

During these events Warwick, although the leader of the Privy Council, was also in its hands. In it he had no majority committed to him, and all knew that it could unseat him as it had unseated Somerset. He maintained his position partly by sowing distrust and inspiring fear and partly by the distribution of plunder. The remnant of the chantry endowments, the rich manors taken from the bishoprics, and the miscellany of plate and valuables rendered unnecessary in the churches by the simplification of services provided the fund for corruption. It was a highly undesirable situation, in which individual members of Council could increase their riches by easy grants under letters-patent, while the Council as a body could shift responsibility to the wide shoulders of its president. Warwick exploited his ascendancy over the King, who became increasingly eager to play his part in the progress of reformation and was kept ignorant of the methods of his mentor. Early in 1550 Warwick permitted Somerset's liberation from the Tower and reinstatement in the Council. It was a move to win over the ex-Protector's following, and it resulted in an uneasy alliance between the two men, with a marriage between two of their children. But Somerset's sense of decency in government could not tolerate all that was going on, and Warwick's critics inevitably gathered to the only alternative leader. In 1551 the differences converged on the meeting of Parliament, which Warwick wished to postpone and Somerset to hasten. It was finally fixed for January 1552, and before that date the personal contest was ended. Warwick got the practice rescinded whereby the King's consent required counter-signing by the councillors, and used this new power to contrive a royal recognition of his faction by the creation of a cluster of peerages and knighthoods. In October 1551 he became Duke of Northumberland; Henry Grey, already Marquis of Dorset, became Duke of Suffolk, having married a daughter of Charles Brandon, Henry VIII's Duke of Suffolk, and thereby connected his family with the Tudor blood; the supple St. John, Earl of Wiltshire, became Marquis of Winchester; and Sir William Herbert, Bedford's assistant in the West, Earl of Pembroke. It is necessary to bear these changes in mind in order to keep track of the persons upon whom the course of events subsequently turned. Among several knighthoods the most notable was that of William Cecil, secretary of state since the previous year.

Having established the prestige of his faction on the royal favour, Northumberland struck down Somerset without delay, since the meeting of Parliament might reverse the situation. He trumped up, as he himself subsequently confessed, a charge that Somerset and his friends had plotted to alter the government and imprison members of the Council. The trial was held in December before a court of peers in which Northumberland and his newly-promoted supporters took their places, and it ended in a half-hearted conviction and sentence of death. The Londoners demonstrated in favour of the accused, and by so doing confirmed Northumberland's decision to get rid of him. On 22 January 1552, the day before the meeting of the Parliament that might have saved him, the Duke of Somerset was executed on Tower Hill. It was a crime committed on pretext of necessity of state by the only ruler of Tudor times who was devoid of any devotion to the state.

Meanwhile the condition of the country continued bad. Henry VIII's debasement of the coinage and extensive foreign borrowings had, as already noted, increased the sales of cloth abroad and so had provided industrial employment as an offset to the agricultural distresses. But such an effect could only be temporary, and by the close of Somerset's protectorate it was wearing off. In 1550 cloth sales at Antwerp ceased to expand, in 1551 they fell heavily. At the same time the inflation meant a great rise of prices in England, a doubling, by some accounts, in the two or three years following the death of Henry. The effect of the inflation was to enrich the profiteers, continually buying for the rise, and to impoverish the generality, while the condition of the very poor grew desperate. The remedy was deflation cautiously applied. Somerset had done nothing. He and his commonwealth advisers were primed with social indignation but not with financial knowledge. Northumberland used deflation with too much suddenness and weight by calling down the value of the debased coinage fifty per cent at one stroke in 1551. The nominal shilling became a nominal sixpence, and chaos and bewilderment increased, while the export trade dipped rapidly into a slump. Unrest verging on rebellion was rife throughout the country, and now the richer sort, such as the Merchants Adventurers and other exporters, began to complain also, and the clothmasters cancelled their orders for the piecework spread among the cottages of the land. The first crude steps in economic control had been taken, and disaster was only averted by the discovery of a financier of genius who became the economic controller. He was Sir Thomas Gresham, a member of the Merchants Adventurers and conversant with the cloth trade and the subtle questions of exchange.

Gresham's work continued over many years, and only its beginnings fall in the government of Northumberland. In that stage, however, one very important step was taken, the breaking of the Hanseatic League's commercial power in England. For Gresham's purposes it was necessary to control the volume and prices of the cloth export and thus to manipulate the rates of exchange to English advantage. The state was to keep a tight hand on the doings of the Merchants Adventurers, and on occasion to dip its hand into their profits. But the Adventurers had by no means a monopoly of the export. A great deal of it had long been conducted by the Hanseatic League from its London headquarters in the Steelyard. The Emperor's arrest of English trade with the Netherlands and Spain in 1545 had allowed the League to increase its share, and its members had thoroughly dug themselves in at Antwerp. The phenomenal exports of cloth in the ensuing years were largely to its profit and not to that of the English merchants.[1] Henry VIII had been unable to interfere, for he depended upon the services of the League to his Navy. Northumberland's knowledge of the Navy made him well

---

[1] Professor Mackie, *op. cit.*, p. 475, records that the customs receipts decreased in Henry VIII's last years. This fact, apparently incompatible with the increase of exports, is partly accounted for by the free trade concession of 1539 and by the arrest of 1545, but it also testifies to the growth of Hanse commerce, which paid lower duties than any other.

aware of that, and also of the fact that the need would arise again; but he yielded to the immediate financial call at the expense of the long-term strategic one. To monopolize the cloth export and to buy the goodwill of the Merchants Adventurers he determined to end the privileges of the Hanseatic League. The process against the League went on concurrently with that against the Duke of Somerset in the winter of 1551-2. There were plenty of good arguments: the privileges were vague and out-of-date; the League had overstepped them and committed illegalities; and it had admitted to its membership cities which were not members when the privileges had been granted. In February 1552 the King resumed into his hands the charters granted by his predecessors, and the German merchants were thenceforward to be reduced to the condition of unprivileged foreigners. The duties that they would thus have to pay would break their hold on the cloth export. The Germans were tenacious men, and negotiations ebbed and flowed in the next eight years; but essentially the decisive step had been taken. English merchants were freed of an unfair competition. The English Navy had yet a price to pay in the loss of the Baltic stores that enabled it to put to sea.

The weak point of the economic position was dependence on the European market, largely the Flemish and German market. A great remedy for unemployment and distress would be provided if trade could be opened up with parts of the world hitherto unexploited. It was no longer a question, as in Henry VII's time, of a short cut to wealth by a western route to tropical spices, but rather of emergence from penury by selling English manufactures to new customers. On this basis began the second impulse of oceanic enterprise, important and continuing on to the Elizabethan greatness. Northumberland was its patron and organizer, a fact that should be, but seldom has been, recorded to his credit when all the rest of his record is condemned. Thus John Dudley, unscrupulous climber and political criminal, originated the continuous movement that grew into the British Empire. No doubt he did it from expediency and with his own interests in view; but he did do it. England was very ignorant of world geography and economic conditions. There were no English books describing the Spanish West or the Portuguese trades with Africa and Asia. Enterprising men like Robert Thorne of Bristol and William Hawkins of Plymouth had sought for knowledge and acted upon it, but their efforts died with them; even Thorne's gorgeous *Declaration of the Indies* lay unpublished in a pigeon-hole. The prosperity of early Tudor days had caused such idleness. Out of the new poverty was to come enterprise. Northumberland as Lord Admiral had had contact with adventurous men and was alive to the possibilities. He realized the need for expert advisers, and obtained two who had the best information at their fingers' ends. One was Sebastian Cabot, who, it may be remembered, had entered Spanish service in 1512 when England had dropped his project of the North West Passage. That discovery was not in the Spanish interest, and he had risen to high office in Spain by his skill in geography and navigation, which had made him the repository of all Spanish information and, as Pilot-Major, the head of the Spanish mercantile marine. He hankered always after the northern discovery which could be made only under English auspices, and in 1548 he accepted the offer of some English councillors and returned to England to be the director of English efforts, although now too old to conduct voyages in person. The other expert adviser was John Dee, a younger man of different qualifications. Just as Cabot knew all that was practically being done on the oceans, so Dee had made himself a master of past learning, and particularly of medieval travels through Asia by European and Arab pioneers. He was also a skilled geographer and mathematician, with ideas for the improvement of navigation, and when he returned in 1551 from his studies at Louvain and Paris, Northumberland recruited him to his service and made him the tutor of his sons.

The first fruit of the new impulse was the inauguration of trade with the nearest non-Christian coast of the Atlantic, the western shore of Morocco, or Barbary without the Straits. Morocco was relatively more important then than now. Its people could purchase English manufactures and pay for them with dates and sugar and the gum-arabic which was a material for cloth-finishing. Its trade was in the hands of resident Jews and had hitherto been monopolized by Lisbon. Cabot had information of all this, and in 1551 collaborated with a syndicate of London merchants to despatch a pioneer expedition to Morocco. The adventure was led by Thomas Wyndham, a rising naval officer, and repeated successfully by him in the following year. Thenceforward the Londoners intensified the trade, which grew steadily in importance, with English factors established in the Moroccan ports, all to the disgust of the Portuguese merchants of Lisbon. Religion coloured their protests, particularly on English impiety in supplying volumes of the Hebrew scriptures to Moroccan

Jews. Wyndham, having established the Morocco trade, went on to something bolder. In 1553, with Northumberland's approval and the loan of two fighting ships from the Navy, he prepared an expedition to the Gold Coast, beyond the West African limit of William Hawkins's former voyages, and never hitherto visited by the English. He did not actually sail until a month after Northumberland's death, and the story belongs to the ensuing period.

The African beginnings were but a crumb of comfort to English distress, and the experts were intent on something greater. Their goal was the Far East, whence Portugal had been drawing riches for half-a-century. There was little public information about it, save its results in the ladings brought by the great carracks to Lisbon and transhipped up Channel to Antwerp. The private knowledge of Cabot and Dee was indispensable. They rejected the Portuguese track by the Cape of Good Hope as too long for the small English shipping, which would need to fill its holds with victuals and water to the exclusion of cargo. There were two possibilities of a shorter cut, the North West Passage which Cabot claimed to have discovered long ago, and the North East Passage round the coast of Asia, unexplored but more attractive. The attraction was undoubtedly put forward by Dee, whose researches in medieval travel had furnished him with information on northern Asia, sound in outline but much too optimistic in the deductions made from it. The tropical East might be the ultimate goal, but its inhabitants had no great use for heavy broadcloth, and the pressing necessity was to sell cloth. The conception was elaborated of a well-peopled northern and central Asia, clad in skins and ready for something better, with great rivers connecting the interior to the northern coast, whence the cloth-bales would pour southwards to be richly paid for; for was not Asia rich? So by the North East it was to be, and Sebastian Cabot with his pilot-major's knowledge drew the plans for a well-conducted expedition worthy of the state that was to sponsor it. In the winter of 1552–3 Northumberland formed a joint-stock company, a new departure in finance, of some two hundred members subscribing £6,000 in £25 shares. Councillors, courtiers, and merchants composed it, and the King promised his letters-patent. The patent, however, did not pass the seals because the King's death prevented completion. In the summer of 1553 it sailed from the Thames for 'the discovery of lands, territories, isles, dominions and seignories unknown'.

Between these bright prospects and Northumberland's actual position the contrast was great. All along he had ruled precariously, juggling with fear, cupidity, and the authority of the young King who obeyed his will. And now the last was failing him. The boy fell seriously ill and was visibly soon to die. Next to him, by Henry's will and the natural order of succession, stood his elder sister the Lady Mary, who had stiffly kept her mass-priests and her allegiance to Rome in spite of all Protestant menaces. With her accession the new Protestantism and its chief author would be laid low. Northumberland's only course was to alter the succession. It was so obvious that he was suspected to be doing it before his plans took shape; and by the close of 1552 various people had been punished for spreading rumours to that effect. But no penalties could stop the talk and the general indignation. Even his natural supporters the Protestants were turning against him, and the councillors whom he had overawed or bribed were growing uneasy.

Northumberland's chosen tool was the new Duke of Suffolk, whose wife was the daughter of Charles Brandon and Henry VIII's sister Mary. The same parents had another daughter who had been married to the Earl of Cumberland. There were thus two ladies of Tudor blood, the Duchess of Suffolk and the Countess of Cumberland, and each had daughters and no sons to inherit their claim; and in the Cumberland case there could be no sons, for the mother had already died. Northumberland had one unmarried son, Lord Guildford Dudley, and in 1552 he had thought of marrying him to the Cumberland heiress. Next year he changed his plan and decided on Lady Jane Grey, eldest daughter of the Suffolks. He could not expect Parliament to assert her claim to the throne in preference to Henry VIII's two daughters, and so could take no overt action until Parliament was dissolved in March. Previous Parliaments had done conflicting things: at one time and another they had declared both Henry's daughters illegitimate and had given Henry the right to dispose of the crown by will, and he had left it to Edward, Mary, and Elizabeth in that order. The last decision clearly predominated, but Northumberland now claimed that without any parliamentary sanction Edward had the right to dispose of the crown by will; and the dying boy, a bigoted Protestant, was ready to ensure a Protestant succession by willing it to Jane Grey. By the end of May Edward had agreed to this 'devise' and Jane was married to Guildford Dudley. The next step was to bring the Council, the judges, and as many notables as possible into line to consent to an act of plain treason; for by statute it was treason to set aside Henry's will. Hardly one of them believed that the 'devise' could succeed—which was no doubt the touchstone to the minds of most—and yet they could not find courage to refuse. The judges were brought into Edward's presence, and he commanded them; and into Northumberland's, and he terrified them. Like certain other persons in our history—Judge Jeffreys is an example—he had the power of inspiring fear in men whose courage was ordinarily good. This personal quality can alone explain the fact that a hundred and more of the leading men in the land set their hands to the letters-patent that tore up Henry's will and imperilled their own heads. They signed, good men and bad, councillors, judges, peers, and aldermen, the wise Cecil, and the guileless Cranmer, the latter on the personal and separate command of the King. One judge alone refused.[1]

It was done on 21 June, and on 6 July King Edward died. The foreign powers knew what was going on, but their situation favoured Northumberland. Charles V, Mary's cousin and supporter, had been defeated by the German Protestants and by the French at Metz, and was in a condition of melancholia that sapped his will-power and threatened his sanity. Victorious France abetted Northumberland, for Henry II judged that a temporary Queen Jane would further his purposes better than a permanent and pro-Spanish Queen Mary.

Northumberland concealed the King's death in order to secure the person of Mary. But she was apprised of his intentions and fled into East Anglia, where, in the most Protestant region of the country, supporters quickly gathered to her, an avowed papist. On 10 July Jane was proclaimed queen in a sullen and silent London which had lost, for the moment, its traditional independence, and where only one young man was found to shout 'The Lady Mary hath the better title!'—for which he lost his ears in the pillory. Northumberland's immediate collapse was due to his inability to be in two places at once. He had to cope with Mary without delay, and yet it was fatal to leave London. He could trust no one to lead a force eastwards, and set out himself with 2,000 men. As soon as he had gone the coun-

---

[1] Professor S. T. Bindoff has kindly pointed out to me that the original draft of the plan in Edward's handwriting excluded all females from the throne, but allotted the succession to the heirs male of Jane and her sisters in order of precedence. The assumption here was that Edward would live long enough for an heir to be born of Jane's prospective marriage. Subsequently, as Edward's health grew worse, the draft was amended to permit of Jane's succession in person. The documents are printed in J. G. Nichols, *Queen Jane and Queen Mary*, Camden Society (1850).

cillors began to desert. In a week it was all over, and Suffolk himself told his daughter that she was no longer Queen. As for Northumberland, he found himself with a dissolving remnant in face of 30,000 men. On 20 July he proclaimed Mary queen and was arrested to ride captive to London. A month later he died on the Tower scaffold, having avowed that he had judicially murdered Somerset and that he himself was, of all things, a Catholic.

I I

THE REIGN OF MARY

IN English history the reign of Mary may appear to have been a reaction that failed, a mere interruption of the national development. This, however, is not entirely true, even in its most obvious application, in the matter of religion; while in some other important aspects it is not true at all. Mary found the Catholics at a low ebb spiritually and devoid of authority and leadership, even in their, own estimation, undecided on vital questions out of communion with Rome, the natural base of their continuance, the Pope abjured by their most active leaders such as Gardiner and Bonner, and by Tunstall their most respected. She failed indeed in her aim of identifying them with the whole nation and extirpating rival creeds; but she left them a minority with a future, as they hardly seemed to be in 1553, reunited in allegiance to the Pope and destined to be a continuing factor in English life. The fact that before Mary's reign the Catholics were schismatic, and after it reconciled, is one that is often overlooked, but it was the governing factor in their survival. It is more common ground that the Protestants also changed. In 1553 they were over-zealous, destructive in action and intolerant in speech, tainted by association with Northumberland, and more unpopular than the Catholics with the peace-loving middle mass of society. After passing through Mary's fire they became broader and more ready for accommodation in the national interest, acceptable to the non-enthusiast majority, and stronger in numbers. But the central fact, it must not be forgotten, is that central majority, which cried plague on extremes and put duty to the commonwealth first. After seeing Northumberland's Protestants and Mary's Catholics in unrestrained action, it had learnt its lesson and knew what it wanted for the future.

Apart from religion, the main lines of development continued without much deviation. The new landowners held their own,

Catholics and Protestants alike—and there were many Catholic holders of Church lands, from the Duke of Norfolk downwards. The social revolution that they had made was confirmed with no prospect of its undoing, and progress lay in accommodating society to it and softening its injustices. In the control of secular business the men who had been influential under Edward were in the main the influential men under Mary, and their proceedings, slow though they appear, give evidence that the bottom of the mid-century trough had been passed. In the new trades and discoveries this is very notable. They and the men who managed them grew steadily in importance. In the oceanic advance there was no break from Northumberland to Elizabeth. Very noticeable is the beginning of a change, not at all promoted by the Queen, in the south-western region of the country, which turned Protestant in spite of its Prayer Book rebellion and coupled Protestantism with militancy at sea. It was as if the life-stream of the nation ignored its government and pursued its own way.

Mary entered London on 3 August, 1553, accompanied by her sister Elizabeth. The new Queen was thirty-seven years old, with a character shaped by her parentage and her unhappy life. From her mother may be traced her sincerity and a natural kindliness, but also a strain of fanaticism capable of overwhelming all other characteristics. Stoical endurance came from that side, and to her father may be accredited a royal quality of command and an active courage that were to prove decisive in an early crisis of her reign. But she had none of Henry's power of radiating a glow of majesty that roused the hearts of the people. It was not to be expected after the long years of sorrow and bitterness, poor health and chilling prospects, and endurance supported only by an inner faith. Repression had crushed the Tudor magnetism that might have been hers if she had grown up in happiness and splendour. She cleared the Tower immediately of many of its prisoners, to make room for Northumberland, Jane Grey and her husband, and a few besides. Among those who came out were the Duke of Norfolk, Gardiner, Bonner, and Tunstall, and Edward Courtenay, an old prisoner but young in years, son of the Marquis of Exeter, beheaded in 1539. Courtenay was important for his Yorkist blood; as a grandson of Edward IV's younger daughter Catherine he had his value in the marriage market. Whatever his father's guilt may have been, he himself had been innocent, and Mary made him Earl of Devonshire.

Northumberland's attempt to subvert the Tudor dynasty was a stroke of fortune for Mary, for it evoked the people's solid loyalty to the Tudors and enabled her to mount the throne with a warmer welcome and more support than she would have received on a normally smooth succession. From the outset, however, she had not the power that her father had wielded or even her grandfather in his first stormy years. She was the first reigning queen in English history, and many supposed that a woman must naturally lack capacity for active sovereignty. Then again she would need to marry, or in default her successor would be another woman with the same problem; and it was obvious that the king-consort of a reigning queen would be in a far more important position than the queen of a reigning king. All had taken it for granted that when Northumberland proclaimed his son's wife queen he was founding a Dudley dynasty; and such in fact was his intention. The English people had no mind to accept any new dynasty without their consultation and consent, and this consideration involved a large limitation of Mary's authority. Thus the Privy Council, which had been the administrative instrument of Henry VIII in his last years, and in the late reign had been something more than that in its exercise of authority that was properly royal, had now a position that compelled the Queen to respect other views besides her own in choosing its membership, and the constitution of her Council influenced the course of her reign. Some of Northumberland's accomplices were naturally excluded, Suffolk and Northampton among them, and some also of his unwilling abettors, including Cranmer and Cecil. In their places Mary put Catholics who had suffered for the cause, Norfolk, Gardiner, Tunstall, and others, but not Bonner, who was never a privy councillor. She appointed also Paget and Rich, who had no ardent convictions but submitted to the royal authority as such. Beyond these she found it advisable or inevitable to include a dozen of the late councillors who had proclaimed Jane Grey queen and had sought, until their hearts failed them, to imprison Mary herself: Winchester, Bedford, Pembroke, Arundel, Shrewsbury, Westmorland, and six commoners. These men had been servants of the Reformation, but were ready to accept the church that the state decreed. The new Council represented all interests but that of the full Protestants, who had no intention of conforming. There were many makeweights, increasing the whole number to fifty, which suggests the older type of institution. Gardiner, restored to his bishopric of

Winchester, became Lord Chancellor. Lord William Howard, a kinsman of the Princess Elizabeth, was made Lord Admiral.

The Queen was bent on restoring not only Catholicism and the monasteries but the Pope's supremacy. For the time she had to go slowly, since her desires were contrary to existing law. She also decided that her marriage should be with Philip, the son of her cousin Charles V, and negotiations began before the summer was out. Here she did not go slowly, and met with trouble in consequence. First, there were the outstanding delinquents to be dealt with. Northumberland, as we have seen, was despatched without delay. Guildford Dudley and Lady Jane Grey were condemned in the autumn and respited in the Tower. Suffolk was not even tried, and was left at liberty. Cranmer was condemned for treason, of which he was not more guilty than Bedford, Pembroke, and the rest of Edward's councillors, but remained in prison to await an ecclesiastical trial when the law should permit. Latimer, Hooper, and other clerics were locked up for alleged sedition to await the same development.

The Protestant divines were allowed the opportunity to escape overseas, and some took it, while the stouter sort preferred to stay and face the issue. Knox and the foreign refugees all left the country. Some historians have held that the emigration of eight hundred Protestants in 1553–4, before any extreme persecution had been begun, was a concerted movement instigated by Cecil, who thereby planned with extraordinary foresight the triumph of Elizabethan Protestantism a few years later. The exiles, it is said, were organized and financed, some in France, the majority in the Rhineland, whence they bombarded Marian England with propaganda and were able to return as a strong party in 1559: 'Study of the organization of this exodus reveals in it the genius of William Cecil planning, very effectively, the first moves in the revolution from which has come the England of modern times.'[1] The cohesion and the propaganda are obvious, but the outcome depended on factors that were hardly foreseeable in 1554; and the financial aid to the exiles sprang rather from spontaneous generosity, in which the merchants trading overseas bore a considerable part.[2] To view the whole movement as a coherent design of Cecil's is unwarranted. Mary was not yet in the mood for burning, and she herself hoped that the Protestant leaders

---

[1] Philip Hughes, *Rome and the Counter Reformation in England* (London, 1942), p. 127. See also Christina H. Garrett, *The Marian Exiles* (Cambridge, 1938).
[2] M. M. Knappen, *Tudor Puritanism* (Chicago, 1939), p. 112.

would emigrate or recant. She was by law supreme head of the Church, in spite of her detestation of the position; and pending its annulment in favour of the Pope she used it to deprive Protestant bishops and restore Catholics. The mass and Catholic ritual were also reintroduced, contrary to law, and some rioting ensued before she had been a month on the throne.

A Parliament was necessary to regularize the position, and it was called without delay. When it met in September 1553 it soon showed that while its collective view was certainly not Protestant it was also not papalist, and broadly it represented the religious position of Henry VIII's last years. This constituted a considerable variation from the Edwardian parliaments, and it indicates the general willingness of the nation to take its religious colour from the crown, which had not as yet shown its full papal intentions. The Parliament passed some but rejected others of the measures desired by the Queen. It repealed Northumberland's tyrannical treason law and the acts establishing Cranmer's prayer book and other Protestant innovations. It declared Catherine of Aragon to have been Henry's lawful wife and repealed the act that had made Mary illegitimate. It granted tunnage and poundage for the Queen's life, as parliaments had done for her three predecessors. Thus her title was fully established and the Catholic forms of worship restored. On the other hand the Houses refused to rescind the royal headship of the Church or make any recognition of the Pope, or penalize those who would not go to mass. A great change on which Mary's heart was set was the restoration of all the lost lands of the Church, including those of the monasteries; and here the will of Parliament was so obviously to the contrary that it was idle even to introduce the proposal in a formal measure. Finally, the Commons remonstrated on the proposed marriage with Philip of Spain and urged the Queen to marry an Englishman; to which she replied in angry terms. The record of this parliament illustrates the constitutional position. In matters of administration and the royal prerogative the Houses could express public opinion, to which the crown was wise to pay attention, but they could not dictate to the crown. The crown on its side could do nothing that required a change in the law without the consent of Parliament, and Parliament, if it did not approve, withheld its consent, as it had often done under Henry VIII. In terms that are familiar to students of British colonial history, Tudor England enjoyed representative but not responsible government.

Some considerations on the Spanish marriage may be mentioned. The Emperor heartily desired it. He was contemplating retirement, with the relinquishment of the Empire to his brother Ferdinand, and of Spain to his son Philip. The Empire, with its Lutherans and its Turkish frontiers, had become a mere encumbrance to him. He thought only of the future greatness of Spain. To ensure the wealth and European predominance of Spain he intended to add to its crown the rule of Naples in the south of Italy and Milan in the north, and that of the seventeen provinces of the money-making Netherlands, together with the County of Burgundy, the Franche Comté lying on France's eastern frontier. Thus the territories of his son Philip would encircle those of the Valois enemy. The weakest part of the circle was the communication through the Channel between the Netherlands and Spain. To maintain it the co-operation of English sea power was indispensable, for if France commanded the Channel it seemed that she might conquer the Netherlands. As things then stood, it appeared that France might even dominate the British Isles and form a block of contiguous kingdoms that would burst the Habsburg ring into fragments and relegate Spain to impotence in the western corner of the continent. To Charles's policy it was therefore essential that his son should marry the English queen and control the English Navy. To some Englishmen, looking with a too cynical eye on the realities of the situation and lacking faith in their country's destiny, it also appeared that the Habsburg and Valois powers were each so mighty that England was bound to become a satellite of one of them; and they of course preferred the Habsburg adhesion with all its commercial advantages. Paget, with his *politique* way of thought, was of this mind. Gardiner, who was both a Catholic and a patriot of Henry's school, was against it, and the sense of the country was with Gardiner. Mary was wholly for the Spanish marriage, not for Paget's political reasons, but for the ideals that filled her soul, of union with her mother's native land, of gratitude to the Emperor who had always been her friend, and, above all else, of the return of England to the Roman communion, hand in hand with the Spain that had never faltered in the faith. Between Mary and her people the Spanish marriage opened a rift that was never to be closed.

The alternative of an English match can be briefly indicated. There were two possibilities, Edward Courtenay, the new Earl of Devon, and Cardinal Reginald Pole, who could have obtained the necessary dispensation. Both had royal blood in their veins. But the first was personally ineligible and the second personally unwilling. Courtenay was no sooner out of the Tower than he began to make up for the lost years by a career of debauchery abhorrent to the Queen's strict mind. Pole, who had for her the merit of being the only living Englishman of note who had never abjured the Pope, was over fifty and felt no vocation for marriage. His temperament was completely sacerdotal, and so exclusively Roman was his allegiance that he looked coldly on the Emperor for his concessions to the German Protestants in the *Interim* of 1548. He wished to see England make submission direct to the fountain-head of the faith and not by any Habsburg mediation, complicated as it was sure to be with mundane politics. He did not wish the Queen to marry at all. He could not yet come to England, for he was still an attainted traitor under sentence of death.

In October the Spanish marriage was agreed in principle, although some important provisos remained to be settled. However hedged with paper safeguards, it was bound to entail a submission to a foreign influence such as Tudor England could not stomach, and the instinct of the country viewed it with alarm and dismay. In January 1554 the ambassadors arrived—their train snowballed through the streets by the youth of London—and the treaty was quickly drawn up. Gardiner as Lord Chancellor had to waive his own opinions and do the best he could. Philip was to observe all English rights and privileges and to introduce no foreigners to English offices. If he should be at war as ruler of any other dominions, it was not to involve England either in fighting or paying. If Mary should die childless Philip's connection with England should cease absolutely. If they had a child it should inherit the Netherlands, Franche Comté, and England, while Spain and the Italian possessions should go to Don Carlos, the son of Philip by his previous marriage. On the face of it the treaty gave England the right to make her own decisions about neutrality and war, and accorded no power of government to Philip. The Emperor, however, was content. He knew that in the next French war, whatever might have been stipulated, Spain would have the services of England.

The English people were ill content, and speedily showed it. Already a conspiracy was being formed for a general rebellion to be timed for the spring of 1554—Courtenay and his adherents to raise the south-west, Sir Thomas Wyatt the men of Kent, Suffolk the midlands, and Sir James Croft the Welsh border. The purpose was to prevent the Spanish marriage, with the interests of Protestantism as a second string, and not professedly to dethrone the Queen. Yet her sister Elizabeth was an obvious alternative, and the plotters talked about her. Elizabeth maintained that they did not communicate with her, and she certainly gave them no countenance. Courtenay was faint-hearted. He blabbed to Gardiner, who was staunch to the Queen. Knowing themselves detected, the others rose in January without due preparation. Suffolk and Croft soon collapsed, and the Devon men did nothing. Wyatt alone produced in Kent a formidable movement which by itself came near to success. The Duke of Norfolk led a force of Londoners to put him down, and these men went over in a body to the rebels, leaving Norfolk to seek refuge in flight. Wyatt then marched on London, reaching the south bank of the Thames on 30 January. Mary saved herself by her courage. Although she knew that half London was disaffected, she stood her ground and called on the citizens to fight. Her leadership decided them, and they held London Bridge against Wyatt. He moved up river and crossed at Kingston, but the delay had been fatal, for it gave time to Bedford and Pembroke to organize the defence. With Lord William Howard, these men, Protestant sympathizers though they had been, saved the situation. Once on the Middlesex bank, Wyatt moved east towards the city. After a skirmish at what is now Hyde Park Corner, he passed through Pembroke's forces and chased another body of Londoners from Charing Cross. If the gates had been opened the city would have been his, so narrow was the margin of its loyalty. But Howard held Ludgate, while Pembroke closed in on the rebels' rear. Wyatt's men, famished and weary, had had enough, and finding himself surrounded he laid down his arms. It was the nearest-run rebellion of the Tudor period and the only one in which London's support of the throne had been doubtful.

Mary had hitherto spared Jane Grey, but was now hardened by the danger, although Jane was innocent of complicity and the rebels had not proposed to make her queen. On 12 February, Jane, aged only sixteen, was executed, together with her husband Guildford Dudley. Suffolk, her father, was beheaded a fortnight later. Wyatt and other leaders, with nearly two hundred of their followers, paid with their lives in due course. Croft was spared, to achieve a long and not too creditable career, as also was Courtenay, destined to a short one. The Princess Elizabeth was in great danger, and her enemies strove hard to implicate her, but could produce no evidence. Simon Renard, the Emperor's ambassador, was urgent for her execution on the ground that Mary's (and Philip's) throne would not be safe while she lived. Lord William Howard, who as Lord Admiral wielded a power that was not to be neglected, was firm that she must be spared, and Gardiner exerted himself on her behalf. Mary sent her to the Tower, and there for two months the matter rested, after which she was removed to live under surveillance out of London. The general effect was to give Elizabeth more prominence than she herself relished as the hope of the anti-Spanish party, which was the nation.

The rebellion had failed, but its expression of the public opinion had been impressive. It was like a vote of censure on a modern administration which just fails by a tiny majority to pass. On the rebound Mary summoned a new Parliament, to which she submitted the marriage treaty. On paper, and if its terms were kept, the treaty was as favourable to England as any such bond could be, and had caused considerable chagrin to many of the Spaniards. Parliament gave its approval, having first enacted that a female sovereign had as complete authority as any of the kings of England, and so having precluded (again on paper) any ground for encroachment by Philip. Still vigilant against encroachment, the Houses rejected a bill that would have made treason such offences against the prospective king-consort as would have been treason if committed against the Queen. They also refused to re-enact the Six Articles and the fifteenth-century *De Heretico Comburendo* that Somerset's first parliament had swept away. On this matter there was a division in the Council itself. Gardiner wished to be empowered to persecute the Protestants, and Paget's party were determined that he should not be; and, for that time, Paget won. It seemed as though both religions were to be tolerated side by side, uneasy as such a situation in practice was. The prayer book and its Act of Uniformity had gone, and the Queen as Supreme Head had restored the Catholic ceremonies, but she had no power to compel conformity, and the Protestants were noisy and recalcitrant. Charles V, fearing for his political aims, advised her to let things rest and give up her ideas of compulsion. From a trusted friend this was a hard saying, but Mary clung doggedly to her purpose. She was able to eject from their livings the married priests and others who would not conform. Their number was from one-fifth to one-quarter of the whole.

This provisional stage was rounded off by the arrival of Philip at Southampton and his marriage to the Queen at Winchester at the end of July 1554. Thus one great matter of debate was settled, and the accomplished fact strengthened the Queen's position. Philip in his stiff way did his best to be popular, and for the moment there was even a pale flicker of general approval.

Meanwhile the secular interests of the nation were moving. Northumberland's oceanic plans were bearing fruit, and the intelligent classes were showing a genuine desire for knowledge of the world beyond Europe. Only a month before Northumberland's fall Richard Eden, a minor official, had published his *Treatise of the New India*, with a dedication to the Duke. The book was a translation of the American part of a Latin cosmography by Sebastian Munster, a German authority. Two years later, in 1555, Eden brought out his *Decades of the New World or West India*, again a translation of the first three Latin Decades written by Peter Martyr of Angleria (not to be confused with the theologian) at the beginning of the century. This work was a history of the first Spanish discoveries and conquests, and although its matter was fifty years old it was unknown to the English public. For them it suggested possibilities that were to conflict with the interests of Philip and Spain. Eden did not obtrude this aspect and was careful to print a fulsome eulogy of Philip to atone for the former patronage by Northumberland. In addition to his translation Eden included full accounts of the first two English expeditions to the Gold Coast, which had only just been accomplished.

The Gold Coast ventures belonged all to the new reign, for it was in August 1553 that Thomas Wyndham sailed from Portsmouth on the first of them. Guided by a Portuguese pilot who had deserted from his country's service, Wyndham rounded Cape Palmas and sailed along the great stretch of African coastline that runs eastwards to the Bight of Benin. His backers were a syndicate of London magnates, three of them knights, who had already opened the Morocco trade, and one of his crew was a boy named Martin Frobisher, who was to be heard of again. Wyndham had his own ship and a ship and a pinnace from the Navy, which, under the rule of Lord William Howard, was to participate in the whole series of the African voyages. The Portuguese claimed monopoly of the coast and had a fortified headquarters at Elmina. Wyndham traded with the negro chiefs on either side of Elmina and obtained gold dust in exchange for his English wares. He then pushed on to Benin for pepper, and there met with disaster in an outbreak of fever that killed him and his pilot and most of his men. The survivors abandoned one ship and came home in the other, with gold enough to yield a profit dazzling to those who held sailors' lives cheap. The London merchants were elated and despatched another expedition without delay. John Lok, the son of a city alderman, commanded it, with a squadron of three ships and two pinnaces. He sailed in 1554 and was home next year with ivory and pepper and no less than four hundredweight of gold, probably a greater amount than private men had ever brought into an English port before. He had skimmed the coast clean of the season's supply, which came not from mines but from alluvial diggings by the Africans, and the indignation of Portugal was extreme. These were the two ventures that Eden publicized before the end of 1555, to set all London talking of Guinea gold and oliphants' teeth. Before long the talk was to be of more than that, of Philip's evil objections and the Pope's iniquity in decreeing such things reserved to Portugal and Spain.

In the summer of 1554 there came news of the north-eastern expedition sent out by Northumberland's joint-stock company in the previous year. It had been commanded by Sir Hugh Willoughby, a soldier of the Scottish wars, and Richard Chancellor, a sea captain of Mediterranean experience, who was perhaps the first scientific English navigator. They sailed with full instructions drawn from the seafaring knowledge of old Sebastian Cabot and the geographical learning of young John Dee. On the Norwegian coast a gale separated them. Willoughby with two ships rounded the North Cape and pushed eastwards until he sighted Nova Zembla, which he took to be a promontory. The season was then too late to round it by the north, and he went back to winter on the coast of Lapland, with a view to completing the discovery next year. So much is known from his own journal, afterwards recovered; but neither he nor any of his men survived the winter, and next summer the ships with the bodies on board were found lying at their anchors by local fishermen with whom the English were later in touch. Later travellers said that Willoughby's crews died through trying to pass the winter on board the ships instead of making snow houses on shore.

Chancellor, making a separate voyage, had better luck. He found the entrance to the White Sea, hitherto unknown, and since it led southwards into the continent he probed it in search of a market for English cloth. At its end he found the Russian village of Archangel

and learned that there was a way to the court of the great Czar ruling
at Moscow in the far interior. The White Sea formed the only coast
of the Czar's dominions, which did not at that time extend to the
Baltic or the Black Sea. The Hanseatic League traded with Russia
overland from the Baltic ports, but allowed no access by Englishmen, to whom all this geography was unknown. Chancellor travelled
to Moscow and presented his credentials to Ivan IV (the Terrible),
who was pleased by the prospect of a direct trade in the English
wares for which the Hanse merchants were making extortionate
charges. In the season of 1554 Chancellor sailed back to England
with a substantial success to report.

The fall of Northumberland involved the dismissal of Sir Thomas
Gresham from his control of English finances; and with Gresham
went the policy of depressing the business of the Hanseatic League.
In September 1553 the Queen restored the League's ancient privileges in England. Its merchants at once began to recoup their losses
by shipping great quantities of cloth to the Netherlands, and by
sending 'white cloths', i.e. undyed and unfinished material, to the
North German ports. The Merchants Adventurers were severely hit,
and their Antwerp trade declined. Whether Mary's motive was the
statesmanlike one of ending a quarrel with the suppliers of naval
stores, or whether it was simply retaliation on the allies of Northumberland, is not apparent; but her policy was soon reversed. The
exchange on the Antwerp bourse turned in England's disfavour and
interest on loans went up, and in November the Queen found
Gresham indispensable and reinstated him. He and the Merchants
Adventurers at once renewed their complaints of the Hanse trade.
They said that the export of white cloths deprived English craftsmen
of employment, that Englishmen had been driven out of the Baltic
ports, that the Steelyard depot was 'colouring' the goods of unprivileged foreigners and passing them out at its own low rates of duty,
and that English shipping was falling out of use and English
mariners starving; so that where thirty or forty ships had been
freighted at one time now only three or four were employed. The
complaints were no doubt exaggerated, but there was something in
them, and the Queen's advisers had to take notice. Early in 1555 the
Council ordered that the Hansa should cease all shipments at privileged rates to the Low Counties, and elsewhere should export only
one white cloth for every three finished ones, any exports in excess
of this paying the unprivileged foreigners' rates.

This was virtually a return to Northumberland's prohibition and Gresham's policy of monopoly and control. The affair was not trivial, but involved the greatest channel of the country's trade. The partial figures that survive give the impression that the annual turnover of the North Sea cloth export was in the neighbourhood of the whole annual revenue of the Crown, and perhaps greater. The Hanseatic League at once protested, and Philip gave his voice in its favour. In 1555 he was over in the Netherlands, where his subjects naturally preferred a competitive supply of cloth to an English monopoly. His attitude gave deep offence to the mercantile interest in London. In 1556 the Queen and her Council made some temporary concessions, allowing the Hanse trade to continue for a year, during which time a diet was to be held to review the whole question. The Hanse traders wanted the whole of their ancient rights and were averse to a diet, which would certainly whittle them down. The year expired without the appearance of their representatives, and they were once more reduced to the status of ordinary foreigners. They answered by declaring full economic war. In August 1557 the Council of the League proclaimed non-intercourse and banished all English ships, goods, and men from its cities. It meant the cutting-off of supplies for the Navy and of the shipments of German and Baltic corn that had been relieving the hunger of a too pastoralized England. The economic war outlived the Queen.

A brief review must suffice for the fortunes of other branches of English trade. That with Spain, mainly at Seville, was the next in importance to the North Sea. It was carried on by resident Englishmen, some of whom married in Spain and became a permanent Anglo-Spanish liaison. Their chief difficulty concerned religious matters, depending on the political relations between the Emperor and England. In 1538 and again in 1545 there had been outbreaks of persecution by the Inquisition which, whatever corporal punishments it inflicted, always accompanied them by confiscation of goods. In Mary's reign the situation naturally improved, and the better conditions extended to the Canary Islands, where English merchants and factors were also in residence. Some even, sailing under the Spanish flag, established themselves in distant Mexico, although they had to ship their cargoes to Seville and not direct to England. The English trade with the Levant through the Mediterranean flourished until the mid-century, when general piracy and the ravages of Turkish fleets caused a decline. In Mary's reign this trade dwindled and ultimately died out for a generation. The Iceland fishery also declined for the economic reason that the Newfoundland banks proved to be the best place for catching cod. The Newfoundland fishery began to preponderate in these years, and the profits were gradually transferred from the east-coast ports to those of the west country, a factor in producing the coming maritime dominance of the west. In general the conditions of trade and national well-being were inexorably changing and forcing England to seek her future on the oceans.

The Spanish marriage had achieved the temporary success of an accomplished fact, and Mary, with Philip at her side, summoned her third Parliament in the autumn of 1554. Her purpose was to obtain the necessary sanctions for the national submission to Rome, and to that end she exerted a perceptible but not extravagant pressure on the choice of members. The Parliament, if not enthusiastically papalist, was certainly Catholic in a fuller sense than were its two predecessors. In this it reflected the predominant doctrine that national unity lay in following the will of the crown, although a foreign observer remarked that the convinced Catholics were nearly all among the middle-aged and elderly. Foreigners usually accorded considerable weight to the Protestant element, but as they were commonly resident in London they did not obtain a true perspective of the whole country.

Cardinal Pole was the papal legate and chosen instrument of the reconciliation. Charles V regarded him as unwise and fanatical and had contrived to keep him out of England until Philip was established. His fellow-cardinal, Granvella, wrote of him in 1554: 'He is a truly learned prelate, very virtuous and indeed of holy life; but he does not understand the first thing about the conduct of affairs.' He was now waiting on the threshold for the word to move in. He hoped to receive not only a spiritual but a temporal submission in the shape of a restitution of the abbey lands. The hope was chimerical after twenty years of sales and resales, leases and sub-leases, exactly as the English cavaliers and the French royalists found similar dreams in 1660 and 1815; and a delegation went over to the Netherlands so to inform the expectant cardinal. With a sore heart he consented to waive restitution and hastened to England, landing on the day before the parliamentary reversal of his attainder. The Queen received him ecstatically, and a week later the two Houses almost unanimously petitioned that the realm should be admitted to the

Roman communion. The Cardinal performed the ceremony of absolution and reconciliation. Parliament next proceeded, not without considerable debate, to some complementary legislation. It included Philip with the Queen in the scope of the treason law, and extended treason to comprise praying to God for the Queen's death or asserting that her title to the throne was defective. It re-enacted the fifteenth-century laws that permitted the Church to condemn heretics and the crown to burn them. It repealed all the legislation of Henry VIII against the powers of the clergy and the papal jurisdiction. But at the same time it declared the ex-Church lands to be, like all other land, within the protection of the common law and not subject to the decisions of any canonical court. This, as Pollard points out, was the heart of the matter: a genuine repentance would have entailed restitution, and without it 'the reconciliation was merely a marriage of convenience'. Renard said as much at the time, and expected its dissolution to follow when the circumstances should change.

Philip had accepted his marriage treaty with mental reservations. He soon began to exercise powers of government and worked persistently to have them recognized. The recording of parliamentary business and royal writs under the joint names of Philip and Mary familiarized the people with the idea, as did the appearance of the two royal effigies on the coinage. On the other hand, Parliament would not consent to his coronation, or to his nomination as regent if Mary should die leaving a child under age. Yet, since the prerogative power was admittedly Mary's and since no one could prevent her from exercising it as her husband desired, he enjoyed in some directions a real authority tempered only by resistance from the cogs of the administrative machine. Broadly, the Queen worked his will in matters temporal, and in matters spiritual placed her own will and conscience above it.

In the matter of the new ocean trades Philip intervened with some effect. In the summer of 1555 a Portuguese ambassador came to complain of the English voyages to the Gold Coast and to demand their prohibition. The merchants concerned were summoned to make their answer to the Council. It is worth quoting:

'We be merchants who, by common usage of the world, do use traffique in all places of the world, as well Asia and Africa and Europa. . . . Amongst other places, our factors did about two years past resort to sundry places where we found several princes or governors, and

with them traffiqued . . . and from them returned quietly, thinking that
without any offence we might use there (where we found no resistance)
the same liberty that we use and do find in all other places of the world.'

In effect the reply was a denial of the monopoly based upon world-
partition by the papal bulls of the fifteenth century, and an assertion
that effective jurisdiction was the title to control: the African chiefs,
said the merchants, were independent sovereigns who could trade
with whom they liked, and the Portuguese were not entitled to call
them their subjects. Philip dissented from this view, for he saw how
it might be applied in the American hemisphere. The Council, it
became fairly evident, did not agree with him, and the result was that
pending further discussion a provisional prohibition for six months
was issued. This would have precluded any voyage for the season of
1555–6, since an autumn sailing was essential to gain favourable
winds and the best conditions on the coast. Philip left in September
for the Netherlands, whence he wrote again commanding that the
voyages should be stopped. The merchants were therefore ordered
to unlade their ships and surrender the trade-goods. In spite of this a
Guinea expedition sailed that autumn and made a prosperous
voyage; and in each succeeding year to the end of the reign the trade
was continued. The Council issued Philip's prohibitions, but took no
great pains to make them effective. Some preparations were forbidden, while others were winked at, and even a great officer of state
like the Lord Admiral defied Philip by allowing the adventurers to
charter the ships of the Navy. A substantial and lucrative commerce
was firmly established, whereby England sold cheap cloth and metal
goods for gold. Also established was the resentment of maritime
England against the King of Spain, as Philip became in 1556.

In the other branch of newly discovered trade Philip was more
complaisant. Chancellor sailed again for Russia in 1555 with full
state approval for the opening of regular commerce by the White
Sea. Before he left, Philip and Mary jointly issued a new charter to
the Company (henceforward commonly known as the Muscovy
Company) superseding the uncompleted grant of Edward VI. The
privileges included discovery to the north-west as well as the north-
east, and Philip's consent is interesting since the north-west was on
the Spanish side of the Pope's line of partition. Probably the king felt
that as the rights had already been substantially granted in 1553 and
did not touch any effective Spanish interest, he might stretch the point
while remaining firm for the monopoly in temperate and tropical

America. The Muscovy trade took root and continued prosperously. Richard Chancellor was wrecked and drowned on the Scottish coast on his second return from Archangel in 1556. He had stayed in Russia for the winter of 1555–6 in order to negotiate with the Czar, and he brought back with him a Russian ambassador who survived the wreck and reached London. The Company had found a new and useful market. It hoped for further eastward advance and sent a small expedition to work along the Siberian coast to the mouth of the great river Ob. The ship did not get so far, and the report was discouraging. The Company then decided to concentrate upon the Russian trade.

When Parliament legalized the burning of heretics its members did not foresee how the power was to be used. The measure was part of the restitution to the Church of its ancient position, and it was permissive, not mandatory. It gave the Church the right to prosecute and the crown to execute, and the effect in the past had been to produce a good many fines and penances and only a few burnings. The circumstances were now different. The Protestants were infinitely more numerous and influential than the Lollards of the past and the pioneers of the New Learning in Henry's middle years. The Queen was determined to suppress them at whatever cost. Gardiner was also determined to strike down the leading Protestant divines, although he showed no great zeal against the humbler folk of his own diocese of Winchester. Bonner, Bishop of London, was rabid against Protestants of all ranks. Pole was wholly with the Queen. He acted through life on the simple principle that allegiance to the Pope alone qualified for survival in this world and the next, and he had no pity for any who would not come within that circle. On the Queen and Pole rests the responsibility for what was done, for all others were their agents. Philip would have been more moderate, not from humanity (in his Netherlands martyrdom was going on at the rate of more than a thousand deaths a year), but for the prudent reason that he did not wish England to be exasperated into revolt. He had read the lesson of Wyatt's rebellion more accurately than had his wife; but in this matter his will could not prevail.

The first victim was John Rogers, the editor of the so-called Matthew's Bible. He suffered at Smithfield on 4 February 1555, having rejected an offer of pardon on recantation. Hooper, the extreme Protestant bishop, was burnt at Gloucester, and three other clerics at different places. Authority then paused to await the effects, and Miles Coverdale was allowed to escape overseas. The effects were disappointing, defiance rather than submission being the general tone. In the spring the persecution became more general, and by the end of the year about seventy persons had been burnt alive. Some were men of note, but the majority were humble people of the sort who had furnished the martyrs for Lollardry. The most prominent sufferers of the year were Latimer and Ridley, who died at Oxford in October, lighting such a candle, in Latimer's famous words, as should never be put out. Latimer had all his life been a fighter for justice as well as religion, and his supreme gift of the memorable phrase endured to the end. His last saying was repeated through the land, and the numbers of the Protestants increased.

Cranmer was still in prison and the Queen hoped to make a better example of him. Unlike the others, he had received his appointment from Rome, and from Rome must proceed his deprivation and degradation. He could have been executed for treason in countenancing Northumberland's plot, but the prevailing interest required that he must die for heresy. Not only that, but he must die repentant, publicly recanting the faith in which he had lived, and presenting to all the world the spectacle of the archbishop of the heretics grovelling in confession of error. Northumberland had recanted on the scaffold, to the confusion of the weaker Protestants; but most men knew that Northumberland had no faith to recant. Cranmer would be different, and his fall would turn thousands. For some months then, there was waged a subtle contest of which the prize was Cranmer's soul and the constancy of many.

The trial itself was the less important matter, for its issue was not in doubt. It was effected in September 1555 by a commission of English clerics nominated by the papal Inquisition. They sent their finding to Rome, which allowed the prisoner to be condemned and handed to the state for punishment, and which also transmitted orders for his formal degradation from clerical orders. Bonner performed the ceremony at Oxford in February 1556, displaying a vulgar glee which moved his own colleague to a gesture of protest. Soon afterwards Cranmer was required to sign a series of documents known as his recantations. The earlier ones were more properly submissions to his sovereign and the existing law, such as his own principles had always enjoined. He distinguished such conformity from a denial of faith, which was next required of him. He was in the hands of practical psychologists who had studied his mentality and temperament. In his Oxford cell he had been virtually present at the burning of Latimer and Ridley, and he knew what burning meant. He remained in the misery of a winter prison until after his degradation by Bonner, and then his keepers tempted him. They transferred him to easy residence in the deanery of Christ Church, where he might walk in gardens and converse with pleasant men of his own breeding. It opened a prospect of declining years spent in some quiet retirement, delivered from the politics he hated, devoted to books and meditation. He was no single-minded fighting-man like Latimer. Astrologers would have judged that he was born under Libra: the balance had always been the symbol of his mind. Truth for him lay not in the shallow syllogisms of the partisan; it was buried deep on bases that were shapeless. There were two sides to every question, and he knew that some, like Pole and the Queen, were completely sincere in convictions opposed to his though based on the same knowledge. Must he be so positive that he was right and they were wrong? He yielded; and no man of our time may scoff save he who has passed unflinching through the subtle rigours of a totalitarian trial. He signed two more recantations, real ones that denied all his faith and affirmed all that he disbelieved. Authority had what it wanted, and gave orders for a final public recantation and the stake.

In his last hours Cranmer saw what he had done, and knew that he could not quit life like that. On the morning of 21 March, the day appointed for the end, he stood up to make his statement. It was a blow to those who had so carefully conditioned him. He denied his recantations, denied the Catholic view of the sacrament, denied the papal supremacy. There was almost an uproar, and they did not let him finish. They had no need to drag him to the stake. He led the way and set the pace. He died with his mind at peace, calmly holding to the hottest flame the hand that had signed away his truth. England has never had much admiration for hard logical strength. Cranmer had been both weak and strong; he had heart as well as brain; and his country loved him, while the Protestants drew courage from his end.

Pole became archbishop and the work went on. Gardiner had died towards the close of 1555. Bonner was active as ever. Some of the bishops were not, perhaps for want of material. The burnings were for the most part in and around London, and in East Anglia and the south-east, the strongest area of Protestantism. From first to last they numbered close on three hundred. The total was small compared with the record of the Netherlands, but it was stupendous for England, which had never seen anything approaching it before. As an attempt to destroy Protestantism it was a failure. The evidence indicates that many of the non-partisan majority were alienated from the state religion and that the numbers of the genuine Protestants increased. They kept no great secrecy about their conventicles, and even preached in the open. Their boldness had something of radical defiance in it, as of the people against rulers of an alien class; for after Cranmer the victims were mostly poor folk, craftsmen and tradesmen, apprentices, and ignorant women. It has been remarked that the gentry, unless they were churchmen, furnished not a single martyr. Neither did the prosperous merchants, their urban counterparts. Property conformed to law and government, but that did not prevent it from being uneasy and ready for a change. On material grounds alone it could have no enthusiasm for Mary's policy. She herself had neither fear nor doubt. A kindly woman in personal relationships, and merciful to political offenders, in religion a ruthless sense of duty possessed her and her heart was of stone. Her health was bad, her unhappiness deplorable, and Pole was her counsellor. These may be mitigations of judgment, though one may doubt if she would have acted otherwise had all been well.

The Queen's unhappiness was due to Philip's departure from England and fading hopes of an heir to carry on the succession, that succession which was the problem of the Tudor dynasty and the nightmare of Tudor England. Philip stayed for more than a year after his marriage, and left for the Netherlands on the call of urgent business in September 1555. He had done his best to conciliate England and had failed; and to insinuate himself into her active government, and had only partially succeeded. He had not advocated the burnings of 1555, but many supposed that they were his work, for Spain was notoriously a burning country, and English residents there were ever conscious of the Inquisition ready to engulf them. Philip and his Spanish household grew steadily more unpopular and more disillusioned with the outcome of his marriage. Unless it should produce issue he had clearly no future in England beyond the life of the Queen. She herself was passionately desirous of an heir. In 1554–5 she persuaded herself that she was with child and unwisely let the world know of her hopes. Dispatches were ready written to notify the courts of Europe of the birth, and in April there was even a premature announcement which caused the ringing of the bells in

London. Before Philip left it was admittedly a delusion, to the comfort of the Protestants at home and overseas. Philip had had enough of it and failed throughout 1556 to return. His wife believed there was still hope and fretted miserably at his absence. Her fourth Parliament, which met in the autumn of 1555, was a disappointment. It would not hear of Philip's coronation or of any restitution of Church land, for which Pole still hoped. Its only concession was one more apparent than real on the payment of firstfruits and tenths. Gardiner died while it was sitting, and Pole, wrapped in his ideals, neglected administration. Public opinion grew more loudly critical and more offensively expressed. The burnings caused many local commotions. Protestant manifestoes from the exiles abroad were widely disseminated. Plots, instigated from France, were hatched and rumoured, with the unwilling Elizabeth as their focus; and members of Parliament were actually or supposedly concerned.

The most dangerous of the plots, early in 1556, had for its object the marriage of Elizabeth with Courtenay and their substitution for Philip and Mary. Courtenay was travelling abroad, and died in Italy later in the year. Elizabeth took pains to dissociate herself and was undoubtedly averse to the plan, although her personal friends and Courtenay's were implicated, together with the French ambassador. Elizabeth's position was thus made difficult, but her danger was less than in Wyatt's time, for the nation was now her protector, and any move to condemn her for treason would have excited a general rebellion led by half the Queen's Council.

Philip's business in the Netherlands was to be present at his father's abdication and to receive the investiture of his sovereignty over the provinces. It was done in October 1555, and in the following January Philip received also the throne of Spain and its Italian dependencies. But there was more than this. The Emperor's last French war was still outstanding, and was ended only temporarily by a truce in February that left Henry II still an enemy on the watch for new advantages. Philip, although a man of peace, thus inherited the French contest. He also inherited a violent quarrel with the Pope. Some months earlier, Paul IV, an aged Neapolitan cardinal, had been elected. In religion he was uncompromising and suspicious of all, including the Emperor and Cardinal Pole, who had made concessions under pressure. In politics he was an Italian patriot, burning to overthrow Spanish power in Italy and especially in his beloved Naples. By the autumn of 1556 he was at war with Spain, and the

Duke of Alva with a Spanish army from Naples was invading the
states of the Church. Paul called on the French for aid, and they
acceded. Once again Europe was engaged in the familiar pattern of
war, with the difference that the Pope and Spain were opposed, and
that the King of Spain, most orthodox of Catholics, was even for a
time under papal excommunication.

To Queen Mary all this caused distress. It kept her husband from
her side, it involved England in the terrible quarrel with Rome, and
it was to involve, in 1557, even her trusted Cardinal Pole in the
deprivation of his legateship and a charge of heresy at the hands of
the bellicose Pope. Events moved inexorably to war with France, for
which Henry II, nothing loath, eased the way by renewed patronage
of English plotters and of maritime exiles from the west-country
who were already preying upon Spanish shipping in the Channel. In
spite of the marriage treaty the Queen joined in Philip's war, the
treaty itself being sapped by a previous obligation to the Emperor,
requiring England to furnish armed forces for the defence of the
Netherlands in return for a similar guarantee of Calais. Without Parliament being called or the country consulted, England found herself
at open war with the French by midsummer 1557.

The Navy, upon which success would turn, was no longer the fine
force that Henry VIII had left. Under Somerset it had turned out
useful squadrons for the Scottish war, and under Northumberland,
who had years of experience as Lord Admiral, the foundations were
laid of the Chatham base and dockyard, while Henry's organization
was rounded off by the creation of a victualling department. But
Northumberland's rule was one of corruption, and there is no doubt
that corruption attacked the Navy. There were great opportunities
for peculation in the purchase and disposal of timber, canvas, and
cordage, and great temptations to slackness in the upkeep of ships
that required unceasing care to prevent them from rotting when laid
up. That these evils were at work in Edward's reign may be inferred
from the prices realized for a number of ships sold as no longer serviceable two years after its close. Among them was a vessel of 450
tons, ten years old, which realized £35, her first cost having been at
least £1,500. Smaller craft at the same time fetched £8 and £10 each.
Mary's government was not to blame for most of that decay, but it
was for the decay that continued. Immediately after the end of her
reign four or five of the largest ships were condemned as beyond
repair, while she had not replaced the *Great Harry*, burnt by accident

in the month of her accession. The evidence does show, in spite of some pleas that have been made to the contrary, that the Navy was corruptly and negligently handled. In addition there was the quarrel with the Hanseatic League. England grew the oaks for building ships' hulls, but not the long pine trunks for their masts and spars. These came from the Baltic, as did the hempen rope, the flax for canvas, the pitch for making seams watertight, and the tar which was the only preservative both for hemp and timber. Without these things a fleet could not be fitted for sea, and in 1557 the Hansa cut off the supply, sending away empty from its ports over fifty English merchantmen that sailed there to lade them. The stocks in England were low, and the Navy, even if otherwise in good state, would have been crippled in consequence.

In general the people gave little support to the Queen in this war. So completely were most men alienated from her that they were inclined to derision of their government's efforts and failures. The country's morale was low after a decade of misrule first by rogues and then by zealots. It gave Mary and her husband no such all-in service as it had given to Henry VIII; and the war was viewed as the work of a faction, parallel to the persecution. In order to ensure England's participation, Philip came over from the Netherlands in the spring of 1557; and, having obtained it, almost solely on the initiative of the Queen, he departed for ever at the beginning of July. He took with him about 7,000 English troops, who joined his army in the Netherlands. There, in August, his forces won the battle of St. Quentin, where the French lost 10,000 men and a number of notable leaders. It might have led to the ruin of France had Philip been enterprising. But he missed the opportunity, captured only a few border strongholds, and retired into winter quarters. The French king recalled his best general, the Duke of Guise, from Italy, and made his north-eastern frontier safe, besides planning a bold stroke of his own.

Mary's treasury was empty, the stores were lacking in the dockyards, and even the stock of gunpowder was almost exhausted. Instead of calling Parliament she levied a forced loan, which evoked no cheerful payment but considerable resistance. Soldiers and seamen mutinied and deserted, and civilians abetted them. Scotland under the queen-mother, Guise's sister, entered the war, and the borders were ill-defended. The most reliable troops to be had were German mercenaries. A force of these were engaged for the border, and as they were crossing the Netherlands Philip detained them and added them to his own army. Neither would he himself declare war on Scotland and so interrupt the Netherland-Scottish commerce. These things made Englishmen regard him as an equal enemy with the King of France. Before the end of the year the Queen was comforted by the patching-up of peace between her husband and the Pope and by a French withdrawal from Italy. She did not foresee that its consequence would be a strengthening of France in the north. The Navy, so much of it as existed otherwise than on paper, was laid up for lack of stores and money, and not a ship of strength was left afloat. Strategically St. Quentin turned out to be a French victory rather than a shattering defeat, for it concentrated the forces of France and lulled her enemies to sleep.

Henry II was an able strategist. He had the courage to give up the Italian dream that had cost his country so dear and to devote himself to more solid aims on his own frontier. In Guise he had a first-class general. Together they devised a sudden stroke in the dead of winter against Calais and its associated strongholds in the English Pale. They concentrated forty-five sail of warships and armed merchantmen at Boulogne, with a siege train and a large army. Such preparations could not have been wholly concealed from a vigilant opponent, but the English government was so ill-served that it knew nothing until too late. Guise marched his men up the coast to Calais, while the ships cut off the doomed town from relief. The English 'ships and barks in the Narrow Seas' were five in number, and their insignificant strength is attested by the total of the men on board, 400 in all. For the first time in half a century sea power was on the side of France. At Dover the Earl of Rutland hastily levied men from Kent and Sussex and embarked them in the local fishing boats, but he had no chance of getting through the blockade. Calais, with crumbling walls of medieval masonry, and a garrison of 800, was invested on the last day of the year by twenty times its numbers armed with heavy battering guns. After an honourable defence it surrendered on 8 January 1558, and Guisnes and the smaller bulwarks of the Pale followed before the end of the month. Ever since the Norman Conquest the crown of England had held some part or other of continental France, and for more than two hundred years its royal standard had floated over Calais. All that was now ended.

The fall of Calais meant three things: the loss of the ancient mart for the sale of raw wool, the loss of the port of entry for invasion of

France, and above all the loss of prestige and a sore blow to the national pride. The wool sales by the merchants of the Staple were no longer of prime importance, for the growth of the cloth industry was extinguishing the amount of raw wool available for export. After the war the export was resumed to Flemish marts, but it gradually died out until in the early Stuart period England became a wool-importing country and export was prohibited. The loss of facility for invading the continent was more serious in the contemporary view than it is to modern judgment. Such military invasions were really of doubtful value to English interests, and in spite of Calais they continued to be made with the aid of French rebels in the period of the wars of religion. The real loss was of prestige. It filled Mary with regret and overflowed her cup of sorrows, it filled the English people with shame and with disgust for her government, and it confirmed their hatred of Philip, in whose cause the war had been undertaken.

Openly or secretly, most people were longing for the end of the reign, treason though it might be to pray for it. Parliament met a fortnight after the fall of Calais and granted a very moderate supply to the treasury. The only warlike undertaking that ensued was the fitting-out of a naval squadron to maintain touch with Philip's army on the Flemish coast at the cost of leaving all the western Channel to the French. The Queen also decided on an extensive programme of building new ships, which was not effective before the war ended. Howard incurred criticism for the Navy's deficiencies and was superseded as Lord Admiral by Clinton, who was to hold the office for close on thirty years. One of Howard's questionable actions had been to lend two of the Navy's middle-sized fighting vessels to the promoters of a Guinea expedition that sailed within three weeks of the fall of Calais. Private adventurers in an illegal trade, it seemed, could get the Queen's ships equipped when she herself could not. It was a concrete example of the divergence between the national activities and those of the government. The Narrow Seas squadron in 1558 took part with its guns in Philip's land victory on the coast at Gravelines, but otherwise England's share in the war was little. In August negotiations for peace were opened at Lille, although they led to no conclusion until the following year. Earlier in the year the young Queen of Scots, long betrothed to the Dauphin Francis, was married to him, and the French tentacles gripping Scotland were strengthened. A Valois Franco-Scottish kingdom, possibly to reach out to Ireland also, was in sight.

England in fact was encircled, with only one ray of hope amid the gloom. As a contemporary described the position, the crown and nobility were poor, captains and soldiers lacking, the people disorderly and divided, prices high and injustice rampant; while the French king with one foot in Calais and the other in Edinburgh bestrode the exhausted realm, which could nowhere look to any steadfast friend. The ray of hope was in the Princess Elizabeth, displaying wisdom in a trying situation. In spite of her seclusion her good qualities were widely known by the spread of opinion from the initiated to their dependants and the people at large. The people looked eagerly to her accession, and poor Mary obliged them. She grew more sickly as summer merged into autumn. Pole was also sick and out of hope. The action of Paul IV had cut him to the heart, nor had Paul's Spanish opponents any good word for him. They blamed him for England's lack of interest in the war and spoke of him as 'the accursed cardinal'. His own countrymen shared the sentiment, and he and his sovereign moved lonely and sad to their end. They died on the same day, 17 November 1558, the Queen in the morning, the cardinal in the evening while the joy-bells were pealing over London. Both were single-minded, honest, and high-principled, and more than any other governors of England had merited the terrible epitaph 'They meant well'.

I 2

THE ACCESSION OF ELIZABETH I

ELIZABETH rode into London on 23 November 1558, amid the genuine plaudits of the people. Her sister had met with the like reception five years earlier. On both occasions the cause of the satisfaction was the same, relief that a hated régime had ended and hope that the new ruler would be better than the last. Mary had taken less than five years to change joyful acceptance into deep disgust. Elizabeth had witnessed the process and was determined not to repeat it. She had had time to measure political forces and effects, to comprehend the emotions and desires of the people, and to assess the characters of the leading men through whom she would have to act. Her own character was formed and her abilities known to herself. For ten years past she had been exposed to acute dangers and insidious approaches, and to hostile watchfulness ready to note compromising words and actions. She had learned to see and say nothing, to speak unconstrainedly whilst revealing nothing, to carry a cheerful countenance, to command easily, to mix a salt of humour in censure, and to show a friendly interest in all people, humble or great. These characteristics she brought ready shaped to her work at the age of twenty-five. She was to live till nearly seventy without much change in them : her *semper eadem* was a true motto. Her personality continued rather than developed, in which respect she was unlike her father. In her own view and in that of her people she was very much his daughter, and she possessed his gift of royal magnetism to rouse the hearts of the multitude.

It would be unjust to imply that Elizabeth's methods of approach to her work constituted the whole of her character or that she was completely materialist in her outlook. From the outset it was apparent that she dedicated herself to the interests of her people and that she placed their freedom first among all considerations and their

prosperity high among the others. If hers was the individual sovereign power to be used always according to her own discretion, it
was always to be used in fulfilment of the public needs. For her, as
for her father and her grandfather, sovereign and people were
but two aspects of the same thing, the English state. A Spaniard
early noted this, saying in effect that she was married to her people;
and it accounts for some of the decisions, not the easiest that could
have been taken, embodied in what it is usual to call the Elizabethan
settlement.

There were in fact several settlements to be accomplished within
a year or two of the opening of the reign, and together they were in
great measure to dictate its course, and even the subsequent fortunes
of the realm for centuries to follow. The first task was to choose
councillors and officers of state. Some of Mary's Council were
reappointed, eleven at first, soon reduced to eight, while fifteen were
left out, and seven new men introduced. Among the high officers
Clinton continued as Lord Admiral and Winchester as Lord Treasurer, together with Arundel and Howard in the royal household.
New ministers who were to wield great influence were Sir Nicholas
Bacon, Lord Keeper of the Great Seal, Sir Walter Mildmay, Chancellor of the Exchequer, and Sir William Cecil, Secretary of State.
Two men destined to prominence and influence, Lord Robert
Dudley and the Earl of Sussex, were at first neither ministers nor
members of the Privy Council. On the whole Elizabeth's corps of
assistants represented the middle opinion of the nation, containing
neither Catholic nor Protestant zealots, and, after the first two
months, not one ecclesiastic of any persuasion.

Cecil, alone of the able men called by the Queen, was to prove
himself a great man, one of the half-dozen greatest ministers who
have served the English state. He was thirty-eight years old and had
made his mark under Somerset and Northumberland. He had disapproved of the latter's plan to alter the succession, but had submitted
to coercion. This caused his dismissal from office by Mary but not
his complete expulsion from government service, in which he had
been intermittently employed on special tasks. His religious bent was
Protestant, but he conformed, like most laymen, to the requirements
of the state, and went to mass until the times should alter. He was
married to a highly educated woman, Mildred Cooke, whose sister
was the wife of the Lord Keeper Bacon, another convinced Protestant. It is evident that Cecil's character and principles were well

known to Elizabeth before she mounted the throne, for she appointed him Secretary without hesitation or delay. It had not been in itself a commanding position, but Cecil with the Queen's approval was to give it a new importance. She told him that she appointed him in the belief that he would be faithful and incorruptible, and time was to show that she was not mistaken.

Elizabeth, having determined the personnel of her administration, had now to deal with her immediate problems. They were: the religion and the ecclesiastical allegiance of the realm; the peace treaty with France and future relations with Spain; the winding-up of the damaging quarrel with the Hanseatic League; a decision about the gold trade with the Guinea coast, and whether the monopoly of Portugal should be respected or denied; and the critical condition of the finances, left in confusion by the late government and continuing to bleed the treasury by the excessive interest payable on foreign loans. These problems were evident from the first day of the reign, and to them was added in the early part of 1559 a flare-up of Calvinism against French domination in Scotland, portending a new 'settlement' in which England would be vitally interested. Altogether, a sufficiency of urgent business confronted an inexperienced queen, who was determined, while listening to advice, to make the decisions her own.

The religious question was the most important. Broadly there were three conceivable solutions: continued allegiance to the Pope, revival of Henry's English Catholicism schismatic from Rome, and re-establishment of a Protestant Church. From the standpoint of foreign policy and good relations with England's neighbours the first appeared much the easiest course, and it would probably have commanded the assent of a sufficient body of English opinion. But it would have done so only on one condition that would ultimately have been fatal to its success, namely that persecution of the Marian sort must cease. It is highly probable that if the new government had decided to continue the burnings a rebellion would have swept it away. The burning campaign had in fact constituted England's war of religion, and it had been decisive. The level of English callousness to suffering had been the crucial factor. The Tudor English were revoltingly callous by the standards of their descendants, but they were tender-hearted by the standards of their own Christendom. Where the Netherlands endured without resistance for a decade a rate of burning from five to ten times that of the Marian persecution, where the French with a taste rather for blood than flame were prepared to indulge in the wild massacre of thousands in a week, and where the Spaniards witnessed with grim approval and no scruple of pity the routine proceedings of the *auto de fé*, the English found Mary's hundred victims a year too much for their stomachs. The persecution had been at a higher rate than England would continue to permit, and it had been at far too low a rate to put an end to Protestantism; and there was no way of bridging the gap between the two requirements. It followed that the Protestants who had withstood it had established their claim to exist and must henceforward be tolerated. That being so, a papalist régime was hardly possible, for contemporary Rome admitted no toleration of heretics. Their existence in large numbers in a country of papal allegiance could only result in chronic instability, potential civil war, and a general condition of unsettlement. Attractive as it might appear to a superficial glance, the papalist solution of the religious question was inadmissible.

The other two solutions, the insular Catholic (if that is not a contradiction in terms) and the Protestant, offered more hope because either of them admitted some possibility of compromise with the other, and the elimination of the worst kind of persecution. For the practical politician of 1558, the *politique* who viewed religion objectively, it was a choice between insular Catholicism and Protestantism, with a maximum blurring of the dividing line between the two.

That was Elizabeth's outlook. Although she did not parade her personal creed, it is evident that she had no mind to submit to Rome. With her parentage it would have been very awkward to do so, since on all Roman arguments she was illegitimate. As she said herself, she was altogether English, and the English of that date were less attracted by the idea of the unity of Christendom than by that of 'England an empire', a body politic containing all its loyalties within itself. Elizabeth meant to be a free sovereign of an independent state. It is evident also from her words and attitude that she was not a zealous Protestant. Zeal was ceasing to abide with the Lutherans, who exalted princes, and transferring itself to the Calvinists, whose aims did not march with royal supremacy over the Church, and whose trumpeter John Knox had just published some unfortunate lucubrations on reigning queens.[1] Elizabeth liked a certain amount

[1] His *First Blast of the Trumpet against the Monstrous Regiment of Women* was published at Geneva in 1558.

of ceremonial, much as a sergeant-major likes it, because it is good for discipline. She shared her father's dislike of a married clergy. She desired the Church to be subordinate to the state and the clergy to be her servants and none other's. She hoped that nearly all her people would be members of the national Church, and she did not intend to commit the error of persecuting those who would not. Subject to these considerations she was indifferent to the precise nature of its practices. There were two models available, Cranmer's first and second prayer-books, and there was no necessity to elaborate a third. The Queen's preference was probably for the first book as more Catholic and more in the mean of opinions. To settle the matter two measures would need to be passed by Parliament, one to transfer jurisdiction to the crown, and another to decree the use of whichever book should be chosen.

It was well known before her accession that Elizabeth did not mean to continue in the Roman allegiance. Foreign diplomats had reported as much, and the expectation of a change was a considerable element in London's enthusiasm for its new queen from the moment of her appearance. There were anti-papal hints in the pageantry that received her in the streets, and they elicited no sign of her displeasure; while a markedly papalist sermon by the bishop who preached at Mary's funeral incurred a reprimand. During that winter the Queen let her attitude be guessed without formally committing herself. Until peace should be made with France and Scotland she could not give flagrant offence to Spain. Moreover, she knew that the nation would approve the decision she had in mind, and it would obviously be strengthened by appearing as a national and not solely a royal decision. Thus she postponed enunciation of religious policy until the meeting of Parliament, and even then it was not the first business dealt with. Meanwhile, though the mass formed part of her coronation service, she herself withdrew during its celebration, and when the abbot and monks of Westminster met her in procession with lighted candles she ordered them away, saying that she could see very well without such illumination. Already before the close of 1558 order had been given for the reading in English of the parts of the service that Henry had anglicized and that Mary had put back into Latin. State documents, also, in which it was necessary to express the Queen's titles, contained an *etcetera* which covered the possibility of a renewal of the royal supremacy and was well known to be inserted for that purpose.[1] Queen Mary had used this device of *etcetera* to draw a veil over the hated supremacy before she had formally got rid of it, and her sister was now copying the example for the opposite purpose.

Parliament met at the end of January 1559. The Commons were normally elected, comprising some thirty per cent of the members of the previous Marian Parliament, and not deliberately packed by the crown except for the usual care taken to secure seats for government spokesmen. But the Tudor Commons, although they always had a will of their own, were responsive to the lead of the crown, and it became evident that the House of 1559 contained a majority for the royal supremacy and also, in excess of the crown's wishes, for a thorough-going Protestant system of worship. In the Lords there was a lay majority for the ending of the papal jurisdiction, although not one bishop was ready to consent. But not only had Mary left six bishoprics vacant at her death, but between that event and the meeting of Parliament four more bishops, including Pole, had died. If these ten places in the House of Lords had been filled by papalist bishops the realization of Elizabeth's intentions would have been much more difficult. She herself did not fill the vacancies before the religious decision was taken, and the gaps in the spiritual representation were sufficient to allow her measures to pass. Parliament thus had in the Commons a large and in the Lords a small majority for the undoing of Mary's work.

It would seem by the most recent weighing of the evidence[2] that the Queen intended to go cautiously in this Parliament, passing only an Act of Supremacy to re-establish the crown's control and postponing a decision on doctrine to another Parliament. As late as March she told de Feria, the Spanish ambassador, that she would restore religion to the condition in which her father had left it. This would have given her a middle position enabling her to hold out hopes of concessions to the Catholic powers on the one hand and to her own Protestants on the other. A Supremacy Bill was accordingly introduced on 9 February. The Protestants in the Commons thereupon asserted themselves by promoting independent bills on doctrine, which were lost, while the Supremacy Bill was so drastically amended by the extreme Protestants, whom we may call Puritans, that a virtually new measure emerged on the 21st, and the

[1] 'Queen of England, France and Ireland, Defender of the Faith, &c.'
[2] By Sir J. E. Neale in *Elizabeth I and her Parliaments 1559-1581* (1953). The exposition is too long for full inclusion on the scale of this book.

Commons tacked to it clauses reviving Edward VI's Act of Uniformity and therefore the book of 1552. They rapidly passed it, but the Lords not only imposed delay but rejected the additional clauses. While the discussion was proceeding the Canterbury convocation, meeting under Bonner's presidency, affirmed the full Roman Catholic position as established by Mary, thus making it evident that changes would be the work of Parliament alone. This impressed the Lords, but the Commons were determined to have their doctrinal enactments. They passed the bill in its amended form and also another making legal the religion established in the last year of Edward VI, thus gaining their point by a different method. The royal decision was usually given on all completed bills at the end of the session. Before that took place the Queen changed her purpose. She had hitherto been against the formal restoration of Protestant doctrine at this stage, but it was being strongly pressed upon her by the Commons. In addition, peace with France was signed on 2 April. She therefore decided to carry both supremacy and uniformity, but to embody them in distinct measures; and the supremacy was not to be that of 'supreme head' but of 'supreme governor'. On 10 April a new and final Supremacy Bill to that effect was introduced in the Commons, to be rapidly completed there and in the Lords a fortnight later. In its wake followed a Uniformity Bill to enforce the use of the 1552 prayer book with minor modifications. In the Lords this bill passed by a majority of only three, all the bishops voting against it. The programme which the Queen had designed for a year of gradual softening of the Catholic position had been put through in three months, and in more decisive form than she had intended, for it was the second prayer book and not the first that prevailed. The Puritan Commons were the determining factor, and they had been stimulated by the exiles returning with radical views from the Rhineland and Switzerland.

The Act of Supremacy made the Queen supreme governor 'as well in all spiritual and ecclesiastical things or causes as temporal', and denied that any foreign prince, prelate, or potentate had any manner of spiritual or ecclesiastical jurisdiction in the realm. An oath of supremacy to that effect was to be sworn by all beneficed clergy and by judges, magistrates, mayors, and office-holders under the crown. A person maintaining the jurisdiction of a foreign prince or prelate was subject to fine and imprisonment and, for the third offence, death. The Queen was empowered to exercise her ecclesiastical jurisdiction through commissioners whom she might appoint. How 'supreme governor' differed from 'supreme head' is a question that has been debated, and the conclusion seems to be that there was no difference of function but a somewhat milder emphasis on the authority conferred. The Act of Uniformity established the use of the prayer book, substantially that of 1552, under the following penalties: clergymen refusing were to be imprisoned for six months, and for life for a third offence; laymen absenting themselves from service at their parish church were to be fined a shilling for each offence.

Such was the religious settlement. That it was more Protestant than the Queen intended was due to the pressure of the returned Puritan exiles and their acceptance by the Commons. It was comprehensive to the extent of satisfying the majority ranging from the surviving Henrician Catholics to the extreme Protestants, for, as has been noted, ceremonial was to the laity a more important matter than doctrine, and in the early years at least the ceremonial emphasis of the services was left largely a matter of local option. The essential and uncompromising decision was that of the royal supremacy, which was desired by the majority of Englishmen. Only the Romanist minority could not conform if it followed its convictions to their logical conclusion. In the early part of the reign most of the Romanists did not do so, and made some show of conformity to avoid trouble. Yet they remained a separate body, a dissident society within the state, capable of being stirred into greater energy and more definite self-assertion. The most admirable part of the settlement was its avoidance of persecution in the sense in which the word was then understood. The Queen expressly stated that she had no wish to probe consciences. Men might believe what they liked and pray as they liked in private as long as they expressed no overt challenge to the national Church. The administration continued even milder than the wording of the law. The fines on laymen were often uncollected, and the beneficed clergy did not in practice incur the severe penalties prescribed for persistent defiance, since before they had reached that stage they had ceased to be beneficed. This last point brings us to the attitude of the clergy, so uncompromisingly expressed in Bonner's convocation. The Marian bishops, with one exception (Kitchin of Llandaff), remained loyal to Rome and were deprived. They were not harshly treated, and some ended their lives in dignified ease, while others preferred to withdraw overseas. Bonner was an exception, as for his conduct to Cranmer if for nothing else he deserved to be; and he died in prison. The parish clergy as a whole did not follow their bishops. There were about 8,000 of them, of whom at least 7,000 conformed to the new dispensation. The figure of one thousand choosing deprivation is, however, only a liberal estimate, for there are no exact statistics; the number may have been smaller but is unlikely to have been larger; a recent authority puts it at no more than 200.[1]

The negotiation of peace to put an end to Mary's disastrous war went on concurrently with the religious transactions; and in this matter Philip II held an important position. The death of Mary deprived him of any status in England other than that of a friendly and allied sovereign. Whatever hopes he may have had of being more than this were speedily dissolved by Elizabeth. When de Feria tried at her accession to assure her that she owed her crown to Philip's good will and implied that she would be wise to deserve his continued favour, she answered that she owed her position to her people; and she soon made it evident that she was paying no marked deference to the Spanish ambassador. He, who had proposed to be always at her ear in the capacity of guide and mentor, could not even get a room allotted to him in the palace and was soon complaining that all the Queen's entourage shunned him. In February 1559 Philip sought to restore his position by offering to marry Elizabeth, on condition that she should become a Catholic and submit to the Pope. She declined, probably to his satisfaction, for his experience as an English king-consort had not been enjoyable, and he had made the offer as a sacrifice to statesmanship.

The peace negotiations were concluded at Cateau-Cambrésis. They were primarily between Philip and Henry II, with England in the humiliating position of a hanger-on at the conference table. The French withdrew entirely from Italy, but kept the three bishoprics (Metz, Toul, and Verdun) which they had seized from the Empire in 1552. At the time it seemed that Philip had the best of it, for his mastery in Italy was impressive. Only in the course of centuries did it appear how the consolidation of her frontier on the Rhine, of which this was the first stage, was to make France the arbiter of Europe. To a similar end Henry II insisted on retaining Calais as a bastion of the flat north-eastern border, where fortified towns counted for much. Elizabeth strove hard to regain Calais, but Philip would fight only in words and declined to break off negotiations

[1] A. L. Rowse, *The England of Elizabeth* (1950), p. 398.

when the French stood firm. In February the Queen was obliged to yield Calais in principle. The French were to restore it in eight years or (at their option) to pay half a million crowns, provided that the peace had been unbroken by England meanwhile. Elizabeth and her ministers wished to recover Calais because the nation was set on it, but they themselves may have doubted whether it was worth the expense of its maintenance. Berwick, on the Scottish frontier, was in a different category. Its defences had been neglected by Mary, and its loss in the war would have been much more serious than that of Calais. Fortunately the Scots did not attempt it, and its refortification was one of the first cares of Elizabeth's government. The French were at this time a powerful but not exclusive element in the ruling of Scotland. The young queen was in France, and her mother, Mary of Lorraine was regent. The Scottish nobles were as keenly aware as English statesmen of the implications of the Stuart-Valois marriage. If it was an ultimate threat to English independence it was a more immediate one to Scottish, and already some men were looking to Anglo-Scottish co-operation in a joint defence against French imperialism. The former Earl of Arran, now Duke of Châtelherault, was of this mind, and he and others made no difficulty in signing peace with England in March 1559. At the same time the outlines of the continental peace were agreed, and on 2 April the Treaty of Cateau-Cambrésis was formally completed. It was not a glorious opening to Elizabeth's reign, but none could blame her for that. The public did blame Philip II, who, having begun his career in English consciousness with the labels of papist and tyrant, continued it under that of traitor. The view was unfair, but the fact that it was held was important.

The Hanseatic League sent representatives to Cateau-Cambrésis, and the English envoys were instructed to treat with them, but no agreement was reached. Cecil had been an ally of Gresham in the original revocation of the Hanse privileges by Northumberland. Cecil and Gresham were once more combining with great plans in view, and they held it essential to confirm the monopoly of the Merchants Adventurers in the Antwerp cloth export. Early in 1559 the Queen was advised not to restore the Hanse privileges, and at midsummer she wrote to the Council at Lubeck inviting the League to state its case. A long haggling ensued and was terminated by an agreement in 1560. By its terms the Hansa retained a privileged position only for goods imported into England from its own cities and exported from

England to them. On its carrying trade it had to pay the same duties as other foreigners. But the most important provision of the treaty was that the Hansa was not to export English cloth to the Netherlands or to Italy, and this was the prize for which the Merchants Adventurers had contended. Finally, it was agreed that Englishmen were to trade freely in the cities of the Hanseatic League. The general effect was that the League lost the excessive privileges it once had enjoyed and lost much of its carrying trade, but still retained some relatively unimportant advantages over other foreigners trading with England. On her side England regained access to the Baltic and the naval stores essential to her survival. It was a winning treaty, as that of Cateau-Cambrésis was a treaty of defeat, and its gains were more substantial than the loss of Calais.

In spite of prohibition by Philip and Mary the Guinea trade had continued to the end of their reign. After Elizabeth's accession it went on as before. There is no record of any immediate decision about it, but it is clear, as one would expect, that there was no effective prohibition, since the expeditions were sufficiently numerous to provoke Portugal to a new protest. In the spring of 1561 a special ambassador arrived from Lisbon with a complaint that English ships were trading on the Gold Coast and elsewhere in West Africa. The coast, he said, had been conquered by the crown of Portugal and was now subject to its dominion, and the king would not permit English trade. The Queen made answer that her subjects should be commanded not to traffic with any part of Africa under the dominion and tribute of the King of Portugal; and the ambassador went away, apparently satisfied. It is evident from the state papers that in this matter Cecil stood at the Queen's side and prompted the English policy. Instructions were issued to the Lord Admiral in May 1561 to see that English merchants conformed with the above decision—and the Guinea voyages went on exactly as before. The Queen and her ministers, it appeared, interpreted the places 'under the dominion' of Portugal as comprising Elmina and one or two other coast fortresses where Portuguese garrisons existed; and maintained, as the merchants had done under Mary, that the African kings and chiefs on the two thousand miles of coastline were independent powers free to trade with the English if they liked. In modern terms Elizabeth and Cecil were acting on the doctrine of effective occupation and denying that the occupation was effective. Portugal relied upon the arguments of prior discovery and conquest, but did make some attempt to show

that the occupation was effective. The Portuguese sent another embassy in 1562 to pursue the matter on these lines, but the Queen
answered that she was informed that the greater part of Guinea did
not obey the authority of the King of Portugal, and that if it did, he
had his own remedy, namely, to forbid its inhabitants to trade with the
English. That of course was to prick the bubble of effective occupation, but in such a manner as the British Empire of after days would
have found very unjust if applied against itself.

So the Queen recognized and regularized the African trade that
her sister and Philip II had attempted to suppress. 'They keep on
sending more ships round Cape Verde,' wrote the Spanish ambassador de Quadra early in 1562; and one squadron of that season contained no less than four vessels chartered from the Navy. The voyages went on in the ensuing years and resulted in a state of war with
Portugal, undeclared but none the less effective, with some sharp
fighting on the African coast and among the adjacent islands. It was
in fact against Portugal and not against Spain that England first declared her repudiation of the claim of the two peninsular powers to
divide between them the maritime exploitation of the world outside
Europe. That claim was based originally on the bulls issued by
fifteenth-century popes, culminating with those of Alexander VI in
1493. It is noticeable that the Portuguese in the 1560s did not appeal
to the bulls in their remonstrances to Elizabeth, and the reason is no
doubt that such an appeal would merely have given an opening for
an anti-papal rejoinder. But the bulls were in men's minds, as appears from a report by de Quadra in 1561 that 'Cecil said to me that
the Pope had no right to partition the world and to give and take
kingdoms to whomever he pleased'. The decision to resist world-
partition and domination was not the least important of the Elizabethan settlements of policy.

The Queen and Cecil, having determined that England should be
independent of foreign powers, began from the outset to remedy the
feeble condition of the national defences. The disgrace of Calais had
evoked some naval energy in Mary's last months, and at least one
large vessel had been completed or purchased, while others were
ordered. Elizabeth rounded off this work by adding four or five ships
to the fleet in her first two years. These did not constitute an increase
of total numbers, but replaced ships that were condemned as hopelessly decayed. Elizabeth's work was therefore that of changing a
paper fleet into a real one. It remained at a modest size, smaller than

that of Henry VIII, until the Spanish war loomed near in later years. The chief base of the Navy was now in the Medway, where Chatham was assuming the position that Portsmouth had held under Henry VIII. Portsmouth under Elizabeth took only minor rank as a naval port.

The new government found the country disarmed in other respects, the coast defences ruinous and their guns dismounted, stocks of powder exhausted, hardly any small-arms and armour, and the county muster-rolls neglected. It determined on immediate rearmament in spite of the cost. In 1559 it was appointing muster-masters in every shire to organize the levies and initiate training, and engineers to renovate the fortifications. The essential munitions were not then manufactured in England but in the Netherlands, where there were regulations impeding export that were likely to be enforced by reason of Philip's disappointment with the turn of affairs in England. Gresham was put in charge of the business. He had the extensive and peculiar knowledge of the Netherlands that the Queen's ministers needed to have of England, and by squaring manufacturers and dealers and bribing customs officers, and above all by mixing as one of themselves with the great financiers, he got the stuff on board English ships, big guns and little, quantities of powder, hackbuts and calivers, and body armour. He was even able by some ingenious practice to steal 2,000 corselets out of the royal armoury at Malines and ship them to London, leaving the king's officials to wonder what had become of them. The success of the rearmament was complete, but it had not been easy, and the fact that in the new warfare England was so dependent on foreigners left an impression on Cecil's mind that led to a remedial policy.

Gresham was a man after Cecil's heart. They shared the conviction that sound finance was the foundation of successful government, while in this matter the Queen was the true granddaughter of Henry VII, with all his acquisitiveness and even more than his zest for economy. For fifteen years past, since Henry's last war, English governments had been anticipating revenue and raising loans, some within the realm and some on the Antwerp bourse, where Mary at the end had been paying as much as 14 per cent interest. Gresham was determined to raise English credit to a better level than that. In 1559 the situation was that the Crown's total debts amounted to £227,000, of which £106,000 was owed at Antwerp with interest from 12 to 14 per cent. The Queen's ordinary revenue, apart from special parliamentary grants, was about £200,000, and by stringent economy she reduced the ordinary expenditure to £135,000. This would have given a surplus of £65,000, which would have more than met the interest on the debts and would in time have paid them off. But rearmament came first, and cost (in 1559–60) £300,000. In the same two years there arose, as will be shown, an emergency in Scotland that had to be dealt with, and it cost £179,000. Parliament in 1559 granted £190,000, and the Queen sold crown lands worth £172,000, but Gresham had to go on borrowing at Antwerp. His difficulties were great, and rumours of Philip's adverse intentions almost stopped his supplies in the summer of 1560, when the creditors were preparing to distrain on the English goods in the Netherlands. But his personal qualities and the growing prestige of the English government carried him through, so that in that year he was renewing loans at 10 per cent. The net result was that by the spring of 1562 Gresham and Cecil had got the Antwerp debt down to just over £100,000, the position at the beginning of the reign, and had paid for rearmament and a Scottish campaign in the interim.

Gresham made unsparing use of the Merchants Adventurers, who had to pay substantially for their monopoly of the Antwerp cloth market. When they sold a shipment of cloth the Flemish currency they received was taken over by the Crown for its own purchases or debts, and the merchants were repaid in English money in London at a different rate of exchange from that obtainable in Antwerp. Thus Gresham was able to improve the rate of exchange by lessening the English demand for it, and at the same time to impose a disguised tax upon the merchants. The reform of the coinage was another measure which he advocated and the government adopted. It was carried out in 1560. The base coins of the previous sixteen years were rated at their true value and received into the mint in exchange for good silver. By this means the holders of the coin paid for the reform, and there was even a small profit to the treasury. These proceedings sound arbitrary. There was, however, no avoiding the fact that the country was in debt, and that everyone would have to pay to get out of it. The general sacrifice was rewarded by general prosperity in the years to come. Within a decade the troublous politics of the Netherlands lowered the position of Antwerp as the financial capital of northern Europe, and London, owing to the work of Gresham and Cecil, was almost ready to take its place. Their policy could not have borne its fruit but for the Queen's integrity. She was as eager as they were for reducing old debts and as reluctant to incur new ones; and she insisted on an economy of expenditure that made her lively court and efficient administration far less costly than Mary's gloomy and incompetent régime. Elizabeth's oft-decried parsimony was the brightest jewel in her crown.

In spite of the peace of Cateau-Cambrésis, France was the dreaded enemy. Henry II was determined to make good the pretensions of Mary Stuart, his daughter-in-law, to the English crown. If Elizabeth's illegitimacy were granted, Mary was the rightful queen. The will of Henry VIII had indeed cut out the descendants of his elder sister, Margaret Tudor (wife of James IV), and had placed next to his own children the offspring of Mary (Duchess of Suffolk), his younger sister, but in international law this will had no validity. The Suffolk claim was represented in 1559 by Lady Catherine Grey, sister of the unfortunate Lady Jane; and even in England she was not taken very seriously as heir to the throne. Everyone supposed and most people hoped that Elizabeth would marry and provide for the succession with children of her own. England certainly did not wish to see her marry Philip II, but rather a minor prince who would be less of a menace to the country's independence. In 1559 the most likely candidate was Philip's cousin, the Archduke Charles, younger son of the Emperor Ferdinand. This would have met Philip's fears of the French threat to England's independence. He was no lover of war and wished to counter that threat by peaceful means, having himself married a French princess (his third wife) as part of the peace settlement. He was also alarmed by the spread of Protestantism in the Netherlands, and perceived that it could best be checked by reviving the Catholic position in England. Henry II was likewise alarmed by the growth of the Huguenot movement in France, and to that extent the two kings were agreed. But otherwise they were not agreed. Henry sought to make the British Isles part of a Valois empire. Philip realized that it would be the ruin of Spain and the Habsburgs. He could best avert ruin by the Habsburg marriage for Elizabeth, which would bring England into the circle of the Habsburg states. But that decision rested with Elizabeth, and if she decided to stand out and maintain her independence, he would still be obliged to support her, or see the French take England.

A few facts of early 1559 may illustrate the position. In February, when the English were claiming the restitution of Calais, the French negotiators remarked that their dauphiness was Queen of England

and asked if they should hand over the town to her. The English northern magnates, who furnished or influenced the wardens of the marches and the defence of the border, were all Catholics and might declare for Mary Stuart and the French. Henry II was in no hurry to disband his forces at the peace, and kept troops and shipping ready for a move in his northern ports, while the talk in Paris was of transferring northern England to the Scottish crown. The French nature, it seemed, needed a dream of conquest, and Italy had been given up for the British Isles to take its place. De Feria from England sent warning to Philip, who did not need it, and ordered his ambassador to dissemble chagrin at the religious tendencies and aid the English to show a united front to France. That last was the crucial factor in the decision of the Queen and Cecil to follow their own policy of English independence. They knew that whatever they did Philip must support them against the French; and secure in that knowledge they proceeded to do things that he greatly disliked. The religious settlement was one, and another was an audacious treatment of the Scottish problem.

Northumberland's withdrawal in 1550 from Somerset's active Scottish policy had left the French to assert their control. Mary of Lorraine, the queen-mother, succeeded Arran as regent, and French troops held most of the strongholds, while the young queen was brought up in France and ultimately married to the dauphin. Scotland remained in the papal allegiance, but its Protestant element was considerable and increasing, a situation in any country, as has been noted, that offered no finality or stability. In 1555 Knox returned and made many converts, and two years later the Calvinist movement took form as 'the Congregation', whose 'Lords' included some of the peers of the realm. Religion was not their only inspiration, and fear of French dominance made them ready to join hands with the new England of Elizabeth. Knox, who had gone back to Geneva, came again to Scotland in the spring of 1559, where his preaching initiated an uprising that was clearly revolutionary, with aims of substituting Protestant for Catholic worship, confiscating church property, evicting the French, and perhaps deposing the French-owned Queen of Scots. The rebels had enthusiasm, but no discipline, munitions, or money. They desired Elizabeth's aid, and their noble leaders had visions of a union of the realms, to be attained by the marriage of Elizabeth with the young Earl of Arran (Châtelherault's son), who had a colourable claim to the Scottish throne.

Elizabeth, young as she was and new to statecraft, showed all the wariness and scepticism of an old hand. She disliked the Calvinist plan of the church governing the state and filling the throne, which was in effect what the Lords of the Congregation had in mind. She had a strong feeling that her position as a monarch required her to maintain the rights of fellow-monarchs and discountenance rebels. She distrusted the new Scottish comradeship for England, coming so suddenly after ages of jealousy and hatred, and doubted if it would last. She desired proof that the Scots were really in earnest and would fight to a finish. One part of the scheme she rejected at an early stage. Young Arran came secretly to London on his passage from Geneva into Scotland. There Elizabeth saw him and decided that he was unbalanced and no husband for her. Her judgment was borne out by the fact that the unfortunate young man did in the event become permanently insane, although in 1559 there were great hopes of him. As for the alliance with the rebels in its broader aspects, although there was so much against it, there was urgent necessity in its favour. Everyone, including the rebels themselves, judged that by themselves they would fail and that the ample forces available in France would make a complete conquest of Scotland. It would be followed by the invasion of a disaffected northern England, after which a tale of ruin would unfold. Cecil was clear that the Scots must be supported, although he was no military adventurer. Neither was his sovereign, but she was constrained to agree with him; and they set about their purpose in a manner that was to be characteristic of many transactions in the course of the reign.

The first stage of the Scottish revolution was achieved by mid-summer, when all central Scotland was in the power of the Congregation and the French troops under D'Oyssel had retreated to Dunbar. On the spot it seemed that Calvinism was triumphant, but Knox and the other leaders knew better. Large forces were preparing to sail from France, there was no means of stopping them on the sea, and no hope of withstanding them on land; for the success had hitherto been that of mobs and rioters against a handful of unpopular foreigners. The mobs had virtually no firearms, no organized food supply, and no money to provide one. Their members turned out for a few days with such victuals as they could carry, and when hunger supervened they could only disperse. At that juncture Henry II of France was suddenly removed by a fatal injury received in a tournament (30 June 1559). In years to come it was to be seen that with him died the vigour of the Valois monarchy, but no one realized that at the time. The dauphin succeeded him as Francis II, with the Queen of Scots as Queen-consort of France and openly claiming to be Queen-regnant of England. Her relatives became the directors of French policy—the Duke of Guise, captor of Calais and saviour of Metz, and the Cardinal of Lorraine, able diplomatist and ultramontane Catholic. They were her uncles, while their sister, her mother, awaited succour in Scotland. There was no doubt that succour would be sent. The accident at the Paris tourney made the peril to Scotland and England more imminent though perhaps less deadly.

D'Oyssel, who at one stage looked like being driven right out of Scotland, managed to hold on while reinforcements began to arrive. He transferred his base to Leith, a better harbour than Dunbar, and in November recovered Edinburgh, which the Congregation had occupied. Next month the French took Stirling and crossed the Forth from Edinburgh into Fife, with the hope of capturing St. Andrews, the spiritual capital. The Lords of the Congregation saw their own forces melt away for the reasons already explained, and the Calvinist enthusiasm damping into depression. Money and munitions were their need, and England alone could supply them.

It was a hard decision for Elizabeth to make, to aid Calvinists and rebels, to risk regular war with France, to imperil the support of Philip the Catholic even while serving the interest of Philip the Habsburg, and to postpone if not destroy the bright prospects held out by the activities of Gresham. To her credit she made it, and by so doing ensured that Scotland and England would take the course of Protestantism, union, and independence. She made the decision, but she prudently disguised it and talked down its significance in order to blind the Catholic world to the fundamental challenge it conveyed. As early as August the mobilization of a small force on the border was considered, but Cecil had to admit that the lack of resources was then so great as to preclude useful action. In the autumn the Queen sent small sums, £3,000 at a time, to the Scots, and one of these consignments was lost when the Earl of Bothwell seized it to his own use. Meanwhile, however, Gresham's munitions were pouring across from Flanders, and Elizabeth was raising dust clouds to dim French vision by talking hopefully of the Archduke Charles and reviving Catholic symbolism in her royal chapel. It began to appear that she was not so Protestant as she had seemed. In fact she was using her growing resources to equip a squadron of the Navy at Chatham. It sailed under William Winter as the year closed, and in a stormy January took three weeks to reach the Forth. But the same weather wrecked French ships and drowned French troops, and on balance profited England.

The English admiral's name was an obvious lead to the sooth-sayers, who immediately discovered a prophecy that when Scotland should see two winters in one year great things would happen. In fact they did, for a fleet in the Forth dominated eastern Scotland as two hundred years later a fleet on the Coromandel coast decided the fate of eastern India. It revived the confidence of the Congregation and brought over waverers to their side and, by cutting their com-munications across the estuary, it caused the French to evacuate Fife. Coupled with English money and munitions, it brought a Scottish army permanently into the field. That winter the war took the pattern of a French occupation limited to Edinburgh and Leith, the latter heavily fortified, and an opposing force, less professional and less well armed, slowly gathering strength to attack.

Hitherto the English help had been informal, and Winter had been left to attack French shipping on his own responsibility. In February 1560 England signed a treaty with the Scots at Berwick, where the Duke of Norfolk had arrived with a small English army. It was agreed that the joint forces should drive out the French, although the monarchy of Mary Stuart was to be preserved; and if the French in-vaded England the Scots were to aid in its defence. Pessimists told Elizabeth that French military power would crush her and that Philip, outraged by her alliance with Calvinists, would connive at her ruin or even take part in it. She, however, relied on her information of some facts to the contrary. Gresham reported that the Spanish govern-ment in the Netherlands was hopelessly in debt and unable to finance a campaign; and that the Queen's support of the Scots had made her more influential in the Low Countries than Philip himself. Sir Nicholas Throckmorton, the English ambassador in France, sent news of a growing Huguenot movement and a conspiracy, not limited to Huguenots, against the ascendancy of the Guises. In mid-March the Tumult of Amboise confirmed the information, with a threat of serious revolt against Guise and the cardinal. Elizabeth saw that she had the enemy on the wrong foot and despatched her troops across the border before the end of the month. Lord Grey, their com-mander, joined the Scots outside Edinburgh, and the venture entered its last stage.

The last stage consisted of the siege of Leith, protracted by the gallantry of the French and the incompetence of their assailants, but decided nevertheless by sea power and Elizabeth's correct reading of the European situation. Cecil went north to negotiate the surrender, and Mary of Lorraine died just before it took place. The Treaty of Edinburgh, signed on 6 July, expressed the result. The French forces were to withdraw from Scotland, and its government was to be by a council of twelve, seven chosen by the absent Queen of Scots and five by the Scottish Parliament that was shortly to meet; and the Queen of Scots was to renounce the use of the royal arms of England and, by implication, her immediate claim to the crown. As often happens in such settlements, the most important consideration was not mentioned, although it was none the less settled by the contingent circumstances. There was no word about religion and the position of the Catholic Church in Scotland; but next month the Scottish Parliament met and repudiated the Pope, abolished the Catholic services, and dissolved the monasteries. In little more than a year Calvinism had effected a complete and final reformation in Scotland, the last and cleanest piece of work in its kind that Europe was to witness.

13

POLITICAL PERILS AND ECONOMIC RECOVERY

IF the Elizabethan settlements can be grouped under one phrase, national independence, the story of the reign is, in one aspect, that of the defence of what had been decided by the autumn of 1560. Just as the Queen's character remained much what it was when she came to the throne, so her life-work continued as the fulfilment of the programme laid down in her first two years. There were, however, other aspects than that. If the essential Elizabeth was static, the nation grew and changed. The national Church, and the national independence, established at the outset, made their marks upon the people. Economical and sensible administration improved their fortunes. Success gave them confidence. The record of Elizabethan England is of a nation rapidly increasing in strength, ceasing to fear this and that and taking its high position for granted, and looking out from its impregnable island upon a world no longer limited to the narrow seas and the coasts of Europe, but stretching east and west to girdle the globe, and north and south beyond the confines of existing knowledge. 'There is no land unhabitable nor sea innavigable': so had written Robert Thorne when the century was young; but the Elizabethans were the first to print his words and seek to make them good. They began slowly and gained speed as they progressed. It may even be argued that the real Elizabethan age did not begin with the reign, but ten years later, and that the first decade was of preparation rather than achievement.

The Church took some time to settle down. There was no haste to get rid of the Marian bishops, who were not all disposed of till near the end of 1559. They were better treated than their Edwardian predecessors had been—no martyrdom, only a spell in the Tower for the more emphatically resistant, and for the others comfortable residence as state guests billeted upon their supplanters. Heath, the Archbishop of York and Mary's Lord Chancellor, lived at large on his own estates. In their places the Queen appointed Protestants. As Archbishop of Canterbury she chose Matthew Parker, a retiring scholar with no wish for high place. He protested his unwillingness, but he had to serve. Elizabeth, as usual, had judged well. Parker, for all his dislike of the high hand, could be firm when duty demanded it, and he helped to seal the new Church with the qualities of toleration and comprehension, while propagating the discipline that springs from good example and unselfish leadership. The other bishops were for the most part moderate men, of middle-class origins and unbrilliant talents, who accepted the settlement and did their best to confirm it. Some of them were exiles of the Marian period, who had lived in the Swiss and German cities and had grown more Protestant than the Queen sometimes liked. With them Puritanism came into England, if we may use the word vaguely to denote a Protestant wing that emphasized direct communion between a man and his God, and disliked intermediaries in the guise of controlling priests with their apparatus of vestment and ritual. This English Puritanism was not identical with Calvinism. Some but not all of the Puritans were Calvinists, with a well-defined doctrine of church government that cut clean across the relations of church and state established in England. They were always a minority, with a narrow strength derived from logical thought pushed to its conclusion. The Puritan majority were not of that sort, but loyal members of the English Church, tolerant and shrewd, with no more liking for uncharitable image-breakers than for priestly image-makers. Cecil was one of them, and Nicholas Bacon, and later Francis Drake and John Hawkins, typical of the whole middle stratum of Englishmen.

The new bishops had much to do in their dioceses. Reports from various sources agree that the parish clergy were in poor state, unspiritual and ignorant, with little hold upon the laity, and that in practical effect church and religion hardly existed. The evidence is good, but it must not be read as of universal truth. There were places where religious teaching was effective. In Plymouth in the 1560s, for example, the restored Protestant services were established in orderly fashion with a real hold upon the people, and were regularly conducted in the ships that sailed out of Plymouth over the

ocean. This we know on chance evidence [1] such as has not survived
for other ports, but may well have been true for them also. In the
north and north-west much genuine Catholicism survived, itinerant
priests still celebrated mass, and the justices, themselves Catholics,
habitually ignored the collection of fines under the Act of Uniformity. In the south there was a period of turmoil in 1559–60, in which
the substitution of communion tables for altars was accompanied by
destruction of images and ornaments, and by other changes effected
by an ebullition of Protestant zeal. Some practical zealots carried off
bells and lead roofing, which had their money value. The Queen
herself, in appointing the new bishops, took possession of lands
belonging to their sees, but her needs were those of the nation and
her profit was not private. In 1563 John Foxe published his famous
work commonly known as the *Book of Martyrs*, of which part had
already appeared in Latin during his exile in Switzerland. Foxe's
book became the history of the Protestants, and four more editions
appeared before the end of the century.

Cecil received little gratitude for the success of the Scottish intervention, which had been his policy more than any man's. He
returned from negotiating the Treaty of Edinburgh to find the
Queen dissatisfied that he had not extorted the restitution of Calais
from the French and, as a mark of her disfavour, declining to allow
him the expenses of his journey. But this was only temporarily true,
and Cecil was fully compensated within a year. The Lords of the
Congregation hoped to round off the treaty by marrying the Earl of
Arran to Elizabeth and so creating in that generation an effective
union of the kingdoms, about which they spoke in terms as enthusiastic as Somerset had used a decade earlier. On personal grounds the
Queen was wise to refuse the offer, although a personal sacrifice on
her part would, to all appearance, have won a glittering political prize;
for Mary Stuart was in France and likely to remain there, and Scotland,
which had not seen her since she was a child of six, was quite ready
to shed its allegiance to her and her Guise maintainers. Cecil, who
knew Arran, was silent about the proposal, but he was anxious to see
the Queen honourably married, and his preference at that time was
for the Archduke Charles.

The tradition of Gloriana, the virgin queen, moving with her
worshipping people through a forty years' honeymoon of increasing

[1] The statements made in the Mexican Inquisition by John Hawkins's men captured
in 1568 at San Juan de Ulua.

mutual love, and, strong in that love, disdaining the aid of any foreign husband, belongs to the latter half of the reign, when queen and people made it. In the earlier years, and particularly among the ruling classes, there was no such feeling, but rather a belief that a woman's reign was a nuisance and would probably be short, and that its best outcome would be that the woman should produce a male successor as speedily as possible, after which she might depart unregretted. The only experience the English had of regnant queens was of Queen Mary. All therefore wished Elizabeth to marry without delay, since if she were to die without issue civil war was almost certain and foreign invasion very probable; and responsible men like Cecil wished her to marry a prince who would bring strength but not dominance to the English throne. The Archduke was the obvious candidate, a younger son of the less powerful branch of Europe's greatest house, an eminent but not a dangerous match.

Cecil's dejection then was great when he returned from Scotland to find his mistress apparently infatuated with Lord Robert Dudley, the younger surviving son of Northumberland, and representative of the most hated family in England.[1] In 1559 there had been talk of the Queen's favour for Dudley, a married man who did not bring his wife to London. In the summer of 1560 she was continually in his company and heaping favours upon him. People said that his wife would be disposed of and Elizabeth would marry him. He had taken Cecil's place as confidential adviser, and Cecil was contemplating retirement from public life. Suddenly in September the scandal became acute when Dudley's wife Amy Robsart was found dead with her neck broken at the foot of a stair. It was probably accident, possibly suicide, possibly murder; and if the last, by no means certainly of Dudley's contrivance, but more likely that of his servants who thought to gain by opening his way to fortune. The effect on the Queen's reputation was damaging, and ultimately it made her marriage to Dudley, if she had ever contemplated marriage, impossible. That could have been foreseen and is enough to acquit both of them. The French took up the tale with glee, for it opened a prospect of a mighty reversal of fortune. Philip's ambassador de Quadra reported that Cecil was virtually dismissed, which was no bad news in that quarter, for Cecil had been too good for Spain as well as for France. But by the end of the year the whole sensation

[1] For the Dudley courtship see Milton Waldman, *Elizabeth and Leicester* (1944).

was cooling down, the Queen remembering her duty, Cecil restored to Council, and Dudley reduced to intriguing with de Quadra to forward his suit.

It is not really likely that Elizabeth meant to marry him or anyone else. To a queen as to any other woman in that time a husband was a master, and she was already a devotee of the great game of governance and statecraft that had to be played from a lone hand. All experience shows that, once having tasted power, neither men nor women are ready to give it up. Elizabeth saw that she had to choose between incompatibles, and she chose power. Some have accounted for her refusal to marry by the supposition that she had a physical defect that forbade it. There was a rumour to that effect in 1559–60, and de Quadra retailed it in his despatches. There was also a rumour that she already had a child. About the alleged disability it can only be said that well-informed men like Cecil and the Earl of Sussex, who must have heard of it, obviously did not believe in it. Cecil took the marriage projects very seriously. Sussex, almost alone of the nobles, was ready to approve the Dudley marriage, because he held that England wanted above all things an heir, and he did not care by whom begotten.

To the end of 1560 Elizabeth's position remained difficult, and in the view of enemies critical. France under the rule of the Guises did not accept the defeat in Scotland. The threat of a Huguenot revolt had prevented the sending of aid to Leith at the vital time, or so the Guises liked to think, forgetting Winter's fleet and the sea power based at Chatham. The Huguenots had since been mastered, with numerous executions and confiscation of estates, and Guisan France was eager to reverse the Scottish decision. The French government refused to ratify the Treaty of Edinburgh, or its queen-consort to renounce the use of the royal arms of England, and French armaments began again to grow ominous. Then, in December, Francis II died after a brief illness, and Mary Stuart was no longer Queen of France. The successor was Charles IX, brother of the dead king and a boy under age. Neither the Duke of Guise nor the Cardinal of Lorraine had any right to the regency, which fell to the queen-mother Catherine de Medici. She was no lover of the Guises, whose ambitions she feared. She had domestic problems to deal with, and the threat to England and to Scotland faded out. For a short season the domestic affairs of England claim chief attention.

Cecil had clear ideas of things that should and should not be done in the interests of prosperity. He worked for the contentment and good order of the people, for the restraint of selfish exploitation of land or anything else, for the promotion and protection of industries that would aid the national defence, and for the expansion of trade and the fisheries. In the Parliament that met in January 1563 he promoted a comprehensive act for social settlement. Craftsmen were to attain their status by an apprenticeship of not less than seven years, covering usually the ages from fourteen to twenty-one. As apprentices commonly lived in their masters' houses, this was designed to keep youth under discipline and to prevent too-early marriages and neglect of children, as well as for the more ostensible object of a thorough learning of the trade. All who had not served their apprenticeship and could not prove themselves tradesmen were obliged to seek work as agricultural labourers. This, provided there were not too many of them, would answer the question of what to do with the vagrants and sturdy beggars: they must, on pain of the stocks and a flogging, hire themselves out to the farmer at wages fixed by the justices in relation to the cost of living. Another enactment dealt with the impotent poor, for whom, for the first time, the parish authority was enabled to levy a rate on the inhabitants.

With regard to the land, Cecil, as a former adherent of Protector Somerset, was in favour of restricting enclosure, and his Act of 1563 took 1528 as the reference year. All land that had been tilled for four years since that date was to be kept perpetually in tillage, and no existing tilled land was to be converted to pasture. The expressed purpose was to prevent the depopulation of villages. Commissions were sent out to watch over the working of the Act, but it is evident that some enclosure continued to be made, especially towards the end of the reign. It must be remembered that although enclosure caused an outcry, there were many people, not alone among the landlord class, who desired it, not only for private gain but for public good. Thomas Tusser, the contemporary poet of agriculture, himself a small farmer, said that enclosed land produced much more than champion or open field and conferred the liberty that made men 'bold of their own'. Local depopulation made vagrants and criminals, greater production benefited the community as a whole. Cecil and a school of active reformers whom we shall meet later in the reign were for avoiding and curing the immediate evil first.

Rearmament had been carried out, thanks mainly to Gresham's ability, but its cost had made an impression on Cecil. England's necessity was Antwerp's opportunity, and the guns and powder and armour had not been cheap. Bronze ordnance was then reckoned superior to iron, and to make it England possessed the tin but lacked copper, to say nothing of the other metals that would pay for it. In 1561 a company was formed, later known as the Society of the Mines Royal, to discover and work gold, silver, copper, and quick-silver, with power to intrude upon the rights of landowners in certain counties. The crown was to receive one-tenth of the metals won and had power to buy the remainder at privileged rates. The Mines Royal got a German engineer to take charge of the work, and from 1564 was producing good quantities of copper and silver, mined chiefly in Cumberland and Westmorland. By the end of the decade the output of copper exceeded the rather limited demand, and the Queen was taking her ten per cent royalty in cash, since the copper was hard to dispose of; but this aspect of the national defence was provided for, and in a few years England became an exporter of artillery. A little later than the Mines Royal another concern known as the Mineral and Battery Works was established, also under Cecil's patronage. It prospected for iron ores and for calamine, the ore of zinc, and not only produced the raw metals but also manufactured iron and brass wire, and such articles as metal wool cards. It found calamine in Somerset, iron in the Forest of Dean, and coal near Bristol. It ran iron wire works in Monmouthshire and brass works in Nottingham and London; and its factories, apart from its mines, employed 8,000 hands. Although the more ancient Sussex iron industry produced a different grade of iron, unsuitable for wire-drawing, it appears to have turned out iron guns. These enterprises were obviously important to the expansion of trade and industry, as well as to defence; and they formed only one department of Cecil's broad policy. His method, as in other matters, was not state owner-ship or even detailed state control, but state encouragement and co-ordination of private enterprise.

Other industries promoted in the 1560s for their value to defence were powder-making and the growing of hemp. It was not forgotten that in Mary's war the bottom of the last powder-barrel had been in sight, and the Elizabethan government did what it could for self-sufficiency. The saltpetre, however, had to be imported, in spite of efforts to obtain a native supply. The imports came from the Levant, and the business was further complicated by the decline of the Mediterranean trade in the first half of the reign. English rope-making and canvas-making were successful to a point, but the products were not so good as those obtained from the Baltic. Gunpowder and naval stores were things that had to be provided, and the necessity had sometimes more influence on policy than historians have accorded it. Timber for shipbuilding had been hitherto obtainable in sufficient quantity in England, although our woodlands did not produce the greater masts and spars. The increase of iron-smelting by means of charcoal was overtaking the native timber supplies by the mid-Tudor period, and a measure of 1559 prohibited the use of oak and other timber growing within fourteen miles of navigable water, with an exception for the iron industry in the Weald of Kent and Sussex. There was a real incompatibility between the needs of the iron industry and those of defence, and the industry had to give way. Until the discovery of methods of iron-smelting by means of coal the greater part of England's raw iron continued to be imported.

In 1560 a notable Englishman came home from Russia. He was Anthony Jenkinson, who had succeeded Richard Chancellor as the leading representative of the Muscovy Company in foreign parts. In the previous year, Jenkinson, who stood well with the Czar Ivan IV, had travelled by boat down the Volga to the Caspian Sea and thence overland eastwards to Bokhara. He was reconnoitring the ancient 'silk route', whereby the products of China and the Far East came through interior Asia to Aleppo and Damascus and thence to the ports of the Levant. His idea was that the English in Russia might tap this trade stream and divert it up the Volga to Moscow and thence to Archangel, thus making it a monopoly of the Muscovy Company. Jenkinson found the overland trade through Asia greatly diminished and hampered by an anarchy of robber chiefs and warring tribes, but he learned that in Persia, to the south of the Caspian, conditions were better. After conference with the English government he went back to Russia, and in 1562, again with the Czar's support, he travelled south to Persia. There he found the elements of a valuable trade and a situation complicated by the fact that all Persian produce for Europe was passing through the hands of the Turks in the Levant. He did however succeed in establishing an English trade. For more than a decade, strange as it may seem, the Muscovy Company was selling English wares in Persia and buying Persian goods, transporting them by the Russian waterways from the Caspian to the White Sea, and thence shipping them through the

Arctic to England, all at a substantial profit. The end came in 1579–80, when Turkish armies overran Persia and turned off the northern 'tap'; whereupon, as will be shown, London enterprise formed the Turkey Company to obtain direct through the Mediterranean what the Muscovy Company had lost by its northern roundabout. These were the seeds of the East India Company. In Elizabethan history they were more than seeds, a vigorous growth of risk-taking initiative practically doing the things that the previous generation had only talked about.[1]

While Chancellor was opening the first English trade with an Asiatic country, John Hawkins was doing the like with Spanish America. He was the son of William Hawkins, the Plymouth pioneer in Guinea and Brazil, and his plan of action differed from his father's. He had made trading voyages to the Canary Islands and was acquainted with influential Spaniards there. He proposed to capture negroes on the African coast and sell them to the Spanish colonists in the Caribbean, having first touched at the Canaries on the outward voyage in order to send word to the colonists of his coming. The existing slave trade was being conducted by contractors who bought the concession from the Spanish crown and made the planters pay highly for the slaves. Hawkins was in a position to undersell the monopolists. He also intended to take out English manufactures, for which there was a good market in the West. He did not wish to do this in defiance of the Spanish government, but rather to induce it to transfer the contract to himself in return for honest and efficient trading and for fighting services which he offered against the Turks in the Mediterranean and, it is fairly evident, against the French corsairs who were raiding the Caribbean in spite of the lately concluded peace. Hawkins's voyages of the 1560's were thus not intended as a challenge to good relations with Spain but as an offer of practical Anglo-Spanish co-operation. It must be confessed, however, that he began them without any permission from Spain, and continued in spite of the Spanish government's prohibition. The Queen had considerable hopes of their utility and invested in them for the profit of her naval funds. Other investors were members of the Privy Council, officials of the Navy Board, and leading merchants of London. The Queen appointed Hawkins her officer and allowed him to sail under her royal standard. Unfortunately Philip II took a

---

[1] In 1525 Henry VIII had entertained an Italian captain named Paolo Centurioni, with exactly this project of trading with Asia through Russia.

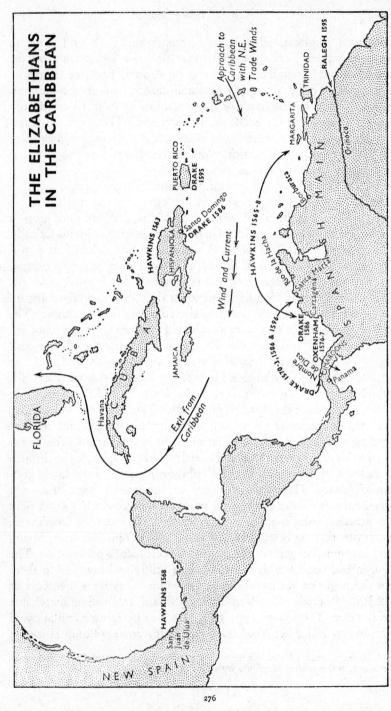

THE ELIZABETHANS
IN THE CARIBBEAN

Approach to
Caribbean with N.E.
& Trade Winds

RALEGH 1595

TRINIDAD

MARGARITA

Orinoco

PUERTO RICO
DRAKE
1595

Santo Domingo
DRAKE 1586

HAWKINS 1565-8

Buenaventura

HISPANIOLA

HAWKINS 1563

Wind and Current

Rio de la Hacha

S   P   A   N   I   S   H   M   A   I   N

Santa Marta
Cartagena
DRAKE
1586
OXENHAM
1576-7
Nombre
de Dios
MAROONS
Panama

DRAKE 1570-3, 1586 & 1596

C   U   B   A

JAMAICA

Havana

Exit from
Caribbean

FLORIDA

NEW   SPAIN

HAWKINS 1568

San Juan
de Ulua

276

less favourable view of the proceedings. He regarded them as an infringement of his sovereignty and a menace of the spread of heresy, and sent orders that trade by the English was not to be allowed. His officers and subjects in the colonies welcomed the supplies that Hawkins brought and made every excuse to disobey their king. This was the pattern of four successive expeditions, three of them commanded by Hawkins in person, that sailed in the period 1562–7. Although Hawkins was conducting a prohibited trade, he was a trader and not a pirate; and Cecil, who would never countenance piracy, took an active part in the management of the voyages and the diplomacy that arose from them. He regarded the new trade as a useful element in the economic recovery for which he was working.

Mary Stuart as a widow found her position in France unpromising, since Catherine de Medici, the queen-mother of Charles IX, disliked her and her Guise relations. In 1561, therefore, Mary decided to return to Scotland, although she knew that as a Catholic sovereign her power would be limited by the Calvinist kirkmen. She sailed to Leith in August, to begin an active reign of which the first four years were relatively peaceful, under an uneasy and mutually suspicious toleration between herself and her subjects. To Elizabeth the presence of Mary in Scotland was unwelcome, for the succession question was undecided and Mary, as a candidate, was in a position to intrigue with Elizabeth's Catholics. At first an ostensible cordiality prevailed between the queens, with suggestions for their personal meeting to come to an understanding. The price of firm peace, however, would have been the formal acknowledgment of Mary as heir to the English throne. To that Elizabeth could not consent, since her safety amid English factions and foreign foes lay precisely in the uncertainty about what would follow her death. She knew also how people were apt to rate favour with the coming sovereign before loyalty to the existing one: she had been an heir-presumptive herself. To refusal of recognition Mary could counter by refusing to ratify the Treaty of Edinburgh, which negatived her claim to be rightful queen of England. The dynastic situation thus remained threatening.

It was only gradually realized that the peace of 1559 was the end of an age and the beginning of another. The Habsburg-Valois contest was over, and the wars of religion were about to begin. Statesmen, not being prophets, could not know that and had painfully to learn it from the events of the following decade. The Tumult of Amboise in 1560 was a warning of civil war in France. The subsequent death of Francis II thrust the Guise party from power and left them to meditate recovery by force, and allowed to the Huguenots a place in Catherine's councils. In March 1562 the Duke of Guise rode with an armed escort to Paris and on the way massacred a Huguenot congregation who were holding a service at Vassy. It was the signal for war, the first of a series that were to rend France for a generation and reduce the Valois monarchy to feebleness. A year later disorder and resistance to Philip's rule began in the Netherlands, never to be effectually ended in the lifetime of any contemporary. These developments, coupled with the problems of Scotland, were to form the conditions of the Elizabethan defence of England and its religion.

Superficially it might appear that the situation in France resembled that in Scotland two years before. In fact there was a considerable difference, which events were to emphasize; for while in Scotland the Calvinists were the majority and their movement an expression of the national patriotism against alien rule, in France the Huguenots never carried the country with them and their movement was that of rebels who weakened the state. In 1562 this was not clear, for reports spoke of Protantism sweeping the country as it had done in Scotland. Throckmorton, the English ambassador, was a friend of the Huguenot leaders, and his information about them was perhaps too sanguine; for he wished Elizabeth to strike a blow against the Valois monarchy and head a Protestant crusade.

Elizabeth had not been very eager for the Scottish intervention, which had been mainly Cecil's work, but she was prepared to give aid and countenance to the Huguenots, and did so against the opinions of the majority in her Council. Her reasons were, firstly, a distrust of Philip II's intentions and a fear that he would aid the Guises to dominate France, reinstate themselves in Scotland and encircle England by an ultra-Catholic ring; and secondly, a hope of recovering Calais or some other port of entry into northern France. As against these motives she had a genuine dislike of rebels and a sense of shame in giving them assistance, and she certainly did not wish them unlimited success. She would have preferred to see the Huguenots neither conquering nor conquered, but sufficiently 'in being' to check Guise ambitions and sufficiently dependent on herself to allow her an effective voice in French policy. These considerations were very similar to those that were shortly to govern her in dealing with the revolt of the Netherlands. They amounted to a defence of

England by keeping the Catholic powers at war or under threat of war on the continent.

In April 1562 the Queen accordingly offered her mediation in the commencing war between Catherine de Medici and the Guise brothers on the one side and the Huguenots on the other. Catherine rejected the offer, perceiving that mediation would make England without expense or risk the patron and supporter of the Huguenots. Elizabeth then treated directly with the Huguenots and in September signed with their leaders a secret treaty whereby she was to send 6,000 troops to their aid and lend them 140,000 crowns, and they were to see that Calais was restored to England. Half of the English force was to garrison Le Havre until the surrender of Calais. This intervention turned out to be a bad investment, because the Huguenots turned out to be the losing side. In October they lost Rouen. In December they were beaten at the Battle of Dreux. In March 1563 they had to lay down their arms and accept the Peace of Amboise, which involved their complete abandonment of their English allies. On the cold view the murder of the Duke of Guise by a Huguenot in February was the only gain to English security from the whole affair. In sending troops to France Elizabeth had been careful to proclaim that she was not at war with the French king, but was assisting those of his subjects who were trying to deliver him from Guise coercion. None the less she held on to Le Havre after the French had come to terms among themselves, since its tenure gave the only hope of obtaining Calais. The reunited French besieged it. For month after month the little English garrison, decimated by plague and continuous attack, held out under Ambrose Dudley, Earl of Warwick, brother of Elizabeth's suitor. Sea power threw in some succours, but the plague was decisive, and Warwick capitulated for the honourable withdrawal of his remnant at the end of July. In the following April England and France signed the Treaty of Troyes, whereby the English claim to Calais was abolished for a French payment of 120,000 crowns.

Elizabeth's venture had failed, and she had spent a good deal more money than she received from the French, thereby retarding once more her emergence from the Marian bankruptcy. She had thenceforward a lower estimate of the Huguenots than they were to deserve. For this first war led to changes in their leadership and their methods. They had lost it because they relied solely on troops in the field, and since they were but a minority among the people of France they were never likely to turn out a preponderant army. Their titular head was the Prince of Condé and their real control was with Admiral Coligny, whose firmness and foresight amounted to genius. Coligny it was who made the Huguenots a maritime power, with a fleet of privateer cruisers based on La Rochelle, a very tough nut for Catholic military power to crack. The results were to be seen before the decade was out.

Parliament was called in January 1563 to grant supplies for the war in France. It passed the social and economic legislation that has already been described, and concerned itself anxiously with the succession to the throne. Lady Catherine Grey, the heiress of Henry VII's younger daughter Mary, had the best claim by existing English law, while Mary Stuart, grandchild of the elder daughter Margaret, had that by the ordinary rules of descent, although debarred by the legalized will of Henry VIII. Between them it seemed that England could not hope to escape the 'regiment of women'. Elizabeth, as we have seen, had no mind to recognize any successor, and had already put Catherine Grey in the Tower for marrying without permission, an offence which she aggravated by giving birth to a son. But three months before Parliament met, Elizabeth had nearly died of an attack of smallpox, and the whole country was insistent that an heir to the throne must be recognized as the only hope of averting civil wars if the vacancy should arise. The Queen was determined not to name an heir, and without positively saying so she put off the decision until the Commons had passed the money bill, and then prorogued them without an answer. There seems to have been no great party at this time in favour of Mary Stuart. The Parliament had in both Houses a Protestant predominance, and enacted the extension of the oath of supremacy to several categories of subjects who had hitherto not been required to take it, including members of the House of Commons.

The attitude of Spain was in these years a serious anxiety to Elizabeth, for Philip's reasons for and against hostility were so evenly balanced that there was no certainty which policy he would follow. The personality of Spanish ambassadors had therefore an unusual interest, since they were sufficiently distant from their master for their day-to-day decisions to be out of his control, and they thus wielded considerable influence on the conduct of Anglo-Spanish relations. The first of the reign was Count de Feria, a stupid and over-bearing man who could not divest himself of the idea that he was the agent of England's overlord, a conception that Elizabeth lost no time in showing him to be out of date. Philip withdrew him in the spring of 1559 and replaced him by Alvarez de Quadra, Bishop of Aquila. De Quadra was clever and plausible, seeking to maintain communications with everyone about the court and to impress his employers with his ability. His letters to Philip and the Regent of the Netherlands are the source of much of our information about the Dudley affair and the privately-expressed views of the Queen's circle, but there is considerable doubt of their veracity. In one of them Cecil is represented as imparting to de Quadra things that we can hardly believe he would have told anyone, least of all a semi-hostile foreigner. It raises the suspicion that de Quadra collected gossip and fathered it on responsible men. In any case there was not much harm done, for de Quadra carried little weight with the Queen and her ministers and not much with his own employers. He died in 1563 of the plague that the English survivors brought home from the siege of Le Havre. His successor was Don Guzman de Silva, a well-balanced and broad-minded man and undoubtedly the most serviceable of the series to the interests of peace. He alone of the five Spanish envoys of the reign conducted his business without making evident the Spanish sense of superiority that England found so irritating, and he was able to remain on friendly terms with Cecil and the Queen while speaking plainly when occasion demanded it.

Spain and England had supported opposite sides in the French civil war, and events at sea made their relations yet more strained. English privateers captured shipping from the Catholic ports of France and claimed, as twenty years earlier, the right to take French goods out of neutral ships. This caused intense indignation in Spain, especially as privateering degenerated into rank piracy coupled with some atrocities inspired by religious hatred. Martin Frobisher robbed Flemish ships in the Channel. Thomas Cobham, brother of a peer, took a Spanish vessel in the Bay of Biscay and deliberately murdered a friar whom he found on board. In one of the captured ships the pirates stole personal property of Philip II, some rich hangings on their way from the Netherlands to Spain. 'Who began it' is generally a futile topic, but it is fair to say that in the minds of their perpetrators atrocities on priests were reprisals. The Inquisition had long been active against Englishmen in Spain. In 1561, for example, there had occurred the case of John Frampton, merchant of Bristol, who was deprived of his ship, goods, and 2,000 ducats in cash, three times racked, and sentenced to live perpetually under surveillance of the Holy Office at Seville, all for having in his cabin an English book suspected to be heretical. At the same time occurred the similar case of Thomas Nicholas, an English factor in the Canary Islands; and these were typical of others.

The mixture of religious and economic tension extended to the Netherlands, where popular wrath was swelling against the civil government and religious persecution. Protestant pamphlets printed in England were smuggled in through Antwerp, and refugees in thousands were already coming over to London. The old disputes about the validity of the Magnus and the Malus Intercursus were revived, to the disquiet of the merchants on both sides. Late in 1563, the plague then raging in England, the Netherlands government made it the occasion to stop commercial intercourse, and this proved to be the first event of a series that broke the ancient bond between England and the Low Countries. The ultimate destination of much of the cloth exported to Antwerp was Germany, and the Merchants Adventurers were quite ready to transfer their activities to a German port. Hamburg offered facilities, but for a first experiment Emden was chosen, and in 1564 a fleet of 40 merchantmen conveyed thither a rich consignment of cloth and many traders and factors to sell it.[1] Antwerp at once gave way and offered resumption on favourable terms. The Merchants Adventurers accepted it, but the old standing of the London-Antwerp trade connection as a law of nature had received a blow that was soon to be repeated. Cecil's papers show that he desired to free England from a relationship that had in the past hampered her liberty of action. His and the Queen's financial ability was breaking one of the bonds. By devoting much of the Parliamentary subsidy of 1563 to the paying-off of foreign debt they had reduced the total owed at Antwerp to less than £25,000 by 1565. Netherland disturbances thereafter made it impracticable to borrow there in any case, while the growing wealth of London ultimately enabled the Queen to raise her loans at home.

Important as were English dealings with the Huguenots and the Netherlands, the most urgent questions in foreign affairs during these years centred on the Queen of Scots. With her claims to the English throne her prospective re-marriage was of vital interest to Elizabeth. At home Mary governed with moderation and wisdom for the first four years after her return in 1561. The Protestant kirk

[1] See E. Lipson, *Economic History of England*, vol. ii (1947 edition), pp. 197–202.

continued free and established with John Knox at its head, Catholics and Protestants sat in the Council, and Mary herself was considered by ardent Catholics to be lukewarm in their religion. Her two most effective ministers were Protestants, Maitland of Lethington, some-times called the Scottish Cecil, and Lord James Stuart, better known by his subsequent title of Earl of Moray, Mary's illegitimate half-brother. It is untrue to represent Elizabeth as the enemy of Mary. She wished her well and, knowing the difficulties of a reigning queen, felt genuine sympathy for a woman in the same position as herself. But she had to guard her position, and fate had placed Mary in the rôle of its assailant. Elizabeth, especially while her own marri-age was still a negotiable proposition, could not afford to recognize anyone as her presumptive successor, because that successor would immediately become the head or the figurehead of a dangerous fac-tion. In Mary's case it was particularly inadmissible, since the threat-ening faction would be the Catholics of England, whom the Queen's policy was seeking to disarm by kindness and convert into loyal and dependable subjects. If everyone were looking to a Catholic succes-sion, all that would be undone. Not only had Mary a general right to what Elizabeth must refuse, the succession, but she had a Catholic right to immediate possession, and had asserted it by assuming the royal arms of England. The Treaty of Edinburgh had stated that she would renounce that right, but she had never ratified the treaty. On the contrary, she was demanding its revision. These questions were tortuously negotiated, without enmity but without result, until 1565. Meanwhile it was evident that if Mary should marry a powerful Catholic prince England would again face a hostile Scotland and the threat of 1559. One proposal for Charles IX of France failed through its inherent unattractiveness, for he was a youngster ten years her junior and also her deceased husband's brother. Another for Philip II's son Don Carlos was more realistic and full of menace for England. Fear of the French gaining Scotland had made Philip sup-port Elizabeth, much as he hated her religious proceedings. The prospect of gaining Scotland himself would make him her active opponent, and for a time in 1563–4 he was ready to offer his son, until the diplomacy of both Elizabeth and Catherine de Medici, who thought alike on the subject, brought the project to nought. The effect of its canvassing was to make evident a diplomatic revolution that was completed by the Treaty of Troyes in 1564. England and France as represented by Catherine de Medici ceased to be hostile, and England and Spain took one more step towards mutual hostility; but it was somewhat uncertain and undecided for some years to come.

It was generally agreed that Mary, who was far less master of Scotland than Elizabeth was of England, would seek support by a marriage. Elizabeth and Cecil wished her to marry an Englishman, provided that he should be of their choosing and a Protestant. As the Don Carlos project cooled off, Elizabeth proposed (in March 1564) Lord Robert Dudley, whom shortly afterwards she created Earl of Leicester; and the fact that she was genuinely eager to see him married to the Queen of Scots is a caution against our sentimentalizing her feelings towards either of them. Mary, however, would only consider Leicester if he were coupled with her desires on the succession and treaty revision, which Elizabeth had no mind to concede, while the Scottish councillors regarded the offer of him as something like an insult; and so this suit also failed to prosper.

An English husband for Mary would not be in Elizabeth's interest if he should be a Catholic, and that was precisely the danger that next raised its head. Henry VII's daughter Margaret, after becoming the widow of James IV, had married a Douglas, and their resulting daughter had married the Earl of Lennox. The Lennoxes had for many years been political refugees in England, and there in 1545 their son Henry, Lord Darnley, was born. Darnley therefore, nineteen years old in 1564, was technically an Englishman; he was also a Catholic, and he was of Tudor descent. There had been doubts and aspersions cast on the Douglas marriage of Margaret Tudor, and the English official view held the Countess of Lennox to be illegitimate. Darnley had nevertheless a Catholic following in the north of England and was a possible Catholic candidate for the throne. In the autumn of 1564 the Earl of Lennox returned to Scotland after long years of exile. Early next year he summoned his son Darnley to join him. Elizabeth, either of her own motion or by Cecil's advice, gave Darnley his passport. The result was that before the summer was out Darnley was married amid Scottish rejoicings to the Queen of Scots. The Scottish claim to the English throne was consolidated, and Mary's husband was a Catholic Englishman. Elizabeth appeared to be, and had ostensible reason to be, greatly chagrined. It seemed that she had blundered in permitting Darnley to go to Scotland when she could have detained him for a while as she had detained Catherine Grey in the Tower. He was her subject, and none could have gainsaid her right to forbid him to leave the country. In fact the Darnley marriage was to result very shortly in the ruin of the Queen of Scots, and some said even at the time that Elizabeth had a foresight that it would be so, and a Machiavellian cunning in facilitating it. The explanation is too far-fetched for credence, and it is sounder to suppose that Elizabeth did make a mistake over Darnley and was genuinely crestfallen at its result. After all, she had no reason to compass Mary's ruin, which was to bring infinite annoyance and danger to herself.

Wide-ranging minds were concerned with more extended ambitions than those of European politics. The Muscovy Company, as we have seen, was pushing its trade through Russia to Persia. Its leading pioneer, Anthony Jenkinson, was intent on making contact with the Far East. His travels into Central Asia had convinced him that there could be no through trade by that route, and he was now seeking to persuade the Company to send another expedition by sea to open up the North East Passage along the Siberian coast. At the same time there was a revival of the North West project. Old Sebastian Cabot, who claimed in his youth to have discovered it, had died in England towards the close of Mary's reign, leaving maps and writings that expressed the nature of his claim. Richard Eden, the translator of the *Decades*, had been the old man's friend and disciple, and he wrote of the Passage as something beyond doubt. A man of action, Sir Humphrey Gilbert, was convinced by the evidence, and sought means to equip an expedition to follow the Passage through to Asia. There were thus two rival schools of thought on the achievement of an all-English route to eastern Asia. Both Jenkinson and Gilbert looked for aid to the Muscovy Company, whose privileges included the monopoly of north-western as well as north-eastern discovery. But the Company was satisfied with its existing business, and did not intend to adventure farther. The Queen and Cecil were interested, but not to the point of spending hard-saved treasure. In 1566 the two captains staged a disputation before the Queen, in which they set forth their proofs and arguments, but there for the time the matter rested. The Queen's policy on discovery and the opening of new trades was simple and consistent throughout her reign. She would give benevolent approval but not public money. If the project were promising enough it could find its own support in the City. Failing that, it was not a proper object for public expenditure. British expansion was to be no pampered nursling born with a silver spoon in its mouth.

Hawkins meanwhile was prospering in his triangular trade with Guinea and the Spanish colonies. He followed his first sale of slaves in Hispaniola with a second and larger expedition to the plantations of the Spanish Main in 1564-5. He worked for Philip's approval but failed to gain it. In 1566, while Hawkins in London was speaking fair to de Silva, the Spanish ambassador, and protesting his readiness to serve the King and not to trade without permission in the Indies, he nevertheless despatched the usual slaving expedition under another captain. Next year he set out in person at the head of a larger squadron than he had ever equipped, comprising two ships of the Queen's and four of his own. This expedition quitted Plymouth in October 1567 on what was to be known as 'the third, troublesome voyage' of John Hawkins. When Hawkins began his ventures in 1562 there was still some semblance of alliance between England and Spain and some hope that it might be revitalized. By 1567 the alliance was almost dead. Philip was determined to have no heretics resorting to his Indies. He had already smitten with a heavy hand a venture of Coligny's Huguenots. They had established a little colony in Florida, and a Spanish force wiped it out in an almost complete massacre. The Huguenots, it is true, were open enemies of Spain, and their Florida post was intended as a base for raids in the Caribbean; but its extinction encouraged Spanish exclusiveness and made it certain that the English, even if they appeared in the guise of friends and behaved as honest traders, would not be admitted.

Sir John Neale's work on Elizabeth's Parliaments is a new passage of history giving a new emphasis to the record. It shows in general that the Puritans were already the most active religious force in the country, and that they were strong not only in the towns which elected them to Parliament, but among the country gentlemen whom the towns were increasingly choosing as their members. It gives the presentation of a House of Commons in which the beginnings of a party organization were taking shape, backed by a vigorous pamphlet propaganda outside, and in which on a division the Puritans commanded a decisive majority. The Commons also were claiming freedom of speech and initiation on topics distasteful to the Queen, although not yet attaining its clear realization. Yet on the great question of the succession in 1566 the Queen did withdraw her veto on debate. Altogether the effect is to date back into the first Elizabethan decade some of the phenomena afterwards prominent under the early Stuarts. But there was this difference: the opposition was completely loyal, and if it questioned the Queen's wisdom on the succession it did not attack the general beneficence of her rule. As a member said, its criticisms were 'the wounds of a lover'. No Puritan was to be moved to say that to Charles I.

Parliament, prorogued from 1563, met again in the autumn of 1566. The Queen's purpose was to obtain supply; that of the Houses, in more Protestant mood than ever, was to get the succession settled, certainly not in favour of the Queen of Scots, but presumably in that of Catherine Grey. Fear of Catholic revival or civil war made the succession now a more urgent question than the Queen's marriage, and the Queen was almost alone in her judgment that the matter was best left unsettled. On her refusal to discuss it the Commons grew mutinous, and Paul Wentworth led an open opposition by questioning her right to limit the subject of debate. A deputation of the Lords met with a hot reception from their sovereign, with general threats and pungent personalities. Finally it all blew over. She withdrew her prohibition of debate and diminished the amount of money she had asked for, and the loyal Commons were content to disperse without being any nearer a decision on the succession. They cannot be blamed for their anxiety about it, for the peace of England hung on the Queen's life. Neither she nor they could know that she was to outlast the century. To her it appeared that, once her successor was known, serious trouble was certain, and in her concluding speech she denied that she was moved by selfish reasons. She had indeed some motives that could not be publicly explained. Foreign affairs were again threatening, and Philip II had to be persuaded that she was not a disturber of his peace. To appear in dissension with her more Protestant subjects was an aid to her general policy. She was renewing, as part of it, her talk of marrying the Archduke, and again a settled succession might tie her hands. Her perennial difficulty with members of Parliament was not that they lacked loyalty but that they knew nothing of diplomacy, and would insist on blaring to the world matters that should have been discussed in whispers. Wentworth and his like were no doubt founders of English liberties, but they were unconscious comforters of the Queen's enemies. The Puritan extremists might have used Katherine Grey as the focus of an intrigue to force the Queen's hand. Their encroachments were unceasing, and Elizabeth, in spite of her concessions, found the session intolerable. She fought hard to avoid any settlement of her marriage or of the succession. It can be seen now that she was right, and that the risks of 'meddling' might have been fatal. Yet no one could be sure, and the decision was a gamble, with the country's life, and the Queen's, at stake.

In these years an opposition to the Queen and to Cecil as her chief counsellor was taking shape and hardening. In one respect it was Catholic, in another conservative. The northern earls, Northumberland and Westmorland, were Catholics, with almost royal authority over their own tenants, and well supported throughout the North. The young Duke of Norfolk, grandson of Henry VIII's Norfolk, was not an avowed Catholic but was sufficiently in sympathy to make it possible that he would conform if the time should come. The Earl of Arundel, of older nobility than the Howards, was also a virtual Catholic, although he had disapproved of Mary's persecution. These two represented the conservative dislike of newly risen men in the Council and of policies that flouted the principles of the time-honoured alliance with Spain and the Netherlands; and with them was connected the Catholic Lord Montague, while there were others more or less in sympathy. The Earl of Leicester hovered between the two sides, jealous of Cecil and anxious to supplant him, yet realizing that he had less than nothing to hope from a victory of Cecil's opponents. Leicester is sometimes found supporting the administration and sometimes intriguing against it. The general purposes of the opposition may be summarized as the elimination from the Council of Cecil, Bacon, and the 'upstarts', the strengthening of the Spanish alliance, and the recognition of Mary Stuart as heir to the throne, the whole tending inevitably to a Catholic restoration. The amount of support that this programme would obtain from the people remained to be seen.

The marriage of the Queen of Scots soon began to turn out badly, for to a woman bred in civilized ways Darnley was an impossible husband, an unlicked cub, arrogant, ignorant, and stupid, who claimed a preponderant share in government while devoting his time to the company of stable-boys. Mary soon regretted having married him, and before six months had passed she was slighting and ignoring him, while he fumed and meditated ways of asserting himself. The emotional disturbance seems to have had a serious effect on Mary, who abandoned the circumspection with which she had hitherto ruled and began to take pronounced and perilous steps in the Catholic direction. Even before this was generally apparent the Kirk party took alarm and Moray headed a rising to keep the Queen under Protestant constraint, only to be defeated and chased south across the border. Elizabeth sent him money, but could give no armed assistance for fear of provoking a French reappearance in Scotland. Mary, on the other hand, requested men and money from the Pope, and appealed, not to France but to Philip II, for advice and protection. It was another step in the diplomatic revolution already noted. As Mary had put down her rebels without much difficulty, it was obvious that papal funds and Spanish countenance were for a further purpose, which was indicated by the dismissal of the English ambassador from Edinburgh early in 1566. Whatever its details, that purpose was in general to stir up a Catholic rising in England and to aid it with an armed force. It was frustrated by the results of Mary's domestic proceedings. She had virtually discarded Maitland in favour of an Italian adventurer David Riccio, who had wandered to Scotland as a musician and found himself promoted to be the Queen's secretary and suspected to be her lover. The fury of Darnley was the opportunity of his former opponents the dissident nobles. Some were in Scotland, Moray and others in England. They agreed with Darnley to advance his power in return for their own restoration to influence and for guarantees to Protestantism. On 9 March, 1566, Darnley and his friends dragged Riccio from Mary's presence and murdered him outside the door, while Moray and the exiles were already on their way back to Edinburgh, where they were readmitted to the Council.

A year of crude melodrama followed, in which statesmanship gave place to passion. Mary fooled her husband by a pretended reconciliation that enabled her to drive the other murderers into exile, although Moray, who had come on the scene after the murder, retained his position. Next, in June 1566, Mary gave birth to a son, who was christened James and was thought by some to be Riccio's.[1] On Moray's advice she adopted a less extreme attitude towards England and made a reasoned plea for her claim to the succession on the ground that Henry VIII's will was invalid. Elizabeth could not have yielded even had she wished, for her Parliament in the autumn was far too Protestant and insistent for a Protestant succession. Darnley meanwhile was again at odds with his wife and seeking the aid of the Catholic powers in his own favour. She now openly sought

---

[1] Long afterwards, when Henry IV of France commented on James VI and I's designation of 'the modern Solomon', he remarked that James was, like Solomon, 'the son of David that played upon the harp'.

to be rid of him, and discussed measures with Moray, Maitland, and others. Divorce was talked of, and resort to the Scottish Parliament with some idea of annulling the marriage without bastardizing the young prince, but murder was at the back of all minds. At the end of 1566 Darnley was ill of smallpox near Glasgow. As he was recovering in January, Mary visited him and brought him to Edinburgh. The Earl of Bothwell, a Protestant of the Council, but always her adherent, lodged him in a house called Kirk o' Field. On 10 February 1567, while Mary was away at a wedding, the house was blown up, and Darnley's body was found strangled in the grounds. There was no doubt that Bothwell had done the murder, and that Mary wished it. That she actually knew that it was to be done is an open question depending on the genuineness of the papers known as the Casket Letters.

For the murder of Darnley alone it is probable that Mary would not have lost her throne. The indignation of the people was aroused by her subsequent proceedings. Lennox, the father of the victim, charged Bothwell with the crime, and the court was so packed and intimidated in favour of the accused that his accuser dared not appear and Bothwell won the case by default. All the world was already commenting on Mary's favour to Bothwell when in April he kidnapped her, with her own connivance, and kept her in his hands while he divorced his wife. When that was done he and the Queen of Scots were married at Edinburgh. The whole country was possessed with fury, and the people spoke of their sovereign in terms unprecedented even in that unbridled age. Moray and the Protestants took the field against her and captured her without a fight on 15 June, 1567. Next month they forced her to abdicate in favour of her son, with Moray as regent. They then imprisoned her in Loch Leven castle, while Bothwell fled overseas, to die later in Denmark. Within a year Mary was out again. In May 1568 she escaped from Loch Leven, raised a force among the Catholic Hamiltons, and tried to make a stand against Moray's troops at Langside. The regent won easily, and Mary rode hard for the border, with death as the alternative to crossing it. On 17 May she was on English soil, demanding English aid but abating not a jot of her claims against Elizabeth.

14

THE ELIZABETHAN AGE TAKES SHAPE

THE entry of Mary Stuart into England was the beginning of a period of crisis, to which other events unconnected in purpose and separated in locality were to contribute. In 1567 the Duke of Alva arrived in Brussels to begin a new treatment of the mutinous Netherlands. In that year also began the second civil war in France, and Huguenot cruisers sailed from La Rochelle to prey upon all Catholic shipping. Four months after Mary's arrival in England an act of treachery and bloodshed took place in the distant Gulf of Mexico, which ended Hawkins's hopes of a peaceful western trade and revealed in a flash the relations that were thenceforward to prevail between aspiring England and possessive Spain. For several years past the old affiliations of the European powers had been slowly breaking down, and it now became apparent that new ones were taking their place.

Twenty years of judicial bloodshed had failed to stamp out Protestantism in the Netherlands, and after the accession of Philip II the Calvinists even grew in numbers and truculence. In 1566 they were openly conducting their worship, assembling in large bodies, and destroying images and desecrating Catholic churches; while at the same time the nobles and gentry, for the most part Catholics, were protesting to the King against the repressive methods of his deputies and the obliteration of the ancient liberties of the provinces. Philip from distant Spain spoke fair but determined on more effective repression: he would rather, he wrote to the Pope, lose his life and his crown than be the sovereign of heretics. In 1567 he sent his best soldier, the Duke of Alva, to collect 10,000 Spanish troops from the garrisons in Italy and to march them north by the Alps and the Rhineland to the Low Countries. There the Spanish regiments formed the *corps d'élite* of a larger army recruited from the Walloons of the Belgian provinces and from German mercenaries beyond the border. The army, drilled and disciplined as Alva knew how, held down the whole country, while its chief proceeded to execute dissentients by the thousand and to assure his King that all was being done without violence. This army of Spaniards and satellites, not existing until 1567, became an international factor of the first importance, not least in the calculations of Cecil and the Queen of England. Its first objective was evidently the extermination of Netherland liberty and Netherland Protestantism, but, having achieved that, it might turn its attention to the liberty and Protestantism of England, and it is not surprising that English statesmen should not view its successes with pleasure or give any aid in promoting them. The English people of London and the east, hearing the tales told by the refugees arriving from the Netherlands, became more anti-Spanish than before, and ready to show sympathy in many practical forms with Alva's victims and opponents.

Suspicion, intolerance, and violence in France led to the second civil war, which began in 1567 when the Huguenots had been foiled in an attempt to seize the person of Charles IX. Both sides engaged German mercenaries, but the results of six months' marching and fighting over central France were indecisive. The really important occurrence was the inauguration of the Huguenot privateering campaign from La Rochelle. That port became the citadel of the Huguenot cause, attracting the Protestant seamen of northern France and, before long, English adventurers also. The war nominally ended in March 1568, but it was only a truce, broken within six months by a Catholic design to capture Condé and Coligny, who escaped and concentrated the Huguenot strength at La Rochelle. The truce scarcely affected the activities at sea, for it was always easier to let loose privateers than to curb them. Some booty was brought into La Rochelle, some into Plymouth or Southampton for sale, and the profits financed the Huguenot cause. Whether at the outset Coligny saw further than that is uncertain, but by the end of 1568 it was apparent that he had called into existence a new weapon not only against the Guises but against Catholicism in general, the weapon of a Protestant sea power that impoverished its opponents, damaged their prestige, and fostered discontent among their subjects. Coligny not only forged the weapon but saw clearly the enemy against whom it must be turned, not essentially the Guise party but the King of Spain. Events were making Philip the commander-in-chief of the Counter-Reformation, in which capacity he was becoming the patron of the rigid Catholics of France. Already there was mutual sympathy between him and the Guisan leaders, a connection destined to ripen into formal alliance in later years. Catherine de Medici, with her son Charles IX, sought to stand firm between Guises and Huguenots, controlling both, but commonly she was too weak to maintain the position. During the wars of 1567–70 she ranged herself with Lorraine and Henry, Duke of Guise (son of Francis, murdered in 1563), but she dreaded the powerful patronage of Philip II, whose growing influence in France boded ill for her boy Charles IX.

The Protestant navy soon had an English element. Where twenty years earlier Devon and Cornwall had been Catholic to the point of rebellion against the Prayer Book, they were now Protestant to the point of war against the Catholic powers. Coligny's brother Châtillon came over to England with commissions from Condé and the Queen of Navarre to distribute to English adventurers, authorizing them to make war not only on the Guisan Catholics but on 'all the enemies of God otherwise called papists', which included Spaniards and Catholic Netherlanders. By the end of 1568 fifty ships, thirty of them English, were cruising with Condé commissions, whose validity the English government recognized and so lifted the plundering out of the category of piracy. Sir Arthur Champernowne, Vice-Admiral of Devon, had two ships at sea with his son in command, Martin Frobisher had three, and William Hawkins, mayor of Plymouth, was owner or part-owner of several. This William Hawkins was the son of Henry VIII's William Hawkins and brother of the John Hawkins then away in the West Indies. The mayor of Plymouth made his port an emporium of captured goods, while farther up Channel the Solent and Southampton were a similar mart more accessible to buyers from London. In all this the profits were more obvious than the religion, but there was an undertaking of 1569 which had no such sordid flavour. The gentry of the south-west equipped a body of horse to fight under Coligny on land. Young Walter Ralegh joined it, and saw a year of hard service with heavy casualties before the third war came to an end. Their standard bore the motto *Det mihi virtus finem*, and to many of them it did.

Sir William Cecil once wrote that piracy was detestable, and he meant it; but he did not regard these proceedings at sea as piracy. To him they were a defensive war against a Catholic attack which he saw maturing against Protestants in all countries, his own included. In 1568 William of Orange and his brother had tried to unseat Alva by leading German mercenaries over the Netherland frontier, but they had been routed and driven out. The Netherlands became uneasily quiet, and the fighting transferred itself to France. To Cecil it was imperative to support Coligny, for if the cause went down on the continent the next scene of conflict would be England. In December he sent a consignment of guns and munitions to La Rochelle. The Queen agreed with Cecil, although with a sigh over the necessity for supporting rebels, a thing which she greatly disliked but had found herself doing, or was about to do, in three several countries. The conservative members of the nobility and the Council regarded the policy as immoral and certain to lead to disaster, and the breach in English ruling circles widened. The advent of a new Spanish ambassador contributed to the same end. In 1568 Philip withdrew de Silva and sent in his place Don Guerau de Spes, a man openly anti-English as England stood then, who conceived it his mission to conspire with treason and stir up discontent in order to force Elizabeth to abandon her Protestant ministers and return to the Marian policy of papalism and subservience to Spain.

Into this England of doubts and perplexities came Mary Stuart, escaping with bare life from her infuriated subjects. She expected Elizabeth's immediate aid in restoring her by force of arms. Elizabeth of course could not do that, for Mary was in a wildly vindictive mood, and the outcome would have been the destruction of Moray and the pro-English Protestant party and the establishment of an ultra-Catholic régime attracting French or Spanish troops to its support. Elizabeth herself was anxious to have Mary restored with safeguards for the security of England, because countenancing rebels, distasteful enough in France and the Netherlands, was a doubly dangerous example in Scotland and might lead to the dissolution of all moral inhibitions against treason in northern England. Yet no safeguard could be devised. Mary was impervious to reason and defiant of restraint. Elizabeth, as one of her advisers said, had the wolf by the ears and could not let go lest she be mauled. Mary at Carlisle held court for all the Catholic gentry of the Marches, who visited her in swarms and went away glowing at her wild femininity, her courage, her misfortunes, and her zeal for religion. At all costs she must be removed from the border, and in July she was taken south to Bolton Castle, in Yorkshire. She claimed a personal interview with Elizabeth for the settlement of a joint policy.

To accord an interview on equal terms would have been incompatible with any subsequent restraint of the Scottish queen; and restraint, for a time at least, was appearing to be the only possible course. Elizabeth could not thrust her over the border undefended, for the kirkmen would have killed her. Cecil pointed out that to let her go to France would revive the whole threat to Protestant Scotland and the English throne, and undo all that had been achieved since 1559. In England she had to stay, and to stay, moreover, not as Elizabeth's equal and the heir to the throne, but as a queen already deposed (as she had been by her own subjects), her sovereignty and heirship transferred to her infant son, with Moray the head of the Protestants as his regent. That, however disguised in kind words, was the essence of Mary's position thenceforward.

In the course of the exchanges of argument Mary had offered to meet Elizabeth and clear herself of the charges made against her by Moray and his party. This undertaking was diverted to the holding of an enquiry at York before commissioners named by the English queen. Mary was represented in the expectation that she was to be restored with or without the consent of Moray. He attended on the summons of Elizabeth to justify himself, which he conceived he had ample evidence to do. The Duke of Norfolk and two others were the English commissioners, appointed to hear information and report it to their Queen, but not to hold a trial or pronounce any sort of judgment. It is therefore no criticism of the conduct of the proceedings that they were inconclusive. It was never professed that they were to constitute a trial, and indeed Mary would not have submitted to the jurisdiction. The business opened at York in October, but hung fire. Moray wanted a guarantee of English support of his regency before he would make public allegations that would entail war to the death between himself and Mary. Elizabeth would not guarantee anything to anybody, but expected all others to commit themselves while she kept a free hand. Norfolk, who had just lost his third wife, was privately contemplating a fourth, the Queen of Scots herself, to be whose fourth husband was a matrimonial risk indeed, but one carrying a gambler's chance of a throne. Norfolk therefore was not anxious to drag damaging evidence into the light; neither were Maitland and others of the Scots, who had had their own fingers in Darnley's murder. The result was that the parties to the enquiry shuffled and intrigued, while Moray confidentially let the English see his trump card, the letters found in a casket belonging to Bothwell and purporting to have been written to him by Mary.

These documents,[1] if genuine, proved that Mary had been a party to the murder of her husband for the sake of Bothwell's love. If forged, they proved nothing. Argument has swayed round them from that day to this, and cannot be summarized here. Every student must make his own choice, and the choice will be mainly influenced by subjective factors. That of the present writer is that they were probably genuine, and that the possibilities of forgery of that type of document were too remote for likelihood. The originals early disappeared, and the controversy has revolved on copies.

The enquiry having got so far, Elizabeth transferred it to London, where it reopened at the end of November before a commission strengthened by the addition of Cecil, Bacon, and Leicester. Here the Casket Letters were formally produced, and were subsequently read to six English peers not included in the commission. Mary denied writing them and withdrew her representative, the Bishop of Ross. A war-scare between England and Spain was looming up, and Guerau de Spes was assuring her of Philip's support. The Spanish king was for the third time a widower, and there was even mention of his marriage to the Queen of Scots; but it was not followed up, and history thereby was deprived of one of its choicest jests. Elizabeth allowed the conference to end in January with the announcement that nothing had touched the honour of Moray and that nothing had been proven against Mary. The letters nevertheless represented a good deal alleged, and most people, including her foreign friends, believed that they told the truth. Mary was committed to the care of the Earl of Shrewsbury and detained at Tutbury in Staffordshire. Her presence in the country, with all her pretensions unabated, served to clarify party aspirations. The loyalty of the majority to Elizabeth became firmer, while northern and Catholic discontent looked for some definite satisfaction. Guerau de Spes, early making contact with the discontented, was writing in November of an approaching restoration of England to the Catholic religion.

Cecil was alive to the Spanish intentions and knew that they could only be carried out by means of armed revolution, aided most likely by the Spaniards in the Low Countries. He, perhaps earlier than other statesmen, had ceased to think of European problems in terms of

---

[1] Eight letters, twelve love sonnets, and two contracts of marriage, all in French.

Habsburg against Valois and was viewing them as of Catholic against Protestant. To him Spain was the citadel of one religion and England of the other, while Scotland, France, and the Netherlands were contested, with results not yet decided. To England it was vital to maintain the Protestant cause abroad, failing which England herself would be assailed by overwhelming forces. Moray must be supported in Scotland, Coligny at La Rochelle, while in the Netherlands Alva was a menace, first as an exterminator of Protestants there, and second as a prospective invader of England. Cecil did not wish to see England at war, but he knew that the Catholic menace must be fought. He was prepared to support the Huguenots with arms, money, and men, unofficially so long as it could be done, in open war if that were the only way; and if the Netherlands should rise in effective revolt he would help them likewise. Intellectually the Queen agreed that he was right, emotionally she had a mystic sense of the sanctity of royalty which forbade her to give more than half-hearted support to rebels; and she had her grandfather's economic dislike of war as not only uncertain but wasteful. She had other counsellors than Cecil, some of them, such as Norfolk, Arundel, and sometimes Leicester, bent on reversing all his policies.

An unexpected affair very nearly fired the Anglo-Spanish combustibles. In the autumn of 1568 Alva's army was in urgent need of money. In spite of the millions brought home annually by the plate fleets, the King had none in his treasury, and was obliged to borrow 450,000 ducats (about £100,000) in silver coin from the bankers of Genoa. This money was shipped up Channel from Spain in November in an unarmed ship and half a dozen pinnaces without escort or even secrecy. Cruisers from' La Rochelle chased the treasure-carriers, which took refuge, the ship in Southampton, the pinnaces in Plymouth and Fowey. As it was probable that the Rochellers would enter the ports and cut out the treasure where it lay, the next step was that the English authorities landed it for its own preservation and got it behind their fortifications. On hearing that the treasure was in English ports Guerau de Spes lost no time in requesting the Queen to turn out an armed force to escort it on its way to Antwerp. She replied that she would consider it. It was indeed a cool request when one remembers that the English feared and de Spes hoped that the use of this money would be to finance an invasion of England. De Spes became deeply suspicious as the days elapsed without the grant of an escort, and when he learned that the treasure had been landed he at once assumed that the English had appropriated it. In the existing situation, indeed, it was only common prudence to prevent it from reaching Alva. Sir Arthur Champernowne at Plymouth, to ease the Queen's action, offered to seize the stuff himself and endure her open displeasure so that he might enjoy her secret favour. Devious courses were, however, not required. The London agent of the bankers revealed to Cecil that the treasure did not become Philip's property until delivered at Antwerp, but remained legally theirs. Upon learning this the Queen borrowed the entire sum herself, much to the relief of its owners, who feared that if it were sent to sea again they would lose it for good. It was a lucky stroke for Elizabeth, at once hampering Alva and strengthening her own finances, at a time when Antwerp had ceased to be a money market and London was hardly ready to take its place. The loan was repaid when it fell due, and whatever term may be applied to the whole transaction, it was not robbery.

The Spanish ambassador was so certain that the English meant to keep the money that before they had actually done so he wrote to Alva that it had been seized, and urged him to arrest all Englishmen and their property in the Netherlands. Alva complied, committing thereby a breach of treaty, since a general arrest was lawful only after complaint of grievance and denial of redress. The Queen countered by arresting all Flemish and Spanish goods in England, to a much greater value, setting forth in a proclamation that she had been thus injuriously treated while considering the forwarding of the treasure to Antwerp. This took place in January 1569, and in February the English were arrested in Spain. Persons were soon liberated, but property was retained and trade was stopped, as it turned out, for years to come.

Guerau de Spes had bungled this affair, in which a man of de Silva's skill might have got the treasure through in spite of Elizabeth's temptations. Cecil had played carefully and kept on the windy side of the law throughout. He had not lost the Antwerp market without having provided for another to take its place. Meanwhile he had inflicted a sharp rap on Spain, which showed Philip that England did not fear his displeasure, and it remained to be seen how Philip would react. As Cecil had no doubt expected, Philip decided not to fight. He had too much to cope with, the sullen Netherlands, the perennial Turkish war in the Mediterranean, the Protestant cruisers in the Channel. He could not openly fight England, but he could make things unpleasant for the Queen by plotting with her malcontents, and Guerau de Spes was the man for that business.

While the arrests of trade were taking place and war appeared possible, at the close of January 1569, a young captain named Francis Drake, hitherto unknown, sailed into Plymouth with a tale that caused the local authorities to send him up to London for examination by the Privy Council; and five days later his employer John Hawkins anchored the Queen's ship *Minion* in Mount's Bay with her crew in so ghastly a state that they could not bring her on to Plymouth, but had to await the sending of fresh men from that port. In due course Hawkins told how on his third tropical expedition he had collected slaves in Africa and had traded successfully along the Spanish Main, supplying black labour and English wares to the colonists with their good-will, although with some resistance on the part of their governors, and how he had refrained from plundering, and had given honest value for the treasure he had obtained. Then, the trade finished, he had made for the exit from the Caribbean by the Florida Channel, but had been driven by a gale into the Gulf of Mexico. His flagship had nearly foundered and was unable to cross the Atlantic without repair. She was the *Jesus of Lubeck*, one of the decayed wrecks of Mary's Navy, which had been condemned to the breakers' yard in 1559 but afterwards reprieved. Hawkins therefore took his fleet into the Mexican port of San Juan de Ulua, whose batteries he occupied as a guarantee against disturbance while he dismantled his flagship. Soon afterwards appeared the incoming Viceroy of Mexico, Don Martin Enriquez, with the plate fleet of thirteen ships to fetch away the annual output of Mexican treasure. Hawkins was Elizabeth's officer, displaying her royal standard, and England and Spain were at peace. He felt it his duty to admit the Spaniards to the port, and did so with misgivings, which were justified three days later when the Viceroy made a sudden treacherous attack on him. The English, though many had been killed unarmed at the outset, made a great defence against odds. Finally Hawkins got away with the *Minion* and Drake with a smaller vessel, while the *Jesus* and several others and a number of men remained in the hands of the Spaniards. Hawkins left San Juan with two hundred men and no food. He landed a hundred in Mexico at their own request and struggled to cross the Atlantic with the remainder, of whom the great majority died on the voyage. Guerau de Spes wrote that only fifteen survived.

Hawkins's men had been recruited in London and Plymouth, and neither east- nor west-countrymen forgot the treachery of San Juan de Ulua. For them it was war with Spain thenceforward. The Queen was angry at the loss of her great ship, and the City interest realized that contact with the western tropics would not in future be by way of trade. In the spring of 1569 Hawkins wrote a short account of the affair which was published as a pamphlet for general information. Its truthfulness has been demonstrated by the recent discovery of Spanish documents that corroborate the essentials. The events of 1568–9 mark the end of all semblance of Anglo-Spanish amity and the beginning of a half-war or cold war of the sort with which the twentieth century is familiar.

The Rochellers continued their scouring of the Channel and its approaches, and rich goods accumulated in English warehouses. In the summer a great convoy sailed from London to inaugurate the new trade with Hamburg that was to replace that lost with the Netherlands. Already in 1567 the Merchants Adventurers under Cecil's direction had made a ten years' agreement with Hamburg for full trading privileges, the advantage to the city being that of serving as port of entry of cloth for all Germany. A few English ships sailed there before the Anglo-Spanish crisis arose, and then in 1569 William Winter with a naval squadron convoyed across the North Sea the richest English trading fleet of the time. Its main cargo was of English cloth, but it carried also the Spanish wines, eastern spices, and western hides and sugars that the Protestant cruisers acquired in the exercise of Condé's commissions. All went without a hitch, and the fleet returned in time to make another successful expedition in the autumn. To Cecil the supersession of Antwerp was in some sort the breaking of a fetter that inhibited English freedom in dealing with Spain.

In March 1569 the Protestant cause received a check at the battle of Jarnac, where the Huguenots were defeated by the Catholics. It was not in the military sense a great battle, but the Prince of Condé was killed with other leaders of note, and the political effect was considerable. It nerved the Catholic party in France to make an effort to overcome Coligny at La Rochelle, and it strengthened Cecil's opponents in the English Council, where they were able to talk of his folly in backing a rebel cause. La Rochelle needed help, and Cecil at first persuaded the Queen to send some ships of her Navy to give it openly. The French ambassador, La Mothe Fénelon, got wind of it and protested so strongly that Elizabeth was afraid of driving the Valois and the Guises to the point of war. She withdrew her official assistance and allowed the project to go forward under private leadership in the guise of a trading expedition. At the end of April fifty ships from London sailed down Channel, to be joined by a dozen out of Plymouth mostly belonging to the Hawkinses. They reached La Rochelle in mid-May and landed victuals, arms, money, and English volunteers, and brought away the plunder stacked on the waterside. Catherine de Medici was angry, but Elizabeth insisted that the business was nothing but normal trade by private merchants; and the fact that Coligny had been effectively strengthened prevented his enemies from fighting England. It must be remembered that Elizabeth and Cecil were countering what they considered to be a concerted Catholic movement to overcome Protestantism. Their policy was an aggressive defence, a calling of bluffs and a probing of weak points, all before that background of pressure at sea that carried the hope of liberty along every rebel coast.

As 1569 drew on, the Anglo-French Protestants at sea were joined by a third ally who ultimately overshadowed both. The Prince of Orange began to issue commissions to Netherland seamen to cruise against Catholic shipping, and the celebrated *Gueux de Mer*, the Beggars of the Sea, were the outcome. In 1569 there were not many of them, but next year they numbered over a hundred sail, many of the ships and men being English. They haunted the North Sea and the eastern Channel, and made Dover their base of supply and mart for the disposal of captured goods. Ships passing between Spain and the Netherlands thus had to elude the English and Rochellers in the western approaches, with Plymouth and La Rochelle as their ports; more Huguenots based on the Solent and Southampton; and lastly the Sea Beggars at Dover. The toll paid by Catholic trade was immense, and it is a wonder that any survived. Philip was convinced that open war with England, bringing the Navy out against him in addition, would entail the loss of the Netherlands; and so, in spite of all provocation, he sought to avoid formal war. He did not forget, however, that a change of sovereign in England could not make his position worse and might be very advantageous.

Whether the Queen or whether Cecil really formulated the policy that England pursued is a question not admitting a simple answer. Cecil gave advice based on the weighing of all factors and alternatives, as may be seen from his memoranda carefully contrasting reasons *pro* and *contra* a decision in debate. He certainly formulated policies, but they were not always those at once adopted, and he was often chagrined and sometimes despairing when they were shelved. The Queen, while respecting his wisdom, never allowed him or anyone to dictate to her. Intellectually she generally agreed with him, but her decisions, so far as can be seen, were not reached by purely rational processes. She had a faculty for which there is no exact definition and consequently no exact term: 'flair', 'hunch', 'intuition' are inexactitudes that serve to indicate it. Its extraordinary run of successes forbids us to describe it as mere gambling. Whatever it was, it sometimes led her to cut across reasoned policies and make illogical decisions, and sometimes to postpone and procrastinate when decision seemed urgent, and to pass weeks in apparent irresolution while difficulties solved themselves and all fell into place for decisive action at the end. Some of her major indecisions, as on marriage, the succession, and the treatment of Mary Stuart, were maintained for years against the pleadings of Cecil and all loyal subjects, and gave better results in the end than the workings of their reasoned wisdom might have done. In many things Cecil's advice prevailed and his influence was evident. On many great matters the Queen listened to others besides Cecil, and when she did not at once follow his counsel men were apt to say that he had lost his hold and that his fall was at hand. Occasionally he appears to have believed it himself, but it never came true. Elizabeth and Cecil were a partnership, a firm, that presided over Elizabethan England; but one partner was very clearly senior to the other.

In the spring of 1569 Cecil's position was strongly assailed by the reactionary nobles who regarded Norfolk as their leader. They desired to overthrow him mainly by reason of class sentiment, disgust that a man of middling rank should wield more power than men of title and lineage. Arundel was emphatic on this point, and others felt the same, and the precedent of Thomas Cromwell and his fall was present in their minds. They could challenge him on a simple issue, the claim of Mary Stuart to the succession. Cecil, like the Queen, was determined not to recognize it. The opposition wanted it recognized, with Mary's marriage to Norfolk as a further development, accompanied, in foreign affairs, by a reconciliation with Spain and abandonment of the foreign Protestants. On hard-contested questions of policy, particularly where foreign powers are concerned, there comes a point where opposition merges into treason. If the Norfolk party did not cross that border in 1569 they came near to it, for they corresponded with Guerau de Spes, who was confident that a revolution would take place. They tried hard to persuade the Queen to abandon her Secretary, and they even meditated a sudden arrest on the Cromwell precedent. But Elizabeth did not play her father's part, and in spite of all pressure she stuck to Cecil. Both realized that there could be no halting at the point where Mary should be liberated and accorded the second place in the kingdom. The end of Elizabeth's reign would follow swiftly unless, as was more likely, a civil war should protract the issue. Having shown that the Queen was on his side, Cecil conciliated his opponents in unessential matters, particularly Norfolk, who virtually took a bribe in the disposition of some disputed northern estates. Norfolk, however, clung to his plan of marrying Mary, not openly avowing it, but carrying on intrigues with the French. Elizabeth knew what he intended and forbade him to think of it. In September he left the court without permission and with rebellion in his mind. He made no attempt to translate thought into action, and was arrested and sent to the Tower in October. Arundel, Pembroke, and Lumley were also arrested. Leicester, who had sided with the men of high descent but had afterwards betrayed them to Cecil, got off with a wigging.

Meanwhile the other wing of discontent, the northern Catholics, had been working themselves up to open rebellion. Their leaders were the Earls of Northumberland and Westmorland, the first a Percy, the second a Neville, with generations of almost royal authority behind them. They and their tenants resented not only the new doings since the beginning of the reign, but also the new bishops, little power as they had in the north country, and the oath of supremacy, although it was scarcely enforced there. The new England was as yet but a threat to northern ways, but a threat that would grow. The North longed for a return to the Catholic world of the past, and the appearance of Mary Stuart gave the obvious opportunity. The people were chafing to be led. The nobles were full of doubt. Treason, even to their independent minds, was an ugly word, and failure meant personal ruin. They wanted to be sure of Norfolk and the southern malcontents. They had the promise of Guerau de Spes that Spain would send aid from Antwerp, a promise that he had no authority to give. In September, when it seemed that Norfolk would rebel, they were ready to join him. Then he faltered and advised them to keep quiet. They debated in irresolution and did nothing. Towards the end of October, with Norfolk a prisoner, the Earl of Sussex, President of the Council of the North, sent Northumberland and Westmorland the Queen's command to repair to court. They expected the journey to end in the Tower, and the order goaded them into rebellion, as perhaps it was meant to do. It was not that the Queen wanted a rebellion, but she (or Cecil) may have reasoned that it was bound to come and would be less dangerous then than later; for with winter setting in it was not likely that Spain would attempt any serious move across the sea.

The earls turned out with several thousand enthusiastic followers. They entered Durham and solemnly restored the Catholic worship in the cathedral. They occupied Hartlepool as a port of reception for Alva's expected aid. They were not strong enough to attempt York, and they failed to rescue Mary Stuart from Tutbury, since she had been removed to Coventry by her custodian the Earl of Shrewsbury. The possession of Mary could alone have prolonged the effort, and with that lost it began to collapse. Moray in Scotland occupied the border and prevented Scottish Catholics from moving to assist. Elizabeth and her Council took measures for raising adequate forces in the south. The test of rebellion showed that many grumblers were loyal and brought them out in support of the Queen. Even Norfolk's sympathizers were released and set to do their parts. Alva in the Netherlands would not send a man. He discerned every appearance of a fiasco and considered de Spes a meddlesome fool for inciting the rising, and his judgment was correct. Sussex, reinforced at York, advanced in mid-December, and the rebels dispersed without a fight. Northumberland fled to Scotland, to be handed over and executed three years later. Westmorland escaped to the Netherlands, never to return. A third northern magnate, Leonard Dacre, who could turn out 3,000 men, had not joined the rebellion. He had been disputing the possession of lands with Norfolk, and on the arrest of Norfolk was taken into favour by the government. He acted against the rebels of November, but himself rose in revolt in January 1570. Lord Hunsdon (Henry Carey, the Queen's cousin) marched against him with an inferior force and routed him, after which all was over but retribution. It was severe, on the principle that an example must be made in every village that had contributed men to the rebel army. Some 800 persons were hanged. Elizabeth has been blamed without stint for cold ferocity. She and England had faced an attempt at civil war and revolution that would have cost lives by thousands had it gone far, and would have ruined the material progress of eighty years. For her England the wars of the fifteenth century were a living and bloody memory; and she had tried mercy and reason first. Northern Catholicism had been most gently handled, and in her eleven years of rule no Englishman had been burnt for religion or beheaded for reasons of state.

Events in the three countries, Scotland, France, and the Netherlands, with whose fortunes England's were interwoven, must be briefly recorded. Before the Rising of the North was fairly over, the settlement in Scotland was imperilled by the death of Moray, who was assassinated by a Hamilton in January 1570. Moray was a wiser and more patriotic man than most of his fellow nobles, and a loyal and trusty ally to England; it must be confessed that Elizabeth sometimes returned him small gratitude for his services. His removal allowed Mary's party to take shape again. It also permitted the Scottish borderers to take the field on behalf of Dacre. Elizabeth punished this by directing her own forces to carry out the usual punitive ravaging beyond the border. She sent support also to the Earls of Morton and Lennox and procured the election of Lennox as regent for the young James VI. Thus Scotland remained in line with the Reformation. In France the latter part of 1569 witnessed a military campaign that at one point came near to a decision. After Jarnac there was a summer of marching and sieges in west-central France, in the course of which the Huguenots were joined by a body of German mercenaries who were able to force their way right across the country from the Rhine. With them were the Orange princes, William and his brothers Louis and Henry, whom Alva had driven out of the Netherlands in 1568. The year might have ended inconclusively but for an encounter in October that developed into the furious battle of Moncontour. Here Coligny was wounded and defeated with heavy loss, but, largely by the good soldiership of Louis of Nassau, the remnants made good their retreat. The victors expected a favourable peace, but La Rochelle was armed and victualled from the sea, and Coligny and the Queen of Navarre had no thought of surrender. Fighting went on through the winter and far into the next year, with an increasing tale of atrocities, until for the third time the parties came to terms in the Treaty of Saint Germain-en-Laye in August 1570. In the Netherlands, which Alva seemed to have completely cowed by his successes in 1568, discontent and potential rebellion gathered head again. The loss of the treasure compelled him to levy exasperating taxes that fell upon the loyal and the disloyal alike, while the rise of the Sea Beggars offered hope to patriots, and their depredations were a continual object-lesson in the principle that sea power can assail land tyranny.

The prospect of a northern rising in the autumn of 1569 was known at Rome, although the news of its occurrence had not been received when Pope Pius V decided to take action at the end of the year. In the greater part of England Elizabeth's policy of comprehension and toleration was bearing fruit, and Catholics were tending to regard it as an obligation of good citizenship to conform openly while semi-secretly receiving the ministrations of their own priests. This dualism was in the interests of peace and of ultimate fusion, but it was not favoured at Rome. In February 1570 Pius V, an austere and narrow man, issued his bull of excommunication and deposition against Elizabeth. It came too late to affect the issue of the rebellion, and it was not until May that copies were smuggled into England and one was found one morning posted on the Bishop of London's door. The effects of the bull were serious but not immediate. In fact it seemed at the time to have completely missed fire. Philip II, the only Catholic prince in any position to contemplate carrying it out, was annoyed at its issue and declared that the Pope had acted without consulting him. He had already decided not to go to war with England in his own quarrel, and had no mind to be the tool of another's. Those Catholics who had joined the northern rising had had their fill of rebellion, while those who had not were more disposed to congratulate themselves than to be moved by this new disturbance. Yet in the long view the Pope had struck a blow at English peace and unity. When in after years his emissaries followed it up, they could call on Catholics to renounce their allegiance and plot or fight against their country's government. Most were to refuse, but some were to comply, and from being loyal subjects to become disloyal. The Protestant majority—and by the 1570s the Protestants were the majority—knew it and did not underestimate the danger. Religious belief was linked with political disaffection; suspicion and harshness supervened on the mutual toleration of the 1560s. The papal power had sown the seeds of hatred, and hatred grew, not soon to die away.

Elizabeth was impressed by the issue of the bull, for she could only believe that the Pope had acted in concert with Spain or France or both. There was precedent for that in the attempt of Paul III to enlist both Charles V and Francis I in the execution of the bull against her father in 1539. Until it became evident that Pius V had no temporal support the Queen therefore resorted to an apparent change of policy in order to avert extremities. She talked of restoring Mary Stuart in Scotland and of ceasing to support the Huguenots in France. In terms of domestic politics it meant rejecting Cecil's views and turning to those of Norfolk and Arundel. The summer of 1570 saw Arundel strong in the Council and Norfolk released from the Tower, Leicester advocating their views, and Cecil seeking to be on good terms with Norfolk and going himself to Mary to discuss the terms of her restoration. How much of this was a sincerely meant reversal of policy and how much was play-acting only the Queen knew and perhaps Cecil guessed; and circumstances were soon to nullify it. The Scottish restoration proposal broke down, not on differences between Mary and the English, but on the refusal of the Protestant Scottish nobles to accept it. They had Mary's own hand to her abdication in 1567 and had given their allegiance to James VI, and they did not mean to go back on the decision. Elizabeth was angry, and Cecil no doubt pleased. As for France, the way to better relations acceptable to all opinions in England was opened by the peace of Saint Germain-en-Laye, and proposals soon began to be heard for a marriage between Elizabeth and Henry of Anjou, brother of Charles IX. The effects of the summer's politics and diplomacy were to relieve Elizabeth of immediate fear of hostility from France or from her malcontents in England. There remained Spain, with a grievance over the treasure and an injury from the Channel privateers, with an enemy of England in her London embassy, and with a king who was the most inveterate foe of Protestantism in Europe. Elizabeth had still to beware of Spain. An Austrian princess was to be Philip's fourth bride, and in the late summer of 1570 she was to sail from the Netherlands to Spain. Alva collected all the ships he could raise, and all the fighting gentlemen and their retinues as a royal escort. It was a necessity as well as a compliment in view of the adventurers then ranging the seas. But the English looked doubtfully on this armament. Scratch force though it was, it might do unpleasant things if suddenly thrown upon the English shore. Elizabeth mobilized her whole Navy under the Lord Admiral, ostensibly to do honour to the lady, in fact to see her escort safely through the Channel. All passed off with civility, and the tension eased. Spain also was not set on the immediate execution of the bull.

The alternative to open war was conspiracy, and here the Pope could take the initiative. A Florentine banker named Roberto Ridolfi had long been settled in London. He had been arrested in 1569 on suspicion of forwarding money to the northern rebels, but had soon been set at liberty. At the end of 1570, after a visit to Italy, he came again to England professing commercial business arising from the Anglo-Spanish arrests of trade. Cecil thought no harm of him, neither did Francis Walsingham, the newly appointed ambassador to France, who had seen him as he passed through Paris and furnished him with a letter of recommendation. In fact Ridolfi was now an agent of the Pope, charged with a task of the first importance, no less than to organize and marshal in one great effort all the actual and potential enemies of Elizabeth and Cecil. Ridolfi's personal qualities made the history of his plot—a talent for persuasive talk, a facility for making unwarranted promises, a self-confidence so excessive as to cloud discrimination between the practical and the chimerical, and a rashness in speech and action that left small play for conspiratorial secrecy. Thus equipped he set to work. He conferred with Guerau de Spes, who shared his propensity for making promises and agreed that Alva should land a force in East Anglia while Philip should send another from Spain to the west country, and that on their appearance the Catholics should rise and join them, having first liberated Mary Stuart. Ridolfi next approached the Bishop of Ross, Mary's ambassador in London, who informed his delighted mistress. Ridolfi was then ready to tackle the Duke of Norfolk, who was to lead the English rising, backed by sixty nobles and prominent gentlemen of whom Ridolfi compiled a list drawn mainly from his imagination. Norfolk had to be carefully handled, since, although he was attracted by the spoils of victory, he did not like the risks or, to do him justice, the guilt. The same was true of Arundel, Lumley, and perhaps half a dozen others, who were the only probables among the sixty. In March 1571 Ridolfi talked over Norfolk with the promise of Mary's hand and the crown matrimonial of two kingdoms. Cecil was to be liquidated, but the fate of Elizabeth was left vague in consideration for tender consciences. Norfolk had consented out of weakness. He was not a whole-hearted traitor, but his position as head of the nobility, the only duke in England, made him indispensable. In April Ridolfi went over to the Netherlands to obtain the consent of Alva to what had already been promised in his name. Philip II also had as yet no knowledge of what was to be done. It was essentially the

Pope's undertaking. Ridolfi was to go from Brussels to Rome and thence to Madrid, so that the late summer would be the earliest time for carrying out the plan.

So far Ridolfi had been dealing with inferior men. Alva was of a different stamp. He at once assessed Ridolfi as a windbag and the plot as likely to end in ruin and probably in the death of Mary Stuart, which would mean the loss of an asset to Spain. His prime care was the Netherland government, and its interests demanded the restoration of trade as soon as possible. Nevertheless, in deference to the Pope and the Catholic cause he could not give a blunt refusal, and so he fixed a condition which he did not think would be met: let Norfolk rise first and take the field with the promised Catholic army, and when it had proved that it meant business, Alva would send troops in support. This decision really pricked the bubble, but Ridolfi in his optimism would not see it. He went on his way to report progress in Rome, where the ecclesiastics, having nothing to lose, received him with enthusiasm.

Whatever might be her fear of the Spanish-Netherland power, Elizabeth's conciliatory steps were nothing more than talk, and she kept the damaging factors of the situation in use or ready for use. Owing to the Hamburg alternative the arrest of trade did more harm to its authors than to England, and their attempts to get intercourse resumed were foiled by the Queen's insistence on stiff conditions. John Hawkins's disastrous expedition had been a disguised state undertaking in which the Queen, her Secretary, and members of her Privy Council had been concerned; and Elizabeth, although her riposte must be thinly disguised, gave Hawkins leave in 1570 to attack the home-coming plate fleet with an armed squadron of his and her providing. He made thorough preparations, but was prevented from sailing by the need to keep every fighting ship in home waters to escort the Austrian bride down Channel. Out of the profits of the privateering war he was at this time building up a formidable fleet of his own, based at Plymouth and independent of the Queen's Navy. A state paper lists sixteen ships, large and small, and heavily armed. The Queen knew Hawkins personally and had formed her judgment of him, and she had no objection to this independent armament. It cost her nothing, and she was able to incorporate it in the national defence, as in the emergency of 1570. From then onwards for some years the regular Navy based at Chatham was ready to meet invasion from the Netherlands, while the Hawkins fleet at Plymouth looked towards Spain.

Hawkins was officially a 'servant' of the Queen, although apart from that he held no precise rank or appointment. William Winter (knighted in 1573) was Surveyor of the Navy and a trusted commander of expeditions in home waters. Sir Edward Horsey was Governor of the Isle of Wight, a post of importance in the event of war. These men, separately and in combination, with the backing of Leicester and the Lord Admiral, began after the treachery of San Juan de Ulua to send out small vessels to harry the coasts of the Spanish Indies and to snap up minor quantities of the treasure as it was being concentrated to lade the plate fleets. Among several captains whom they employed was Francis Drake, who made himself acquainted with the run of the treasure traffic and prepared for something more than a petty raid against it. It is unlikely that the Queen knew the details of these small expeditions, but she undoubtedly knew that they were going on, and as their promoters were her officials she could probably have stopped them had she chosen. Her omission to do so, coupled with her allowance of the use of English ports by the Channel rovers of three nations, forms a side of her policy that should not be overlooked and was often in substantial contradiction to her professions of conciliation.

Partly to obtain supply but mainly in consequence of the papal excommunication, Elizabeth called her fourth Parliament in April 1571. The advanced Protestants were strong in the Commons, and the Queen warned them at the outset not to meddle with matters of state other than those she should propound to them. Her purpose was to obtain an addition to the law, making it treason to introduce a papal bull into the country or to attempt to carry it into effect; or to assert that she was not the rightful queen or that any other person was. This of course was easily passed, but there were other matters of state in which members were interested. Both houses passed a bill legalizing the thirty-nine articles promulgated by convocation in 1563. The Queen vetoed it, foreseeing that it would be a precedent for a parliamentary revision of the articles in future, while her intention was to keep the Church among the 'matters of state' reserved to the royal prerogative. Similarly she vetoed another bill to add compulsory attendance at communion to compulsory church-going; while William Strickland, a Puritan who proposed to reform the prayer-book, was called before the Council and severely admonished. Peter Wentworth first sat in this Parliament, and began a long career of opposition to the crown by speaking for the privilege of members. He became the centre of a group that was vigorous but always numerically small.[1] Neale describes Wentworth's 'passionate conflict with his sovereign, coupled with a love and reverence this side idolatry'. The Parliament in general was far too Protestant for the Queen's taste, with a Protestantism that was becoming critical of many points of Church practice and a disposition to regard the bishops as miniature popes meet to be abolished.

Ridolfi, having found Brussels adverse and Rome favourable, met with a critical but not hostile examination at Madrid. Philip, cautious though he might be, was attracted by the possibility of solving his English problem at a stroke by enthroning a satellite queen whom he would marry suitably to someone of his own choice, not, of course, the Duke of Norfolk or any other Englishman. He consulted Feria and other councillors, who thought well of it and made no bones about rounding off the revolution by the assassination of Elizabeth. Madrid was favourably impressed by a factor that seemed to carry little weight with Alva and had arisen independently of Ridolfi's devices. John Hawkins had learned that some of his men taken prisoners at San Juan de Ulua had been transferred to Spain, and he had asked Guerau de Spes for his good offices in securing their liberation. In the spring of 1571 Cecil, who kept watch on de Spes and Norfolk and the Bishop of Ross, began to suspect that Ridolfi was engaged in more than his innocent commercial business, and found indications that they were all plotting something serious. He knew Hawkins well and trusted his discretion; and with Cecil's and the Queen's consent Hawkins next went to Guerau de Spes and professed himself a traitor who would for a reward use his sea power to facilitate the invasion of his country. De Spes snapped at the bait, and the upshot was that in the course of the summer Hawkins twice sent to Spain an able emissary who had interviews with Feria and with Philip himself and finally came away with an agreement between the king and John Hawkins. By its terms Hawkins was to leave the west open to invasion from Spain by leading his armed squadron from Plymouth to the Netherland coast, and there he was to escort Alva's forces to a landing in eastern England; for which he was to be given a sum of money, the liberation of his men, and a patent of nobility, together with a pardon for his transgressions in the Indies.

---

[1] 'Peter Wentworth', by J. E. Neale, *English Hist. Review*, vol. xxxix (1924, January and April), a detailed account of Wentworth's career which is followed in this and subsequent references.

The movement was timed for the late summer or early autumn, but Philip revealed nothing of Norfolk or the English side of the plot.

Cecil, this year created Lord Burghley, thus knew for certain that Philip intended a surprise invasion. Meanwhile he was gradually solving the rest of the problem. Ridolfi had sent from Brussels a packet of ciphered letters to the Bishop of Ross, and—it was characteristic of Ridolfi—had sent with it the key by which the cipher could be read. The bearer was arrested on landing at Dover, and Burghley thus learned a good deal, but not all; for two ciphers, actually for the names of Norfolk and Lumley, were not given in the key. Burghley could guess that Norfolk was implicated, but the Queen would not allow him to be seized on mere suspicion. She was probably right, for a premature arrest would only have driven the whole conspiracy underground, and Norfolk's peers, who included a sufficiency of Burghley's enemies, would not have condemned him without proof. Patient work through the summer brought its reward. A servant of Norfolk's was caught transmitting a sum of gold to the Marian faction in Scotland, while a search of the Duke's house and the racking of his secretary revealed hidden letters that justified the arrest of the Duke and of the Bishop of Ross. The bishop, titular ambassador though he was, learned that his privilege would not give immunity from the rack. The threat was enough, and he made a full confession of every detail of the great conspiracy, providing damning evidence against Norfolk and also against the Queen of Scots. As soon as Philip and Alva heard that Norfolk was in the Tower they dropped the invasion plan, for which Norfolk in rebellion was to have been the signal. Thus England had escaped a danger, but perhaps not a very great one. Alva's judgment had been just, and the plot, turning on resolute action by the most irresolute politician of his time, had been rickety throughout, an essay of second-rate cleverness against Tudor England.

Retribution was mild. Elizabeth in her cool self-control was satisfied with foiling her enemies and did not choose to press the matter to extremities. She treated the plot as a domestic affair and did not allow Philip to know that Hawkins had deluded him and that his plan for invasion had been detected. Mary's part was revealed, and her continental friends regarded her execution as certain, but Elizabeth took no steps against her other than a tightening of surveillance. The Bishop of Ross earned a contemptuous forgiveness by turning queen's evidence and by a pious admonition to his mistress to eschew 'Italian practices' in future. Ridolfi was safe overseas. Guerau de Spes was summoned before the Council at the close of 1571, told that his dealings with Mary and Norfolk were discovered, and expelled from the country. He retained his faith in Hawkins, and when he reached Brussels continued to urge Alva to proceed with the invasion with Hawkins's aid, even though the English plot was at an end. In the ambassador's imagination all England was longing for a Catholic revolution and would rise in its strength as soon as a Spanish regiment should land. There remained Norfolk. He was brought to trial in 1572 and condemned for treason. Even then the Queen postponed his execution and would have been glad to let him off. But public excitement made it necessary to call a new Parliament in 1572. It was full of angry Protestants who clamoured for Mary's head. To save it the Queen had to give them Norfolk's. He was executed in June, the first notable victim of his kind in fourteen years of Elizabethan rule. In matters of state there was indeed a different atmosphere since the days of Henry VIII.

The Anjou marriage after tedious negotiation failed to come off. Whether Elizabeth sincerely intended it is hard to discern. Burghley certainly desired it. So also did Catherine de Medici, while Charles IX welcomed the opportunity of getting an inconvenient brother out of his kingdom. The obstacle was the stiffness of Anjou about religion. He insisted on being free to practise Catholic worship. Elizabeth after much consideration decided that she could allow no exception to the requirements of her laws; and the difficulty was insoluble. In spite of this, however, Burghley, with Walsingham at the Paris embassy, was able to arrange a promising agreement with France by the Treaty of Blois, signed in April 1572. Its main feature was a defensive alliance whereby either power agreed to aid the other if attacked by a third, Spain being meant. So long as France and England could trust one another—a very limiting proviso—the Treaty of Blois was a guarantee of peace and an answer to such a design as Philip II had entertained by Ridolfi's persuasion. It also marked the tacit abandonment of Mary Stuart by the Valois. But the events of the year were to deprive the treaty of real life, since it was based on a state of affairs in France that was to pass completely away.

For two brief years, from August 1570 to August 1572, the Huguenots were in the ascendant. After the peace of St. Germain-en-Laye they captured the person of the king, not by the armed violence attempted on previous occasions, but by the dominating character of Coligny, who came to court and established a powerful influence over the mind of Charles IX. Coligny saw through the mists of political intrigue to the great issues that governed the fate of nations. His aims were clear, the establishment of Protestantism and the imperial greatness of France, and their attainment was simplified by the fact that the same enemy, Philip II, stood in the way of both. Because Coligny died prematurely and events did not follow the course he would have shaped, we are apt to assume that they could not have done so. But the Huguenot version of Protestantism, based on the teaching of a great Frenchman, had its appeal to the logic of the French mind, and there is no reason why, with better luck, the Calvinist dogma and method of government should not have captured sixteenth-century France as effectively as egalitarian dogma and republican institutions captured its eighteenth-century successor. Coligny's immediate policy was a truce to religious conflict among Frenchmen and an attack on Spain in the Netherlands in collaboration with the Orange princes. He had more distant views also, the building of a transatlantic France in the tropics, growing out of the anti-Spanish raids that the Huguenot sailors had long been conducting; and a trade round the Cape with India, aided by African stations founded at the expense of the Portuguese. The ascendancy of Coligny at court produced an alliance of the Huguenots with the *Politiques* or moderate Catholics, and a depression of the Guises, who were reported in 1571 to have retired in dudgeon. Catherine de Medici watched nervously. She was glad to be relieved of pressure from the ultra-Catholics, behind whom she saw the domination of Philip II, but she was jealous of the new influence of Coligny. She had no ethical motives, little religion and no patriotism, but a strong attachment to the family property, the crown of France, and a determination to control it through her son in whom it was vested.

Threatened, as they knew they had been, by a Spanish invasion from the Netherlands, and not knowing how reluctant Alva was to engage in the attempt, Elizabeth and Burghley had a strong motive for supporting Coligny's aggressive plans. But on the long view no English statesman could wish to see France dominate the Low Countries, and Elizabeth was quite clear that a triumphant France would be a worse neighbour than Spain, however hostile Spain might be. The geographical contrast was inescapable: France in living union with the Netherlands across a land frontier that was nothing but a line on a map; and Spain precariously maintaining herself at the end of a land communication flanked by Protestants in the Alps and the Rhineland, or a sea line assailed by all the private enterprise of the English, French, and Dutch seaports. The Queen was therefore willing to co-operate with France to the extent of making things difficult for Spain, but no farther. She was willing also to assist the Netherland rebels to the same end and with the same limitation. She was then in hope of taking advantage of Spanish embarrassments to come to advantageous terms, cancel the scores on both sides, and begin afresh. It was a juggle with three billiard balls, which the Queen proceeded to execute with skill.

In April 1572 Elizabeth carried out a change of policy which was ostensibly beneficial to Spain but in fact added enormously to Spain's difficulties. She commanded the Sea Beggars operating in the eastern Channel to depart from English ports and enter them no more, and she forbade her own subjects to aid the rovers or buy their plunder. It was on the face of it a rebuff to Spain's enemies, and some have held that nothing else was intended. The effect was that the Beggars concentrated at Dover and thence sailed eastwards to the Dutch coast. It is fairly obvious that they meant to seize a port there, for a port they must have; and they did occupy Brill after a surprise attack, following it by the capture of the more important haven of Flushing. It seems possible that it was not only a foreseen but a concerted move. The Queen had plenty of people to tell her that a cruising fleet needs a base, and the fact that the messenger who conveyed her commands to the Beggars was John Hawkins is a guarantee that she was well informed. There is some indication also that the Dutch leaders had been in consultation with Burghley some time before the event, and had even reconnoitred the defences of Brill.[1] The choice of Hawkins for the warning-off was a delicate touch, since Spanish statesmen were still under the impression that he was devoted heart and soul to their service; and here he was in that character, annoying their enemies.

The Beggars thus carried rebellion to the Dutch coast, and there they lighted a fire that was never put out. Several towns rose in

[1] The full evidence is cited in A. F. Pollard, *Political History of England*, vol. vi (1910), pp. 331–2. For the contrary view, that the Queen's decision was genuinely meant to favour Spain, and that its outcome was not calculated, see 'Queen Elizabeth, the Sea Beggars, and the Capture of Brill', by J. B. Black, *English Hist. Review*, vol. xlvi (1931, January). Professor Black criticizes Pollard's evidence and cites other testimony showing on its face that the Queen was anxious to oblige Spain and was incensed against the Sea Beggars. There is, however, another circumstance that tells in favour of Pollard's contention: there was no parallel warning-off of the Rochellers who were using Plymouth as the Dutch were using Dover. If the Queen had been genuinely benevolent to Spain she would surely have denied her ports to all of Spain's enemies.

succession and evicted Spanish garrisons, and Spain never fully recovered its lost hold. Flushing, a deep-water harbour commanding the entrance of the Scheldt and the access to Antwerp, was very important, and its loss by Spain had strategic effects right up to the campaign of the Armada in 1588. In the following month (May 1572) Louis of Nassau led a force from France into the southern Netherlands, where he took Valenciennes and Mons by a similar surprise, and William of Orange crossed the eastern frontier from German territory and advanced into Brabant. Alva reacted strongly against these converging attacks, and his forces destroyed a body of 5,000 Huguenots advancing to join Louis at Mons. Nevertheless Coligny was preparing a great French effort, and at midsummer the possibility appeared that Spain's days in the Netherlands were numbered. Elizabeth was alarmed at the prospect of a French conquest. She sent Sir Humphrey Gilbert over to the Netherlands with some English levies. His status was that of a volunteer assisting the Dutch of his own motion and not as a servant of the Queen, but he had her secret orders to prevent the French from occupying the ports and not to venture inland himself. His men formed the major element in the garrison of Flushing.

At this juncture all purposes were interrupted by the Massacre of St. Bartholomew in Paris. Catherine de Medici had grown distrustful of the influence of Coligny with Charles IX, and of the war policy which would entrench its Huguenot authors in power. She decided to stop it by encouraging the Guise party to assassinate Coligny. On 22 August a Guisard shot him but failed to kill him. The leaders of the Huguenots were in Paris for the wedding of Henry of Navarre to Marguerite de Valois, from which was expected a permanent peace between the religions. The attempt on Coligny rendered war certain, with the advantage to the side that could strike first. In fear of retribution Catherine at once plotted with Henry of Guise the massacre of the Huguenots in Paris, having won over Charles IX by a tale of a Huguenot plot. The massacre began on 24 August, the action spreading from the Guisan forces to the populace of Paris and thence throughout France. Coligny and thousands of Huguenots were killed, and the survivors took up arms in the fourth civil war.

The news from Paris suggested dire possibilities in London. England and France were indeed on terms of alliance, but it was not unknown for sixteenth-century governments to entertain diametrically opposite policies at the same time and to switch suddenly from one to the other. At first it seemed likely that the French had done this, and that the massacre was the opening move of a holy war of all Catholics against all Protestants, an intention suspected since the Duke of Alva had conferred with Catherine de Medici at Bayonne in 1565. To Elizabeth and her ministers it was grave news, apart from the natural horror with which they viewed the crime itself. That horror was great and unaffected, as the French ambassador was made to know when he sought audience of the Queen; and when news came of satisfaction in Spain and rapture at Rome it did indeed seem likely that the great fight was on. There was no more Huguenot help for Louis of Nassau, who had to surrender at Mons, while his brother retreated on the eastern frontier. Only the Dutch sea towns kept up the fight. But no move developed against England, where it was gradually realized that the massacre was not a prelude to a general war. By the end of the year diplomacy had steadied and Elizabeth was able to resume her own policies.

In the course of the summer her fifth Parliament had met. Elected amid the emotions arising from the Ridolfi plot, it was more Puritan and more intransigent against the Queen's enemies than the last. The Queen herself took no pleasure in belligerent Puritanism, and the tone of the Commons owed nothing to any royal interference with elections. It was the plainest possible evidence of the opinion of the middle classes, and a refutation of the view of Guerau de Spes that England was overwhelmingly Catholic. Philip knew better when he wrote in 1570 of 'the few good Catholics remaining in England'. The general Puritanism of Elizabeth's early years was now, under the influence of Geneva, taking on a Calvinist and Presbyterian definition.[1] This affected men in different ways. The extremists became hardened in their radical and potentially rebellious views, but the majority were in no mood to support a revolutionary movement. In the years to follow they remained Puritan in their way of life and thought, but they remained also in the Church of England and did not actively support the hard core of the Calvinist leadership; and the non-Calvinist kind of Puritanism grew more widespread. During the session a Puritan *Admonition to Parliament* was published, advocating the abandonment of all practices savouring of the old church and the adoption of a virtually presbyterian system of government. Neale describes it as 'one of the most important tracts —perhaps, indeed, the most important—in the history of Elizabethan Puritanism', marking the adoption by the clerical leaders of

[1] Neale, *op. cit.*, p. 181.

the revolutionary policy. The Queen sent the authors to jail and vetoed the discussion of a parallel bill in the Commons. As noted already, she denied the requests for Mary's execution, but consented to Norfolk's, and he was beheaded before the session ended. At its close Peter Wentworth dissented from the motion to thank the Queen, 'the which', he said, 'for my part I did not think Her Majesty had deserved'. The picture presented to the world was of a mild and reasonable sovereign striving to moderate the patriotic and Protestant exuberance of her people; and the picture was none the less useful for being true.

The events of 1572 had produced these effects in international affairs: the Huguenot plan of uniting France in a conquest of the Netherlands was at an end; Spain nevertheless was not free of embarrassment, since the Dutch revolt was in progress and Dutch cities were defying Spanish arms; the massacre had shaken Elizabeth's trust in France, never very great, and had made her feel that the time had come to restore friendship with Spain; while Philip was placing the pacification of the Netherlands before all else, and was convinced that a friendly England and a freeing of the Channel highway were indispensable. Added to these considerations there was another of interest to England. The stimulus to trade caused by the sale of privateer booty to English merchants had been hectic and unhealthy and had already died out. The sea rovers, from killing Catholic trade, were now killing all trade. An economic depression, deepened by some bad harvests, was enfeebling the country, and men of substance were going bankrupt while poor men were starving. English policy faced all these facts. In April 1573 negotiations between England and Alva succeeded in restoring the Anglo-Flemish trade, a restoration that extended shortly to that between England and Spain; and it was agreed that commissioners should assess all the damages committed and strike a balance for settlement. To back the negotiations Elizabeth used her sea power to clean up the trade routes. This time there could be no suspicion of her intentions. William Holstocke, her Comptroller of the Navy, went to sea in February with heavily armed ships that captured privateers right and left and drove their comrades into retirement. He smote the Huguenots as well as the Dutch and gave Spain ample proof of good meaning. And yet, in that same spring, Elizabeth allowed a relief expedition to sail to La Rochelle, where the Huguenots were hard beset by her suitor the Duke of Anjou. She would work for peace, but not at the price of leaving the Catholics triumphant.

15

THE FERTILE SEVENTIES

THE restoration of trade in 1573 marked the end of the four
years' crisis that began in the winter of 1568–9. In the course of
that period certain things had become clear. First, Elizabeth
had brought to a head and dealt with the conservative discontent
that was reactionary rather than Catholic; and thenceforward it was
to be seen no more. As against this, the bull of excommunication had
given point and form to the exclusively Catholic opposition, which
became smaller in volume but more dangerous in quality. If, again,
some Catholics were moving to an extreme, some Protestants were
likewise doing so, and tending to decry Elizabeth's churchmen and
their services as relics of popery. Mary Stuart, revealed by the plot
as a determined enemy of Elizabeth, saw her hopes of a negotiated
restoration vanish. Elizabeth reconciled herself to keeping Mary imprisoned, while the majority of Englishmen were ill content that she
should remain alive. The Valois and even the Guises were now much
less prominent as Mary's friends, having little to spare for her but
lip-service as the effects of the massacre in shattering France made
themselves evident, while Philip II had appropriated the prisoner's
cause, to be promoted or neglected according to his convenience.
The accommodation with Spain, however much Elizabeth might desire to give it reality, was in fact an affair of book-keeping with no
heart in it. English opinion, deeply stirred by the Netherland cruelties
and the French massacre, saw no likelihood of peace, but rather a
world in which Protestants were making a desperate fight for survival
and England was called upon to play her part.

Such being the position, it may seem unreal to speak of the crisis
as ended. But in truth it was. Its most dangerous aspect had been
domestic, and by 1573 the country was more united than ever since
the opening of the reign; for the Puritans, whatever their grumblings,

were not disloyal, and the too-ambitious aristocrats were tamed. In foreign affairs also the position was stronger, for it was Spain that had sought the resumption of trade, and it was France that was eager to conclude a royal marriage. For the moment the foreigners were suitors. The French, deprived of Coligny's inspiration, had given up their hopes of Netherland conquest, while the Spaniards were pinned down and exhausted by sieges of the cities that had defied them since the capture of Brill. In the tortured Netherlands nobody was winning, which was the situation that Elizabeth desired.

The resumption of the Spanish and Netherland trade hastened an economic revival that made the next dozen years a period of marked prosperity. During the arrests of trade England had found compensation elsewhere than in Antwerp and Seville and had suffered less than was expected. With the resumption she recovered her old business while retaining the new. Her fluid capital was also increasing. Part of the profits of the privateering war was in coined wealth, and certain oceanic transactions of the 'seventies were to make notable additions to the stock. Business began to boom and companies to be founded or refounded, while social comfort and luxury increased, and enterprise thus stimulated sought new outlets. The good time lasted until the outbreak of the Spanish war, when a regression ensued. But it was not a regression to the former low level. Elizabethan England had achieved a permanent advance. In the long perspective it can be seen that after 1570 the country's economy emerged from the trough into which it had dipped after 1540, although the symmetry of the curve is masked by shorter fluctuations. The Muscovy Company, the Mines Royal, and the Mineral and Battery Works, which had all been in difficulties during the crisis, were reconstituted with new capital as it began to pass away, while new projects characteristic of an age of hope began to be heard of. It was a sign of the times that in 1574 a patent was granted to a Society for the New Art in Making Copper, the 'art' being the transmutation of iron into the rarer metal. The Society had Leicester and Burghley among its shareholders, and a fraudulent alchemist for its scientific director. The atrocities of Alva caused a large migration of Dutch and Flemish weavers into England, and the French massacre sent Huguenots across the Channel. The Flemings settled chiefly in Norwich and Colchester, where they introduced varieties of cloth-making not hitherto practised in England—the 'new drapery' that played its part in the growing prosperity. By 1572 there were 4,000 foreigners in Norwich, and 6,000 by 1578. Contemporary statements admit their value to the places in which they settled, and yet there were inevitable dissensions, due to the jealousy of the natives and the clannishness of the aliens. Dissension grew also round the French who settled in large numbers in London to practise silk-weaving. They were not the introducers of the industry, but competitors with native craftsmen, and were alleged to break all the rules of the trade and shoulder none of the natives' obligations. They were also settled in Canterbury, Sandwich, Rye, and Southampton. In time the acerbities passed, and the refugees, who on the face of it were a stout stock, were absorbed into the people of England.

A good indication of increasing stability lay in the state of the public debt and the public credit. Elizabeth had begun her reign with an inherited debt, and all the care of herself and Burghley and Gresham had so far been unable to achieve its extinction. Its holders had become to an increasing extent Englishmen rather than foreigners, but much of the indebtedness had remained. In the Parliament of 1576 the Chancellor of the Exchequer was able to announce that within the past two years the internal debt had been entirely paid off. What foreign debt remained seems to have been the obligation to the financiers of Genoa for the treasure diverted to English hands in 1569. Most of this money had not been used, but remained stored in the Tower as a reserve of coin against an emergency. The Queen's credit abroad now stood at 8 or 9 per cent, whereas Philip II could only borrow at 12 to 18 per cent, and was failing to pay his interest.[1]

Philip in fact went bankrupt just as England was emerging from its crisis. In addition to the Netherland revolt he had always a Turkish war, a war of defence against relentless Moslem encroachment in the Mediterranean. The great Spanish-Italian victory in the sea-fight of Lepanto in 1571 had yielded little relief. It was a glorious feat of arms and little more, and within a few months the Turks were again rampant. By 1573 Philip had anticipated the revenues of the Spanish state for five years ahead. His total debts were about twelve million pounds in English value,[2] and in 1575 he suspended the payment of interest. Although his revenues were higher than those of any other sovereign, he lacked financial sense. Meanwhile his wars went on.

---

[1] W. R. Scott, *Joint Stock Companies*, vol. i, pp. 64–5.

[2] Fifty million ducats.—R. B. Merriman, *Rise of the Spanish Empire*, vol. iv, p. 443.

Alva failed to reduce the Dutch cities, and was superseded in 1573 by Luis de Requesens, who was to profess a less harsh policy but to gain little ground by it. This is the background of Philip's pacification with England. In 1573–4 commissioners assessed the damages caused by the arrests of trade and settled the claims in the Convention of Bristol (August 1574). Since the dismissal of de Spes there had been no Spanish ambassador in England, and Spanish business was conducted by a merchant named Antonio de Guaras, resident in London.

Hostilities in the Indies continued in spite of the improvement of Anglo-Spanish relations in Europe. The number of small-scale free-booting expeditions was greater than that of which details survive, as we know from allusions in state correspondence. Small vessels armed with light guns were very cheap, and the men served without regular pay for a share of the plunder. It was called 'adventuring on thirds' from the distribution of the proceeds, one-third to the ship-owners, one-third to the crews, and one-third to the providers of the victuals, usually the owners. The story of one such venture, which may be typical of many, is preserved in the records of the Admiralty Court. It is the story of an 18-ton ship with three small guns, owned by a London merchant otherwise unknown to history. Fifteen of its crew of twenty-five came home to share a pretty little taking worth two or three thousand pounds, obtained by plundering Spaniards in the recognized Tom Tiddler's ground, the angle of coast between the Spanish Main and the Isthmus of Panama. Spanish records are full of complaints of such raids, although the Spanish officials usually did not distinguish between the English and the Huguenots, who were probably more numerous. To the Spaniard they were all 'corsairs and Lutherans'. The Queen must have known of it, but turned a blind eye. It was decently far away, and provided a speculation for moneyed men with a surplus to gamble with; and the participants added to the country's fluid capital and gave employment to a valu-able breed of fighting seamen. No one was hanged for it, except by the Spaniards, although pirates operating in home waters were occa-sionally sent to the gallows.

Francis Drake carried out a much greater raid, achieved by an original departure from the usual practice of snapping up coastal shipping. He was probably equipped by Hawkins and Winter, and sailed in May 1572 with two small vessels and seventy men, just when Gilbert's volunteers were going over to take a hand in the Netherland war. He surprised Nombre de Dios, the Isthmus treasure port, but failed to carry off any booty. He then allied himself with the Cimaroons, runaway negro slaves who lived in the wilds of the Isthmus, and with their aid crossed to within sight of the city of Panama and beheld the Pacific Ocean for the first time. He lost many men by fever and achieved final success in concert with a crew of Huguenots whom he met on the coast. Together they captured a convoy of mules bearing treasure from Panama to Nombre de Dios. There was gold and silver, but the raiders could carry off only the gold. Drake's share was about £20,000, and with it he returned to Plymouth in August 1573, to find that the quarrel with Spain was being patched up. He had made a quick passage, and arrived before the Spanish government had news on which to base a complaint. He retired into obscurity for two years, the winnings presumably being distributed to those concerned. This voyage laid the foundation of Drake's fame as a captain. Its details were known to those in authority and circulated by word of mouth among the public, although nothing was printed at the time.

West Indian treasure-raiding was only one sign of a conviction among active men that England's future was on the oceans, and that it was to be achieved not only by following in Spain's tracks but by discovery in regions still unknown, with a view to opening new trades and founding an English empire of exploitation. The projecting of Edward VI's reign, never wholly laid aside, revived in greater strength. John Dee, with his great learning, formed a link between the 'fifties and the 'seventies, and also in the latter period a link between the court and the seamen, for he was well known in both circles. He wrote memoranda on exploring projects and had interviews with the Queen and her councillors. His cherished design was the opening of an exclusively English route to the trade and learning of far Asia. It might be by the north-west or the north-east, or by Magellan's track in the south-west. He published little, but circulated his ideas confidentially, and this has caused him to be underestimated. Popular tradition remembers only that he was interested in astrology and the occult, and has set him down as in some sort a charlatan. He was not that, but a man of knowledge and public spirit. He gave mathematical and cartographical instruction to sea captains, Frobisher and Davis among them, whereby they were able to enhance the value of their work as discoverers. If the hidden philosophies of Asia were to be his own reward—and he sought no other—

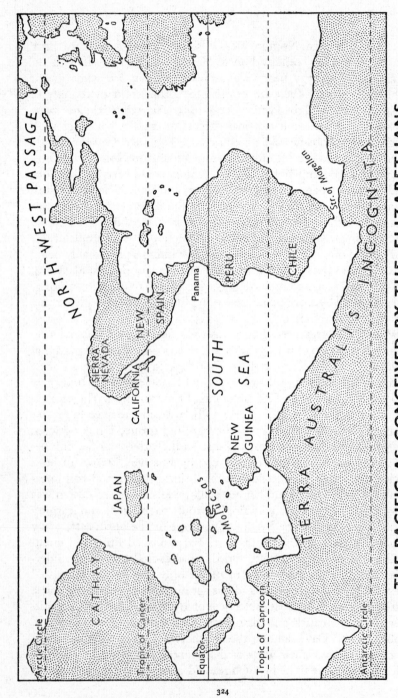

THE PACIFIC AS CONCEIVED BY THE ELIZABETHANS

NOTE: The general outlines are derived from the Atlas of Abraham Ortelius, 1570, used as a standard work in England. The shape of North America is not from Ortelius, but from a contemporary map by Michael Lok, the promoter of Frobisher's voyages. It illustrates the English optimism about the North West Passage.

324

he kept it in mind that his country's would be the rivalling and out-stripping of Spain.[1]

An early revival of the 'seventies was the project of the tropical and southern Pacific, the empire of the South Sea that Robert Thorne had urged half a century before. Biblical students believed that King Solomon's Ophir lay there, and the accepted version of the Travels of Marco Polo represented the thirteenth-century explorer as de-scribing wonderfully wealthy lands away in the ocean to the south-east of China and the Portuguese Indies. A Spanish expedition from Peru had recently discovered an archipelago far out in the Pacific, and had come back to report that they had been in Solomon's Islands and heard of a continent beyond; and this also was known in England. The west country, now that Channel privateering was frowned on, turned to oceanic adventure. In 1573–4 Sir Richard Grenville, William Hawkins, and a group of Devon and Cornish gentlemen moved for a patent from the Queen empowering them to discover and occupy all unknown lands in the southern hemisphere. Their intention was to pass the Straits of Magellan and find the coasts of Terra Australis Incognita, the unknown continent in whose exist-ence men had long believed. The world map of Abraham Ortelius, a Flemish master of geography, had been printed in his Atlas of 1570 and was well known in England. It depicted Terra Australis as bordering Magellan's strait and thence extending in a long slant north-westward across the Pacific towards Indonesia. On that great continental coast the projectors would find peoples and commodities, treasures and spices, and ports fit for English settlement. The Queen listened, and the patent was drafted. Grenville bought ships, and all seemed to be going forward. Then Elizabeth revoked her consent. The reason can only be conjectured. The way to Terra Australis was also the way to Philip's treasure-land of Peru. If Grenville failed to find the first he would doubtless find the second, and privateering was in his record. If he were to raid Peru under her letters patent, it would be a different thing from the Caribbean private adventuring which she could disavow, and might break up her policy of friend-ship with Spain. Such may well have been the Queen's reasoning. At any rate the patent was voided and the project dropped.

There was a task of conquest and colonization waiting to be done nearer home. The anarchic condition of Ireland had been a menace

[1] For a list of Dee's associates and pupils and a reasoned estimate of his position in English life, see E. G. R. Taylor, *Tudor Geography*, 1485–1583 (London, 1930), pp. 76–8.

to England's security in the days of Henry VII, when foreign-aided pretenders used Ireland as a base for the invasion of western England. Henry VII had imposed some stability on Ireland, which Henry VIII maintained and improved before the end of his reign; and French strategy in his wars made no use of Ireland for offensive purposes. Henry's Reformation extended to Ireland so far as to break up the Catholic hierarchy and dissolve the monasteries. But Protestant doctrines had no attraction for the Irish, although equally they evinced at first no passionate adherence to the cause of Rome. Discontent and disturbance were due to family and tribal ambitions, and were as evident under Philip and Mary as under Edward VI. The Earl of Sussex, sent by Mary to govern Ireland, had little success against the chronic disorder. There was no English money to spare for thorough measures, and no sufficient revenue could be raised in Ireland itself. Sussex believed that the settlement of English colonists would be a feasible long-term policy. He tried to make a beginning in the disturbed areas which he shired as King's County and Queen's County, and the names of Philipstown and Maryborough commemorate the effort, but little came of it. In the early years of Elizabeth the area of chief anxiety was in the north, where Shane O'Neill, whose father had been created Earl of Tyrone by Henry VIII, showed the makings of a conqueror and ruler. He neutralized all English jurisdiction and looked like making Ulster and the adjacent areas into an independent principality, until he was murdered by the Scots of Antrim in 1567. He had played for his own hand, without any religious appeal, and although commended by the Pope was described as a heretic by the papal agents who now appeared in Ireland.

The papal emissaries, nuncios, and missionaries were a graver threat to England's safety than sporadic native defiances. They found Ireland a religious desert in which the medieval Catholic rule had been destroyed, while titular Protestant bishops had produced no Protestantism and were as secular in their personal aims as the tribal chiefs. In this fallow field the missionaries worked hard, and in the course of the reign made the Irish a Catholic people in the sense in which the churchmen of the Counter-Reformation used the term. But, like all the missionaries of their time, they could not separate religion from politics, for the age was one of a great religious war. They sought to co-ordinate their religious work with the political aim of Spain and Rome, the overthrow of Elizabethan England; and they did so by welding clan independence into national patriotism, combining widespread risings with foreign aid, and inducing merci-less retaliation from the Queen's ill-supported officers, who struck with the savagery of the weak and committed acts that were to leave their scars for centuries. Elizabethan Ireland was the foundation of the Irelands that have followed it, its pitiful history a product of forces blindly used.

While in Ulster the death of Shane O'Neill produced no peace, for it left no authority in his place, the south and west were distracted by the feuds of the Butler Earls of Ormonde and the Fitzgerald Earls of Desmond. These families were not pure Irish, but of medieval Anglo-Irish origin, which made no difference in their conduct. Sir Henry Sidney, the Lord Deputy who succeeded Sussex, considered Ormonde loyal and sent Desmond a prisoner to London in 1567, whereupon James Fitzmaurice Fitzgerald, the earl's cousin, took the lead in rebellion and appealed to the Pope for countenance. For the time being there was no foreign aid to be had, but the proposal bore fruit at a later date. The policy of planting colonists who should also form a military force was tried on a small scale in Munster in 1568–70, where it alarmed the Irish chiefs and induced them to combine, and again in Ulster by the Earl of Essex in 1573–5. Essex (Walter Devereux) obtained the grant of the lands covered by the present county of Antrim, to be colonized at his own expense and profit. He had to conquer and expropriate the occupants before he could plant, and the attempt broke him. He raised men and ships with the aid of west-country investors, and committed atrocities on the O'Neills and a massacre of the Scots who had long been settled in the area, but was soon at the end of his resources, and died suddenly in 1575 with nothing constructive to his credit. To this Essex venture John Hawkins contributed some shipping, and Drake is found serving in it when he emerges from his two years' disappearance from the record after his Panama raid. Thereafter the luridness of the Irish scene diminished for a brief period.

The idea of strengthening the Catholic faith in Ireland by means of missionaries from without was incidental to a larger plan of recon-verting England by the same means. William Allen, a Catholic priest and formerly head of an Oxford college, had gone into exile at the beginning of the reign. In 1568 he founded an English college at Douai in the southern Netherlands, where he instituted the training of young Englishmen as priests who were to return to their country as missionaries. The youths were enrolled from the age of fourteen upwards, indoctrinated with the necessary beliefs, and conditioned by hard living and ceaseless suggestion to a renunciation of the normal life and a readiness for martyrdom. It is a heroic or a sad story, according to the point of view. From about 1575 the effects began to be seen in the appearance of the missionaries in England, where they travelled in disguise, visited Catholic families, and worked with success to check the easy-going conformity that was changing nominal Catholics into effective Anglicans. The missionary priest would tolerate no such thing. You must cease to conform, he told his hosts, or be cut off from the church; you cannot have it both ways. Faced with the necessity for decision, some broke away and turned Protestant, but many became active Catholics who before had been lukewarm. The crown and its officers and all fully Protestant Englishmen regarded the missionary (or seminary) movement as an insidious and dangerous attack. They could do no otherwise, since the bull of 1570 declared Elizabeth to be deposed and her former subjects to owe her no allegiance. Every person whom the seminary priests converted into an active Catholic was thus also a recruit to the traitors and potential rebels and aiders of the Queen's enemies. The missionary's training was for an exclusively spiritual task, and so he believed it to be, having been taught nothing of the political aspect; yet the bull betrayed him in advance into the ranks of the rebels and plotters, and as a rebel and plotter the state had to treat him, for he was a dangerous man. William Allen never returned to England, but died a cardinal at Rome. His college was later transferred to Rheims. In 1579 another English college was founded at Rome under Jesuit direction, and the following year saw the beginning of an inflow into England of Jesuit missionaries, who were to be even more active and successful than the earlier seminarists.

Elizabeth had a modern mind on the subject of persecution. It made no appeal to her, and she perceived that it could be a weapon more dangerous to its users than to their victims. She was very reluctant to make martyrs of the seminary priests, and at first when captured they were simply imprisoned and sometimes shortly released. Nevertheless their work went on, and their successes were perhaps exaggerated. The Act of 1571[1] brought their offence under the death penalty; and there was the aspect of the example. There was a limit to the toleration a government could afford to show to enemies acting successfully on its soil. Public opinion would grow indignant, or

[1] See p. 310.

worse, contemptuous; and the whole business promised to be a solvent of civil discipline. In 1576 Cuthbert Mayne, one of the Douai men, came into Cornwall and began the usual work of recalling the faint-hearted to their faith and forbidding them to conform. He continued for some months, complete secrecy not being possible, and the authorities taking no action. Then Sir Richard Grenville, the sheriff for 1577, arrested him, and after trial and condemnation Mayne was hanged at Launceston. Two more priests suffered early in the next year. This was the beginning of the application of the death penalty to a matter described by one side as treason and by the other as spiritual persecution.

Puritan opposition to the Elizabethan church was more formidable, as the Queen well knew, than Catholic enmity. The Puritan, although he might derive doctrines from Geneva, drew his strength from England. He advocated no allegiance to a foreign power and looked for no assistance from overseas. He was all English, nationalist, and loyal to the Queen. But he was more loyal still to what he thought the Queen ought to be, a sovereign who would make war on antichrist at the head of all Protestants, behead the dangerous woman who might succeed her and undo all, and tear out the rags of popery that defaced the ritual of the English Church. There are no statistics to provide any idea of the numbers of the Puritans, and in fact there never could have been, for there was never any definition of what constituted a Puritan. A few of them were in clear-cut isolation from the Church, but the majority were members of the Church. Attention has naturally been concentrated on those of them who were clergy and became prominent in dispute. But the importance of the Puritans lay in the fact that they were a large block of the laity, a section of the people whose religious life had a future and was to influence the character and conduct of the whole. The Puritan element had hardly been represented among the Protestants of Henry VIII and Edward VI and the victims of Mary's burnings, whose distinction had lain in doctrine. It came in substantially with the returning exiles of 1559 and was primarily a distinction of practice. To use a phrase that has been much quoted and also refuted, but which is none the less enlightening, Puritanism was 'an attitude of mind rather than a system of theology'.

The first clash had been on the use of vestments and various rituals in the early years of the reign, a matter that Archbishop Parker tried to settle by his 'advertisements' or instructions in 1566.

Their reception showed that already a considerable proportion of the clergy were of Puritan views. The next development was an attack upon the idea of government of the Church by bishops and ultimately by the sovereign who controlled the bishops. It was embodied in pamphlets of 'admonition' to Parliament in 1571 and 1572 and in the writings of Thomas Cartwright and Walter Travers. Cartwright was the outstanding protagonist of Puritanism in the early 'seventies. He was in favour of the Calvinist system of the clergy elected by the congregations, of discipline by presbyteries containing laymen and ministers, and of bishops, who might almost as well be abolished, reduced to the position of senior clergy without any governing functions. The whole system cut right into the Tudor conception of the body politic in its two aspects of church and state ruled equally by the sovereign. Elizabeth's objection was weighty and well-grounded. Puritanism of this sort would mean ultimately a revolution; and she determined not to countenance it. At the same time her conduct of the national business, and especially of foreign policy, was such that the Puritans, find fault as they might with details, had to admit that the results were such as they desired. The Queen was making Puritan England a power in the world. The Puritan challenge thus lost much of the drive that it was to manifest after she was dead. To preserve clearness of thought, it must be emphasized that the active reformers who wanted presbytery and the rest of the Calvinist programme were the ecclesiastical Puritans, insignificant in numbers compared with the Puritanical section of the lay population. Parker died in 1575, understanding well the implications of the Puritan attack, and much more worried by it than by the Catholic movement. The Queen made Edmund Grindal his successor, a man in whom she had apparently been mistaken, for he was soon displeasing her by his sympathy with many of the Puritan contentions.

The dropping of Grenville's South Sea project left the way clear for a rival plan to enter the Pacific by the North West Passage. We have seen Sir Humphrey Gilbert advocating it in the 'sixties, in contention with Anthony Jenkinson, who preferred the North East. Jenkinson had now retired from active adventure, and Gilbert had been employed as a soldier, first in Ireland and then in the Netherlands. When, a little later, he came again into oceanic plans, it was as an advocate of American colonization rather than of the immediate search for the passage. Gilbert, however, had cast his arguments for the North West project into a pamphlet, *A Discourse for a Discovery for a new Passage to Cataia*, which was circulated in manuscript among those interested, and which was widely known before being printed in 1576. Dee read it and was able to back it with learning of his own. Meanwhile a merchant named Michael Lok, one of the family that had pioneered in Guinea voyages in Mary's reign, had independently convinced himself of the existence of the North West Passage, and had joined forces with Martin Frobisher the sea-captain, who was equally a believer. The North West project was not obnoxious to the Queen's policy, since it was for an all-English discovery without any trespass in Spanish waters, and it was to lead, not to Peru and the treasure-coasts, but to Cathay, a name loosely applied to all the eastern end of Asia. The wind thus set fair for Lok and Frobisher. The Muscovy Company tried to assert its monopoly of all northern discovery, but by the Queen's command its objection was over-ruled. The two partners got their licence in 1575, and Frobisher sailed on the first attempt in the summer of 1576. He had an interview with the Queen before he set forth, but no financial support from her. Lok had to raise the money in the City. Dee supplied geographical advice and mathematics for northern navigation.

Frobisher in 1576 rounded the southern point of Greenland and crossed to the western side of Davis Strait. There, in 62° N, he found an opening in Baffin Land rather wider than the Straits of Dover. He assumed that it was a passage leading to the Pacific, although if he had penetrated it far enough he would have found it to be a cul de sac without a western egress. He reached home in October, reporting that the North West Passage was found. Great enthusiasm prevailed, and Michael Lok was able to combine his supporters into the Cathay Company, with a charter from the Queen and a monopoly of trade with Asia by the new route. More than this, a piece of black mineral brought home by Frobisher was thought to be gold ore, and an assayer showed some specks of gold that he declared he had extracted from it. Almost everybody fell for the lure of spice-trading and gold-mining, although Walsingham, perhaps in ironical allusion to Burghley's copper-making speculation, wrote that 'he did think it to be but an alchemist matter'. The general view was that the business was sound and important enough to have the national mantle cast over it. The Queen not only granted her patent but symbolized her support by taking a nominal share, and court and City plunged whole-heartedly. Frobisher sailed again in 1577 with a 200-ton ship that he was to lade with gold ore and send home, and

two small barks with which he was to complete the passage to
Cathay. In fact he made no further discovery, but filled all his shipping with mineral and came home in the autumn. There was further
assaying and experimenting by experts who produced only pinheads
of gold, and it was announced that greater results must await the
construction of large furnaces for the purpose. Meanwhile Frobisher
went off again in 1578 with a fleet of fifteen ships to be laden with
gold-ore, equipped at an expense that exceeded the Company's paid-
up resources. No sooner had he gone than adverse rumours began to
circulate and the boom collapsed. Belief in the ore suddenly vanished,
and there was no more money for furnaces or smelting. Frobisher in
due course returned with hundreds of tons of worthless mineral, to
find the Company bankrupt and the investors screaming for a scape-
goat. They found one in Michael Lok, who was stripped of his
private fortune and sent to jail, although he was not a knave, but
rather, like all the rest, a dupe of his own optimism. Frobisher had
been that year in a new strait, a real one, afterwards known as Hudson Strait; but in the financial recriminations this contribution to
geography was overlooked.

Concurrently with the Frobisher venture a tropical undertaking
went on, without any publicity or letters-patent, but with results that
were to be sensational. Some time in the winter of 1575–6 Drake
returned from Ireland, and was at Plymouth while one of his old
comrades of the Panama raid, John Oxenham, was fitting out a
small expedition there. Drake had conference with Oxenham, but
apart from that fact there is no evidence that he had any hand in
Oxenham's proceedings; it is certain, however, that he knew what
Oxenham meant to do. Oxenham sailed in April 1576 with a 100-ton
ship and a smaller vessel, and arrived about midsummer on the
northern coast of the Isthmus of Panama. He concealed the shipping
and went inland with the men to join the Cimaroons. With their help
he built a rowing-pinnace on a river flowing to the South Sea, and
so was able to appear in the Gulf of Panama early in 1577 and attack
the treasure ships that came up from Chile and Peru. These ships
were unarmed, since the Spaniards expected no enemies in the South
Sea. Oxenham captured a considerable amount of treasure, with
which he retired into the Cimaroon country of Vallano. His movements were leisurely and by no means furtive, for he knew that the
Spaniards at Panama and Nombre de Dios could turn out no great
force against him. Some of his men, bragging to Spaniards whom

they had captured, declared that the present expedition was only an advanced guard and that the English were coming in force to take possession of the Isthmus; while a Spanish officer on the spot reckoned that 300 Englishmen with the support of the Cimaroons could defy all efforts to expel them. Oxenham, however, had only fifty men, and he had underestimated the energy of the Panama authorities. They turned out all their men, sent to Peru for more, defeated the Cimaroons, and hunted him down. It all took a considerable time, and it was towards the end of 1577 that Oxenham was captured. A dozen of his men got away and captured a Spanish coaster, but it is not known whether they reached England.[1]

In 1577, while Oxenham was busy in the Isthmus of Panama, Drake was preparing a new expedition. His intention was to enter the South Sea by passing through the Straits of Magellan, a route so difficult and dangerous that the Spaniards had given up using it, all their communications with Peru and the west coast passing overland across the Isthmus. Drake's ostensible purpose was that of Grenville four years earlier, to discover the continental coast of Terra Australis in the South Pacific. Instructions to that end were made out for him in the summer of 1577, telling him to make friends with the natives of the continent, take note of their commodities, and choose harbours suitable for English trade; after which he was to return by the way he had gone out. This expedition, like those of Hawkins in the 'sixties, was a semi-state undertaking, whose shareholders included the names of Leicester, Walsingham, Hatton, and the Lord Admiral, while the Queen herself was apprised of all that was intended and could have vetoed the whole project had she so pleased. The Terra Australis plan outlined above was not a deep secret and was in all probability known to Burghley, who may possibly have been a participator. Before Drake sailed, however, another and a very secret plan was adopted. Drake was in touch with Walsingham, and Walsingham conducted him to an interview with the Queen, who authorized him to strike a blow against the King of Spain. Times were changed since 1573 and, as will be shown, Spanish proceedings in the Netherlands were growing threatening. Elizabeth's reaction was to strike a heavy but unofficial blow in the distant west to remind Philip of her power of offence. So she told Drake that he might do

---

[1] The Oxenham story has been revolutionized by the discovery of Spanish documents. It was formerly supposed that Oxenham sailed in 1575 and was captured in that year. See I. A. Wright, *English Voyages to the Spanish Main*, Hakluyt Society, (1932).

what he proposed, and Drake went away with a secret plan, not to be revealed to any; and, said the Queen, 'of all men my Lord Treasurer must not know it'.

What the secret plan was that Burghley was not to know, can only be guessed, for no record of it remains. Most people have supposed that it was to be a raid on the Peruvian treasure-coast, since that is what Drake effected. But Drake was an opportunist, and what he did is not necessarily what he set out to do; and the revision of Oxenham's dates, which pushes him into the scene of 1577, gives play to speculations that are unproved but at least legitimate. It is possible that Drake meant to sail up to the Gulf of Panama and join Oxenham in the Isthmus, and that perhaps this was the reinforcement Oxenham expected. When Drake sailed there was no news of Oxenham's disaster. If Drake had found the English ensconced in the Isthmus and providing a base for his armed shipping, the only armed shipping in the South Sea, what a stranglehold he would have had on the treasure route, and what a grip Elizabeth would have had on Philip, and how she would have screwed him to her purposes as her price for letting go! It is all supposition, for there is no direct evidence. Those who knew the secret plan kept silence. Not even Drake's journal of the voyage was allowed to see the light. Of course the Panama plan, if there was one, was dead before he reached the Pacific, for Oxenham was taken prisoner about the time Drake left England.

Drake sailed at the close of 1577 and passed the Straits of Magellan in September 1578 after executing Thomas Doughty for inciting mutiny. Why Doughty tried to ruin the expedition is not clear, but the evidence at his trial showed that he had been revealing plans, or perhaps his guesses, to Burghley. After emerging from the Straits Drake experienced weather that prevented any search for Terra Australis, had he been minded to make one. For weeks he was driven southwards or barely held his ground. He discovered that there was no continent, but open sea to the south of the Straits, and he may have sighted Cape Horn. He lost the company of two of his three ships, of which one turned homewards through the Straits and the other was missing with all hands, and was left with the *Golden Hind* alone to carry out his plans. As soon as the weather permitted he sailed northward along the west coast of South America. There he surprised ports and shipping and captured treasure, and learned from prisoners that Oxenham had been taken. He 'made' his voyage by capturing a treasure-ship bound for Panama, out of which he had a quantity of gold and precious stones and enough silver to provide a heavy lading for the *Golden Hind*. He made no move to approach Panama, although the Spaniards expected him to do so, but disappeared into the Pacific after a final landing on the coast of Guatemala. This was in April 1579, and the news of his depredations began to reach Europe in August. There for the present we leave Drake, as the diplomatists had to, for little could be done about him until he should return to face the music with his spoils.

Drake's departure on this voyage was made possible by a change in the European situation. Although from 1573 onwards Elizabeth was willing to be on good terms with Spain (with the tacit proviso that her seamen might do as they pleased in the Caribbean), she was by no means certain that Spain was sincere in reciprocating the wish for peace. The fitting-out in 1574 of a powerful armament in north Spanish ports with the published intention of reinforcing the Netherlands occasioned much alarm in England. But if Philip really had any anti-English design he did not proceed with it, perhaps on account of the death of Menendez, the able officer who was to have been in command. Elizabeth kept the possibility in mind and maintained relations with France by way of insurance. Here again there were reservations on both sides. The French had sent assistance to the Marian party in Scotland, and Catherine de Medici explained that it had been done by the Cardinal of Lorraine out of sympathy for his co-religionists; whereupon Elizabeth sent help to La Rochelle (in 1573), and explained that it had been done by the Bishop of London out of sympathy for his. Civil war in France was very nearly continuous until 1580, with the Huguenots and the *politiques* contending against the Valois court and the Guises, and with England taking care that La Rochelle should not fall, and subsidizing from time to time the Rhineland count John Casimir to aid the Huguenots with his ritters. Side by side with this, Elizabeth declared her observance of the Treaty of Blois, and renewed it when Charles IX died in 1574 and his brother Anjou succeeded as Henry III. Her aim was to keep the French alliance in being in case of war with Spain, and at the same time to take care that the Huguenots were not destroyed in case France and Spain should combine against her. The purposes of this two-way policy were admirably served by interminable marriage negotiations. The match between Elizabeth and Anjou (Henry III) had broken down on his religious stiffness. It was succeeded by a proposal for her to marry his brother Alençon, the youngest of the sons of Catherine de Medici. Alençon became Duke of Anjou in 1576 and will be referred to under that title. He was under twenty and just half Elizabeth's age when the courtship began, a little pockmarked fellow of no great ability, but—and here was his attraction— a sympathizer with the Huguenots and not sufficiently a rigid Catholic to give trouble on that score if he should come to England. Elizabeth, with her sense of the ridiculous, probably never meant to marry him, but she found the possibility so useful that she kept it alive for nearly a dozen years.

In the Netherlands an unbroken war of independence began with the sea-inspired revolt of Zealand and Holland in 1572. Requesens had no better fortune than Alva, and achieved no substantial reconquest. Yet the casualties in the war of sieges (Haarlem, Alkmaar, Leyden, Zierickzee, and others) were heavy on both sides, and William of Orange was at times out of hope that resistance would continue. Sea power maintained his precarious hold in the two Dutch provinces, but he was convinced that substantial help from England or France was essential, failing which Spain would win in the end. In England, Walsingham was for full assistance to the Dutch, since he believed that Spain meant to conquer all Protestants. Walsingham, it should be noted, had been recalled from the Paris embassy in 1573 and made a Privy Councillor and the Queen's principal Secretary. Burghley, who became Lord Treasurer, was more cautious and thought that limited aid would suffice. Elizabeth disliked the Dutch as rebels and Calvinists, and was only brought to consider helping them by the prospect that they might appeal more successfully to France. To Elizabeth a French occupation of the Netherlands appeared more dangerous than a Spanish. Nevertheless she hardly went beyond 'considering' the plea of the Dutch, and acted as though they could live on hope, which in fact they did. In the critical years 1576–8 her consenting to and rescinding of measures of assistance were the despair of her ministers, who genuinely believed that they were witnessing the ruin of Protestantism and their own country. Yet in the end they were wrong and their mistress right. She did not commit herself, and the cause survived.

The possession of Flushing gave Orange the possibility of blockading the approach to Antwerp up the Scheldt. He used it as a means of putting pressure on the Spaniards, but offended Elizabeth in 1575 by detaining an English merchant fleet bound for Antwerp. The Queen treated him roughly and threatened that if he continued the offence she would side with the Spaniards against him. To some extent both Elizabeth and Orange were bluffing, for both knew that essential community of interest held them together. In the winter of 1575–6 Elizabeth offered her mediation for restoring peace. She sent an envoy to Spain, who was rebuffed uncivilly by Philip. Orange then offered her the sovereignty of the Dutch provinces if she would take up their cause, but all she would do was to talk more mediation. Burghley at the same time spoke in a strongly pro-Dutch fashion to the Spanish agent in London, where a general impression was created that England was growing hostile to Spain. At this juncture (March 1576) Requesens died unexpectedly, leaving no successor but the Council of State (mostly Catholic nobles) to carry on the administration. Philip appointed his illegitimate half-brother Don John of Austria to be Governor, but Don John, who was in Italy, went first to Spain instead of direct to the Netherlands, and there was an interregnum of ten months. In that time the Spanish troops, unpaid and uncontrolled, became bands of robbers living on the country, while Orange unwisely interfered again with English trade and retarded Elizabeth's co-operation. In November, as Don John was approaching by travelling through France in disguise, the Spanish soldiers at Antwerp carried out a massacre of the inhabitants rivalling that of 1572 in Paris. Representatives of all the seventeen provinces thereupon agreed to recognize Don John only if he would immediately send away all the Spaniards and rule through Netherland officials in accordance with the ancient liberties. Don John came in from Luxembourg in January 1577. He had agreed to the terms, having no alternative, and took steps to pay off and send away the Spanish and other foreign soldiers. But he did not regard the situation as final, and neither did Orange, who completely distrusted him.

These events made the perils of the Netherland question appear more imminent to England. Ever since the beginning of the real revolt in the spring of 1572 it had been implicit that England had an interest in the country and could not afford to see a full Spanish despotism established on the ruins of its liberties. Still less could England afford to stand by and witness a French interference and the entrenchment of French power in an area of assembly more threatening than even Ireland could be. It had seemed through those years that English armed intervention was inevitable. But the Queen dreaded the idea of war. She did not on that account shirk her duty to her country's interests, but sought to accomplish it by diplomacy, dishonest and unpromising of success in the minds of forthright men like Walsingham, and yet so far successful. For five years there had been no power in the Low Countries strong enough to be a real threat to England. Now the advent of Don John promised a harder task. Would the Queen's methods be adequate?

Don John was the son of Charles V and did not forget it. The bend sinister was to him no bar to the acquisition of a kingdom, and on that his ambition was set. He was a soldier and the victor of Lepanto, and yet not a disciplined public servant like Alva, but an able man of the commoner type devoted to the service of himself. He regarded the Netherlands governorship as a stepping-stone. Competent work there would provide him with a force and an independent position from which to launch it—and over the narrow sea there were Mary Stuart to be rescued and married and Great Britain a kingdom to be united for an emperor's son to rule. These thoughts were not concealed. Philip knew of them and looked coldly on his brother. Orange knew of them and disbelieved Don John's acceptance of the limitations under which he had promised to rule. Elizabeth knew of them and saw in the brilliant careerist the aggressive military power whose establishment in the Netherlands she must prevent at any cost.

In the first half of 1577 a battle of intrigue went on between Orange, Don John, and Elizabeth, with an alliance of England and the Dutch slowly taking shape. Don John found himself thwarted by the Estates General of any reality of power, reported to Philip that the pledged arrangement would not work, and prepared to take up arms. He raised Walloon soldiery, and in July seized Namur as a fortified base and called on the Estates to aid him against Orange. Elizabeth professed her decision to support Orange, and sent William Davison, Walsingham's colleague in the secretaryship, to treat with him, with the approval of Burghley in addition. The Estates, although jealous of Orange, would not support Don John, and asked for English aid. In September the Queen promised money and men, and then hesitated, fearing that to go too far would mean war with Spain. By that time Drake must have been working on his preparations for the South Sea voyage, and had already had his interview with the Queen. He sailed twice from Plymouth, in November on a false start, and again in December, on what, viewed from the starting point, was a wild gamble. It was, however, a gamble in which the Queen stood to lose nothing—her connection with it was secret—and to win a means of putting pressure on Philip. On second thoughts the Queen sent no aid to the Netherlands, but again talked of mediation, and at the end of the year was once more sending envoys to Philip and Don John to say that the liberties of the Netherlands must be respected, or she would interfere. Don John refused to grant an armistice, already the Spanish regiments were marching back from Italy, and in January 1578 he routed the Estates army at Gembloux. Now or never, it seemed, must Elizabeth strike in. After some weeks delay she decided that her aid should consist of a subsidy to John Casimir to supply German mercenaries. At the same time (March 1578) Philip sent to London his last ambassador, Don Bernardino de Mendoza. Philip no more than Elizabeth wanted war, but he was considerably less wise than she was in recoiling from it; for whereas she was gaining the fruits of a victory without winning one, he was suffering the effects of defeat without being beaten. The elimination of England was indispensable to his success in the Netherlands.

The French factor threatened Elizabeth's satisfaction. Catherine de Medici thought of harking back to Coligny's plans. Henry III disliked his brother Anjou and wished to get him out of France. In March 1578 Anjou was negotiating with the Netherlands Estates with a view to going in with unofficial French aid and carving out a principality for himself. At once Elizabeth encouraged the revival of the courtship. She desired to control Anjou, and he was eager for her countenance. Although the language of love became ever more extravagant, the motives of the principals were quite unsentimental. Jean de Simier, the deputy-lover sent to England on Anjou's behalf, was so caressed by the Queen as to give material for the wilder sort of scandalmongers. In the summer she sent Walsingham to the Netherlands to obtain a sound view of the situation.[1] He was if possible to procure an armistice and peace negotiations between the rebels and Don John; if not, to estimate whether the rebels could hold out with the help of the mercenaries for whom the Queen had already paid £40,000 to John Casimir; and if they could not, to promise English troops, with Sluys and Flushing to be handed over to England as security for the expense. Walsingham reported that the last alternative was the only possibility and that an English army was

---

[1] For all this diplomacy the leading authority is Conyers Read's *Sir Francis Walsingham*, 3 vols. (Oxford, 1925), to which repeated recourse has been made in the writing of this and subsequent chapters.

the only means of keeping out the French. He thought that Elizabeth would at last move, and Orange and the Dutch were led to expect it. But still she did nothing, and in despair they concluded a treaty with Anjou in August. Orange and his friends were indignant, Walsingham aggrieved and disgusted, but nothing would induce her to commit herself. It may have been nervelessness, but was more likely subtlety. She was a judge of men, and did not expect her little suitor to achieve anything more than to keep the situation fluid, as it had been for years past. Whatever the process, the effect was of deep statesmanship of the cold-hearted sort, and there was at least no hypocrisy in it. Elizabeth never professed any altruistic feeling for the Dutch or for any people but her own.

Before returning to England in September 1578, Walsingham had noted how the plague was raging in the Netherland cities, a matter in which, as he remarked, his ambassador's status gave him no privilege over other men. At the end of the month Don John of Austria died suddenly. His heart had never been in his Netherlands task, which he regarded only as a stepping-stone to his further ambitions, and he was already in despair at their frustration. With the new Spanish troops had come an officer of note, Alexander Farnese, Prince of Parma, the son of an illegitimate daughter of Charles V, and Philip appointed him governor. He was at first reported in England as a light-weight, but the estimate was mistaken, and he turned out to be the soundest choice that Philip ever made. In six months, by war and diplomacy, he detached the Catholic southern provinces from the combination against Spain, and left to Orange the leadership of the Dutch, the seven provinces combined thenceforward in the Union of Utrecht. With its outlines clarified from their previous inchoate condition the war went on, as of Dutch against Spaniards, Calvinists against Catholics, with Antwerp and the country near the south bank of the Scheldt as the debatable region between.

The Netherlands question had been treated in some detail because events since 1575 had revealed it as the most absorbing question of policy, the determinant of England's security. In the Privy Council there was a division of opinion. Burghley and Sussex were undoubtedly clear that an absolute Spanish power must not be established, but they recognized that Spain with her best efforts was not in fact establishing it, and so concluded that a cautious encouragement of the Dutch, short of giving mortal offence to Spain, was

meeting the needs of the situation; while they attached great importance to the neutralizing of French designs of penetration, and
thought they could best be met by the marriage of the Queen to
Anjou, which would give England a voice in French policy. Burghley, like the Queen, did not want war with anyone. His heart was set
on peace and prosperity and the expansion of trade. But he was not
a pacifist in the present meaning of the term. He knew well that circumstances might necessitate war, and when the time should come
he would answer the call. His judgment was that the time had not
come, and perhaps might not. Meantime the country was growing
wealthier, and domestic problems, though difficult, were nothing like
so dangerous as at the close of the previous decade. He kept an eye
on the defences. Investigation showed corruption in the Navy under
the rule of Sir William Winter, and neglect of the laid-up ships.
Burghley had not liked the Queen's gamble of letting Drake loose in
the Pacific, but he was strong for naval efficiency. In 1577 he appointed John Hawkins, who had made a report on the matter,
Treasurer of the Navy, and backed him in his efforts for reform.
Walsingham and Leicester, the other two privy councillors of first-
rate influence, were inclined to simplify the issues. They believed
that a general Catholic attack on Protestantism had long been designed and was rapidly maturing, and that war was inevitable. They
thought the French alliance a snare, and opposed the Anjou marriage. They were for full support of the Dutch, however Spain might
take it, and of the Huguenots in opposition to the French court.
Leicester's sincerity is questionable, but Walsingham was an ardent
Protestant, 'the worst of the heretics' as Spain viewed him, whose
policy was dictated by his faith. He would have brought on war
earlier than it actually came. Burghley postponed it until England
was better able to fight. It is a little misleading to describe the contrast between them as that of the war party and the peace party. That
view is derived from Mendoza's despatches, and he, like most of the
Spanish ambassadors, did not understand Burghley as well as
Burghley understood him.

The Anjou marriage proposal reached a new height in August
1579, when the Duke paid a visit to England and Elizabeth saw him
for the first time. They got on well, and she seemed to be bent on the
match. But in the autumn she grew cold again and thrust the blame
on her Council and her people. Now that she was growing older (she
was forty-six) the public were thinking rather of the risk than the

advantage of child-bearing, and were by no means so anxious to see her married as in earlier days. Her death, with Mary Stuart living, would have been a calamity. Religious feeling was also strong against marriage with a Valois. The views of the Puritans were expressed in John Stubbs's *Discovery of a Gaping Gulf*, a pamphlet describing the French marriage as sinful and dangerous. Stubbs lost his hand for writing a libel, but the crowd sympathized with him. Elizabeth, while furious at Puritan presumption, noted that public opinion coincided with her own secret wishes.

Apart from the Netherlands, the events of 1578–9 presaged a storm in international affairs. The young King Sebastian of Portugal led an expedition to invade Morocco in 1578, and was there killed at the battle of Alcazar. His successor was his uncle the Cardinal Henry, an old man not expected to live long, and he was the last legitimate male of his house. After him Philip II had the best genealogical claim to the throne of Portugal, and his preparations to enforce it dominated his policy until the vacancy arose two years later. Such an acquisition would greatly increase Philip's revenues and sea power, and there was much alarm in England and France. Sir Humphrey Gilbert was of those who were not adverse to war with Spain. He had already suggested to the Queen that under cover of a patent for colonization he should lead a squadron to capture the Newfoundland fishing fleets of Spain and Portugal and Catholic France, and with the proceeds equip a strong attack on the West Indies, all this to be disavowed by the Queen if she saw fit. He was not allowed to do it, but he did obtain his patent for colonizing the coast of North America in 1578. In the autumn he prepared a dozen armed ships at Dartmouth and Plymouth. There were contradictory rumours of his destination, which does not seem to have had much relation to his patent. One of them was that he was going to support Oxenham in Panama. He was not going to Newfoundland, for there were no fishermen there when he sailed in November. He was back in the spring of 1579, the voyage a failure, and his force wasted by desertion, shipwreck, and fighting, but where and with whom are unknown. Drake's departure on a distant venture had inspired others, and there are Portuguese reports of a large English expedition (not Gilbert's) on the coast of Brazil in 1579, looking for a site for settlement. There is no English record of it, save that five ships were preparing at Plymouth at the time Gilbert left. The movement for English empire-building was rising strong, and it could only be satisfied by conflict with Spain and Portugal, since they jointly claimed a monopoly.

The Pope, Gregory XIII, not content with training his Jesuit missionaries at Rome, was tempted to try a military invasion. The *empresa*, the enterprise, was pressed upon the Catholic powers by the exiles from England and Ireland. Philip II had the military knowledge to see that it would be a very serious undertaking, and was by no means ready to embark on it, especially after the assimilation of Portugal came within his view. At Rome they were inclined to make light of it and to suppose that some cheap filibustering expedition would suffice. James Fitzmaurice, the Desmond rebel leader, went to Rome and was commissioned by the Pope to invade Ireland in 1577, but his design came to nothing. Then Thomas Stukeley, an English renegade, was given the command next year and set off from Italy with 600 men and a shipload of arms. He changed his purpose on the way, joined Sebastian's Moorish expedition, and was killed at Alcazar. Fitzmaurice resumed the lead, pulled together a cosmopolitan force of adventurers at Lisbon, and landed in Munster in the summer of 1579. He built a fort at Smerwick on the coast of Kerry, and raised an ill-supported rebellion. With him was Nicholas Sanders, papal legate to Ireland, and the affair caused much perturbation in England. It was obviously a movement parallel, with the rôles reversed, to what the English had been doing in the Netherlands. There were Spaniards as well as Italians in the papal force, and men wondered if it was a prelude to war by Philip II. He, however, had no hand in it, and was not to be diverted from his Portuguese designs.

Henry of Portugal died early in 1580, and in the summer Philip's armies moved in to take possession, driving into exile Don Antonio, the illegitimate native claimant. Under Alva's command the invasion went without a hitch, and Philip, his prestige marvellously enhanced, found himself master of the gold of Africa and the spices of the East. It was the first solid success of his reign, and it had a noticeable effect on his character. He became less hesitant and less inclined to overrate the factors against him. Slow he remained, but more actively resolute, with a growing sense of his destiny as the divinely appointed champion of Catholic Christendom, a more dangerous foe than formerly to the destiny of England.

In September, while Philip was still busy with Portugal, a reinforcement of papal volunteers reached Ireland. The English had the rebellion well in hand and the rebels mostly on the run, but the alarm of Spanish intentions redoubled. The reaction was brutal, as always in Ireland. Lord Grey of Wilton, the Lord Deputy, aided by a naval squadron under Winter, battered the intruders into unconditional surrender at Smerwick, and then, finding that they were filibusters with no commission to show from any sovereign recognized by England, put the whole party to the sword. It was what the Spaniards had done to Oxenham's men in Panama; and by the laws of war both nations were within their bloody rights. Fitzmaurice was killed soon afterwards. Nicholas Sanders, hunted through Ireland for two years more, died of hunger in the wilderness to which Munster had been reduced.

It was at this juncture that Drake, in the *Golden Hind*, came into Plymouth Sound, with a first eager question to some fishermen whether the Queen was alive and well. Nothing had been heard of him since he had put to sea with his treasure from the western shore of New Spain. An expedition sent out by the Muscovy Company in 1580 to open the North East Passage to the Pacific had among its objects to look for Drake and guide him home by the new way it should have discovered—so confident was Dee, its scientific adviser, of success. The expedition failed, but Drake needed no guidance. He visited the coast of California and in the Queen's name annexed the country as New Albion. After a refit he sailed across the Pacific and reached the Moluccas, where he laded some tons of the spices that had hitherto been Portugal's monopoly. Thence he threaded the dangerous channels of the great archipelago, stranding once upon a reef and getting off unharmed, gained the Indian Ocean, rounded the Cape, and sailed north through the Atlantic, completing the first English circumnavigation. He brought with him a shipload of silver and a quantity of gold, worth at the lowest estimate nearly twice a year's normal revenue of the English crown, and yielding a profit said to have worked out at 4,700 per cent. No wonder he was anxious to hear about the Queen, upon whom it lay to keep hold of his prize.

16

THE CONFLICT JOINED

FROM 1580 two developments long prepared acquired clearer shape and more visible imminence. One was the war with Spain, the first of the modern-type wars in our history. The other was the foundation of the British Empire. At the outset these two stimulated one another; but it is also true that the Spanish war, once joined, was a deterrent to colonial expansion.

The boom in trade continued, although it did not eliminate the poor. They remained in sufficient numbers to excite the compassion of the liberal-minded and the alarm of all. But in general the community's wealth was increasing, and there is a consensus of observers on the growth of luxury in food, extravagance in dress, and ostentation in building. The emphasis is marked on the way in which the passion for clothes was transcending class distinctions and people of humble station were arraying themselves in a manner previously considered far above them; and this is testimony either to a redistribution of wealth or to its general increase. Since there was no notable redistribution, we may take it as evidence that the early 'eighties were a period of prosperity. So undoubtedly they were. The enterprise and the opportunities existed. Capital had hitherto been short, capital in the mobile form easily applied where needed. The City men had told Wolsey that though rich in stocks they were bare of money, and that was still the complaint until the mid-Elizabethan period. Northumberland's company of 1553 (the later Muscovy Company) represented the City's utmost effort at the time with a subscribed capital of £6,000. Half a century later the East India Company was to raise £68,000 as the joint stock for its first expedition. That is a measure of the growth of the English capital fund upon which much else depended. In the 'eighties John Hawkins estimated that the nation's wealth had grown threefold since the beginning of the reign. It was a testimonial to peace and good government, but to more than that.

The amount of Drake's treasure brought home in 1580 has never been accurately known, since those concerned had reasons for mystification. Different lines of deduction have been applied to the surviving data, and they yield different results, with a minimum of about £400,000, and a possibility of something very much higher, up to $1\frac{1}{2}$ or even 2 millions sterling. In any case it was an enormous accession to the country's fluid capital, a considerably greater sum than the Queen's treasury was collecting as annual revenue. The Queen, that is the treasury, appears to have taken about half of it, Drake became a rich man, and his backers in their various proportions divided the rest after the claims of the sailors had been satisfied. Thus there was, just at the time when relations with Spain degenerated into war, a plethora of capital in the hands of men who knew how to use it in privateering enterprises and in the promotion of new and adventurous trading schemes. At the same time the Queen had the means for a more vigorous policy than had hitherto been possible. The economic importance of Drake's voyage was considerable.

In foreign trade there were two almost simultaneous developments. Hamburg, although friendly to English trade, was a member of the Hanseatic League and subject to its decrees. The League objected to the presence in Germany of the Merchants Adventurers, and when their ten years' contract with Hamburg expired in 1577 compelled that city to refuse renewal and to treat the merchants as unprivileged strangers. It was a shortsighted decision because the retaliation was obvious. Since 1560 the League had been enjoying certain privileges in London, and under Burghley's advice the Queen reduced the Hanse merchants in 1578 to the position of unprivileged strangers. The Merchants Adventurers shifted their German headquarters to Emden, which was not so conveniently located as Hamburg. The danger of a quarrel with the League was that the supply of naval stores might be cut off; but the League was not so strong as it had been in Mary's time, and Burghley promoted the foundation of a new regulated company to include all English merchants trading with Scandinavia and the Baltic. This, the Eastland Company, was chartered in 1579 and was successful in its purpose during the Queen's reign. The Elizabethan Eastland Company had no connection, save in function, with the medieval Eastland merchants, whose separate identity had long been lost by merging with the Merchants Adventurers.

The Levant trade had declined towards 1550, and had been virtually discontinued since that date owing to the general lawlessness that accompanied the increase of Turkish sea power in the Mediterranean. That sea became a closed area to Englishmen, and by 1580 there must have been a dozen of them familiar with the Caribbean for every one who had sailed to the Levant. In the 'seventies, as we have seen, the Muscovy Company had a trade with Persia by the long route through the White Sea and Russia. Although profitable it was precarious, and in fact came to an end in 1580. Before that date some London merchants, headed by Edward Osborne and Richard Staper, had sent agents through Poland into Turkey to seek facilities. The French were already engaged in the trade, having had close connection with Turkey since the days of Francis I. In spite of their jealousy William Harborne, the English envoy, secured a grant of privileges; and it is significant that the Sultan declared that he would exclude no enemies of Spain from his dominions. The English already fell into that category, and there had been hints from their side of an anti-Spanish alliance. In 1581 Elizabeth granted a charter to the Turkey Company, which consisted of twelve merchants working on a joint-stock and gradually building up a fleet of fighting merchantmen less formidable only than the ships of the Navy. Burghley and Walsingham both furthered the formation of the Company, whose importance to the national defence as well as the national economy they both recognized. The Queen in 1582 lent the Company 10,000 lb. weight (over four tons) of silver, undoubtedly of Drake's getting; and for several years the profits were good.[1]

In the spring of 1580 the Jesuit mission sent by the Pope from Rome began its work in England under the leadership of Edmund Campion and Robert Parsons. The presence of both was soon known to the authorities, but over a year elapsed before Campion was taken and Parsons escaped overseas. The fact that they were stirring Catholics into activity and yet could not be caught excited considerable alarm, which was reflected in the acts of the Parliament that met in January 1581. These increased the fines on recusants from their previous trifling amount to £20 a month, and fixed still larger penalties

---

[1] See A. C. Wood, *History of the Levant Company* (Oxford, 1935). It should be noted that the foundation of 1581 was the Turkey Company. It was named the Levant Company in 1592, after amalgamation with the Venice Company of 1583.

for saying and hearing mass. The Queen, however, was less drastic in administration than Parliament in legislation, and recusants who were too poor to pay their fines were not for the most part imprisoned. The hunt was chiefly directed against the missionaries, who were supposed to be organizing a Catholic rebellion to aid a Spanish invasion. Campion was not doing so, and the same may be true of some of the others, although Parsons talked politics while in England. Campion's work was solely spiritual so far as his own intention was concerned. But he was the soldier of the Pope who had invaded Ireland with an armed force, whose bull absolved Catholics from their allegiance, and whose secretary was officially writing that to assassinate 'that guilty woman' would be a meritorious act.[1] While Campion claimed 'we travelled only for souls', Gregory XIII could not say as much. And indeed Campion's claim was in practice a half-truth; for when he gained a soul he made a prospective traitor to the Queen of England. When he was captured in the summer of 1581 the authorities put him on trial, not under recent legislation, but under the simple treason law of 1352, for aiding the Queen's enemies. He was brave and resistant to the torture applied to make him incriminate others, and to the brutalities of a Tyburn execution. But a stainless soldier does not sanctify a cause, and in fact the Jesuit mission was a material attack upon England as formidable as armed invasion and plots against the Queen's life. The invasion by Jesuits and other seminarists continued both before and after open war with Spain began in 1585. By the end of the reign nearly two hundred of them had been executed, although they were a minority of those captured. The majority were simply imprisoned, some were released, and some were even shipped abroad.

After Drake's return there was some discussion on the restitution of his plunder to Spain. Mendoza was naturally insistent on it, and Philip no doubt was extremely indignant at the outrage and alarmed at the extension of privateering to the hitherto inviolate coast of Peru. English merchants trading in Spain and the Netherlands were afraid of another arrest and were willing to see the treasure restored. Influential shareholders in the expedition, such as Walsingham and Leicester, were of course urgent for keeping it. The Queen for some time uttered no decided pronouncement, and let it be supposed that her mind was not made up. It is certain that she meant to keep the treasure if she judged she could do so without war. After six months

[1] In December 1580, in response to an enquiry from English refugees in Spain.

her judgment was that it could be kept. She had a counter-charge to Mendoza's complaints, in the presence of Spaniards among the papal invaders of Ireland. The fact that they had not made half a million pounds out of it was irrelevant to the principle; and she contended that filibustering in Munster was at least as offensive as privateering in Peru. Philip could only answer such argument by war, and for this he was not ready. He had more respect for the difficulty of invading England than any other Spaniard, and infinitely more than had the exiles and churchmen who urged the *empresa* at Rome. He would not give Mendoza the final backing, and on 4 April 1581, Elizabeth announced her decision by knighting Drake on the deck of the *Golden Hind*.

Already Drake was forming plans for English expansion in accord with the new situation created by Philip's conquest of Portugal. Don Antonio, the Portuguese claimant to the throne, having escaped to France, came to England in June. The Azores had declared for him and were refusing to accept Philip's rule. It was thought that the officers of the East Indian possessions would take the same side. Portugal itself was by no means reconciled to its new master. Drake then and afterwards saw Don Antonio as the instrument to the founding of an English tropical empire. Restored by English aid to Portugal, or at least to its colonies, Antonio would rely for his defence on English sea power and would pay for it by opening Brazil and Africa and the Far East to English enterprise. Statesmen might view Philip's seizure of Portugal as a menace to the balance of Europe and the survival of England. Drake saw it as a heaven-sent opportunity. His was the offensive spirit that wins wars, and he infected England with it in the 'eighties, in spite of the non-effectiveness of all his Portuguese plans. In 1581 there was a proposal, not proceeded with, that Drake should be head of a company for trade with countries south of the equator. In place of this a more immediate plan was discussed, for Drake to go with Antonio to the Azores, install English garrisons, and use the islands as a base for attacks on the treasure fleets. This was to be done under the Portuguese flag, with Antonio recognized as King of Portugal, and the English acting as his auxiliaries. Elizabeth, however, expected that it would involve her in war with Spain, and determined not to proceed unless the French would equally commit themselves. Catherine de Medici was afraid of being Elizabeth's tool and of being left to fight a Spanish war from which Elizabeth would extricate herself. Between them they ended in doing nothing, and the plate fleet season slipped away.

An Anglo-French alliance, firmly knit, would have been the best guarantee for either country against the might of Spain. But insincerity and distrust made it impossible. Elizabeth wanted the alliance without paying the price, of marriage to Anjou. Catherine and Henry III wanted Anjou married, and his career thenceforth an English liability, without being prepared to stand firm with England against Spain. In fact Catherine's record was such that no one could trust her, and the French were entitled to say the same of Elizabeth. In the summer of 1581 Walsingham was sent to France on a hopeless mission of creating some sort of compact. Anjou made a second visit to England and raised his wooing to a new sublime of the ridiculous. But his mind was on money, not love, and he simply would not go away without a subsidy for his Netherland adventure. That, and a public promise of marriage, made by Elizabeth in the gallery at Whitehall, were given him; and off he went, not to return. The promise, when reduced to diplomatic form, turned out to be accompanied by conditions that made it certain to be refused. It was not the end of the courtship, which was never formally ended while Anjou lived. Elizabeth liked him better than might have been expected, and when he died she wept tears of genuine regret.

When Drake was in the Moluccas in 1579 he not only collected spices but made an agreement with the Sultan of Ternate whereby the English were to have full facilities for trade with his island. London's ambitions were already set on trade with the East, and much was hoped from this so-called treaty.[1] It was obviously desirable to follow it up without delay. Drake would have been willing to go out again by way of Peru, but that would have been an almost certain step to war. The Queen decided on a strictly mercantile expedition without any treasure-raiding, and to that end put Edward Fenton, who had served under Frobisher, in command of four ships, with orders to sail by the Cape of Good Hope and open trade with the Moluccas. The investors included Drake, Burghley, Leicester, and the Muscovy Company, diverse elements which all had a share in nominating the officers. The result was a divided force and failure. Fenton sailed in 1582 and reached the coast of Brazil, where his expedition virtually broke up. Drake's nominees, including two of his circumnavigators, wished to disregard the orders and pass through the Straits of Magellan. Fenton resisted, and violent quarrels ensued.

[1] No text of it has survived, and it is uncertain whether the arrangement was ever put in writing.

He gave up hope of success and turned back to England. John Drake, nephew of Sir Francis, refused to follow, and went off on a course of his own, to be wrecked and taken prisoner by the Spaniards and never to return to England.

Colonization ran parallel to eastern trade as an expression of the empire-building ambition. The connection between them was close, for settlements in North America were expected to serve as bases for the opening of the North West Passage. In another aspect colonization was bound up with national defence, for the only solution of the Irish problem seemed to lie in providing Ireland with a loyal English population. In yet another it concerned the social improvement that was appealing to broad-minded men, the relief of the chronic poverty of the unfortunate, which continued intractable side by side with general prosperity.

The colonizing movement opened in earnest in 1583 when Sir Humphrey Gilbert at length acted on his patent for North America. He was hard put to it to raise money even for a small expedition, and had to assign the rights over large tracts of virgin America to sub-patentees. The Queen approved, but gave no aid. The colonial party worked for him. Dee had already prepared for the Queen a fine map of the North Atlantic, with a statement of the evidence for her title to North America. Richard Hakluyt, a rising geographer, published in 1582 his *Divers Voyages*, containing documents on John Cabot's original discovery and extracts from foreign books giving the scanty information available about the continent. Michael Lok contributed a map showing the attractiveness of the North West Passage. The Passage was in the minds of most of them, as it had long been in Gilbert's; but it was not the immediate aim of his expedition, which was solely for the purpose of planting a colony and prospecting for precious metals. He sailed with 260 men in the summer of 1583. Early in August, when the fishing fleets were still on the Newfoundland coast, he formally took possession in the harbour of St. John's. He spent some days in prospecting and believed he had found silver ore, and then sailed south-westwards with the intention of planting a settlement on the coast of what is now Nova Scotia. One of his five ships had deserted soon after leaving England, and another was sent home from Newfoundland with sick men and some who were unwilling to proceed. Near Cape Breton the largest of the three remaining was wrecked with the loss of nearly all on board, including the colonists and their equipment. There was nothing for it but to return to England. On the voyage Gilbert was drowned by the foundering of the little pinnace in which he sailed.

Sir Humphrey Gilbert left a deeper mark on English history than his achievements in action warranted. His own qualities are hard to assess, or rather to combine in a consistent estimate. He was brave and active, yet lacked the faculty of command, cruel in Ireland, where all were cruel, yet chivalrous and unsparing of himself in the closing scenes of his life. The secret of his appeal to his countrymen lay perhaps in an indefinable knightliness and a belief in his country's destiny. Men remembered his purposes rather than his failures; and they remembered his words when his ship was soon to sink: 'We are as near heaven by sea as by land'.

The writers of the colonial party expressed the economic, political, and social doctrines of the time. The mid-Tudor depression and the continued unsettlement of Europe showed the inadequacy of the old trades as a basis for England's prosperity. It was held that the country weakened itself and strengthened its rivals by buying goods from them. An increasing knowledge of geography suggested that the outer regions of the world held lands and climates where English factors might buy tropical produce direct from native producers, and so eliminate the toll of profit paid to Spain and Portugal; and where English settlers might produce wines and silk, dyestuffs and naval stores, hitherto obtained from the continent of Europe. Everywhere in the unprospected world lay possibilities of gold and silver: why should it be supposed that Mexico and Peru were the only treasure lands? The advantage of Philip II in financing his European wars by the lading of his plate fleets was present, and exaggerated, in every mind. 'His Indian gold' might yet overthrow England unless she could find gold of her own. New routes to Asia would make England richer than Portugal. Armed settlements on the American coast would be bases from which to raid the Caribbean and attack the returning treasure fleets.

The tide of such ideas had been flowing since the reign of Edward VI, when also, as we have seen, there had been the beginnings of a liberal humanity, in thought if not in action, towards the oppressed and unlucky at the bottom of the social system. The mid-Elizabethans were the first to combine humanitarianism with expansion. Gilbert wrote of inhabiting the countries flanking the North West Passage with the submerged classes in England. Sir Walter Ralegh, his half-brother, took up the plan. Christopher Carleill,

Walsingham's son-in-law, saw the unemployed as the material of
colonies. Granted that it was not all disinterested philanthropy, it is
yet a proof that there was a public opinion to which it was worth
while to appeal. Above all Richard Hakluyt, whose motives at any
rate were pure, since he sought no fortune for himself, put in
eloquent prose the problem of poverty and the colonization of
America as its remedy. To him as to all of them England was over-
peopled, partly by reason of her own good fortune in escaping the
civil wars of the continent. They had no statistics, but they were sure
of the fact. In truth it does seem likely that the population grew in
the sixteenth century from three millions to four, an enormous strain
on a comparatively slow-moving social organism. Better use of the
land, new industries, new commerce, were doing something to meet
the need, but not enough. For the Elizabethan thinkers a British
Empire was the necessity. In 1584 Hakluyt addressed to the Queen,
on Ralegh's urging, a *Discourse of the Western Planting* combining all
the economic, strategic, and social arguments. On the last he said
this:

> 'Truth it is that through our long peace and seldom sickness (two
> singular blessings of Almighty God) we are grown more populous than
> ever heretofore: so that now there are of every art and science so many
> that they can hardly live one by another, nay rather they are ready to
> eat up one another: yea, many thousands of idle persons are within this
> realm which, having no way to be set on work, be either mutinous and
> seek alteration in the state, or at least very burdensome to the common
> wealth, and often fall to pilfering and thieving and other lewdness,
> whereby all the prisons of the land are daily pestered and stuffed full of
> them, where either they pitifully pine away or else at length are miser-
> ably hanged.'

The 'western planting' would cure this canker. To Walsingham's
statesmanlike mind it provided the remedy for another. Puritan
though he was, he viewed the Catholics without hatred as men
lamentably possessed with error. He was no persecutor for religion,
but he was a guardian of the state, and he welcomed the idea of a
Catholic colony to draw off to a harmless distance those who were
dangerous at home. With his approval Sir George Peckham, a
Catholic and one of Gilbert's sub-patentees, proposed to organize a
Catholic settlement as a part of Gilbert's series of American plantings.
It came to nothing on Gilbert's death, but is interesting as an indication of the thought of the time. If Walsingham had hopes from it,

Mendoza had fears. He wrote that it would weaken the Catholic interest, and urged that the seminary priests should forbid their converts to emigrate.

Gilbert left heirs to his two projects, John Davis of Dartmouth for the North West Passage, and Sir Walter Ralegh for America. Davis was distinguished for his scientific navigation, of which he learned much from Dee, and was one of the finest seamen England has produced, a man who thought more of service than of money-getting, a forerunner of James Cook. His expeditions were poorly financed, but with cheap and sometimes rotten outfits he did much. A small syndicate promoted by Dee, Adrian Gilbert, brother of Sir Humphrey, and William Sanderson, a London merchant, sent him out in three successive years, 1585–7. He worked between Greenland and the 'broken lands' north of Labrador that Frobisher had visited. By careful observations he cleared up their geography. In the last voyage of the series, in the summer of 1587, in a leaky pinnace of twenty tons, he reached the record latitude of 73° in Baffin Bay and saw the sea stretching open and free of ice. A contrary wind stopped him, although he beat against it until his victuals were almost exhausted. But he believed that he had found the Passage. He never had the chance to try again, for the next year was the Armada year, and thereafter all the money went into tropical adventures. We shall see him again seeking the East by other approaches.

Ralegh obtained a patent for American colonization in 1584. His idea of the location differed from Gilbert's and he intended to work farther south, where a colony in the latitude of southern Spain might be expected to produce wines and fruits, and would be better placed for Caribbean raids and the waylaying of the plate fleets in the Florida channel. He sent out a reconnaissance in 1584, not to settle but to prospect. His captains reached the coast of the present North Carolina and reported it perfect for the purpose, fertile and temperate, with natives most 'loving' and helpful. Ralegh, a master of words, named it Virginia. The Queen kept him at court, and he appointed Grenville to plant the colony in 1585.

In the minds of Ralegh and Grenville the venture was a move in the Spanish war, which they regarded as then beginning; and they linked Virginia with the West Indies. Grenville sailed out in 1585 by way of Puerto Rico and Hispaniola, on whose coasts he stayed for some time. At the end of June he reached Virginia and settled the colonists on the island of Roanoke. After spending two months in exploring the country, Grenville took the ships back to England, promising to return with supplies in the following year. The men left in Virginia under the governorship of Ralph Lane were rather a military force than a body of colonists. They showed little intention of tilling the ground and establishing themselves as a permanent community. For food they relied upon the Indians and on supplies brought over the sea, as to a garrison. Their achievement was to learn something about the Indians and to make a rough survey of the country and its possibilities. Before a year was out food was becoming scarce and the Indians hostile, while Grenville did not come and the colony was striking no roots. There had been no allocation of separate properties, which might have given an interest in the soil, and no collection of trade goods of any value. To most of the men there could have appeared little object in remaining. Then a great English fleet appeared, not Grenville's, but Drake's, returning from the opening campaign of the war. Drake came to see if he could do anything for the colony, and the colonists prevailed upon him to take them home. He did so in June 1586, and a fortnight after he had sailed Grenville arrived on the coast with ample supplies. Grenville left fifteen men as a token occupation and consoled himself with ravaging the Azores on the voyage back to England.

In 1586, therefore, Virginia was abandoned, for the fifteen men all perished. Ralegh and his associates made new plans for the following year. The attempt of 1587 seems to have carried better promise of founding a colony. The adventurers had more of the settler's and less of the garrison's mentality. Some of them took their wives and children, and there are references to individual grants of land. The governor was John White, who had been in the previous voyage. He reached Roanoke in July and reoccupied the deserted fort, although there were suggestions that the colony should migrate to the mainland. The leading men were determined to plant a permanent settlement. For that purpose they concluded that additional supplies were essential and prevailed upon White, against his will, to go home with the fleet in order to obtain them. He left a hopeful community in good shape on Roanoke, with a promise to be back next year with all things needful. Next year a new Virginia fleet under Grenville was accordingly fitted out, but was forbidden to sail when it was known that the Armada was approaching. In the two following years also White was thwarted of his return to Virginia, and not until 1591 did he reach Roanoke, to find that the settlers had disappeared. No

real news of their fate has ever been learned, although deductions
from slender clues have been attempted. In sum we may say that the
Spanish war had killed the Virginia colony.

Fenton's failure was not the end of Far Eastern projects; and while
the ocean men were meditating fresh expeditions by the Cape and the
Straits of Magellan, the Turkey Company thought of reaching out
through Syria to the Indian Ocean. John Newbery, an associate of
the Turkey merchants, went overland by Aleppo and the Euphrates
to Baghdad and thence to Ormuz on the Persian Gulf in 1580–2. In
1583 he departed in the service of the Company on a longer journey.
With Ralph Fitch he reached India by way of Syria and the Persian
Gulf. After many adventures they agreed that Fitch should remain
to explore Bengal while Newbery should travel home by land and
bring out ships to Bengal to meet Fitch in two years' time. Newbery
perished somewhere on the journey home and was never heard of.
Fitch travelled through Burma, Siam, and Malaya, and ultimately
home in 1591 through India and Syria. His achievement as a traveller
was magnificent, but his report showed that there was little hope of
conducting an overland trade with India. Meanwhile Drake had been
anxious to resume his Moluccas project and to open a spice trade by
the ocean route on the basis of his treaty with Ternate. At the close
of 1584 it was agreed that he should go, and a state syndicate with
the Queen a member set about the equipment of thirty-five ships and
pinnaces with 1,600 men. With such a force Drake would have had
little difficulty in establishing factories in the Spice Islands, and on
the way thither he would have been able to sweep the coast of Peru.
In fact he did not sail. Before he was ready in 1585 the Spanish
situation changed and he was diverted to service in the Atlantic.

Since the beginning of the Queen's reign, and more especially
since the Massacre of St. Bartholomew, many Englishmen had been
convinced that a coalition of the Catholic powers existed for the
purpose of destroying Protestantism. In a formal sense this belief was
long unfounded, and Spain, the Valois, the Guises, the papacy, and
the German Habsburgs were for a long time very much at variance,
and devoid of any common policy. Nevertheless, from the late
'seventies onward, the force of circumstances and the collective will-
power of the Catholic Church did drive the Catholic powers to act
in greater unison, and a coalition of at least Philip II, the Pope, and
the Guises did in practice take shape as England was gradually recognized to be the keystone of Protestantism. Against this development

Elizabeth and her ministers were perpetually vigilant. In no quarter did they need to be more so than in Scotland, the 'postern gate' to the invasion of England.

In the early years of Mary's captivity her Scottish supporters were a considerable force, kept in check with difficulty by Moray and his successors. With the failure of the Ridolfi plot they dwindled. The remnant held the castle of Edinburgh, and in 1573 Elizabeth sent men and guns to aid the Regent Morton and forced them to surrender. Morton had become Regent in the previous year and continued until 1578, giving Scotland a peaceful interval in which she remained steady to the English alliance. A hostile faction ended the regency and declared James VI at the age of twelve fit to govern, but Morton was soon back in power as his leading minister. Then in 1579 the Duke of Guise sent Esmé Stuart, one of the numerous Franco-Scots, as his agent into Scotland. Stuart, created Duke of Lennox, together with James Stuart, Earl of Arran, gained influence with the boy-king and procured the execution of Morton in 1581, a distinct blow to English influence; and at the same time a Jesuit mission appeared in Scotland. Next year the pro-English opponents of Lennox suddenly seized the King and carried him off to Ruthven Castle, near Perth (the 'Raid of Ruthven'), and drove Lennox away to France. Twelve months later James was similarly freed from the Ruthven party by the French faction. By this time, 1583, he was seventeen and seeking to assert himself. With Arran at his elbow he was writing to Guise, Philip II, and the Pope, and was potentially at the disposal of plans for invading England through Scotland. Walsingham went on a mission to him and failed to come to terms. A favourable factor, however, was that James showed no concern for his mother, and her influence in Scotland had ceased to exist. At length after tortuous intrigues Arran was overthrown and Elizabeth established her influence in 1585. By a treaty signed in the next year James entered into a defensive alliance with her and accepted a pension. A condition, unexpressed but understood, was that he should succeed to her throne. The postern gate was closed.

Steps towards the anti-English coalition were taken in 1581–2, when the Jesuit Creighton went to Scotland with a proposal for Lennox to invade northern England with an army to be furnished by the Pope and Philip II, while Guise should land simultaneously in the south. Mary Stuart and Mendoza were informed of the plan, although it is not clear that Philip gave more than a general approval. In detail the provision of the invading army must have been a serious problem. Philip was always brought up against it, while the Roman planners took it lightly. Their remedy for any deficiency of soldiers was always the phantom army of English Catholics, which they were prepared to call out at a moment's notice and to number at ten, twenty, or thirty thousand as occasion demanded. Philip was more realistic, and his greatest admiral Santa Cruz was at that time furnishing him with a very different estimate of the preparations needed for the invasion of England. The Raid of Ruthven and the expulsion of Lennox postponed any action in 1582, and the English government by means of its spy system found out what was being discussed. The discovery to a certain extent misled them for, coupled with the unsatisfactory attitude of James VI in 1583, it fixed their attention on Scotland as the dangerous quarter. In fact the invasion from Scotland was eliminated from the plan as revised in 1583. The intention then was that a body of troops, detached from Parma's forces in the Netherlands and commanded by the Duke of Guise, should land by surprise in Sussex, Arundel being the selected port. Mendoza was to slip out of England in time to join this force at Dunkirk and come over with it, accompanied by Robert Parsons and William Allen. They were to raise the Catholics of England, liberate Mary Stuart, and place her on the throne, she herself being apprised of all and eagerly awaiting the outcome.

Whether this plan would ever have come into effect, and how far it would have gone to success if it had not been detected, cannot be stated. Its essence was evasion of English sea power by surprise. Hawkins was at that time organizing the Navy at Chatham in such wise that he could turn out some of the ships in a very few days and could mobilize the whole fleet within three weeks of the word being given. Could Spanish troops in the spy-haunted Netherlands have gathered at a port, and could shipping have been gathered to carry them, in such short and secret order as to preclude any counteraction from the Medway? It would have needed extraordinary luck with the weather and everything else, including the tongues of ecclesiastics who were prone to babble about their hopes. The plan did not come to trial, for Walsingham detected it. His agents were adepts at obtaining copies of the correspondence of those whom he suspected. In 1583 he thus became possessed of communications between Mary Stuart and the French Ambassador. Beyond the almost normal circumstance that Mary was carrying on an illicit correspondence, they did not tell him much, for Guise was not working through the ambassador of Henry III, who was in fact ignorant of the invasion plan. Walsingham did however learn that one Francis Throckmorton was an agent of Mary's and was deep in some scheme of communications. After six months' watch he arrested Throckmorton in November, and Throckmorton, being racked, confessed a great deal more than had been expected from him, namely the surprise invasion by Guise, the landing at Arundel, the complicity of Mendoza, and much more. Mary's part in the affair was further illuminated next year, when Creighton was captured at sea in possession of a document that gave a full account of it. He tried to throw his papers overboard, but cast them to windward, and they were blown back on deck.

In January 1584 Don Bernardino de Mendoza received a summons to attend the Privy Council, and was there told that his part in the revolutionary plot had been discovered and that it was the Queen's pleasure that he should leave England within fifteen days. Uttering some needlessly heroical bluster, the last Elizabethan tenant of the Spanish embassy duly departed, and the shutters went up at that address for twenty years to come. Mendoza became Philip's ambassador in Paris, where he did his best to maintain his communications with England.

The danger of war, and worse, the danger of the Queen's assassination, came nearer in 1584. First, the Duke of Anjou dropped out. In 1581–3, more or less with Elizabeth's countenance, he had made a show of aiding the Dutch against Parma. But he was no soldier, and the enemy steadily pressed him out of the country, especially after he had compromised himself with his allies by a treacherous attempt to seize Antwerp and use it to make a bargain for himself. He died in July 1584, leaving Elizabeth with no stalking-horse to a task which she would certainly have to undertake without further subterfuge. In France the death of Anjou was of prime importance, for it left the Huguenot Henry of Navarre heir to Henry III, the last of the Valois. The French Catholics swore never to submit to a Protestant king and rallied to the Duke of Guise, who in his turn was closely bound to Philip II. A greater man than Anjou died at the same time, William of Orange, shot by a traitor for a reward publicly offered by Philip II. His death seemed an irreparable blow to the Dutch patriots, not for his military talent, which was not conspicuous, but by reason of his steadfastness and his power of inspiring resolution in others. Meanwhile Parma was mastering the cities and the territory south of Antwerp, and preparing methodically to grasp the great port itself, after which he might go on to reduce the north. It was evident that England would be faced with making a decision whether or not to give open aid to the Dutch, and that war would hang on the answer.

After the death of Orange the assassination of Elizabeth was a danger that haunted her people, and indeed it had been seriously dreaded before. In 1583 the Duke of Guise was in treaty with an Englishman who professed willingness to do the deed for a reward. The plan was made known to Mendoza and to Philip II and to the Pope's secretary, but nothing came of it, as the prospective assassin cried off. His identity is not certain, but he may have been the William Parry who was certainly contemplating the Queen's murder in 1584. This man had a shady record as both a Catholic agitator and a spy of the English government, so that it is difficult to say which he genuinely was. In 1584 he made great play in Catholic quarters with his intention to kill the Queen, but he seems to have claimed afterwards that he did it as an *agent provocateur* to elicit information. Anyhow he talked treason without having any commission to do so, and when denounced was put on trial and executed early in 1585 as if the Queen's ministers believed him to be a traitor. What impressed the public when the story came out was the ease with which he could have done the murder; for on one occasion he was admitted to a private interview with the Queen. Before this, a madman named John Somerville had loudly announced his intention to shoot the Queen, and it was thought necessary to take him seriously so far as to sentence him in due form. He committed suicide in prison.

The Parry case did not become known in 1584, but in that year there were sufficient reasons for public alarm and resentment. It was known that Philip II was ready to pay for the murder of his opponents and that the Pope sanctioned such acts. The plot brought to light by Throckmorton's arrest showed that foreign powers were preparing a surprise attack in Mary's interest and with her knowledge. The expulsion of Mendoza made men expect some signal attempt in retaliation. Of all these things the murder of Orange made the greatest impression, for English values rated him second only to the Queen. For her the people had by the 'eighties the loyalty, comprising almost a religious element, that has shed its glow over the whole reign in retrospect, although in the early years it was only in process of taking shape. To the Protestant Englishman Queen Elizabeth embodied all his hopes and beliefs, much as Queen Victoria did to her subjects three centuries later; and the Tudor feeling was the fiercer in that the surrounding dangers were greater. Men believed that the time had come to be plain with their enemies, and the result was a transaction hitherto unprecedented, a great voluntary combination of all classes of men from all parts of the country for a clearly defined purpose in support of their sovereign. At the instance of the Council a bond of association was circulated for signature. It declared that if the Queen's life were attempted the signatories would revenge it to the uttermost, would prevent the succession of the person in whose favour the attempt was made, and would do their best to put that person to death. Englishmen flocked to join the Association, and the Queen, touched though she must have been by their fervour, was somewhat alarmed at its emphasis. She did not like extremes, and she had a nicer sense of justice in this matter than had her subjects. The Parliament of 1584–5 met a month after the Association was launched, and embodied the bond in a statute, with the modification, at her instance, that the 'person' might only be 'pursued to the death' if privy to the attempt on the Queen's life, and that the process must be by legal trial and not summary violence. The enactment made the terms of plotting plain, and if the 'person' chose to engage in it thereafter she knew what she was in for.

The duties of the Tudor subject in all ranks of life were inescapable and might be onerous. The Earl of Shrewsbury had spent fifteen thankless years as Mary's keeper, treating her by command as a sovereign and a guest, and thus allowing her liberties which she abused by carrying on seditious correspondence; and incurring the suspicion of the Queen's ministers for his laxity, the complaints of Mary for his severity, and the accusations of his own wife for his civility to his charge. At last he got his relief, and Mary was removed in 1585 to the care of Sir Amyas Paulet at Tutbury Castle; and before the end of the year to a pleasanter house at Chartley in Derbyshire. Paulet was a Puritan and a friend of Walsingham, and with him the pretence of the royal guest was dropped, and the prisoner was a prisoner indeed. The opportunities for such secret correspondence as she had carried on through Throckmorton were cut off, and everything she wrote or received passed the scrutiny of the Queen's ministers.

The fortunes of Philip II had been mounting since his seizure of

Portugal, and the summer of 1585 has been described as the apogee
of his reign. In 1582 his fleet under Santa Cruz defeated the French
under Strozzi in a hard fought battle at Terceira and secured the submission of the Azores, hitherto faithful to Don Antonio. In the
Netherlands Alexander of Parma made steady progress in taking
city after city; Brussels and Ghent were among the prizes of 1584,
and Antwerp was on the list for 1585, in which year, in August, it
did punctually fall, and so opened the way for the attack on the
north. Meanwhile Anjou, embodying the threat of French intervention and the screen for English, dropped out, and the murder of
Orange robbed the Dutch of more than an army as the hardest
attack was about to break on them. In France the death of Anjou
precipitated possibilities in Philip's favour. It gave the Guisard
Catholic League a clear issue to fight for, that a heretic must not be
recognized heir to the throne; and Guise and his friends signed a
secret treaty with Philip and took the field against Henry of Navarre
in the spring of 1585 with the formal promise of Spanish support.
Events were making Philip the universal Catholic champion, and he
himself was losing his reluctance to play the part. It needed only that
he should set about breaking England to render the holy war complete and the issue joined on every front. Immediately after Terceira,
Santa Cruz had urged an invasion of England, and Parma also was
confident that it could be done. Philip listened, but allowed Guise to
take the lead with his Scottish and cross-Channel invasion schemes.
The good fortunes of 1584 warmed his slow-moving mind. In 1585
he came to a decision. He probably did not reach it until the end of
the year. His action in the early summer, although in retrospect it
provides the starting-point of the war, was not by the practice of the
time irrevocable and does not indicate that his determination was
fixed.

In the spring of 1585 there was a dearth of corn in Spain, although
it was a season of plenty in England and the north. The Spanish
government offered its safe-conduct to ships bringing cargoes of
grain, and many English vessels availed themselves of the opportunity. In May they were discharging in the northern Spanish ports
when the King issued sudden orders for the arrest and seizure of
ships and men. Elizabeth was at the moment negotiating with the
Dutch, as she had been doing on and off for years, and between them
they had not yet concluded anything to Philip's detriment. The arrest
was therefore an arbitrary act, not forming a stage in an acute quarrel

as the arrest over the treasure seizure had done in 1569. Philip possibly did not appreciate its significance as an extreme step, but it was at once so regarded in England. There the Spanish-trading interest, which had hitherto been reluctant to offend Spain, was eager for counter-measures; and the public, already inflamed with tales of war and atrocity, was clamouring for vengeance and repeating with gusto the story of the *Primrose* of London, whose master, boarded with orders of arrest by no less a dignitary than the Corregidor of Biscay, put up a fight against odds, captured the Corregidor and threw his escort into the sea, and sailed home with his prisoner to England.

Drake's great expedition for the East was still presumably in process of preparation, although there are no records of it after the winter. If it was, it was diverted to form the basis of a new force with which to make reprisals in the Atlantic. The measure was taken in immediate consequence of the arrest, and on 1st July Drake received a commission to visit the Spanish ports and demand the release of ships and men. His fleet was not then ready, neither was the Queen ready to unleash it, and more than two months were to elapse before he actually sailed. Meanwhile the Lord Admiral was issuing letters of reprisal to the aggrieved merchants, and a brisk privateering war was beginning. To the seamen of England its beginning was overdue, and the religious sentiments inspiring it were not all on the Catholic side. The arrest in Philip's ports was not a merely formal affair involving no personal suffering. The *White Bear* of Exmouth was at Lisbon in 1585, and when she was seized her master Andrew Rewell 'was there taken, racked, and tortured to death by the Inquisition'. The statement occurs almost casually in a lawsuit by his widow, and the fact was not rare enough to excite much comment. Such facts did, however, excite hostility among those who furnished the victims.

While Drake was fitting out, the siege of Antwerp was in progress and Elizabeth was bargaining with the Dutch on the terms of her support. As we have noted, the death of Anjou had thrown down the screens both in France and the Netherlands, and Elizabeth was reluctantly convinced that she must aid the Dutch directly or see them overcome, to the ensuing peril of England. She meant her aid to be as limited as might be, and clung to the hope that she might render it without incurring formal war with Spain. Burghley agreed that it must be given, although he too may still have hoped to avoid the full consequence. Dr. Conyers Read gives some evidence suggesting that while Burghley assented in Council to warlike measures he privately advised the Queen to hold back; but this is only a suspicion, and Dr. Read does not hold it proved.[1] On the face of it the Lord Treasurer and all the Privy Council were for aid to the Dutch, while Drake should make himself 'a fearful man' to Philip at sea. It was the policy that Leicester and Walsingham had long advocated. As early as March 1585 Walsingham outlined to the Dutch the Queen's conditions, that she should take them under her protection and give military aid, provided that Flushing and other ports should be placed in her care as pledges. The militant outbreak of the Catholic League in France then caused Elizabeth to hesitate. Guise, it seemed, might have a force to spare for invasion, in which case it would be unwise to send troops to the Low Countries. Burghley advised caution and the further strengthening of the Navy, his general outlook being that of the holder of the card in hand: one can always make war, but, having done so, one cannot as certainly make peace. Walsingham, on the contrary, posed the alternatives of fighting the Spaniards overseas at once or fighting them in England later. In May the Queen leaned to Walsingham's view, and then found the Dutch hesitant to give up Flushing—might she not use it to make a bargain of her own? Philip's arrest of English shipping helped to calm these fears, and at the end of June a Dutch delegation reached England intent on business. It was time, for Parma had encircled Antwerp. The Dutch offered Elizabeth their sovereignty, but were told that it was out of the question; and the negotiations proceeded on the basis of her protection, the haggling turning on how much money and how many men. Before its conclusion, the Queen agreed as a matter of urgency that a force should sail to relieve Antwerp on 15 August; but Antwerp surrendered on the 7th. The main treaty was accomplished after that event. England was to send 5,000 foot and 1,000 horse under a man of note to serve in the field, and to find garrisons for Flushing and Brill, to be occupied as 'cautionary towns'. Elizabeth's councillors were not fools: Flushing was the one port whose possession would have given the Armada a chance three years later.

Drake got his sailing orders as the Dutch negotiation drew to success, and left Plymouth on 14 September, in such haste from fear of a cancellation that he did not wait to fill his water-casks. He had under him what would now be called an amphibious force, twelve companies of soldiers on board a fleet comprising two of the Queen's

---

[1] *Walsingham*, III, ch. xiii, *passim*, which is my general authority for these negotiations.

fighting ships, a few others that could fight, and transports and pinnaces making up a total of twenty-nine sail. The men, soldiers and sailors together, numbered 2,300, and the officers represented many of the families prominent at court and in politics. Frobisher was the vice-admiral, and Carleill commanded the troops. The finance was by a joint-stock syndicate in which the Queen found nominally a third of the capital, while the remainder was subscribed by nobles and privy councillors. The important thing was that the Queen employed her own ships and gave Drake her formal commission. It left no doubt of her position so far as the despatch of the force was concerned. Yet Drake was going out to do more than he was commissioned to do, and for the excess the Queen's answer was ready: 'The gentleman careth not if I disavow him'. He sailed first to Vigo Bay, where he landed men on Spanish soil, captured some booty by way of reprisal, and completed his watering. He found that the Spanish arrest had already been lifted and that Englishmen were free to depart. Nevertheless the comparatively prompt riposte to the arrest, and the landings at Vigo and Bayona, to which there had been no effective opposition, constituted an 'insult' to King Philip which had a prestige effect throughout Europe. Thereafter Drake sailed south into the Atlantic with results that were to be heard of next year.

In the Queen's estimation the aid to the Dutch was a much more serious matter than the despatch of Drake. His expedition cost her comparatively little (£10,000 in cash and the loan of two ships grossly overvalued at another £10,000), and might with luck more than clear itself by the plunder it could take. The army for the Netherlands, small though it appears, was estimated to cost £126,000 a year, or nearly half the crown's normal revenue.[1] It meant putting the finances on a war footing and bidding farewell to the economy that had lifted the country high. Its employment raised the question, which John Hawkins for one answered in the negative, whether armies on the continent represented the proper use of England's strength in war. On the whole the Queen's ministers were of the continental persuasion, as she herself undoubtedly was. She thought of her sea power mainly as a defence of the coastline, and secondarily as a means of financing the land war by capturing booty. She did not believe in her seamen's doctrine that Spain could be beaten by sea power alone. She appointed Leicester to the Netherlands command,

---

[1] 'Elizabeth and the Netherlands, 1586–7', by J. E. Neale, *English Hist. Review*, vol. xlv (1930, July).

but various cavils and hindrances prevented him from crossing the sea until the end of the year.

Leicester took with him the stipulated forces and received a hearty welcome in the Dutch provinces. Their people were not by any means impoverished diehards fighting desperately at the end of all resources. Materially they were well-to-do and had even gained by the war, since their sea power had diverted trade from the south to the Dutch ports. But the Dutch were lacking in governance and in any mechanism for the control of their efforts; and they were less united than patriots should have been. There was a large Catholic element among them, and they were short of soldiers. Their funds were wasted by faulty administration. In general they had not as yet the characteristics of independence, nor did they desire it. They desired to be ruled with full respect to their liberties and customs, and would have been glad for Elizabeth to assume the responsibility. How long they would have been loyal to her is doubtful. Elizabeth utterly declined the sovereignty and was very angry when, soon after his arrival, Leicester accepted the title of Governor-General without consulting her. Her instructions had been that he was to limit himself to the command of the army and to take no part in governing. After much heated writing on her part, Leicester was allowed to continue in office. He realized that the Dutch need was a strong central authority and tried to supply it. But his political competence did not equal his understanding, and he allowed himself to be made the tool of factions. All this clogged military effort, and the Queen had little to show for her money in 1586. Parma was fortunately held back by Philip II, who had determined to invade England and was conserving his forces, leaving the Netherlands to be finished off afterwards. A campaign begun late in the season had small results save the death in October of Sir Philip Sidney, the most gifted of Elizabeth's younger men, mortally wounded in the interception of a convoy near Zutphen. Meanwhile Leicester was proving a poor administrator and wasting the Queen's money and his own private fortune. 'Charges' mounted, soldiers starved, died, or deserted, captains drew pay for non-existent men, and quarrels racked the high command. Elizabeth was disgusted, yet the experience did not cure her propensity to regard the soldiers as the only war-winners. What it did was to foster her notion of extricating herself from the war by making a deal with Philip, which should at the same time satisfy him, preserve England, and be just to the Dutch.

Drake did very much better than Leicester, although he did not capture either of the treasure fleets of 1585. One of them got home just before he left Plymouth, and the other as he was leaving Vigo on 8 October. From Spain Drake went on to touch at the Canaries and to sack the Cape Verdes, which retaliated by infecting his fleet with a fever that killed three hundred men as they crossed to the West Indies. There, at the beginning of 1586 he approached Hispaniola, the greatest island, and captured its capital Santo Domingo by a bold and skilful amphibious attack. Having refreshed his men for a month and collected a ransom, he crossed the Caribbean southwards and attacked Cartagena, the capital of the Spanish Main. This also he took by swift combined operations, and made it pay a larger ransom. The main object, however, was to destroy the local shipping and to disarm the defences by carrying off all the guns. Drake had thought of going on to the Isthmus and marching across it to take Panama, which would have cut the treasure-route; but losses by sickness precluded it. He passed out of the Caribbean by the Florida Channel, took St. Augustine in Florida, and brought away Ralegh's first colony from Virginia, as already described. The booty just failed to cover the expenses, although the Queen should have been pleased, seeing that she had all this service for virtually nothing. The service itself was great. Drake had impoverished the Indies and captured 240 guns. Philip had to spend money on replacing them and refortifying all the colonial ports. It was money he could ill spare, with the result that the Italian financiers stiffened their terms and Spanish trade was severely hit. The ultimate effect in lightening pressure on the Dutch was considerable, and would have been cumulative had the oceanic offensive been kept up. But the Queen viewed it only as a demonstration of English power, and having made it, waited for the enemy to propose peace. He did not, and as no following western blow was struck in 1586, he made good the damage sooner than was expected and even got plate fleets home in that year. Philip had no doubt that he was at war, and was determined to make peace only with a beaten England. Elizabeth would hardly admit that there was a war, and conceived of Drake and Leicester as aids to negotiation. She was mistaken, but not foolishly; for the cause of her disappointment was an unnoticed change in her enemy. The Philip of 1586 was a different man from the Philip who had swallowed the loss of Alva's treasure-chests seventeen years before.

To Burghley and Walsingham and all men of judgment there was no doubt that a very serious war had begun. They had to look to the defences, in which the weakest point was the existence of the English Catholics and the possibility that they would rise in aid of foreign invaders. In fact they did not, but there had been so much bragging from those who hoped that they would, and so much effort to ensure that they should, that the main body of the people were justifiably anxious. The focus of a possible Catholic rising was Mary Stuart, in whose name it would be conducted, and whose existence also was the principal incentive to the plans for Elizabeth's assassination. Walsingham was convinced that Mary would never cease to join in such enterprises. The transferences to Tutbury and then to Chartley enabled him to stop her underground correspondence. He knew that she would contrive to reopen some secret line, and he provided her with facilities. He had arrested one of her agents and had come to terms with him. This man arranged that the brewer at Chartley should take in and bring out packets of letters concealed in the household beer-barrels, and informed Mary that the line was open. Mary at once began to use it, and her every letter was opened, copied, and duly forwarded by Walsingham's people. In the summer of 1586 the minister was on the track of a plot. John Ballard, a Jesuit priest, came over from France to arrange for a Catholic rising. He returned to Paris and concerted measures with Mendoza, who informed Philip and received his approval. Then Ballard came again to England and recruited, among others, a young gentleman named Anthony Babington, who had already done services for Mary and was known to her. Ballard talked largely of invading armies which the Catholics must be ready to join. In June he introduced the question of assassinating Elizabeth, often discussed among the hotheads of the movement. Babington took it up and agreed with five friends to do it. He wrote of it to Mary through the secret post, and she replied in terms that clearly revealed her cognizance. The 'person' was privy to the murder plot. Walsingham arrested the men, and Ballard, Babington, and the others were executed in September. Such is the merest outline of a very complicated story. As with other stories concerning Mary, its truth has been denied by those who assert that Walsingham fabricated the plot and forged the letters. But, as Pollard remarked, he could not have forged the letters in which Mendoza reported the plot, before its detection, to Philip, and which did not come to light till the nineteenth century. In the judgment of most historians Walsingham's villainy has not survived a close investigation of the evidence, and his part as an *agent provo-cateur* is no more than this, that he made sure that when a clandestine correspondence did begin he should know what was in it.

Elizabeth was at last brought face to face with a question she had shirked : what to do with Mary Stuart? It needed a sustained effort of nearly four months before the answer was beyond doubt, an effort on the part of her councillors and her people. Mary was tried in October at Fotheringay Castle and found guilty by a court consisting of peers, privy councillors, and judges. Elizabeth intervened to have the whole case reconsidered by the Star Chamber, with the like result, and then again by Parliament, summoned to meet at the end of October. The Houses urged the Queen to allow execution to follow sentence, and she would give no answer, save to publish the sentence. Meanwhile rumours swept the country, that the Spaniards had landed, Guise had landed, Mary had escaped, new plots against the Queen's life had been detected, even that the Queen was dead; and through it all came an ever more passionate demand that Mary must die, for if she survived the Queen, England was lost. At length Elizabeth signed the death-warrant, but gave no order to despatch it to Fotheringay. The Privy Council sent it without her knowledge, and Mary was beheaded on 8 February 1587. Philip II was privately pleased, since he did not desire to conquer England for anyone but himself. The Guisard French were wildly indignant and threatened extremities, but Henry III, between his Huguenots and Leaguers, had little time for resentment at the fate of his sister-in-law. James VI displayed formal grief, which was easily allayed by the reflection that his succession was the clearer. The only sovereign whose regrets were real and deep was Elizabeth.

17

THE ARMADA AND PORTUGAL

ALTHOUGH Santa Cruz urged the invasion of England soon after
the fall of the Azores, Philip did not then take any decision.
Like Elizabeth, he attached great importance to the attitude of
France, and he knew that France would be as much opposed to his
conquest of England as he had been to French designs at the opening
of Elizabeth's reign. The progress of Guise and the Catholic League
in 1585 began the removal of this fear. The Leaguers were putting up
a fight and becoming a real power, and they were bound first to Philip
and only secondarily to the long-term interests of France. The
existence of Mary Stuart was another deterrent to a war for the
conquest of England. So long as she lived she was the Queen of
England in Catholic eyes, and a Catholic crusade must be for the
purpose of seating her on the throne. It would not suit Philip at all,
for success would mean that in Mary and Guise he would have two
satellites more closely bound to one another than to himself. He had
his own genealogical claim to England, and he desired that his
daughter should take Elizabeth's place. The news from England in
1585 showed, however, that the English were determined that Mary
never should succeed; and Philip dispassionately calculated that the
Queen of Scots was unlikely to survive an invasion and a revolution,
however fatal those events might be to Elizabeth. In a sense the
Bond of Association was a solution of one of his difficulties. In the
closing months of 1585, with Drake's insult at Vigo to digest, and
news of the levying of Leicester's little army for the Low Countries,
Philip at last made up his mind. Invasion it was to be, and thenceforward he never looked back.

It was high time, from the point of view of his interests. If he could
have brought off this invasion twenty or even ten years before, how
different would his position have been, with his rebels in Holland
and his enemies in France alike beaten down, and the Counter-

Reformation triumphant over Christendom. It was what Walsingham dreaded through the years, but to Elizabeth and Burghley falls the credit of averting it. It was they who staved off the war while they were weak, who made good use of the respite, and accepted the necessity at last when their England was rich, united, and well armed. In detail their statecraft may have been inglorious, in result it was magnificent.

In January 1586 Philip asked Santa Cruz for a plan of the invasion campaign, but on receiving it did not adopt it; for Santa Cruz recommended a fleet of 77,000 tons of shipping, sailing direct from Spain to southern England and there landing 60,000 soldiers, the fleet itself being manned by 30,000 mariners. The estimated cost was nearly four million ducats, and Philip saw little hope of raising the money. The proposed numbers of soldiers and sailors were greater than Spain or any other European power had ever mustered at one time, and the provision of victuals and equipment would have been a staggering problem. Philip rejected this plan and went to work on something smaller. He was right, for it turned out that the utmost effort was needed to victual even 30,000 men on shipboard. Philip's solution proved just feasible as a matter of supply. A fighting fleet and a convoy of hulks or merchantmen with 8,000 seamen was to carry 20,000 soldiers up Channel to the Flemish coast, where it was to make contact with Parma and cover the crossing to Kent of the pick of his army of 30,000 men. A large proportion of the soldiers brought from Spain would not be among the actual invaders, for they were allotted to permanent service in the ships. In Spanish fleets the gunners and small-arms men were all soldiers, and the sailors had only the duty of working the ship. If the plan had gone well, it would have landed perhaps 30,000 men in England, for Parma would have been obliged to leave some in the Netherlands. In England the county musters accounted for greater numbers. But they included the physically unfit and the unarmed, and old men up to sixty. The trained bands of London were comparatively well exercised. For the countrymen it was mainly a matter of fighting spirit and the countryman's common sense. England had some coast defences, but no strongly fortified cities inland. Even the walls of London were mainly symbolic and would have fallen rapidly under bombardment. The invasion was designed for the late summer of 1587.

In 1586 the English began to hear talk of the Spanish plans, but could discern no preparations that threatened special danger that

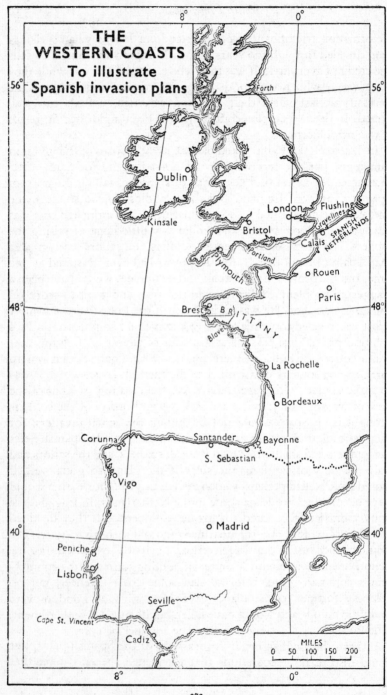

THE
WESTERN COASTS
To illustrate
Spanish invasion plans

year, when it seemed that Guise rather than Philip might attempt a landing. A small English squadron crossed the Atlantic to capture the Spanish and Portuguese fishermen on the Newfoundland banks, and thereby damaged the Spanish victualling arrangements, which rested largely on the accumulation of salted fish. John Hawkins was sent to sea in August with four of the Queen's best ships and several others. His probable design was to intercept the plate fleets or the carracks with the East Indian trade for Lisbon, but the arrest of the Babington plotters and the rumours of a Guisan landing in Sussex caused a general panic, and the Council ordered him to 'ply up and down' in the Channel until it was too late for anything else.

Philip's preparations were as yet preliminary. His first concern was financial. All his European revenues were allocated to expenditure which they failed to cover. Only the western treasure and the eastern spices offered relief. The King's income from these sources was exaggerated, and the reality was insufficient to finance the wars. It was nevertheless indispensable to survival, even in the crippled condition in which Philip halted along from loan to default and promise to loan; and without the treasure his collapse would have been speedy. For a special effort he had to seek additional supplies, and he turned to the Pope. Sixtus V, who succeeded Gregory in 1585, was not easy to deal with. He had an unpontifical admiration for the ability of 'Jezebel', and hoped for her conversion as much as her conquest; and it seemed to him that if Philip did win it would make Rome subject to all-powerful Spain. However, the war was represented as a Catholic crusade, and Sixtus had to make a show of co-operating. Parsons and Allen were at his ear, doing their utmost to procure the invasion of their country. They told him that the English Catholics would rise 25,000 strong, that the English Navy was so consumed with rot that no more than four ships could put to sea, that a landing of 15,000 Spaniards would be sufficient to overturn a corrupt régime hated by most of its subjects. Sixtus yielded to the extent of granting Philip the right to collect some substantial church revenues, and of promising a direct payment of a million crowns, but only after the Spanish army should have landed in England. It was much less than Philip hoped for, and he had to lay heavier taxes on his impoverished subjects and to deal with money-lenders who raised their terms as the story of Drake's West Indian raid came in.

With such resources the work at last took shape in the winter of

1586–7. Philip's best ships were twelve galleons that he had acquired with the crown of Portugal. To these he added by building in all the Spanish shipyards, by purchase and requisitioning of Italian merchantmen and Flemish and German hulks, and by adapting these vessels as well as might be to the purposes of war. The collection of the victuals went very slowly. Above all, artillery was short, and the ships were being concentrated long before there were guns to arm them.

In 1586 Elizabeth attempted no follow-up of Drake's blow in the Caribbean. As we have seen, she regarded it less as a stroke of war than of diplomacy, and waited for its results in the shape of overtures for peace. They were not forthcoming, and the news from Spain next winter was serious. The invasion fleet was undoubtedly being prepared, and was to sail in 1587. The English spy system, very effective in the later stages of the war, was not yet fully developed, and the reports exaggerated the forwardness of Spanish preparations. From England, on the other hand, the Spaniards got very little military information. Mendoza in Paris was trying to organize a service of spies, but he had to admit that it was impossible to plant them where they were needed: any stranger near a seaport was taken up and questioned, travellers had to carry permits signed by a magistrate, and even in London the keepers of inns and lodging-houses reported all their guests to the justices. Public spirit was aroused, and every man was his own policeman. The effort was justified by the success of Drake's campaign of 1587; for he prepared his fleet in unbroken secrecy, and it was only as his guns were opening fire in Cadiz harbour that Philip received a warning from Mendoza that he was coming.

Drake was sent out to thwart the invasion plans. He was 'to impeach the gathering' of the Spanish squadrons; and the Queen took a further step towards acknowledged war by permitting him to enter Spanish ports in order to destroy the shipping. On second thoughts she withdrew the last permission, but Drake had sailed before her change of orders reached him. He left Plymouth on 2 April with a fleet stronger than that which he had led to the Caribbean: four of the Queen's large galleons, one belonging to the Lord Admiral, four of the Turkey Company's fighting merchantmen, and other less formidable private ships. The expenses were paid, as before, by a joint-stock syndicate in which the Queen was the largest shareholder. As Drake sailed down the enemy coast questioning prisoners and neutrals he learned that Santa Cruz was in Lisbon with a number of Philip's best ships, that another division was in Cadiz, and that the Armada as a whole was not ready, since it lacked guns, men, and victuals, and many ships had yet to come round from the Mediterranean. In a short campaign he proceeded to cause the utmost damage and confusion. The fleet in Cadiz was unready for action, and some of its impressed vessels had no sails, for they had been taken ashore as a precaution against desertion; but the anchorage was commanded by forts and batteries and defended by twelve galleys, which were supposed to be very formidable in land-locked waters. Drake disregarded the obstacles and sailed in, destroying all the large shipping with very little loss to himself. His rout of the galleys made a great impression, for these craft fought hard and took their punishment again and again, yet could make no stand against the fire of the new-style English galleon. Apart from the galleys, it was thought extraordinarily bold for Drake to risk his fleet against the batteries. His reward was the capture or destruction of thirty-seven sail according to his own claim, or twenty-four by the admission of the Spaniards, including a great galleon built for Santa Cruz himself.

After this Drake cruised off Cape St. Vincent, while his small craft captured fishing boats and coasters conveying supplies to Lisbon. At St. Vincent Drake needed a place to land for water and secured it by the capture of Sagres castle, which defended a good anchorage. Having made sure of this he went north to Lisbon, where Santa Cruz had some fine ships lacking guns and men. Drake judged that to enter Lisbon as he had Cadiz was an unjustifiable risk, since the city was twelve miles up a difficult channel flanked by forts and swept by a strong tide. He remained at the entrance, failed to induce Santa Cruz to come out, and then returned to Cape St. Vincent. He had stopped the concentration of the Armada, which would not be resumed for some time, and had effected all the damage then possible. The time limit to his own proceedings was in sight, for he was under-victualled, and hunger and sickness were already weakening his crews, so that another three or four weeks must see the end of the campaign. Instead of waiting at St. Vincent he sailed suddenly westward to the Azores. Near the island of St. Michaels on 8 June he found what he had hoped for, a great carrack from India with a lading that more than paid the whole cost of his expedition. With this brilliant prize Drake was back at Plymouth before the end of June, less than three months from his setting forth.

There was still time for the Armada to get ready and sail that year. Philip was intent upon it, as the best answer to the singeing of his beard. Drake knew it, and came home hoping to refit and revictual and sail again for the Spanish coast. But he was not allowed to move. Peace overtures were still the Queen's hope. Now that we have shown our strength, she argued, Philip must see reason. She even 'disavowed the gentleman' who had done her fighting to the extent of explaining to the enemy that the entry into Cadiz was contrary to her orders and that she was greatly displeased with it. It was of no avail. The Armada did not, however, sail for England that year. The most decisive result of Drake's campaign occurred after he had ended it. When Santa Cruz and his sovereign heard of the capture of the carrack they were tortured with anxiety for other rich shipping that was shortly due at the Azores, and imagined Drake established there collecting plate fleets and East Indiamen. Santa Cruz worked hard to get his Lisbon ships equipped, and in August he led them out to the Azores to seek an enemy who had long departed. He did not regain Lisbon until October. Philip then ordered him to carry out the invasion, but there was the usual delay for repairs and revictualling, and winter set in to preclude further action. The Armada's voyage was postponed to 1588.

Leicester, who had returned to England at the close of 1586, did not resume his command in the Netherlands until the following June, when Drake's campaign was nearly finished. Leicester was ill supplied with money and at odds with the Dutch. His second campaign effected nothing, and at its close he came home for good. Although Parma was fortunately being starved of money and men by Philip, whose Armada demanded everything, he was able nevertheless to capture Sluys. During all this time Elizabeth was keeping up a more or less secret and unofficial negotiation with Parma for a general peace. It was done by disavowable intermediaries and did not reach the formal stage until late in 1587. This business appeared to take a promising turn while Drake was away, which accounted for the Queen's coldness towards his successes. She was almost alone in her pursuit of a negotiated peace at that stage. Burghley wanted peace no less than she, but he was convinced that it was only to be won now with sword in hand. So also were all her advisers except Sir James Croft, who was a Spanish pensioner. Meanwhile Elizabeth allowed such fancies to stay her warlike hand, for she held back her Navy while the Armada took shape unmolested. She yielded the initiative to Philip, with whom it lay to choose between fighting and peace, and when and how the next military move should be effected. He allowed Parma to negotiate, since it kept the Queen in doubt of his intentions. He never meant the negotiation to succeed.

Through the autumn of 1587 Parma was expecting and hoping that the Armada would come up Channel to break the blockade and escort his invasion barges across to England. At that time he could see good hopes of success. Only small Dutch craft were blockading his coast. Drake was at Plymouth with only the ships he had used in his 'singeing' raid—not more than nine or ten of serious fighting value; and he would be unable to stop Santa Cruz at the strength the Armada had now attained. Hawkins and the Lord Admiral were now at Chatham with four-fifths of the English fleet, but they had not been allowed to mobilize it, and the ships lay at their moorings without crews or stores. By very efficient preparatory measures Hawkins had made it possible to get the whole Navy to sea within three weeks of the word being given. Parma probably made a longer estimate and was convinced that the invasion would meet with no serious opposition until he should be landed on England's soil. But his proviso was that it must be done at once: all depended on catching the English with their fleet unready. Meanwhile he was perturbed by the fact that the Spanish plan and his own part in it were being noised all over Europe and that England knew just what to expect.

Walsingham had that year organized the spy service in Spain and was getting more exact information at its close than at its beginning. By this means the Queen knew of Philip's purpose that the invasion should be made in October and consented to all precautionary measures except the final stages in mobilizing the fleet. The county militias were mustered, and the lords-lieutenants and county justices were urged to see that they were armed. All this cost the Queen's treasury nothing, but the Navy would be a different matter. She was straitened for ready money, even for sufficient to pay for victuals and gunpowder. She was not heavily in debt, but had nowhere to borrow. Antwerp had long been ruined and closed as a money-market, and the Italian bankers were bound to Philip. She could only look to her own subjects. The City was already impoverished by the stoppage of trade, which was causing distress throughout the country. Loans in London yielded little, and Parliamentary subsidies came in slowly, while the yield from the customs had dropped heavily. The Queen therefore did not turn out the fleet in the autumn. In December, when the foreign intelligence was not more alarming, she at last gave the orders, and Howard and Hawkins called up their crews and got their ships down the Medway with a speed and smoothness that testified to the efficiency of the Navy Board. Why the Queen mobilized at this juncture is not clear on the score of passive defence, for Philip had given up hope of action for the winter. But January showed that offensive moves were within her scope. Drake at Plymouth was to be strengthened to thirty sail, including seven of the Queen's galleons, and with that force he was to make a winter attack on the Spanish ports and land Don Antonio to start a Portuguese rebellion. Soon, however, the aggressive mood changed, and by the end of the month negotiation was again uppermost. It was now known that Philip had postponed the Armada's sailing. The Lord Admiral got orders to discharge half his men, and Drake to stand fast, while a diplomatic mission went over to Flushing to deliberate with Parma's spokesmen and the Dutch. The hope lasted until March, when it was seen to be illusory. The negotiations continued even after that, and were still in progress when the Armada was coming up Channel.

By the end of March the Armada was concentrated at Lisbon and nearing its greatest strength. Drake was eager to attack it. He wished to have fifty sail under his command with which to seek regular battle on the coast of Spain, for he held very strongly that the fight should be there and that the Armada should not be allowed to approach the Channel unchallenged. Drake's demand faced the Queen's ministers with a problem, for if granted it meant that he would be in supreme command of the main force of the Navy, while the Lord Admiral would be left behind in the Thames with only a nominal authority. This, it was evident, would not do. By Tudor practice, when the whole Navy went to sea the Lord Admiral must be in command. The officers expected it, and men like Hawkins and Winter, who were older than Drake, and Frobisher, who disliked him intensely, would not have given cheerful obedience to him, or indeed to any other whom they regarded as no more than their equal. That had been shown even in the small expedition of 1587, when William Borough, the vice-admiral, had openly repudiated Drake's authority and caused a dangerous schism in the service. The only possible commander-in-chief was the Lord Admiral, Charles, Lord Howard of Effingham, who had succeeded the Earl of Lincoln three years before. He was an able man, tolerant, friendly, and modest, accessible to advice, and yet withal the superior, so sure of himself that his authority was never questioned, even by the strong-natured individualists who composed his following. Weighing these things, the Queen and Council solved the problem raised by Drake's fighting programme. They ordered Howard to sail westward to Plymouth with the bulk of the fleet, there to join Drake and take over the command. Hawkins and Frobisher went with Howard. Winter and Lord Henry Seymour were left in the Narrow Seas with a quarter of the fleet to back up the Dutch blockaders and ensure that Parma should not emerge of his own initiative. Howard reached Plymouth towards the end of May. He made Drake his vice-admiral and Hawkins rear-admiral, and added five other senior officers to form a small council from which he sought advice.

Early in 1588 the Marquis of Santa Cruz died. He was succeeded by the Duke of Medina Sidonia, who protested his incapacity for the command and was appointed against his will by Philip II. The Spaniards had learnt one lesson from Drake at Cadiz by which they profited, and during the winter they increased the numbers and weight of the guns in their fighting ships. The English were fairly well informed of the numbers and description of the Spanish ships, but in the matter of the guns they were not, and it was to have a considerable effect on the fighting in the Channel. Medina Sidonia, like Santa Cruz, worked hard to improve his fleet, but was not hopeful of the outcome. It was barely possible to maintain the strength in men, for death and desertion balanced all efforts at recruitment. Parma also in the Netherlands was no longer hopeful of success. The winter had diminished his army to 17,000, and since the English fleet had been mobilized he saw little chance of breaking the blockade. For him the conditions were entirely changed since the autumn. Philip was the driving force. He would listen to no tales of doubt or difficulty. Mainly through his determination the Armada sailed from Lisbon at the end of May. For more than a fortnight it was pinned to its own coast by contrary winds, and then Medina Sidonia went into Corunna for food and water. As he was doing so a gale inflicted damage that called for further delay.

The English at Plymouth did not learn for some time that the Armada had put back. Howard and his captains were concerned to get southward and fight it on its own coast. They were prevented first by the Queen. She thought that it might slip past them and find

England undefended, and she preferred to have her fleet located at
the mouth of the Channel. Howard, backed by Drake, protested
vigorously against this inhibition and at length secured a free hand.
Two other factors stopped him, victualling and the weather. He was
victualled scantily for less than a month at a time with supplies that
had mostly to be sent down Channel. It was a summer of strong
westerly winds, and the victuallers were seriously delayed. Then,
when he had the food and could get to sea, the same weather prevented him from reaching Spain. This happened three times in June
and early July. On the last occasion he almost gained the Spanish
coast, only to be forced back. He re-entered Plymouth on 12 July
short of food and with many men sick. The English had heard by
now that the Armada had been out and had put back. Reports exaggerated its damages, and they had the impression that it would not
try again. They were busy at Plymouth refitting, for attacks on
Spanish ports and attempts on the plate fleets. There was in fact at
this stage a distinct tendency to rate the enemy low. And then on the
19th the Armada was in the Channel, seen that day off the Lizard,
and due off Plymouth in a matter of hours; and as if to emphasize
that a new act had opened in the year's drama, the violent weather
ceased and gentle breezes blew mainly from the westward to move
the combatants slowly up Channel.

The Armada had altogether 130 ships, of which it is reckoned that
thirty-seven were of serious fighting value, the rest being transports
and small craft. The Queen's Navy was small. It contained only
twenty-one fighting vessels of 200 tons and over; and of these sixteen were with Howard at Plymouth and five with Seymour in the
Downs. In addition there were the fighting merchantmen of the
Turkey Company and one or two large ships belonging to individuals. Whether any other merchant vessels, of which great numbers
were in attendance, had much fighting power is unknown. The naval
officers had little to say for them, save that they helped to make a
show. It is probably true that the campaign was fought by less than
forty ships on either side, and that in the earlier stages Howard was
considerably outnumbered. In guns the English expected to be superior, and here they were disappointed; for Medina Sidonia's best
ships had more and heavier guns of the short-range types than had
the Queen's, and in longer-ranged weapons were almost as good. In
general, the idea that the Spaniards neglected artillery and expected
to win victory by boarding and a hand-to-hand fight has been proved

erroneous by the research of recent years.[1] We should not, however, swing our statements too far in the opposite direction: the Spanish guns were good, but the same may not have been true of their gunnery, for they inflicted few casualties on the English while suffering heavily themselves. The Spaniards reckoned that their best ships were good to sail and manœuvre, but in this quality they were far outclassed by the best of the English. There is considerable truth in the traditional contrast between the high-charged, unhandy Spanish galleons and the low-built galleons which Hawkins turned out. The former held more guns and men, but the latter could sail round them. The Spanish transports, the hulks or *urcas*, were slow and unweatherly, and many of them also were unseaworthy through defective hulls and gear.

When Medina Sidonia sighted the English coast he checked his speed to allow all his ships to come up and form the determined battle-order. It was devised for the protection of the transports carrying most of the soldiers on the way up Channel. In front sailed the Duke himself and the best of his fighting ships in a line abreast. Next came the hulks in a series of lines in close order. Behind them and overlapping them on either flank were four smaller squadrons of fighting ships, also in lines abreast. With a multitude of vessels of various types it could not have been an easy order to keep, and its forward movement had to be extremely slow. Partly for this reason and partly through the lightness of the weather the average speed up to the Straits of Dover was less than two miles an hour. The Spaniards did not know that the main English fleet was at Plymouth, for they had only heard of Drake's minor force there. Philip's orders were that the Armada was not to attack ports or seek battle before it had reached the Flemish coast and made junction with Parma; but that if it met with Drake's small squadron it might scatter them or drive them up Channel. While still to the westward some of the Spanish officers urged Medina Sidonia to go for Plymouth, since, not having met with Drake, they concluded that he was still within the Sound and might be annihilated in close action by the weight of the Armada. The Duke felt bound to refuse, and that night learned from captured fishermen that Howard's fleet was there.

The English, surprised by the enemy's approach, made haste to get their fleet out to sea, and took a considerable time to do it, for many

---

[1] See *Mariner's Mirror*, 1949, April, p. 90: 'The Elizabethan Navy and the Armada Campaign', by Lieut. Commander D. W. Waters, R.N.

of the ships were refitting. By the afternoon of the 20th Howard had
the best part of his fleet out east of the Eddystone, while others were
still coming from the port. In the evening they saw the Armada to
the westward. In the night Howard worked to windward outside the
Armada, while the ships late out of Plymouth did the same between
the Spaniards and the land; and in the morning of the 21st all joined
with the advantage of the windward position and the Armada to the
east of them. It was a feat of seamanship which revealed the sailing
quality of the English galleons to the Spanish officers, who knew
that their own fleet could not have done it.

That morning Howard attacked, his galleons sailing in lines ahead
along the Spaniards' rear, firing their broadsides and seeking to
cripple individual ships. The Spaniards retaliated with a fire whose
weight was a surprise and precluded hope of a quick and easy victory.
The English could not close to a decisive range, and the bulk of the
Armada kept its formation and sailed forward while Medina Sidonia
and the best of his ships turned against their assailants. 'We durst not
adventure to put in among them,' wrote Howard, 'their fleet being so
strong.' Another captain spoke of the attack as 'coldly done'. However, the Armada was seen safely past Plymouth, whose capture
would have been a sore blow to England. Neither side had reason to
exult. The English had found the enemy more formidable than they
had expected. The Spaniards were dismayed by the manœuvring
powers of the English, who could inflict casualties while keeping out
of serious trouble themselves. On the following night an injured
Spanish galleon fell behind and had to surrender to Drake. Soon
afterwards another was crippled by an explosion and also fell to the
English.

The Armada continued its course up Channel, with the English
closely following and seeking a favourable chance for an attack. It
was by no means a chase, for the initiative was with the Armada, and
it set the pace, a very slow one. On the morning of 24 July the fleets
were just east of Portland Bill when a breeze sprang up from the
north-east and gave the Spaniards the advantage of the windward
position which they had lost off Plymouth. The English fleet was
now in four groups or squadrons, under Frobisher nearest the land,
the Lord Admiral next to him, Hawkins farther to seaward, and
Drake farthest out of all. With the wind in their favour the Spaniards
moved a press of ships to overwhelm Frobisher, while Medina
Sidonia engaged Howard to prevent him from going to the rescue.

Frobisher fought hard against odds, and Howard's squadron fired hotly against Medina Sidonia. Then the wind went round to south-west, Hawkins and Drake were able to get into action, and the Armada broke off the fight and sailed on its way. Not a ship was lost by either side, although both had fired away more ammunition than they could spare.

Again there was a day of slow sailing eastward and on the morning of the 25th both fleets were becalmed off the southern point of the Isle of Wight. The English believed that Medina Sidonia would try to seize the Solent and the Spithead anchorage between the Wight and the Hampshire coast. Forty-three years before, the French had attempted it and had landed their troops in the Isle of Wight. It was a favourable place to begin an invasion, and there was in fact some talk of it among the Spanish officers, but the Duke refused, since the King's orders forbade it. It was with the possibility in mind that Howard and Hawkins, seeing some Spanish ships drifting apart from their fleet in the morning calm, had themselves towed within range by their boats, and began an attack. Later a south-west wind blew and the battle became general, with a movement before wind and tide past the Wight and towards the Owers shoals to the east of it. Drake and Hawkins as before worked round the Armada to seawards, with some hope of driving it on the Owers. But the tide was finished before this could be done, and the Armada's solid defence and formidable fire-power enabled it to keep the English at a distance and continue on its way. It had lost a first-class galleon, so badly hit as to be obliged to leave the fleet and make for the French coast, there to be wrecked. The English counted this battle a victory because it had put the Armada to leeward of the last suitable port on the south coast. If the Spaniards were to land farther up Channel it would have to be on open beaches, with consequently greater weather risks.

For the present the weather continued light, and more than two days were needed to cover the hundred miles to the Straits of Dover. It may be asked why Howard did not keep up a continuous attack on the Armada, since he could do so with some damage to the Spaniards and little loss to himself. The answer was simple; he had not the powder and shot. He now had ammunition for no more than one day's hard fighting, and he had to reserve it for a fight that would be really decisive. So far the circumstances had not permitted that. The time was now at hand when the English must create the

circumstances or find themselves in a critical situation. The
Armada was reaching its objective.

So the position appeared to Howard and his captains, but to
Medina Sidonia and his it was full of doubt and discouragement.
They also were short of ammunition. The English could outsail
them and were dogging them closely. How could they expect to get
Parma's defenceless barges out of the Flemish ports and across the
sea, and land his soldiers on the English beach under the nose of an
enemy who could at any moment deliver a major attack? The whole
undertaking moreover was a gamble on the weather. It had so far
been kind, but what would become of the Armada's cherished order
in a gale? With such questionings the Spaniards came to anchor in
the open sea off the little port of Calais on the afternoon of 27 July,
and Medina Sidonia sent messengers by land to Parma asking what
he meant to do. East of Calais the coast was lined with dangerous
shoals, between and over which only small craft could sail. Parma's
barges must come out to open sea to effect a junction, and small
Dutch fighting craft were blockading them closely. Philip's plan had
assumed this junction in the open, but now the men who had to
effect it did not find it easy. If a large deep-water port had been available it would have been different. The only such port was Flushing.
If Parma had held it, the Armada could have entered and the junction
could have been made, and for the next act they could have waited
indefinitely until the English were obliged to leave the seas open.
But Flushing was in Dutch Zealand and held by an English garrison.
There was to be no indefinite waiting in the open anchorage of
Calais.

At Calais Howard anchored a mile to windward of the Spaniards.
Next day Seymour and Winter crossed the Straits and joined him
with thirty ships in all, including five of the Queen's galleons.
Howard's modern critics have failed to emphasize that he had up to
this point been seriously outnumbered. Short of food as well as
powder, he determined to force a battle without delay. He had eight
medium-sized merchantmen prepared as fireships, and set them ablaze
about midnight on 28 July to be driven by wind and tide upon the
Armada. It was not a new idea, but it was none the less effective. The
Spanish captains cut their cables and made off in confusion, which
they were unable to remedy during the remaining hours of darkness.
At dawn the English saw that Medina Sidonia and two or three others
had anchored again close to their original position, but that the rest of

the Armada was dispersed over miles of sea to the north-eastward along the fringe of outlying sands, while one of the greatest ships had run ashore near Calais. By breaking up the close order the fireships had done what was required of them, and the English fleet attacked while the advantage was good. The Spanish leader at once weighed anchor and sought with some success to pull his scattered fleet together. The ensuing battle is known as that of Gravelines. It continued all the day of 29 July, the English squadrons working separately under their own leaders and seeeking to crush individual victims by their fire. In the main the Armada survived the day, although with much damage and loss of lives. It lost altogether four large ships which, with the three previously lost, was a deduction of about one-fifth from its initial strength. The damage, the casualties and the expenditure of powder were decisive. The Armada could not fight again. If it had had Flushing it might have taken refuge and recuperated; but its nearest friendly port was in Spain. The fighting at Gravelines ended in the evening, when the wind began to blow hard from north-west and to drive the Spaniards towards the shoals. The English hoped that the night would see the end of the Armada, but it was saved by a shift of wind to south-west which enabled it to escape into the North Sea. Howard's fleet was intact, but out of ammunition and very nearly out of food. He also could not fight another battle without supplies, but he had more prospect of getting them than had Medina Sidonia.

Medina Sidonia decided that the Armada must return to Spain, and that the way was not through the Channel but northward round the whole circuit of the British Isles. Parma, who had not yet moved a man, now knew that he had no chance of doing so. By consent of its leaders, the great invasion plan was therefore dead. The English were not yet so certain. They had undoubtedly won, but they had not won so easily as they had expected, and their prevailing mood was rather of thankfulness than of exultation. Howard still thought on the morrow of Gravelines that the Armada might turn south again, or perhaps seek a port of refuge and refit in Scotland, and he was also concerned lest Parma's troops should yet put to sea. Howard assumed 'a brag countenance' to cover his lack of powder and shot, and saw the Spaniards past the Firth of Forth. He returned to the Thames estuary, there to pay off the fleet and send the Queen's ships up to Chatham. Typhus and putrid food were now killing by hundreds, and even thousands, the men who had saved the country;

and Howard, summoned to court to tell his tale, had no heart for glory and quickly got away again to rejoin his men and aid Hawkins in getting them relieved and sent home. The Queen and Burghley also were in no jubilant mood. Their dismay was of the purse, for the cost of the campaign, £160,000, had emptied the treasury and left a heavy debt with which to face the next round in the war.

If these were the troubles of the victors, those of the Spaniards were worse. Before reaching the Biscayan ports in September the Armada lost half its ships and two-thirds of its men. Many ships were wrecked, with few survivors, on the Scottish and Irish coasts. As many as thirty-five of the original 130 simply disappeared at sea, leaving no record of their fate, which was largely due no doubt to the English gunnery at Gravelines. Medina Sidonia got home, a sick man, reviled by public opinion but not by the King, who avowed that his admiral was not to blame. The disaster was immense, but Philip met it with dignity and turned at once to new measures of war without a thought of suing for peace. His people followed him, and the long-term effect was bracing rather than weakening. On England the effect of the victory was permanently stimulating. The seamen knew that it had been a difficult fight and might well have ended otherwise—'All the world,' said Howard, 'never saw such a force as theirs was'; but the public at large became imbued with the impression circulated by Ralegh in a famous pamphlet, of an inherent English superiority and a braggart Spanish ineptitude, emphasized further by the divine favour in sinking the beaten Armada: *flavit Deus et dissipati sunt*. This mood endured long and gave the nation a confident outlook on the war and the efforts of the Counter-Reformation. The authors of the Armada had certainly appealed to the deity, and sixteenth-century Protestants did not forbear to point out the apparent answer.

As early as September, before the last battered Spaniard had made Santander, the English were discussing the exploitation of the victory. If pressed home it could bring speedy peace, but how best to do it? Broadly there were two very different plans put forward. The first, devised by Hawkins, was purely naval. He had so organized the naval administration that it was possible to equip and victual the Queen's ships to remain continuously at sea for four months and more, although the mixed expeditions of regulars and merchantmen, victualled by joint-stock investors, seldom lasted more than two. Hawkins considered the Queen's Navy as containing twenty-four fighting vessels besides pinnaces. He would allot twelve to the defence of the Channel, and the other twelve to an oceanic blockade. The fleet for this purpose was to be in two squadrons, each of six great ships and six pinnaces. Each squadron should stay out four months and then be relieved by the other, and they were to cruise about the Azores or between those islands and the coast of Spain. By this means a continuous lookout would be kept for the plate fleets and the East Indiamen, and even if the treasure was not captured it would be prevented from getting through to Spain. Hawkins claimed, and no one gainsaid him, that with the treasure stopped Philip would be obliged to make peace. The result would be rapid, and there would be no need to send Englishmen to the continent to fight on land. He expressly said that land operations should be eschewed as both expensive and profitless. The naval blockade, on the other hand, would pay for itself by its captures. This plan was never put into operation. If successful, it would have avoided a dozen or fifteen years of war. If it had failed, its failure would not have been more harmful than that of the policies and no-policies that in fact prevailed.

The alternative plan was Drake's. Drake would have utilized the Azores, and much more, but by a different approach. He proposed to invade Portugal and set Don Antonio upon the throne. That done, the Azores would certainly renounce their unwilling allegiance to Philip and would be at the service of the Anglo-Portuguese allies; and Antonio, moreover, was ready to grant trading facilities in Brazil, Africa, and the East. There was little doubt that Philip would have been brought down by a successful revolt of Portugal, which would have interrupted the treasure stream as effectively as the direct oceanic blockade. Drake's plan demanded two things besides naval power: the creation of an English army, and the raising of a Portuguese rebellion to co-operate with it. Without giving much thought to these necessities the Queen and her councillors decided to employ Drake, but to make his plan secondary to a more immediate purpose of their own; for the Queen's primary object was not to win Portugal but to destroy the surviving ships of the Armada in the northern Spanish ports.

The treasury was unequal to financing a large expedition, and the method was that of a joint-stock syndicate putting up £60,000, the Queen contributing six of her ships included in a nominal share of £20,000. Private vessels constituted the remainder of the fleet, but were not available in numbers to carry the large force of soldiers, and Dutch merchantmen were impressed in addition. The military force was hastily recruited, with the exception of a handful of old soldiers brought from the Netherlands, and the majority were untrained, undisciplined, and of poor quality. On muster parades they were recorded as numbering about 18,000, but probably never reached that figure. Some of those actually present at Plymouth took no part in the expedition, for certain of the impressed transports, alleging various deficiencies, turned back soon after putting to sea. Speedy action was desirable, and it was at first hoped to make a start in January 1589, but fluctuations of policy and administrative delays postponed it to April. Drake was the commander of the fleet and Sir John Norreys of the army, in which there were several distinguished officers from the Netherlands. As usual in these part-private ventures the victualling was bad, and the force set out with food for less than a month.

The instructions to the commanders ordered them to attack the northern Spanish ports and destroy the Armada shipping in them, then to do the like at Lisbon and, if it were there found possible, to install Antonio as king; and if not, to go to the Azores and conquer some of the islands. The emphasis of these orders was quite different from that of Drake's plan. The primary purpose was to mop up the remains of the Armada, and Don Antonio came in as an optional secondary objective. It has been customary to tell the story of the expedition from the standpoint of Drake and his career and to show how he was hampered by an order that should never have been given, to attack the Spanish ports before going to Lisbon. It is legitimate, however, to view the undertaking from the Queen's standpoint[1]; for hers was the supreme authority and responsibility, and her officers should have done their best to obey her. She had information that in and near Santander were forty ships of the previous year's Armada, in bad condition probably, but equally probably capable of repair and further service. Philip, she also knew, had not renounced hope of naval success and was already collecting victuals and stores for a new enterprise, of which these ships would be the basis. On the face of it the Queen was reasonable in desiring their destruction and the completion of the victory of 1588. That accomplished, Drake might follow his designs on Lisbon and the Azores. Viewing matters as they appeared to the Queen at the opening of 1589, we must realize

[1] See 'Queen Elizabeth and the Portugal Expedition', by R. B. Wernham, *English Hist. Review*, vol. lxvi (1951, January and April).

that a stroke on Santander, comparable to that on Cadiz two years before, was a more feasible objective than that of making Don Antonio King of Portugal. Elizabeth's weakness lay perhaps in allowing any encouragement to the Portuguese plan in the instructions for 1589; but there finance constrained her. There was little money profit to be hoped for at Santander, and the investors would have been less ready to come forward without the attraction of a gamble infinite in its possibilities. Drake and Norreys before sailing did not face the problem of conflicting purposes and stand out for a revision of their instructions. Instead they sailed with the Queen's orders and disobeyed them.

On 18 April 1589 they left Plymouth, and arrived five days later in sight of Cape Ortegal, near the north-west corner of Spain. Unfavourable winds may have prevented them from going deeper into the Bay of Biscay, but the testimony on the winds is conflicting. There was at any rate no subsequent attempt to remedy the matter, and the expedition spent the next fortnight in attacking Corunna, where there was only one Armada ship.

The landing at Corunna has never been explained save on the ground that it constituted an 'insult' to the King of Spain. The English took the lower town, but failed in an assault on the upper, which held out to the end. There was a positive gain in the capture of many guns and of large quantities of victuals that might have remedied the unsatisfactory condition of the force in that respect. But such was the negligence and disorder that most of the ships were not revictualled and their companies were hungry soon afterwards. Along with the food there was wine in the Corunna storehouses, and the undisciplined troops drank themselves sick and were permanently weakened. When it was seen that the upper town could not be taken the commanders deliberated on the next step. A council of sea officers gave opinion that with the prevailing wind it would be unwise to make for Santander, where the fortifications were formidable and they might find themselves on a lee shore. It was what Drake and Norreys wanted, and they set their course for Lisbon, notifying the Queen of their reason. The reasoning would have been equally valid if advanced in England before the start, and the Queen was wrathful, the more so because her young favourite the Earl of Essex had run away from court to join the expedition and had not yet been sent back as she had ordered. It was not only among drunken pikemen that discipline was slack.

The fortnight lost at Corunna was a fortnight presented to the

Spanish commander at Lisbon, and it was perhaps decisive of the whole campaign. The Cardinal Archduke Albert at Lisbon, Philip's nephew, made good use of the time. He had only a small force of Spanish troops, and he had the disaffected population of one of the great cities of Europe to overawe. Had there been a rising in Lisbon he would have been lost. He prevented it by ruthless arrests and executions of prospective leaders, successfully sitting on the safety-valve until the crisis was past. Portuguese patriotism was not at full pressure. It was anti-Spanish, but religion worked the other way and was anti-heretic.

Drake landed Norreys and Don Antonio and the army at Peniche, forty-five miles from Lisbon. The plan was that Norreys should march to the capital while Drake should enter the Tagus with the fleet and appear off the Lisbon waterfront to co-operate in the siege. Drake's part was essential because the army had no wheeled transport and its guns and victuals were carried in the ships. With what food they could bestow on their persons the soldiers set off, weak with the Corunna drinking and the prison conditions of life in the crowded ships. Antonio promised a Portuguese rising in aid, and Norreys forbade plundering to avoid giving offence; but hardly a man stirred, and no assistance was given to the invaders. For six days the unfortunate army stumbled forward in drought and burning heat, losing 200 men a day. It arrived outside the walls of Lisbon to find that the fleet was not there. Drake had reached Cascaes, outside the narrows of the channel leading up to Lisbon, with a fair wind for entering. He did not take the chance, but landed men to seize Cascaes as a port giving a much shorter line of access to the army. On the following days the wind was unfavourable. The passage up to Lisbon was not much more than twelve miles, but it was commanded by batteries, and the tides ran fiercely. Drake was impressed by the risks, but at length determined to take them on the first good wind. When the day arrived he learned that the army was in retreat and on its way down to Cascaes. Norreys had waited to the limit of endurance, and had retired from walls which he had no guns to breach. He and Essex and the troops had fought gallantly against Spanish sorties, but they lacked all essentials for a siege.

The commanders lingered at Cascaes, but had little prospect of making another attempt on Lisbon, for sickness was now so rife that the army was down to 5,000 men fit for duty. After further delay, during which a Hanse fleet of merchantmen bearing warlike stores for Philip was captured, the force moved north to Vigo and burned it. The effectives were now 2,000. It was agreed that Drake should sail with the best men to the Azores while Norreys should take the remainder home. Drake set off, but at once a gale scattered his fleet. His crews were too weak for further work, and he had to turn about for England. He arrived at Plymouth just over two months after setting out, having lost great numbers of men, variously computed as from 3,500 to 11,000.

The counterstroke to the Armada had failed. Drake's idea had been bold, and possible if carried out with his old vigour and with a singleminded concentration on the Lisbon objective. But the organization of the expedition was bad, and there was a divergence of purpose between the Queen and the commanders that should have been resolved before the start. The result was that the war, which success would have ended, was to drag on without end in sight. Drake was heavily discredited with the Queen, and with Drake the Navy, which was illogical. But so it was, and for years afterwards Elizabeth held back her deadliest weapon and spent her resources on armies on the continent, doing work that the Navy might have rendered needless if used at its full strength.

18

THE ELIZABETHANS AT WAR

A

FTER the Armada there was a change in the aspect of Elizabeth's reign. It was mainly a change of mood and outlook, caused by the overthrow of a menace against which the nation had braced itself in a spirit of supreme achievement. All men of good will had stood together, with differences of party and religion laid aside. Now the effort was over, and the nation knew instinctively that the peril would not recur. The war henceforward was less a fight for survival than one for warlike profit and a favourable peace. The people were loyal and keen to win, but could not remain at the patriotic height of 1588. The Queen and her councillors, disappointed of an early peace, continued somewhat wearily, hoping always for an end, not seeing how it was to be won, and resenting the prolongation of a war they hated; and there was a good deal of nagging, dissension, and frustration of effort in consequence. So far as the war was concerned, the climax of the Armada campaign was followed by fifteen years of anticlimax. In home politics and domestic affairs the progress of the Tudor century continued, while certain problems suggested that the Tudor revolution was not the prelude to a long static period for the body politic.

There had been no major change in the Privy Council since Cecil had become Burghley and Lord Treasurer, and Walsingham had taken his place as Secretary in the early 'seventies. Howard had become Lord Admiral in 1585, and Hatton Lord Chancellor in 1587, but the work of both was mainly departmental, as also was that of Archbishop Whitgift, who became a Privy Councillor in 1586. Now the Council was radically changed by the deaths of Leicester after the Armada in 1588 and of Walsingham in 1590. Leicester had outlived his scandalous phase and grown respectable, ending as a public servant whose influence was mainly for sound courses although his talents were mediocre. Walsingham had been a first-rate home secretary and foreign secretary combined, and efficiency could only suffer by his loss. Hatton died in 1591, having made a good Chancellor, although esteemed a mere courtier and light-weight. Younger men came in, the young Earl of Essex and Burghley's son, Robert Cecil, whom his father in his declining years trained and brought forward to take his place. Essex, strong in the Queen's favour, had been Burghley's ward, but the Cecils had no mind to yield him the primacy that he sought. The sentimental bond between Essex and the Queen was of political importance, but Elizabeth, fifty-five in the Armada year, when Essex was twenty-one, was not philandering with him as with Leicester in earlier days. The clue to their relations was rather that of adoptive mother and son. The Queen loved the boy in that sense, and could use him to fill Leicester's later position as the Queen's personal friend of high rank, undertaking the sort of work that might have been done for her by an obedient consort. In this Essex failed her by reason of his own windy egotism. He entered the Privy Council in 1593, but Robert Cecil had a seat two years earlier and became Secretary of State in 1596.

The Puritan question had grown more important with the years. Ralegh estimated that there were 20,000 Puritans in the country, using the word evidently in the narrow meaning of those who were prepared to dissent actively from established practices. Ralegh's estimate was of course the vaguest guess, without any statistical foundation. It was a small number compared with the whole population, but a large one compared with the total of those who devoted thought to religion. Whitgift in 1585 declared the non-conforming clergy to number about 6 per cent of the whole. When Edmund Grindal succeeded Parker at Canterbury in 1575 a movement known as 'the prophesyings' was becoming important in the Church. It consisted of meetings of the clergy and sometimes of prominent laymen for study of the Bible and discussion of Christian practice. Such meetings helped the spread of practical Christianity, and the new archbishop, with some of his colleagues, strongly favoured them. But the prophesyings might obviously lead to criticism of the existing order and undermining of authority. The Queen viewed them as a danger to the royal prerogative, ordered Grindal to suppress them, and suspended him from his administrative functions when he refused. Grindal remained suspended until his death in 1583. By that time a fresh challenge was in progress. Travers's book on church discipline

(1574) suggested the conversion of the Church of England to Presbyterian methods of government by a movement from below, and where, as in the eastern counties and the midlands, there were sufficient numbers of Puritan clergy, they were holding presbyterian classes or synods and agreeing upon matters of practice without regard to the authority of the bishops. It is difficult for us to appreciate the significance of such a movement as it appeared to the Queen. For her the church and the state were but two aspects of one solid body, the body politic. Any challenge to authority in one was a challenge in the other, with the prospect of chaos if it should succeed. In the 1580s, with the Spanish thunder rumbling over the horizon, she could not tolerate such a threat of internal disruption. Grindal died opportunely, and Elizabeth's answer to the presbyterian movement was to appoint John Whitgift, a man in whom she was not mistaken, to suppress it.

Archbishop Whitgift showed that in England at any rate it was possible for a Calvinist to be an episcopalian, for he was a Calvinist in his belief in predestination and other Genevan doctrines. He completely rejected the Calvinist system of church government and was firm for the royal authority exercised by the bishops. Burghley and other councillors might sympathize with the Puritans and urge the Queen to go gently with them, but Whitgift was entirely of the Queen's mind on the danger of such a course. They were probably right. For Elizabethan England to be given over to a strife of sects would have been most perilous, and crude Puritanism needed to be refined in many fires before it became a dominant element in the national life. Whitgift took the sting out of the contentious professional Puritanism of the clergy. For discipline he required them to subscribe to the supremacy, the prayer-book, and the thirty-nine articles, and he enforced it by means of the High Commission, a strengthened and permanent form of the successive commissions that had already been exercising the power of the supremacy in the Queen's name. This court offended against ideas of English liberty by compelling the accused to incriminate himself, and was likened by Burghley to the Spanish inquisition. Whitgift was successful, and by the end of the 'eighties church discipline was improved, while practical Puritanism on the other hand was spreading its leaven in English life. In Parliament the brothers Wentworth linked the Puritan cause with that of resistance to royal restraints on topics of debate. Peter Wentworth had already in the session of 1576 been stopped by his fellow-members while attempting a speech on the Queen's auto-cracy in religion. In the Parliament of 1587 he supported his friend Sir Anthony Cope in promoting a bill to abolish the Prayer Book and substitute a Calvinist service, and then converted the whole question into one of Parliamentary privilege. The ten questions which he asked the House to answer would have constituted rulings on the nature of the constitution. But the Speaker did not put them, and Wentworth was committed to the Tower. He probably had more sympathizers in the Commons than appeared, but with the Armada getting ready it was no time for sensible men to start a controversy of that sort. The Parliament of 1593 rounded off Whitgift's measures by enacting that those who refused to attend church or frequented un-lawful conventicles might be banished. A handful of separatists ac-cordingly went into exile, while the mass of the Puritans conformed.[1] Peter Wentworth's final phase in opposition turned on the succession question. For demanding that it should be formally decided without delay he was committed to the Tower in 1593 and died there four years later.

A final flare-up preceded the lull consequent on Whitgift's success. In 1588–9, beginning a few weeks after the defeat of the Armada, appeared the series of tracts written under the pseudonym of Martin Marprelate. They were a scurrilous and hilarious indictment of the bishops and their faults and failings. The author's identity was never discovered, although some of the producers were prosecuted and punished when their secret press was hunted down. John Penry, the chief of them, escaped for the time to Scotland. The Marprelate Tracts caused sensation, indignation, and amusement. If they in-flicted discredit on the bishops they probably did the Puritan clergy no service; for Martin was a ribald fellow who was patently enjoying himself, which was out of character with the humourless severity of the clerics. One of them complained that he had made sin ridiculous when he should have made it odious.

The Armada year saw the effective beginning of one more of the various attempts to colonize Ireland with English settlers. The colon-izing movement, whether in Ireland or in North America, attracted the same projectors, and it is no mere coincidence that the most active leaders in the Irish scheme were the Virginian pioneers Ralegh and Grenville. Munster had been devastated and depopulated

---

[1] M. M. Knappen, in *Tudor Puritanism* (Chicago, 1939), pp. 282–3, etc., holds that the Queen herself was the insuperable obstacle to the success of Puritanism.

by the Desmond rebellion and the papal invasion of 1579–80. It was said that outside the few towns there were no human inhabitants or domestic animals to be seen and that wolves ranged over the land. The Earl of Desmond was killed in 1583, when the other leaders were already dead or in exile. The Desmond lands were forfeited to the Crown, and their extent was over-estimated. The Queen's ministers and the colonial projectors agreed on a scheme for re-population with English settlers. The large units were to be 'seignories' of 12,000 acres of productive land with unlimited mountain and waste, to be sub-divided by their grantees to gentlemen-tenants and planted with working colonists. Such a plan was easier to frame on paper than on the ground, for there were no accurate surveys on the basis of which boundaries could be described, and there followed years of delay and litigation on titles. During that time the Irish filtered in and began to reoccupy the land in pastoral fashion under various tribal claims that could not be made to fit into English ideas of land law. At length the Queen, seeing that the condition of Munster was an invitation to Spanish invasion, appointed in 1588 a commission which settled some of the questions of title; and Ralegh, Grenville, and Sir Warham St. Leger were among those who took up seignories. The legal extent of the Desmond forfeitures was found to be less than half of the area first estimated, so that a great deal of Munster was still left to the Irish, and the resulting population would in any event have been more Irish than English. In fact the English never amounted to more than a handful. Ralegh, who had three-and-a-half seignories, sent over 300 men with their families. Grenville was in Munster in 1589–90, intent on founding a patrimony for a branch of his family that should be permanently based on its Irish estates and rank with the senior line in Devon and Cornwall. But Grenville planted fewer men than did Ralegh, and none of the others planted as many. There were twenty-three seignories in all, including one granted to Edmund Spenser, but altogether the men, women, and children probably did not exceed fifteen hundred.

All depended on a vigorous and prolonged effort of leadership. The Elizabethans did not realize, as the Lords Baltimore were to do in the following century, that founding a colony was a full-time job to which a man must devote himself to the sacrifice of all other interests. Ralegh's location was not mainly in Munster but at court, where, moreover, he got into trouble for his marriage in 1592, with resulting imprisonment in the Tower. Grenville took a command at sea in 1591 and was killed in the last fight of the *Revenge*. Direction in most of the grants fell to stewards and factors, and the patriotic empire-building ideas of the originators degenerated into land-jobbing and the extraction of revenue. The Munster colony after a promising infancy withered in its childhood. Its end was to come before the close of the reign.

With the war the maritime activities of the age reached their greatest intensity, not only in regular expeditions against the enemy but in projects of exploration and extension of trade, with a large privateering enterprise between the two. There were thoughts in plenty on American colonization, although these bore little fruit in action until peace was restored. With the exception of Ralegh's plunge into Guiana, the notable exploring and pioneering expeditions were chiefly connected with the aim of opening trade with eastern Asia. That had been a project never long at rest since the days of John Cabot and Henry VII, inspiring all the Arctic explorations and to some extent the work on the North American coast, and drawing a new reality from the actual visit of Drake to the Spice Islands. Drake's route by the Straits of Magellan proved more attractive than the shorter possibility in the north, because it skirted the Peruvian treasure-ground. Drake was naturally followed by others, whose varying fortunes illuminate by contrast his own great powers of leadership.

The first was Thomas Cavendish, a Suffolk man who had served under Grenville in the Virginia voyage of 1585. Although he made his departure from Plymouth, he appears to have fitted out in 1586 in the Thames and to have had no connection with the west-country adventurers. He sailed with three small ships and passed through the Straits of Magellan in January and February 1587. Then, after Drake's example, he raided Chile and Peru, but found the Spaniards alert and better armed. For a small capture of treasure he had to fight hard and lost thirty men. Still following the classic model he went north to California, and off that coast met with a rich Spanish ship returning from the Philippines with gold and Chinese wares. The great ship's crew outnumbered the English and fought for six hours, and her lading was too much for the English vessels to carry. Cavendish took the most valuable goods and burnt the rest. He had already abandoned his smallest ship for lack of hands. Shortly after the great capture he lost sight of the second, which was never heard of again. With the surviving ship he crossed the Pacific, reconnoitred the

Philippines and the coast of Java, and came home by the Indian
Ocean and the Cape. In Java he was on friendly terms with the Portuguese officers, who said that the Eastern possessions were at Don
Antonio's disposal if he would come out and take them. Cavendish
reached the Channel in September 1588, his track crossing that of
Medina Sidonia on his way round Ireland to Santander. The voyage
had been immensely profitable and had revealed much information
about Eastern trade; and more of it was made public than after
Drake's circumnavigation.

The publication was effected by Richard Hakluyt (probably pronounced Hacklit), a clergyman belonging to an ancient family of the
Anglo-Welsh border, who made himself the greatest English historian of discovery and maritime enterprise. We have already seen
him aiding Gilbert with *Divers Voyages*, and Ralegh with the *Discourse of the Western Planting*. In 1583 Walsingham sent him to Paris as
chaplain to the English embassy and unobtrusive observer of the
spies and intriguers who frequented it. He remained till the close of
the Armada year, and busied himself with collecting from French
captains and Portuguese refugees all the information he could gain
on the geography and trade of the world outside Europe. He was
also gathering books, manuscripts, and narratives from his own
countrymen. On his return to England he cast the whole into a close-
packed quarto volume published at the end of 1589: *The Principal
Navigations, Voyages and Discoveries of the English Nation made by Sea
or over Land to the most remote and farthest distant Quarters of the Earth
at any time within the Compass of these 1500 Years*. It is a rolling, full-
bodied title worth quoting, for it covers a great book, which became
greater still as the years produced new 'worthy acts of our nation'
and necessitated an enlarged edition in three volumes published in
1599–1600. The prefaces and dedicatory epistles of the volumes con-
tain Hakluyt's doctrine that England must develop her sea power
and make her future by commerce and colonization. Some of the
narratives are extracts from books, but most are the unpublished
stories of participators in the adventures, all carefully edited and co-
ordinated by Hakluyt to tell the history of achievement, most of
which, despite the title, falls within his own century, and indeed
within his own lifetime. Hakluyt's *Voyages* compares with Foxe's
Martyrs as a maker of English character and a director of the English
outlook; and Hakluyt has outlived Foxe, for he is still read
to-day.

The success of Cavendish, following that of Drake, made adventurers look on the Straits of Magellan as the gateway to fame. It was no easy approach, and a large expedition that left Plymouth in 1589 failed to get through and returned after suffering heavy casualties. Then Cavendish set out again in 1591, with John Davis in company. They intended to pass the Straits and sail together up to California, whence Cavendish was to cross the Pacific while Davis searched for the North West Passage back to Europe. The voyage was disastrous. A first attempt to pass the Straits failed, after which the two captains parted company at sea. Cavendish died, and his ship returned to England. What he had done with the winnings of his circumnavigation does not appear, but he had not spent much on the equipment of his second expedition. Davis had never made money by his voyages, and the result was that now he was left with a rotten ship, deficient in sails and gear, short of food, and with men nearly naked in the bitter weather of the south. In spite of all he persisted. He got through the Straits and out into the Pacific, only to be blown back and narrowly escape destruction for lack of canvas fit to withstand the wind. After dreadful sufferings from hunger and scurvy he returned to an Irish port in 1593 with sixteen survivors of the seventy-six who had sailed with him. Davis's purpose was to open trade with the Far East, by whatever route it might be possible. He still had hopes of the North West Passage, but was never able to attempt it again himself. In 1595 the Dutch began a resolute effort to gain an eastern trade by way of the Cape, and Davis took service with them to learn the navigation by that route.

To initiate the most distant trade that the world had to offer required more capital than England was yet prepared to risk, more especially as warlike expeditions in the Atlantic were making semi-compulsory calls on court investors, and privateering in the same area was a very profitable use for merchants' capital. An eastern trade would need to finance itself by plunder obtained from the enemy, and broadly there were two schools of thought on how it should be done. The Devon school followed Drake in supporting the claims of Don Antonio and proposing to establish themselves in the East in friendship with the Portuguese. Their financing was therefore to be sought from the plunder of Peru, and their approach to the East was by the Straits of Magellan and the Pacific. The London school, on the other hand, sought success by attacking and plundering the Portuguese in the East and expropriating them from their trading stations; and the Londoners' route to the scene of action was by the Cape of Good Hope and the Indian Ocean. Ultimately the London plan resulted in the foundation of the East India Company. If the Devon plans had succeeded, the result might have been that the East India Company would have become a west-country concern based on Plymouth, with a considerable difference in the after-history of England. The two plans were seen at rivalry in the dissensions that ruined Fenton's expedition of 1582.

The merchants who formed the Turkey Company were the main promoters of the London ambition. It was probably they who petitioned in 1589 for leave to trade by the Cape of Good Hope and proposed to use three of the Turkey Company's ships. Two years later they obtained their permission and sent out James Lancaster in command. Lancaster made a terrible pioneer voyage. When he reached the Cape he had so many sick that he had to send one ship home with the worst cases. Soon after he entered the Indian Ocean his other consort was lost with all hands. Left alone, he coasted to Zanzibar, crossed the Indian Ocean, and reached the Malay archipelago. There he cruised for some months taking rich cargoes from Portuguese ships and learning the conditions of the trade. He was also losing men so fast that it became doubtful whether he could work his ship home. In attempting to do so the crew became so weak when they reached the North Atlantic that they had to run before the trade wind to the West Indies in the hope of obtaining food. There Lancaster lost the ship by the sheer debility of the crew, and was brought home with a handful of survivors by a French privateer. Still another terrible voyage was that of Benjamin Wood, who sailed in 1596 and reached the coast of Burma, where he was wrecked and lost his life. Seven survivors recrossed the Indian Ocean in a small native vessel. They landed on Mauritius, whence one was ultimately rescued by a Dutch ship in 1601.

The west-country pioneers made one more serious effort with the expedition of Richard Hawkins, son of Sir John, in 1593–4. His purpose was to sail by the Straits, raid the coast of Peru, and thence cross the Pacific and make a thorough mercantile examination of the countries of eastern Asia, including Japan and China, which no Englishman had yet seen. There are indications that his successful return would have been followed by the foundation of a Plymouth company for East Indian trade. But he never reached Asia. Drake had found the Peruvian Spaniards unarmed, Cavendish had found them ready and able to fight, Hawkins found them in overwhelming strength. His single ship with seventy-five men was chased by six Spaniards with two thousand. Escaping them, he was brought to action by two strong ships with 1,300 men and plenty of guns. For three days he held out, but in the end was forced to surrender with his ship sinking and only fifteen men unhurt. His was the last of the Elizabethan voyages into the South Sea, where the Spaniards had profited by disaster and taken adequate measures to defend their wealth.

An enterprise completely new to Englishmen was characteristically initiated by Ralegh. By reading all the Spanish accounts of South America that he could find, and by questioning Spanish prisoners, Ralegh had learnt that the Spaniards believed a civilized empire to exist in the interior of the continent, extraordinarily rich in gold. Further, he had quite up-to-date information of the searches made by Antonio de Berrio for the golden state, and of Berrio's conviction that the city of Manoa, ruled by Eldorado the gilded king, lay in the highlands of Guiana and was best approached by ascending the Orinoco. In 1594 he sent out a pinnace to reconnoitre the island of Trinidad at the mouth of the river, where Berrio had established a settlement. In 1595, still out of favour with the Queen, Ralegh sailed in person to the Orinoco. He captured Berrio and dispersed his settlement, then went up the Orinoco with the ships' boats. More than any leader of his time he had a talent for friendship with savages, and the river Indians were soon at his service. They confirmed the Spanish story of a rich empire up country, best reached by way of the Caroni, a tributary of the Orinoco. Ralegh found the Caroni, but its passage was barred by falls. The season was late, and flood-waters were making the rivers difficult. He returned to his ships and to England, convinced that he was on the verge of a discovery that would reverse the relative positions of England and Spain—Elizabeth's revenue of half-a-million as against Philip's of ten times as much. Ralegh was persuaded of the golden empire, England's for the seeking. He did not advocate its conquest, but its defence in friendly alliance against the Spaniards who were preparing to invade it. He had also seen on the banks of the Orinoco what he took to be gold mines waiting to be dug. On his return he published his *Discovery of Guiana*, cogent in argument, beautiful as Elizabethan prose; but the Queen was sceptical, the great men disliked him, and nothing was done. It was as well, for Manoa did

not exist. Twenty years were to elapse before Ralegh should fit out
for Guiana again.

After the Portugal venture of 1589 and the failure of military invasion, it should have been John Hawkins's turn, and for a moment
he hoped it was. In the latter half of 1589 two small squadrons were
at sea which could have formed the basis for his plan of a continuous
oceanic blockade for the stoppage of the treasure traffic. The Earl of
Cumberland with one of the Queen's ships and three of his own
cruised about the Azores, while Frobisher with four ships took the
inner station off the coast of Spain and Portugal. Between them these
two commanders inflicted great loss on the returning West Indian
trade and more than repaid the expense of sending them out. It was
at this time that the Spaniards were making a radical change in their
treasure-transit. The great convoys still sailed with the bulky cargoes,
but the bullion no longer went with them. It was conveyed instead
in small fast vessels sailing independently. These were so designed as
to be able to run from heavy assailants, while well enough armed to
fight small ones. The English called them 'the King's treasure
frigates'. Their use, coupled with a system for the rapid despatch of
orders across the ocean, enabled Philip to get the treasure through in
the intervals between the English operations, and made more essential than ever the continuous blockading effort that Hawkins demanded. Philip was this year unable to send out a fleet to engage the
English or escort the convoys home. He was taking measures to
build one, but their result depended on his receipt of the treasure.
This was the position when Hawkins got his plan sanctioned at the
end of the year and equipped his first squadron of six ships in order
to sail in February 1590.

Hawkins found to his sorrow that he was dealing with people who
could not be made to comprehend his scale of values. Privy Council
agenda on 23 February included the question: 'Whether it be convenient that Sir John Hawkins shall proceed in his voyage?'; and the
answer noted in the margin, 'Thought unmeet for him to go'. Those
few words were the death-sentence on the ocean blockade. News had
been received that Philip was preparing an expedition to occupy
Brittany in conjunction with the League in France, and to use the
Breton ports as a base for the invasion of England. Any such expedition could not possibly be a large one, and it was for such con-
tingencies that Hawkins was allotting only half the Navy to his
blockade, leaving the other half to look after the Channel. However,

he was stopped, and a month after he should have sailed five million ducats from the West came safely into Spanish ports, the last consignment to be carried in a full plate fleet. Some of that money went to the making of a new Spanish navy which, without it, could never have come into being. As for Brittany, the Spanish troops did not sail till October, and then there were less than 3,000 of them. Hawkins was at length allowed to sail at the end of May, for the main purpose of watching for the Brittany expedition, which in the end eluded him. Frobisher was sent out to the Azores in July, too late to intercept another consignment of treasure in the new carriers. Since the Azores had been unwatched for eight months its despatch was not a surprising move on the part of the Spaniards. Frobisher went home in September and Hawkins was recalled at the end of October, after which many more months elapsed with the ocean routes completely open. Hawkins had taken a few minor prizes, but did not pretend to have made a successful voyage. The Queen apparently blamed him, and he joined Drake on the shelf for some years to come, so far, that is to say, as active command was concerned. He continued to work at high pressure as Navy Treasurer, and in these years turned out the finest ships of the Elizabethan fleet, designed on the battle experience of the Armada year.

The Queen and the Council continued their version of the blockade, that of cruises at intervals, by sending out Lord Thomas Howard in 1591 with six ships of the Queen's and smaller auxiliaries. Sir Richard Grenville went as vice-admiral. They sailed to the Azores with much at stake; for Philip had held back the great convoy of the previous season, sending only the treasure carriers, and for 1591 there was a double fleet to come home from the West. It was nearly three years since the defeat of the Armada, and not one season's treasure had been missed. Thanks to this money the equipment of a fighting fleet, embodying Armada experience, was nearly complete. The western convoys were due in the late summer, and the fleet from Spain would then be ready to meet them at the Azores. Howard and Grenville were about the islands, and Cumberland with a mainly private force on the coast of Spain. It was not till the last day of August that the clash occurred, when Howard, five months out and with sickly crews, was caught in the process of cleaning his ships by Alonzo de Bazan with the new Spanish fleet. Howard was heavily outnumbered and short of many men. He retreated out of the Flores anchorage and just managed to sail clear of the Spaniards to the open sea, except that his last ship the *Revenge*, with Grenville in command, was stopped and cut off. Surrounded by the whole Spanish fleet and hopeless of escape, Grenville fought the epic battle that has made his name live in history. When both he and his ship were mortally wounded the survivors surrendered. Grenville died a day or two later, and the *Revenge* sank before she could be repaired. The great convoys reached the Azores, 140 ships, many in bad order through long exposure to the worm of tropic anchorages. A violent gale swept the islands and wrecked so many ships that less than half of the rich trade came into Spanish ports.

The ominous development of 1591 was that Philip had a navy. Its effect on the English government was the opposite of what might have been expected. They sent fewer of the Queen's ships to sea and had the majority laid up, 'keeping Chatham church'. It was evident now that the blockade would require greater force than two years earlier. But if Philip could build a new navy out of defeat what might not Elizabeth have done out of victory? She was spending money enough on soldiers to have paid for an overwhelming ocean force in days when the men were ready and eager and a ship like the *Revenge* could be built for less than £3,000. In 1592 she sent only two of her ships out to the Azores, in 1593 two, in 1594 none, while the treasure came regularly to Philip's hands. Elizabeth feared that she would have to face another invasion. She was content to await it, with Drake employed in fortifying Plymouth and Hawkins doing dockyard work. Before leaving this topic the illustrative figures may be quoted. From 1588 to 1603 the state spent £550,000 on the Navy and sea expeditions, and £3,300,000 on land armies.[1] The figures are capable of different rendering owing to the fact that some operations were both naval and military, but on the lowest proportion the expenditure on armies was more than four times that on the Navy. There was of course an enormous weight of tradition behind the view that soldiers alone won wars and that fleets were only coast defences. Drake and Hawkins were prophets who are honoured now more than they could expect to be in their own day when, as it happened, their greatest victory had been in sight of the English coast.

There was another side to the naval war than that of the regular expeditions. Privateering was carried on to a greater extent than ever before. In the older French wars it had been in home waters. Against

---

[1] Computed by W. R. Scott in *Joint Stock Companies*, I, 95.

Spain it was chiefly on the ocean, the two main cruising grounds
being the Caribbean and the vicinity of the Azores. Spanish records
recently discovered show an almost incredible concourse of small
English vessels in West Indian waters,[1] and the Spaniards, although
they were unpleasantly quick in creating a fighting fleet, were slow
to produce light forces to cope with the privateering plague. Their
fortification of the ports was effective, but it did not prevent steady
and serious losses at sea. Merchants, courtiers, and officials invested
in privateers. Alderman John Watts of London was a large-scale
operator reputed to be very successful. Drake, Ralegh, Hawkins,
the Howards, and the Privy Councillors in general all sent their own
privateers to sea. The Earl of Cumberland was especially active
and persistent, and himself often sailed with his ships. One voyage
with another it was highly profitable, and the winnings provided
the wherewithal to invest in the joint-stock expeditions under
the Queen's orders, which were usually not a financial success.
When the Queen's ships went to the Azores the privateers followed
in the hope of sharing in larger game than they could bring down
alone. In 1592 they brought off the richest capture of the war, the
great East Indian carrack *Madre de Dios*. She was assailed and
taken by a number of private vessels belonging to Ralegh, Hawkins,
and Cumberland, while the Queen, having a ship in the neighbourhood, claimed a predominant share. The choicest part of the lading
was plundered by the privateer crews, and what was left to be brought
into port was valued at £140,000.

Statesmen who did not believe that the war could be quickly won
by sea had justification for their land campaigns, which seemed
indeed essential to the defence of England. If Spain were victorious
in the Netherlands she would gain the ports from which a continuous threat of invasion might be maintained until at length it
found its opportunity. If Spain and the Catholic League were
victorious in France the menace would be doubled. No one forgot
how near a French army had come to landing in 1545. England was
bound by treaty to aid the Dutch on land. She was bound by interest
to see that Henry of Navarre did not succumb in France. Events in
that country conspired to draw Elizabeth into the field. Henry III,
the last of the Valois, had procured the murder of the Duke of Guise
in 1588. In August 1589 he was himself assassinated by a fanatic of

[1] Irene A. Wright, *Further English Voyages to Spanish America*, Hakluyt Society
(1951), *passim*.

the League. Navarre was the rightful heir, and assumed the title as
Henry IV, a Huguenot king recognized by perhaps a minority of the
French, repudiated by the League and its Spanish ally. A hard fight
lay before him, and it was a fight for England and the Dutch as well
as for France. Elizabeth had to aid him. She did it with a better heart
since she was now combining with a lawful king and not with rebels
with whom her lot had always hitherto been cast. The Protestant
coalition that Walsingham had longed for was in being, and its
members spoke of 'the common cause'.

The details of the land wars were involved and the military results
inconclusive. The campaigns were protracted year after year, mainly
by reason of the existence of numerous fortified towns, and of the
very small numbers of men that the combatants were able to put into
the field at a financial cost that strained them to the uttermost. The
Dutch indeed were growing richer by the trade of their seaports, but
Henry IV required continuous subsidies in the form of loans that he
could not repay. In 1589 Elizabeth furnished him with £60,000, and
when she raised English troops to be paid by him they seldom were
paid. In the autumn of that year she sent Lord Willoughby to
Normandy with 4,000 men. They served well in a campaign of petty
incidents that helped at least to save Henry's cause from extinction.
At the end of the year a mere remnant was left to return to England.
Willoughby had been Leicester's successor in the Netherlands
command, and when he went to France his place was taken by Sir
Francis Vere, who worked well with Maurice of Nassau and made
a great name as a fighting soldier. In 1590 the war took more definite
shape. In January Philip made a new treaty with the League, whereby
he promised 20,000 men and large sums of money and was to have
possession of French towns and the use of seaports against England.
It was the alarm consequent on the knowledge of these plans that
caused Hawkins, as we have seen, to be interdicted from beginning
his blockade of the treasure route. The alarm was exaggerated, for it
was not until October that Philip landed 3,000 Spaniards at St.
Nazaire. He did however instruct Parma to strike in against Henry
from the Netherlands. Some of Parma's men were with the League's
army that Henry routed at Ivry, his first notable victory, and when
in the summer Henry laid siege to Paris, Parma marched in person
and effected its relief. Parma obeyed Philip's orders against his own
judgment, for the diversion of effort enabled the Dutch and English
in the Netherlands to capture important towns and improve a

position which had been discouraging. From this date in fact the salvation of the Dutch became ever more certain.

Spaniards in France were a spur to the Queen and her Council, who sent two small armies, one to Brittany and the other to Normandy, in 1591. Altogether it was computed that England had over 10,000 men on the continent in this year. First Sir John Norreys went with 3,000 to Brittany, landing at Paimpol in May. He spent the season fighting the local forces of the League, but had no battle with the Spaniards, who had established themselves on the Blavet river in the south of the province. Brest, in which the English were chiefly interested for its strategic value to Philip, was held for Henry IV, and the object of Norreys's expedition was to prevent any threat from developing against it. At the end of the year Norreys had barely a third of his men left, a common result of these campaigns, in which sickness and privation were terribly costly to the small numbers engaged. Elizabeth was dissatisfied at Henry's lack of co-operation, which was due to his own weakness. She was nevertheless determined to support him, and her favourite Essex was clamouring for a chance to show his quality. In August she sent Essex to Normandy with 4,000 men to join Henry in besieging Rouen. By October, when Henry was ready, Essex had only 1,500 men fit. The siege lasted for six months, until Parma again came to the rescue and relieved the place in April 1592. It was his last service to his somewhat ungrateful sovereign, and he died, worn out with disappointment, at the end of the year. Essex was active and always eager to take personal risks, but showed little sign of generalship. The Queen, disliking the risks, recalled him in January, but a remnant of his men continued in Henry's service.

From this time onwards the English interest was mainly in Brittany. In May 1592 the English and Huguenot forces there were defeated with severe loss by the Leaguers and Spaniards at Craon. Elizabeth blamed Henry's commander and threatened withdrawal, but new rumours of an armada preparing in Spain convinced her that she must keep her foothold in Brittany. Burghley agreed, and a new treaty bound Elizabeth to keep 4,000 men in the province and Henry not to make a separate peace with Spain. Norreys went over with these men in November, while at the same time the Spaniards at Blavet were reinforced to 5,000. Nothing of lasting effect was done before midsummer 1593, when Henry IV altered the whole aspect of the war by changing his religion. In July he attended mass at St.

Denis, on the threshold of the capital which that ceremony was to gain him. A truce followed between him and the League, and although a few irreconcilables held out, the war became a national contest of France against Spain, with the eviction of the Spaniards from Brittany as its first object. Philip determined not to quit his hold, on which depended any hope he might have of invading England. He reinforced his Blavet troops, and in April 1594 moved them north to the shore of Brest water. There they built the strong fort of Crozon, threatening the anchorage and ultimately Brest itself. The Queen met the threat by sending new troops to Norreys, including 1,000 veterans from the Netherlands under Sir Thomas Baskerville. With them went a naval squadron with 1,200 sailors commanded by Frobisher. The troops fought their way to Crozon and found the ships waiting to co-operate. After a month's siege Norreys and Frobisher stormed Crozon and drove the remaining Spaniards back to the Blavet, a minor haven unsuitable for the assembly of an armada. Frobisher was mortally wounded at Crozon. Early next year the Queen withdrew her forces from Brittany, judging that Henry was now strong enough to look after himself.

The capture of Crozon relieved for the time the fears of a new invasion project. Although the little armies sent to France had in effect done the work required of them, the fighting had in the main been inglorious and disappointing, the sufferings of the troops had been great, and the unpopularity of the service such that impressment had been the only means of raising men. The result was that English opinion veered again to Hawkins's way of thinking on the conduct of the war, 'that we have as little to do in foreign countries as may be, but of mere necessity, for that breedeth great charge and no profit at all'. Hawkins and Drake were ready with a new plan for striking at the treasure route, and the Queen gave her consent at the close of 1594.

Hawkins, who brought a financial and statistical sense to his appreciations of strategy, was convinced that the stoppage of the treasure meant the end of Philip's power to fight; but the plan now to be followed was not his of intercepting it at the Azores, but Drake's of capturing Panama and thereby plugging the neck of the bottle. This required a military force to march across the Isthmus, and Baskerville, a noted fighting man, was appointed to command it. The preparations were prolonged for months, to the accompaniment of much careless talk that was reported in Spain. Finance was by a joint-stock subscribed by numerous adventurers, the Queen's share being the contribution of six of her galleons, while about twenty private ships were added. Drake and Hawkins were joint commanders with equal authority, and so far was their mutual independence carried that each had direct command of half of the fleet, each engaged his own officers and men, and each separately victualled his ships according to his own ideas of what was necessary. Their methods and temperaments were entirely different, and the officers were grouped in rival followings. It was of no good augury, and neither was the intriguing and whispering that went on in court circles while the expedition slowly concentrated at Plymouth. A spy reported to Philip that there was little to fear, since the venture would be overthrown before its start. It very nearly was. When all was ready at Plymouth the Blavet Spaniards made a sudden raid with four galleys on the Cornish coast, burning villages and getting away before the Plymouth fleet could intercept them. It was the first Spanish landing on English soil, and the Queen was much perturbed. She took it as the harbinger of an invasion, and ordered Drake and Hawkins to give up their plans and cruise instead on the Spanish coast. On their protest she relented so far as to permit them to sail westward if they would promise to be back within six months. It was hardly enough for the Panama plan, which was accordingly exchanged for something simpler. A disabled treasure-ship was reported to be lying in the harbour of San Juan de Puerto Rico, unable to continue her voyage to Europe. Drake and Hawkins sailed in August 1595 with the sole object of raiding Puerto Rico and taking this one ship's lading, said to be worth two million ducats. Once again far-seeing strategy had been replaced by something not so good.

Success depended on speed and secrecy, and there was neither. A few days out of port, Drake declared that he was short of victuals and insisted on attacking Grand Canary to obtain some. Hawkins objected, and was overruled after a bitter wrangle. The Canary attack was a failure and no foodstuffs resulted. Drake then consented to cross the Atlantic without them. Some Englishmen had been captured at Grand Canary and questioned by the governor, who immediately sent a warning to Puerto Rico. Meanwhile Philip ordered five of his treasure-frigates to fetch the bullion home. These ships overtook the English in the Caribbean, captured a straggler, and learned the destination. They raced for Puerto Rico, and their

speed took them there before the English could appear. The English
in fact did not hurry, for Hawkins insisted on putting everything in
readiness for a battle with a Spanish fleet that was known to be
following. At this point Hawkins fell ill, and died as the fleet
approached Puerto Rico. The place had been doubly warned and was
well prepared. Drake made an attack, but was beaten off with loss.
The expedition had failed in the object for which it had set out.
Drake was determined not to go home empty-handed, and reverted
to the Panama plan. He landed Baskerville with 700 men at Nombre
de Dios to march across the Isthmus. In four days the troops came
back to the ships, foiled by a well-posted Spanish force. It was ten
years since Drake had been in the Indies, and all was greatly changed.
He lingered on the Central American coast, but there was nothing
more to be done. Fever was raging, and Drake caught it. He died in
January 1596 and was buried in the bay of Porto Bello, not far from
Nombre de Dios, the scene of his first great enterprise. Baskerville
brought the expedition home after beating off the pursuing Spanish
fleet. The loss of Drake and Hawkins at sea, like the deaths of
Leicester and Walsingham near the throne, altered the character of
the time. Burghley was left, but he was soon to follow.

Year after year Philip had been reported to be gathering a new
armada and nothing had come of it. In the winter of 1595–6 the news
became more circumstantial, and it seemed that an invasion really
was in preparation. Active-minded men held that an offensive move
was the best prevention, and at length brought the Queen to consent.
Broadly speaking, the strategy adopted was that of Drake, to seek
battle on the coast of Spain and inflict loss and destruction before the
threat matured. Six of the Queen's galleons were at sea with Drake,
and most of the remainder were to be employed in the new expedition, which was therefore a command for the Lord Admiral in
person. An army was also to be shipped, and its inevitable commander was Essex, who was joined to Howard with equal authority
over the whole expedition. This was the third occasion of the
employment of two joint-commanders, an idea that had an attraction
for the Queen. Of secondary rank were Lord Thomas Howard,
Ralegh, and Sir Francis Vere, after whom came a multitude of well-
known officers and gentlemen. The troops numbered about ten
thousand, fewer than on the Portugal expedition, but infinitely
better equipped, supplied, and disciplined. A Dutch contingent—a
new portent on the sea—was a prominent part of the force.

Before the start Spain took an initiative as in the previous year, but a more serious one. In April 1596 a Spanish army from Flanders laid siege to Calais, which Henry IV found himself unable to succour. Essex was eager to go to the relief, but before anything could be done the place surrendered. Calais in Spanish hands was regarded as a serious threat to England's security, but this was an exaggeration, for the port was small and shallow and not available for first-class fighting ships. The English decision was to let Howard and Essex go forward with their Spanish voyage. Essex was less than half the Lord Admiral's age and a turbulent young man. There were skirmishes between them at the outset, but on the whole Essex seems to have shown unexpected deference to his senior, and Howard was a man who could manage anyone. Their joint command was reasonably harmonious. Essex nevertheless had a private plan which he did not disclose to the Queen before sailing, to hold a Spanish port, preferably Cadiz, with a permanent garrison, and thereby create a base for a close blockade of the whole coast—one more version of the theme of strangling the treasure traffic.

On 1 June the armament sailed from Plymouth, and only after getting well out to sea did the commanders reveal that Cadiz was to be the point of attack. The result was that the defence had only twelve hours' warning of their arrival on 20 June. A heavy sea prevented an initial landing on the outer beaches, and on Ralegh's urging the fleet entered the harbour to attack the shipping first and the town second. In the port there were four of the 'apostles' class, the greatest Spanish galleons, of which two were burnt and two were captured, the first important prizes permanently added to the Queen's Navy. Next day Howard turned to the merchant shipping, which included an out-going fleet for the Caribbean. The Spaniards offered two million ducats as ransom, which was not accepted; and then burnt the whole concourse of fifty vessels with ladings worth ten millions. The English saved a little from the flames, but not much. Meanwhile the troops were landing to storm the city. They broke in after a light resistance and soon occupied the important points. There was some killing in the streets, chiefly by the Dutch, but Howard and Essex were determined on humanity and restored order without much trouble. The Queen's instructions had forbidden unnecessary bloodshed, and particularly the use of violence to women. At the time they were written, it may be said, prospective invaders of England were talking of dragging her by the hair

through the streets of London. The English commanders sent the
civil population out of Cadiz and then systematically gutted the place
of its artillery, munitions of war, and miscellaneous wealth, which
was considerable. The value of the goods carried off on official
account probably paid the costs of the expedition, and the officers
and men are known to have taken large personal plunder.

After a fortnight all was done, and the question of the next move
arose. Essex wished to be left in Cadiz with a permanent garrison.
The others refused to allow it, knowing that the Queen would not
consent. In the exhausted condition of Spain the evacuation of Cadiz
was probably a mistake, for if Philip had made the effort to recover
the place against a well-led garrison it would have been at the cost of
his collapse elsewhere. After a minor landing near Cape St. Vincent
it was determined that the fleet should sail for the Azores. A foul
wind prevented it, and all were really eager to get home with their
booty and their credit; for this had been a creditable affair—well-
disciplined, healthy, successful—different indeed from the unhappy
Portugal voyage of seven years before. Howard entered Plymouth
on 8 August, and Essex two days later. The Queen was at first
appreciative, but soon grumbled at the small spoil in comparison
with what might have been collected, and at the disproportionate
amounts retained by private individuals. The grumbling grew into a
storm, and congratulation on the best managed stroke of war since
the defeat of the Armada was overwhelmed by accusation and
recrimination over pounds, shillings, and pence. Out of it all the
stock of Essex had risen. His well-known personal hardihood was,
it was now acknowledged, adorned by humanity, moderation, and
generosity, and a wisdom that had so far been to seek. He became
England's favourite as he was the Queen's. His growth in grace may
have been partly due to the Lord Admiral, the best senior colleague
a man like Essex could have had. Four months after the sack of
Cadiz the exchange at Florence published its periodical list of debtors
who had failed to meet their obligations. Among them was the King
of Spain.

In spite of all, the Armada of 1596 was sent to sea. It was a cheaply
and hastily equipped force under Don Martin de Padilla, who
gathered ninety sail at Lisbon and shipped an army whose quality
was far below that which had given the Spaniards their fame. The
army, however, did not fight. The expedition sailed from the Tagus
on 13 October, and was struck by a heavy gale off Cape Finisterre

four days later. Nearly half the ships were driven on the coast and wrecked with great loss of life. Those which came to safe anchorage were at once deserted by as many of the troops as could contrive to get away, and the whole undertaking was thus rapidly ended. In England there had been much levying of county forces, overhaul of fortifications, and despatch of troops to Ireland, but not a full naval mobilization. There was no great need for that, since Padilla's fleet included few fighting ships, and men of sea experience like Ralegh did not take the threat too seriously on account of the lateness of the season. Its proposed destination, England or Ireland, was never revealed, but Ireland was the more probable goal of the two.

19

THE CLOSING YEARS

ALTHOUGH, as there is little doubt, the ability of government declined from the Armada to the end of the reign, the condition of England, the good order, spirit, and confidence of the people, improved. In the 1590s there was no *fin de siècle* depression or disillusion. On the contrary there were unbounded pride in the country's achievement and hope for the future. The defeat of the Armada was decisive to that generation. It was not only the vindication of sea power as a mode of national life, but a sentence of the Almighty in the cause of the islanders against their assailants. *Flavit Deus*, however inadequate as a description of events in the Channel, was an article of faith to Protestants of puritanical tone, who were ready to apply the doctrine of election to their nation even though, as charitable men, they preferred to hold it vaguely as individuals. England was never so high and aspiring as in the last years of Elizabeth. The Queen herself, by contrast, was past her best, and her best councillors were going. Her talents were such as had made her kingdom prosper in peace, and she was out of her element in war. The same is true of the administrative machine and its methods, which allowed of no outstanding war minister, no swift decisions and concentrations. Between Elizabeth and England there was in the last years a rift, though not a great one. She was old, and her character had always been fixed. Her people's was developing, and they felt young.

The war was the period of great Elizabethan literature, which was not in any narrow and direct sense connected with politics. There were as yet no politics of the sort that inspired literature in later times. There was criticism of the Queen's actions and of the advice that her councillors gave, or were supposed to have given, to her. But there was no questioning of the political and social system, no

party of reform and party of reaction. The connection between literature and events, which was not very extensive, was that some writers
were interested in action, warlike or conspiratorial for the most part,
and in the characters of men and women who made it. A sufficient
public was also interested in these things and would pay for books
and drama that reflected them. The new society that succeeded the
generation of religious turmoil, and took itself so much for granted
that it did not realize that it was new, made this demand, which was
supplied by a generation of professional writers who made letters
their living. They also were new, for the writing of the past had been
done by men who lived mainly for other pursuits and wrote as a
recreation or to express their beliefs. Lyly, Marlowe, Shakespeare,
Jonson, and the minors of their time were men of a new profession,
of whom some did well and some poorly. Shakespeare, as actor and
playwright, made an income comparable in value to that of a best-
selling novelist of our day, and his transcendent genius, uninhibited
by any evident bonds, was mated without friction to a businesslike
nature that made, saved, and invested money and raised its owner in
the social scale to his own obvious satisfaction. To catalogue the
writings of these men is not useful in a brief survey of their time. The
books with which such a survey is concerned are those that made
history then and there, whereas Marlowe and Shakespeare were long-
term creators for the future. The only play of Shakespeare's that
made any Tudor history was *Richard II*, and that only to the slightest
degree, as will be recorded.

It was an age also of novels, romances, pamphlets, and poems.
Their historical significance, taken in the mass, is that they were
largely concerned with secular subjects and not with religious controversy. They were the reading of a generation for which the
problems of the mid-century were settled and other interests predominated. Notable was the timeless interest of sheer beauty, of
imagery, rhythm, and free fancy, served by Spenser's poems and enjoyed by a generation that was fancy free. That chord had been
struck only by rough ballads a century earlier, and was not greatly
evident in the grim Tudor winter after the dissolution of the monasteries. Now wealth and success were calling it to life. Self-awareness
again, and introspective examination, formerly an affair of religion,
grew merely sentimental in the last two decades of the age, and produced the crop of sonneteering for which the 'nineties were remarkable.

All that represents but one side, the cultured and perhaps not very deep-feeling side, of the last Elizabethans. There was also the puritanical undercurrent, deep and wide, for whom its great literature was all in one cover, the Bible Englished by Tyndale. To its readers the connection between events and the scriptures was evident. Rome and Spain were antichrist and his armies, and the English, marked to fight the battles of God, were equated with the chosen people of old. This attitude, so characteristic of the seventeenth century, was well developed in the closing decades of the sixteenth. It is seen even among courtiers and public officials as well as in the ranks of the public. If Bunyan had lived in the 1590s he would not have been out of his world.

As the war settled into its stride, trade and dependent industry had to accommodate themselves to its conditions. English cloth-fleets no longer went to Antwerp, but Flushing was open, and so also was Amsterdam, while the direct export to Germany continued. Antwerp never recovered, since, though undisturbed in Spanish hands, its access from the sea was blockaded by its enemies' possession of Flushing. By war or treaty the Scheldt remained closed for two hundred years to come. Many of the merchant firms, the craftsmen, and the contractors migrated northwards into free Dutch territory, and there built up the commercial enterprise characteristic of the following century. English disputes with the German Hansa recurred during the war, mainly on the carrying of contraband to Spain by the hulks of the German and Baltic ports. One such quarrel caused in 1598 the expulsion of the Hansa from England and the confiscation of its London premises at the Steelyard above London Bridge. But the Hanseatic League was no longer the power it had been, and the merchants of the Eastland Company were able to increase the Baltic trade while the Merchants Adventurers dealt with North Sea Germany. Southwards, the direct and open trade with Spain and Portugal ceased, a loss that was financially compensated by the gains of privateering in the ocean war, while there was still some indirect disposal of English cloth in those countries. In the Mediterranean the English trade was well established. When the short-term privileges of the Turkey Company ended it was reconstituted as the Levant Company in 1592. Its chief mart was at Aleppo, and its change from joint-stock to regulated company methods of business was a sign that conditions were easier and more settled.

Ocean trades were feeling their way to greater expansion. The East

Indian attempts have already been noticed. In West Africa, slaving was at a discount for lack of the western market, but the late Elizabethans maintained touch with the Guinea coast for the sake of its commodities. In 1588 some Exeter merchants, in collaboration with Don Antonio, obtained from the Queen a charter to monopolize for ten years the trade of the Gambia and Senegal coastline; and on a scale that is now obscure the trade went on during that period, the charter being renewed in 1598. In 1592 another group received a similar grant for the Sierra Leone region. Westward, English ships were beginning to enter the Gulf of St. Lawrence and thereby extend the area of the Newfoundland fishery. On the Guiana coast speculative merchants were entering the river mouths to collect cotton and tobacco from the Indians, the way having been pioneered by pinnaces that Ralegh sent out after his own penetration of the Orinoco. In spite of the war, a new trade was arising on the eastern part of the Spanish Main. It was quite distinct from Hawkins's old business, consisting chiefly in the exchange of English manufactures for tobacco and in the lading of salt at the great natural salt-pan of Punta de Araya for the use of the Newfoundland fisheries. Finally men began to talk again of Ralegh's lost colonists, and small craft once more coasted the future United States and sampled its commodities. All this was far from being a final flicker of Tudor enterprise. It was more in the nature of a crescendo, and an anticipation of the greater doings of the future.

On the whole the war, especially with privateering taken into account, was by no means ruinous to English prosperity. There were nevertheless hard times for many of the people, and the steady increase in well-being characteristic of the early and middle periods of the reign was not maintained. The changes in foreign commerce naturally prejudiced some while profiting others. New commodities made new industries and caused some decline in old. Socially, if the times were stimulating and exciting for the active, intelligent people, they were not always so for the masses. The calls for military service were considerable. The county militias were frequently embodied for training or on alarms of invasion, and their members served without pay. The forces sent overseas were compulsorily levied, and although they were small they were drawn from a small population: one must multiply by twelve to obtain the proportion of to-day's figures, and the casualties then appear heavy enough. Soldiering was very unpopular, as sea service was not, and discontent and desertion were serious.

In 1592–3 Francis Bacon declared that England had a surplus of food, and Parliament referred to the great plenty and cheapness of grain. Thereupon immediately ensued five consecutive years of scarcity amounting almost to famine, of which 1596 was the worst. Wet summers were the cause, and breadstuffs rose to excessive prices, while deaths from starvation were many. Town corporations, county justices, and the Privy Council all did their best to mitigate suffering by arranging for grain imports, shifting supplies from good districts to bad, distributing cheap or free to the poor, and punishing profiteers. It was a good illustration of the efficacy of an administration that relied on public spirit rather than on salaries to get its work done, but it could not alter the grim fact that food was short. Perhaps the central administration itself was less able than it had been. The war occupied too much of its attention, and the great Elizabethan lights were going out. Enclosure was still complained of, though its extent was small. In any region in which it had recently taken place it was naturally blamed for dearth and scarcity. In Oxfordshire in the autumn of 1596 there was threat of a serious rising for the destruction of enclosures and the seizing of corn stocks. The energy of the local justices and the Privy Council nipped the affair in the bud. The contrast between the good reports of 1593 and the ill conditions of 1596 shows how dependent on the chances of the weather were Elizabethan England and all other countries at the time. Famine and pestilence were common and uncontrollable, and men were so used to the fact that it did not excite them to questionings of the goodness of their government. They might riot to pull down fences and rob granaries, but they were not moved to demand political reforms.

Essex came home from Cadiz ambitious to dominate the government. Against him he had the Cecils, Burghley and his son Sir Robert; and the younger Cecil had been made Secretary in Essex's absence. Ralegh was also a rival, but of less weight. The Queen had never truly forgiven him for his unpermitted marriage and had never esteemed him as in the statesman's class. He was now forty-five and could expect little higher advancement. The chief allies of Essex were the brothers Anthony and Francis Bacon, sons of the Lord Keeper of the early part of the reign. They had hoped for promotion from Burghley, whose wife was their aunt, but he was solely concerned with the future of his son. The Bacons were young and ambitious but temperamentally far apart from Essex. Francis Bacon—an embodiment of cool intellect if ever there was one—urged him not to base his position on military achievement (sound advice, for Essex was not a great general), but to seek 'domestical greatness' by devoting himself to the civil administration. Essex listened to Bacon but could not bring himself to eschew adventure; and in three years Bacon's counsel was vindicated. Meanwhile Essex assiduously attended Council, spent much money on building up a private information service in foreign countries, and urged the vigorous prosecution of the war, with himself in a commanding rôle. The Queen sentimentally doted on him like a fond mother, but politically distrusted his counsels and was of the Cecils' way of thinking. They wanted to see the war ended, since England and Protestantism were reasonably secure, and that for them had been its object. Essex and the 'men of blood', on the other hand, favoured its continuance, chiefly, it would seem, as a field for the display of their prowess. There is something of a paradox between the sentimental hold of Essex upon the Queen and the fact that in most contested questions she acted on the Cecils' advice. This held good even in the filling of appointments by the personal adherents of the rivals. Essex uniformly failed to get his men promoted, while the Cecils successfully pushed theirs.

The indefatigable Philip was still working on invasion plans. He had one foot in the grave and was bent on destroying England before the other followed. In the spring of 1597 he gathered yet another armada at Corunna and the adjacent ports. In England it was known, and Essex desired to lead a fleet to make a preventive attack. The Queen sanctioned it, with Lord Thomas Howard and Ralegh as his subordinates; and ultimately nineteen of her ships, large and small, were mobilized, with some good armed merchantmen, a Dutch contingent, and a host of transports for a military force. They all sailed from Plymouth in July and were scattered by a south-west gale of a violence exceptional for the season. It was late in August before Essex was able to sail again with a diminished force. Adverse winds prevented him from attacking the Spanish ports, and he made for the Azores to intercept the plate fleets. Among the islands his behaviour was not that of an inspired commander. He quarrelled violently with Ralegh for capturing a useful landing-place when he, Essex, was not present, and consented to overlook the offence only on condition that Ralegh's exploit should not be mentioned in the official account of the expedition. Then, having placed his fleet to guard the approach to Terceira from the westward, he changed his purpose and attacked an island to the east. While he was doing so, the great Spanish convoy from the west arrived safely at Angra in Terceira and was then unassailable. Essex's fatal absence in the wrong direction had resulted in the loss of the nearest chance that ever occurred in these wars of taking a plate fleet. When his supplies were consumed he had to sail home almost empty-handed. This was bad enough, but something else confirmed the Queen's disgust for oceanic expeditions. In October, while Essex's fleet was straggling back in scattered groups believing that all was over for the year, Philip's armada issued from Ferrol and Corunna in their path. With luck Philip might have scored a victory and have gone on to achieve an unopposed landing on the English coast. It did not come to that, for the usual gale smote his armament and drove it home in confusion. But when Elizabeth learned all, she is said to have determined not to let her fleet out of the Channel again.[1]

Essex with the Lord Admiral in 1596 had shown promise. Essex in sole command in 1597 had shown himself unfit for the position. Such was the Queen's judgment, and she said so plainly, while at the same time still yearning over him as a son, or a lover or a friend, however one decides to describe him. It was a curious situation. He himself withdrew in dudgeon from court, and took to his bed. The others, Burghley, Cecil, Howard, Ralegh, did not press their advantage, but behaved as good comrades to a man out of luck, urging him in kindly letters to return and resume his place. In all appearance their attitude was generous, in effect it was as deadly as the subtlest malice, for it emphasized Essex in the posture of a wilful fool. Ostensibly his quarrel was on a question of precedence, for the Queen had created Howard Earl of Nottingham which, with his office of Lord Admiral, placed him before Essex. The solution was found by appointing Essex Earl Marshal, of equal authority to the Admiral, which, with his senior earldom, put him in front again. These things did not seem so childish to the Elizabethans as they do now, but they must to some extent have caused ridicule of the great man's pettishness.

Whitgift had temporarily settled the Puritan question, although by methods that were to arouse rancour against the Church in time to come. The penal laws against Catholics continued, and laymen were fined and Jesuits executed, although in smaller numbers than formerly. The lower rate of executions testified to the lessening of

---

[1] E. P. Cheyney's account in his history of Elizabeth's last years: but M. Oppenheim, in his comments on *Monson's Tracts*, did not rate highly the chance of a Spanish victory.

the danger since the previous decade; and many of those caught were let off lightly. The Catholic laymen were anxious to end the situation which made them suspect as rebels, and to testify allegiance to the Queen while preserving their creed. The Jesuits were keenly against it, though some of the secular priests favoured it. One of them as early as 1590 declared that Catholics could rightfully serve the Queen in arms against Spain and that Rome erred in stating the contrary. This was heresy to the Jesuits and opened the way to a further dispute on the English succession, the Jesuits, inspired by Robert Parsons, declaring for Philip II's daughter, and the seculars and the mass of the Catholic laymen for James Stuart. In 1598 the Pope appointed George Blackwell arch-priest of the Catholics in England, with instructions, although not himself a Jesuit, to enforce the Jesuit points of view. The secular priests protested. They did more, entering into negotiations with the English Church for a toleration based on their declaration of allegiance to the Queen in all save the spiritual supremacy. Elizabeth herself refused this. She would no more recognize dissent by Catholics than by Puritans. But tacitly there was a considerable accommodation, and a relaxation of the penal laws. The Catholics were loyal, as indeed they had shown themselves from the beginning of the war, and open-minded men like Robert Cecil saw no advantage in persecution. The fact that a Catholic priest had sat in conference with a Protestant bishop, which would have been an impossibility in the 1580s, showed whither affairs were trending.

The Parliament of 1593 had been mainly occupied with religious affairs. Another met in the autumn of 1597, when economic difficulties and social distress were the chief concern. All these Parliaments had of course the business of voting supplies, for the war demanded them. The Commons were satisfied that the Queen's administration was not wasteful, and granted what was needed without the complaints and accusations that marked provision for war expenditure in other periods both before and after the Tudor. The figures for the several Parliaments are less important than the total, which for the period 1588–1601 amounted to approximately two million pounds. The cost of warlike operations during the same period was about four millions. The Queen thus provided half of the war expenditure from sources for which she had not to apply to Parliament, besides financing from them the whole cost of the court and the civil administration. Those sources of income were the

profits from crown lands, the customs and other duties on trade, and
the feudal dues recoverable from landowners on various occasions.
But the total income did not meet the expenditure, and the Queen,
much as it grieved her prudent nature, had to sell crown lands to
meet the deficit. She made no attempt to levy taxes without consent
of Parliament. Some of the loans that she obtained from individuals
and corporations were to a certain extent forced, but they were short-
dated and were repaid when due.

The period of dearth and distress that began in 1593 was happily
nearing its close in 1597–8, although the fact was unknown to the
Parliament that met in October 1597. At the outset Francis Bacon
spoke strongly on enclosures and the depopulation of villages, which
he declared to be still going on after a century of preventive legislation. The only remedy was more legislation, especially as some of the
previous enclosure law had been repealed in 1593. He introduced
two bills for that purpose, and they were duly passed into law, to
have little permanent effect on an economic process that defied them.
Enclosure for pasture was uppermost in men's minds in a season of
famine in corn, but some of the enclosure of the time was for more
efficient tillage, and to prevent it was of doubtful benefit. Depopulation of villages was connected with another matter that this Parliament was much concerned with, namely, vagabondage, beggary, and
honest poverty. Detailed acts were passed for dealing in the usual
drastic manner with wandering rogues and sturdy beggars, who
cloaked in many guises their aversion from honest toil. The wars had
produced a new problem of this kind in the old soldiers with long
service in France or the Netherlands, discharged for wounds or
sickness, and unable to find employment suited to their disabilities.
The new legislation made some attempt to provide for them, chiefly
as licensed beggars.

But it was in provision for the normal poor, the unlucky though
honest persons who could not earn a living, that this Parliament did
memorable work. The problem had grown from the break-up of the
medieval economy and its remedial institutions in the earlier part of
the century. At first there had been neither understanding nor
sympathy. The reaction to poverty of the mid-Tudor legislature had
been to treat it well-nigh as crime and punish accordingly. This
happened on the national scale, where Parliament discussed beggary
in the mass. But on the local scale, where men knew their neighbours
and perceived the causes of distress, there was more humanity from

the outset; and towns and cities, London not least, established relief institutions and were proud of them. The Elizabethan Parliaments gradually expressed this tone, and step by step built up a code by tentative measures until the time came in 1597 for their consolidation. By the Act of that year each parish was to appoint four overseers of the poor who, with the churchwardens, were to collect contributions payable compulsorily by men of substance. With the money they were to buy materials to be worked upon by the able unemployed and to support the impotent, and in some cases to build cottages for them. They might also give licences to beg, and were to see that the children of the poor were apprenticed to trades. The overseers were made to do their work by the county magistrates, supervised in their turn by the Privy Council. It was always possible for a man complained of to be called up before the Council to give an account of himself, a process sufficiently unpleasant to be deterrent to slackness. This Act had been substantially forty years in the making. It was to remain the fundamental measure for three centuries to come. It was given some amendments in 1601; but the effective date of the great Elizabethan Poor Law is 1597-8.

In August 1598 died Lord Burghley after forty years continuous service of the Queen. His influence in creating the success of the reign is of its nature difficult to assess. What would the Queen have been without him? Probably little different, for hers was a nature that received small impress from others. But that is not to say that she would have been equally successful. Burghley in his love of economy and dislike of irrevocable courses was the expression of herself, but in his moderation, his intellectual balance, his capacity for seeing both sides of a question, his constructive policies, and his good temper (or more truly, the control of his ill-temper), he supplied what she lacked. In the first generation of a new, post-revolutionary age he was exactly the minister the country needed, with domestic oscillations to be damped down, industry to be fostered, and foreign wars postponed as long as possible. His services to English mankind did not stop at the negative. Like his Queen he placed reason and humanity before violence and bloodshed, and unlike her he was in tune with the religious outlook of a Protestant England that was growing amid the cold ashes of earlier fires; and we need no religious bias of our own to appreciate that English Protestantism was one of the characteristics that were to make the country great. Burghley had his share in it. His work has been generally appraised with greater emphasis on his foreign than on his domestic labours. That may be mistaken, for while he achieved much in preserving the new England he achieved more in designing and building it. Elizabeth held him for a true servant and an old friend, and the record of her visiting him in his last illness and coaxing him to eat gives a lower value to the hard words and political tantrums that were the lot of all her followers.

Three months before Burghley's death the French, now reunited under Henry IV, made a separate peace with Spain at Vervins; and in September Philip II died, worn out with labour rather than disappointment, but seeing at the last that English expansion was not to be restrained. The French peace, against which English envoys protested in vain, was an act of self-regarding desertion on the part of Henry IV. His conversion had disarmed the Catholic opposition, and the League was virtually dead; and he hankered for a chance to rebuild disintegrated France. There was, of course, no hint of his joining Spain, and his falling-out was not disastrous to England. That summer of 1598 there was a possibility of a general peace. But Spain would not concede a recognition of Dutch independence, the Dutch would accept nothing less, and Elizabeth to her credit would not abandon them. So the war went on, although for England its issue was really decided. It had been a defensive war, and the defence had won. England and Protestantism were secure. The last phase was to concern Ireland, which was by no means secure, but the principal part there was not to be played by the Spaniards.

The last and greatest revolt against Tudor rule in Ireland began almost imperceptibly and swelled in volume during the middle 'nineties. The province of Ulster was then the region least penetrated by English influence. Hugh O'Neill, Earl of Tyrone, was at once the holder of a peerage from the crown, instituted by Henry VIII, and the recognized chieftain of a congeries of Irish clans that had never been conquered, and possessed the substance of independence and the will to maintain it. His chief strength lay on the southern borders of Ulster, and the importance of his fidelity to the crown was obvious, since he was in a position to maintain or disturb the peace of the north. He was an able man, educated in England, acquainted with the court and politics, and trained in the modern methods of warfare with firearms. Hugh Roe O'Donnell, a younger man, was the strongest chief in the north-western part of Ulster. He had been seized by the English and detained for five years in Dublin. At the close of 1591 he escaped to his own country and sought immediately to begin an anti-English war, looking to O'Neill for countenance and support. O'Neill took his time to decide, but ultimately agreed with O'Donnell in 1593, determining to proceed quietly and make full preparations before declaring himself. The most promising preparation was to seek Spanish aid. There were Irish exiles in Spain, and through them the malcontents approached King Philip. He was nothing loth to serve Elizabeth in Ireland as she had served him in the Netherlands, but he also took his time. He sent some money in 1594, and on the strength of it O'Neill and O'Donnell with several subordinate chiefs took the field and began ravaging beyond the borders of Ulster. The Queen's representatives in Ireland did not appreciate the importance of what was going on, and it was not until 1595 that she was apprised that a serious rebellion had begun.

The rebel demands were for recognition of the Catholic religion and the exemption of tribal areas from the intrusion of English officials, in other words for complete autonomy. Ulster to a great extent enjoyed it already, and the danger of its formal expression was that the movement would extend to the rest of Ireland. The Queen naturally refused, but had insufficient troops to enforce her decision. The rebels had received little but promises from Spain, and waited to see whether real aid would follow. An interval of negotiation alternating with skirmishes thus extended to 1596, when Philip sent emissaries, having hitherto sent only letters, with promises of armed force. In spite of the blow delivered at Cadiz in that year by Howard and Essex, Philip did despatch an armada of invasion, which was foiled by storms at sea and never reached England or Ireland. The prospect, however, was sufficiently exciting to decide the rebels to fight. As had been foreseen, the contagion spread into Connaught and Munster and into Leinster outside the narrow confines of the Pale. By the middle of 1598 all Ireland was in revolt. It was then that the Munster colony begun by Ralegh and Grenville came to its end. The handful of settlers were driven off their lands. Many perished, and the rest escaped to the sea-ports and thence to England. Edmund Spenser reached London only to die soon afterwards. In Connaught Sir Conyers Clifford was holding out with a single company of foot and no ammunition. On the Ulster border Sir Henry Bagenal was defeated and killed by O'Neill with the loss of more than a thousand men at the battle of the Yellow Ford. In the Pale the English element was gloomy and demanding the retention for its own defence of what forces remained.

It was the moment for Spain to strike in, but Spain was not equipped for the task. A large expedition was wrecked on its own coast in the autumn of 1597, while Essex and Ralegh were returning from their Islands Voyage. The next armada, in the summer of 1599, got as far as being driven on the Brittany coast. Not until 1601 did a Spanish army reach Ireland, when, as will be shown, it was too late.

The events of 1598 showed the Queen that stronger measures were needed in Ireland. There was in that year no Lord Deputy or Lord Lieutenant, the previous holder of office, Lord Burgh, having died soon after appointment. Someone of the Queen's great men had to take up the task, which was more than likely to result in his ruin. Essex, in whose ability public opinion, if not the Queen, still believed, was half willingly manœuvred into the job. He was made Lord Lieutenant early in 1599, and sailed in April with a brilliant company of officers and the largest army the Tudors had yet sent across the Irish Sea. Altogether, with those already in the country, he had a paper strength of 17,000 men, which diminished from the outset by the usual processes of privation, sickness, and desertion. But he was no longer the Queen's favourite. She was beginning to distrust him, not only as a general but as a loyal subject, and her treatment of him throughout the year was coloured by a sarcastic captiousness that verged on hostility. He was too sensitive to be unaffected by it, and before the campaign was over it was driving him to thoughts of self-assertion by violent action against the Queen's other ministers, to whose influence he ascribed her attitude.

Essex, whose health was not good, failed from the outset to display the energy and judgment expected of him. His difficulties were great, but instead of rising to them in the style of a great leader he spent the summer of 1599 in following side-issues that yielded no hope of an early finish of the war. Such proceedings incensed the Queen, who had spent heavily for a decision. She expected him to strike first at O'Neill as the keystone of the rebellion; but since his victuals in the wilds of Ulster would be driven cattle from the south, and the beasts were neither strong enough to drive nor fat enough to kill after the winter scarcity, he postponed the Ulster campaign to midsummer. He undertook instead a reinforcement of Connaught and a military progress through Leinster and Munster, where supplies were better. It was intended to be completed in a month, but

DERRY
ANTRIM
O'DONNELL
ULSTER
Carrickfergus
Blackwater
Yellow Ford
O'NEILL
Dundalk
Drogheda
CONNAUGHT
BURKE
PALE
Galway
Shannon
KING'S COUNTY
KILDARE
Dublin
LEINSTER
QUEEN'S COUNTY
ORMONDE
MUNSTER
Wexford
DESMOND
Waterford
Smerwick
Cork
Kinsale
Castlehaven

ELIZABETHAN
IRELAND

MILES
0 10 20 30 40 50 60
*Lands of magnates and
chiefs underlined*

occupied two, and there was little permanent conquest to show for it. On the debit side were the losses inevitable from long marches in difficult country and the further weakening of his force by leaving garrisons in the south. So small was his field army when he returned to Dublin that he doubted the wisdom of attacking O'Neill that year, and his officers agreed with him. Essex stated the difficulties to the Queen, who ordered him to proceed. Before he could do so, Clifford was defeated and killed in Connaught with the loss of several hundreds. Even so, the Queen's order stood, and at the end of August Essex advanced to the Ulster border with less than 3,000 men. The Queen considered that her fine and costly army had been frittered away by bad generalship before it had even approached its task; and she made caustic play with Essex's objections, first that it had been too early in the season to invade Ulster, and next that it was too late.[1]

The unlucky man gained touch with the rebel forces early in September. O'Neill had twice his numbers and greater mobility. He did not use them to win a battle, but kept Essex marching up and down the frontier seeking an opportunity that he could not find. O'Neill was almost as disillusioned with the war as Essex was, because he knew that England was ultimately capable of an effort great enough to beat him. He had taken up arms in the hope of Spanish aid, and Spain had sent none. O'Neill therefore held Essex off from attacking him and at the same time made offers to treat. After a few days Essex consented to parley and unwisely met O'Neill at a river-ford between the armies. By talking to the rebel without having any witnesses in earshot, he gave a golden opportunity to his detractors to call him a traitor. The exasperated Queen might well give credence to them, for the result of the conversation was a truce to be renewed periodically by agreement of the commanders. Essex, brave as he personally was, had been conquered by circumstances which a greater general would have controlled. By irresolution and lack of persistence he had allowed the adverse circumstances to enmesh him. The truce was a sorry outcome to the great expedition for the conquest of Ulster.

Elizabeth's determination to show no sympathy or understanding goaded not only Essex but his officers. They thought of it in terms of evil influences at court that must be poisoning the Queen's mind. Essex himself was popular with the army. He was generous in his appreciation of merit, to the extent of having conferred a number of knighthoods disproportionate for such a campaign. He had an army party ready to follow him in dubious courses. At one instant he thought of leading the whole army to England to remove his enemies —which meant primarily Cecil, Ralegh, and Nottingham—by force. He gave that up, not without having talked about it, and went himself with a select party, returning from Dublin contrary to an explicit

[1] See *Elizabeth's Irish Wars*, by Cyril Falls, (London, 1950), especially Ch. xvi. Professor Falls traces the story in detail from original sources, and his conclusions unfavourable to Essex must be accepted in preference to Cheyney's more charitable account.

order that he was not to do so without leave. He reached court unannounced at the end of September and was immediately placed under arrest.

The Queen had to decide whether to make the Irish truce a basis for a peace unaccompanied by the surrender of the rebel, or to appoint a new commander, spend her money on a new army, and continue the war. She chose the second, and appointed as Lord Deputy a man who had never displayed the thrust and exuberance of Essex but in whom she discerned solid qualities, Charles Blount, Lord Mountjoy.

Mountjoy took up his post early in 1600, to find that O'Neill had profited by the collapse of Essex to make himself a national Irish leader in the twin causes of Catholicism and independence. O'Neill had moved south for the winter and had undone much of Essex's work in Munster. Mountjoy distrusted the policy of deep penetration of hostile country, which never brought an unwilling enemy to action, and always lost a number of men. He worked instead by fortifying and garrisoning as many points as possible and wearing out the Irish by remorseless attrition in the destruction of foodstuffs and the hunting down and killing of local leaders. It was not quick work, but the Queen had reconciled herself to that, and she treated Mountjoy better than she had treated Essex, giving him the necessary backing during the seasons of 1600 and 1601.

At length, in the autumn of 1601, Philip III achieved what his father had always failed to do, and landed a substantial Spanish force in Ireland. It was late in the war, for Mountjoy's policy had quieted Munster, and he was about to attack Ulster with a larger army than Essex had had. He was called off by the news that the Spaniards were in the south, Juan de Aguila having landed at Kinsale with 4,000 men in mid-September. Mountjoy swiftly concentrated his forces and laid siege to Kinsale in October, the southern Irish not having risen in any numbers to join the Spaniards. They, lacking sea supremacy, were cut off. Their ships could not stay by them or supply them, while an English squadron speedily dominated the coast. Aguila's only hope lay in O'Neill, O'Donnell, and the Ulster rebels. They duly marched south, and were heavily defeated by Mountjoy on Christmas Eve in an attempt to raise the siege. O'Neill retired northwards, O'Donnell escaped to Spain, and Aguila capitulated on easy terms on 2 January 1602. The rebellion had been on the down grade before the Spaniards landed. Their failure took the heart out of it.

Mountjoy applied his devastating and garrisoning policy to Ulster, where suffering was dreadful and depopulation far advanced. At last, in March 1603, Hugh O'Neill, Earl of Tyrone, surrendered, on pardon and restitution of his personal property, but otherwise unconditionally. The contest between England and Rome for the body of Ireland was decided, whatever might be the disposal of its soul.

Essex remained under restraint, confined to his own London house, for several months after his return. He was not brought to trial, for his offences were unknown to the law, but in 1600 he was called before a special commission which suspended him from his offices for military disobedience to the Queen's orders. He was then at liberty, save that he was forbidden to go to court. The wiser councillors wished the Queen to forgive him, since they foresaw some scandalous outbreak if he were driven to desperation; but she remained hard, considering his conduct to have been that of an over-mighty subject. His general popularity, due to his lack of guile and his kindness to all subordinates, continued unabated, and led to a good deal of seditious talk in sympathy with his misfortunes. From being the favourite of Elizabeth he had become the favourite of the people. He and his friends, notably the Earls of Southampton and Rutland, formed the nucleus of an opposition such as had not existed since the Ridolfi Plot; and he corresponded with James of Scotland, offering support for his succession, and hinting that the Cecil party were secret favourers of the Spanish claim. In January 1601 the friends of Essex, including officers from the army in Ireland, gathered at Essex House in the Strand. Early in February they planned a rising for the capture of the court and the Queen and the removal of her ministers. To condition public opinion in London they paid the Globe Company to revive Shakespeare's *Richard II* with its obvious implication of the course they meant to pursue. On the 8th they took arms and marched into the City, professing loyalty to the Queen, and declaring that the crown was sold to the Spaniard and that Essex's life was in danger. There were only two hundred of them, and the issue turned on the action of the Londoners. The citizens made no move, amazed that mere discontent should be thus translated into armed rebellion. The court's forces were soon on the spot, and Essex had nothing for it but to surrender. He was found guilty of treason by a court of his peers. The Queen remained implacable, and he was executed with five others on 25 February. Southampton was found guilty, but remained in the Tower until the

Queen died. The other ringleaders escaped with fines, Rutland paying £30,000. The Earl of Essex had in many respects a noble character, incapable of deceit or spite, courageous and gifted. His misfortune was that he never grew up, and remained to his death at thirty-three an ungovernable schoolboy and a nuisance to the older men with whom his lot was cast. Robert Cecil, who had reason to fear him, or perhaps in his cool way concluded that he had no reason, was not vindictive and even regarded him kindly. It was Elizabeth more than any who decided on his death. In her old heart glowed the Tudor suspicion of a popular noble; he had once lost all control of his temper in her presence, and he was reported to have made an unpardonable personal remark about her. Her former affection was dead.

While the Essex tragedy moved to its conclusion the East India Company was born. The voyages of Lancaster and Davis, the success of the Dutch since 1595, and the publication in English (through Hakluyt's energy) of Linschoten's account of India and the way thither, all combined to bring the project to the point of action. The leaders were mostly merchants of the Levant Company, the secretary was common to both, and the early East Indian minutes were kept in the Levant Company's book. The organization was, however, distinct and independent. After negotiations covering more than a year, the Queen issued the East India Company's charter on 31 December 1600. It created a company of named members, who alone were permitted to engage in the trade. They were not to do so with their individual ships and goods, but by subscribing to a joint stock for the fitting-out of an expedition under the management of the committees[1] or directors. The joint stock for each voyage was to be wound up and distributed with the profits at its conclusion, a new joint stock being raised for the next venture. On a first joint stock of nearly £70,000, the Company sent out its first expedition in 1601, comprising a large private ship-of-war bought from the Earl of Cumberland, and three armed Levant traders, all under the command of James Lancaster, with John Davis as his chief pilot. They were bound by the Cape of Good Hope for Sumatra and Java to obtain spices by trade with the natives or capture from the Portuguese. Thus the London plan of East Indian trade was at length in operation. The expedition was highly successful, but its return did not take place in the Tudor period.

---

[1] Committee (probably with accent as in legatee) meant an individual, not a modern committee.

Elizabeth's last Parliament met in October 1601, summoned principally to vote supplies for the war, which was now the costly Irish war
and little else. As usual, the Commons had their own wishes on
further policy or legislation. The old topics on which their ideas had
caused friction with the Queen were now dead or less active: her
marriage, the succession, ultra-Protestant moves to reform the
Church. The succession was tacitly agreed as destined for James VI,
and had ceased to strike fire since Wentworth's suppression. Whitgift
had disciplined the reformers, and their party, recognizing the
Queen's decision, were resigned to wait for other times. Yet friction
there was of the gravest, and the subject was monopolies. Throughout the Tudor period it had been customary for the crown to favour,
pay, or reward individuals at the public expense by granting them
letters patent to perform some act which otherwise the law would
not permit them to perform. A common form of grant had been of
licence to export forbidden commodities, such as wool by non-
members of the Staplers' Company, corn in time of scarcity, or undyed cloth. These were not monopolies, but they furnished plenty of
precedent for the power of the royal prerogative in trade regulation
to suspend the law in favour of individuals. Trade monopolies had
long existed in the privileges of companies like the Staplers and the
Merchants Adventurers, usually justifiable in the public interest.
With the economic changes of the mid-century and the growth of
oversea enterprise, monopolies held by companies became more
numerous, reaching about a dozen in the half-century between the
foundations of the Muscovy and the East India Companies. Individuals also, such as Gilbert and Ralegh, received monopoly rights
in American exploitation. They could claim, like the companies, that
monopoly was necessary to protect them in the prosecution of enterprise for their own and the public good. Monopolies of a different
sort became common from the middle years of the reign, consisting
in the sole right to sell some article that had hitherto been commonly
dealt in. These became more numerous and grievous to the generality in the 1590's. They obviously caused enhanced prices and restraint of trade. As the prerogative stood, the Queen had power to
grant them and the courts of law no power to disallow them: when
a person brought a suit against the exercise of a monopoly the case
was stopped by order of the Privy Council.

The Commons of 1601 demanded reform. As a member read a
long list of monopolized articles, another member interjected: 'Is not

bread there?' and declared that it would be by next Parliament if
remedy were not found. There were in fact some twenty-four
monopolies that could be considered objectionable. Some of these,
such as that for the sale of playing cards, caused no heavy grievance,
and the really oppressive ones were few. That made them none the
less offensive, and indignation was increased by high-handed methods
of enforcement. Parliament had two means of proceeding: either by
legislation limiting the prerogative, legislation that would require
the royal assent; or by petitioning the Queen. There was an evident
majority for ending the monopolies, and debate on the method of
doing so went on hotly for a week. The proceedings were supposed
to be secret, but were of course made known to the Queen. Her
reactions to former questionings of the prerogative had been uncompromising, and the Commons on this occasion prepared with
trepidation for a tussle. She probably surprised them when she sent
for the Speaker and told him that she had learned with indignation
how injurious to her subjects some of the monopolies were. She had
not known, she said, that this was so, and she would immediately
suspend and investigate the grants complained of. Three days later a
royal proclamation was published revoking at once and unconditionally the letters patent for ten of the most objectionable monopolies,
and leaving the validity of the others to be tested at law without any
interference by the Privy Council. Thus the Queen did justice to her
subjects, but she did it herself by the same prerogative power that
had done the injustice. Her Commons had debated the matter, and
she had not even waited for a formal approach from them. The royal
prerogative and the popularity of the sovereign were preserved, but
the unwritten authority of the Commons was enhanced. One can
imagine that if Peter Wentworth had survived to plunge into this
affair it might have taken a less happy turn.

A few days later Elizabeth made her last great speech to Parliament, or rather to a select hundred and fifty members of the Commons summoned to wait on her at Whitehall. It was a declaration of
her unity with her people and of her single-minded pursuit of their
happiness: 'Though God hath raised me high, yet this I account the
glory of my crown that I have reigned with your loves. . . . In
governing this land I have ever set the last judgment day before
mine eyes, as so to rule as I shall be judged and answer before a
higher judge, to whose judgment seat I do appeal that never thought
was cherished in my heart that tended not to my people's good.' She

thanked the members for apprising her of the evil of the monopolies, touched on the dangers through which she had passed, and ended: 'For myself I never was so much enticed with the glorious name of a king, or the royal authority of a queen, as delighted that God hath made me his instrument to maintain his truth and glory and to defend this kingdom from dishonour, damage, tyranny, and oppression.' The speech throughout was tinged with valediction, like that of her father's last address some sixty years before. It was her last Parliament, and perhaps she guessed it.

This was in November 1601, and the reign was ending. The Queen was sixty-eight, almost the last survivor of her generation among the great, surrounded now by younger people among whom she felt lonely. The only question at issue in politics was the succession, and it hardly was a question, for there was little doubt of the answer. On all grounds of public interest the successor must be the Stuart James VI. Two other candidates were mentioned, but without a hope of success: the Infanta of Spain, and Arabella Stuart, who represented the Lennox claim that had substantially perished with Darnley. The Spanish claim was supported only by the Jesuits, and not even by the Catholic secular priests. Essex had thought to make use of it as a bogey in his hare-brained rising, but it had caused fear to none. Arabella Stuart represented a claim obviously inferior to that of James VI, and she was a nonentity devoid of weight. James it had to be, and the practical question became that of ensuring the transition with smoothness and decency when Elizabeth should die. The men who did it, Sir Robert Cecil and his party, were not guilty of any disloyalty to the Queen. The task was a necessity, and she most likely knew that they were negotiating, although she would never discuss the subject, much less agree to any open recognition of her successor.

Essex had determined on open recognition and had asked James to send a mission to London to take a prominent part in the new order that was to follow Essex's capture of the court. The Earl of Mar, the Scottish representative, arrived to find Essex dead, and transferred his addresses to Cecil. They agreed that there should be no premature move and that James should rely on Cecil's assurance that his succession should be effected when the time came. So it was done. The Queen's health fluctuated in 1602, without physical ill, but with a sadness and depression of spirit that pulled her down. During the winter it increased, and in March came the end, a slow death due mainly, as it seemed, to lack of will to live. Early in the morning of 24 March, 1603, Elizabeth died, and the Tudor Age was ended.

Fifty-six years had passed since the death of Henry VIII. The political fluctuations that followed it had long been smoothed, and with Elizabeth there came at length a stability that made the nation stronger and greater than it had been. Her own contribution lay in governance, in alleviating feuds, in managing men, in substituting tolerance for cruelty and law for violence. Her Elizabethans became notably a litigious people, which was an improvement on the intimidation and injustice that the habit of litigation replaced. In the methods of politics her reign saw an advance in civilization, exemplified by the cessation of the state executions that had gone on for a century since the wars of Lancaster and York. Her few high-ranking victims of the scaffold were all fairly convicted of rebellion or of substantial plotting to overthrow the state. They were indeed few compared with those of her father; and the milder atmosphere of court and council established itself in the English tradition. Against such change for the better must be set the two hundred executions of Jesuits and other missionaries. But that, after the bull of 1570, was war, and the priests were the agents of a power that was bent on subduing the existing England. Morality had not reached the height of condemning such executions: neither has it to-day, as the examples of our own wars testify. Beggary and destitution claimed infinitely more victims. They had long done so, but here again the beginnings of a social conscience were seen in the poor-law and the plans of the colonial projectors, in the founding of charitable schools and alms-houses, and in Hakluyt's plea that there was something better to be done with starving pilferers than hanging them. All things considered, the Elizabethans were more humane than their fathers.

In relations with the outside world it was an age of enterprise and new ideas. They had existed under the Henries, but there had been little national drive behind them. After the mid-century real and fruitful steps were taken to base prosperity on contacts with the whole world instead of merely Europe. England as a world-power grew from the generation after Henry's revolution. Elizabeth approved but did not initiate. She was more occupied with securing the conditions for advance than with promoting it. She left it to her people, while making it her own task to ensure that they survived to achieve their ambitions. There lay her prime contribution to the success of her age, in the diplomacy, neither feeble nor flamboyant, that founded the position of our country in relation to the continental powers.

APPENDICES

I. THE CONSTITUTION

To appreciate the mode of government in Tudor England we need to divest our minds of the facts of the present-day constitution—electorate, elected House of Commons, ministers drawn from the elected majority and responsible to the Commons, the formal Crown, the wisdom-giving House of Lords—and realize that such relationships had no place in the thoughts of the Tudor English. We need also to abandon a prejudicing approach to the subject that was long current, the conception that the Tudor monarchy was 'new', in anything but ability, and that the 'new monarchy' was the expression of a 'Tudor despotism'. The idea of the despotism dies hard; yet, dispassionately read, every chapter of the story embodies some contribution to the killing of it.

The Tudor monarchy began under the conception of a king who did everything in the then limited field of executive government, with institutions and officers appropriate to the achievement of his work; and of a people free to say and do as they liked within a known framework of law and custom, their practical freedom being in many respects more extensive than that of their descendants in the modern state of to-day. A nice harmony between the monarchical executive and popular liberty was requisite. If the monarchy was in feeble hands liberty became disorder and 'lack of governance' the complaint of the weak. If the monarchy overstepped what inherited and instinctive thought held to be its proper functions, the popular protest made itself felt, not by indignant speeches in a parliament that was in any case unlikely to be sitting, but by riot and rebellion. Popular risings from the Jack Cade affair in the mid-fifteenth century to that of the Kentish men under Wyatt in the mid-sixteenth may almost be regarded as a function of the constitution, the counterpart of the votes of censure moved in the parliaments of a more modern age: all were expressions of popular liberty or opinion.[1] The beginning of the change-over from tumultuous protest to parliamentary protest may be seen as the Tudor period advanced and Parliament became a relatively more important ingredient of the constitution. But the two methods overlapped, and the earlier took long to die out. In the light of this spirit of

---

[1] One may exclude the numerous revolts led by magnates inspired by their personal grievances, but in the early Tudor period the slaying of the Earl of Northumberland and the Cornish risings against Henry VII, the Pilgrimage of Grace, the Prayer Book rebellion of 1549, Ket's rebellion, and Wyatt's, were all popular movements.

the constitution, monarchy-cum-liberty, the institutions of the Tudor period must be viewed.

The King's chief instrument in the more personal exercise of his powers was the Council. Henry VII's Council presented no novelty of form. It was large, chosen by himself, contained members of various origins and qualifications and fitted for widely differing duties, and had no clear rules on location, attendance, or the scope of its work. Some of its members were continuously prominent and concerned with the highest affairs, others are obscure. In general the councillors advised the King when their advice was asked, carried out executive tasks delegated by him to them, and acted as a judicial body for cases best decided by the central authority. There are no extant records of the proceedings of the early Tudor Council, but it seems probable that the advisory and adminis-trative functions were more generally performed by the members as individuals than by the Council as a body, and that a select few did the important work. The judicial function was gradually becoming defined, to be exercised ultimately in the Star Chamber and the Court of Requests.

Parliament was not a regularly working part of the constitution. Its meetings were at undefined intervals and depended largely on the needs of the Crown for revenue, but also, after 1529, on its wish for legislation and on the necessity for mutual understanding between the King and his people at times of crisis. Until 1529 the duration of Parliaments was brief, usually a single session of little more than a month, and several years might elapse without the calling of a Parliament and without any public demand for one. From 1485 to 1528 the sessions of Parliament averaged about one in three years and a quarter; from 1529 to 1559, the years of reformation, counter-reformation, and final settlement, one in one-and-a-third years; from then on to 1603, one in three years. In the central period of great frequency, legislation was the predominant motive for summons. The initiative was with the King,[1] and in the first genera-tion the constituencies were reluctant rather than eager for a meeting which would probably result in taxation, or in legislation that only some limited interest had any desire to promote. The early Tudor Commons numbered a little under 300 members, the large majority being returned by the corporate towns without any uniformity of method. The method was not considered a vital matter, and the elections were unexciting and usually uncontested. The early borough members were probably for the most part local burgesses, although there was an element of lawyers and official persons. As the period progressed and Parliament grew more important the gentry began to seek seats for the boroughs. This becomes very noticeable in the reign of Mary, when the gentry as a whole were opposed to the Queen's religious policy. The county members, two each for most of the English shires, were always knights or gentlemen elected

[1] The word is used, as Elizabeth I used it, to include herself.

by the freeholders of land worth at least forty shillings a year. The Commons were already a recognized House of Parliament, and their Speaker was a royal nominee (although in form chosen by themselves) whose duty was to exercise some control in the royal interest. In 1523 Sir Thomas More as Speaker claimed the privilege of free speech in the Commons, and this in after years came to be regarded as an ancient privilege, but its extent remained limited and was somewhat grudgingly allowed by Elizabeth. The Lords were still in process of attaining the definition which later attached to them. Their origin, in the medieval great councils of magnates of all kinds, still permitted persons to sit by virtue of the positions they held as well as by rank and title, but the process of limiting seats to the hereditary nobles and the senior members of the Church was almost completed in the period. Until the Reformation the greater abbots as well as the bishops sat as lords spiritual, after it the bishops alone. Legislation was on the request or assent of both Houses, completed by the royal assent. Judicially, the assembly was the High Court of Parliament, but the greatest judicial function, that of impeachment, was in abeyance during the whole Tudor period, its place being taken by the bill of attainder, an act of legislation whose accompanying debate had sometimes the elements of a trial.

Courts of various kinds were the framework of the constitution and in some aspects the guardians of liberty and effective barriers to despotism. From their early medieval origin in the King's Court or household of close servants and advisers they had long ago proliferated into well-rooted separate institutions, and were still doing so. The trio of great common-law courts were those of the Exchequer, the King's Bench, and the Common Pleas. The common law was so called because it was the growth, recognized among lawyers, of centuries of enunciations of principle by the judges and of judicial interpretations of statutes; and it was an English growth, not greatly influenced by the Roman law prevalent in continental Europe. The Court of Exchequer tried financial causes between the Crown and the subject, the King's Bench other civil and criminal matters between Crown and subject, the Common Pleas cases between subjects. The Court of Chancery had originated somewhat later and was finally taking shape as the organ of 'the King's conscience' in matters of justice, where justice was alleged to have miscarried in other courts. In addition to this function of equity, it had that of decision in cases not cognizable in the common law, such as wrongs done among Englishmen overseas. In the seventeenth century we find it used as a tribunal for cases between Englishmen in the early colonies. The High Court of Admiralty, reorganized by Henry VIII, took account of cases of maritime law. Its criminal jurisdiction over piracy was for the most part orally conducted and has left few records. Its civil jurisdiction in claims for damage, loss, and insurance of ships and goods, and breaches of contract, was conducted by written pleas and evidence and decision by judge without jury, in the manner common in foreign courts, for the maritime law was of continental origin. The Star Chamber and the Court of Requests were aspects of the work of the Council and were known as prerogative courts, since they exercised the royal prerogative and not the common law. They were not however informal, but produced a body of lawyers and a written procedure of their own. The Council used drastic methods, even to torture, to extract evidence, but in the Star Chamber it did not impose the death penalty.

Outside the capital the judges travelled the country, holding periodical assizes at the county towns and trying by common law the criminal and civil cases remitted to them by the county magistrates. Juries, very much subject to the judge's authority, were employed, and the jurors had not lost all trace of their original status of witnesses. The justices of the peace or county magistrates had originated in the fourteenth century and they increased greatly in importance under the Tudors. They were unpaid, appointed by the Crown, and removable at any time, and their duties were considered incidental to the position of a 'worshipful' or respected gentleman. The shire was the unit within which the justices were grouped, and the lord-lieutenant, originating in Henry VIII's last years, was the head of the county bench as well as the commander of the county militia. In their own neighbourhoods the justices arrested suspects and imposed minor corporal punishments and fines in petty sessions held at any time. The bench of the shire justices met in quarter sessions and dealt with serious offenders, with power to hang the worst; but murder and the greater crimes were reserved for the assizes. Another branch of the justices' duties was administrative, the execution of instructions from the King's Council on the great variety of things that had to be done locally in the course of government. Besides taking orders from the Council they had also to report to it, and so were the regular informants of the Council on the state and opinion of the country. The administrative work of the justices increased greatly as the Tudor period progressed and the central authority became more comprehensive. They were at the height of their importance during the Spanish war, with its continual military preparations, complicated by watchfulness on plotters and the seminary priests, and control of the Puritan malcontents.

The sources and collection of revenue were intricate but must be briefly stated. The ordinary revenue was within the Crown's unmodified right of collection. Revenue authorized by Parliament and consisting of short-term taxes was considered extraordinary and justifiable only by war or misfortune. Between the two stood the tonnage and poundage, part (but only part) of the duties on foreign trade, granted indeed by Parliament, but for the duration of the sovereign's life, and therefore part of his ordinary revenue. The ordinary revenue, collected without reference to Parliament, comprised the customs or permanent duties on trade, together with the tonnage and poundage; the income from Crown lands; the profits of justice in the shape of fines and fees; and the feudal fees and dues levied on most of the owners of landed property, together with the profits of the Court of Wards administering the property of minors, and the farms or annual sums paid by the boroughs in respect of their chartered privileges. Of these the first two, customs and Crown lands, provided the major part of the income whereby the King was expected 'to live of his own' without in time of peace troubling his subjects for any more. The Exchequer was the department into which originally all revenue was paid. Its procedure became so elaborately developed against fraud, and by what is in modern slang termed 'empire-building' by officials, that it grew too rigid and slow-moving, so that governments found it very difficult to ascertain their true financial position. In the later medieval centuries the magnates grasped control of the Exchequer, and the kings countered this by having parts of the revenue paid directly into departments of their own household or court, the Wardrobe first, and later the Chamber. The weaker monarchy of the fifteenth century allowed the Exchequer to regain control. Henry VII revived the Chamber as a financial instrument and personally supervised its accounts, thus keeping his own hand directly on the growing Crown lands revenue, while the customs remained with the Exchequer. This system continued to the 1530's, when the great accession of revenue from Church sources was handled by a new institution, the Court of Augmentations, active until abolished by Mary in 1554. There were also other financial courts dealing with specified minor sources of income. In the last year of Edward VI and the first of Mary (1552–4) the Lord Treasurer, the Marquis of Winchester, reorganized the financial mechanism by bringing nearly all the revenue into a reformed Exchequer, which continued for the rest of the period; and the Chancellor of the Exchequer grew into an important officer in the administration.[1] Farming of the customs for rents paid by financiers who collected the dues was practised before, during, and after the Tudor period.

The Tudor constitution demanded a hard-working and efficient head, the monarch himself, or a great minister, or a close-linked combination of the two. In an undisciplined and unscrupulous society the machine would not run of itself, and any relaxation of personal control would soon produce disorder and weakness. Henry VII and then Wolsey worked the early Tudor constitution as outlined above. With the Reformation came changes amounting to a revolution in practice, although one to some extent disguised under the apparent continuance of institutions. The changes can be considered under the following heads: (1) the exten-

---

[1] For full details of these changes see G. R. Elton's *Tudor Revolution in Government*, Ch. iii.

sion of the Crown's effective jurisdiction over the Church and over hitherto imperfectly ruled parts of the country such as the North and Wales and its Marches, the subjection of the Church extinguishing all foreign authority and making England a true sovereign state; (2) the increased importance of Parliament and the use of its statutes in a flood of legislation to effect the above changes, making it clear that the sovereign authority was the King in Parliament, but always with the continuance of the royal prerogative, extensive though not comprehensively defined; (3) the conversion of the large body of individual councillors into the compact and smaller Privy Council, usually with more than a dozen but less than a score of members, sitting regularly, deliberating and advising the sovereign as a body, issuing administrative orders, and questioning suspects and witnesses, persons who for one reason or another were 'called before the Council' to give an account of their doings or the things they knew.

The story of the achievement of the first of the above headings is embodied in the general history of the generation from 1529 to 1559. It is summed up in the phrasing of the oath prescribed by the Elizabethan Act of Supremacy in the latter year: 'I do utterly testify and declare that the Queen's highness is the only supreme governor of this realm . . . as well in all spiritual and ecclesiastical things or causes as temporal; and that no foreign prince, person, prelate, state or potentate has or ought to have any jurisdiction, power, superiority, pre-eminence, or authority, ecclesiastical or spiritual, within this realm. . . .'

The new phase in the importance of Parliament began with the assembly of 1529, which continued, against former practice, to sit un-dissolved in six sessions until 1536, and was used by Henry VIII and Cromwell to embody their revolutionary measures in statute law. Henry went into alliance with the Commons against the papal supremacy and the abuses existing in the Church, and since the greater part of the articulate opinion of the country wanted what the King wanted, namely complete English sovereignty, the Commons of this Parliament were more truly representatives than many had been in the past. The old-time borough corporations had often regarded Parliament as involving them in a distasteful duty: someone has to go, had been the thought: let us send X and Y: it is their turn, although of course we shall have to pay their expenses. From 1529 the bearing of the matter rapidly altered, and X and Y became ambitious or public-spirited men, often from outside the borough, who were eager to serve as its representatives. Not that this led to many contested elections, for the choice was that of a local oligarchy and was generally made before the formal election day. Having arrived at Westminster, the members were not the subservient tools of despotism that they have sometimes been represented. Even under Henry VIII they were influenced but not baldly commanded by the Crown, and they had a will of their own in rejecting measures that it sought to promote. The Parliaments of Mary's reign refused to do several important things that she desired. The first Parliament of Elizabeth decisively modified her wishes on the religious settlement, and throughout her reign both Lords and Commons criticized and influenced her policy on serious matters. In both the Queens' reigns religion was the main subject of contention; but under Mary the Commons resisted an initiative of the Queen's, whereas under Elizabeth they took the initiative in seeking to make the Queen go farther than she desired. The Commons of Elizabeth would undoubtedly have been bolder still but for the perils of the time and their own confidence in her wisdom. Their potential demand for further power was reserved for expression under the Stuarts. The intrusion of the gentry into the borough representation became more strongly marked as the century progressed, while the element of the plain burgesses diminished. The number of seats increased, not only by the representation of Wales and the inclusion of former palatinate regions of England, but by the creation of many new parliamentary boroughs, to a total of 467 by 1603.

The new Privy Council was evolved under Cromwell and in the last years of Henry VIII. Its efficiency was displayed in the management of the French and Scottish war of 1543–6 and the foiling of a serious threat of invasion by France. It is surprising that the Council's activities in warlike administration at this time have been generally passed over, for the material for their study is plentiful. Under Edward VI the Council grew larger and its power, in the absence of an active sovereign, greater. Mary employed the large and inchoate Council of the old type, but with an inner ring of more trusted ministers. Under Elizabeth the true Privy Council returned, and settled down as the effective organ of administration and executive until the Puritan revolution of the seventeenth century. The leading councillors occupied ministerial positions, not only in the household offices but as Lord Treasurer, Lord Chancellor, Lord Admiral, Chancellor of the Exchequer, and above all Principal Secretary, who evolved during the Henrician revolution from a personal assistant of the sovereign into the permanently prominent minister he became when the post was held first by Cecil and then by Walsingham. The Elizabethan privy councillors, it need hardly be added, were appointed solely at the sovereign's discretion, and owed nothing to parliamentary support.

II. THE NAVY

THE Royal Navy is one of the great creations of the Tudor period, ranking with the constitution as a moulder of the national destiny. The word navy had two meanings. In one sense it meant the entire shipping and all the mariners of the realm. By ancient principle the ships and seamen were in a peculiar sense at the King's direct disposal, and he required no parliamentary authority to use them as he saw fit; and this was linked with the parallel principle that the royal prerogative covered the regulation of trade and the passage of subjects overseas. The term Royal Navy referred commonly to the King's own ships, acquired and maintained at his expense. In thinking of these ships there was a 'household' point of view, the neglect to appreciate which has caused some misapprehensions about their history. They were regarded as in the same category of royal property as the King's houses on land. If a royal palace were burnt or dismantled the new edifice arising in its place would still be called the palace of the same name. In the same way, if a King's ship was lost or broken up, another might be built to fill its place in the establishment under the same name, an entirely new vessel, although referred to as, for instance, 'the *Mary Rose* new builded'. It is misleading always to interpret 'new building' as merely a rebuilding or major repair of an existing ship; although it might have that meaning.

The Yorkist kings had a handful of ships which did little or no service as a fleet and were probably used to carry cargoes on the royal account. Henry VII took over these vessels and built two large fighting ships, the *Regent* and the *Sovereign*, together with some smaller ones. An officer called the Clerk of the King's Ships had been appointed since the thirteenth century, and under Henry VII the Clerk was in administrative charge of the small fleet. Henry VIII expanded his Navy from the beginning of his reign by building and buying large ships. At the outset the ship-of-war was still in conception the adapted merchantman, formidable by reason of a large crew of armed men rather than by an equipment of heavy guns. The merchant type most suitable was the carrack of southern Europe, a vessel of large size, great beam in proportion to length, and high superstructures in poop and forecastle, enabling the maximum number of men to fire the numerous light weapons provided. Decisive fighting by such vessels entailed grappling and boarding and perhaps, as in one notable instance, the loss of both the combatants by fire. That incident, in 1512, caused Henry VIII to improve the carrack by installing a tier of heavy guns low down near the waterline, so that his ship could batter and sink the enemy without grappling. Thus, before the Reformation, was created Henry VIII's first Navy, of which the largest ship was the first *Great Harry* of 1,500 tons, a carrack-built monster that gave his admirals considerable anxiety in the shallow waters and anchorages of the English coast.

The Navy did what was required of it in the French wars of 1512–14 and 1522–5, but the administration was not perfect, and waste and delay were apparent. The enlarged fleet had outgrown the simple administration of the Clerk of the Ships, and new officers had to be created. The first was that of Keeper of the Storehouses for supplying the ships, and this officer developed into Treasurer of the Navy. As he did so, and acquired an accountant's duties, another officer, first mentioned in 1524, took over the provision and issue of materials, and he was entitled the Comptroller of the Ships. Meanwhile the Lord High Admiral, more commonly styled the Lord Admiral, formerly not a sea-going officer, was made one by Henry VIII, and it became the rule that when the whole fleet was mobilized the Lord Admiral should take command.

There were ten years of peace after the second French war, breaking down into a sort of cold war with the Catholic powers as the English Reformation revealed its meaning. During the peace years the Navy had less spent on it and the ships were ageing. When the foreign situation grew menacing in the late 'thirties, Henry built a virtually new Navy. He did it with the wealth taken from the monasteries, a 'new builded' *Great Harry* of 1,000 tons, *Mary Rose*, *Minion* and others taking the places of broken-up vessels of the same names, all up-to-date Henrician versions of the carrack-built type, with the big superstructures but also with the big guns. In addition he built a quite new type named galleasses;[1] of medium-sized ships with low superstructures or none at all, long in proportion to beam ($4\frac{1}{2}$ to 1), with a full rig of masts and sails, but also with long oars, pulled by several men each, for propulsion in calms and manœuvre in battle. Some of these galleasses were as large as 450 tons, while smaller examples descended into a pinnace class known as rowbarges. The oared vessels were classified as 'the rowing pieces,' but they were essentially sailing ships with auxiliary power. The 'great ships' or purely sailing carracks were regarded as the main strength of the fleet, and ran to higher tonnages. There was only one decade of English galleass building, *c*. 1535–45. The type evidently had disadvantages. The Spaniards used four great galleasses in the Armada and did little good with them.

Thus equipped and administered, Henry's Navy waged its last war in 1543–6. A squadron of it helped to deliver the heavy blow to Scotland in 1544, and it kept the Channel for the King's crossing to France later

---

[1] The galleass was new in the English service, but the design had long been developed in the Mediterranean. The so-called Flanders Galleys that came from Venice to England were in fact galleasses.

in the year. Its greatest service was in foiling the invasion threat of 1545. That year must have been the highlight in the traditions of the seamen who witnessed it, and as late as the Armada year there were at least two of them still serving, Sir William Winter at sea and William Holstocke in the dockyards. The intensity of the war and the growth of the fleet necessitated more elaborate administration. In 1545 the King appointed three new officers, the Lieutenant of the Admiralty, the Master of the Ordnance for the Ships, and the Surveyor of the Ships. The first served as the deputy of the Lord Admiral, the second title explains itself, and the Surveyor concerned himself with rigging and equipment for sea. When the ships were laid up in peace time, most of the guns were not kept on board, but were stored together with those for the army in the Tower of London, where there was also a Master of the Ordnance for the land. In the Tower there were workshops for the repair of artillery and the making of the wooden mountings. All these officers were known collectively as the Principal Officers of the Navy—the Lieutenant, the Treasurer, the Comptroller, the Surveyor, the Master of the Ordnance, the Clerk of the Ships—and from 1546 they sat in regular meeting as the Navy Board, destined to endure until 1832. It should not be confused with the Board of Admiralty, which did not exist in Tudor times and began much later as the delegation of the Lord Admiral's functions to a commission. The Principal Officers were administrative officials, but they were also (the Treasurer at one time excepted) combatant officers who commanded at sea. The explanation is that each member of the Navy Board had sufficient general competence to take over the duties of any other who might be absent, and also that each had behind him a staff of subordinates who could carry on for a time without him. In the Armada campaign the entire Navy Board went on active service with the exception of the aged Holstocke, who seems to have borne the whole burden at Chatham and who died next year.

As already noted, all the merchant shipping of the realm and every man categorized as a mariner were at the King's direct disposition. Merchant vessels served in every fleet with the King's ships. Their owners were paid at a traditional rate of 3d. per ton per week, and since this was below the current rates for chartering there was an element of taxation in the arrangement. The men were paid 5 shillings a month and their victuals, but generally received no clothing. The 5 shillings a month was raised to 6s. 8d. (half a mark) in Henry's last war, and to 10 shillings under Elizabeth. Privateering against enemy trade was on a large scale. Shipowners received licence 'to annoy the King's enemies' at their own expense and profit, and no less than sixty privateersmen operating in the Channel were called in to assist the Navy at Portsmouth when the French invasion was imminent in 1545. The word privateer was not yet coined, and the ships and men engaged were known as the freebooters or simply as men of war, a term not then applied to the Navy.

Henry VII's dockyard was at Portsmouth. With France as the opponent Portsmouth was convenient, but it was also unsafe for laid-up ships, which might be destroyed by a sudden raid. Henry VIII used the Thames for dockyard work, at Woolwich and Deptford, although he assembled his fleets at Portsmouth. Under Edward VI the Duke of Northumberland, who had been Lord Admiral, laid the foundations of the yard at Gillingham on the Medway which grew into Chatham dockyard. Under Elizabeth this was the headquarters of the Navy, not only for laying-up and repairs but for mobilization, since during most of her reign the greatest danger was of invasion from the Spanish Netherlands. Portsmouth declined, but Plymouth rose to second place as the western base for the active fleet looking towards Spain; and Plymouth began to develop dockyard facilities in the Hamoaze anchorage, which long afterwards received the name of Devonport after existing for two centuries under the plain appellation of The Dock. One other administrative post was created by Northumberland, that of Surveyor of the Victuals, but he was never a member of the Navy Board. Elizabeth in 1562 discontinued one of the Principal Officers, the Lieutenant of the Admiralty, and no successor was appointed during the rest of the period.

When Henry VIII died there were 53 ships in the Navy, most of them built during the previous twelve years. Twenty-five of these ships were of over 200 tons, and the total tonnage was 11,268. The efficiency characteristic of the late king and his councillors did not at once wear off, and a naval squadron did good work in Somerset's Scottish campaign, while the foundation of the Medway dockyard was a very wise decision. But the reign of Edward VI was one of lowered tone and increasing corruption, and the Navy did not escape. The results of a deterioration that must have been going on for years are to be seen in the reign of Mary, when a number of decayed ships were sold at breaking-up prices and it became difficult to turn out even a moderate force for Channel service. Apart from the ships sold off, others remained on the books but were in such condition that they could not go to sea; and the whole Navy, reduced at Mary's death to 7,110 tons, was more a paper than a fighting force. In the first twenty years of Elizabeth there was a good recovery in fighting efficiency, although this was a period in which only minor squadrons went to sea and the whole Navy never fought under the Lord Admiral's command.[1] The Queen was apparently being well served, although it afterwards came out that a good deal of peculation and graft was going on in the dockyards. Elizabeth did not at this period increase the numbers of her ships, but she did build or buy new vessels to replace those left hopelessly decayed by Mary, and the paper fleet became a real one.

[1] The whole Navy was mobilized once, in 1570, but there was no fighting.

From 1562 the roll of the Principal Officers remained unaltered until 1577. Lord Clinton, afterwards Earl of Lincoln, was the Lord Admiral, having been appointed by Mary a year before her death. Benjamin Gonson, a landsman, was Treasurer and the presiding officer at the Navy Board. Sir William Winter filled the two offices of Master of the Ordnance and Surveyor. His brother, George Winter, was Clerk of the Ships. William Holstocke was Comptroller. Following the recognized practice of the time, none of these men devoted themselves exclusively to their official duties. They all engaged in mercantile pursuits and owned or managed merchant shipping in their private capacities. Gonson was a merchant in business on his own account. As Navy Treasurer he seems to have been honest and industrious, but, lacking the experience and technical knowledge of the other Officers, who were all seamen, he was overruled by them in important matters. The two Winters, filling three of the five seats on the Board, had the chief influence, and Sir William, a dominant man, was the real director of the administration. His character and conduct exhibit two aspects not often found together: he was efficient and public-spirited enough to give the Queen a reasonably good fleet, equal to the modest demands made upon it; and he was at the same time greedy and corrupt to the extent of making her pay twice as much as she should have done for the service rendered, he and his allies pocketing the difference. One question arises. Who, in the Privy Council, was the minister of marine? He should have been Clinton, the Admiral; but Clinton appears to have been easy-going and devoted to other affairs. The real minister was Cecil (Burghley from 1571), a wise man, but of no nautical knowledge. He could judge only by results, and they were that the minor campaigns of the 'sixties and 'seventies were successfully conducted. He may have had suspicions that beneath the surface all was not well, but he had to await the advent of an independent professional adviser before taking action.

Upon this set-up impinged the personality of Sir John Hawkins, who was to be the creator of the fleet that saved the country in the Spanish War and made England an oceanic power. And here a divergence is necessary to the question of strategy. The whole outlook of the Tudor Navy and the whole of its service had hitherto been limited to the coastal waters of northern Europe, the Channel, the Bay of Biscay, the North Sea. No Tudor fleet had ever been more than a few days' sail from Portsmouth or Chatham. The Navy was built and organized with this employment in view. The carrack-built great ships took the sea only in the summer, in fine-weather cruises with shelter close at hand. The two *Great Harry's* never went west of Plymouth or north of the Thames. The Channel guard in winter and the expeditions to the Scottish coast were work for the smaller craft. The manning and victualling were in conformity with this. The ships were crowded to capacity with soldiers and sailors, living so close in quarters where cleanliness was impossible that they died wholesale of typhus and dysentery. Victuals and drink for such numbers could endure only for short periods. But the compensating factor was proximity to the English coast, whence new men and supplies could be drawn. And so the Henrician Navy did what was needed in the French and Scottish wars, and the early Elizabethan in the like circumstances was also successful. The measure of their competence is supplied by the failure under Mary. The Principal Officers, all of them men bred in this phase of naval effort, were satisfied that they were on the right lines.

John Hawkins was a man with a different past, an ocean seaman who had sailed repeatedly to the Canaries, West Africa, and the Caribbean. On his last West Indian voyage he had taken one of the Queen's great ships, the 700-ton *Jesus of Lubeck*, and twice she had nearly foundered at sea, while her defects occasioned the entry into San Juan de Ulua which entailed the ruin of the expedition. He was thoroughly dissatisfied with the high-charged type as a ship of war. Hawkins worked for the future of England as an oceanic power, and in the 1570's foresaw the war with Spain, now become the enemy instead of the ally of Tudor England. He was for winning this war by campaigns in the Atlantic, attacking the Spanish colonies and stopping the plate-fleets that brought Philip II the money for his armies and his anti-Protestant crusade. Hawkins wished to convert the English Navy of the narrow seas into an ocean-going Navy. There is no doubt that Drake's thoughts were similar, but in the 'seventies Drake had yet his position to make, and it was only after his return in 1580 that his voice was powerful in naval affairs. Even so, Drake had little to do with administration, for he was never a member of the Navy Board. Meanwhile Hawkins had married Gonson's daughter and gained inside information of what was going on in the dockyards under Winter's control. Hawkins was already known and trusted by the Queen and Burghley. He revealed to the minister the corruption and extravagance of the Principal Officers, and in 1577 wrote a detailed report on it. His father-in-law died that year, and by Burghley's choice John Hawkins succeeded him as Treasurer of the Navy. It was in effect a censure of Winter who, but for his ill-doings, would naturally have had the appointment.

Hawkins began work with two main purposes: to stop peculation and give the Queen a better fleet for her money, and to convert the ships and men into an ocean-going force able to keep the sea for months in place of the weeks that had been the endurance of the old squadrons. He encountered opposition to both purposes. Winter was a powerful man, able to pull many strings, and for seven years he fought Hawkins tooth and nail. The exposure of roguery rankled, and the Winter alliance countered it with accusations that Hawkins was himself corrupt. But the

Treasurer held on and achieved both a sensational saving of money and a fleet that all acknowledged to be in perfect condition when it fought the Armada; and Burghley throughout supported the reformer. For some years indeed Hawkins, in order to have a free hand, was allowed to farm the Navy, receiving ultimately a fixed annual sum for the performance of the whole of the dockyard work, minutely specified, with his opponents the Principal Officers to report on any shortcomings they could find. It was a gruelling test of the Treasurer's work, to which he knew he could stand up. For the ships Hawkins favoured a new type, the galleon, which superseded the carrack-built great ship. The galleon, contrary to a widely held impression, was not the clumsy vessel commonly associated with Spanish practice, but was the new advanced design of the late sixteenth century, and England built galleons with radical and not conservative intent. The essential of the galleon was the proportion of beam to length, one to three-and-a-half, which was found to yield a fast, weatherly and easily handled ship. The superstructures had nothing to do with the galleon characteristic. Spain built galleons with high superstructures, Hawkins built galleons with low ones, and his proved to be the better ships. At the outset he had little money allowed him for additional ships, but he converted $2\frac{1}{2}$ to 1 carracks into $3\frac{1}{2}$ to 1 galleons by cutting them in two amidships and building in new structure between the halves. The dockyards did surprising work of this sort; and Peter Pett and Matthew Baker,[1] the two Master Shipwrights under Hawkins, deserve remembrance. At the same time they cut down the superstructures to improve sailing quality and the general resistance to strains endured in a violent sea. Hawkins also diminished the numbers of men in the crews, for he had never seen sense in cramming excessive numbers into a space so unavoidably filthy that many of them died of disease. Smaller numbers meant greater sea endurance by lessening the demands on the victuals. In a paper on this reform he explained that fewer men would be better men, with less dirt, vermin, sickness, and starvation, and he pointed out to the Queen that if she would raise the pay to ten shillings a month the total wage bill would be no greater; and she agreed. The old coastal Navy men were outraged by the reshaping of the ships and grumbled loudly; but a new school of ocean sailors was arising, with Drake at its head, and they were for the low-built galleons.

The turning-point in Hawkins's work came in 1585. He had fought and beaten Winter, and Winter was a big enough man to shake hands on it; and thenceforward they worked in amity. The appointment that year of a new Lord Admiral, Howard of Effingham, always Hawkins's friend, probably brought about the reconciliation. The war was beginning, and

---

[1] Some working drawings by Matthew Baker preserved at Cambridge constitute the earliest designs for English ship construction known to exist. There are reproductions of them at the Science Museum, South Kensington.

there was money for enlarging the fleet. Before and after the Armada Hawkins built fine new galleons and ocean-going pinnaces. When he died in 1595 the Navy was entirely transformed from the service of twenty years earlier. Winter had played his part with the guns, making the long-range 18-pounder culverin the standard heavy piece. By the date of the Armada there were 25 modern or modernized fighting ships of over 100 tons, and 18 ocean-going pinnaces. These formed the core of the whole national marine which turned out in 1588, in which year the Queen's ships bore the brunt of the fighting.

The Hawkins impulse continued to the end of the reign, only to be submerged in a tide of corruption under James I. The fact that the great Armada fights took place in sight of the English coast has tended to obscure the permanent significance of the new Elizabethan Navy. For it made England an oceanic power, a development retarded under the early Stuarts but resumed with vigour by the Commonwealth; and by consequence a colonial and imperial power. This could not have happened without the naval doctrine and the public outlook as well as the material force requisite for the task; and Hawkins at Chatham and Drake at sea were pre-eminently the men who laid the foundations.

III. THE PRINCIPLES AND ADMINISTRA-
TION OF OCEANIC EXPANSION

FROM its beginning under Henry VII until the Puritan Revolution of the seventeenth century the founding of the British Empire was controlled by the royal prerogative; and, at least to the end of the Tudor period, there was little parliamentary discussion of its processes.[1] The legal instrument for many of the chief transactions was the royal letters-patent under the great seal. The prerogative covered the movement of English subjects into and out of the realm: it might forbid them to leave, and it could recall them. Empire-building included not only the founding of colonies but the initiation of new trades in regions hitherto unfrequented, and in the latter aspect it was sometimes permitted informally by the prerogative without the issue of letters-patent. The prerogative was often used to confer a monopoly of a new trade or a colonial area upon specified persons or companies. Such monopolies were justified by the fact that their recipients were taking risks to create something new, and were not encroaching on existing business, as were the domestic monopolists whom Parliament did attack towards the close of the period. A fundamental European assumption, a law of Christendom such as Sir Thomas More spoke of at his trial, should be noted as a background feature. It was that Christians were *ipso facto* at war with infidels, and that it was therefore lawful to appropriate the lands and goods of the heathen and to take them captive. In practice it was often expedient to let this principle sleep in order to make treaties with the infidel, but in law it existed. It was invoked as late as 1647 in a speech by counsel to a committee of the House of Commons, and it had an obvious bearing on the slave trade.

Henry VII issued three important patents. The first, in 1496, permitted John Cabot, his sons, and their deputies to discover and annex in the King's name any lands hitherto unknown to Christians, and to enjoy, subject to conditions, the monopoly of trade with them. The second in 1501, to a Bristol syndicate of three English merchants and three Portuguese captains from the Azores, permitted likewise the discovery and annexation of lands unknown to Christians and must therefore have had different lands in view from those discovered by Cabot in 1497–8. The

---

[1] The Act of 1566 for the Muscovy Company is a borderline exception. It is explanatory of the patent of 1555, designed to remedy abuses that have arisen in the operation of that instrument; and in part it is of the nature of a Navigation Act. This procedure by statute was presumably for legal convenience in prosecuting those who had been infringing the intention of the patent. There was a parallel bill, not proceeded with, in 1586 to amplify Ralegh's patent for Virginia.

third, in 1502, to a syndicate of four containing three of the 1501 grantees and one new one, was of a different purport, permitting them to 'discover and recover' any lands, without the proviso of their being unknown to Christians, but with the limitation that the lands must not be 'now in the possession' of any Christian power in amity with the King. This is the first statement of what became a standard English principle, that the Crown did not recognize the rights of other states based solely on prior discovery, but made actual possession the test—the doctrine of effective occupation. There was another basis of claim, covering areas yet to be explored as well as those discovered, embodied in the fifteenth-century papal bulls of partition and donation to Portugal and Spain, resting on the papal right to administer the law of Christendom already noted. Henry VII ignored the papal decision and proceeded as if he had never heard of it. It is just possible that in 1496 he had not, since we do not know how far these bulls were communicated to others than their recipients. The grantees of the 1502 patent admitted others and were known as the Company Adventurers to the New Found Lands. They were amply empowered to found, govern and defend colonial possessions, and may have done so; but the achievement was not permanent, unless it was the continuous frequentation of the Newfoundland fishery from this date.

Throughout the Tudor period enterprise was almost wholly at the expense of the projectors, with little royal expenditure, none indeed after the reign of Henry VIII. Henry VII was fairly liberal in granting rewards and pensions to successful adventurers, and there is a statement that he equipped one of the five ships of John Cabot's second expedition; but on what terms we do not know. He probably contributed also to Sebastian Cabot's expedition of 1509. Henry VIII and Wolsey attempted to found a national company for exploration and trade in 1521, but it is evident that they expected the merchants to find the money. The only purely royal expedition on record is that of John Rut with two of the King's ships in 1527.

The achievements under the Henries were the establishment of the Newfoundland fishery and of the dyewood trade on the coast of Brazil. William Hawkins of Plymouth is known to have conducted a Brazil trade for ten years, working at his own financial adventure. The Southampton merchants also had a fortified post in Brazil in 1542. The subsequent silence of the records is not conclusive proof that the trade was then discontinued. William Hawkins acted with the encouragement of Henry VIII and Cromwell, but neither he nor the Southampton men received any formal grant by letters-patent. The Portuguese Crown objected to intrusions in Brazil and Africa, but permitted direct trade between England and the Azores and Madeira. Spain also made Englishmen free of the Canary Islands, which were included in the dominions covered by the commercial clauses of the Treaty of Medina del Campo in 1489.

Until the middle of the Tudor period efforts at expansion were promoted by a few individuals adventuring from a prospering England not greatly interested in the ocean. From the reign of Edward VI national necessity became the spur, necessity to open new trades for an England in economic distress. The promoters felt that they were serving the country as well as themselves, and the movement widened its appeal until it became a truly national interest. The Duke of Northumberland opened the new phase with his patronage of the Merchants Adventurers for the Discovery of New Trades, subsequently known as the Muscovy Company. It was novel in organization, being the first English joint-stock company, with a permanent working capital subscribed by 240 investors in £25 shares. A charter of incorporation by Edward VI was agreed but not completed at the time of his death, and the legally valid grant was that of Philip and Mary in 1555. The original intention was to open the north-east passage to Asia, and the substantial achievement was a new trade with Russia by the White Sea. At the same time syndicates of London merchants, also with Northumberland's approval, were opening a West African trade with Morocco and were preparing to extend it to the Gold Coast. These men received no formal recognition for the monopoly of their new trade. The Gold Coast trade became extensive in Mary's reign, purely as private London enterprise prohibited by the Queen. Highly placed men were interested in promoting it, and they contrived to defy the prohibition.

The reason for Philip's objection, which inspired Mary's prohibition, is worth considering. It was at bottom the fact that Spain and Portugal had a joint interest in maintaining their tropical monopolies; but on the surface it was no more than that a friendly sovereign the King of Portugal complained of trespass in his dominions. There was no mention of the papal bulls of partition. Neither had there been, so far as we know (but we know very little), any mention of them in the Spanish objections to Henry VII's promotion of John Cabot. Some have thought that the importance of the bulls of partition as a basis of the policy of Spain and Portugal has been overestimated, and that these powers really based their claims on prior discovery and occupation. Certainly Philip could not have considered the line of partition as extending into the north, for it was in his name as well as his wife's that the 1555 charter of the Muscovy Company was issued; and by that instrument the Company was granted the monopoly of all discovery and new trade to the north, the north-east, and the north-west of London. In the first decade of Elizabeth again, when the Portuguese protested against the continuance of the English trade with Guinea, they made no mention of the papal bulls. On the other hand, official Spanish maps of this period mark the line of partition as a meridian extending to the north pole, and Cecil in 1561 protested to the Spanish ambassador that the Pope had no right to partition the world; while Charles V had cited the bulls when objecting to the French voyages to Canada under Jacques Cartier. It would seem that the bulls lay at the back of policy, although the appeal was generally to prior discovery and occupation when they could be alleged. The English doctrine was that of effective occupation, stated at the beginning by Henry VII, restated by the London merchants under Mary, and again decisively by Elizabeth in the 1560's, when she told the Portuguese ambassador that if his master really possessed the African coast his command to his subjects there would prevent them from trading with the English. The Queen implied that effective resistance would alone exclude her merchants, and that she would respect no claim based only on prior discovery. In one respect, however, the Tudor sovereigns left the argument open. Until the Spanish war had actually begun, none of them issued patents of incorporation to oceanic pioneers for the regions frequented by Spain and Portugal. Under Elizabeth there were vigorous tropical enterprises, but she did not before 1585 give her formal sanction to any of them. In the same period projects for North America and the northern passages to Asia received chartered rights.

The pre-war part of Elizabeth's reign witnessed the semi-official state enterprise, ostensibly in private hands and disavowable by the Queen at need, but directed by the Secretary of State and the Lord Admiral and numbering the Queen and some of her privy councillors among the investors. This was the nature of John Hawkins's trade with West Africa and the Caribbean from 1564 to 1569. It was also the nature of Drake's outstanding expedition to the Pacific in 1577–80. Hawkins had no formal commission from the Queen, although he had an interview with her before sailing in 1564. Drake claimed that he had a commission, but failed to produce it at Doughty's trial, and it is possible that her authorization was only verbal. In any case, it fell short of a patent. Grenville, earlier than Drake, had planned a Pacific enterprise, but gave it up on failing to obtain the Queen's sanction. After Drake's return, other enterprises to the Far East and the Pacific were discussed, and one, Fenton's expedition, started; but there was no incorporation. The West African trade of the same period was sanctioned only by the Queen's instructions to the Lord Admiral. The traders were competing syndicates and individuals and were not combined in a corporation. On a lower scale of authority were the raiding attacks on the Spaniards in the Caribbean, Drake's of 1572–3 being the most notable. These had no formal sanction of any kind, but were certainly permitted in the sense that no punitive action was taken against the investors and leaders.

For enterprise in non-Spanish latitudes the Queen's letters-patent, conferring definite rights, were freely granted: Frobisher and Lok's

Cathay Company in 1577, Humphrey Gilbert's colonizing patent in 1578, Ralegh's in 1584, Adrian Gilbert's patent for the North West Passage in 1585. The colonial patents, it is true, contained no geographical limitations of the territories to which they applied, but it was understood that the objective was North America, and the grantees made no attempt to colonize anywhere else. In this respect they were quite under the Queen's control, since her authority was as good for modifying the patent as for granting it. Two charterings of mercantile companies without any exploring element complete the tale of activity of the pre-war years: the regulated Eastland Company of 1579, bringing the Baltic trade under organization; and the joint-stock Turkey Company of 1581, reviving a trade, previously lost, with the Ottoman dominions by way of the Mediterranean. The Turkey Company was refounded in 1592 as the Levant Company, and continued as a regulated company. There was no state financing of any of these chartered bodies, and of the semi-official non-chartered undertakings only in the sense that they were allowed to hire ships of the Navy. The interests of the Muscovy and Turkey Companies required the maintenance of ambassadors from the Queen at Moscow and Constantinople, but the Companies and not the Queen defrayed the costs of their services.

With the war began the issue of patents for regions which Philip II could regard as the monopoly of his Portuguese subjects: to the Barbary merchants as an incorporated company in July 1585, to the merchants of Exeter for trade with the Gambia in 1588, and most notably to the East India Company in 1600. In South America Ralegh was urgent for a royal and national undertaking for the acquisition of Eldorado, which he believed to be accessible by the Orinoco; but he failed to secure the Queen's support.

The enterprises of the Tudor period, besides embodying intrusion on the Spanish and Portuguese monopolies, represent the dual aspect of the British Empire that grew out of them: colonies in the West and a mercantile dominion in the East, with the quest of a western or northern passage to Asia as a connecting link between the two. They may be regarded as the first chapter in the history of the Empire, to which the medieval chartered companies had formed the introduction.

NOTE ON BOOKS
compiled by D. M. Palliser

Mr Williamson corrected and added to this volume until 1964, but died before being able to make further changes in a fourth edition. Inevitably, the spate of research on the Tudor period, which shows no signs of abating, has over the past fifteen years added new facts and modified old interpretations. Fortunately, guidance on further reading is provided by three excellent bibliographies. Conyers Read's *Bibliography of British History: Tudor period, 1485-1603* (2nd edn., 1959) includes almost all works of value published before 1957. This can be supplemented by the shorter but more recent *Tudor England 1485-1603* by M. Levine (1968), and within its chosen field by W. H. Chaloner and R. C. Richardson, *British Economic and Social History: a bibliographical guide* (1976). The present note is therefore confined to a select list of major recent publications, together with a very few older books which have not been superseded

GENERAL Outstanding recent textbooks covering all or part of the period include C. Russell, *The Crisis of Parliaments: English history 1509-1660* (1971); D. M. Loades, *Politics and the Nation 1450-1660* (1974); C. Cross, *Church and People 1450-1660* (1976); and C. S. L. Davies, *Peace, Print and Protestantism 1450-1558* (1976). S. T. Bindoff's *Tudor England* (1950) in the *Pelican History of England* is a brilliant survey in brief compass. G. R. Elton provided a masterly volume in the *Methuen History of England* (*England under the Tudors*, 1955), which he himself has now significantly revised and partly superseded in *Reform and Reformation: England 1509-1558* (1977) in Arnold's *New History of England*. Extended narrative accounts of shorter periods include W. K. Jordan's *Edward VI: the young king* (1968) and *Edward VI: the threshold of power* (1970), though both have been challenged by recent work, and a useful analysis of the whole mid-century period is W. R. D. Jones, *The Mid-Tudor Crisis 1539-1563* (1973). W. T. MacCaffrey's *The Shaping of the Elizabethan Regime* (1970), covering the period 1558-72, is invaluable. Finally, A. L. Rowse's *The England of Elizabeth* (1950) is a brilliant panorama of the Elizabethan age which covers almost everything except narrative history.

GOVERNMENT, POLITICS AND THE CONSTITUTION
B. P. Wolffe, *The Crown Lands, 1461-1536* (1970) and S. B. Chrimes,

Henry VII (1972) are valuable on the early Tudor period. G. R. Elton, *The Tudor Constitution: documents and commentary* (1960) has not only an excellent selection of printed documents but also, in the introductions to each section, the best guide to Tudor government. He has also contributed a series of extremely important books: *The Tudor Revolution in Government* (1953); *Policy and Police: the enforcement of the Reformation in the age of Thomas Cromwell* (1972); and *Reform and Renewal: Thomas Cromwell and the Common Weal* (1973), though their argument for a 'revolution in government' in the 1530s is controversial. The best guide to the controversy remains the attacks by G. L. Harriss and P. H. Williams, and Elton's replies, in *Past and Present* nos. 25 (1963), 29 (1964), 31 and 32 (1965). Elton's other important articles, covering a wide range of subjects, are now conveniently available in his *Tudor and Stuart Politics and Government* (2 vols., 1974). In 'Was there a Tudor despotism after all?', an article now reprinted in his important collection of essays *Freedom, Corruption and Government in Elizabethan England* (1973), J. Hurstfield forcefully restates an older view of the 1530s, and especially of government by proclamation. The proclamations themselves, much neglected compared to parliamentary statutes, are discussed in R. W. Heinze, *The Proclamations of the Tudor Kings* (1976) and F. A. Youngs, *The Proclamations of the Tudor Queens* (1976). Detailed studies exist of over half the Tudor parliaments: S. E. Lehmberg, *The Reformation Parliament* (1970) and *The Later Parliaments of Henry VIII* (1977), and Sir John Neale, *Elizabeth I and her Parliaments* (2 vols., 1953-57). Unfortunately the two last are confined almost entirely to the lower house, as well as concentrating somewhat pathologically on clashes between crown and commons. There is still no satisfactory history of the upper house (certainly of at least equal importance to the Commons) except J. E. Powell and K. Wallis, *The House of Lords in the Middle Ages* (1968), which terminates in 1540. Nor are there good modern accounts of the main organs of central government except for J. Hurstfield. *The Queen's Wards* (1958), D. E. Hoak, *The King's Council in the Reign of Edward VI* (1976), and W. J. Jones, *The Elizabethan Court of Chancery* (1967). The provincial councils are, however, usefully discussed by F. W. Brooks, *The Council of the North* (Historical Association Pamphlet, 1953), and P. H. Williams, *The Council in the Marches of Wales under Elizabeth I* (1958): the latter is outstanding. Finally, the cult of royalty is admirably discussed by R. Strong, *Portraits of Queen Elizabeth I* (1963) and *Holbein and Henry VIII* (1967), and by F. Yates, *Astraea* (1975), and the relationship between ideas and politics in J. K. McConica, *English Humanists and Reformation Politics under Henry VIII and Edward VI* (1965).

WARFARE, FOREIGN POLICY AND OVERSEAS EXPAN-
SION R. B. Wernham, *Before the Armada: the growth of English*
foreign policy, 1485-1588 (1966) is a useful survey, while G. Mattingly,
Renaissance Diplomacy (1955) is invaluable on diplomatic relations.
Recent views of the warfare and armed forces of the first four Tudors
are still mostly confined to articles and unpublished dissertations,
apart from C. G. Cruickshank, *Army Royal: Henry VIII's invasion of*
France, 1513 (1969). Elizabeth's reign is better served, e.g. by C. G.
Cruickshank, *Elizabeth's Army* (2nd edn., 1966); L. Boynton, *The*
Elizabethan Militia 1558-1638 (1967); K. R. Andrews, *Elizabethan*
Privateering: English privateering during the Spanish war, 1583-1603
(1964) and *Drake's Voyages* (1967); and C. Wilson, *Queen Elizabeth*
and the Revolt of the Netherlands (1970). M. Lewis, *The Spanish*
Armada (1960), is excellent, while G. Mattingly, *The Defeat of the*
Spanish Armada (1959), is a brilliant picture of west European politics,
diplomacy and warfare in 1587-88, going far beyond the promise of its
title. Conyers Read's *Mr Secretary Walsingham and the Policy of*
Queen Elizabeth (3 vols., 1925), *Mr Secretary Cecil and Queen Eliza-*
beth (1955), and *Lord Burghley and Queen Elizabeth* (1960) are massive surveys of government (especially foreign) policy rather than biographies. On overseas expansion generally there is Rowse's *Expansion*
of Elizabethan England (1955), supplemented for Ireland by D. B.
Quinn, *The Elizabethans and the Irish* (1966); N. Canny, *The Eliza-*
bethan Conquest of Ireland (1976); and *A New History of Ireland:*
Volume III: Early Modern Ireland 1534-1691, ed. T. W. Moody,
F. X. Martin and F. J. Byrne (1976); and for America by D. B. Quinn,
England and the Discovery of America, 1481-1620 (1974). Internal
revolts are well surveyed in A. Fletcher, *Tudor Rebellions* (2nd edn.,
1974), and S. T. Bindoff, *Ket's Rebellion 1549* (Historical Association
Pamphlet, 1949) is a brilliant brief analysis of the Norfolk rising of
1549. There are full-length studies of the mid-century revolts in
J. Cornwall, *Revolt of the Peasantry 1549* (1977) and D. M. Loades,
Two Tudor Conspiracies (1965), which considers Wyatt's rebellion and
other crises of Mary's reign.

CHURCH, RELIGION AND BELIEF There is no recent survey
of the pre-Reformation church as a whole, but parts are well covered
by D. Knowles, *The Religious Orders in England* (Vol. III, 1961), and
P. Heath, *English Parish Clergy on the Eve of the Reformation* (1969).
A. G. Dickens's brilliant *The English Reformation* (1964) is the standard account, though unfortunately the detailed narrative is taken only
to 1559; and one controversial aspect of the Reformation is judiciously
treated in J. Youings, *The Dissolution of the Monasteries* (1971). For
Elizabeth's reign, the religious 'left' and 'right' are well served by

P. Collinson, *The Elizabethan Puritan Movement* (1967) and J. Bossy, *The English Catholic Community 1570-1850* (1975), and brilliantly summarised in more popular form in P. McGrath, *Papists and Puritans under Elizabeth I* (1967), but there is still no satisfactory treatment of the silent majority in between. However, C. Cross, *The Royal Supremacy in the Elizabethan Church* (1969) is useful, and her *Church and People 1450-1660* (1976) is especially illuminating on the post-Reformation period. Two valuable collections of articles embodying recent research are *Continuity and Change: personnel and administration of the Church of England, 1500-1642* (1976), and *Church and Society in England: Henry VIII to James I* (1977), both edited by F. Heal and R. O'Day. Among some excellent local studies of the Reformation are A. G. Dickens, *Lollards and Protestants in the Diocese of York* (1959) and C. Haigh, *Reformation and Resistance in Tudor Lancashire* (1975). K. Thomas's *Religion and the Decline of Magic* (1971) is a masterly survey of popular culture and beliefs, including astrology and witchcraft, supplemented by A. Macfarlane, *Witchcraft in Tudor and Stuart England* (1970); most other work on witchcraft should be ignored. E. M. Tillyard, *The Elizabethan World Picture* (1943) remains the best short account of the prevalent 'World view' from literary sources.

ECONOMY AND DEMOGRAPHY P. Ramsey, *Tudor Economic Problems* (1963), remains the best introduction to Tudor economic history, but for a more up-to-date context see D. C. Coleman, *The Economy of England 1450-1750* (1977), and for a brilliant and detailed picture of the early period W. G. Hoskins, *The Age of Plunder: King Henry's England 1500-1547* (*Longman Social and Economic History of England*, 1976). Macmillan's *Studies in Economic and Social History* include four excellent guides to aspects of the economy: R. B. Outhwaite, *Inflation in Tudor and Early Stuart England* (1969); R. Davis, *English Overseas Trade 1500-1700* (1973); D. C. Coleman, *Industry in Tudor and Stuart England* (1975); and J. Chartres, *Internal Trade in England 1500-1700* (1977). C. E. Challis, *The Tudor Coinage* (1977) supersedes previous work in that field, and the *Journal of European Economic History*, iv (1975) contains important revisionist articles on inflation by Challis and H. A. Miskimin Recent research on urban history is summarised in P. Clark and P. Slack, *English Towns in Transition 1500-1700* (1976), and work on many towns is gathered usefully in their *Crisis and Order in English Towns 1500-1700* (1972) and in Clark's *The Early Modern Town: a reader* (1976). The standard work on agriculture and related topics is the massive and comprehensive *The Agrarian History of England and Wales: Volume IV: 1500-1640*, ed. J. Thirsk (1967), and on the manor and tenurial relationships the most useful guide is E. Kerridge, *Agrarian Problems in the Sixteenth Century and After* (1969). Dr Thirsk has also, in *Economic Policy and Projects: the development of a consumer society in early modern England* (1978), re-evaluated the success of government economic policy, including patents and monopolies.

The extensive recent literature on population, now being accorded a central role in Tudor history, is best approached by way of P. Laslett, *The World We Have Lost* (2nd edn., 1971) and J. D. Chambers, *Population, Society and Economy in Pre-Industrial England* (1972), while L. A. Clarkson, *Death, Disease and Famine in Pre-Industrial England* (1975) provides a useful popular account. There is no satisfactory book on the demographic history of the Tudor period as such, but good recent surveys of two different kinds of demographic crisis are P. Slack *et al.*, *The Plague Reconsidered: a new look at its origins and effects in sixteenth and seventeenth century England* (1977) and A. B. Appleby, *Famine in Tudor and Stuart England* (1978).

SOCIETY AND CULTURE Laslett, *The World We Have Lost*, gives a clear outline of the ladder of social status, and different strata are analysed in L. Stone, *The Crisis of the Aristocracy 1558-1641* (1965); M. Campbell, *The English Yeoman under Elizabeth and the Early Stuarts* (1942); and the chapters on landlords and labourers in *The Agrarian History of England and Wales: Volume IV*. There is no detailed study of the Tudor gentry at a national level, but local studies include J. T. Cliffe, *The Yorkshire Gentry from the Reformation to the Civil War* (1969). The problem of poverty is well summarised in J. Pound, *Poverty and Vagrancy in Tudor England* (1971), and the series of studies by W. K. Jordan on charitable bequests is summarised in his own *Philanthropy in England, 1480-1660: a study of the changing pattern of English social aspirations* (1959). The best recent surveys of education are K. Charlton, *Education in Renaissance England* (1965) and J. Simon, *Education and Society in Tudor England* (1966).

Much of the best work on Tudor society has been conducted at the local or regional level, and has emphasised the great divergences between local communities. The pioneering study was A. L. Rowse's *Tudor Cornwall* (1941), and some of the more outstanding recent con-tributions include W. T. MacCaffrey, *Exeter 1540-1640: the growth of an English county town* (1958); R. B. Smith, *Land and Politics in the England of Henry VIII: the West Riding of Yorkshire: 1530-46* (1970) A. D. Dyer, *The City of Worcester in the Sixteenth Century* (1973); A. H. Smith, *County and Court: government and politics in Norfolk, 1558-1603* (1974); M. Spufford, *Contrasting Communities: English villagers in the sixteenth and seventeenth centuries* (1974); and P. Clark, *English Provincial Society from the Reformation to the Revolu-*

tion: religion, politics and society in Kent, 1500-1640 (1977).

It is impossible to do justice to the arts in a brief space, but attention should be drawn to the relevant volumes of the *Oxford History of English Literature* (vol. III, by C. S. Lewis, 1954: vol. IV, part 1, by F. P. Wilson, 1969) and of the *Oxford History of English Art* (E. Mercer, *English Art 1553-1625*, 1962), as well as to R. Strong, *The English Icon: Elizabethan and Jacobean portraiture* (1969). A. L. Rowse, *The Elizabethan Renaissance: the cultural achievement* (1972) is stimulating but patchy, and not always reliable. M. Airs, *The Making of the English Country House 1500-1640* (1975) is stimulating, while H. M. Colvin, D. R. Ransome and J. Summerson, *The History of the King's Works: Volume III: 1485-1660*, part 1 (1975) is the first instalment of the definitive work on palaces, fortifications and other royal buildings.

BIOGRAPHIES S. B. Chrimes, *Henry VII* (1972) is really more an account of the reign than a true biography. H. F. M. Prescott, *Mary Tudor* (2nd edn., 1952) is good, and J. J. Scarisbrick, *Henry VIII* (1968) is outstanding. There is no real biography of Edward VI, but his Lords Protector are considered in M. L. Bush, *The Government Policy of Protector Somerset* (1975), and B. L. Beer, *Northumberland: the political career of John Dudley, Earl of Warwick and Duke of Northumberland* (1973). Sir John Neale's classic *Queen Elizabeth I* (1934) errs on the side of Elizolatry, contains no footnotes, and is in need of major revision, but B. W. Beckingsale, *Elizabeth I* (1963) and P. Johnson, *Elizabeth I* (1974) are good recent portraits, while A. Fraser, *Mary Queen of Scots* (1969) has performed the same service for her rival. The best biographies of Wolsey and More remain A. F. Pollard, *Wolsey* (1929) and R.W. Chambers, *Thomas More* (1935), supplemented on More's ideas by J. H. Hexter, *The Vision of Politics on the Eve of the Reformation* (1973). None of Elizabeth's leading councillors and courtiers has yet a wholly satisfactory biography, except C. Cross's *The Puritan Earl: the life of Henry Hastings third Earl of Huntingdon 1536-1595* (1966), though B. W. Beckingsale, *Burghley, Tudor statesman* (1967) is a useful account. Two good lives of archbishops are J. Ridley, *Thomas Cranmer* (1962), and V. J. K. Brook, *Whitgift and the English Church* (1957). In a class of its own is S. Schoenbaum, *William Shakespeare: a documentary life* (1975), which marries the narrative to facsimiles of over 200 documents.

INDEX

Acts, Companies, Treaties, are grouped under those headings respectively